New perspectives on the
American community

The Dorsey Series in Sociology
Consulting Editor
Charles M. Bonjean
The University of Texas at Austin

New perspectives on the

American community

Edited By

ROLAND L. WARREN

Professor Emeritus
Brandeis University

and

LARRY LYON

Baylor University

First Edition

1983

THE DORSEY PRESS
Homewood, Illinois 60430

ISBN 0-256-02869-9

Library of Congress Catalog Card No. 82–72876

Printed in the United States of America

1 2 3 4 5 6 7 8 9 0 KP 0 9 8 7 6 5 4 3

3/4/83 Baker & Tylr 14.95

Dedicated to
Margaret Hodges Warren
and
Carol Townsend Lyon

PREFACE

This fourth edition of *New Perspectives on the American Community* differs in several ways from its three predecessors. First, approximately one third of the selections are new, with special emphasis on the early holistic classics as well as more recent economic concerns. There is a coeditor—Larry Lyon—and a new publisher—the Dorsey Press—for this edition.

Still, the purposes of this edition are the same as those of previous editions. In many ways, the ideas set forth in the prefaces to the first three editions apply even more to this new collection. For example, in the first edition:

> In a way, this book of readings represents the record of a journey—a journey through the enormously rich and varied literature on the American community, a journey which the editor invites the reader to retrace with him by this means. It reproduces some of the major points of interest in the territory covered. Most of the towering landmarks are here, either in complete or in excerpt form. In many cases, of course, the important points of interest are represented only sketchily. The reader may want to go beyond the brief sample of this or that aspect of the itinerary which is given in these pages. And, of course, the seasoned traveler may well raise questions about why this or that favorite point of interest was not included at all.

The most towering of all landmarks in the literature on the American community can be found in the holistic studies added to this edition.

In the second edition:

> As in the original edition, many of the selections treat issues of intense current interest and controversy. But this book was not compiled simply to respond to current topics of interest or as a handbook for social change. Rather, it gathers together some of the more important attempts to conceptualize community life and some of the more generalizable analyses of community processes.

The two new selections on the fiscal difficulties besetting many of our largest cities reflect our desire to be topical, but we feel also that they provide two important and contrasting approaches to analyzing numerous other community issues.

Finally, in the prefaces to the second and third editions:

> The more fateful the problem grows of how daily life is experienced where one lives and labors, the more important it becomes to seek a valid understanding of why things are as they are, so that we may go on to consider how they may become worthy of the best that is in us.

The new coeditor wholly supports that proposition. Further, he welcomes this opportunity to collaborate with the editor of the first three editions in this attempt to add to that understanding of community.

As in all collections such as this one, we owe a large debt to the authors whose writings constitute this volume, but in this instance, a more substantial debt is acknowledged. Many of the writers represented in this edition developed the initial concepts of community, refined them and gave them acceptance, even preeminence, in academic inquiry. Now, several other authors included here are extending, evaluating, redefining these concepts, while continuing to make more relevant the questions we ask about the American community. We acknowledge this tremendous intellectual debt, which is also shared by all who join in the inquiry into the community in America.

Financial support from Baylor University's Faculty Development Program and University Research Committee have eased and speeded our efforts. And on a more personal note, several individuals have assisted in the preparation of this book. Charles M. Bonjean has provided able and welcome editorial support that is reflected throughout this volume. Paulette Edwards, Linda Compton, and Susan Lewis have helped in requesting permissions, typing, revising, and general organization. Finally, on an even more personal level, the support and encouragement of our wives is gratefully acknowledged, and it is to them this book is dedicated.

Roland L. Warren
Larry Lyon

CONTENTS

SECTION FOUR
Metropolis, city, suburb, neighborhood, and village

SECTION FIVE
Community politics and economics

SECTION SIX
Social change at the community level

SECTION SEVEN
Alternative communities

Basic approaches to the community

SECTION ONE

INTRODUCTION

Although there has been a rich succession of studies using the "city" or the "community" as their field of focus, it is still possible to raise the most fundamental questions: What is a city? What is a community? A number of circumstances contribute to the difficulties of definition and conceptualization.

First, even the most superficial consideration indicates the serious problems involved: the lack of a formally structured organization corresponding to the unit of study, the lack of clear geographic boundaries to delineate the locus of study, and especially the spilling over of social relationships beyond political boundaries.

Second, there are a number of different kinds of dimensions which all seem appropriate to the question of definition but which do not coincide as an aggregate: types of social relationships and behavior patterns, types and distributions of people and functions, means of sustenance, relationships to other population clusters, and so on through a long list. Depending on which dimensions are chosen as the crucial ones, different conceptions emerge.

The selections in Section One all speak to this question of fundamental conceptualization. They are not so much concerned with definitions as with a systematic examination of one or another fundamental aspect of the city or the community. In aggregate, they indicate some of the important ways of thinking about the community. They illustrate that there are many such ways, and suggest that no single way can be expected to account for all of the varied strands which make up their object of study.

Ferdinand Tönnies did not make a special study of geographic communities as such, but his basic work is highly illuminating for an understanding of geographic communities past and present, small and large. His primary concern was with two ways in which people relate to each other. In one way, characteristic of families, neighborhoods, and friendship groups, they relate to each other in a sense of mutuality, common destiny, and the common bonds and obligations that arise therefrom. Tönnies uses the German term *Gemeinschaft* (roughly, community) to designate such relationships, and he associates them with a term which has been translated as "natural will." In contrast, people may relate to each other in a means-end relationship, entering into various rationally-thought-out types of relationship characterized by various forms of exchange and represented by the market. In such relationships, each person "trades" or exchanges with other persons for what each of them wants. Rationality is high, in that each is serving his own best interests as that person sees them. There is little sentiment involved. These are associated with the "rational will." Tönnies employs the term *Gesellschaft* (roughly, society) to designate such relationships.

Tönnies states that both types of relationships usually exist simultaneously, but he indicates that Gemeinschaft is likely to prevail in small rural communities, Gesellschaft in larger urban communities. He also indicates a historical development from relationships characterized primarily by Gemeinschaft to those in which Gesellschaft is prevalent.

Although he does not focus his analysis on the geographic community, Tönnies' theoretical approach has direct relevance to most if not all of the many works presented in this volume of readings.

The excerpt from Tönnies' works included here is taken not from his book *Gemeinschaft und Gesellschaft* but from an article he wrote several decades later summarizing his theoretical approach.

Which way of thinking captures the essence of the social reality which we term the city? Max Weber, in his famous work *The City,* had a stimulating answer: The city is essentially a settlement with a market. It is the market that characterizes urban life, rather than size, degree of impersonality, or other physical or social characteristics. Two things stand out about Weber's approach. It is a definition essentially in terms of social processes—the processes surrounding the exchange of goods and money in the market. And it is a definition which seeks the essence of the city in its historical origins.

One can approach the nature of city life from an examination of the differences in experience, attitude, and behavior which characterize urban life as differentiated from rural. This approach was taken by Georg Simmel, a German sociologist who had great influence on the development of sociological theory in Europe and America, and especially on the development of a theory of urbanism. His purpose was not so much to define the metropolis as to explore the relationship between the urban environment and the psychic experience of the inhabitants. Thus, his approach was mainly social-psychological. He showed how such characteristics as intensification of nervous stimulation, intellectuality, pecuniary evaluation, emphasis on a precise time schedule, a blasé attitude, individuality, division of labor, and casualness of contact are all interrelated in the life of the metropolis.

Although Simmel's paragraphs are tightly reasoned, they are also replete with rich and colorful images and penetrating observations. Thus, in indicating the tendency to evaluate things in monetary terms, he wrote, "All things float with equal specific gravity in the constantly moving stream of money." Speaking of reserve in connection with the multiplicity of casual contacts, he observed, "What appears in the metropolitan style of life directly as dissociation is in reality only one of its elemental forms of socialization."

Simmel was dispassionate in his analysis, asserting that "it is not our task either to accuse or to pardon, but only to understand." He pointed out that "today metropolitan man is 'free' in a spiritualized and refined sense, in contrast to the pettiness and prejudices which hem in the small-town man," but "it is obviously only the obverse of this freedom if, under certain circumstances, one nowhere feels as lonely and lost as in the metropolitan crowd."

The selection by Robert Ezra Park on "Human Ecology" may seem somewhat abstract and not sufficiently explicit to help capture substantial parts of the significant social aspects of the city. Based largely on Park's ecological conceptualization of city life, there developed over a period of two decades an intensive and exciting series of research investigations into the life of the great city of Chicago. This is of historical importance in the development of urban sociology. More than that, though, Park's ecological approach still has relevance as a valid way of conceiving the human community. Just as plants and animals occupying the same habitant come into competing but reciprocally meaningful relationships to each other and to the surrounding natural environment—relationships which constitute a "community" in that their activities quite inadvertently become intertwined in a "natural economy" —so also do the human inhabitants of a city. The nature of this interrelationship, associated especially with the division of labor, is in itself an important aspect of the urban scene. Park was particularly emphatic that although the concept "balance of nature" may be useful as a heuristic device at any particular moment of investigation, changes in the interrelationships of the habitants are taking place almost constantly, changes which can be examined using such basic ecological concepts as competition, dominance, and succession.

But beyond the economy of the biotic human community there is the cultural community. "In human as contrasted with animal societies, competition and the freedom of the individual are limited on every level above the biotic by custom and consensus."

It is precisely in this dynamic interplay between cultural values, controls, and behavior patterns and the ecological processes involving sustenance and the "natural economy" that the way opens for an ecology of urban community life. "Human ecology is, fundamentally, an attempt to investigate (1) the processes by which the biotic balance and the social equilibrium are maintained once they are achieved, and (2) the processes by which, when the biotic balance and the social equilibrium are disturbed, the transition is made from one relatively stable order to another."

If Park's explanation of human ecology seems too biological to have relevance for social phenomena in the community, the classic application of these ecological principles by Louis Wirth should prove otherwise. Note that Park defined the "human community" as consisting of two fundamental elements: a population and a culture. Wirth, a student and colleague of Park's in the Sociology Department of the University of Chicago, distinguished three community population characteristics (size, density, and heterogeneity) and explained how they determined the cultural patterns of the community. It is Wirth's position that these three population variables combine to create gesellschaft-like relationships similar to those described by Tönnies and Simmel.

Norton E. Long, a political scientist, has contributed a colorful and imaginative perspective on the community by combining the ecological approach with the concept of local activities as a series of different, interrelated games. His use of the "game" analogy is not related directly to the recent developments in "game theory" as a method of calculation and decision making. Rather, it is closer to the current theoretical formulation which sees the community as a social system, itself comprised of various subsystems, many of which have important ties to systems outside the locality. In such terms, Long seems to be saying that there are a number of identifiable social systems operating at the locality level, each with its own values, goals, norms, and behavior patterns. These systems stand in symbiotic relationship to one another and support each other in largely inadvertent ways. But Long is quite sufficiently explicit in his own terms: "The ecology of games in the local territorial system accomplishes unplanned but largely functional results. The games and their players mesh in their particular pursuits to bring about over all results; the territorial system is fed and ordered. Its inhabitants are rational within limited areas and, pursuing the ends of these areas, accomplish socially functional ends."

Long is able, without belaboring his points, to integrate his line of discourse with major recent developments in ecological, power structure, and social system theory. Thus, although the text reads like an engaging article by an expert stylist and storyteller, his incisive remarks are interwoven with important theoretical considerations.

Principally, the analogy with a series of games and their players and rules provides a readily understandable means of getting at specific areas of community interest and acknowledging their interrelations, while escaping the need for saying everything at once.

Israel Rubin takes a still different approach—in many ways a much more radical one. He asks for a thorough reexamination of the concept of community. He takes as his point of departure a widely recognized historical trend in the Western world generally and in American communities specifically. This trend has been for the element of residence and locality to become progressively less important as the determinant of significant social ties. Division of labor, increased transportation and communication facilities, and the consequent exchange of ideas and material goods lessen the dependence of people on their immediate surroundings and bring them into social contacts and relationships extending far beyond their immediate geographic localities. Social ties spring up around foci other than common residence, such as occupational role, ethnic identification, political or religious persuasion, and so on. These affiliations serve as links between individuals and the larger society, thus performing functions which in times past were to a much larger extent performed by the local community.

Rubin seizes on this widely acknowledged circumstance and draws from it the conclusion that the concept of community must be redefined without any necessary reference to locality. Rather, community must be conceived and defined in terms of those ties which link the individual meaningfully to the larger society, a set of ties which may or may not involve residential locality, and a set of ties which need not reproduce in miniature the larger social macrocosm. Such ties are to be found in concrete organizations, situated in important institutional areas, and characterized by primary and secondary interaction of the members.

The next two articles in this section might well have been placed in the section on Social Change, for their primary focus relates directly to the process of, or need for, community change and development. Yet they are included here because each adds an important alternative theoretical conception of the local community to those already considered.

Following in the tradition of Harold Kaufman, Kenneth P. Wilkinson presents a strong case for considering local communities as fields of interaction, and he characterizes such fields as emergent, dynamic, and unbounded. The conceptualization is somewhat reminiscent of Long's ecology of games, but Wilkinson places more emphasis on two characteristics: the locality-oriented nature of the field interaction characterizing community and the distinguishing characteristics of community development as "improving" the structure of the community field in the sense of "contributing to increased generalization potential in the relationships among actors."

Although Marxist analysis has long been applied at national and international levels, only recently has it focused on local phenomena as well. William Tabb and Larry Sawers, in the excerpts provided here, explain why a Marxist, or conflict perspective, is being developed only now for the urban community, and they contrast their Marxist political-economy approach with more traditional "mainstream" views. Not all conflict analyses of the community are such a direct application of Marx and Engles as this selection from Tabb and Sawers; nor do they all provide such a clear and emotional call for radical social change. However, this selection provides a straightforward statement of a general Marxist approach to community analysis and change which is echoed in only slightly more muted tones in other local studies of this genre.

The concluding selection of this section is a recent presentation that Roland L. Warren made to the Community Section of the American Sociological Association. In his paper, Warren acknowledges the multiplicity of approaches to community that are shown throughout Section One. He argues that these conflicting approaches, or paradigms, are not a temporary problem that will be solved by the development of a more powerful and inclusive paradigm. Rather, Warren maintains that the existence of several approaches to community will continue in the foreseeable future. Further, he sees the multiple and often conflicting approaches not as a problem to be solved, but as signifying a vibrant field that includes a flexible assortment of approaches, or tools, for social inquiry.

Warren's view of multiple approaches to the study of community is reflected throughout this edition of *New Perspectives on the American Community*. This collection of readings is deliberately eclectic because the editors believe that: (1) community sociology has been and will continue to be a multiparadigm field, and (2) more can be learned by studying communities from several viewpoints than from an exclusive focus based on a single approach.

1

Gemeinschaft and Gesellschaft

Ferdinand Tönnies

We return to the simple problem and thought: what, why, and how do thinking human beings will and want? The simple and most general answer is: they want to attain an end and seek the most appropriate means of attaining it. They strive toward a goal and seek the correct way leading thereto. This is the action, the behavior, which in the affairs of practical life, of daily work, of struggle, of trade, has through the ages been directed and made easier by pleasure and devotion, by hope and fear, by practice and habit, by model and precept.

Human volition. The general human volition, which we may conceive as natural and original, is fulfilled through knowledge and ability and is also fundamentally conditioned through reciprocal interaction with them. The whole intellect, even in the plainest man, expresses itself in his knowledge and correspondingly in his volition. Not only what he has learned but also the inherited mode of thought and perception of the forefathers influences his sentiment, his mind and heart, his conscience. Consequently I name the will thought of in this latter sense natural will (*Wesenwille*), contrasting it with the type of rational will (*Kürwille*), in which the thinking has gained predominance and come to be the directing agent. The rational will is to be differentiated from intellectual will. Intellectual will gets along well with subconscious motives which lie deep in man's nature and at the base of his natural will, whereas rational will eliminates such disturbing elements and is as clearly conscious as possible.

Deliberation, the thought form of ends and means, can separate the two, one from the other. From this results the inference that the means are not fundamentally connected to the end; that is to say, the means and end are not allied, interwoven, or identical. The means may rather be completely isolated and therefore possibly even stand in strong opposition to the ends. In this case the end under consideration requires that the means be as suitable to it as possible, that no means or segment thereof be used which is not conditioned by the end, but that the means most suitable for the attainment of a given end be chosen and used. This implies a definite divorce and differentiation of end and means which, therefore, permits no consideration of means other than that of their perfect suitability for the attaining of the end. The principle of the rationalization of the means develops everywhere as a necessary consequence the more thought, in accordance with the desire and intention, is intensively focused on the end or the goal. This signifies, therefore, an attitude of indifference to the means with respect to every consideration other than their greatest effectiveness in attaining the end. This indifference is frequently attained only by overcoming resistance resulting from motives other than the consideration of the end, which motives may hinder, dissuade, or frighten one from the application of this means. Thus, action which adjusts the means to the end desired may be viewed with definite reluctance, also with fear and anxiety, or, more characteristically, with aversion and, what is akin thereto, with feelings of opposition such as come with remorse. With some exaggeration,

Reprinted with permission of the editors and Michigan State University Press from *Community and Society*, by Ferdinand Tönnies, translated and edited by Charles P. Loomis, pp. 247–59. Copyright © 1957 by Michigan State University Press.

Goethe says the acting man is always "without conscience." In reality, the acting person often finds it necessary, if he "unscrupulously" follows his goal, to repress or overcome his conscientiousness. On account of this necessity, many consider themselves justified in despising or disowning such feelings, and sometimes they even find their satisfaction in bravado and arrogance, making themselves free from all such considerations.

This means, therefore, that on the one hand there is the simple emotional (impulsive) and, therefore, irrational volition and action, whereas on the other there is the simple rational volition and action in which the means are arranged, a condition which often stands in conflict with the feelings. Between these two extremes all real volition and action takes place. The consideration that most volition and action resembles or is inclined toward either one or the other makes it possible to establish the concepts of natural will and rational will, which concepts are rightly applied only in this sense. I call them normal concepts. What they represent are ideal types, and they should serve as standards by which reality may be recognized and described.

Gemeinschaft and Gesellschaft. It is not a question of contrasting the rational will with the nonrational will, because intellect and reason belong to natural will as well as to rational will. Indeed, intellect in natural will attains its fruition in the creative, formative, and artistic ability and works and in the spirit of the genius. This is true even though in its elementary forms natural will means nothing more than a direct, naïve, and therefore emotional volition and action, whereas, on the other hand, rational will is most frequently characterized by consciousness. To the latter belongs manufacturing as contrasted with creation; therefore, we speak of mechanical work (as expressed in the German and other languages) referring to forging plans, machinations, weaving intrigues, or fabrications which are directed to the objective of bringing forth the means, the exclusive determination of which is that of producing the outward effects necessary to attain our desired ends.

When these concepts are applied to associations, it should not be understood that we are thinking only of the regular motives leading to the entrance into an association, creating of a confederation, or organizing of a union or special interest group, or even the founding of a commonwealth. It is, however, of importance to recognize what motives lie at the basis of and explain the existence of all kinds of association or cause their persistence, and while we are here interested only in positive bases, this holds also for negative motives upon which persistence may be based. In this connection it is not to be understood that the bases belong fundamentally and persistently either to the one or the other category, that is, of natural will or rational will. On the contrary a dynamic condition or process is assumed which corresponds to the changeable elements of human feeling and thinking. The motives fluctuate so that they are now of one category, then of the other. However, wherever such development takes place a certain regularity or even "law," in the sense of a tendency toward abstract rational forms, may be observed.

I call all kinds of association in which natural will predominates Gemeinschaft, all those which are formed and fundamentally conditioned by rational will, Gesellschaft. Thus, these concepts signify the model qualities of the essence and the tendencies of being bound together. Thus, both names are in the present context stripped of their connotation as designating social entities or groups, or even collective or artificial persons; the essence of both Gemeinschaft and Gesellschaft is found interwoven in all kinds of associations, as will be shown.

SOCIAL SYSTEMS

1. Relationships, collectives, social organizations. As social entities or forms, I differentiate: (1) Social relationships *(Verhältnisse)*, (2) Collectives *(Samtschaften)*, (3) Social organizations or corporate bodies *(Körperschaften)* (leagues, fellowships, associations, or special-interest groups).

The third form is always thought of as a kind of human person capable of creating a definite unified will which, as the will of the natural or artificial persons belonging to it, binds and constrains them to act in conformity with such will, which may be directed inwardly or outwardly. In the social relationship it is not the relationship itself which is so considered, even though it be designated by a special name. However, it is essential that its subjects or bearers, who may be considered as "members" of the relationship, are conscious of it as a relationship which they will affirmatively and thus establish as an existing reality. This manner of establishing a social relationship represents in embryonic or emergent form what is evolved to perfection in the establishment of a social organization or corporation capable of willing and acting.

The collective lies between the social relationship and the social organization. It is thought of as a plurality which, like the social organization, includes a multitude of persons so held together that there result common intentions, desires, inclinations, disinclinations—in short, common feelings and ways of thinking. However, the collective is not capable of real volition. It can reach no decision as long as it does not "organize" itself into a committee, special-interest group, or council.

2. The social relationship. The social relationship is the most general and simplest social entity or form. It also has the deepest foundation, because it rests partly upon the original, natural, and actual conditions as the causes of connections, of mutual dependence, and of attachment among men, and because it rests partly on the most fundamental, most universal, and most necessary requirements of human beings. The one basis, like the other, is raised to consciousness with different effects. If a natural relationship exists, as for example between my brother and me, on one hand, or between my brother-in-law, my stepbrother, adopted or foster brother and me, on the other, I have the feeling that we are intimate, that we affirm each other's existence, that ties exist between us, that we know each other and to a certain extent are sympathetic toward each other, trusting and wishing each other well. This is true although in the latter case, involving persons who are not blood brothers, the relationship is not so natural as in the first where I know the same mother gave birth to both my brother and me. From this it follows that we have certain values in common, whether it be that we are obliged to manage an estate together, or that we divide possessions as inheritances between us, or that the matter of intellectual goods or ideals is involved. At any rate, out of each such relationship, even between two, there results the recognition and acknowledgment of the social relationship as such on the part of each and therefore the knowledge of each that definite mutual action must regularly result therefrom. This action is expected and demanded of each by the other, and each expects and demands of himself that it be carried out in relation to the other. In this lies the embryo of "rights" which each claims for himself but also concedes to the other, as well as "duties" to which one feels obligated but which one puts upon oneself knowing that the other party wills that he be and considers that he is so obligated.

However, when I become conscious of my most urgent needs and find that I can neither satisfy them out of my own volition nor out of a natural relation, this means that I must do something to satisfy my need; that is, engage in free activity which is bound only by the requirement or possibly conditioned by the need but not by consideration for other people. Soon I perceive that I must work on other people in order to influence them to deliver or give something to me which I need. Possibly in restricted individual cases my mere requests will be granted, as, for example, in the case of a piece of bread or a glass of water. However, as a rule when one is not receiving something in a Gemeinschaft-like relationship, such as from within the family, one must earn or buy it by labor, service, or money which has been earned previously as payment for labor or service.

I now enter or have already entered into a social relationship, but it is of a different kind. Its prototype is barter or exchange, including the more highly developed form of exchange, the sale and purchase of things or services, which are the same as things and are therefore thought of as capable of being exchanged for things or for other services. All action which is of an intellectual nature, and consequently oriented by reason, is of this type because comparison and thinking are necessary to it and furnish a basis for it. Social relationships which result from such barter or exchange are primarily momentary in that they involve a momentary common volition. However, they come to have duration partly through repetition resulting in regularity of the exchange act and partly through the lengthening of the individual act by the postponement of fulfillment on the part of one or both sides. In this latter case there results a relationship, the distinguishing characteristic of which is a one-sided or mutual "promise." It is a real social relationship of obligation or mutual dependence resulting first of all from mutual promises, even though they may be expressly stated by one side and only tacitly understood by the other as such an eventual promise.

Also, the relationships which come to

us from nature are in their essence mutual, are fulfilled in mutual performance. The relations produce this mutuality and demand, require, or make it necessary. Having these characteristics, they resemble the exchange relationship. However, the natural relationship is, by its very essence, of earlier origin than its subjects or members. In such natural relationships it is self-evident that action will take place and be willed in accordance with the relationship, whether it be what is contained on the one hand in the simplest relationships resulting from desire and inclination, from love or habit, or on the other hand from reason or intellect contained in the feeling of duty. These latter types of natural will change into one another, and each can be the basis of Gemeinschaft.

On the other hand, in the purest and most abstract contract relationship the contracting parties are thought of as separate, hitherto and otherwise independent, as strangers to each other, and perhaps even as hitherto and in other respects inimical persons. *Do, ut des* (I give, so that you will give) is the only principle of such a relationship. What I do for you, I do only as a means to effect your simultaneous, previous, or later service for me. Actually and really I want and desire only this. To get something from you is my end; my service is the means thereto, which I naturally contribute unwillingly. Only the aforesaid and anticipated result is the cause which determines my volition. This is the simplest form of rational will.

Relationships of the first type are to be classified under the concept Gemeinschaft, those of the other type under the concept of Gesellschaft, thus differentiating Gemeinschaft-like and Gesellschaft-like relationships. Gemeinschaft-like relationships differ to the extent that there is assumed, on the one hand, a real, even if not complete, equality in knowledge or volition, in power and in authority on the part of the participants, and on the other hand, an essential inequality in these respects. This also holds for the relations of Gesellschaft. In accordance with this distinction we shall differentiate between the fellowship type and the authoritative type of social relationship. Let us now consider this difference.

A. In Gemeinschaft-like relationships.
a. Fellowship type. The simplest fellowship type is represented by a pair who live together in a brotherly, comradely, and friendly manner, and it is most likely to exist when those involved are of the same age, sex, and sentiment, are engaged in the same activity or have the same intentions, or when they are united by one idea.

In legend and history such pairs occur frequently. The Greeks used to honor such friendships as those of Achilles and Patroclus, Orestes and Pylades, Epaminondas and Pelopidas, to the extent that to Aristotle is ascribed the paradox: He who has friends has no friend. In the German language and literature it is customary to designate such sentiments, the nature of which the Greeks glorified as mutual happiness and sorrow, as a brotherly relationship. This characterization is based more on the thought of the ideal than on actual observation, but it is correct in so far as brothers actually make the most natural as well as the most probable pairs of friends, more because of their origin than because of a motive.

b. Authoritative type. The relationship of father to child, as observations in everyday life will prove, is to be found in all the strata of society in all stages of culture. The weaker the child and the more it is in need of help, the greater the extent to which the relationship is represented by protection. Protection of necessity always carries with it authority as a condition, because protection regularly can be carried out only when the protected party follows the directions and even the commands of the protector. Although all authority has a tendency to change into the use of force, in the case of the father as well as the mother relationship such a tendency is arrested by love and tenderness. These sentiments, being of animal and vegetative origin, are more likely to be regularly accorded to a child born to a parent than to any other possessed and protected person. The general character of the father relationship can be easily extended to include similar relationships involving protection, examples of which are the stepfather, foster father, the general house father, and the guardian, even though these, as representatives of the father, do not necessarily legally stand in Gemeinschaft-like relation to the ward. The authority of the father is the prototype of all Gemeinschaft-like authority. It is especially true in the case of the priesthood, even though the basis may be different. This rests primarily upon mythological conceptions which place the father in Olympus or in heaven and perhaps ascribe numberless children to the father of the gods and men. Or in a less sensual, more refined form, the father may be represented by an only son whom the struggle against polytheism tends almost to identify with the father. Little wonder that the title Pope (*Papa*, literally "father") in the original church of all bishops was raised to the pinnacle of spiritual dignity in the Roman Church and that in the Oriental Church the especially high priests are called fathers (*Popen*) in the language of the common people. Also, world and political authority, which is often mixed with and may not be less sanctified than the spiritual, easily takes on the character of the well-wishing father, as is most plainly expressed in the term "father" of a country. The fatherly authority, however, is the special case of authority of age, and the prestige-giving quality of age expresses itself most perfectly in the authority of the father. This easily explains the eminence which is attributed to the senator in the worldly and the presbyter in the spiritual commonwealth.

c. Mixed relationships. In many Gemeinschaft-like relationships the essence of authority and that of fellowship are mixed. This is the case in the most important of the relationships of Gemeinschaft, the lasting relation between man and woman which is conditioned through sexual needs and reproduction, whether or not the relationship is called marriage.

B. In Gesellschaft-like relationships. The difference between the fellowship and authoritative types is also to be found in the Gesellschaft-like relationships. It can, however, be derived only from the fact that the authority is based upon a free contract whether between individuals, as service contracts, or by agreement of many to recognize and place a master or head over them and to obey him conditionally or unconditionally. This may be a natural person or a collective person which results directly from individuals uniting in a society, social organization, or corporate body which is capable of volition and action and can be represented through its own totality. The Gesellschaft-like authority attains its consummation in the modern state, a consummation which many predecessors strove to attain until the democratic republic came into existence and allowed for development beyond the Gesellschaft-like foundation. The actual authority results, however, in the simple Gesellschaft-like relationship, from the difference in the power of two parties, as in the labor contract. Such authority results from contracts made between the individual "employer" and individual "employee," and also from the condition out of which come "peace treaties" between victor and conquered. Apparently it is a contract, but in actuality it is coercion and abuse.

3. The collective. The second concept of social entity or form is that of the collective. I make distinctions between natural, psychical, and social collectives. Our concept concerns only social collectives but these rest partly on natural and partly on psychical collectives, partly on both. This is because the essence of a social collective is to be found in the natural and psycho-logical relationships forming the basis of the collective and are consciously affirmed and willed. This phenomenon appears everywhere in the life of a people and in many forms of mutualities, as, for example, in forms of life and customs, superstitions and religion. It is especially in evidence in the distinguishing characteristic through which a segment of a people, that is, certain classes, are given prominence, nobility, and authority. A distinguishing characteristic which has this function is partly an objective phenomenon and partly something positive in the people's consciousness. The consciousness of belonging to a controlling estate makes its appearance in a distinct manner as pride and haughtiness—feelings which in turn are coupled with the submission and modesty of those "lower" classes over which authority is exercised so long as the controlling estates, as such, are honored, and so long as their excellence, or even their divinity, is believed in.

In the case of the collective the concepts of Gemeinschaft and Gesellschaft should also be applied. The social collective has the characteristics of Gemeinschaft in so far as the members think of such a grouping as a gift of nature or created by a supernatural will, as is expressed in the simplest and most naive manner in the Indian caste system. Here, to be fixed to a given calling is just as necessary and natural as being born, and the professional estate or group has the same significance as a large family for which the pursuit and means of making a livelihood, even if this should be accomplished by thievery, is represented as something inherited which it is a duty to retain and nurture. In all systems of ranks or estates, traces of this condition are to be found because (and to the extent that) a complete emancipation from the social relationships established at birth seldom occurred and was often impossible. Thus, man as a rule submits to the social status in which parents and forebears, or, as it is wont to be expressed, "God," has placed him as if it were his lot to bear, even though it be felt as a burden, which, however, is habit and is lightened by the recognition that it cannot be changed. Indeed, within these limits there can exist an intellectual self-consciousness which affirms this estate (rank) even though it be recognized as one of the less significant. This intellectual basis manifests itself partly as the group extols itself for certain superiorities or virtues, the lack of which in the dominating estate is noticed and complained about. Also, the intellectual basis is to be found partly in the consciousness of special knowledge and skill of the group, as, for example, its art, craftsmanship, and skill, which are thought of as being at least the equivalent of the other honored or ruling estates.

Consciousness of a social collective has different results when directed toward the attainment of definite and important ends which it knows to be and claims are its own characteristics. This happens in a pronounced way in the political and intellectual struggle in which the social strata of a people stand against each other as classes. The more the consciousness of authority as a feeling of superiority results in putting one class in such a position of power as to force the lower class to stay in its place, the more this latter will strive toward the attainment of equality and therefore the more indignant it becomes concerning oppression and arrogance on the part of the controlling class, which it attempts to restrict and displace.

Whether this process is called class struggle (*Klassenkampf*) or struggle of estates (*Ständekampf*) is not important. The struggle among the estates usually takes place earlier, is less radical, and can be allayed. The lower estates strive only for the opportunity to participate in the satisfactions of life and fundamentals of authority, allowing the controlling estate to remain in power. This latter remains in

power by proclaiming its own fitness and disparaging that of the lower estates and by exerting effort to reduce these lower strata to submission.

The class struggle is more unconditional. It recognizes no estates, no natural masters. In the foreground of the consciousness of the whole class which feels that it is propertyless and therefore oppressed, stands the ideal of the Gemeinschaft of property in field and soil and all the implements of labor. These latter have been acquired through the art of trade or as inherited property belonging by "law" to the small minority which, as the propertied class, is set off against the propertyless class. Therefore, the class struggle becomes more conscious and general than the struggle among the estates. However, even though there be no definite form of struggle there is a corresponding consciousness which makes itself felt in many ways. The great propertyless masses prefer to think of themselves as the people (*Volk*), and the narrow class which is in control of property and its use thinks of itself as society, even though each expression is all inclusive. "The" people (*Volk*), as in the case of the estate, resembles the Gemeinschaft; "the" society, like the class, has, in the sense in which it is here used, the basic characteristic of Gesellschaft.

4.   *The social organization.*   The third and most important category of pure or theoretical sociology is the social organization or corporate body, a social body or union known by many other names. It is never anything natural, neither can it be understood as a mere physical phenomenon. It is completely and essentially a social phenomenon and must be considered as composed of several individuals. Capacity for unified volition and action, a capacity which is demonstrated most clearly as competency to pass resolutions, characterizes it. Just as the thinking individual is capable of making decisions, so is a group of several individuals when they continuously agree or agree to the extent that there prevails and is recognized a definite will as the will of all or sufficient consensus to be the will of the social organization or corporate body. Thus, the volition of such a group can be represented by the will of a natural person behind whom the will of the whole social organization or corporate body stands. Continuing our discussion of social organizations or corporate bodies, we may make the following observations:

(1) A social organization or corporate body can originate from natural relationships provided these are social relationships. In this connection, kinship, the most universal and natural bond which embraces human beings, comes to our attention. The most important social organization or corporate body which originates therefrom and which among all known peoples occurs as the original form of a common life is the kinship group, the gens, clan, or whatever name is applied to designate this ancient union or unity.

Whether or not the totality of adult persons includes the women, whether their council ends in agreement which is sanctioned by a supposed will of God, or whether they rejoice in and willingly accept the decisions of a leader and head, it is under these conditions that there is formed the embryo of a consciousness which matures into something beyond a mere feeling of belonging together, and there is established and affirmed an enduring self or ego in the totality.

(2) A common relation to the soil tends to associate people who may be kinsfolk or believe themselves to be such. Neighborhood, the fact that they live together, is the basis of their union; it leads to counseling and through deliberations to resolutions. Here again the two principles of fellowship and authority will be involved. The outstanding example of an association of this type is the rural village community, which attains its consummation in the cultivation of the soil practiced

in common and the possession of common property in village fields or land held in common by the village, and in the Mark-community which comes to represent the unity of several neighboring village communities which originally may have formed one unit.

The rural village community is frequently identical with a great family or clan but the more alien elements are taken in the more it loses its kinship characteristics. The bond of field and soil and living together first takes its place along with and later more and more supplants the bond of common ancestry. Especially when an alien tribe and its leaders become the conquerors of a territory and establish themselves in the seats of control without extirpating or driving out all the former residents and owners does this tendency manifest itself, molding a new people *(Volk)* from the two groups, even though the one was subjected to new masters. The existence of the village community as a social organization or corporate body ordinarily continues in the form of a fellowship. Such a village community, however, may be modified by the power and rights of feudal lords.

(3) In the more intimate and close living together in the town, the fellowship and cooperative quality attains a new level. Living together tends to depend less on common nature. People not related by blood tend to assemble in the towns since these originally were walled-in villages or strongholds whose inhabitants were forced to cooperate for defense and for the maintenance of peace and order among themselves and thereby to form a political community, either under the rule of a lord or as citizens of equal rights. This was the great mission and service of the town *(Stadt)* community, the *"Polis"* which grew to be that commonwealth which later in Europe and elsewhere up to our time has bequeathed its character and name to the state *(Staat)*, the mightiest of all corporate bodies. That assembly of the sovereign

people, the religious association *(Ekklesia)*, the other great commonwealth of the Roman and post-Roman period, loaned its name to the Church and spread its glory throughout the world in a similar manner.

These social bodies and communities retain their common root in that original state of belonging together, which according to our concept is the Gemeinschaft. Indeed, although the original state of common being, living, and working is changed, it retains and is able to renew its mental and political form and its cooperative functions. Thus, a people *(Volk)* which feels itself bound together by a common language, when held together within a national association or even when only striving to become a nation, will desire to be represented in a unity or *Volksgemeinschaft*, which may become intensified by national consciousness and pride, but may also thereby lose its original genuineness.

5. Capitalistic, middle-class, or bourgeois society (bürgerliche Gesellschaft). During this development, the original qualities of Gemeinschaft may be lost because there takes place a continued change in the original basis upon which living together rests. This change reaches its consummation in what is frequently designated as individualism. Through this development social life in and of itself is not diminished, but social life of the Gemeinschaft is impaired and a new phenomenon develops out of the needs, interests, desires and decisions of persons who previously worked cooperatively together and are acting and dealing one with another. This new phenomenon, the "capitalistic society," increases in power and gradually attains the ascendancy. Tending as it does to be cosmopolitan and unlimited in size, it is the most distinct form of the many phenomena represented by the sociological concept of the Gesellschaft.

A great transformation takes place. Whereas previously the whole of life was nurtured and arose from the profoundness of the people *(Volk)*, the capitalistic society

through a long process spreads itself over the totality of this people, indeed over the whole of mankind. As a totality of individuals and families it is essentially a collective of economic character composed primarily of those who partake in that wealth which, as land and capital, represents the necessary means to the production of goods of all kinds. Within narrow or far-flung borders which are determined by actual or supposed kinship bonds, of the existence of which the language group is the most valuable sign, it constructs its state, that is to say, a kind of unity resembling a town community which is capable of willing and acting. It develops as the capitalistic middle-class republic and apparently finally attains its perfection in the social republic. It considers the state a means of attaining its ends, of which not the least important is protecting its person and property as well as the intellectual attitude which gives status and honor to its supporters.

However, since this capitalistic middle-class society cannot, without betraying itself, admit its uniqueness as a collective of Gesellschaft in contradistinction to the people *(Volk)* or, so to speak, herald this difference by raising its own flag, it can only assert its existence through claiming to be identical with, as well as representative and advocate of, the whole people to which it furnishes guidance. This process, which does not stop with conferring equal political rights on all citizens, to a certain extent closes the always widening hiatus between the wealth monopoly of the narrow and real Gesellschaft and the poverty of the people, but it cannot change the essential character of the hiatus. Indeed, it deepens it, spreading and strengthening the consciousness of the "social question."

By means of political and other intellectual organization promoted by town and, to a greater extent, by city life, the consciousness of the Gesellschaft gradually becomes the consciousness of an increasing mass of the people. The people come more and more to think of the state as a means and tool to be used in bettering their condition, destroying the monopoly of wealth of the few, winning a share in the products. Thus, the laborer would be allowed a share in proper proportion to his reasonable needs and the leaders in pro-duction their share of certain goods which are to be divided for consumption, and those things suitable for continued common utilization would be retained as common property of the Gesellschaft, which is to say of the people or their organized association, the state.

2

The nature of the city

Max Weber

ECONOMIC CHARACTER OF THE CITY: MARKET SETTLEMENT

The many definitions of the city have only one element in common: namely that the city consists simply of a collection of one or more separate dwellings but is a relatively closed settlement. Customarily, though not exclusively, in cities the houses are built closely to each other, often, today, wall to wall. This massing of elements interpenetrates the everyday concept of the "city" which is thought of quantitatively as a large locality. In itself this is not imprecise for the city often represents a locality and dense settlement of dwellings forming a colony so extensive that personal reciprocal acquaintance of the inhabitants is lacking. However, if interpreted in this way only very large localities could qualify as cities; moreover it would be ambiguous, for various cultural factors determine the size at which "impersonality" tends to appear. Precisely this impersonality was ab-

Reprinted with permission of the editors and Macmillan Publishing Co., Inc., from *The City*, by Max Weber, translated and edited by Don Martindale and Gertrud Neuwirth, pp. 71–74. Copyright © 1958 by The Free Press, a Corporation. Footnotes have been renumbered.

First published in *Archiv für Sozialwissenschaft und Sozialpolitik*, vol. 47, p. 621 ff. (1921). Last edition: *Wirtschaft und Gesellschaft* (Tübingen: J. C. B. Mohr, 1956) vol. 2, p. 735 ff. —All the notes in this translation are those of the editors.

sent in many historical localities possessing the legal character of cities. Even in contemporary Russia there are villages comprising many thousands of inhabitants which are, thus, larger than many old "cities" (for example, in the Polish colonial area of the German East) which had only a few hundred inhabitants. Both in terms of what it would include and what it would exclude size alone can hardly be sufficient to define the city.

Economically defined, the city is a settlement the inhabitants of which live primarily off trade and commerce rather than agriculture. However, it is not altogether proper to call all localities "cities" which are dominated by trade and commerce. This would include in the concept "city" colonies made up of family members and maintaining a single, practically hereditary trade establishment such as the "trade villages" of Asia and Russia. It is necessary to add a certain "versatility" of practiced trades to the characteristics of the city. However, this in itself does not appear suitable as the single distinguishing characteristic of the city either.

Economic versatility can be established in at least two ways: by the presence of a feudal estate or a market. The economic and political needs of a feudal or princely estate can encourage specialization in trade products in providing a demand for which work is performed and goods are bartered. However, even though the *oikos* of a lord or prince is as large as a city, a colony of artisans and small merchants bound to villein services is not customarily called a "city" even though historically a large proportion of important "cities" originated in such settlements.[1] In cities of such origin the products for a prince's court often remained a highly important, even chief, source of income for the settlers.

The other method of establishing economic versatility is more generally important for the "city"; this is the existence in the place of settlement of a regular rather than an occasional exchange of goods. The market becomes an essential component in the livelihood of the settlers. To be sure, not every "market" converted the locality in which it was found into a city. The periodic fairs and yearly foreign-trade markets at which traveling merchants met at fixed times to sell their goods in wholesale or retail lots to each other or to consumers often occurred in places which we would call "villages."

Thus, we wish to speak of a "city" only in cases where the local inhabitants satisfy an economically substantial part of their daily wants in the local market, and to an essential extent by products which the local population and that of the immediate hinterland produced for sale in the market or acquired in other ways. In the meaning employed here the "city" is a market place. The local market forms the economic center of the colony in which, due to the specialization in economic products, both the nonurban population and urbanites satisfy their wants for articles of trade and commerce. Wherever it appeared as a configuration different from the country it was normal for the city to be both a lordly or princely residence as well as a market place. It simultaneously possessed centers of both kinds, *oikos* and market and frequently in addition to the regular market it also served as periodic foreign markets of traveling merchants. In the meaning of the word here, the city is a "market settlement."

Often the existence of a market rests upon the concessions and guarantees of protection by a lord or prince. They were often interested in such things as a regular supply of foreign commercial articles and trade products, in tolls, in moneys for escorts and other protection fees, in market tariffs and taxes from law suits. However, the lord or prince might also hope to profit from the local settlement of tradesmen and merchants capable of paying taxes and, as soon as the market settlement arose around the market, from land rents arising therefrom. Such opportunities were of especial importance to the lord or prince since they represented chances for monetary revenues and the increase in his treasure of precious metal.

However, the city could lack any attachment, physical or otherwise, to a lordly or princely residence. This was the case when it originated as a pure market settlement at a suitable intersection point *(Umschlageplatz)*[2] where the means of transportation were changed by virtue of concession to nonresident lords or princes or usurpation by the interested parties themselves. This could assume the form of concessions to entrepreneurs—permitting them to lay out a market and recruit settlers for it. Such capitalistic establishment of cities was especially frequent in medieval frontier areas, particularly in East, North, and Central Europe. Historically, though not as a rule, the practice has appeared throughout the world.

---

[1] For the place of the household or *oikos*-economy cf. Max Weber, *General Economic History,* trans. Frank H. Knight (Glencoe: The Free Press, 1950) pp. 48, 58, 124 ff., 131, 146, 162; and Johannes Hase Broek, *Griechische Wirtschaftsgeschichte* (Tübingen: J. C. B. Mohr, 1931) pp. 15, 24, 27, 29, 38, 46, 69, 284.

[2] Charles H. Cooley's theory of transportation took the break in communication, either physical or economic, as the most critical of all factors for the formation of the city.

Without any attachment to the court of a prince or without princely concessions, the city could arise through the association of foreign invaders, naval warriors, or commercial settlers or, finally, native parties interested in the carrying trade. This occurred frequently in the early Middle Ages. The resultant city could be a pure market place. However, it is more usual to find large princely or patrimonial households and a market conjoined. In this case the eminent household as one contact point of the city could satisfy its want either primarily by means of a natural economy (that is by villein service or natural service or taxes placed upon the artisans and merchants dependent on it) or it could supply itself more or less secondarily by barter in the local market as that market's most important buyer. The more pronounced the latter relation the more distinct the market foundation of the city looms and the city ceases by degrees to be a mere appendaged market settlement alongside the *oikos*. Despite attachment to the large household it then became a market city. As a rule the quantitative expansion of the original princely city and its economic importance go hand in hand with an increase in the satisfaction of wants in the market by the princely household and other large urban households attached to that of the prince as courts of vassals or major officials.

3

The metropolis and mental life

Georg Simmel

The deepest problems of modern life derive from the claim of the individual to preserve the autonomy and individuality of his existence in the face of overwhelming social forces, of historical heritage, of external culture, and of the technique of life. The fight with nature which primitive man has to wage for his *bodily* existence attains in this modern man its latest transformation. The 18th century called upon man to free himself of all the historical bonds in the state and in religion, in morals and in economics. Man's nature, originally good and common to all, should develop unhampered. In addition to more liberty, the 19th century demanded the functional specialization of man and his work; this specialization makes one individual incomparable to another, and each of them indispensable to the highest possible extent. However, this specialization makes each man the more directly dependent upon the supplementary activities of all others. Nietzsche sees the full development of the individual conditioned by the most ruthless struggle of individuals; socialism believes in the suppression of all competition for the same reason. Be that is it may, in all these positions the same basic motive is at work: the person resists to being leveled down and worn out by a social-technological mechanism. An inquiry into the inner meaning of specifically modern life and its products, into the soul of the cultural body, so to speak, must seek to solve the equation which structures like the metropolis set up between the individual and the superindividual contents of life. Such an inquiry must answer the question of how the personality accommo-

Reprinted with permission of the editor and Macmillan Publishing Co., Inc., from *The Sociology of Georg Simmel*, edited by Kurt H. Wolff, translated by H. H. Gerth and C. Wright Mills, pt. 5, chap. 4, pp. 409–424. Copyright 1950, renewed 1978, by The Free Press. The footnote has been renumbered.

dates itself in the adjustments to external forces. This will be my task today.

The psychological basis of the metropolitan type of individuality consists in the *intensification of nervous stimulation* which results from the swift and uninterrupted change of outer and inner stimuli. Man is a differentiating creature. His mind is stimulated by the difference between a momentary impression and the one which preceded it. Lasting impressions, impressions which differ only slightly from one another, impressions which take a regular and habitual course and show regular and habitual contrasts—all these use up, so to speak, less consciousness than does the rapid crowding of changing images, the sharp discontinuity in the grasp of a single glance, and the unexpectedness of onrushing impressions. These are the psychological conditions which the metropolis creates. With each crossing of the street, with the tempo and multiplicity of economic, occupational, and social life, the city sets up a deep contrast with small town and rural life with reference to the sensory foundations of psychic life. The metropolis exacts from man as a discriminating creature a different amount of consciousness than does rural life. Here the rhythm of life and sensory mental imagery flows more slowly, more habitually, and more evenly. Precisely in this connection the sophisticated character of metropolitan psychic life becomes understandable—as over against small town life which rests more upon deeply felt and emotional relationships. These latter are rooted in the more unconscious layers of the psyche and grow most readily in the steady rhythm of uninterrupted habituations. The intellect, however, has its locus in the transparent, conscious, higher layers of the psyche; it is the most adaptable of our inner forces. In order to accommodate to change and to the contrast of phenomena, the intellect does not require any shocks and inner upheavals; it is only through such upheavals that the more conservative mind could accommodate to the metropolitan rhythm of events. Thus the metropolitan type of man—which, of course, exists in a thousand individual variants—develops an organ protecting him against the threatening currents and discrepancies of his external environment which would uproot him. He reacts with his head instead of his heart. In this an increased awareness assumes the psychic prerogative. Metropolitan life, thus, underlies a heightened awareness and a predominance of intelligence in metropolitan man. The reaction to metropolitan phenomena is shifted to that organ which is least sensitive and quite remote from the depth of the personality. Intellectuality is thus seen to preserve subjective life against the overwhelming power of metropolitan life, and intellectuality branches out in many directions and is integrated with numerous discrete phenomena.

The metropolis has always been the seat of the money economy. Here the multiplicity and concentration of economic exchange gives an importance to the means of exchange which the scantiness of rural commerce would not have allowed. Money economy and the dominance of the intellect are intrinsically connected. They share a matter-of-fact attitude in dealing with men and with things; and, in this attitude, a formal justice is often coupled with an inconsiderate hardness. The intellectually sophisticated person is indifferent to all genuine individuality, because relationships and reactions result from it which cannot be exhausted with logical operations. In the same manner, the individuality of phenomena is not commensurate with the pecuniary principle. Money is concerned only with what is common to all: it asks for the exchange value, it reduces all quality and individuality to the question: How much? All intimate emotional relations between persons are founded in their individuality, whereas in rational relations man is reckoned with like a number, like an element which is in itself indifferent. Only the objective measurable achievement is of interest. Thus metropolitan man reckons with his merchants and customers, his domestic servants and often even with persons with whom he is obliged to have social intercourse. These features of intellectuality contrast with the nature of the small circle in which the inevitable knowledge of individuality as inevitably produces a warmer tone of behavior, a behavior which is beyond a mere objective balancing of service and return. In the sphere of the economic psychology of the small group it is of importance that under primitive conditions production serves the customer who orders the good, so that the producer and the consumer are acquainted. The modern metropolis, however, is supplied almost entirely by production for the market, that is, for entirely unknown purchasers who never personally enter the producer's actual field of vision. Through this anonymity the interests of each party acquire an unmerciful matter-of-factness; and the intellectually calculating economic egoisms of both parties need not fear any deflection because of the imponderables of personal relationships. The money economy dominates the metropolis; it has displaced the last survivals of domestic production and the direct barter of goods; it minimizes from day to day the amount of work ordered by customers. The matter-of-fact attitude is obviously so intimately interrelated with the money economy, which is dominant in the metropolis, that nobody can say whether the intellectualistic mentality first promoted the money economy or whether the latter determined the former. The metropolitan way of life is certainly the most fertile soil for this reciprocity, a point which I shall document merely by citing the dictum of the most eminent English constitutional historian: throughout the whole course of English history, London has never acted as England's heart but often as England's intellect and always as her moneybag!

In certain seemingly insignificant traits, which lie upon the surface of life, the same psychic currents characteristically unite. Modern mind has become more and more calculating. The calculative exactness of practical life which the money economy has brought about corresponds to the ideal of natural science: to transform the world into an arithmetic problem, to fix every part of the world by mathematical formulas. Only money economy has filled the days of so many people with weighting, calculating, with numerical determinations, with a reduction of qualitative values to quantitative ones. Through the calculative nature of money a new precision, a certainty in the definition of identities and differences, an unambiguousness in agreements and arrangements has been brought about in the relations of life-elements—just as externally this precision has been effected by the universal diffusion of pocket watches. However, the conditions of metropolitan life are at once cause and effect of this trait. The relationships and affairs of the typical metropolitan usually are so varied and complex that without the strictest punctuality in promises and services the whole structure would break down into an inextricable chaos. Above all, this necessity is brought about by the aggregation of so many people with such differentiated interests, who must integrate their relations and activities into a highly complex organism. If all clocks and watches in Berlin would suddenly go wrong in different ways, even if only by one hour, all economic life and communication of the city would be disrupted for a long time. In addition an apparently mere external factor, long distances, would make all waiting and broken appointments result in an ill-afforded waste of time. Thus, the technique of metropolitan life is unimaginable without the most punctual integration of all activities and mutual relations into a stable and impersonal time schedule. Here again the general conclusions of this entire task of reflection become obvious, namely, that from each point on the surface of existence—however closely attached to the surface alone—one may drop a sounding into the depth of the psyche so that all the most banal externalities of life finally are connected with the ultimate decisions concerning the meaning and style of life. Punctuality, calculability, exactness are forced upon life by the complexity and extension of metropolitan existence and are not only most intimately connected with its money economy and intellectualistic character. These traits must also color the contents of life and favor the exclusion of those irrational, instinctive, sovereign traits and impulses which aim at determining the mode of life from within, instead of receiving the general and precisely schematized form of life from without. Even though sovereign types of personality, characterized by irrational impulses, are by no means impossible in the city, they are, nevertheless, opposed to typical city life. The passionate hatred of men like Ruskin and Nietzsche for the metropolis is understandable in these terms. Their natures discovered the values of life alone in the unschematized existence which cannot be defined with precision for all alike. From the same source of this hatred of the metropolis surged their hatred of money economy and of the intellectualism of modern existence.

The same factors which have thus coalesced into the exactness and minute precision of the form of life have coalesced into a structure of the highest impersonality; on the other hand, they have promoted a highly personal subjectivity. There is perhaps no psychic phenomenon which has been so unconditionally reserved to the metropolis as has the blasé attitude. The blasé attitude results first from the rapidly changing and closely compressed contrasting stimulations of the nerves. From this the enhancement of metropolitan intellectuality, also, seems originally to stem. Therefore, stupid people who are not intellectually alive in the first place usually are not exactly blasé. A life in boundless pursuit of pleasure makes one blasé because it agitates the nerves to their strongest reactivity for such a long time that they finally cease to react at all. In the same way, through the rapidity and contradictoriness of their changes, more harmless impressions force such violent responses, tearing the nerves so brutally hither and thither, that their last reserves of strength are spent; and if one remains in the same milieu they have no time to gather new strength. An incapacity thus emerges to react to new sensations with the appropriate energy. This constitutes that blasé attitude which, in fact, every metropolitan child shows when compared with children of quieter and less changeable milieus.

This physiological source of the metropolitan blasé attitude is joined by another source which flows from the money economy. The essence of the blasé attitude consists in the blunting of discrimination. This does not mean that the objects are not perceived, as is the case with the half-wit, but rather that the meaning and differing values of things, and thereby the things themselves, are experienced as insubstantial. They appear to the blasé person in an evenly flat and gray tone; no one object deserves preference over any other. This mood is the faithful subjective reflection of the completely internalized money economy. By being the equivalent to all the manifold things in one and the same way, money becomes the most frightful leveler. For money expresses all qualitative differences of things in terms of "how much?" Money, with all its colorlessness and indifference, becomes the common denominator of all values; irreparably it hollows out the core of things, their individuality, their specific value, and their incomparability. All things float with equal specific gravity in the constantly moving stream of money. All things lie on the same level and differ from one another only in the size of the area which they cover. In the individual case this coloration, or rather discoloration, of things through their money equivalence may be unnoticeably minute. However, through the relations of the rich to the objects to be had for money, perhaps even through the total character which the mentality of the contemporary public everywhere imparts to these objects, the exclusively pecuniary evaluation of objects has become quite considerable. The large cities, the main seats of the money exchange, bring the purchasability of things to the fore much more impressively than do smaller localities. That is why cities are also the genuine locale of the blasé attitude. In the blasé attitude the concentration of men and things stimulate the nervous system of the individual to its highest achievement so that it attains its peak. Through the mere quantitative intensification of the same conditioning factors this achievement is transformed into its opposite and appears in the peculiar adjustment of the blasé attitude. In this phenomenon the nerves find in the refusal to react to their stimulation the last possibility of accommodating to the contents and forms of metropolitan life. The self-preservation of certain personalities is bought at the price of devaluating the whole objective world, a devaluation which in the end unavoidably drags one's own personality down into a feeling of the same worthlessness.

Whereas the subject of this form of existence has to come to terms with it entirely for himself, his self-preservation in the face of the large city demands from him a no less negative behavior of a social nature. This mental attitude of metropolitans toward one another we may designate, from a formal point of view, as reserve. If so many inner reactions were responses to the continuous external contacts with innumerable people as are those in the small town, where one knows almost everybody one meets and where one has a positive

relation to almost everyone, one would be completely atomized internally and come to an unimaginable psychic state. Partly this psychological fact, partly the right to distrust which men have in the face of the touch-and-go elements of metropolitan life, necessitates our reserve. As a result of this reserve we frequently do not even know by sight those who have been our neighbors for years. And it is this reserve which in the eyes of the small-town people makes us appear to be cold and heartless. Indeed, if I do not deceive myself, the inner aspect of this outer reserve is not only indifference but, more often than we are aware, it is a slight aversion, a mutual strangeness and repulsion, which will break into hatred and fight at the moment of a closer contact, however caused. The whole inner organization of such an extensive communicative life rests upon an extremely varied hierarchy of sympathies, indifferences, and aversions of the briefest as well as of the most permanent nature. The sphere of indifference in this hierarchy is not as large as might appear on the surface. Our psychic activity still responds to almost every impression of somebody else with a somewhat distinct feeling. The unconscious, fluid and changing character of this impression seems to result in a state of indifference. Actually this indifference would be just as unnatural as the diffusion of indiscriminate mutual suggestion would be unbearable. From both these typical dangers of the metropolis, indifference and indiscriminate suggestibility, antipathy protects us. A latent antipathy and the preparatory stage of practical antagonism effect the distances and aversions without which this mode of life could not at all be led. The extent and the mixture of this style of life, the rhythm of its emergence and disappearance, the forms in which it is satisfied—all these, with the unifying motives in the narrower sense, form the inseparable whole of the metropolitan style of life. What appears in the metropolitan style of life directly as dissociation is in reality only one of its elemental forms of socialization.

This reserve with its overtone of hidden aversion appears in turn as the form or the cloak of a more general mental phenomenon of the metropolis: it grants to the individual a kind and an amount of personal freedom which has no analogy whatsoever under other conditions. The metropolis goes back to one of the large developmental tendencies of social life as such, to one of the few tendencies for which an approximately universal formula can be discovered. The earliest phase of social formations found in historical as well as in contemporary social structures is this: a relatively small circle firmly closed against neighboring, strange, or in some way antagonistic circles. However, this circle is closely coherent and allows its individual members only a narrow field for the development of unique qualities and free, self-responsible movements. Political and kinship groups, parties and religious associations begin in this way. The self-preservation of very young associations requires the establishment of strict boundaries and a centripetal unity. Therefore they cannot allow the individual freedom and unique inner and outer development. From this stage social development proceeds at once in two different, yet corresponding, directions. To the extent to which the group grows—numerically, spatially, in significance and in content of life—to the same degree the group's direct, inner unity loosens, and the rigidity of the original demarcation against others is softened through mutual relations and connections. At the same time, the individual gains freedom of movement, far beyond the first jealous delimitation. The individual also gains a specific individuality to which the division of labor in the enlarged group gives both occasion and necessity. The state and Christianity, guilds and political parties, and innumerable other groups have developed according to this formula, however much, of course, the special conditions and forces of the respective groups have modified the general scheme. This scheme seems to me distinctly recognizable also in the evolution of individuality within urban life. The small-town life in Antiquity and in the Middle Ages set barriers against movement and relations of the individual toward the outside, and it set up barriers against individual independence and differentiation within the individual self. These barriers were such that under them modern man could not have breathed. Even today a metropolitan man who is placed in a small town feels a restriction similar, at least, in kind. The smaller the circle which forms our milieu is, and the more restricted those relations to others are which dissolve the boundaries of the individual, the more anxiously the circle guards the achievements, the conduct of life, and the outlook of the individual, and the more readily a quantitative and qualitative specialization would break up the framework of the whole little circle.

The ancient *polis* in this respect seems to have had the very character of a small town. The constant threat to its existence at the hands of enemies from near and afar effected strict coherence in political and military respects, a supervision of the citizen by the citizens, a jealousy of the whole against the individual whose particular life was suppressed to such a degree that he could compensate only by acting as a despot in his own household. The tremendous agitation and excitement, the unique colorfulness of Athenian life, can perhaps be understood in terms of the fact that a people of incomparably individualized personalities struggled against the constant inner and outer pressure of a de-individualizing small town. This produced a tense atmosphere in which the weaker individuals were suppressed and those of stronger natures were incited to prove themselves in the most passionate manner.

This is precisely why it was that there blossomed in Athens what must be called, without defining it exactly, "the general human character" in the intellectual development of our species. For we maintain factual as well as historical validity for the following connection: the most extensive and the most general contents and forms of life are most intimately connected with the most individual ones. They have a preparatory stage in common, that is, they find their enemy in narrow formations and groupings the maintenance of which places both of them into a state of defense against expanse and generality lying without and the freely moving individuality within. Just as in the feudal age, the "free" man was the one who derived his right merely from the narrow circle of a feudal association and was excluded from the larger social orbit—so today metropolitan man is "free" in a spiritualized and refined sense, in contrast to the pettiness and prejudices which hem in the small-town man. For the reciprocal reserve and indifference and the intellectual life conditions of large circles are never felt more strongly by the individual in their impact upon his independence than in the thickest crowd of the big city. This is because the bodily proximity and the narrowness of space makes the mental distance only the more visible. It is obviously only the obverse of this freedom if, under certain circumstances, one nowhere feels as lonely and lost as in the metropolitan crowd. For here as elsewhere it is by no means necessary that the freedom of man be reflected in his emotional life as comfort.

It is not only the immediate size of the area and the number of persons which, because of the universal historical correlation between the enlargement of the circle and the personal inner and outer freedom, has made the metropolis the locale of freedom. It is rather in transcending this visible expanse that any given city expands in a manner comparable to the way in which wealth develops; a certain amount of property increases in a quasiautomatical way in ever more rapid progression. As soon as a certain limit has been passed, the economic, personal, and intellectual relations of the citizenry, the sphere of intellectual predominance of the city over its hinterland, grow as in geometrical progression. Every gain in dynamic extension becomes a step, not for an equal, but for a new and larger extension. From every thread spinning out of the city, ever new threads grow as if by themselves, just as within the city the unearned increment of ground rent, through the mere increase in communication, brings the owner automatically increasing profits. At this point, the quantitative aspect of life is transformed directly into qualitative traits of character. The sphere of life of the small town is, in the main, self-contained and autarchic. For it is the decisive nature of the metropolis that its inner life overflows by waves into a farflung national or international area. Weimar is not an example to the contrary, since its significance was hinged upon individual personalities and died with them; whereas the metropolis is indeed characterized by its essential independence even from the most eminent individual personalities. This is the counterpart to the independence; and it is the price the individual pays for the independence, which he enjoys in the metropolis. The most significant characteristic of the metropolis is this functional extension beyond its physical boundaries. And this efficacy reacts in turn and gives weight, importance, and responsibility to metropolitan life. Man does not end with the limits of his body or the area comprising his immediate activity. Rather is the range of the person constituted by the sum of effects emanating from him temporarily and spatially. In the same way, a city consists of its total effects which extend beyond its immediate confines. Only this range is the city's actual extent in which its existence is expressed. This fact makes it obvious that individual freedom, the logical and historical complement of such extension, is not to be understood only in the negative sense of mere freedom of mobility and elimination of prejudices and petty philistinism. The essential point is that the particularity and incomparability, which ultimately every human being possesses, be somehow expressed in the working-out of a way of life. That we follow the laws of our own nature—and this after all is freedom—becomes obvious and convincing to ourselves and to others only if the expressions of this nature differ from the expressions of others. Only our unmistakability proves that our way of life has not been superimposed by others.

Cities are, first of all, seats of the highest economic division of labor. They produce thereby such extreme phenomena as in Paris the remunerative occupation of the *quatorzième*. They are persons who identify themselves by signs on their residences and who are ready at the dinner hour in correct attire, so that they can be quickly called upon if a dinner party should consist of 13 persons. In the measure of expansion, the city offers more and more the decisive conditions of the division of labor. It offers a circle which through its size can absorb a highly diverse variety of services. At the same time, the concentration of individuals and their struggle for customers compel the individual to specialize in a function from which he cannot be readily displaced by another. It is decisive that city life has transformed the struggle with nature for livelihood into an inter-human struggle for gain, which here is not granted by nature but by other men. For specialization does not flow only from the competition for gain but also from the underlying fact that the seller must always seek to call forth new and differentiated needs of the lured customer. In order to find a source of income which is not yet exhausted, and to find a function which cannot readily be displaced, it is necessary to specialize in one's services. This process promotes differentiation, refinement, and

the enrichment of the public's needs, which obviously must lead to growing personal differences within this public.

All this forms the transition to the individualization of mental and psychic traits which the city occasions in proportion to its size. There is a whole series of obvious causes underlying this process. First, one must meet the difficulty of asserting his own personality within the dimensions of metropolitan life. Where the quantitative increase in importance and the expense of energy reach their limits, one seizes upon qualitative differentiation by playing upon its sensitivity for differences. Finally, man is tempted to adopt the most tendentious peculiarities, that is, the specifically metropolitan extravagances of mannerism, caprice, and preciousness. Now, the meaning of these extravagances does not at all lie in the contents of such behavior, but rather in its form of "being different," of standing out in a striking manner and thereby attracting attention. For many character types, ultimately the only means of saving for themselves some modicum of self-esteem and the sense of filling a position is indirect, through the awareness of others. In the same sense a seemingly insignificant factor is operating, the cumulative effects of which are, however, still noticeable. I refer to the brevity and scarcity of the inter-human contacts granted to the metropolitan man, as compared with social intercourse in the small town. The temptation to appear "to the point," to appear concentrated and strikingly characteristic, lies much closer to the individual in brief metropolitan contacts than in an atmosphere in which frequent and prolonged association assures the personality of an unambiguous image of himself in the eyes of the other.

The most profound reason, however, why the metropolis conduces to the urge for the most individual personal existence—no matter whether justified and successful—appears to me to be the following: The development of modern culture is characterized by the preponderance of what one may call the "objective spirit" over the "subjective spirit." This is to say, in language as well as in law, in the technique of production as well as in art, in science as well as in the objects of the domestic environment, there is embodied a sum of spirit. The individual in his intellectual development follows the growth of this spirit very imperfectly and at an ever increasing distance. If, for instance, we view the immense culture which for the last 100 years has been embodied in things and in knowledge, in institutions and in comforts, and if we compare all this with the cultural progress of the individual during the same period—at least in high status groups—a frightful disproportion in growth between the two becomes evident. Indeed, at some points we notice a retrogression in the culture of the individual with reference to spirituality, delicacy, and idealism. This descrepancy results essentially from the growing division of labor. For the division of labor demands from the individual an ever more one-sided accomplishment, and the greatest advance in a one-sided pursuit only too frequently means death to the personality of the individual. In any case, he can cope less and less with the overgrowth of objective culture. The individual is reduced to a negligible quantity, perhaps less in his consciousness than in his practice and in the totality of his obscure emotional states that are derived from this practice. The individual has become a mere cog in an enormous organization of things and powers which tear from his hands all progress, spirituality, and value in order to transform them from their subjective form into the form of a purely objective life. It needs merely to be pointed out that the metropolis is the genuine arena of this culture which outgrows all personal life. Here in buildings and educational institutions, in the wonders and comforts of space-conquering technology, in the formations of community life, and in the visible institu-

tions of the state, is offered such an overwhelming fullness of crystalized and impersonalized spirit that the personality, so to speak, cannot maintain itself under its impact. On the one hand, life is made infinitely easy for the personality in that stimulations, interests, uses of time and consciousness are offered to it from all sides. They carry the person as if in a stream, and one needs hardly to swim for oneself. On the other hand, however, life is composed more and more of these impersonal contents and offerings which tend to displace the genuine personal colorations and incomparabilities. This results in the individual's summoning the utmost in uniqueness and particularization, in order to preserve his most personal core. He has to exaggerate this personal element in order to remain audible even to himself. The atrophy of individual culture through the hypertrophy of objective culture is one reason for the bitter hatred which the preachers of the most extreme individualism, above all Nietzsche, harbor against the metropolis. But it is, indeed, also a reason why these preachers are so passionately loved in the metropolis and why they appear to the metropolitan man as the prophets and saviors of his most unsatisfied yearnings.

If one asks for the historical position of these two forms of individualism which are nourished by the quantitative relation of the metropolis, namely, individual independence and the elaboration of individuality itself, then the metropolis assumes an entirely new rank order in the world history of the spirit. The 18th century found the individual in oppressive bonds which had become meaningless—bonds of a political, agrarian, guild, and religious character. They were restraints which, so to speak, force upon man an unnatural form and outmoded, unjust inequalities. In this situation the cry for liberty and equality arose, the belief in the individual's full freedom of movement in all social and intellectual relationships. Freedom would at once permit the noble substance common to all to come to the fore, a substance which nature had deposited in every man and which society and history had only deformed. Besides this 18th-century ideal of liberalism, in the 19th century, through Goethe and Romanticism, on the one hand, and through the economic division of labor, on the other hand, another ideal arose: individuals liberated from historical bonds now wished to distinguish themselves from one another. The carrier of man's values is no longer the "general human being" in every individual, but rather man's qualitative uniqueness and irreplaceability. The external and internal history of our time takes its course within the struggle and in the changing entanglements of these two ways of defining the individual's role in the whole of society. It is the function of the metropolis to provide the arena for this struggle, and its reconciliation. For the metropolis presents the peculiar conditions which are revealed to us as the opportunities and the stimuli for the development of both these ways of

allocating roles to men. Therewith these conditions gain a unique place, pregnant with inestimable meanings for the development of psychic existence. The metropolis reveals itself as one of those great historical formations in which opposing streams which enclose life unfold, as well as join one another with equal right. However, in this process the currents of life, whether their individual phenomena touch us sympathetically or antipathetically, entirely transcend the sphere for which the judge's attitude is appropriate. Since such forces of life have grown into the roots and into the crown of the whole of the historical life in which we, in our fleeting existence, as a cell, belong only as a part, it is not our task either to accuse or to pardon, but only to understand.[1]

---

[1] The content of this lecture by its very nature does not derive from a citable literature. Argument and elaboration of its major cultural-historical ideas are contained in my *Philosophie des Geldes* (*The Philosophy of Money*; München and Leipzig: Duncker und Humblot, 1900).

4

Human ecology

Robert Ezra Park

I. THE WEB OF LIFE

Naturalists of the last century were greatly intrigued by their observation of the interrelations and coordinations, within the realm of animate nature, of the numerous, divergent, and widely scattered species. Their successors, the botanists and zoölogists of the present day, have turned their attention to more specific

inquiries, and the "realm of nature," like the concept of evolution, has come to be for them a notion remote and speculative.

The "web of life," in which all living organisms, plants and animals alike, are bound together in a vast system of interlinked and interdependent lives, is nevertheless, as J. Arthur Thomson put it, "one of the fundamental biological concepts" and is "as characteristically Darwinian as the struggle for existence."[1]

Reprinted from Robert Ezra Park, "Human Ecology," *American Journal of Sociology* 62, no. 1 (July 1936), pp. 1–15, by permission of the University of Chicago Press. Copyright 1936 by The University of Chicago.

[1] *The System of Animate Nature* (Gifford Lectures, 1915–16), II (New York, 1920), 58.

Darwin's famous instance of the cats and the clover is the classic illustration of this interdependence. He found, he explains, that humblebees were almost indispensable to the fertilization of the heartsease, since other bees do not visit this flower. The same thing is true with some kinds of clover. Humblebees alone visit red clover, as other bees cannot reach the nectar. The inference is that if the humblebees became extinct or very rare in England, the heartsease and red clover would become very rare, or wholly disappear. However, the number of humblebees in any district depends in a great measure on the number of field mice, which destroy their combs and nests. It is estimated that more than two thirds of them are thus destroyed all over England. Near villages and small towns the nests of humblebees are more numerous than elsewhere and this is attributed to the number of cats that destroy the mice.[2] Thus next year's crop of purple clover in certain parts of England depends on the number of humblebees in the district; the number of humblebees depends upon the number of field mice, the number of field mice upon the number and enterprise of the cats, and the number of cats—as someone has added—depends on the number of old maids and others in neighboring villages who keep cats.

These large food chains, as they are called, each link of which eats the other, have as their logical prototype the familiar nursery rhyme, "The House that Jack Built." You recall:

The cow with the crumpled horn,
    That tossed the dog,
    That worried the cat,
    That killed the rat,
    That ate the malt
    That lay in the house that Jack built.

Darwin and the naturalists of his day were particularly interested in observing and recording these curious illustrations of the mutual adaptation and correlation of plants and animals because they seemed to throw light on the origin of the species. Both the species and their mutual interdependence, within a common habitat, seem to be a product of the same Darwinian struggle for existence.

It is interesting to note that it was the application to organic life of a sociological principle—the principle, namely, of "competitive cooperation"—that gave Darwin the first clue to the formulation of his theory of evolution.

"He projected on organic life," says Thomson, "a sociological idea," and "thus vindicated the relevancy and utility of a sociological idea within the biological realm."[3]

The active principle in the ordering and regulating of life within the realm of animate nature is, as Darwin described it, "the struggle for existence." By this means the numbers of living organisms are regulated, their distribution controlled, and the balance of nature maintained. Finally, it is by means of this elementary form of competition that the existing species, the survivors in the struggle, find their niches in the physical environment and in the existing correlation or division of labor between the different species. J. Arthur Thomson makes an impressive statement of the matter in his *System of Animate Nature.* He says:

The hosts of living organisms are not . . . isolated creatures, for every thread of life is intertwined with others in a complex web. . . . Flowers and insects are fitted to one another as hand to glove. Cats have to do with the plague in India as well as with the clover crop at home. *. . . Just as there is a correlation of organs in the body, so there is a correlation of organisms in the world of life.* When we learn something of the intricate give and take, supply and demand, action and reaction between plants and animals, between flowers and insects, between herbivores and carnivores, and between other conflicting yet correlated interests, we begin to

[2] J. Arthur Thomson, *Darwinism and Human Life* (New York, 1911), pp. 52–53.

[3] Ibid., p. 72.

get a glimpse of a vast self-regulating organization.

These manifestations of a living, changing, but persistent order among competing organisms—organisms embodying "conflicting yet correlated interests"—seem to be the basis for the conception of a social order transcending the individual species, and of a society based on a biotic rather than a cultural basis, a conception later developed by the plant and animal ecologists.

In recent years the plant geographers have been the first to revive something of the earlier field naturalists' interest in the interrelations of species. Haeckel, in 1878, was the first to give to these studies a name, "ecology," and by so doing gave them the character of a distinct and separate science, a science which Thomson described as "the new natural history."[4]

The interrelation and interdependence of the species are naturally more obvious and more intimate within the common habitat than elsewhere. Furthermore, as correlations have multiplied and competition has decreased, in consequence of mutual adaptations of the competing species, the habitat and habitants have tended to assume the character of a more or less completely closed system.

Within the limits of this system the individual units of the population are involved in a process of competitive cooperation, which has given to their interrelations the character of a natural economy. To such a habitat and its inhabitants—whether plant, animal, or human—the ecologists have applied the term *community*.

The essential characteristics of a community, so conceived, are those of: (1) a population, territorially organized, (2) more or less completely rooted in the soil it occupies, (3) its individual units living in a

relationship of mutual interdependence that is symbiotic rather than societal, in the sense in which that term applies to human beings.

These symbiotic societies are not merely unorganized assemblages of plants and animals which happen to live together in the same habitat. On the contrary, they are interrelated in the most complex manner. Every community has something of the character of an organic unit. It has a more or less definite structure and it has "a life history in which juvenile, adult and senile phases can be observed."[5] If it is an organism, it is one of the organs which are other organisms. It is, to use Spencer's phrase, a superorganism.

What more than anything else gives the symbiotic community the character of an organism is the fact that it possesses a mechanism (competition) for (1) regulating the numbers and (2) preserving the balance between the competing species of which it is composed. It is by maintaining this biotic balance that the community preserves its identity and integrity as an individual unit through the changes and the vicissitudes to which it is subject in the course of its progress from the earlier to the later phases of its existence.

II. THE BALANCE OF NATURE

The balance of nature, as plant and animal ecologists have conceived it, seems to be largely a question of numbers. When the pressure of population upon the natural resources of the habitat reaches a certain degree of intensity, something invariably happens. In the one case the population may swarm and relieve the pressure of population by migration. In another, where the disequilibrium between population and natural resources is the result of some change, sudden or gradual, in the conditions of life, the preexisting cor-

---

[4] "Ecology," says Charles Elton, "corresponds to the older terms Natural History and Bionomics, but its methods are now accurate and precise." See article, "Ecology," *Encyclopaedia Britannica* (14th ed.).

[5] Edward J. Salisbury, "Plants," *Encyclopaedia Britannica* (14th ed.).

relation of the species may be totally destroyed.

Change may be brought about by a famine, an epidemic, or an invasion of the habitat by some alien species. Such an invasion may result in a rapid increase of the invading population and a sudden decline in the numbers if not the destruction of the original population. Change of some sort is continuous, although the rate and pace of change sometimes vary greatly. Charles Elton says:

The impression of anyone who has studied animal numbers in the field is that the "balance of nature" hardly exists, except in the minds of scientists. It seems that animal numbers are always tending to settle down into a smooth and harmonious working mechanism, but something always happens before this happy state is reached.[6]

Under ordinary circumstances, such minor fluctuations in the biotic balance as occur are mediated and absorbed without profoundly disturbing the existing equilibrium and routine of life. When, on the other hand, some sudden and catastrophic change occurs—it may be a war, a famine, or pestilence—it upsets the biotic balance, breaks "the cake of custom," and releases energies up to that time held in check. A series of rapid and even violent changes may ensue which profoundly alter the existing organization of communal life and give a new direction to the future course of events.

The advent of the boll weevil in the southern cotton fields is a minor instance but illustrates the principle. The boll weevil crossed the Rio Grande at Brownsville in the summer of 1892. By 1894 the pest had spread to a dozen counties in Texas, bringing destruction to the cotton and great losses to the planters. From that point it advanced, with every recurring season, until by 1928 it had covered practically all the cotton producing area in the United States. Its progress took the form of a territorial succession. The consequences to agriculture were catastrophic but not wholly for the worse, since they served to give an impulse to changes in the organization of the industry long overdue. It also hastened the northward migration of the Negro tenant farmer.

The case of the boll weevil is typical. In this mobile modern world, where space and time have been measurably abolished, not men only but all the minor organisms (including the microbes) seem to be, as never before, in motion. Commerce, in progressively destroying the isolation upon which the ancient order of nature rested, has intensified the struggle for existence over an ever widening area of the habitable world. Out of this struggle a new equilibrium and a new system of animate nature, the new biotic basis of the new world-society, is emerging.

It is, as Elton remarks, the "fluctuation of numbers" and "the failure" from time to time "of the regulatory mechanism of animal increase" which ordinarily interrupts the established routine, and in so doing releases a new cycle of change. In regard to these fluctuations in numbers Elton says:

These failures of the regulating mechanism of animal increase—are they caused by (1) internal changes, after the manner of an alarm clock which suddenly goes off, or the boilers of an engine blowing up, or are they caused by some factors in the outer environment—weather, vegetation, or something like that?[7]

and he adds:

It appears that they are due to both but that the latter (external factor) is the more important of the two, and usually plays the leading rôle.

The conditions which affect and control the movements and numbers of populations are more complex in human societies than in plant and animal communities, but they exhibit extraordinary similarities.

The boll weevil, moving out of its an-

---

[6] "Animal Ecology," ibid.

[7] Ibid.

cient habitat in the central Mexican plateau and into the virgin territory of the southern cotton plantations, incidentally multiplying its population to the limit of the territories and resources, is not unlike the Boers of Cape Colony, South Africa, trekking out into the high veldt of the central South African plateau and filling it, within a period of 100 years, with a population of their own descendants.

Competition operates in the human (as it does in the plant and animal) community to bring about and restore the communal equilibrium, when, either by the advent of some intrusive factor from without or in the normal course of its life-history, that equilibrium is disturbed.

Thus every crisis that initiates a period of rapid change, during which competition is intensified, moves over finally into a period of more or less stable equilibrium and a new division of labor. In this manner competition is superseded by cooperation.

It is when, and to the extent that, competition declines that the kind of order which we call society may be said to exist. In short, society, from the ecological point of view, and in so far as it is a territorial unit, is just the area within which biotic competition has declined and the struggle for existence has assumed higher and more sublimated forms.

III. COMPETITION, DOMINANCE AND SUCCESSION

There are other and less obvious ways in which competition exercises control over the relations of individuals and species within the communal habitat. The two ecological principles, dominance and succession, which operate to establish and maintain such communal order as here described, are functions of, and dependent upon, competition.

In every life-community there is always one or more dominant species. In a plant community this dominance is ordinarily the result of struggle among the different species for light. In a climate which supports a forest the dominant species will invariably be trees. On the prairie and steppes they will be grasses.

Light being the main necessity of plants, the dominant plant of a community is the tallest member, which can spread its green energy-trap above the heads of the others. What marginal exploitation there is to be done is an exploitation of the dimmer light below this canopy. So it comes about in every life-community on land, in the cornfield just as in the forest, that there are layers of vegetation, each adapted to exist in a lesser intensity of light than the one above. Usually there are but two or three such layers; in an oak-wood for example there will be a layer of moss, above this herbs or low bushes, and then nothing more to the leafy roof; in the wheat-field the dominating form is the wheat, with lower weeds among its stalks. But in tropical forests the whole space from floor to roof may be zoned and populated.[8]

But the principle of dominance operates in the human as well as in the plant and animal communities. The so-called natural or functional areas of a metropolitan community—for example, the slum, the rooming-house area, the central shopping section and the banking center—each and all owe their existence directly to the factor of dominance, and indirectly to competition.

The struggle of industries and commercial institutions for a strategic location determines in the long run the main outlines of the urban community. The distribution of population, as well as the location and limits of the residential areas which they occupy, are determined by another similar but subordinate system of forces.

The area of dominance in any community is usually the area of highest land values. Ordinarily there are in every large city two such positions of highest land value—one in the central shopping district, the other in the central banking area. From these points land values decline at first precipitately and then more gradually

---

[8] H. G. Wells, Julian S. Huxley, and G. P. Wells, *The Science of Life* (New York, 1934), pp. 968–69.

toward the periphery of the urban community. It is these land values that determine the location of social institutions and business enterprises. Both the one and the other are bound up in a kind of territorial complex within which they are at once competing and interdependent units.

As the metropolitan community expands into the suburbs the pressure of professions, business enterprises, and social institutions of various sorts destined to serve the whole metropolitan region steadily increases the demand for space at the center. Thus not merely the growth of the suburban area, but any change in the method of transportation which makes the central business area of the city more accessible, tends to increase the pressure at the center. From thence this pressure is transmitted and diffused, as the profile of land values discloses, to every other part of the city.

Thus the principle of dominance, operating within the limits imposed by the terrain and other natural features of the location, tends to determine the general ecological pattern of the city and the functional relation of each of the different areas of the city to all others.

Dominance is, furthermore, in so far as it tends to stabilize either the biotic or the cultural community, indirectly responsible for the phenomenon of succession.

The term "succession" is used by ecologists to describe and designate that orderly sequence of changes through which a biotic community passes in the course of its development from a primary and relatively unstable to a relatively permanent or climax stage. The main point is that not merely do the individual plants and animals within the communal habitat grow but the community itself, i.e., the system of relations between the species, is likewise involved in an orderly process of change and development.

The fact that, in the course of this development, the community moves through a series of more or less clearly defined stages is the fact that gives this development the serial character which the term "succession" suggests.

The explanation of the serial character of the changes involved in succession is the fact that at every stage in the process a more or less stable equilibrium is achieved, which in due course, and as a result of progressive changes in life-conditions, possibly due to growth and decay, the equilibrium achieved in the earlier stages is eventually undermined. In such case the energies previously held in balance will be released, competition will be intensified, and change will continue at a relatively rapid rate until a new equilibrium is achieved.

The climax phase of community development corresponds with the adult phase of an individual's life.

In the developing single organism, each phase is its own executioner, and itself brings a new phase into existence, as when the tadpole grows the thyroid gland which is destined to make the tadpole state pass away in favour of the miniature frog. And in the developing community of organisms, the same thing happens —each stage alters its own environment, for it changes and almost invariably enriches the soil in which it lives; and thus it eventually brings itself to an end, by making it possible for new kinds of plants with greater demands in the way of mineral salts or other riches of the soil to flourish there. Accordingly bigger and more exigent plants gradually supplant the early pioneers, until a final balance is reached, the ultimate possibility for that climate.[9]

The cultural community develops in comparable ways to that of the biotic, but the process is more complicated. Inventions, as well as sudden or catastrophic changes, seem to play a more important part in bringing about serial changes in the cultural than in the biotic community. But the principle involved seems to be substantially the same. In any case, all or most of the fundamental processes seem to be

---

[9] Ibid., pp. 977–78.

functionally related and dependent upon competition.

Competition, which on the biotic level functions to control and regulate the inter-relations of organisms, tends to assume on the social level the form of conflict. The intimate relation between competition and conflict is indicated by the fact that wars frequently, if not always, have, or seem to have, their source and origin in economic competition which, in that case, assumes the more sublimated form of a struggle for power and prestige. The social function of war, on the other hand, seems to be to extend the area over which it is possible to maintain peace.

IV. BIOLOGICAL ECONOMICS

If population pressure, on the one hand, cooperates with changes in local and environmental conditions to disturb at once the biotic balance and social equilibrium, it tends at the same time to intensify competition. In so doing it functions, indirectly, to bring about a new, more minute and, at the same time, more territorially extensive division of labor.

Under the influence of an intensified competition, and the increased activity which competition involves, every individual and every species, each for itself, tends to discover the particular niche in the physical and living environment where it can survive and flourish with the greatest possible expansiveness consistent with its necessary dependence upon its neighbors.

It is in this way that a territorial organization and a biological division of labor, within the communal habitat, is established and maintained. This explains, in part at least, the fact that the biotic community has been conceived at one time as a kind of superorganism and at another as a kind of economic organization for the exploitation of the natural resources of its habitat.

In their interesting survey, *The Science of*

Life, H. G. Wells and his collaborators, Julian Huxley and G. P. Wells, have described ecology as "biological economics," and as such very largely concerned with "the balances and mutual pressures of species living in the same habitat."[10]

"Ecology," as they put it, is "an extension of Economics to the whole of life." On the other hand the science of economics as traditionally conceived, though it is a whole century older, is merely a branch of a more general science of ecology which includes man with all other living creatures. Under the circumstances what has been traditionally described as economics and conceived as restricted to human affairs, might very properly be described as Barrows some years ago described geography, namely, as human ecology. It is in this sense that Wells and his collaborators would use the term.

The science of economics—at first it was called Political Economy—is a whole century older than ecology. It was and is the science of social subsistence, of needs and their satisfactions, of work and wealth. It tries to elucidate the relations of producer, dealer, and consumer in the human community and show how the whole system carries on. Ecology broadens out this inquiry into a general study of the give and take, the effort, accumulation and consumption in every province of life. Economics, therefore, is merely Human Ecology, it is the narrow and special study of the ecology of the very extraordinary community in which we live. It might have been a better and brighter science if it had begun biologically.[11]

Since human ecology cannot be at the same time both geography and economics, one may adopt, as a working hypothesis, the notion that it is neither one nor the other but something independent of both. Even so the motives for identifying ecol-

---

[10] Ibid.

[11] H. H. Barrows, "Geography as Human Ecology," *Annals of the Association of American Geographers* 8 (1923), 1–14. See Wells et al., *Science of Life,* pp. 961–62.

ogy with geography on the one hand, and economics on the other, are fairly obvious.

From the point of view of geography, the plant, animal, and human population, including their habitations and other evidence of man's occupation of the soil, are merely part of the landscape, of which the geographer is seeking a detailed description and picture.

On the other hand ecology (biologic economics), even when it involves some sort of unconscious cooperation and a natural, spontaneous, and nonrational division of labor, is something different from the economics of commerce; something quite apart from the bargaining of the market place. Commerce, as Simmel somewhere remarks, is one of the latest and most complicated of all the social relationships into which human beings have entered. Man is the only animal that trades and traffics.

Ecology, and human ecology, if it is not identical with economics on the distinctively human and cultural level, is, nevertheless, something more than and different from the static order which the human geographer discovers when he surveys the cultural landscape.

The community of the geographer is not, for one thing, like that of the ecologist, a closed system, and the web of communication which man has spread over the earth is something different from the "web of life" which binds living creatures all over the world in a vital nexus.

V. SYMBIOSIS AND SOCIETY

Human ecology, if it is neither economics on one hand nor geography on the other, but just ecology, differs nevertheless in important respects from plant and animal ecology. The interrelations of human beings and interactions of man and his habitat are comparable but not identical with interrelations of other forms of life that live together and carry on a kind of "biological economy" within the limits of a common habitat.

For one thing man is not so immediately dependent upon his physical environment as other animals. As a result of the existing world-wide division of labor, man's relation to his physical environment has been mediated through the intervention of other men. The exchange of goods and services have cooperated to emancipate him from dependence upon his local habitat.

Furthermore man has, by means of inventions and technical devices of the most diverse sorts, enormously increased his capacity for reacting upon and remaking, not only his habitat but his world. Finally, man has erected upon the basis of the biotic community an institutional structure rooted in custom and tradition.

Structure, where it exists, tends to resist change, at least change coming from without; while it possibly facilitates the cumulation of change within.[12] In plant and animal communities structure is biologically determined, and so far as any division of labor exists at all it has a physiological and instinctive basis. The social insects afford a conspicuous example of this fact, and one interest in studying their habits, as Wheeler points out, is that they show the extent to which social organization can be developed on a purely physiological and instinctive basis, as is the case among human beings in the natural as distinguished from the institutional family.[13]

In a society of human beings, however, this communal structure is reinforced by custom and assumes an institutional character. In human as contrasted with animal

---

[12] Here is, obviously, another evidence of that organic character of the interrelations of organisms in the biosphere to which J. Arthur Thomson and others have referred. It is an indication of the way in which competition mediates the influences from without by the adjustment and readjustment of relations within the community. In this case "within" coincides with the orbit of the competitive process, at least so far as the effects of that process are substantive and obvious. See Simmel's definition of society and the social group in time and space quoted in Park and Burgess, *Introduction to the Science of Sociology*, 2d ed., pp. 348–56.

[13] William Morton Wheeler, *Social Life among the Insects* (Lowell Institute Lectures, March 1922), pp. 3–18.

societies, competition and the freedom of the individual is limited on every level above the biotic by custom and consensus.

The incidence of this more or less arbitrary control which custom and consensus imposes upon the natural social order complicates the social process but does not fundamentally alter it—or, if it does, the effects of biotic competition will still be manifest in the succeeding social order and the subsequent course of events.

The fact seems to be, then, that human society, as distinguished from plant and animal society, is organized on two levels, the biotic and the cultural. There is a symbiotic society based on competition and a cultural society based on communication and consensus. As a matter of fact the two societies are merely different aspects of one society, which, in the vicissitudes and changes to which they are subject, remain, nevertheless, in some sort of mutual dependence each upon the other. The cultural superstructure rests on the basis of the symbiotic substructure, and the emergent energies that manifest themselves on the biotic level in movements and actions reveal themselves on the higher social level in more subtle and sublimated forms.

However, the interrelations of human beings are more diverse and complicated than this dichotomy, symbiotic and cultural, indicates. This fact is attested by the divergent systems of human interrelations which have been the subject of the special social sciences. Thus human society, certainly in its mature and more rational expression, exhibits not merely an ecological, but an economic, a political, and a moral order. The social sciences include not merely human geography and ecology, but economics, political science, and cultural anthropology.

It is interesting also that these divergent social orders seem to arrange themselves in a kind of hierarchy. In fact they may be said to form a pyramid of which the ecological order constitutes the base and the moral order the apex. Upon each succeeding one of these levels, the ecological, eco-nomic, political, and moral, the individual finds himself more completely incorporated into and subordinated to the social order of which he is a part than upon the preceding.

Society is everywhere a control organization. Its function is to organize, integrate, and direct the energies resident in the individuals of which it is composed. One might, perhaps, say that the function of society was everywhere to restrict competition and by so doing bring about a more effective cooperation of the organic units of which society is composed.

Competition, on the biotic level, as we observe it in the plant and animal communities, seems to be relatively unrestricted. Society, so far as it exists, is anarchic and free. On the cultural level, this freedom of the individual to compete is restricted by conventions, understandings, and law. The individual is more free upon the economic level than upon the political, more free on the political than the moral.

As society matures control is extended and intensified and free commerce of individuals restricted, if not by law then by what Gilbert Murray refers to as "the normal expectation of mankind." The mores are merely what men, in a situation that is defined, have come to expect.

Human ecology, in so far as it is concerned with a social order that is based on competition rather than consensus, is identical, in principle at least, with plant and animal ecology. The problems with which plant and animal ecology have been traditionally concerned are fundamentally population problems. Society, as ecologists have conceived it, is a population settled and limited to its habitat. The ties that unite its individual units are those of a free and natural economy, based on a natural division of labor. Such a society is territorially organized and the ties which hold it together are physical and vital rather than customary and moral.

Human ecology has, however, to reckon with the fact that in human society competition is limited by custom and culture.

The cultural superstructure imposes itself as an instrument of direction and control upon the biotic substructure.

Reduced to its elements the human community, so conceived, may be said to consist of a population and a culture, including in the term culture (1) a body of customs and beliefs and (2) a corresponding body of artifacts and technological devices.

To these three elements or factors—(1) population, (2) artifacts (technological culture), (3) customs and beliefs (nonmaterial culture)—into which the social complex resolves itself, one should, perhaps, add a fourth, namely, the natural resources of the habitat.

It is the interaction of these four factors—(1) population, (2) artifacts (technological culture), (3) customs and beliefs (nonmaterial culture), and (4) the natural resources—that maintain at once the biotic balance and the social equilibrium, when and where they exist.

The changes in which ecology is interested are the movements of population and of artifacts (commodities) and changes in location and occupation—any sort of change, in fact, which affects an existing division of labor or the relation of the population to the soil.

Human ecology is, fundamentally, an attempt to investigate (1) the processes by which the biotic balance and the social equilibrium are maintained once they are achieved and (2) the processes by which, when the biotic balance and the social equilibrium are disturbed, the transition is made from one relatively stable order to another.

5
Urbanism as a way of life
Louis Wirth

In the rich literature on the city we look in vain for a theory of urbanism presenting in a systematic fashion the available knowledge concerning the city as a social entity. We do indeed have excellent formulations of theories on such special problems as the growth of the city viewed as a historical trend and as a recurrent process,[1] and we have a wealth of literature presenting insights of sociological relevance and empirical studies offering detailed information on a variety of particular aspects of urban life.

But despite the multiplication of research and textbooks on the city, we do not as yet have a comprehensive body of competent hypotheses which may be derived from a set of postulates implicitly contained in a sociological definition of the city, and from our general sociological knowledge which may be substantiated through empirical research. The closest approximations to a systematic theory of urbanism that we have are to be found in a penetrating essay, "Die Stadt," by Max Weber,[2] and a memorable paper by Robert E. Park on "The City: Suggestions for the Investigation of Human Behavior in the Urban Environment."[3] But even these excellent contributions are far from constitut-

Reprinted from Louis Wirth, "Urbanism as a Way of Life," *American Journal of Sociology* 44, no. 1 (July 1938), pp. 1–24, by permission of The University of Chicago Press. Copyright 1938 by the University of Chicago. Footnotes have been renumbered.

[1] See Robert E. Park et al., *The City* (Chicago, 1925), esp. chaps. 2 and 3; Werner Sombart, "Städtische Siedlung, Stadt," *Handwörterbuch der Soziologie*, ed. Alfred Vierkandt (Stuttgart, 1931); see also bibliography.

[2] *Wirtschaft und Gesellschaft* (Tübingen, 1925), pt. 2, chap. 8, pp. 514–601.

[3] Park, et al., *The City*, chap. 1.

ing an ordered and coherent framework of theory upon which research might profitably proceed.

In the pages that follow we shall seek to set forth a limited number of identifying characteristics of the city. Given these characteristics we shall then indicate what consequences or further characteristics follow from them in the light of general sociological theory and empirical research. We hope in this manner to arrive at the essential propositions comprising a theory of urbanism. Some of these propositions can be supported by a considerable body of already available research materials; others may be accepted as hypotheses for which a certain amount of presumptive evidence exists, but for which more ample and exact verification would be required. At least such a procedure will, it is hoped, show what in the way of systematic knowledge of the city we now have and what are the crucial and fruitful hypotheses for future research.

The central problem of the sociologist of the city is to discover the forms of social action and organization that typically emerge in relatively permanent, compact settlements of large numbers of heterogeneous individuals. We must also infer that urbanism will assume its most characteristic and extreme form in the measure in which the conditions with which it is congruent are present. Thus the larger, the more densely populated, and the more heterogeneous a community, the more accentuated the characteristics associated with urbanism will be. It should be recognized, however, that in the social world institutions and practices may be accepted and continued for reasons other than those that originally brought them into existence, and that accordingly the urban mode of life may be perpetuated under conditions quite foreign to those necessary for its origin.

Some justification may be in order for the choice of the principal terms comprising our definition of the city. The attempt has been made to make it as inclusive and at the same time as denotative as possible without loading it with unnecessary assumptions. To say that large numbers are necessary to constitute a city means, of course, large numbers in relation to a restricted area or high density of settlement. There are, nevertheless, good reasons for treating large numbers and density as separate factors, since each may be connected with significantly different social consequences. Similarly the need for adding heterogeneity to numbers of population as a necessary and distinct criterion of urbanism might be questioned, since we should expect the range of differences to increase with numbers. In defense, it may be said that the city shows a kind and degree of heterogeneity of population which cannot be wholly accounted for by the law of large numbers or adequately represented by means of a normal distribution curve. Since the population of the city does not reproduce itself, it must recruit its migrants from other cities, the countryside, and—in this country until recently—from other countries. The city has thus historically been the melting pot of races, peoples, and cultures, and a most favorable breeding ground of new biological and cultural hybrids. It has not only tolerated but rewarded individual differences. It has brought together people from the ends of the earth *because* they are different and thus useful to one another, rather than because they are homogeneous and like minded.[4]

There are a number of sociological propositions concerning the relationship between (a) numbers of population, (b) density of settlement, (c) heterogeneity of inhabitants and group life, which can be

---

[4] The justification for including the term "permanent" in the definition may appear necessary. Our failure to give an extensive justification for this qualifying mark of the urban rests on the obvious fact that unless human settlements take a fairly permanent root in a locality the characteristics of urban life cannot arise, and conversely the living together of large numbers of heterogeneous individuals under dense conditions is not possible without the development of a more or less technological structure.

formulated on the basis of observation and research.

SIZE OF THE POPULATION AGGREGATE

Ever since Aristotle's *Politics*,[5] it has been recognized that increasing the number of inhabitants in a settlement beyond a certain limit will affect the relationships between them and the character of the city. Large numbers involve, as has been pointed out, a greater range of individual variation. Furthermore, the greater the number of individuals participating in a process of interaction, the greater is the *potential* differentiation between them. The personal traits, the occupations, the cultural life, and the ideas of the members of an urban community may, therefore, be expected to range between more widely

separated poles than those of rural inhabitants.

That such variations should give rise to the spatial segregation of individuals according to color, ethnic heritage, economic and social status, tastes and preferences, may readily be inferred. The bonds of kinship, of neighborliness, and the sentiments arising out of living together for generations under a common folk tradition are likely to be absent or, at best, relatively weak in an aggregate the members of which have such diverse origins and backgrounds. Under such circumstances competition and formal control mechanisms furnish the substitutes for the bonds of solidarity that are relied upon to hold a folk society together.

Increase in the number of inhabitants of a community beyond a few hundred is bound to limit the possibility of each member of the community knowing all the others personally. Max Weber, in recognizing the social significance of this fact, pointed out that from a sociological point of view large numbers of inhabitants and density of settlement mean that the personal mutual acquaintanceship between the inhabitants which ordinarily inheres in a neighborhood is lacking.[6] The increase in numbers thus involves a changed character of the social relationships. As Simmel points out:

[If] the unceasing external contact of numbers of persons in the city should be met by the same number of inner reactions as in the small town, in which one knows almost every person he meets and to each of whom he has a positive relationship, one would be completely atomized internally and would fall into an unthinkable mental condition.[7]

The multiplication of persons in a state of interaction under conditions which make their contact as full personalities impossi-

---

[5] See esp. vii. 4. 4–14. Translated by B. Jowett, from which the following may be quoted:

"To the size of states there is a limit, as there is to other things, plants, animals, implements; for none of these retain their natural power when they are too large or too small, but they either wholly lose their nature, or are spoiled. . . . . [A] state when composed of too few is not as a state ought to be, self-sufficing; when of too many, though self-sufficing in all mere necessaries, it is a nation and not a state, being almost incapable of constitutional government. For who can be the general of such a vast multitude, or who the herald, unless he have the voice of a Stentor?

"A state then only begins to exist when it has attained a population sufficient for a good life in the political community: it may indeed somewhat exceed this number. But, as I was saying, there must be a limit. What should be the limit will be easily ascertained by experience. For both governors and governed have duties to perform; the special functions of a governor are to command and to judge. But if the citizens of a state are to judge and to distribute offices according to merit, then they must know each other's characters; where they do not possess this knowledge, both the election to offices and the decision of lawsuits will go wrong. When the population is very large they are manifestly settled at haphazard, which clearly ought not to be. Besides, in an overpopulous state foreigners and metics will readily acquire the rights of citizens, for who will find them out? Clearly, then, the best limit of the population of a state is the largest number which suffices for the purposes of life, and can be taken in at a single view. Enough concerning the size of a city."

[6] Weber, *Wirtschaft und Gesellschaft*, p. 514.

[7] Georg Simmel, "Die Grossstädte und das Geistesleben," *Die Grossstadt*, ed. Theodor Petermann (Dresden, 1903), pp. 187–206.

ble produces that segmentalization of human relationships which has sometimes been seized upon by students of the mental life of the cities as an explanation for the "schizoid" character of urban personality. This is not to say that the urban inhabitants have fewer acquaintances than rural inhabitants, for the reverse may actually be true; it means rather that in relation to the number of people whom they see and with whom they rub elbows in the course of daily life, they know a smaller proportion, and of these they have less intensive knowledge.

Characteristically, urbanites meet one another in highly segmental roles. They are, to be sure, dependent upon more people for the satisfactions of their life-needs than are rural people and thus are associated with a greater number of organized groups, but they are less dependent upon particular persons, and their dependence upon others is confined to a highly fractionalized aspect of the other's round of activity. This is essentially what is meant by saying that the city is characterized by secondary rather than primary contacts. The contacts of the city may indeed be face to face, but they are nevertheless impersonal, superficial, transitory, and segmental. The reserve, the indifference, and the blasé outlook which urbanites manifest in their relationships may thus be regarded as devices for immunizing themselves against the personal claims and expectations of others.

The superficiality, the anonymity, and the transitory character of urban-social relations make intelligible, also, the sophistication and the rationality generally ascribed to city-dwellers. Our acquaintances tend to stand in a relationship of utility to us in the sense that the role which each one plays in our life is overwhelmingly regarded as a means for the achievement of our own ends. Whereas, therefore, the individual gains, on the one hand, a certain degree of emancipation or freedom from the personal and emotional controls of intimate groups, he loses, on the other hand, the spontaneous self-expression, the morale, and the sense of participation that comes with living in an integrated society. This constitutes essentially the state of *anomie* or the social void to which Durkheim alludes in attempting to account for the various forms of social disorganization in technological society.

The segmental character and utilitarian accent of interpersonal relations in the city find their institutional expression in the proliferation of specialized tasks which we see in their most developed form in the professions. The operation of the pecuniary nexus leads to predatory relationships, which tend to obstruct the efficient functioning of the social order unless checked by professional codes and occupational etiquette. The premium put upon utility and efficiency suggests the adaptability of the corporate device for the organization of enterprises in which individuals can engage only in groups. The advantage that the corporation has over the individual entrepreneur and the partnership in the urban-industrial world derives not only from the possibility it affords of centralizing the resources of thousands of individuals or from the legal privilege of limited liability and perpetual succession, but from the fact that the corporation has no soul.

The specialization of individuals, particularly in their occupations, can proceed only, as Adam Smith pointed out, upon the basis of an enlarged market, which in turn accentuates the division of labor. This enlarged market is only in part supplied by the city's hinterland; in large measure it is found among the large numbers that the city itself contains. The dominance of the city over the surrounding hinterland becomes explicable in terms of the division of labor which urban life occasions and promotes. The extreme degree of interdependence and the unstable equilibrium of urban life are closely associated with the division of labor and the specialization of occupations. This interdependence and instability is increased by the tendency of each city to specialize in those functions in which it has the greatest advantage.

In a community composed of a larger number of individuals than can know one another intimately and can be assembled in one spot, it becomes necessary to communicate through indirect mediums and to articulate individual interests by a process of delegation. Typically in the city, interests are made effective through representation. The individual counts for little, but the voice of the representative is heard with a deference roughly proportional to the numbers for whom he speaks.

While this characterization of urbanism, in so far as it derives from large numbers, does not by any means exhaust the sociological inferences that might be drawn from our knowledge of the relationship of the size of a group to the characteristic behavior of the members, for the sake of brevity the assertions made may serve to exemplify the sort of propositions that might be developed.

DENSITY

As in the case of numbers, so in the case of concentration in limited space, certain consequences of relevance in sociological analysis of the city emerge. Of these only a few can be indicated.

As Darwin pointed out for flora and fauna and as Durkheim[8] noted in the case of human societies, an increase in numbers when area is held constant (i.e., an increase in density) tends to produce differentiation and specialization, since only in this way can the area support increased numbers. Density thus reinforces the effect of numbers in diversifying men and their activities and in increasing the complexity of the social structure.

On the subjective side, as Simmel has suggested, the close physical contact of

numerous individuals necessarily produces a shift in the mediums through which we orient ourselves to the urban milieu, especially to our fellowmen. Typically, our physical contacts are close but our social contacts are distant. The urban world puts a premium on visual recognition. We see the uniform which denotes the role of the functionaries and are oblivious to the personal eccentricities that are hidden behind the uniform. We tend to acquire and develop a sensitivity to a world of artifacts and become progressively farther removed from the world of nature.

We are exposed to glaring contrasts between splendor and squalor, between riches and poverty, intelligence and ignorance, order and chaos. The competition for space is great, so that each area generally tends to be put to the use which yields the greatest economic return. Place of work tends to become dissociated from place of residence, for the proximity of industrial and commercial establishments makes an area both economically and socially undesirable for residential purposes.

Density, land values, rentals, accessibility, healthfulness, prestige, aesthetic consideration, absence of nuisances such as noise, smoke, and dirt determine the desirability of various areas of the city as places of settlement for different sections of the population. Place and nature of work, income, racial and ethnic characteristics, social status, custom, habit, taste, preference, and prejudice are among the significant factors in accordance with which the urban population is selected and distributed into more or less distinct settlements. Diverse population elements inhabiting a compact settlement thus tend to become segregated from one another in the degree in which their requirements and modes of life are incompatible with one another and in the measure in which they are antagonistic to one another. Similarly, persons of homogeneous status and needs unwittingly drift into, consciously select, or are forced by circumstances into,

[8] E. Durkheim, *De la division du travail social* (Paris, 1932), p. 248.

the same area. The different parts of the city thus acquire specialized functions. The city consequently tends to resemble a mosaic of social worlds in which the transition from one to the other is abrupt. The juxtaposition of divergent personalities and modes of life tends to produce a relativistic perspective and a sense of toleration of differences which may be regarded as prerequisites for rationality and which lead toward the secularization of life.[9]

The close living together and working together of individuals who have no sentimental and emotional ties foster a spirit of competition, aggrandizement, and mutual exploitation. To counteract irresponsibility and potential disorder, formal controls tend to be resorted to. Without rigid adherence to predictable routines a large compact society would scarcely be able to maintain itself. The clock and the traffic signal are symbolic of the basis of our social order in the urban world. Frequent close physical contact, coupled with great social distance, accentuates the reserve of unattached individuals toward one another and, unless compensated for by other opportunities for response, gives rise to loneliness. The necessary frequent movement of great numbers of individuals in a congested habitat gives occasion to friction and irritation. Nervous tensions which derive from such personal frustrations are accentuated by the rapid tempo and the complicated technology under which life in dense areas must be lived.

HETEROGENEITY

The social interaction among such a variety of personality types in the urban milieu tends to break down the rigidity of caste lines and to complicate the class

structure, and thus induces a more ramified and differentiated framework of social stratification than is found in more integrated societies. The heightened mobility of the individual, which brings him within the range of stimulation by a great number of diverse individuals and subjects him to fluctuating status in the differentiated social groups that compose the social structure of the city, tends toward the acceptance of instability and insecurity in the world at large as a norm. This fact helps to account, too, for the sophistication and cosmopolitanism of the urbanite. No single group has the undivided allegiance of the individual. The groups with which he is affiliated do not lend themselves readily to a simple hierarchical arrangement. By virtue of his different interests arising out of different aspects of social life, the individual acquires membership in widely divergent groups, each of which functions only with reference to a single segment of his personality. Nor do these groups easily permit of a concentric arrangement so that the narrower ones fall within the circumference of the more inclusive ones, as is more likely to be the case in the rural community or in primitive societies. Rather the groups with which the person typically is affiliated are tangential to each other or intersect in highly variable fashion.

Partly as a result of the physical footlooseness of the population and partly as a result of their social mobility, the turnover in group membership generally is rapid. Place of residence, place and character of employment, income and interests fluctuate, and the task of holding organizations together and maintaining and promoting intimate and lasting acquaintanceship between the members is difficult. This applies strikingly to the local areas within the city into which persons become segregated more by virtue of differences in race, language, income, and social status, than through choice or positive attraction to people like themselves. Overwhelmingly the city-dweller is not a homeowner, and since a transitory habitat does not generate

---

[9] The extent to which the segregation of the population into distinct ecological and cultural areas and the resulting social attitude of tolerance, rationality, and secular mentality are functions of density as distinguished from heterogeneity is difficult to determine. Most likely we are dealing here with phenomena which are consequences of the simultaneous operation of both factors.

binding traditions and sentiments, only rarely is he truly a neighbor. There is little opportunity for the individual to obtain a conception of the city as a whole or to survey his place in the total scheme. Consequently he finds it difficult to determine what is to his own "best interests" and to decide between the issues and leaders presented to him by the agencies of mass suggestion. Individuals who are thus detached from the organized bodies which integrate society comprise the fluid masses that make collective behavior in the urban community so unpredictable and hence so problematical.

Although the city, through the recruitment of variant types to perform its diverse tasks and the accentuation of their uniqueness through competition and the premium upon eccentricity, novelty, efficient performance, and inventiveness, produces a highly differentiated population, it also exercises a leveling influence. Wherever large numbers of differently constituted individuals congregate, the process of depersonalization also enters. This leveling tendency inheres in part in the economic basis of the city. The development of large cities, at least in the modern age, was largely dependent upon the concentrative force of steam. The rise of the factory made possible mass production for an impersonal market. The fullest exploitation of the possibilities of the division of labor and mass production, however, is possible only with standardization of processes and products. A money economy goes hand in hand with such a system of production. Progressively as cities have developed upon a background of this system of production, the pecuniary nexus which implies the purchasability of services and things has displaced personal relations as the basis of association. Individuality under these circumstances must be replaced by categories. When large numbers have to make common use of facilities and institutions, an arrangement must be made to adjust the facilities and

institutions to the needs of the average person rather than to those of particular individuals. The services of the public utilities, of the recreational, educational, and cultural institutions must be adjusted to mass requirements. Similarly, the cultural institutions, such as the schools, the movies, the radio, and the newspapers, by virtue of their mass clientele, must necessarily operate as leveling influences. The political process as it appears in urban life could not be understood without taking account of the mass appeals made through modern propaganda techniques. If the individual would participate at all in the social, political, and economic life of the city, he must subordinate some of his individuality to the demands of the larger community and in that measure immerse himself in mass movements.

THE RELATION BETWEEN A THEORY OF URBANISM AND SOCIOLOGICAL RESEARCH

By means of a body of theory such as that illustratively sketched above, the complicated and many-sided phenomena of urbanism may be analyzed in terms of a limited number of basic categories. The sociological approach to the city thus acquires an essential unity and coherence enabling the empirical investigator not merely to focus more distinctly upon the problems and processes that properly fall in his province but also to treat his subject matter in a more integrated and systematic fashion. A few typical findings of empirical research in the field of urbanism, with special reference to the United States, may be indicated to substantiate the theoretical propositions set forth in the preceding pages, and some of the crucial problems for further study may be outlined.

On the basis of the three variables, number, density of settlement, and degree of heterogeneity, of the urban population, it appears possible to explain the characteristics of urban life and to account for the differences between cities of various sizes and types.

Urbanism as a characteristic mode of life may be approached empirically from three interrelated perspectives: (1) as a physical structure comprising a population base, a technology, and an ecological order; (2) as a system of social organization involving a characteristic social structure, a series of social institutions, and a typical pattern of social relationships; and (3) as a set of attitudes and ideas, and a constellation of personalities engaging in typical forms of collective behavior and subject to characteristic mechanisms of social control.

6

The local community as an ecology of games

Norton E. Long

The local community whether viewed as a polity, an economy, or a society presents itself as an order in which expectations are met and functions performed. In some cases, as in a new, company-planned mining town, the order is the willed product of centralized control, but for the most part the order is the product of a history rather than the imposed effect of any central nervous system of the community. For historic reasons we readily conceive the massive task of feeding New York to be achieved through the unplanned, historically developed cooperation of thousands of actors largely unconscious of their collaboration to this individually unsought end. The efficiency of this system is attested to by the extraordinary difficulties of the War Production Board and Service of Supply in accomplishing similar logistical objectives through an explicit system of orders and directives. Insofar as conscious rationality plays a role, it is a function of the parts rather than the whole. Particular structures working for their own ends within the whole may provide their members with goals, strategies, and roles that support rational action. The results of the interaction of the rational strivings after particular ends are in part collectively functional if unplanned. All this is the well-worn doctrine of Adam Smith, though one need accept no more of the doctrine of beneficence than that an unplanned economy can function.

While such a view is accepted for the economy, it is generally rejected for the polity. Without a sovereign, Leviathan is generally supposed to disintegrate and fall apart. Even if Locke's more hopeful view of the naturalness of the social order is taken, the polity seems more of a contrived artifact than the economy. Furthermore, there is both the hangover of Austinian sovereignty and the Greek view of ethical primacy to make political institutions seem different in kind and ultimately inclusive in purpose and for this reason to give them an over-all social directive end. To see political institutions as the same kind of thing as other institutions in society rather than as different, superior, and inclusive (both in the sense of being sovereign and ethically more significant) is a form of relativistic pluralism that is difficult to en-

Reprinted, Norton E. Long, "The Local Community as an Ecology of Games," *American Journal of Sociology*, 64 (November 1958), pp. 251–61, by permission of The University of Chicago Press. Copyright © 1958 by The University of Chicago.

This paper is largely based on a year of field study in the Boston Metropolitan area made possible by grants from the Stern Family Foundation and the Social Science Research Council. The opinions and conclusions expressed are those of the author alone.

tertain. At the local level, however, it is easier to look at the municipal government, its departments, and the other agencies of state and national government as so many institutions, resembling banks, newspapers, trade unions, chambers of commerce, churches, etc., occupying a territorial field and interacting with one another. This interaction can be conceptualized as a system without reducing the interacting institutions and individuals to membership in any single comprehensive group. It is phychologically tempting to envision the local territorial system as a group with a governing "they." This is certainly an existential possibility and one to be investigated. However, frequently, it seems likely, systems are confused with groups, and our primitive need to explain thunder with a theology or a demonology results in the hypostasizing of an angelic or demonic hierarchy. The executive committee of the bourgeoisie and the power elite make the world more comfortable for modern social scientists as the Olympians did for the ancients. At least the latter-day hypothesis, being terrestrial, is in principle researchable, though in practice its metaphysical statement may render it equally immune to mundane inquiry.

Observation of certain local communities makes it appear that inclusive overall organization for many general purposes is weak or nonexistent. Much of what occurs seems to just happen with accidental trends becoming cumulative over time and producing results intended by nobody. A great deal of the communities' activities consist of undirected cooperation of particular social structures, each seeking particular goals and, in doing so, meshing with others. While much of this might be explained in Adam Smith's terms, much of it could not be explained with a rational, atomistic model of calculating individuals. For certain purposes the individual is a useful way of looking at people; for many others the role-playing members of a particular group is more helpful. Here we deal with the essence of predictability in social

affairs. If we know the game being played is baseball and that X is a third baseman, by knowing his position and the game being played we can tell more about X's activities on the field than we could if we examined X as a psychologist or a psychiatrist. If such were not the case, X would belong in the mental ward rather than in a ball park. The behavior of X is not some disembodied rationality but, rather, behavior within an organized group activity that has goals, norms, strategies, and roles that give the very field and ground for rationality. Baseball structures the situation.

It is the contention of this paper that the structured group activities that coexist in a particular territorial system can be looked at as games. These games provide the players with a set of goals that give them a sense of success or failure. They provide them determinate roles and calculable strategies and tactics. In addition, they provide the players with an elite and general public that is in varying degrees able to tell the score. There is a good deal of evidence to be found in common parlance that many participants in contemporary group structures regard their occupations as at least analogous to games. And, at least in the American culture, and not only since Eisenhower, the conception of being on a "team" has been fairly widespread.

Unfortunately, the effectiveness of the term "game" for the purposes of this paper is vitiated by, first, the general sense that games are trivial occupations and, second, by the preemption of the term for the application of a calculus of probability to choice or decision in a determinate game situation. Far from regarding games as trivial, the writer's position would be that man is both a game-playing and a game-creating animal, that his capacity to create and play games and take them deadly seriously is of the essence, and that it is through games or activities analogous to game-playing that he achieves a satisfactory sense of significance and a meaningful role.

While the calculability of the game situation is important, of equal or greater importance is the capacity of the game to provide a sense of purpose and a role. The organizations of society and polity produce satisfactions with both their products and their processes. The two are not unrelated, but, while the production of the product may in the larger sense enable players and onlookers to keep score, the satisfaction in the process is the satisfaction of playing the game and the sense in which any activity can be grasped as a game.

Looked at this way, in the territorial system there is a political game, a banking game, a contracting game, a newspaper game, a civic organization game, an ecclesiastical game, and many others. Within each game there is a well-established set of goals whose achievement indicates success or failure for the participants, a set of socialized roles making participant behavior highly predictable, a set of strategies and tactics handed down through experience and occasionally subject to improvement and change, an elite public whose approbation is appreciated, and, finally, a general public which has some appreciation for the standing of the players. Within the game the players can be rational in the varying degrees that the structure permits. At the very least, they know how to behave, and they know the score.

Individuals may play in a number of games, but, for the most part, their major preoccupation is with one, and their sense of major achievement is through success in one. Transfer from one game to another is, of course, possible, and the simultaneous playing of roles in two or more games is an important manner of linking separate games.

Sharing a common territorial field and collaborating for different and particular ends in the achievement of overall social functions, the players in one game make use of the players in another and are, in turn, made use of by them. Thus the banker makes use of the newspaperman, the politician, the contractor, the ecclesias-

tic, the labor leader, the civic leader—all to further his success in the banking game—but, reciprocally, he is used to further the others' success in the newspaper, political, contracting, ecclesiastical, labor, and civic games. Each is a piece in the chess game of the other, sometimes a willing piece, but, to the extent that the games are different, with a different end in view.

Thus a particular highway grid may be the result of a bureaucratic department of public works game in which are combined, though separate, a professional highway engineer game with its purposes and critical elite onlookers; a departmental bureaucracy; a set of contending politicians seeking to use the highways for political capital, patronage, and the like; a banking game concerned with bonds, taxes, and the effect of the highways on real estate; newspapermen interested in headlines, scoops, and the effect of highways on the papers' circulation; contractors eager to make money by building roads; ecclesiastics concerned with the effect of highways on their parishes and on the fortunes of the contractors who support their churchly ambitions; labor leaders interested in union contracts and their status as community influentials with a right to be consulted; and civic leaders who must justify the contributions of their bureaus of municipal research or chambers of commerce to the social activity. Each game is in play in the complicated pulling and hauling of siting and constructing the highway grid. A wide variety of purposes is subserved by the activity, and no single overall directive authority controls it. However, the interrelation of the groups in constructing a highway has been developed over time, and there are general expectations as to the interaction. There are also generalized expectations as to how politicians, contractors, newspapermen, bankers, and the like will utilize the highway situation in playing their particular games. In fact, the knowledge that a banker will play like a banker and a newspaperman like a newspaperman is an important part of what makes the situation calculable and permits the players to estimate its possibilities for their own action in their particular game.

While it might seem that the engineers of the department of public works were the appropriate protagonists for the highway grid, as a general activity it presents opportunities and threats to a wide range of other players who see in the situation consequences and possibilities undreamed of by the engineers. Some general public expectation of the limits of the conduct of the players and of a desirable outcome does provide bounds to the scramble. This public expectation is, of course, made active through the interested solicitation of newspapers, politicians, civic leaders, and others who see in it material for accomplishing their particular purposes and whose structured roles in fact require the mobilization of broad publics. In a sense the group struggle that Arthur Bentley described in his *Process of Government* is a drama that local publics have been taught to view with a not uncritical taste. The instruction of this taste has been the vocation and business of some of the contending parties. The existence of some kind of overall public puts general restraints on gamesmanship beyond the norms of the particular games. However, for the players these are to all intents as much a part of the "facts of life" of the game as the sun and the wind.

It is perhaps the existence of some kind of a general public, however rudimentary, that most clearly differentiates the local territorial system from a natural ecology. The five-acre woodlot in which the owls and the field mice, the oaks and the acorns, and other flora and fauna have evolved a balanced system has no public opinion, however rudimentary. The cooperation is an unconscious affair. For much of what goes on in the local territorial system cooperation is equally unconscious and perhaps, but for the occasional social scientist, unnoticed. This unconscious cooperation, however, like that of the five-

acre woodlot, produces results. The ecology of games in the local territorial system accomplishes unplanned but largely functional results. The games and their players mesh in their particular pursuits to bring about overall results; the territorial system is fed and ordered. Its inhabitants are rational within limited areas and, pursuing the ends of these areas, accomplish socially functional ends.

While the historical development of largely unconscious cooperation between the special games in the territorial system gets certain routine, overall functions performed, the problem of novelty and breakdown must be dealt with. Here it would seem that, as in the natural ecology, random adjustment and piecemeal innovation are the normal methods of response. The need or cramp in the system presents itself to the players of the games as an opportunity for them to exploit or a menace to be overcome. Thus a transportation crisis in, say, the threatened abandonment of commuter trains by a railroad will bring forth the players of a wide range of games who will see in the situation opportunity for gain or loss in the outcome. While overall considerations will appear in the discussion, the frame of reference and the interpretation of the event will be largely determined by the game the interested parties are principally involved in. Thus a telephone executive who is president of the local chamber of commerce will be playing a civic association, general business game with concern for the principal dues-payers of the chamber but with a constant awareness of how his handling of this crisis will advance him in his particular league. The politicians, who might be expected to be protagonists of the general interest, may indeed be so, but the sphere of their activity and the glasses through which they see the problem will be determined in great part by the way they see the issue affecting their political game. The generality of this game is to a great extent that of the politician's calculus of votes and interests important to his and his side's success. To be sure, some of what Walter Lippmann has called "the public philosophy" affects both politicians and other game-players. This indicates the existence of roles and norms of a larger, vaguer game with a relevant audience that has some sense of cricket. This potentially mobilizable audience is not utterly without importance, but it provides no sure or adequate basis for support in the particular game that the politician or anyone else is playing. Instead of a set of norms to structure enduring role-playing, this audience provides a cross-pressure for momentary aberrancy from gamesmanship or constitutes just another hazard to be calculated in one's play.

In many cases the territorial system is impressive in the degree of intensity of its particular games, its banks, its newspapers, its downtown stores, its manufacturing companies, its contractors, its churches, its politicians, and its other differentiated, structured, goal-oriented activities. Games go on within the territory, occasionally extending beyond it, though centered in it. But, while the particular games show clarity of goals and intensity, few, if any, treat the territory as their proper object. The progatonists of things in particular are well organized and know what they are about; the progatonists of things in general are few, vague, and weak. Immense staff work will go into the development of a Lincoln Square project, but the 22 counties of metropolitan New York have few spokesmen for their overall common interest and not enough staff work to give these spokesmen more substance than that required for a "do-good-ing" newspaper editorial. The Port of New York Authority exhibits a disciplined self-interest and a vigorous drive along the lines of its developed historic role. However, the attitude of the Port Authority toward the general problems of the metropolitan area is scarcely different than that of any private corporation. It confines its corporate good citizenship to the contri-

bution of funds for surveys and studies and avoids acceptance of broader responsibility. In fact, spokesmen for the Port vigorously reject the need for any superior level of structured representation of metropolitan interests. The common interest, if such there be, is to be realized through institutional interactions rather than through the self-conscious rationality of a determinate group charged with its formulation and attainment. Apart from the newspaper editorial, the occasional politician, and a few civic leaders the general business of the metropolitan area is scarcely anybody's business, and, except for a few, those who concern themselves with the general problems are pursuing hobbies and causes rather than their own business.

The lack of overall institutions in the territorial system and the weakness of those that exist insure that coordination is largely ecological rather than a matter of conscious rational contriving. In the metropolitan area in most cases there are no overall economic or social institutions. People are playing particular games, and their playgrounds are less or more than the metropolitan area. But even in a city where the municipal corporation provides an apparent overall government, the appearance is deceptive. The politicians who hold the offices do not regard themselves as governors of the municipal territory but largely as mediators or players in a particular game that makes use of the other inhabitants. Their roles, as they conceive them, do not approach those of the directors of a TVA developing a territory. The ideology of local government is a highly limited affair in which the officeholders respond to demands and mediate conflicts. They play politics, and politics is vastly different from government if the latter is conceived as the rational, responsible ordering of the community. In part, this is due to the general belief that little government is necessary or that government is a congery of services only different from others because it is paid for by taxes and provided for by civil servants. In part, the separation of economics from politics eviscerates the formal theory of government of most of the substance of social action. Intervention in the really important economic order is by way of piecemeal exception and in deviation from the supposed norm of the separation of politics and economics. This ideal of separation has blocked the development of a theory of significant government action and reduced the politician to the role of register of pressure rather than responsible governor of a local political economy. The politics of the community becomes a different affair from its government, and its government is so structured as to provide the effective actors in it neither a sense of general responsibility nor the roles calling for such behavior.

The community vaguely senses that there ought to be a government. This is evidenced in the nomination by newspapers and others of particular individuals as members of a top leadership, a "they" who are periodically called upon to solve community problems and meet community crises. Significantly, the "they" usually are made up of people holding private, not public, office. The pluralism of the society has separated political, ecclesiastical, economic, and social hierarchies from one another so that the ancient union of lords spiritual and temporal is disrupted. In consequence, there is a marked distinction between the status of the holders of political office and the status of the "they" of the newspapers and the power elite of a C. Wright Mills or a Floyd Hunter. The politicians have the formal governmental office that might give them responsible governing roles. However, their lack of status makes it both absurd and presumptuous that they should take themselves so seriously. Who are they to act as lords of creation? Public expectation neither empowers nor demands that they should assume any such confident pose as top community leaders. The latter position is reserved for a rather varying group (in some communities well defined and clearcut, in others vague and amorphous) of holders for the most part of positions of private power, economic, social, and ecclesiastical. This group, regarded as the top leadership of the community, and analogous to the top management of a corporation, provides both a sense that there are gods in the heavens whose will, if they exercise it, will take care of the community's problems and a set of demons whose misrule accounts for the evil in the world. The "they" fill an office left vacant by the dethronement of absolutism and aristocracy. Unlike the politicians in that "they" are only partially visible and of untested powers, the top leadership provides a convenient rationale for explaining what goes on or does not go on in the community. It is comforting to think that the executive committee of the bourgoisie is exploiting the community or that the beneficent social and economic leaders are wearying themselves and their digestions with civic luncheons in order to bring parking to a congested city.

Usually the question is raised as to whether *de facto* there is a set of informal power-holders running things. A related question is whether community folklore holds that there is, that there should be, and what these informal power-holders should do. Certainly, most newspapermen and other professional "inside dopesters" hold that there is a "they." In fact, these people operate largely as court chroniclers of the doings of the "they." The "they," because they are "they," are newsworthy and fit into a ready-made theory of social causation that is vulgarized widely. However, the same newspaperman who could knowingly open his "bird book" and give you a rundown on the local "Who's Who" would probably with equal and blasphemous candor tell you that "they" were not doing a thing about the city and that "they" were greatly to be blamed for sitting around talking instead of getting things done. Thus, as with most primitive tribes, the idols are both worshiped and beaten, at least verbally. Public and reporters alike are relieved to believe both that there is a "they" to make civic life explicable and also to be held responsible for what occurs. This belief in part creates the role of top leadership and demands that it somehow be filled. It seems likely that there is a social-psychological table of organization of a community that must be filled in order to remove anxieties. Gordon Childe has remarked that man seems to need as much to adjust to an unseen, socially created spiritual environment as to the matter-of-fact world of the senses.

The community needs to believe that there are spiritual fathers, bad or good, who can deal with the dark: in the Middle Ages the peasants combated a plague of locusts by a high Mass and a procession of the clergy who damned the grasshoppers with bell, book, and candle. The Hopi Indians do a rain dance to overcome a drought. The harassed citizens of the American city mobilize their influentials at a civic luncheon to perform the equivalent and exorcise slums, smog, or unemployment. We smile at the medievals and the Hopi, but our own practices may be equally magical. It is interesting to ask under what circumstances one resorts to DDT and irrigation and why. To some extent it is clear that the ancient and modern practice of civic magic ritual is functional—functional in the same sense as the medicinal placebo. Much of human illness is benign; if the sufferer will bide his time, it will pass. Much of civic ills also cure themselves if only people can be kept from tearing each other apart in the stress of their anxieties. The locusts and the drought will pass. They almost always have.

While ritual activities are tranquilizing anxieties, the process of experimentation and adaptation in the social ecology goes on. The piecemeal responses of the players and the games to the challenges presented by crises provide the social counterpart to the process of evolution and natural selection. However, unlike the random mutation of the animal kingdom, much of the behavior of the players responding within the perspectives of their games is self-conscious and rational, given their ends in view. It is from the overall perspective of the unintended contribution of their actions to the forming of a new or the restoration of the old ecological balance of the social system that their actions appear almost as random and lacking in purposive plan as the adaptive behavior of the natural ecology.

Within the general area of unplanned, unconscious social process technological areas emerge that are so structured as to promote rational, goal-oriented behavior and meaningful experience rather than mere happenstance. In these areas group activity may result in cumulative knowledge and self-corrective behavior. This problem solving in the field of public health and sanitation may be at a stage far removed from the older dependence on piecemeal adjustment and random functional innovation. In this sense there are areas in which society, as Julian Huxley suggests in his *The Meaning of Evolution*, has gone beyond evolution. However, these are as yet isolated areas in a world still swayed by magic and, for the most part, carried forward by the logic of unplanned, undirected historical process.

It is not surprising that the members of the "top leadership" of the territorial system should seem to be largely confined to ritual and ceremonial roles. "Top leadership" is usually conceived in terms of status position rather than specifiable roles in social action. The role of a top leader is ill defined and to a large degree unstructured. It is in most cases a secondary role derived from a primary role as corporation executive, wealthy man, powerful ecclesiastic, holder of high social position, and the like. The top-leadership role is derivative from the other and is in most cases a result rather than a cause of status. The primary job is bank president, or president of Standard Oil; as such, one is naturally picked, nominated, and recognized as a member of the top leadership. One seldom forgets that one's primary role, obligation, and source of rational conduct is in terms of one's business. In fact, while one is on the whole pleased at the recognition that membership in the top leadership implies—much as one's wife would be pleased to be included among the ten best-dressed women—he is somewhat concerned about just what the role requires in the expenditure of time and funds. Furthermore, one has a suspicion that he may not know how to dance and could make a fool of himself before known elite and unknown, more general publics. All things considered, however, it is probably a good thing for the business, the contacts are important, and the recognition will be helpful back home, in both senses. In any event, if one's committee service or whatever concrete activity "top leadership" implies proves wearing or unsatisfactory, or if it interferes with business, one can always withdraw.

A fair gauge of the significance of top-leadership roles is the time put into them by the players and the institutionalized support represented by staff. Again and again the interviewer is told that the president of such-and-such an organization is doing a terrific job and literally knocking himself out for such-and-such a program. On investigation a "terrific job" turns out to be a few telephone calls and, possibly, three luncheons a month. The standard of "terrific job" obviously varies widely from what would be required in the business role.

In the matter of staffing, while the corporation, the church, and the government are often equipped in depth, the top-leadership job of port promotion may have little more than a secretary and an agile newspaperman equipped to ghostwrite speeches for the boss. While there are cases where people in top-leadership posi-

tions make use of staff from their own businesses and from the legal mill with which they do business, this seems largely confined to those top-leadership undertakings that have a direct connection with their business. In general, top-leadership roles seem to involve minor investments of time, staff, and money by territorial elites. The absence of staff and the emphasis on publicity limit the capacity of top leadership for sustained rational action.

Where top leaderships have become well staffed, the process seems as much or more the result of external pressures than of its own volition. Of all the functions of top leadership, that of welfare is best staffed. Much of this is the result of the pressure of the professional social worker to organize a concentration of economic and social power sufficient to permit him to do a job. It is true, of course, that the price of organizing top leadership and making it manageable by the social workers facilitated a reverse control of themselves—a control of whose galling nature Hunter gives evidence. An amusing side-light on the organization of the "executive committee of the bourgeoisie" is the case of the Cleveland Fifty Club. This club, supposedly, is made up of the 50 most important men in Cleveland. Most middling and even upper executives long for the prestige recognition that membership confers. Reputedly, the Fifty Club was organized by Brooks Emery, while he was director of the Cleveland Council on World Affairs, to facilitate the taxation of business to support that organization. The lead time required to get the august members of the Fifty Club together and their incohesiveness have severely limited its possibilities as a power elite. Members who have tried to turn it to such a purpose report fairly consistent failure.

The example of the Cleveland Fifty Club, while somewhat extreme, points to the need on the part of certain activities in the territorial system for a top leadership under whose auspices they can function.

A wide variety of civic undertakings need to organize top-prestige support both to finance and to legitimate their activities. The staff man of a bureau of municipal research or the Red Feather Agency cannot proceed on his own; he must have the legitimatizing sponsorship of top influentials. His task may be self-assigned, his perception of the problem and its solution may be his own, but he cannot gain acceptance without mobilizing the influentials. For the success of his game he must assist in creating the game of top leadership. The staff man in the civic field is the typical protagonist of things in general—a kind of entrepreneur of ideas. He fulfills the same role in his area as the stock promoter of the 20s or the Zeckendorfs of urban redevelopment. Lacking both status and a confining organizational basis, he has a socially valuable mobility between the specialized games and hierarchies in the territorial system. His success in the negotiation of a port authority not only provides a plus for his taxpayers federation or his world trade council but may provide a secure and lucrative job for himself.

Civic staff men, ranging from chamber of commerce personnel to college professors and newspapermen, are in varying degrees interchangeable and provide an important network of communication. The staff men in the civic agencies play similar roles to the Cohens and Corcorans in Washington. In each case a set of telephone numbers provides special information and an effective lower-echelon interaction. Consensus among interested professionals at the lower level can result in action programs from below that are bucked up to the prestige level of legitimatization. As the Cohens and Corcorans played perhaps the most general and inclusive game in the Washington bureaucracy, so their counterparts in the local territorial system are engaged in the most general action game in their area. Just as the Cohens and Corcorans had to mobilize

an effective concentration of top brass to move a program into the action stage, so their counterparts have to mobilize concentrations of power sufficient for their purposes on the local scene.

In this connection it is interesting to note that foundation grants are being used to hire displaced New Deal bureaucrats and college professors in an attempt to organize the influentials of metropolitan areas into self-conscious governing groups. Professional chamber of commerce executives, immobilized by their orthodox ideology, are aghast to see their members study under the planners and heretics from the dogmas of free-enterprise fundamentalism. The attempt to transform the metropolitan appearance of disorder into a tidy territory is a built-in predisposition for the self-constituted staff of the embryonic top metropolitan management. The major disorder that has to be overcome before all others is the lack of order and organization among the "power elite." As in the case of the social workers, there is a thrust from below to organize a "power elite" as a necessary instrument to accomplish the purposes of civic staff men. This is in many ways nothing but a part of the general groping after a territorial government capable of dealing with a range of problems that the existing feudal disintegration of power cannot. The nomination of a top leadership by newspapers and public and the attempt to create such a leadership in fact by civic technicians are due to a recognition that there is a need for a leadership with the status, capacity, and role to attend to the general problems of the territory and give substance to a public philosophy. This involves major changes in the script of the top-leadership game and the self-image of its participants. In fact, the insecurity and the situational limitations of their positions in corporations or other institutions that provide the primary roles for top leaders make it difficult to give more substance to what has been a secondary role. Many members of present top leaderships are genuinely reluctant, fearful, and even morally shocked at their positions' becoming that of a recognized territorial government. While there is a general supposition that power is almost instinctively craved, there seems considerable evidence that at least in many of our territorial cultures responsibility is not. Machiavellian *virtu* is an even scarcer commodity among the merchant princes of the present than among their Renaissance predecessors. In addition, the educational systems of school and business do not provide top leaders with the inspiration or the know-how to do more than raise funds and man committees. Politics is frequently regarded with the same disgust as military service by the ancient educated Chinese.

It is possible to translate a check pretty directly into effective power in a chamber of commerce or a welfare agency. However, to translate economic power into more general social or political power, there must be an organized purchasable structure. Where such structures exist, they may be controlled or, as in the case of *condottieri*, gangsters, and politicians, their hire may be uncertain, and the hired force retains its independence. Where businessmen are unwilling or unable to organize their own political machines, they must pay those who do. Sometimes the paymaster rules; at other times he bargains with equals or superiors.

A major protagonist of things in general in the territorial system is the newspaper. Along with the welfare worker, museum director, civic technician, etc., the newspaper has an interest in terms of its broad reading public in agitating general issues and projects. As the chronicler of the great, both in its general news columns and in its special features devoted to society and business, it provides an organizing medium for elites in the territory and provides them with most of their information about things in general and not a little of inside tidbits about how individual elite

members are doing. In a sense, the newspaper is the prime mover in setting the territorial agenda. It has a great part in determining what most people will be talking about, what most people will think the facts are, and what most people will regard as the way problems are to be dealt with. While the conventions of how a newspaper is to be run, and the compelling force of some events, limit the complete freedom of a paper to select what events and what people its public will attend to, it has great leeway. However, the newspaper is a business and a specialized game even when its reporters are idealists and its publisher rejoices in the title "Mr. Cleveland." The paper does not accept the responsibility of a governing role in its territory. It is a power but only a partially responsible one. The span of attention of its audience and the conventions of what constitute a story give it a crusading role at most for particular projects. Nonetheless, to a large extent it sets the civic agenda.

The story is told of the mayor of a large eastern metropolis who, having visited the three capital cities of his constituents—Rome, Dublin, and Tel Aviv—had proceeded home via Paris and Le Havre. Since his staff had neglected to meet the boat before the press, he was badgered by reports to say what he had learned on his trip. The unfortunate mayor could not say that he had been on a junket for a good time. Luckily, he remembered that in Paris they had been having an antinoise campaign. Off the hook at last, he told the press that he thought this campaign was a good thing. This gave the newsmen something to write about. The mayor hoped this was the end of it. But a major paper felt in need of a crusade to sponsor and began to harass the mayor about the start of the local antinoise campaign. Other newspapers took up the cry, and the mayor told his staff they were for it—there had to be an antinoise campaign. In short order, businessmen's committees, psychiatrists, and college professors were mobilized to press forward on a broad front the suppression of needless noise. In vindication of administrative rationality it appeared that an antinoise campaign was on a staff list of possibilities for the mayor's agenda but had been discarded by him as politically unfeasible.

The civic technicians and the newspapers have somewhat the same relationship as congressional committee staff and the press. Many members of congressional committee staffs complain bitterly that their professional consciences are seared by the insistent pressure to seek publicity. But they contend that their committee sponsors are only impressed with research that is newsworthy. Congressional committee members point out that committees that do not get publicity are likely to go out of business or funds. The civic agency head all too frequently communicates most effectively with his board through his success in getting newspaper publicity. Many a civic ghostwriter has found his top leader converted to the cause by reading the ghosted speech he delivered at the civic luncheon reported with photographs and editorials in the press. This is even the case where the story appears in the top leader's own paper. The need of the reporters for news and of the civic technicians for publicity brings the participants of these two games together. As in the case of the congressional committee, there is a tendency to equate accomplishment with publicity. For top influentials on civic boards the news clips are an important way of keeping score. This symbiotic relation of newsmen and civic staff helps explain the heavy emphasis on ritual luncheons, committees, and news releases. The nature of the newspapers' concern with a story about people and the working of marvels and miracles puts a heavy pressure for the kind of story that the press likes to carry. It is not surprising that civic staff men should begin to equate accomplishment with their

score measured in newspaper victories or that they should succumb to the temptation to impress their sponsors with publicity, salting it to their taste by flattering newspaper tributes to the sponsors themselves. Despite the built-in incapacity of newspapers to exercise a serious governing responsibility in their territories, they are for the most part the only institutions with a long-term general territorial interest. In default of a territorial political party or other institution that accepts responsibility for the formulation of a general civic agenda, the newspaper is the one game that by virtue of its public and its conventions partly fills the vacuum.

A final game that does in a significant way integrate all the games in the territorial system is the social game. Success in each of the games can in varying degrees be cashed in for social acceptance. The custodians of the symbols of top social standing provide goals that in a sense give all the individual games some common denominator of achievement. While the holders of top social prestige do not necessarily hold either top political or economic power, they do provide meaningful goals for the rest. One of the most serious criticisms of a Yankee aristocracy made by a Catholic bishop was that, in losing faith in their own social values, they were undermining the faith in the whole system of final clubs. It would be a cruel joke if, just as the hard-working upwardly mobile had worked their way to entrance, the progeny of the founders lost interest. The decay of the Union League Club in *By Love Possessed* is a tragedy for more than its members. A common game shared even by the excluded spectators gave a purpose that was functional in its time and must be replaced—hopefully, by a better one. A major motivation for seeking membership in and playing the top-leadership game is the value of the status it confers as a counter in the social game.

Neither the civic leadership game nor

the social game makes the territorial ecology over into a structured government. They do, however, provide important ways of linking the individual games and make possible cooperative action on projects. Finally, the social game, in Ruth Benedict's sense, in a general way patterns the culture of the territorial ecology and gives all the players a set of vaguely shared aspirations and common goals.

7

Function and structure of community: Conceptual and theoretical analysis

Israel Rubin

INTRODUCTION

If we begin with the truism that a scientific concept is useful to the degree that it enables the isolation of a distinct phenomenon or unit worthy of study and analysis, we are led to serious doubt concerning the continued utility of the concept of "community" in social science. The difficulty clearly emerges when it comes to assessing the modern scene in developed societies, especially the United States. A cursory examination of the mainstream of community literature reveals three general tendencies, occasionally overlapping with each other, all of which are, in my view, unsatisfactory. First, we detect the Tönniesian tendency to link community with the small town or village of traditional society, a tendency that leads into the futile path of

romantic revery and the bewailing of the fate of modern man, who has "lost his community."[1] Then, we find application of the concept to almost any form of social organization that is territorially bounded, especially if the size of the unit renders it accessible on a daily basis to its members.[2]

With this loose perspective, it becomes virtually impossible to even approach a realistic evaluation of how modern industrial man is faring community-wise.[3] And finally, we notice a degree of restlessness on the part of some students who feel unhappy with either of the two aforementioned views and are, hence, inclined to

Reprinted with the permission of the author and publisher from Israel Rubin, "Function and Structure of Community: Conceptual and Theoretical Analysis," *International Review of Community Development*, no. 21–22 (1969), pp. 111–119.

This is a revised version of a paper entitled "A Revision of the Concept of Community" that I read at the annual meeting of the American Sociological Association, August 1968, Boston, Massachusetts. I am grateful to my colleague of the History Department at Cleveland State University, Professor Julius Weinberg, who read an earlier version of the paper and offered valuable comments. I am equally indebted to all participants in the round table discussion at Boston. They have been of considerable assistance in clarifying my ideas.

[1] See Ferdinand Tönnies, *Community and Society (Gemeinschaft and Gesellschaft)*. Trans. and ed. by C. P. Loomis (Ann Arbor, Michigan, 1957). R. A. Nisbet, *Community and Power* (New York, 1962). A somewhat modified approach, but within the same basic tradition, is offered by J. S. Coleman under the title "Community Disorganization" in R. K. Merton and R. A. Nisbet, eds., *Contemporary Social Problems*, 2d ed. (New York, 1966), pp. 670–722.

[2] Cf., for example, C. M. Arensberg and S. T. Kimball, *Culture and Community* (New York, 1965), esp. pp. 15–16, 102; B. M. Mercer, *The American Community* (New York, 1956); I. T. Sanders, *The Community, an Introduction to a Social System* (New York, 1958); and L. F. Schnore, "Community" in *Sociology, an Introduction*, ed. N. J. Smelser (New York, 1967), pp. 79–150, esp. p. 95.

[3] For an admission of this problem see J. Bernard, "Community Disorganization" in *International Encyclopedia of the Social Sciences*, 1968, vol. 3, pp. 163–169.

cease insisting on geographic boundaries as necessary for community.[4] However, while this negation, as we shall later see, is a welcome departure from orthodoxy, the alternatives offered are equally lacking in rigor, often leaving us with such intangible framework as "community of interest," thus searching for community anywhere from the psychiatrist's couch to the state.[5] It is, hence, no wonder to find that a leading student of the subject has, after long years of research in this area, recently appealed for discontinued use of the term because it "has become an omnibus word."[6]

In this paper I shall endeavor to argue that the mess contains a healthy residue worthy of retrieval, that careful scrutiny points to an area of reality appropriately termed community. I shall then argue that if carefully used, the concept of community may direct our attention to a highly important aspect of social life and, especially, to the way this aspect has been affected by modern conditions.

SEARCH FOR STRUCTURE VIA FUNCTION

It seems appropriate, for our purpose, to approach the problem of community structure through the back door, i.e., by first clarifying the function of the structure we are seeking. Without such clarification, discussion of whether or not modern man's community has been going through disorganization or reorganization is bound to remain academic in the worst sense of the term. A sampling of the literature on community function at once reveals the confusion that beclouds the entire community literature. For example, we are told by leading students that the function of community is to provide for the daily needs of the individual,[7] help preserve culture and society,[8] or provide specialized services.[9] The obvious difficulty with these general and diffuse claims is that they lack not only data to substantiate that these functions cannot be performed by any structure other than that termed "community" by the respective authors, but they actually lack any sound theoretical basis that would at least lend logical support for these theses. Why should one assume that satisfaction of daily needs must take place within a community? Unless, of course, one chooses, as some do, to define the term as the territory within convenient daily reach of the individual. But then we fall into tautological reasoning, for each individual who manages to survive has, by definition, access to sources that provide for his daily necessities. Hence, what purpose does it serve to search for the nature of

---

[4] Most outspoken along this line has been D. Martindale. See chap. 5 "The Community" in his *American Social Structure* (New York, 1960), pp. 131–50. Also, A. K. Basu, "The Concept of Community in Developing Nations" in *Sociology and Social Research*, 1968, pp. 193–202. As noted, these trends overlap. Many continue to insist on territoriality and, at the same time, search for new dimensions. See Arensberg and Kimball, *Culture and Community*; M. R. Stein, *The Eclipse of Community: an Interpretation of American Studies* (Princeton, 1960); M. Freilich, "Toward an Operational Definition of Community" in *Rural Sociology*, 1964, pp. 117–127; and W. A. Sutton and J. Kolaja, "The Concept of Community" in *Rural Sociology*, 1960, pp. 197–203. Others merely note difficulties without indicating new approaches. See N. Anderson, "Rethinking our Ideas about Community" in *International Review of Community Development*, 1962, pp. 143–53 and R. L. Simpson, "Sociology of Community" in *Rural Sociology*, 1965, pp. 127–49.

[5] See especially Basu, *Concept of Community*, Stein, *Eclipse of Community*, p. 130 and ff. and H. Zentner, "The State and the Community: A Conceptual Clarification" in *Sociology and Social Research*, 1964, pp. 414–27.

[6] G. A. Hillery, Jr., "Villages, Cities, and Total Institutions" in *American Sociological Review*, 1963, pp. 779–91.

---

[7] Mercer, *The American Community*; Sanders, *The Community*. Also implied in Schnore, *Community*, and in R. Warren, *The Community in America* (Chicago, 1963), esp. pp. 9–10.

[8] Most explicit on this point are Arensberg and Kimball, *Culture and Community*. The view is partially echoed in Mercer, *The American Community*, Schnore, *Community*, and Zentner, *State and Community*.

[9] Mercer, *The American Community* and Schnore, *Community*.

modern man's community beyond the obvious observation that unlike his predecessor, urban-industrial man has daily access to a larger chunk of territory and greater variety of goods and services that came, by virtue of their availability, to be included in the list of one's "daily needs?" With minor variations the argument could be repeated with regard to the claimed functions of providing "specialized services" or the preservation of culture and society.[10]

It seems, therefore, justifiable to first search for a need or a set of needs the satisfaction of which is more specifically linked to a structure reasonably termed "community" and then proceed to examine the necessary (from the point of view of the claimed need-satisfaction) parameters of such a structure. Such an examination will have to be characterized by open-mindedness with regard to the exact form of the structure. We shall assume that the necessary elements may be found in a variety of structural forms, as the latter may be a function of the sociocultural context. Only then shall we be ready to attempt an assessment of the modern scene: whether or not (or to what degree) modern man has managed to satisfy his need for community.

Over a half century ago, Durkheim provided the theoretical nucleus for the present approach. He stated:

A society composed of an infinite number of unorganized individuals that a hypertrophied State is forced to oppress and contain, constitutes a veritable sociological monstrosity. For collective activity is always too complex to be able to be expressed through the single and unique organ of the State. Moreover, the State is too remote from the individuals; its relations with them too external and intermittent to penetrate deeply into individual consciences and socialize them within. Where the state is the only environment in which we can live communal lives, they inevitably lose contact, become detached, and thus society disintegrates. A nation can be maintained only if, between the State and the individual, there is intercalated a whole series of secondary groups near enough to the individuals to attract them strongly in their sphere of action and drag them in this way, into the general torrent of social life.[11]

Thus, it is this need for intermediary structures through which individuals feel meaningful related to the larger society of which they are members, the need not to feel alienated, that gives rise to what Nisbet has called "the quest for community."[12]

Let us now examine socio-logically what properties such a structure would need to possess if it is to fulfill this mediating function between individual and society. Five structural characteristics readily come to mind.

1. Intermediate size. We are, obviously, searching for structures that are, on the one hand, small enough to enable individuals to experience what is commonly called a "sense of community" and are, on the other hand, large enough to give members a feeling of meaningful incorporation into the larger societal structure, a feeling that the small friendship group cannot provide.

2. Presence of significant primary and secondary interaction. Although we are aware of the fact that virtually every real human group or organization is characterized by some measure of both primary

---

[10] Many writers on the subject (e.g., Bernard, Coleman, Freilich, Martindale) avoid the problem of function altogether.

[11] E. Durkheim, *Division of Labor in Society*, trans. by George Simpson (Glencoe, Ill.; 1964), "Preface to the Second Edition: Some Notes on Occupational Groups," p. 28.

[12] *The Quest for Community* was the earlier title of the above-cited *Community and Power*. It is interesting that Nisbet, who uses the mediating function of community as the central theme of this book and cites Durkheim frequently on the nature of anomie, fails to credit Durkheim with the basic idea of community function. It is also ironic that despite its basically romantic view, Nisbet's book is, as far as I could establish, the only contemporary explicit statement that accepts that Durkheimian view, which, as we shall see, militates heavily against the romantics' gloominess.

and secondary interaction,[13] we also recognize that in some structures, one or the other tends to dominate. However, in order to fulfill the community function, an organization must be the scene of both varieties of interaction that are, furthermore, inextricably intertwined. For a "sense of community" implies a feeling that the organization provides simultaneously both a sphere of congeniality and an opportunity to partake in social processes that affect some vital area (or areas) of existence.[14]

3. Key institutional setting. Unless an organization focuses around an area of behavior considered to be of central importance within the culture, it cannot possibly convey to its members a sense of significant incorporation in society via membership in the organization. It follows that we may expect community organizations to vary in their institutional setting from culture to culture, as well as from one subculture to another.

4. Relative stability. There are two aspects of stability and both seem necessary for a community. First, we barely need to belabor the point that the organization must endure for a considerable stretch of time, than an ad hoc structure cannot function as a community. Then, the individual must belong to the organization for a significant portion of his adult life. Organizations (e.g., a typical modern urban neighborhood) with a high rate of membership turnover cannot be expected to assume a high level of significance for the individual.[15]

5. Concreteness. Finally, it should by now be clear that we are speaking of concrete social structures within which individuals recognize at least a significant

number of fellow members with whom they interact and identify. A mere aggregate of people who constitute some "community of interest" will, obviously, not serve our purpose.

Equally important for the purpose of enabling identification of communities is the isolation of unnecessary characteristics. Since we have settled on mediation between individual and society as the core function of community and rejected the necessity of such functions as provision of daily needs or preservation of culture, we should be able, as a concomitant, to strike from our required list those structural features that are frequently associated with community but which are tied to the functions that we have judged as nonessential. Of central importance here are two items, institutional microcosm and territorial focus.

There is no apparent reason why a community should contain a cross section of all major institutions, why the community ought to encompass family or religious behavior. Such a claim would especially be difficult to defend with regard to Western-style developed societies with highly developed institutional division of labor. If such functions as economic production or education have proven to be feasibly (in fact, necessarily) accomplished in functionally specific structures, why insist that the community function require a diffuse setting?

Even more important is the issue of territorial boundaries, a characteristic on which most community students insist.[16] This insistence is clearly associated with

---

[13] Cf. S. Greer, *Social Organization* (New York, 1962), p. 33 and ff.

[14] Obviously, many organizations are the scene of such dual interaction for some members and not for others. The implications will be noted later.

[15] What was said in n. 14 also applies with regard to stability.

[16] In an early article entitled "Definition of Community: Some Areas of Agreement" (*Rural Sociology*, 1955, pp. 111–23), Hillery analyzed over 90 definitions of community and found that with few exceptions there is agreement on inclusion of territory in the definition. Of the more recent statements that I have examined, the territorial element is either explicitly or implicitly included in the above-cited writings of Anderson, Arensberg and Kimball, Bernard, Coleman, Freilich, Sanders, Schnore, Simpson, Stein, Sutton and Kolaja, and Warren.

the assumed function of daily-need-provision, which, by its very nature, takes place within a geographic unit or a set of units (neighborhood, township, metropolitan area). The territorial view of community is probably responsible for most of the fuzzy theorization that we have discussed above. For example, the romantic theme that modern man has "lost" his community is fed by the common observation that the neighborhoods, towns, and cities have ceased to serve as significant foci of identification for the mobile man of industrial society. However, from our vantage point we see no reason for saddling the concept with the territorial element. Individuals may meaningfully relate to their respective societies through nonterritorial as well as through territorial substructures. In fact, this is the very heart of the present thesis and there is ample support for this view in both theory and research.

BACKGROUND OF THE PRESENT APPROACH

Durkheim has not only provided the theoretical foundation for understanding the function of community, but he also laid the groundwork for the analysis of community structure in modern conditions, indicating that "as advances are made in history, the organization which has the territorial groups as its base (village or city, district, province, etc.) steadily becomes effaced." We are further cautioned against confusing persistence with adequate function. "To be sure, each of us belongs to a commune or department, but the bonds attaching us there become daily more fragile and more slack. *These geographical divisions are, for the most part, artificial and no longer awaken in us profound sentiments. The provincial spirit has disappeared never to return; the patriotism of the parish has become an archaism that cannot be restored at will"*[17] (italics mine).

And finally, avoiding the romantic despondence, Durkheim visualized not only the possibility but the probability of substitute structures that would emerge to replace the outdated territorial units.

This early statement, which contains most of the theoretical elements of the present proposition, has, curiously, gone unnoticed by most students of the subject. The few exceptions, especially Martindale, have not been specific enough in their suggestions of alternative approaches and have occasionally even reinforced views of those who remained in the mainstream of community study.[18]

In 1957, Goode drew our attention to the possibility of regarding professions as "communities within communities," indicating that a profession may be a community despite its lack of a "physical locus."[19] Thus, Goode, after a half-century lapse, attempted to renew Durkheim's erstwhile plea (though, like Nisbet, not specifically acknowleging the ancestry) for the abolition of the territorial crutches, and even looked in the direction indicated by Durkheim, the occupational sphere, for the emergence of nonterritorial communities. Although Goode's effort goes beyond Durkheim's general and abstract statement, the plea being more specifically directed at community theorists, his statement has also been largely ignored.

Fortunately, assistance has been forthcoming from the world of empirical research. Data, though widely scattered, have been accumulating that do not allow us to ignore the subject for another half-century.

Several types of data are relevant to our theme.

---

[17] Durkheim, *Division of Labor*, pp. 27–28.

[18] For example, Schnore uses the intangible nature of the "community of interest" alternative in his argument for viewing community in terms of geographic boundaries. *Community*, pp. 90–92. We shall soon see that this is not necessarily the case.

[19] W. J. Goode, "Community Within a Community: The Professions." *American Sociological Review*, 1957, pp. 195–200.

First, research has consistently substantiated the common observation that in the modern setting territorial units have been strained by the emergence of structures that cut across town, city, or state boundaries. This has become clear from the early investigations by Warner et al.,[20] to subsequent studies such as the ones by Vidich and Bensman,[21] or Lois Dean.[22] Aside from bolstering our impressions with facts, these studies have two additional advantages over our casual observations: they extend the view to the small town, and they point not only to strain experienced by the "local," but also to the concurrent adaptive advantage of the "cosmopolitan."

Reinforcement for this view comes from studies that focus on various aspects of elite and leadership structure. For example, Photiades found small-town businessmen to feel more alienated than those of larger cities.[23] And in a pair of articles Young and Larson report findings that show (a) the importance of membership in large voluntary organizations, (b) that the high prestige organizations are those that transcend local boundaries, and finally (c) that significant primary interaction occurs within the confines of large-scale organizations.[24] The latter finding, particularly important on account of its indication of the large organization's potential for community function, ties in to still another series of studies that concentrated on primary interaction and/or political function

of associations traditionally dubbed "secondary."

In a pioneering study over a decade ago, Bell and Boat[25] attempted to pierce the stereotype image of the impersonal nature of urban life. Their data showed not only the existence of widespread informal interaction within the city, but also that some of the so-called secondary associations often provide the framework of such interaction. Inching a bit closer to our mark, Greer and Orleans found in St. Louis that certain associations serve as "parapolitical structures," i.e., they contain cells of important political activity.[26] Even more important for our purpose is their finding that these parapolitical structures serve mainly the "cosmopolites" who are "unengaged in the local area as a community" and are, instead, politically active "through organizations based upon occupational, class and ethnic interests."[27] Hall and Schwirian, confirming these observations in a recent study, consequently conclude that in mass society occupational situs is a more significant determinant of political behavior than locality of residence.[28]

Finally, turning our attention to a different cultural setting, Rubin,[29] analyzing the pietist Chassidic movement among Jews, suggests that the apparent tenacity of the Chassidic community may, at least in part, be attributed to the nongeographic structure of that community type which rendered it less vulnerable to the frequent uprootings experienced by Jews. The implication is offered that wherever residen-

[20] W. L. Warner and J. O. Low, "The Factory in the Community" in W. F. Whyte, ed., *Industry and Society* (New York, 1946), pp. 21–45.

[21] A. J. Vidich and J. Bensman, *Small Town in Mass Society* (Garden City, N.Y., 1960).

[22] L. Dean, *Five Towns: A Comparative Community Study* (New York, 1967).

[23] J. D. Photiades, "Social Integration in Varied Size Communities" in *Social Forces*, 1967, pp. 229–36.

[24] R. C. Young and O. L. Larson, "A New Approach to Community Structure" in *American Sociological Review*, 1965, pp. 926–34 and "The Contribution of Voluntary Organizations to Community Structure" in *American Journal of Sociology*, 1965, pp. 178–86.

[25] W. Bell and M. D. Boat, "Urban Neighborhood and Informal Social Relations" in *American Journal of Sociology*, 1957, pp. 391–98.

[26] S. Greer and P. Orleans, "Mass Society and Parapolitical Structures" in *American Sociological Review*, 1962, pp. 634–46.

[27] Ibid., p. 646.

[28] N. E. Hall and K. P. Schwirian, "Occupational Situs, Community Structure, and Local Political Participation" in *Sociological Focus*, 1968, pp. 17–30.

[29] I. Rubin, "Chassidic Community Behavior" in *Anthropological Quarterly*, 1964, pp. 138–48.

tial continuity is strained, a successful adaptation to the strain may involve transition to a community type with a focus other than residence.

It is now time to integrate these bits and pieces into a comprehensive set of propositions.

THE PRESENT FORMULA

Proposition 1. There is a need for intermediate-size structures—communities—to serve as buffers between the individual and the larger society. It is understood that the assumption of this need is made with respect to virtually every society, excepting only some simple societies that are not larger in size than we would consider to be the optimal size of a community. It is not important for our purpose to establish the exact nature of this need. It may be an objective need, as Durkheim claims. It may also be that the claim that such a need exists constitutes a value judgment, as Nisbet would have it. The main point to be kept in mind is that if alienation is to be prevented, community needs to exist.

Proposition 2. In order to fulfill its function, a community must be a concrete organization that is relatively stable, situated in a central institutional area, and within which members of the organization interact significantly on both the primary and secondary level.

Conversely, there is no need that the community provide for the daily needs of its members and, hence, there is no reason that it constitute a microcosm of the larger sociocultural system.

There is no need to further belabor these points that have been discussed in detail.

Proposition 3. Communities may be organized either along residential lines or along other, nonresidential boundaries, as the necessary functional and structural elements do not appear to require territorial focus.

Proposition 4. While limited communication technology of preindustrial societies may favor territorial communities, modern conditions appear to encourage the formation of communities that, though occasionally located within a geographic boundary, are focused on other than territorial or residential factors.

This is, of course, not suggesting that nonterritorial communities are confined to modern societies, or that modern conditions absolutely preclude the possibility that some territorial units will continue to serve as communities, at least to some individuals. And certainly we do not overlook the fact that territorially based structures continue to exist and perform a category of important functions (in the general area of "daily needs" that we discussed). I merely suggest that due to increased mobility in modern societies, we should expect a relative shift in importance away from the neighborhood or town community; that, as Durkheim pointed out, the mere existence of, say, a town, does not automatically mean that it continues to elicit from its inhabitants the strong sense of identification required for a community. The assumption seems warranted in the light of studies such as the ones by Goode, Greer and Orleans, Hall and Schwirian, Rubin, or Young and Larson, that were cited previously.

QUESTIONS AND PROBLEMS

Obviously, the above outline constitutes, at best, no more than a series of guesses, albeit warranted by available scant knowledge. We are in need of systematically focused and far more extensive validating data before we accept this as a realistic view. Furthermore, the model has serious gaps that need to be filled with further empirical research.

Thus, we do not know what proportion of the population in our society, and in equally developed societies, have either made the transition to nonterritorial communities or are in the process of doing so. Nor do we have an idea as to which segments of society are involved; whether the selective process follows along class, ethnic, religious, or any other lines. Similarly, we are in dire need of comparable data with regard to societies in various stages of development. Another uncharted area concerns the complexity of modern community life. The view presented here points to the probability of partial as well as multiple community. In other words, we have some reason to believe that, on the one hand, some organizations may serve as communities to some but not all members[30] and, on the other hand, some individuals probably relate to their society through several rather than a single community. Which organizations and what category of individuals are respectively involved and what patterns the processes follow are currently open questions.

Paralleling our lack of data, present theory shows considerable lag in most of these areas and will probably not advance significantly before fresh data are in. For example, should we find that working-class individuals have been lagging behind their middle-class contemporaries in adapting to the mobile conditions of modern life, we would be capable of no more than guessing concerning the aspect of working-class existence to which we ought to attribute the lag. We would be at a similar loss with respect to ethnic or religious variables should the latter appear to be significant factors in the process.

---

[30] See notes 14 and 15.

SUMMARY AND CONCLUSION

In this paper I have argued for a view of community in terms of its mediating function between individual and society and suggested an open-minded approach regarding structure, with particular emphasis on the necessity to discard the territorial crutches. I have, further, stressed the desirability of research for testing the validity of the presented view as well as for reducing our current gaps in both empirical data and theory. It seems to me that the approach has significant potential for the human sciences. As far as modern man is concerned, we might be able to pinpoint realistically the extent and locus of alienation, isolate the variables involved, and, perhaps, indicate avenues toward solution of alienation problems that may be found to exist in our midst. We may even be able to shed new light on some specific problems such as union behavior (are some problems of unions associated with their local focus?) or the current controversy about "community control" (to what extent and for whom do the black and other ethnic ghettos serve as real communities?). As for developing societies, a clear view of the changing nature of community and an understanding of correlates of adaptation should enable anticipation of emerging alienation problems and, hence, preventive planning. However, as a first step, we need to exchange loose theory and romantic daydreaming for rigorous open-minded research on community structure and process.

8

A field-theory perspective for community development research

Kenneth P. Wilkinson

The purpose of this paper is to outline a conception of community development from the perspective of social field theory, drawing upon and extending earlier studies (Kaufman, 1959; Kaufman and Wilkinson, 1967; Wilkinson, 1969, 1970a) in which the community was defined as a social field. The notion of the community field will be reviewed briefly and extended to encompass a notion of community development. This will then be explicated through discussion of selected contemporary issues in community development practice. The aim in this discussion will be to identify fundamental theoretical issues underlying the practical concerns. Research needed to deal with these issues will be indicated.

THE COMMUNITY FIELD

Field theory (see Wilkinson 1970a:311–314, which draws upon Maxwell, 1890: 532–533; Lewin, 1951; Fagan, 1964; Yinger, 1965; and Kaufman, 1959) is concerned with the emergent dynamics of unbounded wholes, which are termed fields. Fields have been identified and examined at many levels of analysis, including first the physical and biological and more recently the psychological, cultural, and social. Fields are emergent in the sense that they differ from the sum of the characteristics of their components. They are dynamic in that they are constantly changing. "Unbounded" means literally without boundaries—fields shade into one another and must be distinguished according to their core properties rather than according to the characteristics of their perimeters. A field is holistic in the sense of having a configurational or systemic unity. How a field can be emergent, dynamic, and unbounded and still have sufficient internal unity to constitute a single, holistic thing is one of the problems with which field theory deals.[1]

Groups, organizations, communities, and other forms of social organization may be treated as social fields. A social field is "a process of interaction through time, with direction toward some more or less distinctive outcome and with constantly changing elements and structure" (Wilkinson, 1970a:317). The main components are behavioral roles of actors as these are more or less tenuously organized through time relative to one another and relative to the collective interests being pursued. The emergent, dynamic, and boundless qualities of a social field derive in large part from the objective contingencies of behavioral events. One never knows *exactly* what will happen next as many variables and forces, each with "multiple possibilities" (Yinger, 1965), converge to interact at the moment of behavior. The holistic characteristics of a social field, while man-

Reprinted with permission of the author and the publisher from Kenneth P. Wilkinson, "A Field Theory Perspective for Community Development Research," *Rural Sociology* 37, no. 1 (March 1972), pp. 43–52. The footnotes have been renumbered.

This is a revised and extended version of a paper presented at the annual meeting of the Association of Southern Agricultural Workers in Jacksonville, Florida, February 3, 1971.

[1] In contrast to both extreme phenomenology, which assumes that the universe is disintegrating, and teleology, which assumes that there is a basic, pervasive force toward order, field theory assumes that both order and disarray, both "system" and "turbulence" (Turney-High, 1968) are essential characteristics of reality.

ifested in behavioral regularities, result on the other hand primarily from individual and collective processes of conceptualization.

Among the social fields in a given locality are some which are locality-oriented, meaning (Wilkinson, 1970b: 56–57) that the principal actors and beneficiaries are local residents, the goals of action represent interests of local residents, and the action is public as opposed to private in that beneficiaries include persons in addition to the actors. In many instances the actions and structures which constitute one of these fields are oriented toward a single interest or category of interests. Such fields may be grouped for purposes of study along institutional-interest lines.

The community field (Kaufman, 1959: 10) is a locality-oriented social field through which actions expressing a broad range of local interests are coordinated. It emerges from the institutional-interest fields and acts upon them.[2] The essential, distinctive process of the community field is that of generalization across interest lines. It is through the community field that comprehensive community "improvement" efforts are conducted.

The community field is manifested in the acts of generalized leaders which contribute to the accomplishment of goals in a variety of community projects over the course of time and in the structure and activities of groups and organizations which seek to coordinate and muster resources for these projects. It includes unorganized as well as organized activities and informal as well as formal associations. Government may or may not be involved, and if involved it may or may not play a central role. The community field is in a constant process of change as actors, associations, and actions move into and out of contact with the generalization process.

COMMUNITY DEVELOPMENT

Development is a problem to which the assumptions of field theory are especially relevant. Social organization is seen from this perspective not as a given in either its present or its future condition but as a dynamic, inherently unstable phenomenon existing largely, as it were, on a thread of memory consensus connecting crudely related real moments. Order and unity are forever in jeopardy. There is no assurance of continuity and balance. There are inherent problems of organization for which there are no inherent solutions. Development must be regarded not as a natural unfolding of some predetermined or evolutionary sequence of forms but as a process set against powerful tendencies in nature. Unity, order, meaning, and purpose—the directional features of social change—stem not so much from the nature of things as from the interests (that is, the wills, values, ideas, attitudes, sentiments, and concerns) of men.

Community change is a much broader process than community development, and community development is only one factor in the emergence of the community field. Sometimes, in the configuration of ecological, cultural, social, psychological, and chance factors which figure in change in the local society, there is a category of actions which reflect the intentions of actors to create or strengthen the relationships and patterns through which they seek collectively to express the range of their common interests and to solve their community problems. It is this category of purposive, structure-building activities which constitutes community development. This is only one of many factors, and often its influence on the local society and on the community field is slight or none. Given the openness of the field-the-

---

[2] The community field is, of course, an abstraction from the other social fields, but these are also abstractions. Detailed criteria for identifying actions in the community field have been given by Kaufman (1959: 13; cf. Green and Mayo, 1953; Sutton and Kolaja, 1960).

ory concept of causation, however, purposive action such as community development can, under certain conditions, have far-reaching consequences.

Community development, thus conceived, is always purposive. Unintentional actions may have as much or even more influence on the community field and certainly should not be ignored in a comprehensive study of community change. But a serious error in causal assessment can be made if intentional and unintentional actions are grouped together as dependent variables and "explained" in terms of the same set of independent variables. The causes of "purpose," which is at the heart of the concept of development, emanate from distinctive roots.

Community development is also always positive. This means that the intentions of the actors have to do with what is subjectively defined as improvement. In community development, as in any social context of development, consensus between at least two actors on an operational definition of improvement is required. Consensus is an adequate criterion when treating development in strictly ideational terms. When dealing with development of a specific form, such as a community field, a more stringent criterion of what is "positive" may be used. The purpose is then designated as positive only under conditions which may be objectively defined.

Although community development is always purposive and positive, it does not follow that it is always successful. In fact, it is not necessary, for definitional purposes, that it ever be successful. The same is true of development of any social form. It is precisely on this point that the scientific legitimacy of the concept turns. To require that development be "successful" in an ontological sense is to require more than can be delivered. Success is a mental construct based in part on an abstraction from reality. To say that community development has been successful in an absolute sense is to overestimate grossly man's ac-

tual control over reality and to ignore many of the forces in the causal field.[3] Trying is enough to qualify as community development. Nothing is ever finally "developed" nor are there degrees or stages of a fully "developed" state. The development is nothing more than the action undertaken with positive purpose. It is true and proper that both the science and the practice of community action are oriented toward understanding as many of the causal variables as possible. It is also true, however, that distinctive forces such as community development must be ferreted out for special investigation if sense is to be made of the patterns of change which are observed.

Community development is primarily structure-oriented. Kaufman (1959) has drawn a distinction between development *in* the community and development *of* the community. The former, referred to in the literature as differentiation, modernization, and community growth, treats the community only as a context within which special-interest programs of change, usually of a highly technical nature and with extra-local direction, are conducted. Development *of* the community requires that attention be given to the integrative, generalizing structures in the local society.

Every act in a social process, whether in a community field or elsewhere, has structural as well as task-accomplishment consequences. Community development is purposive action which is oriented in a positive way toward the structure of the community field. Such action is probably less frequent empirically than that purposive action which is oriented in a positive way toward task accomplishment. The consequences go both ways; that is, both task accomplishment and community structure are affected by all community ac-

---

[3] By the same token, of course, though admittedly in an oblique way, community development as described here never fails to have some influence in and on the community field.

tions. But consequences aside, it is the orientation of the actors which is the distinctive quality of community development.

The general social-psychological literature on actor involvement in social organizations contains suggestions for a conception of leader orientation. The concept of structural orientation has been used effectively in recent treatments of leadership in small groups (Mills, 1967) and complex organizations (Katz and Kahn, 1966). The essential notion, which has also been used by Mead, Piaget, and others, is that individuals may be classified at a given time and compared with themselves over the course of time in terms of the concept of structure embodied in their self-definition of their own roles and those of others in a group or organization. At one level are those who have only a vague awareness, if any, of structure and little or no interest in it. Their behaviors are relevant to structure but they have no awareness of this. At another level are those for whom structure is viewed as a given—an inherent order to be adapted to but not something to be modified or challenged. At yet another level are those who "subordinate structure" (Katz and Kahn, 1966) by viewing it as a manipulatable tool for expressing interests, something to be changed and modified as necessary to conform to the "meta-group" image (Mills, 1967) held by the actors. Leaders are those who operate at this last level. They, in the present context, are the participants in community development. They orient their behavior in a positive way to the structure of the community field, acting in immediate situations to effect changes in structure in line with a desired image.[4] Structurally ori-

ented behavior is that in which an attempt is made to alter structure. It is positive if it attempts to "improve" the structure.

There are special problems of dealing with structural orientations of the actor within the context of community. Although structure is an emergent phenomenon in any social field, it is even less apparent to actors in the community than in a formal organization or in most small groups. The same is true concerning boundaries, which in all cases are basically ideational in character, but which in the case of community action structures are even less clearly related to empirical referents. It is the interplay of authority structures, normative systems, and presumably bounded units, among other things, with which one must contend as either an actor or a student approaching the community. There is seldom a pervasive, clearly delineated set of structural cues such as one finds in the organization or group. The structural features of interorganizational and intergroup fields have received little attention in sociology (see Warren, 1967) and the relation of the individual to these structures even less. It is an assumption of the approach described here that these two phenomena—interstitial field structure and the actor's orientation thereto—not only exist but also have critical bearing within social processes. The critical factor and the central concern of the social-psychological study of the community field is structurally oriented behavior of actors in which an attempt is made to alter the field structure in a positive way.

There is no escaping the value connotations of positing a "positive" direction of social change. Any set of proposed or attempted changes might be regarded as positive relative to the unique values of a given grouping of actors. The only way to transcend this relativism in community study is to adopt a given definition of community structure and evaluate given alterations, in terms of whether they move the structure toward or away from the

[4] Leadership is thus a symbolic process in precisely the sense that symbolic processes have been defined by students of Mead and Cooley (see, most recently, Lyman and Scott, 1970; Warriner, 1970; and Denzin, 1970). It involves behavior relevant to an existing social process which has meaning in a shared context of co-actors. It is "constructed," in Blumer's sense of the word, and it is structurally situated.

state delineated in the definition. Community structure is defined here in terms of generality or comprehensiveness of interest scope. There is no absolute way to determine whether such a state is good apart from a value reference. But acts which move the structure toward greater generality may be designated as positive, given the end of creating or maintaining community.

In the case of the community field, "improving" the structure means contributing to increased generalization potential in the relationships among actors. This might occur in many ways. An example would be helping to establish and maintain a comprehensive organization to sponsor and coordinate community action projects. Another might be such a simple act as introducing a leader in one interest field to a leader in another. Structure of the field is altered positively by any act which increases generalization potential in the field in any way, to any degree. If such is attempted purposively it is community development.

It has been noted (Wilkinson, 1970b) that few acts have an exclusively structural orientation and, indeed, that structural consequences usually must be inferred in behavioral analysis from observations of task-related behavior. Exclusiveness, however, is not necessary for community development, and actual consequences are less relevant than are orientations. In the usual case, the critical issue in operationally defining communty development is whether an actor in a community action project who is primarily concerned with getting a job done tries to do so in such a way as to improve the structure as described above. If so, what he is doing is community development.

COMMUNITY DEVELOPMENT ISSUES

Recent policy debates and discussions of such topics as "balanced growth" (National Goals Research Staff, 1970) and "environmental quality" (Perloff, 1969) have revived a number of old issues in community development and perhaps have articulated a few new ones. Groups in several parts of the country have been debating issues in "community and human resources development" as part of an attempt to generate new research in "rural development." Questions noted in some of these debates include the following: Should we try to save all the little towns or only those with growth potential? How can "growth" be the criterion, when it is cancerous growth of the cities that we are up against? How can we get away from the fruitless controversy over rural-urban distinctions and get on with the business of area development? In community development should we stress "process" or technical skill? What good is it to work out a plan for suboptimization in various sectors of a local economy if the people won't buy it? Who should be the planners, the elite or the masses? How is a multicounty area like a community? What should be the role of volunteer groups? How can we make community development relevant to the fundamental problems of society? There are many other questions. The fact that they are frequently being raised may be part of a significant social trend.

Many of the practical questions may be summarized in terms of four general types of issues. These are issues of value, capability, responsibility, and commitment. The value issue has to do with the kind of community desired, capability with the range of the possible, responsibility with the locus of initiative, and commitment with the psychological bases of participation and leadership.

Genuine value issues cannot be resolved through research, although they can be clarified and they should be taken into account in behavior studies. Value positions on issues about the quality of life at both the task and the social relational levels are rooted in culture, personality, and unique circumstances. All that a relativistic, nonteleological science can do is to help resolve questions of the effectiveness and efficiency of alternative means for reaching valued goals. This holds with regard both to material goals and to the quality of relationships among people. A problem for basic research is to evaluate the effectiveness and efficiency of generalization relative to other means of reaching goals in the local society at both the material (task) and the social relationship levels. What is called for is a test of whether the community field is more or less useful than other means for pursuing the two kinds of values (Warren, 1965, 1970).

A major research problem relating to the issue of capability is to determine the effect of purposive action, here called community development, upon the level of generality actually achieved in the community field. It is perhaps characteristic of Western man that he tends to overestimate his control over himself and the rest of the universe in both his anticipation of the future and his after-the-fact accounting for events. The relationship between purposive action and actual outcomes can, however, be measured with some accuracy through carefully designed research. It would seem to be especially important to consider in research on community behavior the level of the actor's awareness of the dominant forces affecting community structure. Through such research it may be possible to develop more realistic strategies of purposive change and more valid criteria for evaluating programs.

The question of whether responsibility for community development should lie in the community or elsewhere is partly a question of values, but it has an important dimension which is directly subject to research. That is the question of the structural consequences of community development efforts initiated from outside the community. Within the narrow definition of community development presented here, these efforts are probably rare. More often, community structure is ignored by external agencies (for a case study, see Wilkinson, 1969). But where local initiative is lacking and community development is desired, intervention is sometimes attempted. Very little is known about the consequences.

The issue of commitment is central to community development and is clearly subject to research. The various types and levels of commitment which result in community development need to be identified and their causes and consequences assessed. One important line of research would be to identify and map the interplay of self-seeking and community-service motives underlying the various types of structural orientation noted above. Such research might be geared toward clarifying the distinction and the relationship between power and leadership in community action. Commitments of the individual, as these are manifested behaviorally within a situational context, provide an important link between theories of personal and social organization.

CONCLUSION

The discussion of research issues has only been suggestive, as has the presentation of the field-theory concept of community development. The major point being made is that attention in research needs to be given to purposive attempts by actors in the community field to increase the generalization potentials of their interactional relationships. This is an area of research about which little systematic knowledge has been generated despite much study of seemingly related topics. But it is one area which, from the perspective of field-theory, should be expected to yield insights into important forces in social change. Part of the importance of these forces is that they are things about which something presumably can be done.

REFERENCES

Denzin, Norman K.
1970   *The Research Act: A Theoretical Introduction to Sociological Methods.* Chicago: Aldine.

Fagan, Edward R.
  1964   *Field: A Process for Teaching Litera-
          ture.* University Park: Pennsylva-
          nia State University Press.
Green, James W., and Selz C. Mayo
  1953   "A framework for research in the
          action of community groups." *So-
          cial Forces* 31 (May), pp. 320–327.
Katz, Daniel, and Robert L. Kahn
  1966   *The Social Psychology of Organiza-
          tions.* New York: John Wiley &
          Sons.
Kaufman, Harold F.
  1959   "Toward an interactional concep-
          tion of community." *Social Forces*
          38 (October), pp. 8–17.
Kaufman, Harold F., and Kenneth P. Wilkinson
  1967   *Community Structure and Leader-
          ship: An Interactional Perspective in
          the Study of Community.* State Col-
          lege: Mississippi State University,
          Social Science Research Center,
          Bulletin 13.
Lewin, Kurt
  1951   *Field Theory in Social Science: Se-
          lected Theoretical Papers.* Ed. by
          Dorwin Cartwright. New York:
          Harper & Row.
Lyman, Stanford M., and Marvin B. Scott
  1970   *A Sociology of the Absurd.* New
          York: Appleton-Century-Crofts.
Maxwell, James Clerk
  1890   *The Scientific Papers of James Clerk
          Maxwell.* Vol. I. Ed. by W. D.
          Niven. Cambridge, Eng.: Cam-
          bridge University Press.
Mills, Theodore M.
  1967   *The Sociology of Small Groups.* En-
          glewood Cliffs, N.J.: Prentice-
          Hall.
National Goals Research Staff
  1970   *Toward Balanced Growth: Quantity
          with Quality.* Washington, D.C.:
          U.S. Government Printing Office.

Perloff, Harvey S., ed.
  1969   *The Quality of the Urban Environ-
          ment: Essays on "New Resources" in
          an Urban Age.* Washington, D.C.:
          Resources for the Future.
Sutton, Willis A., and Jiri Kolaja
  1960   "The concept of community."
          Rural Sociology 25 (June), pp.
          197–203.
Turney-High, Harry Holbert
  1968   Man and System: *Foundations for
          the Study of Human Relations.* New
          York: Appleton-Century-Crofts.
Warren, Roland
  1965   *Types of Purposive Change at the
          Community Level.* Waltham, Mass.:
          Brandeis University Papers in So-
          cial Welfare, No. 11.
  1967   "The interorganizational field as a
          focus for investigation." *Admin-
          istrative Science Quarterly* 12 (De-
          cember), pp. 396–419.
  1970   "Toward a non-utopian norma-
          tive model of the community."
          American Sociological Review 35
          (April), pp. 219–228.
Warriner, C. K.
  1970   *The Emergence of Society.* Home-
          wood, Ill.: Dorsey Press.
Wilkinson, Kenneth P.
  1969   "Special agency program accom-
          plishment and community action
          styles: The case of watershed de-
          velopment." *Rural Sociology* 34
          (March), pp. 29–42.
  1970a   "The community as a social
          field." *Social Forces* 48 (March),
          pp. 311–22.
  1970b   "Phases and roles in community
          action." *Rural Sociology* 35
          (March), pp. 54–68.
Yinger, J. Milton
  1965   *Toward a Field Theory of Behavior:
          Personality and Social Structure.*
          New York: McGraw-Hill.

9

Marxism and the metropolis

William K. Tabb and Larry Sawers

One may ask why suddenly in the 1960s and 1970s have so many Marxists begun studying cities and so many urbanologists turned to Marx. Indeed, why did not Marxists pay attention to urban problems before the 1960s? Marx's followers prior to the last decade or so have tended to focus on the core relations of capitalism. While cities were often considered to be the site of class struggle, the space itself hardly seemed important or worthy of special study. Marxists focused their attention instead on problems of unemployment, low wages, arbitrary management, and unsafe working conditions. They have worked to build a class-conscious workers' movement on the factory floor, the place where the primary contradiction of capitalism was seen to be most intense.

This changed in the 1960s. The middle-class exodus from the cities and consequent loss of the tax base, the civil-rights movement, and the urban conflagrations all drew attention to the cities. Struggles over urban space intensified as community groups fought for their homes against highways and urban renewal. Many came to see these struggles over "turf" as forms of class struggle. It became evident that the inner-city poor were being relocated not to eradicate the slums but to move the slums, to "reclaim" valuable land now occupied by the poor and convert it to use for luxury housing, office buildings, convention centers, commuter expressways. The poor working class families, who suffered with little compensation the loss of their homes and communities, were excluded from the benefits of this development.

From *Marxism and the Metropolis: New Perspectives in Urban Political Economy* by William K. Tabb and Larry Sawyers. Copyright © 1978 Oxford University Press, Inc. Reprinted by permission. Pp. 4–19.

Similarly, the class nature of struggles for community control of schools, the police, and other urban services, became apparent.

Concern over the fate of U.S. cities was widespread. Yet not surprisingly, the approach of analysts varied with their ideological predilections and prior methodological and political commitments. A conventional wisdom has developed, and within that view a more conservative and a more liberal approach can be distinguished. In the next section these approaches are briefly described and contrasted with the Marxist position.

THE ALTERNATIVE VIEWS

The mainstream viewpoint holds that the urban crisis is the result of the operation of urban land, job, and commodity markets as they satisfy household preferences and react to various outside stimuli. Even though the results of this process are on occasion deplored, at least by the liberal wing of the orthodox school, they are ascribed to consumers' tastes and various inevitable technological and economic forces.

For conservatives, the policy implication that flows from this stance is to do nothing, inasmuch as the urban crisis results from individual maximizing behavior in a market context and therefore is either optimally efficient or so close to it that a corrupt and bungling government could only make matters worse if it tried to improve upon the market. Conservatives tend to see the solution in less government.

Liberals are more likely to acknowledge the undesirable consequences of the market, such as racial polarization, urban blight, pervasive poverty, and the city's fiscal crisis. During "liberal" administrations, government obliges with a panoply of fragmented programs, each designed to ameliorate a specific problem as though it were unrelated to other programs or to the larger system. The results have been disappointing. There is some debate over why this is the case. Is it that we do not know enough, and have only "thrown money at problems"?

The Marxist political economist finds not only liberal solutions but liberal analysis to be inadequate and believes that it will be virtually impossible to remedy urban ills without a fundamental alteration of the political economic system. The liberal reformers' programs are destined to fail not because we do not know enough but because their programs do not address the systematic nature of the problem. The wealthy find it in their interest that the status quo be maintained. While the powerful can by no means always get what they want, they can generally exercise disproportionate influence within broad situational constraints. If their ability to manipulate the state goes unchallenged, they will continue to frustrate liberal intentions. Mainstream social scientists assume in their explanatory models that capitalism is a permanent system; their analysis fails to explain how it changes over time. For the most part they fail to explore the process of its unfolding. Marx saw capitalist growth culminating inevitably in its demise from causes the system itself creates. The Marxist argues that the crisis the city now faces is the symptom of deep-seated tensions lying within capitalist social relations. Even the most liberal of mainstream thinkers, however, take as given the basic contours of the political economy. The specifically capitalist character of production is taken as given and they presume that it must continue to be organized by the owners of capital. Therefore, in their view, the best that can be done is some redistribution or reform—to patch over

the most obvious evils of the system. This necessarily limits reforms to redistribution of resources only after the fundamental array of power and income has already taken shape. By so doing they miss, according to Marx, the central problem: that one group of people, the workers, has to sell for a portion of each day their ability to work (their *labor power*, as Marx termed it) to a far smaller group, which controls labor, the product of labor, and the means of producing the goods and services society needs.

In Marx's view, this simple relationship, the sale of labor power by workers and the control of the investible surplus by capitalists, lies at the root of almost all economic and social problems in a capitalist system. We therefore must pause to describe this process more fully, and then we will talk about its significance.

Marxist analysis begins with a perspective that sees all things in a state of continuous change and evolution—nothing is static. Thus it views traditional social science, which attempts to take "snapshots" of society through a focus on equilibrium and harmony, as unable to treat reality in its essential form. The analysis of any society is rooted in material phenomena rather than in the idealistic theories of conventional social science ("it's human nature," "it was a historical accident"). The most essential material base for any society, Marxists argue, lies in the way production is organized. In every society except the most primitive, the bulk of the population is engaged directly in production, while a tiny minority controls their labor and the things they produce. For example, the slave owner or the feudal lord controls the labor and the product of the slave or serf. In a modern free-enterprise economy, the owners of factories, offices, trucks, and so forth—the owners of capital—direct the labor of wage workers and own the fruit of their labor. The arrangements whereby one class controls the labor of another are called the *social relations of production.* This relationship between a ruling class and a subservient one is inherently conflictual; this class conflict becomes the primary source of social change.

A second defining dimension of society relates to the size and skill of the labor force, the level of technology, the instruments or tools of production, and so forth, which are together termed the *forces of production.* Together with the social relations of production, they are known as the *mode of production.* Marxists divide history into several epochs defined by the prevailing mode of production: primitive communist, ancient, feudal, capitalist, and social societies. The rest of society—from the legal structure, parts of which are little more than codification of the social relations of production, to the family structure and even the prevailing personality structure—flows ultimately, though not mechanically, from the mode of production. With reference now to the subject of the present volume, the physical and social structure of the city is seen by Marxists as the evolving product of the social forces of production and the class relations they engender.

Since capitalists make decisions based on their desire to make profits, they try in every way possible to pay workers only part of the value their labor produces, an amount just sufficient to sustain life and to reproduce more workers for the next generation. Value produced by workers in excess of what they are given, Marx called *surplus value;* this is the basis for profit and other property income in our society. Even though wages, or the price of labor power, rises—perhaps a better education comes to be required or the automobile becomes necessary to get to work or a higher standard of living is attained through workers' struggles and becomes the socially acceptable norm—only the capitalist accumulates capital. The vast majority must sell their ability to work, must get a job to eat. A tiny minority, by virtue of its ownership of the means of production, the factories

and the office buildings where work takes place, directs the labor of the first group and owns what is produced. One group sells labor power and the other decides how production takes place. In the next section, we describe some of the ways that capitalist social relations affect the social and spatial structure of the metropolis.

THE CLASS STRUGGLE AND SPACE

General Motors, General Electric, and all the other generals whose corporate headquarters impressively rise above our large cities were once small companies with a few employees. But because they are able to plow the surplus back into the firm, they could steadily hire more workers and grow larger. Their machines were produced by past generations of workers, and are in this basic sense the embodiment of workers, of "dead labor."

Living labor confronts the power of these corporate giants. The power that stands over them is a power created by workers; yet is seen as belonging to the corporations, to capital. Thus when workers demand higher wages and better working conditions, and the corporate power refuses, relying on its size, financial and political strength, and most of all on its ability to deny the workers a means of living, it has appropriated this strength from the sweat and blood of past workers. When a company moves from a city to a place where it can find labor that will work for less, it takes the productive capacity built by its workers away from them—creating unemployment, eroding the tax base, leading ultimately to the urban crisis. From the firm's point of view, it must do this in order to survive; if other sellers lower their costs and they do not, they will lose out in the competitive struggle. Capitalists have to expand to survive; they must seek new markets, cheaper raw materials, and lower wage labor or die. The large capitalists—at first the merchants, then the railroads and the banks, and later the multinational corporations—spread their dominion over the hinterland in an ever-expanding outward movement until few places in the world are untouched. In short, the inevitable, incessant struggle to maximize profits shapes the fundamental framework within which industrial location and therefore economic geography is formed.

In capitalism, where the class struggle permeates every segment of society, some sectors of the working class find themselves in a position in relation to their employers that is more favorable than other sectors of the working class. This allows the advantaged sectors greater success in their struggles for higher wages and better working conditions. Moreover, the employers also have an interest in paying their workers a range of wages. These wage differentials, by dividing workers and granting nominal rewards for those working within the system, militate against the formation of a strong class-consciousness and working-class militancy. Thus there is a relatively wide range of incomes found within the working class. This income hierarchy within the working class, as well as the much greater differences between the working class and the ruling class, expresses itself in the spatial arrangements of residence within the modern metropolis. Divisions between and among classes are reflected in conflicts between and within political jurisdictions.

A pattern of residential segregation by income exists within capitalist cities and is often identified with the concentric growth patterns modeled by sociologists such as Burgess and Park and by economists such as von Thünen and Alonso. The sociologists note that similar land uses tend to agglomerate, and that zones take on a pattern of homogeneous land use that gird the city's core in a series of belts.

The first ring from the central business district is a zone of transition, of warehouses and the residences of the very poor. Then comes a ring of the more solid working class; then the white-collar pro-fessions, with the richest pushing outward to escape the intrusion of the other groups as the city grows. (When the city declines, as many in the Northeast have begun to do, areas of blight spread outward.) Such an analysis is not new. But as presented by mainstream urbanologists it does not tell us much about the social determinants of such a ring pattern of growth. By far the best explanation and description is over 100 years old and is found in Friedrich Engels's classic study, *The Conditions of the Working Class in England in 1844*, which contains a rich understanding of the process that Burgess was to describe a half century later.

* * * * *

THE FETISHISM OF SPACE

Sociologists and economists have engaged in seemingly endless debate about the precise nature of the spatial dispersion of various income groups. But what difference does it really make whether the income segregation is concentric-zonal, sectoral, or any other particular spatial form? Since the relation is really one between classes or subclasses, and not one between areas, such a discussion obscures what is really at issue. This mis-specification can be termed "the fetishism of space." It mistakes the surface manifestation of social divisions—spatial segregation—for the social division itself.

This stress on surface concepts in traditional approaches to the city is paralleled by a use of language that obfuscates the class nature of urban society and incorporates implicit ethical judgments. For example, the classical urbanologists have adapted the terminology of plant ecology to the urban scene. In 1925 Burgess, in his paper "The Growth of Cities," characterized the "zones of deterioration" encircling the central business districts as containing "submerged regions of poverty, degradation, and disease," with "their underworlds of crime and vice," the "purgatory of lost souls." "The next zone," wrote

Burgess, "is also inhabited predominantly by factory and shop workers, but skilled and thrifty." The notion of social control, of socializing the "inferior" immigrant workers—the Italians, the Poles, the Jews —is largely what was on Burgess's mind. He noted: "Where mobility is the greatest, and where in consequence primary controls break down completely, as in the zone of deterioration in the modern city, there develop areas of demoralization, of promiscuity and of vice."

Engels, a half-century earlier, had a clearer sense of the cause-and-effect relationships behind the urban concentric configuration. He saw the workers as victims, not as inferior beings. He knew that retail merchants are forced by competition to open their shops along thoroughfares, and that the rich shut the poor away from their sight, cutting large swaths through working-class neighborhoods so that they can more speedily get to the financial district without seeing the "grimy misery that lurks to the right and the left." The self-regulating market leads to such results. The hierarchy of capitalist structure is mirrored in the segregated living arrangements by occupational status of the metropolitan area.

When the subject turns to the racial hierarchy within the working class, the language used is even more explicitly slanted. As we examine the contemporary mainstream literature on race and land use, we find models which speak of "invasion," "conquest," "retreat." Whites are "ejected" as blacks "invade.". . .

In short, the class struggle under capitalism, unfolding in a complex and contradictory fashion, has shaped the nature of urban space. Unlike the mainstream theorists, who see harmony and equilibrium in the allocation of space, Marxists see the class struggle as affecting where corporations build their factories and stores, and where various residential areas are located.

In the next part, we detail how "inevitable" urban processes result from the profit-seeking criteria of decision makers in the market.

PROFITS, COMPETITION, AND CAPITALISM

One of the defining characteristics of capitalism is that business enterprise is motivated by the drive to gain profits. This is not a matter of choice for the individual capitalist. Unless profits are earned and reinvested in the company, it will not grow and thus will fall behind in the competitive race. Sooner or later it will be gobbled up by the larger firms, fade away, or if it does survive, become irrelevant because of its small relative size. The competitive drive for profit affects every facet of our society, and its impact on spatial organization is profound. A few examples will illustrate the point.

Artists and other creative people locate in a poor area of town where rents are low. Soon their needs are met by coffee houses, art galleries, organic food instead of processed chemicals, and handcrafted products instead of plastic ones. As a market is developed, corporate capitalism and the consumer society move in. Chain stores drive up rents, and the coffee houses where one could sit playing chess over a cup of coffee are driven out. High-rise structures are built in place of the small buildings of the previous century, which had stonework, intricately inlaid woodwork, and handmade glass. What happens to the way space is consumed is essentially the same as what happens in other areas of a market economy: production is dominated by profit-seeking firms.

Another example of the way in which the profit-seeking character of enterprise has shaped urban geography has to do with the transportation system. The shape of the metropolis is, of course, crucially affected by the nature of the transportation network. The latter has been formed by profit-seeking businesses. In the 1930s General Motors formed various subsidiaries whose sole function was to buy up trolley-car companies, sack the existing rolling stock and other facilities, convert the system to motorbus—GM was already at that time the largest bus manufacturer—and then sell the franchise to whomsoever would promise to buy GM bus replacements. By this method GM destroyed over 100 trolley systems in 45 of the nation's largest cities. Even a federal court conviction on antitrust charges failed to stop GM from changing the nature of transportation in cities. The bus is poor competition for the trolley, so this process served to drive Americans to the automobile; and there too GM stands to profit. To a very significant extent, then, the very structure of the modern American metropolis has been shaped by one company's relentless search for profits.

An earlier generation of urban transportation was also molded by the profit motive. While trolley lines "made sense," the way they were built did not. The first trolley-car lines were frequently built out from the cities into empty farmland. The trolley companies made their profits in speculating on the land adjacent to the trolley lines. When the land along the trolley lines was sold off, the trolley companies could no longer sustain the nickel fare. Desperate commuters then forced the city government to subsidize the lines or to buy them outright.

General Motors has profited handsomely from its policy of destroying trolleys at the expense of trolley-car owners and urban dwellers. But capitalist competition for profit may lead to results which are harmful not only to the capitalist class as a whole and to the working class, but also to the individual capitalist. If, for example, an area becomes desirable, land values rise, new dense patterns of land use create congestion, and the environmental amenities which attracted economic activity in the first place are destroyed. The process repeats itself, and still newer, more desirable areas are developed—with the same result. The old abandoned areas degenerate still further. At first it was only the seashore resorts, like Coney Island and Miami Beach, where the overbuilding, congestion, pollution, overcrowding, and then decay became noticeable. Then followed the central business districts and the older suburbs, the fringe areas of central cities. Now it is said that there is no hope for the entire industrial Northeast. The principle is the same in all of these cases. The profit motive puts profit before social need.

The competition that dominates the world of business has spread to the public sector; one finds that the competition among governments has a significant impact on the spatial arrangements of the metropolis. While smaller capitalists may still be tied to a single locality, larger ones are not. This means that manufacturers can play off a government in one potential location against another, seeking better terms. Jurisdictions, knowing that their survival depends on attracting new jobs and holding onto old ones, compete against each other in offering costly incentives, rent-free, specially constructed buildings, utilities at below cost, new roads, tax abatement for several years, and help in discouraging trade-union activities.

In a less than full-employment economy, the gains of one city must come at the expense of others. Not only does this lead local governments to offer location incentives with their inevitable costly competitiveness, but also to minimize local taxes to make their location attractive. Repelling low-income immigrants becomes as important as attracting industry with high taxpaying ability and low public-service requirements. Just as attracting high-wage, tax-contributing firms is not a net gain to the nation, so keeping out the poor is not a program without cost in the aggregate view.

When businesses find ways to use the state in their pursuit of profit, they do so. The logic of the market asserts that the best use of resources is measured not by need but by ability to pay. The poor, of course, have the most limited ability to pay and are thus at the end of every queue, and are offered only society's leftovers. Normally, if the well-to-do desire the land that the poor have been allotted, they merely outbid them in the marketplace and the poor are pushed aside.

* * * * *

CONCLUSION

A Marxist approach to the study of urban economics offers a fruitful avenue of study because it begins by asking why cities exist in the form they do, what their evolution has been, and what the tendencies embodied in contemporary production forms are. By examining how the productive relations and ownership patterns yield a particular income distribution and how the social divisions are reflected spatially in terms of residence areas and public services, the Marxist approach is able to show how urban economic problems are created, perpetuated, and re-created over time and how their form changes to reflect development in the mode of production and its superstructural relations.

Once one examines the patterned inequality and class nature of oppression, "policy recommending" takes on a very different meaning. The key questions become what works and what does not work in the redistribution of resources and the

establishment of a movement capable of compelling further change. In reply to mainstream economists who argue for a value-free social science, radicals see that the research people choose to do and the selection of initial assumptions and methodology are in essence political decisions.

The decay of urban America continues apace. The alienation and cynicism that assert that "nothing can be done" spread. So too do the slums and the poverty. The grief lies untouched by reforms. . . .

The popular forces for change are building even as the crisis of capitalism deepens. We do not await this "inevitable" occurrence. We put our scholarship at the service of the class forces which will bring about this transition.

REFERENCES

Alonso William. *Location and Land Use: Toward a General Theory of Land Rent.* Cambridge, Mass.: Harvard University Press, 1964.

Burgess, Ernest W. "The Growth of the City: An Introduction to a Research Project." *Publications of the American Sociological Society,* 1924.

Engels, Friedrich. *The Conditions of the Working Class in England in 1844.* 1845; rpt. Moscow: Progress Publishers, 1973.

————. *The Housing Question.* 1872; rpt. Moscow: Progress Publishers, 1975.

Park, Robert E. et al. *The City.* Chicago: University of Chicago Press, 1925.

Wilson, James Q. *Urban Renewal: The Record and the Controversy.* Cambridge, Mass.: MIT Press, 1966.

10

Observations on the state of community theory

Roland L. Warren

While few of us are completely satisfied with the present state of community theory, it is nevertheless quite apparent that many alternative approaches to the subject have arisen. Some are more developed, theoretically, than are others. Nearly two decades ago I described six of these alternative approaches under the heading of the community as people, as spatial arrangements, as shared institutions, as interaction, as power structure, and as social system. More recently, Jessie Bernard (1973) based her intriguing book on different theoretical approaches as alternative paradigms, pointing out the anomalies and other deficiencies which each alternative community paradigm had developed. Neither her list nor mine completely exhausts the different facets of the community phenomenon which have been singled out as the focus of analysis by one investigator or another.

It would benefit us all to have further critiques of these different approaches, pointing out the relevant aspects of communities which they illuminate as well as their inherent limitations, along with the many aspects of communities which each of them tends to ignore. I think, for example, of the illuminating critiques of community power studies given us by John Walton (1976) and Manuel Castells (1973).

The lack of complete satisfaction with any of these theoretical approaches leads quite understandably to the aspiration for a new theoretical approach which will take such weaknesses and strengths into account and serve as an adequate, definitive

theoretical approach to the community. My view is that this quest is a vain one.

I believe it is important for us to realize, as we avail ourselves of Thomas Kuhn's (1962, 1970) penetrating treatment of the paradigmatic nature of investigation in the natural sciences and apply it by inference or analogy to the social sciences, that Kuhn seemed to be wrong on two crucial points. The first was the suggestion that the social sciences had probably not reached the paradigm stage at all. Yet it is apparent that in the social sciences in general, and sociology and community studies in particular, a multitude of paradigms abound, meeting both Kuhn's loose definition of paradigms and his descriptive account of the functions paradigms serve in the natural sciences.

The second point on which Kuhn's analysis is wrong if applied to the social sciences has to do with his contention that, in the natural sciences, at least, one paradigm must displace another. They cannot exist for any extended period of time as acceptable alternative approaches. Nevertheless, anyone familiar with the controversies raging between social-system theorists and conflict theorists, or between each of these and symbolic interactionists, can testify to the less than peaceful coexistence of a plurality of vigorous paradigms over extended periods of time.

I draw certain epistemological implications from this circumstance. Namely, regardless of how natural scientists may look upon the eternal and exclusive validity of their scientific paradigms (and fewer of them have remained sanguine about these characteristics since the past century or so), the social sciences must rest content with paradigms which cannot lay such

---

Paper presented to the Community Section of the annual meeting of the American Sociological Association, Boston, 1979.

claim to comprehensiveness and hence ex-clusiveness. They must recognize that each is useful for certain aspects of the subject under investigation, but each is inadequate to account for all aspects. Therefore, rather than displacing one another they must be considered as tools for analysis, some more useful than others in specific investigations, but none of them, present or future, justifying a claim to exclusiveness. I have tried to make this point recently in arguing for the advantages to be derived from considering communities as arenas of interaction rather than as collectivities in the Parsonian sense, which I believe has characterized most community paradigms in the past. But to argue its advantages is not to assert that it can replace the type of analysis which considers the community as a single entity, behaving as it behaves, as an entity. We need both, and just as Dahrendorf (1959) so ably pointed out the difficulty if not impossibility of developing a more inclusive paradigm which would incorporate both system theory and conflict theory, so I would suggest the theoretical impossibility of a more inclusive theory which adequately synthesizes the things which are done best by interaction-arena and collectivity paradigms, respectively. Therefore, let us have a multiplicity of paradigms. Those which endure, despite their shortcomings, will find supporters and utilizers only because they can do some things—though not all things—better than can their alternatives. Let us have a kit of good tools; but why use a screwdriver when we need a saw, or why use a hammer when we need a foot rule?

Be all that as it may, a cynic might look at what could be considered fadism in community theory. The community as shared institutions had its heyday. So did the ecological approach. (Remember when ecology meant something to sociologists other than preserving endangered species and recycling soft-drink bottles?) Then there came the flood of social class studies, the social system whirl, the power structure fling, and so on and on. As we turn so rapidly away from one paradigm and toward another, we are likely to think of the first paradigm as being fully exploited and exploded. There is much explanatory power, and there are many interesting facets yet to explore in each of these paradigms which enjoyed an earlier limelight.

I think we still have much to learn about the structure and exercise of power in local communities, and their relationship to the larger surrounding society. The concept of community power still presents important challenges. Interest has waned, quite rightly in my opinion, in only one narrow facet of power structure conceptualization and methodology. Incidentally, I do not think *comparative* community power structure studies will add much to what we already know until they get off the dead center of bare empiricism.

Likewise, I believe the intriguing notion of studying communities as systems of action has been far from fully exploited. Closely related to this, the symbolic interactionists still have a great, as yet unmade contribution to make to our understanding of communities.

We still have much to learn about the nature of the ties between various parts of local communities and organizations and other types of groupings in the surrounding society. In particular, an approach to the community which views it as the stage on which these extra-community organizations and groupings of various kinds interact has yet to be fully exploited. In many ways, actions taking place locally can be more adequately explained from this paradigm than from the alternate paradigm of viewing them simply as locally generated phenomena. Again, must we choose the one and discard the other? I hope not.

Withal, many of us tend to neglect the excellent work done in studies of communities by other disciplines—not only anthropologists, with whom we are usually somewhat conversant, but by geographers, economists, and in some respects psychologists.

My own feeling is that we have done a relatively lackluster job of benefiting by the mass of data concerning community change generated in the past two decades. What we have here is a veritable smorgasbord of undeveloped paradigms, captivating ideas, unsystematic pontificating, and little more.

In these days, attention is turning to two new paradigms. One is network theory. We are off and running in this new direction. Will the bubble grow larger and larger and finally burst, much like community power studies? It may leave a more permanent and significant residue if, as now seems apparent, there emerges a strong effort to develop a theoretical base which takes it out of pure sociometry and provides a common conceptualization for both the quantitative matrix approaches and the more qualitatively rich studies of the structure, function, and meaning of these networks to the people involved.

The other rising star on the community horizon is provided by neo-Marxist theory. It will be interesting, and should be enlightening, to see how far one can get in deriving community structure and function from the needs of those who control production in a private profit economy, especially in connection with the asserted need for cheap labor and for a market of consumers willing or forced to pay high prices in order to assure high private profits, and of social services as increasingly being called upon to smooth over the difficulties and to enable the system to endure. These circumstances must be relevant to the nature and function of American communities. But so far, it seems to me, we have had only descriptions, special terminology, and largely unsupported assertions. Whether this young tree will bear fruit still remains to be seen.

My final point is an old one, conjuring up those timeworn oldsters, *Gemeinschaft* and *Gesellschaft*—the Waldorf and Sheraton of all sociological muppet shows. They keep rearing their ugly heads largely because they are powerful analytical concepts. Analytically they are distinct, but in most social situations they coexist. Because they are a dichotomy analytically, we tend to fasten on one or another of them in investigating various social phenomena, to the neglect of the other. So many of the social relationships and processes apparent in communities have elements of both *Gemeinschaft* and *Gesellschaft*. Yet we have not so far developed any mode of systematic analysis into this mixture of oil and water in so many important social relationships on the local level. How do they apply to relationships between social classes, ethnic groups, formal organizations? How do they apply, more microscopically, to the role relationships between employer and employee, salesman and customer, old-timer and newcomer? One recalls Parsons' (1951, 1964) brilliant analysis of the doctor-patient relationship in terms of the pattern variables, themselves derived from Toennies' seminal work. But unfortunately, Parsons showed little interest in communities as such, and his contributions in this area are relatively insignificant. Meanwhile, we content ourselves with referring, often with malice, to the alleged old *Gemeinschaft*-like community, and tell each other ponderously that modern industrial communities are more *Gesellschaft*-like. Is this the last word? I hope not!

One final note: One may quite rightfully look for the functions provided by communities in the past in other types of institutional settings today—in the fraternal club, in the ethnic group, in the brotherhood of baseball card collectors, or in the religious orders, or the Klu Klux Klan. Well and good; and greatly important. But this does not gainsay the importance of localities, and their social organization, to individuals and families. Anyone who thinks that the local community is a matter of little importance needs only to read tomorrow's newspaper.

REFERENCES

Bernard, Jessie
    1973   *The Sociology of Community.* Glenview, Ill. Scott, Foresman.

Castells, Manual
    1973   *La Questione Urbaine.* Paris: Francois Maspero.

Dahrendorf, Ralf
    1959   *Class and Class Conflict in Industrial Society.* London: Routledge & Kegan Paul.

Kuhn, Thomas
    1962, 1970   *The Structure of Scientific Revolutions.* Chicago: The University of Chicago Press.

Parsons, Talcott
    1951, 1964   *The Social System.* New York: Free Press of Glencoe.

Walton, John
    1976   "Community Power and the Retreat from Politics: Full Circle After Twenty Years?" *Social Problems* 23 (February); pp. 292–303. Also reprinted in this book.

Holistic community studies

SECTION TWO

INTRODUCTION

For many social scientists, community sociology is conceptualized mainly in terms of the community studies discussed in this section. The landmark descriptions of Middletown, Yankee City, and Chicago have become classics in American sociology. They can still be found on required reading lists in courses such as stratification, deviance, and theory. As such, they remain among the most widely known works of American sociology. In fact, these holistic community studies may be more appreciated *outside* community sociology today than they are in the field itself. Some current books that focus on community sociology scarcely refer to them at all, and many of the recent articles published in the field do not cite the classic holistic studies. Thus, the time for descriptive analyses of entire communities appears to have passed,[1] giving way to *national* studies of groups based not on community of residence, but rather on extracommunity variables, such as age, race, sex, and social class.

What, then, is the contribution of these holistic studies? To answer this question, we begin this section with an excellent summary of the three most influential community studies: Robert and Helen Lynd's pioneering studies of Middletown, W. Lloyd Warner and associates' exhaustive, controversial examination of Yankee City, and the many ecological, often problem-oriented studies of neighborhoods in Chicago under the direction of Park, Burgess et al. at the University of Chicago.

Collin Bell and Howard Newby begin their insightful summary by acknowledging the tremendous influence of the Lynds' research in Middletown. The continuing importance of the two classic Middletown volumes to subsequent community research and theory is impressive. Thus, it is no coincidence that this section will conclude with a research report from Muncie (Middletown) that replicates the Lynds' original efforts of over 40 years ago. Bell and Newby are slightly less positive in their treatment of the Chicago studies; although it is with these studies of ethnic neighborhoods, urban deviance, and ecological patterns and processes that community research reached a predominance in American sociology that it had been unable to obtain previously, and has been unable to maintain subsequently. Bell and Newby are more critical still of Warner's five volumes of analysis in Yankee City. They refer to Warner's analysis as often being "wrongheaded" and "silly."

This ranking of the "big three" in community studies probably conforms to that held by most community scholars. Still, it would be incorrect to infer from their summary that Warner's Yankee City volumes represent a massive, but ultimately inconsequential set of community studies. While it is true that Warner's analysis has received more criticism than the research in Muncie or Chicago, it is also true that his six-class, multidimensional, stratification model, with its emphasis on prestige, continues to have considerable effect on how American sociologists conceptualize and measure social class position. Additionally,

---

[1] One major exception is the Middletown III project described later in this section.

Warner's research team went on from Yankee City to add impressive studies of "Jonestown," and "Deep South." Thus Warner's analysis of Yankee City, flawed though it may be, has had considerable influence on sociology in general as well as on community research in particular.

The community studies summarized by Bell and Newby provide valuable analyses of community life in America. The subsequent studies of places like "Springdale," "Old City," and "Crestwood Heights" that they inspired also added to our understanding of different communities in America. But, taken as a whole, what can they tell us about American communities? Can we infer more than the effects of the depression on Muncie from *Middletown in Transition?* What of other communities? Did they too experience a centralization of power in an X, Y, or Z family? Do the six classes of Newburyport exist in all communities? In short, can these case studies of different communities somehow be combined into a cumulative set of findings that helps us to understand the structure and dynamics of *all* American communities?

Maurice Stein directly confronts these questions in his book, *The Eclipse of Community*. It is Stein's contention that these classic case studies can be combined to illustrate and explain three powerful forces that reshaped the structure of American communities: urbanization (as illustrated in the Chicago studies), industrialization (Middletown), and bureaucratization (Yankee City). The "mass society" these forces produce reduces the distinctiveness and independence of American communities. Thus Stein finds the American community being "eclipsed" by a "mass society" similar to the *Gesellschaft*-like descriptions made earlier in the selections by Tönnies, Weber, Simmel, Wirth, and Rubin.

The role of the community in a mass society is a debatable one. Of course, even Stein recognizes that the community remains important and that the concept of "a monolithic conception of mass society" can be overstated. But Stein also concludes that the community, and by inference, community studies are no longer "at the center of the stage."

The proper place of the community in American society is the focus of the subsequent selection from *Small Town in Mass Society* by Arthur J. Vidich and Joseph Bensman. It is a holistic community study that illustrates clearly the dependency the local community now has on the larger mass society described by Stein. The excerpt included here deals with several aspects of this dependency. It points out how certain people through their connections with outside organizations constitute channels through which ideas, customs, and usages flow into the locality. A wide variety of organizational and personal channels provide "bridges" to the larger society and "gatekeeper roles" with regard to it, roles from which persons having special access to one system or another in the larger society derive local power.

Finally, this section concludes with a return to the site of arguably the most influential of all the community studies, Muncie, Indiana. The Middletown III project, under the direction of Theodore Caplow, has received considerable media attention, especially in regard to the lack of substantial change in values among citizens of Muncie in the 50-year period between Middletown I–II and III. In this selection, however, Caplow and Bruce Chadwick examine a more complex issue: inequality. By traditional, objective criteria of occupational inequality, a small, slow shift toward greater class inequality is uncovered in their analysis—much like the national pattern based on similar measures. But when the *lifestyles* of the two basic occupational classes are compared, a totally opposite picture emerges. Recreating the detailed, descriptive data originally gathered by the Lynds, Caplow and Chadwick find "that most of the differences in life-style between business-class families and working-class families reported in 1924 had diminished or disappeared by 1978."

It is interesting to note that when the objective measures of inequality commonly used in national stratification research are employed in Middletown, the local class dynamics reflects national trends. On the surface, this implies support of the "mass society" hypothesis. But something very important has occurred in Middletown—an equalization of lifestyles between classes—that may well have also occurred throughout the United States. National data, however, do not have the intensive, descriptive quality of community studies necessary to find out. It may be, then, that we can extend Stein's conclusion about the role of holistic community studies. Communities "do provide a meeting ground . . . which the depersonalizing forces of mass society can diminish but never destroy." But beyond that, communities may provide a research site that allows the discovery of mass society characteristics that are not readily observable at the national level.

11

The American community studies

Collin Bell and Howard Newby

No pretence can be made that it is possible in a relatively short chapter comprehensively to survey and assess all American community studies. What can be done is to take some of the unquestionably most important studies and consider their contribution. . . . The sociological purposes served by community studies can be broadly divided into two. First, they provide a basis for a general understanding of a society—though, as will be shown below, the extension of findings particular to one community to the whole of society is a besetting sin of American community studies. Second, community studies allow the exploration of the effects of the social setting on human behaviour, that is, treating the community as an independent variable. This again is a pervasive tendency of American community studies.

MIDDLETOWN

Middletown is for the sociologist of the community what Durkheim's *Suicide* is for sociology as a whole. It represents a mag-

Reprinted with permission of the authors and publisher from Collin Bell and Howard Newby, *Community Studies* (London: George Allen and Unwin, Ltd., 1972), pp. 82–111.

nificent and imaginative leap forward. The Lynds' contribution is such that, just as *Suicide* has shaped the development of the whole discipline, *Middletown* has shaped the development of community studies. Both studies have provided a model for sociological analysis and many later achievements were only possible because of the innovations of both Durkheim and the Lynds. We are now on the shoulders of giants. Whereas it is all too easy, with hindsight, to belittle these achievements, especially in the light of later advances, their seminal contribution should be remembered. The Lynds set the style for future community studies. Their approach, techniques, and analysis have been followed remarkably closely by many later sociologists of the community. The problems that they encountered and to which they posed solutions are the same, in many cases, as those faced by all community sociologists, only those who followed the Lynds into other communities had the benefit of the Lynds' monographs to guide them. This is by no means to suggest that they were always right (nor for that matter was Durkheim), but they were both first in the field and often right.

In a way the community study came about by accident. The Lynds originally had no intention of giving a total picture of the town of Muncie. In the early 1920s the Lynds—Robert and Helen, husband and wife—were working for a small institute of social and religious research which decided to survey religious provision and practices in a typical small American town. The Lynds sought a suitable frame of reference into which to put their study and were attracted by the then current work of Clark Wissler and W. H. R. Rivers, who both presented *n*-fold classifications under which the activities of any *culture* (key term) could be classified. It was the latter's classification that was adopted and which provided the organisational framework for the Lynds' analysis. The classification is: Getting a Living, Making a Home, Training the Young, Using Leisure, Engaging in Religious Practices, and Engaging in Community Activities. The Lynds found that just as a study of primitive religion requires an understanding of a primitive society in all its aspects, so the methods and approach of social anthropology can legitimately be applied to the study of American religion in its *total* setting. It did not prove posible to study one social institution in a locality—religion in this case—in isolation, but rather it proved necessary to examine its interrelations with other institutions. And so it might be said that the modern community study was born.

The Lynds described what they were doing as "studying synchronously the interwoven trends that are the life of a small American city." They go on to face the continually besetting problem of the *typicality* of any community. They claim that "a typical city, strictly speaking does not exist" but add that Muncie "was selected as having many features common to a wide group of communities." One other point mentioned in their first paragraph has continued to be a matter of some contention, seen alternatively as the main strength or the chief weakness of the field of community studies: "Neither fieldwork nor report has attempted to prove any thesis: the aim has been, rather, to *record* observed phenomena, thereby raising questions and suggesting fresh points of departure in the study of group behaviour."[1] This is either to be attacked as smacking of some casual empiricism, or praised as being unbiased and for letting the data speak for themselves. This duality of reception for community studies has, of course, continued, and was exemplified in the Introduction to this book.

The Lynds' books were extraordinarily successful by any standards—*Middletown* went through six printings in 1929 alone.

---

[1] Robert S. Lynd and Helen M. Lynd, *Middletown: A Study in Contemporary American Culture* (New York: Harcourt, Brace, 1929), p. 3 (our emphasis) (London, Constable).

Its achievement has been summed up by John Madge when he said that it was "the first scientific and ostensibly uncritical, objective description of smalltown life. Here for the first time, without reformist overtones and without dramatization was a mirror held up to the ordinary American."[2] Their achievement is in fact even greater for they returned to Muncie almost a decade later, in 1935, to ascertain what had happened to the community during the Depression and produced an equally good, some would say better, community study, *Middletown in Transition*.

The second study, however, is markedly different in tone. For example, whilst in *Middletown* the Lynds had, it would seem almost instinctively, divided the community into two groups, the "working class" and "business class" they maintain a somewhat deadpan "getting at the facts" approach. In *Middletown in Transition*, Robert Lynd adopted within a similar basic structure (the anthropological classification detailed above) what has been seen as a hard-hitting exposure of the sources of power in what he regarded as a typical American small town. Though it will be shown below[3] that some of his evidence is open to alternative explanations, he packed into *Middletown in Transition* all his militant and evangelical feelings about what was wrong with American society. The two Middletown monographs illustrate well that it is a relatively short step from the community study as empirical description to the community study as normative prescription.

The Lynds also set the style for future community research by going to live in their community. The fieldwork for *Middletown* took 18 months and was completed by 1925. There is an appendix, "Note on Method," describing their fieldwork techniques. They tried to be unobtrusive but not covert and said they had just come to "study the growth of the city." They had no general questionnaire, just the anthropological conceptual scheme around which they organized their data. This is prior to the days when sociologists sampled, and it is clear that they may well have been biased in those they talked to. Under the heading "interviews" in their appendix, they write." These varied all the way from the most casual conversations with street-car conductors, janitors and barbers, to chance associates at luncheon or club meetings to carefully planned interviews with individuals especially qualified to give information on particular phases of the city's life."[4] These included, for example, leading ministers and club secretaries. In order "to test in individual families certain hypotheses as to trends observed in the behaviour of the community" they interviewed 124 "working class" families and 40 "business class" (called "just good substantial folks") families. It is clear that these were not samples in the scientific sense (in that all families in Muncie stood an equal chance of being selected for study)—for example it is explicitly said that they would only interview those members of the business class who were willing to cooperate.

It is necessary to consider carefully how Muncie was chosen in the first place (this information is always vital for community studies and is frequently omitted from the published monograph). The Lynds say that they had no ulterior motive and they appear to have listed the characteristics a city should possess so as to be representative of contemporary America.[5] These characteristics were: a temperate climate, a rapid expansion rate so that the community should feel the stresses of social change, an industrial culture with a fair amount of modern high-speed machine production, it should *not* be a one-plant

[2] John Madge, *The Origins of Scientific Sociology* (London: Tavistock, 1963), p. 128.

[3] See Chapter 7.

[4] Lynd and Lynd, *Middletown*, p. 507.

[5] Compare Warner's approach discussed below.

town (they were wrong in equating a single-plant town with a single-industry town—as will be seen below the whole of Muncie, not just its industry, was dominated by the activities of one family), a substantial and autonomous local artistic life and a location in the Midwest. It also had to be small enough to study—this criterion which is central to so many community studies has meant that we are forever being told that relatively small towns are typical even though the majority of the population in most industrialized societies live in large towns. Madge for one has been suspicious of the apparent complete rationality of their selection criteria. Lynd came from Indiana and so probably already knew something about the community.[6]

The Lynds, once they were established in Muncie and organizing their data under the six headings borrowed from anthropology, began to concentrate on two key dates, 1890 (when the population was 11,000) and 1924 (when the population was 35,000). They clearly aimed to describe and explain the differences that had taken place in Muncie between these dates. The dichotomous class classification used has been mentioned above, the working class were those who dealt with things, the business class were those who dealt with people. It is marvellously simple but totally atheoretical, and in detail empirically difficult to apply. The Lynds are the first community participant observers, accepting all invitations and going to all meetings. Unlike Lloyd Warner, they also made extensive use of locally produced documentary data, the census, court and school records, and the newspapers. They also used diaries, club minutes, and scrapbooks. These data were of course especially valuable for the 1890s. By the standards of the time, the Lynds were scrupulous in describing the sources of their data in the body of their monographs.

It is to be expected that the anthropological classification adopted by the Lynds for analysing the community would not fit in easily with their data. Yet there is no strain apparent when reading their monographs. The classification performed the function of letting the authors describe in a "value-neutral" way a style of life acidly etched by Sinclair Lewis. At least in *Middletown* their objective, which by and large they attain, was systematic description and not external judgment. The chapter on "The Organization of Leisure" (which is within the general section "Using Leisure") points out, for example, that the family is declining as a unit of leisure-time pursuits, and that friends are becoming more important. It was discovered that more working class women had "no friends."[7] There are many verbatim comments which give a richness to their analysis, but as in the more recent work of, for example, the Institute of Community Studies in Britain, it is not always possible to exactly attribute these quotations to an individual whose characteristics are known. The Lynds, like the much later writers on suburbia (see below), go on to discuss the effects of propinquity (what the Lynds call "vicinage") on the pattern of social relationships. The Lynds point out the effects of informal groups, like the neighbourhood, on the one hand and formal groups, like the church on the other, in "acquainting members of the community with each other"[8]—and how this varies by their two classes. They similarly discuss sex differences in friendship patterns. They contrast the number of parties reported in the local press in 1890 with

---

[6] It is interesting to note that when in the early 1950s Katz and Lazarsfeld were looking for a locale for their study that became *Personal Influence* Muncie got onto their short list as being nearly average by some quite vigorous criteria and yet was rejected on the grounds of being a one-industry town. This factor must be remembered when the substance of the Lynds' findings are recounted below.

[7] Lynd and Lynd, *Middletown*, p. 272.
[8] Ibid., p. 275.

1924 (the population had increased three-and-a-half times and the parties over ten-fold). "Dropping-in" had decreased. They work their way through a large number of voluntary associations describing (but not quantifying) their activities and their membership, concluding that "the unorganized social occasions of the neighbourhood in 1890 have given way increasingly to semi-organized dances and clubs."[9] In fact they located 458 active clubs—one for every 80 people, whereas in 1890 there were 92—one for every 125 people. They note, without comment, that there was a growing tendency for the business class to make club life serve other than recreational ends, notably those of getting a living,[10] and there is a particularly perceptive account of the activities of the Rotary Club. Their concluding sentence to this chapter, however, hints at what was to come in *Middletown in Transition*. "In view of the tightening of social and economic lines in the growing city, it is not surprising that the type of leisure-time organization which dominates today tends in the main to erect barriers to keep others out."[11] However, the Lynds' methods in *Middletown* are well illustrated by this chapter, for by and large they muster facts in order to convey impressions. What now appears so surprising is that these facts, or rather the accumulation of facts like these, over nearly 30 chapters were horrifying to cultured metropolitan America: *Moronia* in Mencken's memorable metaphor. The point remains, though, that for the modern sociologist, the Lynds' handling of their data in *Middletown* is elementary and there is nothing approaching what Madge calls "a well-ordered theoretical structure."[12]

However, by the time Robert Lynd produced *Middletown in Transition*, he knew quite clearly what he was doing. The number of man-days of fieldwork was about one tenth of that for the first study. Simplicity was their aim the second time, not elaboration. As Robert Lynd wrote, "Here was an American city which had been the subject of 18 months of close study in 1924–25. During the following decade the conditions of its existence had been unexpectedly altered in a way which affected every aspect of its life. Its growing population had been tossed from prosperity beyond any experienced prior to 1925 to an equally unprecedented depression. The opportunity thus presented to analyse its life under the stress of specific interrupting stimuli, whose course can be traced, offered something analogous to an experimental situation."[13] This time precise questions were posed of Muncie: had the basic culture remained intact? Had the trust in self-help and belief in the future been maintained? Had the old faiths survived and were the young adopting them? Had the sense of community developed further or had the latent cleavages become "sharper"?

The changes that are described in *Middletown in Transition* can be epitomized by the villains of that book, the "X" family. They are not mentioned in *Middletown*. The Lynds say that they themselves were blind and that the "X" family was invisible. But in 1935 "after ten years' absence from the city, one thing struck the returning observer again and again: the increasingly large public benefactions and the increasing pervasiveness of the power of this wealthy family of manufacturers, whose local position since 1925 is becoming hereditary with the emergence of a second generation of sons."[14] Though from their own evidence when one of the brothers "X" died in 1924 "the entire business of

[9] Ibid., p. 283.
[10] Ibid., p. 286.
[11] Ibid., p. 312.
[12] Madge, *Origins of Scientific Sociology*, p. 147.

[13] Robert S. Lynd and Helen M. Lynd, *Middletown in Transition* (New York, Harcourt, Brace, 1937), p. 4.
[14] Lynd and Lynd, *Middletown in Transition*, pp. 74–75.

the city stopped during his funeral."[15] In 1935 business ran Middletown and the "X" family dominated business; in the words of one of the Lynds' informants: "The one big point about this town. . . [is] that the "X" dominate the whole town, are the town, in fact."[16] Another Middletowner told Robert Lynd in 1935 that "If I'm out of work I go to the X plant; if I need money I go to the X Bank, and if they don't like me I don't get it; my children go the X college; when I get sick I go to the X hospital; I buy a building lot or house in an X subdivision; my wife goes down town to buy clothes at the X department store; if my dog strays away he is put in the X pound; I buy X milk; I drink X beer, vote for X political parties, and get help from X charities; my boy goes to the X YMCA and my girl to their YWCA; I listen to the word of God in X subsidized churches; if I'm a Mason, I go to the X Masonic Temple; I read the news from the X morning newspaper; and, if I am rich enough, I travel via the X airport."[17] There is an interesting contrast in "Government" between Middletown and Middletown in Transition. In the first book there is only a short 20-page chapter, whereas in the second it is 54 pages, and much of the chapter on the "X" family is devoted to government.[18] The Lynds concluded that the lines of leadership and related controls were highly concentrated and were more concentrated than in 1925. However, it is also shown that at many points this control was unconscious and when conscious, well-meaning or "public-spirited." But so long as the owners of such vast personal resources as the "X" family exhibited a public-spirited, willing-

ness to help with local problems, leadership and control would be forced upon them by circumstances and their patterns would tend to become the guiding patterns, or so runs Lynd's analysis.

There is, of course, much more to Middletown in Transition than the "X" family, and the changing patterns of social activity of the rest of the population are examined, though not in as much detail as in the earlier volume. The last chapter, however, requires special attention as it was an ambitious attempt to sum up the ideology of Middletown. The chapter is called "The Middletown Spirit." The technique of exposition used by Lynd is first to list what Middletown was for, and then what it was against. Middletown was for being honest, kind, friendly, loyal, successful, average, simple, sound, traditional, and courageous. It valued "character" above "brains." It believed in progress, but not too much too quickly, in individualism, and that one got what one deserved. It was convinced American ways were best and that American business was the core of society; the family was the fundamental institution and schools should stick to teaching the facts. Leisure was great but work came first. American democracy was the ultimate and ideal form of government and Christianity was the final form of religion. To give charity was good, to receive bad. Middletown was against the opposite of this list and also divergent personalities, innovations in ideas, art, literature, government, religion, education, the family. It was against Washington, or more exactly centralized government and planning that curtailed the making of money. It was against foreigners, minorities, deviants, frills and the weak.

As Robert Lynd points out, this complex of beliefs naturally favoured the contribution of the businessman in the community. "As . . . the chief contributor to the community's welfare, the successful businessman in Middletown elicits from his fellow citizens whole-hearted praise,

---

[15] Ibid., p. 75.

[16] Ibid., p. 77.

[17] Ibid., p. 74.

[18] The chapter that most increased in length between the two studies was "Caring for the Unable." This was clearly an area of major institutional reorganization, since most working-class and some middle-class families had suddenly found themselves involuntarily thrust into the "unable" category.

as well as envy and emulation. Since Middletown's values are regarded as leading to "success," it follows easily that those who are successful must obviously have these values to have become successful. So by this subtle and largely unconscious process, Middletown imprints to the successful businessman the possession . . . of the qualities of . . . the city's other values."[19] The greatest achievement of this ideology lay in its ability to reconcile the apparent contradictory qualities of ruthlessness on the one hand and consideration for others on the other. The successful businessman was licensed to be harshly enterprising in his strictly business relations in order that he might enjoy the luxury of friendliness out of business hours.

Between the time of the two studies tolerance increased in some directions, for instance religion, but decreased in others, particularly with regard to political and economic affairs. This was especially true in relation to Middletown's attitude to organized labour. The Middletown spirit was the businessmen's ideology and it dominated Middletown—for example it was repeatedly claimed that there were no class differences in Middletown. This was a denial by both the business and the working class, because the latter adopted the former as a reference group. The conclusion of the Lynds was "that the line between the working class and business class, though vague and blurred still, is more apparent than it was ten years before."[20] However, the Lynds did not develop a satisfactory tool to analyse social class, and their contemporary in the field, Lloyd Warner, tried much harder. Unlike him, though, the Lynds do not make much use of their class distinctions for analytical purposes. Nevertheless their usage of class is based on objective measures whereas Warner's is based on subjective.

The Lynds' conclusion is that despite the shock of the Great Depression the basic texture of Middletown's culture had not changed between 1925 and 1935. The Depression was viewed as an "interruption" to be "waited out." In 1935 the community was still living by the same values. Robert Lynd hardly bothers to conceal his regret that Middletown had as he puts it "learned nothing." The paradox is that Muncie was better off than neighbouring communities, largely through the activities of the "X" family. He was of course writing against a background of Fascism in Europe, and whereas the return of Roosevelt in 1936 secured the New Deal, he concluded with a deeply pessimistic sentence that this did not preclude the possibility "of a seizure of power carefully engineered as *by* the business class and *for* the business class and publicized in the name of Americanism and prosperity."[21] This last sentence shows the strengths and weaknesses of *Middletown* and *Middletown in Transition* in particular and community studies in general. At best the Lynds' contribution was to write meaningfully on significant issues, and they do so against a detail of vividly reported empirical fact. And yet their political interpretation of the community and their far-reaching forecasts have not only been overtaken but seem out of place.

The "Lynds in transition" demonstrate the path that community sociologists have often found it necessary to follow. They started work in a condition of almost total theoretical naiveté, and having set out to collect the facts adopted a current anthropological framework into which to fit them. It must be stressed that they did indeed collect these facts with a rare rigour. It is also to their credit that they came to recognize a need for a theory— Lynd admits to reading Marx between the two studies. They adopted a "stratification" model of the community, though

---

[19] Ibid., p. 422.
[20] Ibid., p. 451.

[21] Ibid., p. 510.

without Lloyd Warner's insistent use of it as almost the only analytical variable in analysis. And they became interested in what two decades later would have been called "community power." They remained to the end, though, better field-workers than theoreticians, for as Polsby has shown[22] they collected data that allowed their own model of the community to be shown as in some ways mistaken if not false. Their first volume does, however, contain the main conceptions necessary for interpreting the effects of industrialization on American communities, and their second for interpreting the effects of the Depression. However, unlike so many community sociologists, Warner for instance, they were reluctant to make sweeping generalizations from Middletown to America. This first major community study is distinguished by the fullness with which the social structure before industrialization is described, indeed it has a historical grasp rarely equalled in many later community studies.[23]

THE CHICAGO SCHOOL

The theoretical ideas behind the "human ecologists" of the Chicago school of community sociologists were discussed in Chapter 2. The concern here is to discuss both their methods and their substantive contributions through their empirical monographs. Don Martindale has called the Chicago school "urbanism incorporated."[24] The founder of the firm was Robert Park and his associates were Ernest

Burgess, Niels Anderson, Frederick Thrasher, Roderick McKensie, Harvey Zorbaugh, Paul Cressey, Clifford Shaw, Walter Reckless, and Louis Wirth. Their products were not only a marvellous series of monographs but they also had a distinctive style and approach to the community. The titles of their books are peculiarly evocative: *The Hobo: the Sociology of the Homeless Man* (1923), *The Gang* (1927), *The Gold Coast and the Slum* (1929), *The Taxi Dance Hall* (1932), *The Jack-Roller: A Delinquent Boy's Own Story* (1930), *Six Boys in Trouble* (1929) and *The Ghetto* (1929). The author of the last was also the author of arguably the single most famous paper ever written in sociology: "Urbanism as a Way of Life."[25]

In toto the production from Chicago in less than a decade is very impressive. No other city has ever been studied in such detail. The methods used in each monograph prove on inspection to be diverse: participant observation in the case of Anderson who became a hobo (though both his fieldwork and that of Zorbaugh seem shallow in the light of William Whyte's *Street Corner Society*), the collection of life histories in the case of Shaw studying the "Jack-Roller," official statistics in the case of Reckless on organized vice. They are unified not so much by their methods, though they all tended at some stage to tramp the streets, as by the general ecological model of the city, first formulated by Park and elaborated by Burgess and by their field of interest: Chicago. This is both the school's greatest strength, for their data is wonderfully rich, and its greatest weakness, for all their data is on one city at one time. Despite their historical investigations, like many other American community studies they can be charged with "localism," with having a curious local ethnocentricity notwithstanding the fact that they were the most cosmopolitan and

---

[22] See the detailed discussion in chap. 7, pp. 232–33.

[23] In writing about the Lynds' work we are only too aware of the wealth of detail that has been left out, and clearly it must not be thought for one moment that the above account is a substitute for reading the originals. This point will not be frequently reiterated but applies to most of the community studies discussed in this book.

[24] p. 28 of his "Prefatory Remarks" to his translation of Max Weber's *The City* (New York: Free Press, 1958).

[25] Originally published in the *American Journal of Sociology*, 1938.

worldly-wise of men. They failed to work out the relations between the special conditions existing in Chicago during the first 30 years of this century and other possible patterns of urbanisation during that time and after.

Whilst much of the work of the Chicago School is primarily descriptive (how else can Thrasher's location of 1,313 gangs be justified?) It has the advantage of being written from within a common framework. The techniques of the school can be approached from this autobiographical remark of Park's, "I expect that I have actually covered more ground, tramping about cities in different parts of the world, than any other living man. Out of all this I gained, among other things, a conception of the city, the community, and the region, not as a geographical phenomenon merely, but as a kind of social organization."[26] Soon after Park went to Chicago, he published an article in 1916 in the *American Journal of Sociology* called, "The City: Suggestions for the Investigation of Human Behavior in the Urban Environment."[27] This was the manifesto and programme of what was to become the Chicago school. It is a long article, of 46 pages and contains the origins of many of the ideas which saw empirical fruition in the later monographs. He relates what he calls "local organization" to the city plan and introduces the term *natural areas* for areas of "population segregation." These natural areas became the locale for specific studies, e.g., *The Gold Coast* or the *Ghetto*. He quotes with approval the old German adage that "city air makes men free" (*Stadt Luft macht frei*). Here is a central paradox in the formulations of the Chicago school: they stress the freedom that results from living in large, dense, socially heterogeneous and anonymous cities (the elements of urbanism as a way of life) and yet also posit a rather

narrow determinism that is too crude for geographers let alone sociologists. They most certainly relate types of social behaviour in communities to a precise and specific ecology—hence the Chicago monographs are spattered with maps of this or that activity against the "concentric ring" pattern of Chicago (see Figure 11–1). Park puts is like this: "Because of the opportunity it offers, particularly to the exceptional and abnormal types of man, a great city tends to spread out and lay bare to the public view in a massive manner all the human characters and traits which are ordinarily obscured and suppressed in smaller communities. The city, in short, shows the good and evil in human nature in excess. It is this fact, perhaps, more than any other, which justifies the view that would make the city a laboratory or clinic in which human nature and social processes may be conveniently and profitably studied."[28] Clearly Park believed that he could study the city as an object and the methods he favoured were the "same patient methods of observation that anthropologists like Franz Boas and R. H. Lowrie had expended on the life and manners of the North American Indian." He also began the collection of statistical data, i.e. relating to the city, and began the trend that culminates in the "neo-ecologists," Shevky and Bell, Leo Schnore, and Otis Dudley Duncan. Park was not free from community being used as normative prescription for he clearly cherished a vision of a developed science of the community which could chart patterns of change so that men might finally fashion their social environments to conform more closely with their ideals. Park wanted to preserve unity in the face of diversity, instead of the custom-bound homogeneity of rural life.

Burgess's famous diagram (adapted in Fig. 11–1) represents an elaboration of Park's formulation of the ecological idea on which the Chicago studies are based.

---

[26] R. E. Park, *Human Communities: The City and Human Ecology* (New York, Free Press, 1952), p. 5. (London, Collier-Macmillan).

[27] Reprinted in Park, ibid.

[28] Ibid., p. 51.

FIGURE 11–1

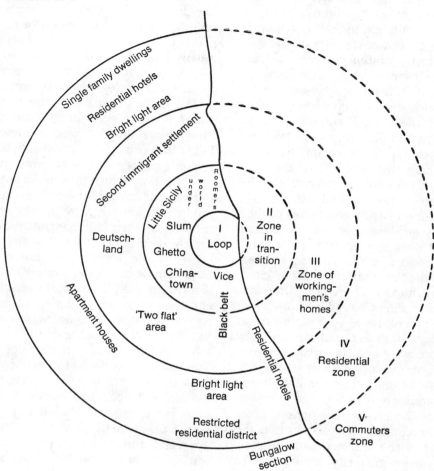

The key point is that it is what would now be called a "dynamic model" and the central concept is that of *succession*. Succession is used to describe the fact that these concentric rings, built up one after another historically as a city grows, are also invaded successively from the inside: for example, when an area which has been occupied by wealthy families begins to run down the homes are taken over as rooming houses, while the wealthy former residents move to a more suburban locality. They leave behind the now familiarly titled "twilight zone." Until Rex and Moore's[29]

work in Birmingham, though, the approach of pursuing ecological studies of the community in conjunction with detailed fieldwork seemed almost to stop after the early 1930s. Perhaps by this time Chicago has been overstudied. It will now be seen that it is no longer sufficient to identify a community as, say, located in the zone of transition or in suburbia. Common location in the physical structure of a community may be a starting place for an investigation, though few modern sociologists would now treat this factor as a sole, or at least as a very important independent variable, or for that matter as an independent variable at all.

---

[29] See below.

The actual social experience of Chicago was not that of every other city—it increased in population by half a million in each of the first three decades of this century and many of the newcomers were immigrants from Eastern and Southern Europe. To a quite remarkable extent Chicago was also the creation of the railway: towns that developed either earlier or later, Boston and Los Angeles to take two American examples, have an ecological structure markedly different to that of Chicago. So, like many community sociologists, those who worked in Chicago became bound by the peculiarities of their community and assumed that the rest of the world was similar if not identical. When a Chicago sociologist writes generally about the "community" or the "city," he means Chicago. There was little concern for comparing Chicago with any other city to see differences as well as similarities in their adaptations to population influxes.

What precisely was the urban community? It "turns out, upon closer scrutiny, to be a mosaic of minor communities, many of them strikingly different one from another, but all more or less typical. *Every City* has its central business district; the focal point of the whole urban complex. *Every City*, every great city, has its more or less exclusive residential areas of suburbs; its areas of light and of heavy industry, satellite cities, and casual labour mart, where men recruited for rough work on distant frontiers, in the mines and the forests, in the building of railways or the borings and excavations for the vast structures of our modern cities. *Every American City* has its slums; its ghettos, its immigrant colonies, regions which maintain more or less alien and exotic culture. Nearly every large city has its bohemias and bohemians, where life is freer, more adventurous and lonely than it is elsewhere. These are the so-called natural areas of the city."[30]

Such natural areas were studied by Zorbaugh in *The Gold Coast and the Slum*. Not only is this one of the finest of the many good Chicago monographs but it also raises, in particular, interesting and crucial questions about the whole school's approach to and view of the community.

The Gold Coast and Little Sicily (the slum) have few common customs and "there is certainly no common view which holds the cosmopolitan population of this region together in any common purpose . . . the laws which prevail are not a communal product, and there is no organized public opinion which supports and contributes to their enforcement.[31] So Zorbaugh doubts whether "in any proper sense of the word" the "Lower North Side" can be called a community at all. "It is a region . . . an area of transition, the character of its populations and the problems which it presents are at once a reflection and a consequence of the conditions which this period of transition imposes."[32] The test for this book, indeed of the Chicago school, might well be "everywhere the old order passeth, but the new order hath yet to come." Underlying this is a very Durkheimian view of society which appreciated that the old forms of mechanical solidarity had broken down and that organic solidarity is ever precarious.

The area that interested Zorbaugh was one of extremes, not just of contrasts. The Gold Coast "has the highest residential land values in the city, and among the lowest are to be found near by . . . the Lower North Side has more professional men, more politicians, more suicides, more persons in *Who's Who*, than in any "community" in Chicago."[33] The Gold Coast was on the lake side, the blocks behind were rooming houses—Anderson's "hobohemia" was located here, and still further inland, but in most cases only a

---

[30] Park, *Human Communities*, p. 196 (our emphasis).

[31] Harvey W. Zorbaugh, *The Gold Coast and the Slum* (Chicago, University of Chicago Press, 1929), p. vii (London, Chicago U.P., 1929).

[32] Ibid., pp. vii–viii.

[33] Ibid., p. 6.

couple of dozen blocks away from the Gold Coast, were "Little Italy" and "Little Sicily"—the slums. In common with the other Chicago monographs Zorbaugh begins with a detailed physical description of the locality, for example of Lake Shore Drive, "the Mayfair of the Gold Coast . . . rise the imposing stone mansions, with their green lawns and wrought-iron-grilled doorways, of Chicago's wealthy aristocracy and her industrial and financial King."[34] In contrast, "The slum is a bleak area of segregation of the sediment of society; an area of extreme poverty, tenants, ramshackle buildings, of evictions and evaded rents; an area of working mothers and children, of high rates of birth, infant mortality, illegitimacy, and death; an area of pawnshops and second-hand stores, of gangs, of "flops" where every bed is a vote,"[35] and "it harbours many sorts of people: the criminal, the radical, the bohemian, the migratory worker, the immigrant, the unsuccessful, the queer and the unadjusted."[36] Everywhere there is movement—the strength of the Chicago school is their feeling for describing urban processes: Zorbaugh noted for example that "the Negro, too, is moving into this area and pushing on into "Little Hell" (the core of "Little Italy")."[37] Within the slum, but not of it, was "Towertown," a considerable colony of artists and would-be artists.

Zorbaugh's methods are indicated by the number of paragraphs that begin "As one walks"—for example, "One has but to walk the streets of the Near North Side to sense the cultural isolation beneath these contrasts."[38] Some of the individuals that once lived in the slum "have succeeded in climbing" but for the rest "the district east of State Street exists only in the newspapers."[39] Similarly the "Gold Coaster"

knows little except through sensational newspaper reports of what happens in the slums. In a key passage Zorbaugh sums up his impressions: "The *isolation* of the populations crowded together within these few hundred blocks, the *superficiality* and *externality* of their contacts the *social distances* that separate them, their absorption in the affairs of their *own little worlds*— these and not mere size and numbers, constitute the problems of the inner city. The community, represented by the town or peasant village where everyone knows everyone else clear down to the ground, is gone. Over large areas of the city "community" is little more than a geographical expression. Yet the old traditions of control persist despite changed conditions of life. The inevitable result is cultural disorganization."[40] There is, of course, a posture of nostalgia here for the rural community, but integration may be possible on another basis than *Gemeinschaft*. Chicago in the 1920s appears, though, to be classical *Gesellschaft*.

The greater part of Zorbaugh's book is devoted to a detailed examination and description of each area in the Near North Side. He begins with the Gold Coast itself, but first makes a detailed historical examination of the changes that had occurred in the area over the previous century. The Chicago school were always aware that they were observing the latest stage, that could only be understood in relation to the past growth of the city. The Gold Coast was "society" but membership, unlike in the recent past and in smaller communities like Newburyport,[41] was no longer based entirely on birth. Wealth rather than hereditary social position was the criterion. Zorbaugh collected a document from a female member of one of Chicago's "oldest and most aristocratic families" in which she wrote, "The society of today is topsy-turvey. No doubt it is due to the growth of the city. Great fortunes and great wealth

[34] Ibid., p. 7.
[35] Ibid., p. 9.
[36] Ibid., p. 11.
[37] Ibid., p. 11–12.
[38] Ibid., p. 12.
[39] Ibid., p. 13.

[40] Ibid., p. 16.
[41] See below, pp. 98–105.

have led to ostentation and display. The city is so large that society can no longer hold together."[42] And as Zorbaugh describes: "One no longer is born to social position; one achieves social position by playing "the social game."[43] This game is described in some detail—for example the techniques of breaking into *The Social Register*. Zorbaugh demonstrates that the Gold Coast families were not one group but were internally differentiated into cliques.

"Back of the ostentatious apartments, hotels, and homes of the Lake Shore Drive, and the quiet, shady streets of the Gold Coast lies an area of streets that have a painful sameness, with their old, soot-begrimed stone houses, their none-too-clean alleys, their shabby air of respectability."[44] This is the next area that Zorbaugh describes: the world of furnished rooms. Demographically this area is interesting: 52 percent were single men, 10 percent were single women, while the remaining 38 percent were married "without benefit of clergy." It was also a childless area.[45] The whole population turned over every four months.[46] In this social situation Zorbaugh argues that "there can be no community tradition or common definition of the situation, no public opinion, no informal social control."[47] The exaggerated mobility and astonishing anonymity "are the direct antithesis of all we are accustomed to think of as normal in society." It should be noted that the stereotype "community" has been taken to be "normal." One typical weakness of the Chicago school is exhibited here: their concentration on "natural areas" prevented them always from viewing the city as a whole. If they had stepped back a bit, as it were, it might have been possible for them to consider

where those who were living in the rooming house district had come from and where they were moving to. It is then conceivable that the sheer temporality of their stay should have suggested that this district was meeting temporary needs, in many cases reflecting a particular stage in the life cycle. They had come from and would return to a community thought of by Zorbaugh as "normal in society." The Chicago school's contribution to our knowledge of urban processes is surer on "intergeneration" mobility processes: "children" moving "out" and "up" from Little Sicilies, than on "intra-generational" processes: leaving home to live in a rooming house, or flat, or bedsitter, and later moving to suburbia after marriage to have and rear children.

The bohemia of "Towertown" is described next, demonstrating that many who lived there were seeking an escape from the "repressive conventions" of the smaller community. This is at the same time as the "X" family in Middletown are preventing "modern" literature and "modern" art being found in the public libraries and galleries. He then moves to discuss what he calls "The Rialto of the Half World"—the world of bright lights, restaurants, and jazz. Here are hobos, squawkers (pedlars and street salesmen) and the "Wobbly" headquarters, cabarets and brothels, tea-rooms and homosexuals. That most large cities have areas such as this is indisputable (one thinks of the juxtaposition of radical publishing houses and stripclubs in Soho), but few people live there: it is a "service" area for the wider community.

Behind these bright lights were the slums and "one alien group after another had claimed this area. The Irish, the Germans, the Swedish, the Sicilians have occupied it in turn. Now it is being invaded by a migration of the Negro from the south."[48] The Negroes have come from

[42] Zorbaugh, *Gold Coast and Slum*, p. 48.
[43] Ibid., p. 49.
[44] Ibid., p. 69.
[45] Ibid., p. 71.
[46] Ibid., p. 72.
[47] Ibid., p. 82.

[48] Ibid., p. 127.

communities like those described in a later section. Here the immigrant to the city "meets with sympathy, understanding and encouragement . . . (and) . . . finds his fellow-countrymen who understand his habits and his standards and share his life-experience and viewpoint. In the colony he has a status, plays a role in a group. In the life of the colony's streets and cafés, in its churches and benevolent societies, he finds response and security. In the colony he finds that he can live, be somebody, satisfy his wishes—all of which are impossible in the strange world outside."[49] This looks extraordinarily like the usual view of the traditional community, for indeed these are what Herbert Gans later was to call "urban villages."[50] Zorbaugh located 28 district nationalities in the Near North Side Slum. He wants to call the specific areas "ghettos" and like the medieval Jewish ghetto they form a more or less independent community with their own customs and laws. It was out of "Little Sicily" that the Mafia emerged—they had mostly come from around Palermo. It seems that in "Little Sicily" it was possible for many Sicilians to remain *encapsulated*—to use Mayer's term[51]—in Chicago: they continued in almost every respect the mores, especially those relating to sexual relations, of the village areas from which they had migrated. And the Mafia continued the fierce and persistent feuding between families.

So the contrasts within the area described by Zorbaugh are tremendous and yet there was a common theme in the very great difficulty found by all groups in maintaining or reconstructing any *sense* or *feeling* of community. The Gold Coasters, we are told, had no sense of community apart from sharing a good address; the rooming-house people as described by Zorbaugh were completely detached from society and the hobos by definition were isolates and wanderers. The only place where there was any rootedness was in Little Sicily, but they would be displaced by the next wave of immigrants.

The one important ingredient in all the Chicago monographs is the concept of ecology and the practice of relating (if not determining) community structure to geographical and spatial realities. Otherwise their theoretical advances were slight: they provided a truly impressive amount of factual detail on Chicago, but little else. Take for example Zorbaugh's theoretical chapter, "The City and the Community," and it will be seen that this adds little to the theory of community. True, he rejects idealized notions of community and stresses "that the life of a local area has a natural organization which must be taken into account,"[52] but this is little more than a plea for yet more empirical work "to discover how the community acts, how it sets up standards, defines aims and ends, gets things done; and to analyse what has been the effect of the growth of the city upon the life of local areas, what changes have come with the industrial city." The village still represents the example *par excellence* of the community and he writes that in the city "an area becomes a community only through the common experiences of the people who live in it, resulting in their becoming a cultural group, with traditions, sentiments and attitudes and memories in common—a focus of belief, feeling and action. A community, then, is a local area over which people are using the same language, conforming to the same mores, feeling more or less the same sentiments, and acting upon the same attitudes."[53] However, he clearly feels that though this may have existed in European peasant villages or early American towns, communities like this are not found in the modern

[49] Ibid., p. 141.

[50] H. J. Gans, *The Urban Villagers* (New York, Free Press, 1962) (London, Collier Macmillan, 1962).

[51] P. Mayer, "Migrancy and the Study of Africans in Towns', *American Anthropologist*, 1962.

[52] Zorbaugh, *Gold Coast and Slum*, p. 221.

[53] Ibid., pp. 222–23.

city ". . . as glimpse of the life (this may be the true contribution of many Chicago monographs) of the Gold Coast, of Little Hill, of Towertown, or the world of the furnished rooms so vividly shows, local areas of the city are vastly different from the village and over great areas of the city the last vestiges of the community are disappearing."[54] This would seem to be denied by his own data, especially on the migrant colonies. He goes on to use Burgess's concentric zone typology of urban growth and repeats Burgess's claim that these are displayed (only modified by physical features) in every city. Within each zone of these broader zones "competition, economic and cultural, segregates the population."[55] The local consequence of this competition, a reflection of the division of labour, is an exaggeration of social distance in the residential locality. In the constantly idealized village practically everybody has some economic and cultural relationship with everybody else. In the city, however, such relationships no longer occur in the local community and social distance consequently increases. There is in the city, he argues, a replacement of face-to-face and intimate relationships by casual, transitory, disinterested contacts and as there is "no common body of experience and tradition, no unanimity of interest, sentiment and attitude which can serve as a basis for collective action, local groups do not act. They cannot act, local life breaks down."[56]

The Chicago school in general, and Zorbaugh in particular, fail to take account of the general tendency in industrial societies towards individuation and the extent to which people positively *choose* city life for what it can offer. If the sociologists approach the study of community with an ideal typical community in mind, it can but only be always disintegrating. If the Chi-

cago school were presiding over the total eclipse of some past rural community, then later sociologists have presided over the collapse of city communities into suburbia (see below). It is not helpful to identify a particular way of life with a particular ecological space. Yet what ecology can do is to give some indication of the spatial *constraints* within which choices are made. The particular contribution of the Chicago school was an appreciation of *how* cities changed. Their dynamic model of successions and areas of change has very wide applicability, and not just to large cities. As will be shown in the next section Lloyd Warner's assumption about the stability of "Yankee City" seriously misled him about that community's past. A careful reading of Zorbaugh's *The Gold Coast and the Slum*, which had been published six years before Warner entered the field, would have sensitized him to urban processes and perhaps allowed a more realistic analysis of "Yankee City."

YANKEE CITY

The Yankee City project must rank as the most intensive, exhaustive, and expensive single study ever made of a small American community, or anywhere else for that matter.[57] The first of the five volumes that reports the findings of Lloyd Warner and his colleagues lists a research staff of 30: 4 were writers, analysts and fieldworkers, 9 were analysts and fieldworkers, 5 were just fieldworkers and 12 were just analysts, i.e. 18 people, at least, had done fieldwork in Newburyport, the small New

---

54 Ibid., p. 228.
55 Ibid., p. 232.
56 Ibid., p. 251.

57 W. Lloyd Warner and Paul S. Lunt, *The Social Life of a Modern Community*, Yankee City Series, I (New Haven, Yale University Press, 1941); *The Status System of a Modern Community*, 1942; Warner and Leo Srole, *The Social Systems of American Ethnic Groups*, 1945; Warner and J. O. Low, *The Social System of a Modern Factory*, 1947; Warner, *The Living and the Dead*, 1959. These five volumes will be referred to respectively as Yankee City I (YCI), YCII, YCIII, YCIV, and YCV. Students may like to know that Warner has abridged the series into one volume published in 1963 (New Haven, Yale University Press).

England town for which Yankee City is the pseudonym (the use of pseudonyms are a verbal manifestation of his assumptions of the broader generalization of his study). The project was conceived as part of a research programme conducted from Harvard, and it was originally aimed to examine the "non-work" aspect of the lives of the workers being studied by Elton Mayo at Western Electric (the famous Hawthorne experiments). Warner found this prospect impossible. He had just returned from three years fieldwork among Australian aborigines and wanted to apply the same techniques used there to the study of American communities. Unfortunately "Cicero and Hawthrone (the location of the Western Electric factory) and other industrial sub-communities in Chicago . . . seemed to be disorganized; they had a social organization which was highly disfunctional if not in partial disintegration. If we were to compare easily the other societies of the world with one of our own civilization, and if we were readily to accommodate our techniques, developed by the study of primitive society, to modern groups, *it seemed wise to choose a community with a social organization which had developed over a long period of time under the domination of a single group with a coherent tradition.*"[58]

New England and the Deep South seemed likely locations for such a community. Warner's fatal error was that his anthropological orientation and techniques misled him into believing Yankee City was, in fact, like that. It has been shown that he had serious misconceptions, particularly about the community's history, that his ahistorical functionalist conceptual framework and methods never allowed him to realize. Warner's strength was his lack of ethnocentricity which certainly allowed him to see and report phenomena long ignored in American society, for example, stratification, and yet he was blind

to other aspects of the community. Warner wrote that "to be sure we were not ethnocentrically biased in our judgements, we decided to use no previous summaries of data collected by anyone else (maps, handbooks, histories etc.) until we had formed our own opinion of the community."[59] In the fifth volume, *The Living and the Dead: The Symbolic Life of a Community,* Warner, commenting on the "history" portrayed in Yankee City pageants, said that it "was what community leaders now *wished* it were and what they *wished* it were not. They ignored this or that difficult period of time or unpleasant occurrence and embarrassing group of men and women; they left out awkward political passions; they selected small items out of large time contexts, sizing them up to express today's values."[60] It is unfortunately true that Warner's own words quoted above can be used as a similar indictment against his work in Yankee City as a whole. His unwillingness to consult the historical record and his complete dependence on materials susceptible to traditional anthropological analysis, i.e., the acts and opinions of living members of the community, served to obliterate the distinction between the actual past and current myths about the past. This is particularly ironic, as the determination of the Yankee City investigators to escape the ethnocentric biases of culture-bound history led them to accept uncritically the community's legends about itself. This is, as Stephen Thernstrom, Yankee City's historian, has remarked, "surely the most ethnocentric of all possible views."[61]

Warner's view of the community is explicitly and rather crudely functionalist, for he admits that "the analogy of the or-

---

[58] YCI, p. 4 (our emphasis).

[59] Ibid., p. 40.

[60] YCV, p. 110.

[61] Stephen Thernstrom, *Poverty and Progress: Social Mobility in a Nineteenth-century City* (Cambridge, Mass., Harvard University Press, 1964), p. 230 (London, Harvard University Press—Oxford University Press, 1965).

ganism was in our thinking when we looked at the total community of Yankee City and the various parts of its internal structure."[62] Elsewhere the community is called a "working whole in which each part had definite *functions* which *had* to be performed or substitutes acquired, if the whole society were to maintain itself."[63] His functionalism is of an evolutionary variety and he refers to "higher" and "lower" cultures. The community was defined as "a body of people having a common organization or common interests and living in the same place under the same laws and regulations."[64] The ordered social relations of this locally bound group he calls the social structure and "all local groups differ sufficiently everywhere for the individuals in them to be aware of belonging to one group and not to another, even though the other may be but little different from their own."[65] This would seem to belie the geographical mobility of Americans. Warner had a two-dimensional geometrical view of the community: Social space was seen as having two dimensions, the vertical which is a hierarchical order in which people occupy higher and lower positions, and the horizontal which is the social differentiation at any given level.

The community is variously called a "convenient microcosm for field study" and a "laboratory" by Warner. "In my research," he wrote, "the local community was made to serve as a microscopic whole representing the total American community."[66] It is therefore particularly important to know how Yankee City was chosen. Twenty-two variables were used to categorize many communities and Newburyport was chosen because it was the one that "most nearly approached the

ideal-typical expression" of the central tendencies of American society. These "tendencies" are expressed rather vaguely when Warner wrote ". . . we know America is a large industrial nation, founded on a vast agricultural base, that it constantly assimilates and fails to assimilate large numbers of immigrants from different European cultures, that its religious life is largely Protestant, but that it has a strong Catholic minority, that it has powerful political and economic hierarchies, that its associational and civil enterprises are deeply pervasive, and that there is a considerable distance from the bottom to the top levels of the socioeconomic heap."[67] He uses the community study both as a "sampling device," i.e. a method to get at these tendencies (which we should note are assumed, not proven), as empirical description, and as an object, for he refers to varieties and sorts of communities.

So above all "we sought a well integrated community,"[68] but he had already commented on the lack of integration in Chicago—did that city *not* represent the central tendencies of American society? But they "did not want a community where the ordinary daily relations of the inhabitants were in confusion or conflict." They did, however, want a community "where the social organization had become firmly organized and the relations of the various members of the society [are] exactly placed and known by the individuals who made up the group." And what is more, that is what they found, or appeared to find. Warner also specified that the community should have a few industries and several factories because "we wished to see how the factory and the workers were geared into the life of a larger community."[69] It should be autonomous and not a metropolitan satellite,

[62] YCI, p. 12.

[63] Ibid., p. 14 (our emphasis).

[64] Ibid., p. 16.

[65] Ibid., p. 17.

[66] W. Lloyd Warner, *Structure of American Life*, Edinburgh, Edinburgh University Press, 1952, p. 33.

[67] Ibid., p. 34.

[68] YCI, p. 38.

[69] Ibid., p. 39.

which implied that the anthropologist in Warner was yearning for "isolated wholes." It is questionable whether this is a reasonable approach to communities in advanced industrial societies. The community also had to be small "since, if [it] were too large, our detailed methods of observation could not be applied." Such a community, we believed would manifest much of the complexities of modern life but would be beyond the possibilities of detailed examination." The final condition that the community had to meet makes one wonder whether the other conditions were so many *post facto* legitimations, "the community had to be near enough to Cambridge (Mass.) so that [we] could go back and forth without difficulty or loss of time."[70]

Their techniques were in the first place to do "a Robert Park": they walked round the town and produced a map of the physical nature of the community. They introduced themselves to prominent individuals who introduced them to their friends," which shortly spread our sources of information from the top to the bottom of the community." This is diametrically opposed to Warner's main substantive conclusion on "social classes" in Yankee City which by (his) definition are discrete and bounded friendship groups. If early informants could in fact introduce Warner to friends from the top to the bottom of the community, this is important data in its own right and contradicts his main conclusions on stratification in the community. In any case they used the local stratification system to enter and one frequently voiced criticism is that Warner was in fact captured by his key informants, the Lower Uppers and Upper Middles, as he calls them. Certainly right from the start of the project there appears to be no attempt to ensure and demonstrate that informants covered the whole social range in Yankee City. The investigators appeared to have

had no real entry problems and "assumed that everyone would have the good sense to know that what we were doing was important and deserving of confidence."[71] They appear, though, to have made no attempt to really explain their aims, but then you probably would not to Australian aborigines either. They let Yankee City define their role and give them a place in the social structure: as social historians and economists and genealogists and "to the members of the varied ethnic groups were we fair-minded gentlemen interested in seeing that their groups received their rightful place in the economic and historical study we were making."

Their techniques were eclectic: observation (as has been shown in the previous chapter, this is not a single technique), interview, documents, newspapers, and even an aerial survey. They felt the need to use many and varied techniques for "the general objective of our research was to determine the *complete* set of social relations which constituted Yankee City society."[72] Their first task was to "place" (their term) the person being interviewed and in a very revealing remark Warner says that this was not difficult as "common knowledge provides a good rough general framework within which a given individual can be placed."[73] So not only did Lloyd Warner make insupportable assumptions about what sort of community Newburyport was, but he also made initially rather cavalier assumptions about its internal structure, or maybe he believed that his early informants had told him all there was to know. The community was both very thoroughly and somewhat eccentrically covered by any standard—they "had an observer to complete a list of those who bought magazines and papers to find out what journals were purchased," and they sampled traffic to get those just passing

---

[70] Ibid., p. 43.

[71] Ibid., p. 48.
[72] Ibid., p. 48 (our emphasis).
[73] Ibid., p. 48.

through! The health office told them who had venereal disease in the community.[74] Warner rejects the sample survey as a research tool—in the great Boothian tradition he wanted to know all the facts, though the survey's main advantage of obtaining systematic facts appertaining to individuals would surely have allowed Warner to defend himself against some of his critics.

All these data were collated on what must be seen as the centre of Warner's research—the Social Personality Cards. There was one card for each adult in the community. On them were recorded, name, residence, age, sex, social status, occupation, maiden name of wife, names of children, membership of cliques and associations, church affiliation, type of house, newspapers and magazines taken, movies attended, his doctor and undertaker, and summary budget data (which *was* apparently from some sort of sample, the details of which we are not told). Also any information from public welfare and police records relating to each individual was added. These data were punched on to machine-readable cards and described statistically, though precious little of it is reported in the five Yankee City volumes. These data were collected over the four years from 1930–34 and so it is not a *real* population study for the 16,785 individuals do not correspond to the population of Yankee City at any one time. Warner appreciates that the key problem about his Social Personality Cards is that they are "data . . . centred on individuals." So whilst they lend "themselves readily to statistical compilation and correlation of attributes and relational characteristics of individuals . . . difficulties arose, however, when it became necessary to compare one relation between individuals with another."[75]

The Yankee City volumes are well

	Percent	Percent in full employment
Upper upper	1.44	90.00
Lower upper	1.56	94.44
Upper middle	10.22	83.14
Lower middle	28.12	62.26
Upper lower	36.60	41.48
Lower lower	25.22	27.57
Don't know	0.84	

known for their characterization of the population of Newburyport into six distinctively named classes. Warner claims that he started with a general economic interpretation of human behaviour. He does not say that it was a marxist orientation but it would seem to have been very similar. Yet while in Yankee City he discovered that some people were ranked low even when they had higher incomes than people ranked above them, and that others with low incomes were ranked high. People with the same jobs were ranked differently, for instance doctors, and this was *not* related to how good a physician he was. The famous Warner definition of social class is two or more orders of people who are believed to be and are accordingly ranked by the members of the community in socially superior and inferior positions."[76] This had consequences for the physical structure of Yankee City as different areas had a different status: Hill Street was top, Side Street in the middle, and Riverbrooker low. These "class" differences are reflected in Yankee City cliques, clubs, and associations. The titles of the "classes" and their sizes are shown in the table. It is relevant to point out that in 1933 Newburyport had an unemployment rate of nearly 19 percent: the proportion in full employment of each "class" is shown in the second column of the table. Lloyd Warner's procedure for "classing" a community [may be summed up] like this: "All the types of social structure and each of the thousands of families, thousands of

---

[74] Ibid., p. 63.
[75] Ibid., p. 73.

[76] Ibid., p. 82.

cliques, and hundreds of associations were, member by member, interrelated in our research. With the use of all structural participation, and with the aid of such additional testimony as the area lived in, the type of house, kind of education, manners and other symbols of class (sic), it was possible to determine very quickly the approximate place of any individual in society. In the final analysis, however, individuals were placed by the evaluations of the members of Yankee City itself, by such explicit statements as "she does not belong" or "they do not belong."[77] Imagine trying to use this technique in a city! Warner clearly believes that a community has a social structure with "classes" as "real entities" (not categories) into which *all* the inhabitants can unambiguously be placed, that people use their local community as a reference group, and that people agree on their criteria of ranking and can classify each other by them. This definition of class led to an extraordinary outburst from other social scientists that will be considered in the later chapter on local stratification. All that should be noted here is that, in the words of C. Wright Mills, "Warner's insistence upon merely one vertical dimension led to the consequent absorbing of three analytically separable dimensions [economic, status, and power] into one "sponge" word "class".[78] Mills adds that most of the confusions and inadequacies of Warner's study flow from this fact. Warner has threaded *all* the many coloured beads on one vertical string.

Having said what he means by class and categorized the population, Warner then adopts the technique of drawing up what he calls "profiles." Though compulsive reading if one has a taste for Thirties American prose ('. . . on that autumn evening Mrs. Henry Adams Bredken-

ridge. . .')—should they really be confused with social science? They are admittedly fictionalized and indeed they could have been written by Sinclair Lewis. Warner even makes one of his characters refer to *Babbitt* (Chapter 15) with reference to the class system in Zenith. "No one actual individual or family in Yankee City is depicted, rather the lives of several individuals are compressed into that of one *fictive* person"[79] and similarly "the persons and situations in some of the sketches are entirely imaginary." The central damning limitation of these "profiles" is that they were all constructed without regard for the scientific canons of verifiability and in a manner which allowed the biases of the authors to operate unchecked. We have no idea how typical they are, and so stylistically similar are they to Sinclair Lewis that we could be forgiven for thinking them fiction. After the profiles, however, "the remainder of the volume is concerned solely with this quantitative problem of how many, etc."

All data on Yankee City are presented "by class." Class is the major analytic variable and so there are chapters on "sex and age, birthplace, ethnic minorities, ecology, all "by class," i.e. the six status groups enumerated by Warner and listed above. The confusion between class and status is everywhere evident, for example, we are told that in "Yankee City houses are (thus) symbols of *status*, in the society. The cultural differences in the family life of the several *classes* are reflected in house type and symbolized by it. The house is, moreover, the paramount symbol of the unequal distribution of the valued things of life among the several *classes*"[80] and "age of marriage is in direct relation to *the status* [to be consistent he should have written class] of an individual, the upper class marry late, the lower class marry young."[81]

---

[77] Ibid., p. 90.
[78] C. Wright Mills, review of YCI in *American Sociological Review*, 7, 1942, reprinted in his collected essays edited by I. L. Horowitz, *People, Politics and Power*, London, Oxford University Press, 1965.

[79] YCI, p. 127 (our emphasis).
[80] Ibid., p. 215 (our emphasis).
[81] Ibid., p. 252.

He continues his analysis "by class" of the economic life of the community, the control of property, and how individuals spend their money. The approach of the principal investigator and the general style of the volumes are well depicted in this passage: "When an individual in Yankee City spent money for articles which could be purchased, he was acting in accordance with his system of values and thereby satisfying certain of his desires. The desires of all those who spent money for the things they wanted were basically physical, but the values which dominated the expression of their wants were social. All men and women in Yankee City as physical organisms needed food and shelter, but the values which dictated their choice of a house or of food for a meal were socially determined and also expressed the demands, needs and limitations of their social personalities in a status [sic] system."[82] Here the community, through its status system (or as Warner usually calls it, class system) is seen as an independent variable affecting individual behaviour. Treating the "association" as one of the foremost mechanisms of integration of Yankee City society, Warner presents an analysis "by class," similarly with church and school, the political structure, and reading.

Volume II of the Yankee City series, *The Status System of a Modern Community*, is a descriptive statistical extravaganza. There is a concern to tabulate 19 varieties of "class types of associational membership" against the six classes. This gives 54 "positions" to which are added varieties of family and clique membership giving 89 "positions." The 89 "positions" are described separately and contain 71,149 memberships which are tabulated (the famous Table 18 lasts for 86 pages!). We are almost completely baffled by this volume, especially as its authors admit they cannot say anything about the strength or intensity of the relationship involved.[83] Volume III, *The Social Systems of American Ethnic Groups* relates in more detail their position in the social structure of Yankee City. The social history of each ethnic group is traced from its arrival up to the 1930s. This volume, together with Volume IV, *The Social System of the Modern Factory*,[84] contains Warner's important statements on the "blocked mobility hypotheses."[85] Warner computes the "social position" (average occupational status) of the Irish for 1850, 1864, 1873, 1883, and 1893 and goes straight on to talk about their "moderate and slight mobility." Thernstrom, in a magnificent piece of historical research into 19th century Newburyport has shown though that (1) the Irish were not an "entity" in that "to compute overall occupational status indices for all Irish names in the community in 1864 and 1883 was of dubious value, because in fact a majority of the Irishmen living in Newburyport in 1864 had left the community by 1883 and the bulk of the 1883 group consisted of newcomers to the city"[86] and (2) manual Irish immigrants who stayed in the community, though they begat manual sons, also bought property and so certainly should have been seen as socially mobile. Warner's techniques do not allow him to differentiate between different dimensions of social mobility (nor do most other techniques for that matter). Thernstrom shows that paradoxically Yankee City may in fact have been a "sample" of the main trends of American society, though Warner was wrong about what they were. A host of critics have attacked the assumption that seemingly small and static communities like Newburyport and Morris (Jonesville)[87]

---

[82] Ibid., p. 287.

[83] YCII., p. 200.

[84] Note in passing the use of the definite rather than the indefinite article.

[85] YCIV, pp. 87–89, 182–85.

[86] Thernstrom, *Poverty and Progress*, p. 238.

[87] Studied by Warner and his colleagues and reported in the community study, *Democracy in Jonesville* (New York, Harper & Row, 1949; London, Harper Torchbooks).

are adequate laboratories for observing American social life. Thernstrom has shown that Newburyport was far less deviant than Warner made it out to be. Newburyport was not the dormant, self-contained, predominantly old American *Gemeinschaft* village portrayed in the Yankee City volumes.[88]

In the abridged version of *Yankee City* it is interesting to note that what was Volume IV is now called "the transition." It is from this volume that Maurice Stein pulls his message about the destructive effect of bureaucratization on the community.[89] It is the study of a strike which broke the "open shop" and led to unionization. The extension "upwards" out of the Yankee City of the factory hierarchy (i.e. absentee ownership), and "outwards" through manufacturing associations and unions increased the breakdown of communication between management and labour. This, and the breakdown of the old skill hierarchy with modern methods of mass production, replaced by task anonymity, were the underlying causes of the strike. This was interpreted by Warner as an attempt on the part of the workers to gain a new and different sense of status through unionization. As the old mobility of workers up the factory skill hierarchy was blocked this, and the acquisition of the factory by New York Jews, removed the social constraints against striking. Lipset and Bendix, though, argue that the strike sentiments were an expression of anti-semitic attitudes on the part of a large part of the population. Jews with high economic position and low status were, they argue, a threat to the whole value system of the

community.[90] The fifth and final volume, *The Living and the Dead*, is about the symbolic life of Yankee City, about political myths and "dead heroes."

There have been so many criticisms of Warner that it might well be time to call for a moratorium on them. Never in the history of community studies has so much effort been expended by so many people with such wrongheaded assumptions and with such inappropriate concepts and techniques. Yet Lloyd Warner did break the academic taboo and open up the debate about stratification in the United States. Occasionally he was just silly: "Jonesville is in all Americans and all Americans are in Jonesville, for he that dwelleth in America dwelleth in Jonesville, and Jonesville in him,"[91] and his work suffers throughout from the basic delusions that the ahistorical, functionalist assumptions of the old equilibrium school of social anthropology provided an adequate framework for studying a complex modern community in an industrial society. The details of Warner's study can be used to document the changes occurring in some American communities in the 30s, for example, it is difficult not to conclude that "the transition" and the strike described in Volume 4 shows a breaking down of the old status hierarchies— though they may not have been so old, as Thernstrom has shown—and the rise to some considerable power of the working class. What Warner calls the "classes" of Yankee City, which are described in Volume 1, as joint participants in a common community system, increasingly confront each other as embodiments of collectivities under the control of remote power centres which determine their relationships to each other far more than factors arising in the local community.

---

[88] Warner describes the Upper Uppers as having lived in Yankee City for generations but in fact a close examination of his data shows that less than 60 percent had been born in or near Newburyport and almost a quarter had been born outside New England (YCI, p. 209).

[89] Maurice Stein, *The Eclipse of Community* (New York, Harper & Row, 1964), chap. 3.

[90] S. M. Lipset and R. Bendix, "Social Status and Social Structure: A Reexamination of the Data and Interpretations," *British Journal of Sociology* 1 (1951), p. 232.

[91] *Jonesville*, p. xv.

12

The eclipse of community

Maurice Stein

After these selective summaries of three sets of American community studies [Chicago, Middletown, Yankee City] the remaining task is to show how they provide the basis for developing a generalized theoretical approach to the field. This theory should be able to account for the main patterns of change found in each of these communities so as to facilitate exploration of the same patterns under quite different circumstances. In other words, the theory has to point toward further cumulative research. It is just this problem of accumulation that has made theorizing in this area so difficult. Community studies are always confined in time and space so that the relevance of any particular investigation for understanding later or earlier studies is always in question.

Even if one assumes that time can be held in abeyance, it is doubtful that the student of any particular American community can reasonably claim to generalize his distinctively sociological findings so as to imply descriptive validity for all or even most American communities. The search for "representative" communities on the basis of which generalization about all of them or about the society itself can be developed is doomed to failure. Yet Park, the Lynds, and Warner all made this assumption about the objects of their research. The point is not that Chicago, Muncie, and Newburyport were representative communities in any statistical sense but rather that they were undergoing processes of structural transformation that affected all

American cities and towns to one or another degree, and therefore could be used as laboratories in which to study these representative social processes.

* * * * *

Theorizing from such a vast amount of empirical material as is represented by the three sets of studies already reviewed, as well as from the entire body of American community studies, is a challenging and even frightening task. The person who would do so has to be prepared to omit much that seemed important to the authors of the studies he is working from as well as much that seems important in them to him but which does not yet fit into his evolving theoretical framework. Finding an adequate level of generality is an ever-present problem, as is remaining satisfied with any given level once it has proved useful. This theory attempts to stay as close to the empirical materials as it can while still establishing the relationship of the trends they reveal to the major social processes of our time. Thus, the choice of urbanization, industrialization, and bureaucratization as processes shaping American community life was based on the findings of general sociological theorists like Marx, Weber, Durkheim, and others. That each of these three sets of studies exemplifies one of the processes as they manifest themselves at the level of the community suggests that the field workers were able to detect major forces of change even though they did not always interpret them with these concepts.

The theory to be developed will block out an approach to *American* community development. Whether the same interpretations could be applied to community development in other national or cultural contexts will not be explored here. It is admittedly an historically limited theory. For that matter, one of its main requirements is that the historical context of any community study be carefully examined as a shaping force.

The problem of generalizing from community studies having a specific locus in time and space is to be met at least in part by explicit incorporation of the relevant historical events as structural influences. The Lynds' *Middletown in Transition* is an excellent example of a study that directly meets this requirement by building the research around the impact of a major historical crisis. Warner never succeeds in bringing the depression explicitly into his interpretations until the fourth volume, and even there he does not consider all of its important structural effects. In any event, the kind of theory being developed here emphasizes the "decade experiences" so that any American community study during the early 40s would have to assess the impact of World War II, while one completed in the early 50s would be committed to including as one variable the effects of the cold war and, finally, the Korean War. The national and international events of the decade must be studied as they impinge on the community and the underlying forces shaping its structure.

This means that every community study is to be viewed as a case study. We can go even further and maintain that they should all be studies of the effects of basic processes and historical events on changing social patterns. This means that the state of affairs before the change as well as while it is in progress should be carefully specified. Every good community study is a study of transitional processes.

* * * * *

It may prove helpful to block out some of the more formal aspects of the theory of community development growing out of the first three chapters. First, every community study must start with a description of the social structure as this has changed over a period of time. Whenever possible, attention should focus on aspects of the structure deemed problematic by the participants as well as by the observer. Earlier studies provide a set of models indicating possible structural patterns but they cannot be projected onto any unique situation without first testing to determine whether or not they fit. Park sensitizes us to the constellation of urban subcommunities found in Chicago in the 20s; yet this certainly cannot be taken as an accurate map of the subcommunity constellation in any other American community, either now or then. Similarly, the Lynds' pictures of Muncie social structure, whether as two-class or three-class conceptions, must be applied with caution. They sensitize us to class subcommunities of considerable importance and indicate possible relationships between such subcommunities—especially differential power—which should not be neglected in any field work. Warner's stratificational model goes even further by suggesting that prestige, power, and economic position are not necessarily correlated and thereby calls attention to "old family" aristocracies as well as the "nouveauriche." In addition, he points to the possibility of complicated interplay between ethnic status and the social hierarchy which demands exploration in each instance. All of these models imply special bases for structuring likely to be found in any American community. But the task of the field worker is to use these models to identify the actual structures in the particular community under investigation. In other words, specification of the social structure, though not undertaken in a theoretical vacuum, remains a creative task.

Once the picture of the social structure has begun to emerge, patterns of change should also be carefully noted. How did the observed structure come into being and what are the forces conducive toward its modification in determinate directions?

Here the internal social system of each subcommunity has to be investigated. Is it divided along generation lines into "orthodox" traditional practices upheld by the older members, in contrast to "heterodox" novel tendencies among the youngsters? What are the "problems" felt by the whole community as differentiated from those felt only by particular subcommunities and even by its segments?

This preliminary structural "sizing up" of the community and its subcommunity constellation should pay close attention to directions of change. Ecological and demographic data can sometimes be helpful in this connection. Are there any coherent "neighborhoods" in the city and if there are do their residents so identify them? Can a pattern of distribution of disorganized behaviors be identified and if so how is this related to the subcommunity constellation? It is important to remember that the social structures must always be determined by examination of institutional patterns and the problematic behavior fitted into this. Analyses in this theory always move through the several levels: the whole community, a subcommunity, subcommunity strata, and individual role-playing. Warner provides a different kind of problem-centered model in his analysis of the strike. Here, tensions in a specific social system, the factory, are interpreted as reflecting changes in the relations between various strata in Yankee City which, in turn, reflect the assumption of control by absentee owners as part of the nationwide bureaucratization of industry. It is very important to distinguish these various levels so as to identify the point at which any particular analysis falls.

Once the social structure has been provisionally charted, Park's theory of urbanization should prove an excellent starting point. It forces attention toward the elements making up the population and raises questions about their coalescence into subcommunities over the period of the growth of the city. Current disorga-nization can be studied in the context of the subcommunities in which it appears and the control mechanisms related to the behaviors they are supposed to contain. Novel subcommunities not anticipated by the theory should be carefully noted for further study. Again, the absence of any that might have been expected is equally significant and must be explained. Thus the decline of Bohemias in some American cities like Boston is as important as the proliferation of many different kinds of suburbs.

When the effects of urbanization have been assessed, our two other environmental pressures, industrialization and bureaucratization, should be inspected. Here it is difficult to know clearly whether one is studying the system or its environment, but this ambiguity haunts all "field-theoretical" interpretations. Though few communities today will still be undergoing the transition from craft to industrial economy that were discerned in Muncie, the Lynds give us the tools for analyzing industrialization. Except in isolated "backward" areas, industrial technique in production and consumption will already have taken a deep hold. Most jobs are mechanized and employ some degree of assembly-line specialization while most families depend mainly on mass-produced goods to provide the necessities and status insignia that make up life in our time. But this general view obscures the many pressures on community life arising from regularly occurring technological innovation in methods of production which destroy some jobs and create new ones. Perhaps the spread of automation heralds the next major phase of industrialization. Its effects on community life, both directly through changes in work roles and indirectly through the increased leisure it will make available, are incalculable. Consumption patterns are still being modified in line with the quest for an ever-expanding standard of living as the Lynds emphasized, and this, in turn, leaves the identification of consequent changes in every area of institutional life an open area for investigation. Perhaps the much-debated effects of television are a case in point, though recent studies seldom attain the sophistication of the Lynds' work because they do not locate the ramifying consequences of television in the context of *changing* total community patterns.

Middletown in Transition provides a valuable model for placing the community in the context of the historical period so as to pinpoint the effects of the decade experiences on the main patterns of change. The Lynds' contribution is not so much that they decide to study the effects of the depression, but that they studied its effects on the changes resulting from industrialization. Thus, the short-term (decade) historical context is introduced so as to maximize its analytic relevance. We learn that the depression did not diminish the impulse toward conspicuous acquisition but that it did create an awareness on the part of workers that large-scale agencies like trade unions and political parties could help in securing this. Similarly, any community study undertaken today would have to consider the implications of "prosperity," "recession" and the cold war as a context for observed internal changes.

Aside from calling our attention to additional bases for social structuring, Warner documents the effects of bureaucratization, the organizational concomitant of industrialization. He does this first by showing the effects of centralized absentee ownership on the attitudes of local workers who see the "outsiders" as alien and opposed to their interests. Then he shows how some degree of stabilization of the authority system in the factory is attained by acceptance of union bargaining. The traditional owner-managers in Yankee City have lost their power and wealth, and loss of their prestige is likely to follow. It is also likely that the stratum which Warner called "lower-upper" in 1935 has by now

raised its status while the old "upper-uppers" continue downhill. Most American communities have probably accepted the fact of absentee ownership of large industry and the integration of corporate managers into community power structures is undoubtedly much more advanced. Furthermore, the legitimacy of such managers and owners could hardly be challenged on the same grounds as it was during the strike, if only because the circumstances in which factory manager-owners are also community leaders with the closeness to the workers that existed during the early period in Yankee City is no longer part of the American experience.

If we use these three sets of studies as points of departure, the foregoing should suggest an interpretive framework for examining other community studies as well as for formulating new ones. The conceptual model rests on the examination of change and assumes that urbanization, industrialization, and bureaucratization, as defined earlier, plot most of the key dimensions. Since the historical period of these three fundamental studies is confined to the 20s and 30s, we would expect that research completed today will deal with later stages. In field-theoretical terms, the problem today is as much one of identifying the contemporary stages of urbanization, industrialization, and bureaucratization through their manifestations as environmental pressures as it is of discovering the new patterns of community social structure that they call forth.

There is one underlying community trend to which all three of the studies refer. That is the trend toward increased interdependence and decreased local autonomy. Park referred to this process as urban or metropolitan dominance, and the Chicago sociologists did much to delineate its operations. Lynd noted the parallel phenomenon of dominance by centers of technological diffusion so that Muncie came to depend increasingly on Hollywood and New York for its entertainment, as it did on Detroit for industrial advance in the automotive plant. Warner dealt with this specifically in his discussion of the impact of absentee ownership, by which Yankee City shoe factories became the lowest echelon in a chain of command reaching upward to New York City. All of these studies during the 20s and 30s, then, show increasing standardization of community patterns throughout the country with agencies of nationwide diffusion and control acting as centers of innovation. Intimate life patterns become susceptible to standardized change as the mass media begin to inform each age group about new fashions and styles. Thus, the conditions for formation of a mass society were found in these previously examined social processes, even though more advanced forms had not yet appeared.

It is the study of problems like this for which the community theory being developed is singularly well adapted. For here is one junction point between macroscopic social theories and microscopic social research. The Lynds achieve such a juncture in *Middletown in Transition* when they show that the Muncie working class did not react to the depression as Marxist theories about class consciousness would have predicted. Their achievement, however, is not so much measured by this simple negative finding as it is in terms of their report on the institutional accommodations which preserved the dominant wish for mobility intact despite widespread unemployment. Since Marx's hypothesis referred to a national proletariat and not to that segment found in a small Midwestern American town, Lynd's findings can hardly negate any more than they could confirm this broad Marxist hypothesis. What they can do is give us some insight into the workings of the process whereby class consciousness is generated and shaped by focusing on its specific determinants in this particular context. If we could gather enough data on reactions to the depression in other community con-

texts, then we would have some conception as to the circumstances under which the Marxist form of consciousness appears as against those under which it does not.

This is the most clear-cut example and one peculiarly well adapted for showing the possible uses of community studies to clarify our understanding of basic social processes. The whole issue of social stratification in America, which is so central to social theory, can clearly be interpreted in terms of systems of community stratification as well as in terms of strata that presumably cut across the whole national social structure. Warner is as much in error when he projects the rather unique stratificational system of Newburyport onto the entire United States as are students of national stratification when they project some simplified "national" system onto the complicated communities and subcommunities of which our country is made up. The point here is not to discourage speculation at either level but rather to identify the kinds of problems that can best be handled by each as well as to see where they can fruitfully interpenetrate.

* * * * *

There are, of course, many central sociological problems that fall outside the purview of the community study. An important instance would be the interpretation of national power like that offered by C. Wright Mills in *The Power Elite*. Similarly, the community study can hardly hope to throw much light on the origins of the environmental pressures which it takes for granted. While it can show the effects of urbanization, industrialization, bureaucratization, and even the depression in a specific context, it can hardly explain these supralocal processes themselves. Broad problems of social structure such as the dispute between "mass" and "class" theories can be dealt with only fragmentarily, though the evidence in the studies reported thus far suggests that both models apply in varying degrees.

Some comments on the nature of modern communities might help to clarify the scope of this theory of communities. Park distinguished between three aspects or levels of community—the biotic, the moral, and the spatial. *Biotic* refers to functional interdependence, *moral* to group identification and loyalty, while *spatial* implies distinctive location. In a simpler society, these three levels of community would probably coexist so that the group with which one lived would be the one with which one worked and to whom one's loyalties were paid. As Park well knew, these concepts could not be readily applied to community life in the city. Here, people often distinguish between their work community, their neighborhood, and their social circle. There is nothing that demands that these separate spheres of institutional participation include the same individuals or in any sense constitute a coherent social whole. Spatial neighborhoods may have no significant social meaning and true communal congeniality may exist between people scattered throughout a city.

Unlike role analyses which focus on a specific aspect of an individual's social participation, community sociologists always consider the full range of institutional participation as each aspect of it affects every other aspect. Thus, Lynd's analysis of the functional interconnections of the emerging industrial community in Muncie is distinguished exactly by this sense of institutional reciprocity so that changes in family consumption requirements can be seen as central for motivating industrial role playing. The individual's total life space—his modes of participating in major institutional areas—are always at the focus of attention. Changes in this life space receive careful study. The life history can provide essential data on the respondent's changing life space as he perceives it throughout his life. These changes have to be studied within the context of changes in his community systems.

One central methodological problem of community studies lies in learning to coordinate these orders of data.

But it is impossible to take up all of the substantive and methodological problems raised by this theory in a single chapter. The word *toward* in the title must be underscored. It is included as a way of emphasizing the intention of the chapter—to indicate the elements of a theory and to block out an approach to its application. But it should also suggest the tasks that remain. There is a broad field open for anyone inclined to work out the systematic relations between urbanization, industrialization, and bureaucratization more carefully than has been attempted here.

* * * * *

Before a comprehensive theory of community comparable to the synthesis achieved by Park in the 20s can be put together, a far more complete picture of the levels of participation in and response to mass society must be obtained. This is a prerequisite for reformulation of Park's theory of natural areas. No amount of theorizing can identify the range of urban subcommunities in the modern city, nor can it describe their structures or their interrelations. Ecological and demographic data help to provide starting points for explorations into metropolitan social structures. Park's injunction to "get out and look" bears repeating. The single category "suburbia" contains at least three subtypes as exemplified by Park Forest, Crestwood Heights, and exurbia. There is good reason to suppose that many others will be found. Our cities obviously contain working-class suburbs, occupational communities, new kinds of business districts like the huge peripheral shopping centers, and even Bohemias.

Though we can no longer be certain that the "freedom of the city" is as meaningful as Park assumed, urban settings do provide opportunities for individual expression and association hardly possible in the small town. And theories about mass society should not be allowed to obscure the problems that this remaining diversity presents. It is likely that diffusion of standardized entertainment and information through the mass media exerts a homogenizing influence; however, this influence differs according to the community context in which it operates. Perhaps in some communities it affects public life styles, leaving intimate manners less affected. In others the reverse may hold true. Marginality is obviously still a common urban phenomenon, but its character has changed since the 20s. Fewer people are caught between two clearly defined cultural systems as were the immigrants and their children. Instead, the bulk of the population is exposed to many competing directives, none of which evoke very deep responses. But again the really interesting questions arise when the problem is posed in terms of specific subcommunity contexts and the styles of marginality encountered in each of them.

Aside from its substantive inaccuracies, a monolithic conception of mass society stifles the research impulse. Why bother going to all the trouble involved in field work if the findings are known in advance? The main reason for carefully confining theoretical formulations to community contents in this volume is to avoid such premature closure. Sociologists have to learn to let their theorizing and their observations range freely among various levels of abstraction without getting "fixated" at any single point. This is easy to recommend but hard to achieve. Theorizing at a highly abstract level usually evokes a lingering sense of guilt over the differentiating features that must be temporarily ignored. And, vice versa, discussions of the distinctive features are haunted by the impulse toward underlying generalities. There is no formula for avoiding the twin hazards of excessive generality and excessive specificity other than cultivating responsiveness to the conscience pangs aroused by excess in either direction.

Rather than concluding with any final formulations about American community life, it seems appropriate to end by again mentioning two perspectives. The first is constituted by the series of community studies summarized and interpreted in this volume. It serves to identify the historical processes shaping American community life and points to an outcome summarized in the conception of mass society. Paradoxically, this conception is most useful when it is pushed downward to lower levels of abstraction—mass society in its suburban embodiment or mass society in its small-town embodiment. The second perspective attempts to further "humanize" the first. No matter how tremendous the pressure to treat oneself and others as objects in mass society, vital human dramas are still enacted. Anthropology and psychoanalysis help to illuminate these dramas, as do the traditional "humanistic" disciplines. It is the special responsibility of the community study to keep these dramas continually in focus. No matter how far from the center of the stage, they do provide a meeting ground for people within a community which the depersonalizing forces of mass society can diminish but never destroy. There is even a possibility that sociologists will contribute to the enlargement of these meeting grounds, but this can happen only if we keep reminding ourselves that we are studying *human* communities and if we mold our theories and methods accordingly.

━━━━━ *13* ━━━━━
Small town in mass society
Arthur J. Vidich and Joseph Bensman

Springdale is connected with the mass society in a variety of different forms. The cumulative effect of these various connections makes possible the continuous transmission of outside policies, programs, and trends into the community, even though the effects of the transmission and the transmitting agents themselves are not always seen. Outside influences can be transmitted directly by a socially visible agent such as the extension specialist who lives in the community for the purpose of acting upon it. Outside interests and influences can also be expressed indirectly through members of the community: policies and programs of relatively invisible outside interests are transmitted by *heads* of local branches of state and national organizations, by *heads* of local businesses dependent on outside resources, and by *heads* of churches attached to larger organizations. In some instances the community is affected by the consequences of decisions made by business and government which are made with specific reference to the community, i.e., the decision to build a state road through the community or the decision to close down a factory. Plans and decisions that refer directly to the community are made from a distance by invisible agents and institutions. Perhaps most important are the mass decisions of business and government which are transmitted to the rural scene by the consequences of changes in prices, costs, and communications. These affect the town even though they are not explicitly directed at

it, and they comprise the invisible social chain reactions of decisions that are made in centers of power in government, business, and industry. The invisible social chain reactions emanating from the outside no doubt alter the life of the community more seriously than the action of visible agents such as the extension specialist.

These types of transmission do not represent mutually exclusive channels, but rather exist in complex interrelationship with each other. They merely suggest the major ways in which the community is influenced by dynamics which occur in the institutions of mass society. How these combined dynamics in their various combinations affect the fabric of life in Springdale can be seen by examining the way in which cultural importations and economic and political connections shape the character of community life. In their net effect they influence the psychological dimensions of the community.

CULTURAL IMPORTATIONS FROM MASS SOCIETY

The external agents of cultural diffusion range from specific observable individuals placed in the local community by outside institutions to the impact of mass media of communications and successive waves of migration. The consequence of these modes of diffusion lies in the effect which they have on local styles of living.

Formal importing organizations

The adult extension program of the land grant college is mediated at the local level by the county agent and the home demonstration agent who are concerned respec-

Reprinted from Arthur J. Vidich and Joseph Bensman, *Small Town in Mass Society: Class, Power and Religion in a Rural Community*, rev. ed. Copyright © 1958 by Princeton University Press; Princeton Paperback, 1968, pp. 81–100 and 122–36. Excerpts reprinted by permission of Princeton University Press.

tively with farming methods and production, and patterns of homemaking and family life. These agents carry out their program through the Farm and Home Bureau organizations. In Springdale township these agencies have a membership of 300–400 adults. The county agent is primarily concerned with introducing modern methods of farm production and operation and with fostering political consciousness among the farmers. As a type of executive secretary to the local Farm Bureau whose officers are local farmers, the agent acts as an advisor in planning the organization's program, which includes such items as production and marketing problems, parity price problems, and taxation problems.

The organizational structure of the Home Bureau parallels the Farm Bureau. From skills and techniques and personnel available at the extension center, local programs consist, for example, of furniture refinishing or aluminum working as well as discussions on such topics as child-rearing, nutrition, penal institutions, and interior design. The Home Bureau extension specialist trains a local woman in information and techniques which are reported back to the local club. This program, geared as it is to modern home-making, child-rearing, and the feminine role, has the effect of introducing new styles and standards of taste and consumption for the membership.

Other institutional connectors similar to the above in organizational structure account for the introduction of still other social values and social definitions. The 4-H Club, the Future Farmers of America, and the Boy and Girl Scouts, as well as the Masons, Odd Fellows, American Legion, Grange, and other local branches of national organizations and their auxiliaries, relate the Springdaler to the larger society through the social meanings and styles of activity defined in the programs, procedures, and rituals of the national headquarters. State and national conventions,

but not office holding, of these as well as church organizations directly link individuals to the outside. In effect these arrangements regularize and institutionalize the communication and organizational nexus between the small town and the point of origin of new ideas and values.

New cultural standards are also imported by agents who are not permanent residents of the town or who have only a transient relationship with it. These include the teachers at the central school, many of whom view their jobs as a temporary interlude in a progression of experience which will lead to a position in a city system. The other agents of contact are a wide variety of salesmen and "experts" who have a regular or irregular contact with business, government, and private organizations. From the surrounding urban centers and the regional sales offices of farm implement and automobile manufacturers and nationally branded products, modern methods of merchandizing and business practice are introduced. Experts in civil defense, evangelism, fire-fighting, gardening, charity drives, traffic control, and youth recreation introduce new techniques and programs to the local community. This great variety and diversity of semipermanent and changing contacts in their cumulative effect act as a perpetual blood transfusion to local society. The net effect that these agents have as transmitter of life styles depends in a measure on their position and prestige in the community. The differential effect of these cultural contacts is treated below.

The ubiquity of mass media

Social diffusion through the symbols and pictorial images of the mass media of communications has permeated the community, reducing the local paper to reporting of social items and local news already known by everyone. Few individuals read only the local weekly paper; the majority subscribe to dailies published in surrounding cities and in large metropolitan areas. This press, itself part of larger newspaper combines, presents an image of the passing scene in its news and nationally syndicated features to which the population of an entire region is exposed.

The mass culture and mass advertising of television and radio reach Springdale in all their variety. Television, particularly, is significant in its impact because for the first time the higher art forms such as ballet, opera, and plays are visible to a broad rural audience. National events such as party conventions, inaugurations, and investigative hearings are visible now to an audience which was previously far removed from the national centers of action and drama. . . . The state department of education syllabus defines minimum standards and content for subject matter instruction. Courses of Sunday school instruction are available for all age levels, and each faith secures its material from its own national religious press. In each of these major institutional areas the standards and *content* of instruction are defined in sources available only in standardized form.

The immigrant as cultural carrier

Specific individuals are carriers of cultural diffusion, and the volume and extent of migration in and out of the community suggests the degree and intimacy of its contact with the mass society. In a community which is regarded as stable and relatively unchanging by its own inhabitants, only 25 percent of its population was born locally. Another 25 percent has moved into the community since 1946 and 55 percent are new to the community since 1920. Moreover, of the 45 percent who have moved to the community since 1932, more than 30 percent have lived for a year or longer in cities with populations in excess of 25,000; 7 percent in cities with populations in excess of one-half million. . . .

The cumulative consequences of these

channels of diffusion and the quantity and quality of the "material" diffused denies the existence of a culture indigenous to the small town. In almost all apsects of culture, even speech forms, and including technology, literature, fashions and fads, as well as patterns of consumption, to mention a few, the small town tends to reflect the contemporary mass society.

Basically, an historically indigenous local culture does not seem to exist. The cultural imports of each decade and generation and the successive waves of migration associated with each combine to produce a local culture consisting of layers or segments of the mass culture of successive historical eras. In the small town the remaining elements of the gay-90s culture are juxtaposed against the modern central school. The newer cultural importations frequently come in conflict with the older importations of other eras. The conflict between "spurious" and "genuine" culture appears to be a conflict between two different ages of "spurious" culture.

THE ECONOMIC NEXUS: OCCUPATIONAL GATEKEEPERS TO THE MASS SOCIETY

Simply because individuals pursue given occupations, their interconnections with mass society follow given patterns. They may be direct employees of specific organizations of the mass society; they may be the objects and targets of the programs of mass organizations; they may be trained by and in great institutions or their skills may be utilized only in urban areas. Because of these occupational characteristics they are specially qualified, accessible, and available as transmitters of specific organizational and cultural contacts and contents. . . .

The professionals

A number of institutional representatives who are residents of the town receive their position in the community by virtue of their connections with outside agencies. Their position in the community is secured in part by the institution to which they are connected and by the evaluation of the role they are imputed to have in the agency which they locally represent.

The group of individuals who possess a borrowed prestige based on their external affiliations fall largely in the professional category. They are individuals who uniformly possess a college education. Among their ranks are included lawyers, ministers, doctors, teachers, engineers, and a variety of field representatives of state and federal agencies who settle in the community for occupational purposes. All of these individuals, except one or two, have migrated to the community as adults. In addition to the prestige which they are accorded by virtue of being "educated," their overwhelming characteristic as a group lies in the influence which they have in mediating between the town and the larger society. They possess the knowledge and techniques necessary for connecting the small town to the intricate organization of the mass bureaucratic society. They possess "contacts" with outside agencies and their role requires an ability to understand "official" documents and forms, and to write appropriate letters to appropriate bureaus. Thus, for example, the lawyer is counsel to political bodies as well as to free associations and other local organizations, in which capacities he gains an extensive and intimate knowledge of affairs of the town and thereby acquires a position of influence. In like manner the technical knowledge of state educational regulations and policies possessed by the high-school principal is indispensable to the locally constituted school board. . . .

Moreover, this professional group as a whole, including the relatively transient teaching staff, are felt to have access to styles of taste and consumption which are considered different from those available to the rest of the community. As a result these institutional connectors are considered outside the ordinary realm of prestige assignments and social stratification. That is, their social position in the community is not guaranteed by conforming to standards which are indigenous to the community but, rather, by imputed conformance to "alien" or "exotic" standards of urban life.

As a result of this dual position, individuals in this group, especially those who have come from or have resided for some time outside the community, are able to influence styles of consumption and thought in the community. They do this in three main areas of activity: in organizational activities, community projects, and social fashions. They have been prime movers in setting up a formal program of youth recreation and in vigorously participating in and supporting local cultural activities such as plays, recitals, and educational talks. In the PTA they constitute the block favoring those modern methods and programs which bring the outside world to the small town—talks by foreign university students, race relations discussions, and sociodramas in dating and parent-child relationships. Ideas for the development of a community center and adult education programs emanate from and are supported by them. In terms of dress styles and personal adornment as well as home furnishings and styles of party giving, this group is in the forefront of innovation.

This innovating group of middle-class newcomers is supported by a group of college-educated locals who act as a bridge between the new standards and local society. In supporting these new standards, the local group absorbs some of the resentment which is directed at the innovating group by both the farmers and merchants.

It must be noted that the professionals' psychological orientation to accentuate the "elite" cultural values of mass society is more than merely a product of their residence, education, or background in the mass society. The limitations on economic success and the limited professional opportunities in the community mean that the drive toward success through work and investment is not fully available to them. The possession of alien cultural standards makes it possible for the professionals to reject the success drive by accepting meaningful standards alternative to those available to the rest of the community; they distinguish themselves in the community by their identification with external values.

Businessmen

For storekeepers, filling station operators, appliance dealers, automobile and farm equipment dealers, and feed mill operators, the external world is a source of supply for the goods and commodities which they sell on the local market. Their position in relation to their source of supply and the overall condition of the national economy determines the level of their business activity, ceilings on their potential income, and hence indirectly their style of life. . . .

Industrial workers

Industrial workers represent a curious gap in the relationship of the rural community to mass society. Individuals who live in Springdale but work outside on products which are geared to a national market are not understandable to other members of the community because the rural community lacks the perceptual apparatus necessary to understand industry and the industrial process. The industrial worker lives in the community, but the occupational basis of his existence is not subject to the social pigeonholing by others necessary to making judgments and assessments of him. . . .

Farmers

As noted earlier, there are two classes of farmers, the rational and the traditional. A major difference between them is the way they organize their production in relation to the mass market and government regulations.

Those who gear themselves to the mass market address themselves to favorably pegged prices, subsidies, and quotas. As a consequence when prices and regulations are favorable they accept the favorable environment as a condition for their operations. They invest and expand, work hard and are successful. Their success stimulates confidence and buoyancy and produces an expansionist psychology.

In a peculiar way the traditional farmers who as a group do not gear themselves to the mass market do this specifically because of their relations with the mass market. As older farmers they have learned from the depression that they can be economically vulnerable, and they have learned that they can survive in the community by being immune to the market. The depression experience was so bitter for them that they have learned nothing since. Thus it happens that at the time of the study they were still living in the market of the early 30s. . . .

THE POLITICAL SURRENDER TO MASS SOCIETY

Local political institutions consist of a village board, a town board, and local committees of the Republican and Democratic parties. The jurisdiction of the village board includes powers of control and regulation over a variety of community facilities and services—street lighting, water supply, fire protection, village roads, street signs, and parks. To carry out the functions empowered to it, it possesses the power of taxation. The town board is concerned chiefly with fire protection and the construction and maintenance of roads; through its participation on the county board of supervisors, it participates in programs connected with welfare, penal, and other county services.

However, at almost every point in this seemingly broad base of political domain the village and town boards adjust their action to either the regulations and laws defined by state and federal agencies which claim parallel functions on a state wide or nationwide basis or to the fact that outside agencies have the power to withhold subsidies to local political institutions.

Local assessment scales and tax rates are oriented to state equalization formulas which partially provide the standardized basis on which subsidies are dispersed by the state. State highway construction and development programs largely present local political agencies with the alternative of either accepting or rejecting proposed road plans and programs formulated by the state highway department.

The village board, more than the town board, is dependent on its own taxable resources (taxes account for almost half its revenues) and best illustrates the major dimensions of local political action. The village board in Springdale accepts few of the powers given to it. Instead, it orients its action to the facilities and subsidies controlled and dispensed by other agencies and, by virtue of this, forfeits its own political power. Solutions to the problem of fire protection are found in agreements with regionally organized fire districts. In matters pertaining to road signs and street signs, action typically takes the form of petitioning state agencies to fulfill desired goals "without cost to the taxpayer." On roads built and maintained by the state there is no recourse but to accept the state traffic bureau's standards of safety. A problem such as snow removal is solved by dealing directly with the foreman of the state highway maintenance crew through personal contacts: "If you treat him right,

you can get him to come in and clear the village roads." In other areas of power where there are no parallel state agencies, such as for garbage collection or parks, the village board abdicates its responsibility.

As a consequence of this pattern of dependence, many important decisions are made for Springdale by outside agencies. Decisions which are made locally tend to consist of approving the requirements of administrative or state laws. In short, the program and policies of local political bodies are determined largely by acceptance of grants-in-aid offered them—i.e., in order to get the subsidy, specific types of decisions must be made—and by facilities and services made available to them by outside sources.

Psychologically this dependence leads to an habituation to outside control to the point where the town and village governments find it hard to act even where they have the power. Legal jurisdictions have been supplanted by psychological jurisdictions to such an extent that local political action is almost exclusively oriented to and predicated on seeking favors, subsidies, and special treatment from outside agencies. The narrowing of legal jurisdictions by psychologically imposed limits leads to an inability to cope with local problems if outside resources are not available.

Power in local political affairs, then, tends to be based on accessibility to sources of decision in larger institutions. Frequently this accessibility consists merely of the knowledge of the source, or it may mean a personal contact, or an ability to correspond to get necessary information. Under these circumstances, power in the political arena is delegated to those with contacts in and knowledge of the outer world and to those who are experts in formal communication with impersonal bureaucratic offices. These are, on the individual level, the lawyer and, on an institutional level, the political party. The lawyer gains his paramountcy through technical knowledge and personalized nonparty contacts up the political hierarchy with other lawyers. He is the mediator between the local party and the party hierarchy, and transforms his personalized contacts into political indispensability in the local community. His access to outside sources of power determines his power and predominance in the local community. . . .

PUBLIC INTERESTS AND POLITICAL PARALYSIS

The village board and the Republican committee do not represent all the community views. There exist other groups who would be interested in "desirable" social expenditures, who lament the do-nothing attitude of the village board, and who would be interested in a revision of assessment evaluations. Residents of Back Street, as well as residents of several other streets, constitute an interest group who want paved roads and street lights. More recent migrants from cities (particularly professionals and industrial workers) would like recreational facilities and swimming instruction for their children and a community building as a center for social activities. The village as a whole is interested in snow removal and a garbage and trash removal service. The entire community is interested in better fire protection (replacement of obsolete equipment) and increased water pressure in the kitchen spigots. Individual businessmen and home owners have grieved to the board for a reassessment of their property "to bring it in line with other assessments." A large but unorganized group of individuals is interested in bringing industry to the community. No action was taken on any of these measures in the years preceding and during the field work of the study.

These desires for improvement, change, and increased expenditures are held by individuals who have no stake in or control over the village board and who are beyond the purview of party politics—

they do not vote and only when they have a special cause or a special complaint or request do they attend meetings of the village board. Their efforts to secure the action they desire remain at the level of private complaining or of occasional attendance at a board meeting as individuals who represent themselves or a specialized organization with a specialized request. The most frequent complaint of local citizens, including board members themselves, concerns alleged inequities in the assessment structure of taxable property. In the entire history of the community, assessments have not been reviewed and great differences exist in assessments of equivalent properties. . . .

The paralysis of the board in not being able to cope with this and other problems reflects an underlying paralysis of organized political action in the village at large, except for individual efforts among those groups which desire action. The groups and the individuals who want political action lack the tradition, the specialization, and the organization to make their views felt. The complexity of organizing political support; the necessity for historical, legal, and technological knowledge in defining an issue clearly; the lack of knowledge of procedure; the lack of time—all these factors lead to inaction and a complaining but dissatisfied acceptance of the "business as usual" ideology of the village board. . . .

THE CONSEQUENCES OF POLITICAL PARALYSIS

Reliance on experts

. . . The legal counsel acts and is regarded as a source of information and as an authority not only on legal questions but also on general matters of procedure, precedent, and history. When he speaks he is listened to with attention, and his suggestions and recommendations are ordinarily accepted without question.

In addition to the board's reliance upon

the technical skill of its counsel, it is frequently unable to act without the expert advice of outside experts. When it comes to erecting street signs, for example, the board must deal directly with a sergeant in the state traffic bureau who is familiar with the type of sign required and the regulations about its placement. In matters of youth recreation, the board was advised by a state representative with respect to its legal part in the administration of the program. The reliance of the board on outside experts is seen most clearly, however, in the fact that a large part of its business is conducted by correspondence with state agencies. In this process the village counsel who possesses the necessary skills is the connecting link to the outside agency and it is through him as he acts on the village board that the reliance of the board on experts is demonstrated most clearly.

The social basis of unanimity

The dominating influence of Flint on the board does not deny the possibility of conflict among the members. Beneath the public unanimity of the board, there exist small but important differences of interest between board members. For one, who lives on a street without light, there exists a potential impulse to secure street lighting in needed places. Another who is superintendent of the fire district is more inclined than the others to spend money on fire equipment. The clerk who owns no business property and is not a voting member of the board would be favorably disposed to a reassessment program. The mayor tends to be more "economy-minded" than some of the trustees. Each participant of the board has a pet interest which serves as a potential basis for conflict. Yet this conflict is never openly apparent and the principle of unanimity of decision is never broken. When board business touches on issues of potential conflict, each board member brings up for subliminal assessment the position of

other members on the issue in question— i.e., who would be apt to oppose the measure and with what intensity—and avoids further mention of the topic.

Since the board member has neither skill nor knowledge nor a constituency to support him, he lacks confidence in his own opinion and his own cause. Instead of pushing an idea, he retreats to more familiar territory, the espousal of "economy-mindedness" on which he knows all members agree. When an issue comes up on which the positions of all board members are not known—when some new problem presents itself, for instance—a long process of discussion, during which board members frequently contradict themselves, ensues. This discussion, which appears so strange to the outsider, takes place for the purpose of finding a common ground on which all can agree and in which no opinion stands out. In this way no member irrevocably commits himself on an issue and, hence, does not alienate himself from the other members of the board with whom he must deal from month to month and in his daily living on a "friendly" basis. These dynamics explain the lengthy and poorly directed discussion which occupies the time of the board and provide a partial explanation for the phenomenon of unanimity.

In addition, however, there is always the danger that, should an issue come into the open, conflicting parties will appeal to outside individuals or groups or to the more important figures in the machine. Public sentiment could easily be mobilized around the issues of assessments, street lighting, and snow removal. There is the ever-present possibility that an issue can be taken directly to the leaders of the machine since the link between the board and the machine is intimate.

As a consequence of these dynamics, in any situation which suggests that differences of opinion exist, action is postponed or delayed to a subsequent meeting or indefinitely. Between meetings, interested parties are consulted, board members meet and talk informally, and some type of "understanding" is reached before the next meeting. If the item at issue is small (where to place a street light), several important individuals in the neighborhood are talked to, and opinion is sounded in other neighborhoods which do not have street lights. If the issue is large (such as a several thousand dollar bank loan to repair a broken water main—the issue being how good a job is to be done), Howard Jones is consulted directly. In many cases this activity between meetings settles the issue so that it comes up for perfunctory approval at a subsequent meeting; or, if a *modus vivendi* cannot be worked out, nothing further is heard of the issue.

In the ordinary conduct of business in this manner, potential issues and conflicts never become visible at a public level. Undisciplined appeals to outside groups which would threaten the monopoly of power of the controlling group do not occur. The board, especially the trustees who alone possess the voting privilege, openly state that they do not want "to stir up trouble." Since the board members themselves carry responsibility for their actions, they do not take action until the appropriate individuals are consulted and until it is apparent that responsibility is diffused into unanimity. There is the continuous effort to seek the formula by which unanimity can be achieved. Until unanimity is reached, there is a tacit agreement to discuss the proposal and to postpone the decision until the time comes when either by wearing down, time limitations, or accident a formula is found. The formula itself takes many forms. Typically it is indefinite postponement. Frequently it is arrived at by "doing what we did last year or ten years ago." Sometimes it is reached by taking the "only legal course open to us according to the law of the state." In no instance is a formula based on a recognition of conflicting interests which require balancing.

Dependence on extra-legal bodies

As a consequence of this structure of decision making, the village board is not usually in a position to act when pressing action is required. When special problems arise which require nontraditional solutions or quick decisions and quick action, extra-legal bodies take over the functions of village government and meet the problem by extra-legal, quasi-legal, or private means. . . .

POLITICAL CEREMONIES AND POLITICAL PARTICIPATION

The pattern of village politics can be summarized in terms of an analysis of the meaning of the political ceremony. The political ceremony consists of the endless and indecisive talk which occurs in formal meetings of the village board. The formal meeting itself is a social ritual in which discussion serves the purpose of avoiding decision making. . . .

As a further result of these dynamics all opposition groups in the village are, and can only be, organized around a single issue at any one time. All such groups in the past have been temporary and the machine has survived, even though in the process a number of local programs have been accomplished which otherwise might never have happened.

It is in this, perhaps minimal, way that outside interest groups are represented and that to some degree a democratic process is carried out. For, no matter what their own interests may be and no matter how reluctantly they acquiesce, the village board and the political machine, in order to maintain political control, must find some method of accommodating these pressures which, if avoided, would result in their loss of control. The reluctant acceptance of these issues and the programs which they entail constitute the foundations of democracy in the rural village.

14

Inequality and lifestyles in Middletown, 1920–1978

Theodore Caplow and Bruce A. Chadwick

When Robert and Helen Lynd (1929) reported the results of their 1924–25 study of
the small industrial city they called Middletown, they described the boundary between the business and working classes as
a "watershed" and emphasized how much
difference it made to be born on one side
or the other (Lynd and Lynd, 1929: 23–24):

The mere fact of being born upon one or the
other side of the watershed roughly formed by
these two groups is the most significant single
cultural factor tending to influence what one
does all day long throughout one's life; whom
one marries; when one gets up in the morning;
whether one belongs to the Holy Roller or Pres-
byterian church; or drives a Ford or a Buick;
whether or not one's daughter makes the desirable high school Violet Club; or one's wife
meets with the Sew We Do Club or with the Art
Students' League; whether one belongs to the
Odd Fellows or to the Masonic Shrine; whether
one sits about evenings with one's necktie off;
and so on indefinitely throughout the daily
comings and goings of a Middletown man,
woman, or child.

In 1935 the Lynds (1937) went back to
Middletown to see how the community
had weathered the Depression. On this
second visit, they refined their description
of the two classes by dividing each of them
into three occupational subdivisions but
found nothing to modify their opinions
about the importance of the "watershed."
Indeed, they argued that the unequal burden imposed by the economic crisis had
caused the two main classes to drift further
apart.

In 1976, the Center for Program Effectiveness Studies, University of Virginia,
undertook another study of the same community, called the Middletown III project.[1]
The question of whether class stratification
had increased or decreased in Middletown
was one of the first to be addressed. In the
effort to answer it, we have discovered
some interesting patterns of change that
are probably not confined to Middletown.

In this paper we shall first examine the
changes in the relative size of Middletown's business class and working class
from 1920 to 1970, based upon six decennial censuses. Then, still using census
data, we will examine the trend of occupational inequality in Middletown during the
same period. Finally, comparing survey
data gathered in 1978 with survey data
obtained by the Lynds in 1924, we shall try
to assess what happened to the lifestyles
of Middletown's two major classes between those years.

WORKING CLASS AND BUSINESS CLASS

The Lynds' distinction between working class and business class was the earliest formal differentiation, so far as we can
discover, between what are now called
blue-collar and white-collar occupations.
"Members of the first group," they wrote,
"by and large, address their activities in
getting their living primarily to *things*, utilizing material tools in the making of
things and the performance of services,
while the members of the second group

Reprinted with permission of the authors and
publisher from Theodore Caplow and Bruce A.
Chadwick, "Inequality and Life-Styles in Middle-
town, 1920–1978," *Social Science Quarterly* 60, no. 3
(December 1979). © 1979 by The University of Texas
Press.

[1] Supported by the National Science Foundation,
grant #SOC 75-13580. The investigators are Theodore Caplow, Howard M. Bahr, and Bruce A. Chadwick.

address their activities predominantly to *people* in the selling or promotion of things, services, and ideas" (Lynd and Lynd, 1929:22). This classification, as they noted, is not entirely satisfactory. Aside from the twilight zone where occupations overlap, there seem to be some professional occupations largely concerned with things and some service occupations largely concerned with people. The scheme makes no provision for the social placement of families in which husband and wife are employed on opposite sides of the watershed, and it has no real place for farmers. Nevertheless, it is the best single scheme of social class that we have, and much more is known now about white-collar/blue-collar differences than when the Lynds introduced it.

The Lynds considered and rejected a "conventional tripartite division" in their first study for two reasons: "(1) Since the dominance of the local getting-a-living activities impresses upon the group a pattern of social stratification based primarily upon vocational activity, it seemed advisable to utilize terms that hold this vocational cleavage to the fore. (2) Insofar as the traditional three-fold classification might be applied to Middletown today, the city would have to be regarded as having only a lower and a middle class; eight or nine households might conceivably be considered as an upper class, but these families are not a group apart but are merged in the life of the mass of the business folk" (Lynd and Lynd, 1929:23).

Contrary to a widespread impression, they did not abandon this position in their second report. *Middletown in Transition* (Lynd and Lynd, 1937:74) gives a great deal of attention to one dominant family but the principal chapter on that topic is titled "The X Family: A Pattern of Business Class Control." They did, however, subdivide the business class into groups 1, 2, and 3 in descending order of status from wealthy manufacturers, bankers, and managers to small proprietors and clerical

workers and for good measure, they subdivided the working class into groups 4, 5, and 6, descending from foremen and craftsmen to poor white itinerant workers. The entire treatment of these matters in *Middletown in Transition* reflects their impression that the compartmentalization of classes had increased sharply from 1925 to 1935.

In order to assure ourselves that we could separate the 1970 population of Middletown into business and working classes by the Lynds' method, we replicated their coding of the occupational distribution of Middletown as reported in the 1920 census. They classified families for this purpose by the occupation of a male head, and additional wage earners were not taken into account. Female-headed families were appropriately classified by the occupation of the female head, but were not weighed in the overall estimate of class size. The distortions introduced into the estimates by these peculiarities are rather small, since the two principal sources of error—the greater proportion of the female labor force in business-class occupations and the greater proportion of female-headed households in the working class—tend to cancel each other out. Although their account of how they assigned an occupation to a given class is not totally clear and they shifted some individuals from one class to another on the basis of personal knowledge, our coding achieved a high degree of agreement with theirs, with the difference in classification being only 0.1 percent.

Table 14–1 shows the distribution of Middletown's labor force by major occupational category in the six decennial censuses from 1920 to 1970, and the division of population into business class and working class according to these categories. The 50-year trends revealed by Table 14–1 are clear, and parallel those for the entire United States. We note a slow but steady increase in the relative size of the business class—from 29 percent of Mid-

TABLE 14–1
Distribution of Middletown's labor force by major occupational categories, 1920–1970

Occupational category	1920 Number	1920 Percent	1930 Number	1930 Percent	1940 Number	1940 Percent	1950 Number	1950 Percent	1960 Number	1960 Percent	1970 Number	1970 Percent
Professionals	892		1,396		1,398		2,036		2,766		5,189	
Managers	581		679		1,637		2,010		1,914		1,811	
Clerical	1,662		1,925		3,377		2,792		3,547		7,865	
Sales	1,659		2,305				1,891		1,780		2,264	
Subtotal												
"Business class"	4,794	29.9	6,305	33.2	6,412	35.7	8,729	37.7	10,007	40.7	17,129	47.0
Craftsmen	3,404		3,927		3,031		3,420		3,314		3,232	
Operatives	3,144		3,827		4,937		6,967		6,455		7,865	
Laborers	3,278		3,032		1,366		1,265		1,471		1,363	
Service	807		1,100		1,527		2,203		2,661		6,031	
Household	602		726		663		519		688		840	
Subtotal												
"Working class"	11,235	70.1	12,612	66.8	11,524	64.3	14,374	62.2	14,589	59.3	19,331	53.0
Total	16,029	100.0	18,917	100.0	17,936	100.0	23,103	99.9	24,596	100.0	36,460	100.0

Source: Decennial Censuses of 1920, 1930, 1940, 1950, 1960, 1970. For comparable data on the entire United States, see Rothman (1978), Table 3.2, page 48.

dletown's population in 1920 to 47 percent in 1970. (This shift becomes even more impressive when we discover that the ratio of business-class to working-class occupations had been quite stable in Middletown during the previous 50 years, 1870–1920. The respective proportions of business and working class in 1870 were 24 percent and 76 percent, only two points away from the 1920 figures.[2]) The largest part of this increase was accounted for by professionals, whose relative number more than tripled. The percentage of clerical workers also increased substantially, but the percentages of managers, proprietors, and officials and of salesmen were about the same in 1970 as in 1920, despite some intermediate fluctuations. The percentage of craftsmen declined from each census to the next and the percentage of laborers declined even more. Semiskilled workers, after some intermediate fluctuations, were relatively more numerous at the end of the period than at the beginning, but the "industrial" section of the labor force (craftsmen, operators, and laborers taken together) declined from 71 percent in 1920 to 42 percent in 1970. (Fifty years earlier, in 1870, it had been 72 percent.) The proportion of service workers increased from 4 percent in 1920 to 14 percent in 1970. To the extent that many of the service occupations have as much to do with people as with things, the business class/working class dichotomy probably *understates* the shift from occupations dealing with things to occupations dealing with people that occurred between 1920 and 1970.

OCCUPATIONAL INEQUALITY

As Middletown's population approaches an equal division between business-class and working-class occupa-

tions, occupational inequality might be expected to diminish were it not for the uneven distribution of trends *within* the major categories. The greatest increase in business-class occupations has occurred toward the top among professionals and the greatest increase in working-class occupations has occurred toward the middle of that category, among service workers.

If we assign one of the standardized occupational prestige scores like Siegel's (1971) adaptation[3] of the Duncan-Hatt scale to the nine occupational categories included in the table and allow ourselves the large assumption that the scores may be applied retroactively to these occupational categories all the way back to 1920, we can measure changes in occupational inequality during the 50-year period.

The prestige scores for every occupation listed by Siegel within each of the nine major categories were averaged to obtain a mean prestige score for each category. These mean scores were then multiplied with the number of labor force participants in each of the nine categories as reported by the census. The scores were then averaged to provide a mean occupational prestige score for each decade. By measuring the slope of linear regression from the lowest to the highest decile of the labor force at each census from 1920 to 1970, we can derive the trend. The results are shown in Table 14–2. A state of perfect occupational equality, i.e., the whole population engaged in occupations having the same prestige, would have a slope of 0.00 by this method. The higher the slope, the greater the inequality. The absolute value of the slope has no significance, being a function of the essentially arbitrary scoring of the occupational prestige scale, but if

---

[2] Based on a recoding of the original enumerators' reports for the Census of 1870 by Alexander E. Bracken. See his "Middletown as a Pioneer Community," Center for Program Effectiveness Studies, Middletown III Project, Paper No. 10, 1978.

[3] The mean scores calculated for the nine categories of Table 14–1 are as follows:

Professional	.. 60.3	Operators	.... 29.0
Managers	.... 51.7	Laborers	..... 20.5
Clerical	...... 41.8	Service	.... 27.8
Sales	.... 35.4	Household	
		workers	.... 19.3

TABLE 14–2
Decile-slope measurement of occupational inequality in Middletown, 1920–1970

	Male labor force	Female labor force	Total labor force
1920	3.30	3.89	3.54
1930	3.54	4.31	3.54
1940	3.44	4.12	3.70
1950	3.58	3.91	3.76
1960	3.62	3.95	3.77
1970	3.77	4.25	3.85

Siegel scores of occupational status plotted by deciles of the male, female, and combined labor forces.
Source: Bruce A. Chadwick and C. Bradford Chappell, *Inequality, 1920–1976*, Working Paper, Center for Program Effectiveness Studies, November 1977, Figures 2–19.

the scoring system remains the same from T_1 to T_2 comparison may be made between them.

Table 14–2 shows a moderate increase in the inequality of occupational prestige in the male labor force over the 50-year period and a trendless oscillation in the female labor force. These combined to produce a very slow accentuation of inequality for the total labor force; between 1920 and 1970, the decile slope increased by about 9 percent.

We find, in sum, that the conspicuous equalization from 1920 to 1970 in the relative proportions of the labor force in business-class and working-class occupations did not imply any mitigation of occupational inequality. For the system as a whole, and for the male labor force, inequality was somewhat greater in 1970 than in 1920; for the female labor force it did not appreciably change.

The slight increase of occupational inequality was accompanied by an unmistakable increase in the average level of occupational prestige. The mean Siegel score for the male labor force rose from 32.8 in 1920 to 37.5 in 1970—equivalent to more than half the difference between semiskilled operators and craftsmen. The occupational prestige of women showed a nearly identical increase. In other words, the average level of occupational prestige

increased concurrently with an increase in the inequality of occupational prestige.[4]

This increase is unsurprising, especially in view of its general congruence with the changes that occurred in the entire United States labor force during the same period (Rothman, 1978). Except for a minor overlap between sales workers and craftsmen, all white-collar occupational categories are scored higher than all blue-collar occupational categories by this scale. Thus, given the relative increase in the white-collar component of Middletown's labor force from 1920 to 1970, noted above, an increase in mean occupational prestige was inevitable. But it was not inevitable that the mean prestige scores of business-class and working-class occupations should move further apart between 1920 and 1970—as actually occurred. Using grouped data, the differences between the mean occupational prestige of white-collar and blue-collar workers was 18.6 points in 1970 compared to 15.6 in 1920.

Clearly, there was no conspicuous equalization of occupational prestige between Middletown's two classes during the period. But when we turn to the lifestyles of Middletown's business and working classes, and compare them over time, we see another picture entirely.

CLASS DIFFERENCES IN LIFESTYLES

Most of the Lynds' (1929) conclusions about class differences in lifestyles in *Middletown* were based on their 1924 interviews with 122 working-class wives and 44 business-class wives who had at least one child at home between the ages of 6 and

---

[4] Of course, we cannot be sure that the scale of occupational prestige we have used, or any of the other available scales, really permit valid comparisons of inequality to be made over so long an interval of time. However, we know that the rank order of occupational prestige ratings is remarkably stable over time. See Counts (1925); Deeg and Patterson (1947); and Hodges, Siegel, and Rossi (1964) for an interesting line of replicative research.

18. In order to obtain comparable data, we collected interviews with a similar sample during the summer of 1978. We drew a systematic random sample of 2,192 married women from the Middletown city directory. Every 15th married woman was selected after the random drawing of an initial number between 1 and 15. We wrote to each of those selected explaining the purpose of the study. A reply postcard was enclosed for the recipient to indicate whether she had a child of the required age and whether she was willing to be interviewed. Two hundred and 65 women replied that they did have a child, and of this number, 178 agreed to be interviewed and 87 refused. Those who expressed a willingness to be interviewed were telephoned, an appointment was made, and an interview conducted. Three hundred and 44 returned the postcard indicating that they were not eligible to be interviewed. Most reported they did not have a child of the appropriate age, while in a few cases family members indicated that the respondent had died.

The 1,583 women who did not return the postcard were telephoned, the study explained, the presence or absence of children ascertained, and those who were eligible were invited to be interviewed. Of those telephoned, 518 turned out to be eligible and 155 were scheduled for an interview. The remaining 353 refused. The overall response rate was 42 percent; 793 of the 2,192 women contacted were eligible, and 333 of those were interviewed.

The interviews were conducted by six well-trained interviewers, all of whom were mature married women. The interview schedule used by the Lynds in 1924 was followed as closely as possible. Most questions were worded exactly as they had been in the earlier study, and it does credit to the Lynds' sociological insight that the questions were still relevant and comprehensible to our respondents 54 years later.

Needless to say, we can think of many questions the Lynds did not ask that we would like them to have asked. The items reported below do not give us a comprehensive picture of business-class and working-class lifestyles, either then or now, but they are what we have to work with and, fragmentary or not, the data for 1924 are incomparably better than the data usually available to sociologists attempting to describe the typical behavior of a past era. Indeed, the quality of the data is confirmed by the nonobviousness of the findings. They are not what we expected and not at all what we would have obtained by the usual method of comparing an empirical study of present behavior with an imaginative reconstruction of past behavior. The usual method is persuasive but essentially defective, and we learn much more by comparing a few bits of real information about the past with comparable bits about the present, particularly when, as in this case, the information obtained in the past was sought for the same intellectual purpose as ours—to describe class differences in lifestyles in Middletown.

The information available from these two surveys concerns the working day, the unemployment of family heads, the employment of married women, housing quality, the marital relationship and the parental role.

The working day. In 1924, as Table 14–3 shows, the great majority (93 percent) of working class families rose at or before 6:00 A.M. on working days, while the great majority (85 percent of business-class families stayed in bed past that hour. By 1978 this spectatcular difference had vanished. Only 38 percent of working-class families now rise at or before 6:00 in the morning but 31 percent of business-class families do so. The Lynds' retroactive information seemed to shown that in 1890, most Middletown families rose at or before first light on working days. Late rising is one of the benefits of modernization, and

TABLE 14–3
Middletown families Rising by 6 A.M. on a typical work day, by social class, 1924 and 1978

	Working class*		Business class†			
	Number	Percent	Number	Percent	X^2	P
1924‡	(112)	93	(40)	15	89.4	.001
1978	(141)	38	(192)	31	1.5	NS

* The difference between the working class in 1924 and in 1978 is significant at the .05 level, X^2 = 3.8.
† The difference between the business class in 1924 and in 1978 is significant at the .001 level, X^2 = 82.8.
‡ Lynd and Lynd, 1924:53.

we can say that it reached the business class first and the working class later but we are not able to explain why so many more business-class families rose early in 1978 than their predecessors did in 1924.

Unemployment. The threat of unemployment was a dominant feature of the working-class lifestyle in the 1920s. Nearly 70 percent of the working-class wives interviewed at that time reported that their husbands had been unemployed during the previous five years; 28 percent of them had encountered unemployment during the previous year, 1923. In sharp contrast, unemployment had been negligible in the business class. Only one instance of a husband's unemployment was reported by the 40 business-class wives interviewed by the Lynds.

We obtained nearly identical results in 1978. Table 14–4 shows that about one in four of the male heads of the working-class families in our sample were unemployed at some time during 1977, while unemployment was negligible for the heads of business-class families in the sample. The class difference was significant at the .001 level in 1977 as it had been in 1923, although neither year saw any economic disturbance. Job security continues to be a major advantage that white-collar workers enjoy over blue-collar workers and, as these surveys indicate, that advantage has not significantly diminished in Middletown in the past half-century.

What Table 14–4 does not show is that the implications of involuntary unemployment were very different in 1978 than they were in 1924. These differences show up in the more extended thematic responses obtained in both surveys. The Lynds referred repeatedly to the dread of unemployment that prevailed among working-class housewives in 1924 and to the disturbance of family life that occurred when the fear became an actuality (Lynd and Lynd, 1929:58–67). Of those families in the earlier

TABLE 14–4
Middletown housewives reporting husbands unemployed during previous year, by social class, 1924 and 1978

Previous year	Working class*		Business class†			
	Number	Percent	Number	Percent	X^2	P
1923‡	(165)	28	(40)	1	64.3	.001
1977	(141)	25	(192)	4	29.0	.001

* The difference between the working class in 1923 and in 1977 is not significant, X^2 = 0.4.
† The difference between the business class in 1923 and in 1977 is not significant, X^2 = 0.0.
‡ Lynd and Lynd, 1929:57 and 512.

sample who experienced unemployment, most had made drastic readjustments, reducing their expenditures on food and clothing, removing their telephones, taking children out of school, canceling life insurance, and giving up their homes. Many of the wives had gone out to look for work in direct response to their husband's joblessness. In the present era of unemployment insurance, multiple forms of public assistance, abundant credit, and larger savings, Middletown's working-class families no longer live in constant dread of unemployment and most housewives do not change their routines or react strongly when their husbands are unemployed. Unemployment is still regarded as a hardship in Middletown's working class, but it is not the life-threatening crisis that it used to be.

Employment of married women. In the 1920s, the unemployment of husbands was almost the sole reason why Middletown wives with children took jobs outside the home, and they generally remained in the labor force only as the harsh necessity persisted. The Lynds (1929:27) were definite that the husbands' unemployment was the leading reason for the employment of married women. Only one of the business-class housewives in their sample had held a full-time outside job during the previous five years, she being apparently also the only business-class wife whose husband had suffered unemployment.

By 1978 this situation had changed out of all recognition. The unemployment of husbands was seldom the reason for the entry of wives into the labor force and when it was, the reemployment of the husband was unlikely to be followed by the wife's return to the home. An unexpected effect of this change, as Table 14–5 shows, has been to equalize the propensity to work of business-class and working-class wives despite the persistent class difference in husbands' unemployment. If their testimony is believed, the married women with children who worked full-time in 1978 did so because they wished to, for the extra income or the independence or the experience, and the attraction of these incentives was not noticeably affected by social class. In 1978, about half the respondents in our sample, who it will be remembered were married women living with their husbands and with children aged 6 to 18, reported having held full-time outside jobs within the previous five years; the difference between working-class and business-class wives had almost disappeared. Against the background of 1924, it is striking that the incidence of employment of working-class wives showed no significant increase at all from 1924 to 1978, while the incidence of employment of business-class wives increased from a very low level to nearly the same level as the working class. This is perhaps the most important change we discovered in the relative situation of the

TABLE 14–5
Middletown housewives holding full-time outside jobs during 1919–1923 and 1973–1977, by social class

	Percent who have worked					
	Working class*		Business class†			
	Number	Percent	Number	Percent	X^2	P
1919–1923‡	(124)	44	(40)	3	23.9	.001
1973–1977	(141)	48	(192)	42	7.7	.01

* The difference between the working class in 1919–23 and 1973–77 is significant at the .05 level, $X^2 = 5.0$.
† The difference between the business class in 1919–23 and in 1973–77 is significant at the .001 level, $X^2 = 22.8$.
‡ Lynd and Lynd 1929:27.

two classes. Whereas the full-time employment of wives was a penalty of working class membership in 1924, it had ceased by 1978 to be a class identifier and was no longer regarded as a penalty. So far as we know, this striking pattern of change has not been reported for the United States as a whole, but we shall be surprised it if turns out to be unique to Middletown.

Quality of housing. The Lynds (1929:99) described in vivid images the dilapidated housing of the poorer working-class family in 1924:

The poorer working man, coming home after his nine and a half hours on the job, walks up the frequently unpaved street, turns in at a bare yard littered with a rusty velocipede or worn-out automobile tires, opens a sagging door, and enters the living room of his home. From this room the whole house is visible—the kitchen with table and floor swarming with flies and often strewn with bread crusts, orange skins, torn papers, and lumps of coal and wood; the bedrooms with soiled, heavy quilts falling off the beds. The worn green shades hanging down at a tipsy angle admit only a reflected half-light upon the ornate calendars or enlarged colored portraits of the children in heavy gilt frames tilted out at a precarious angle just below the ceiling. The whole interior is musty with stale odors of food, clothing, and tobacco. On the brown varnished shelf of the sideboard the wooden-backed family hair brush, with the baby bottle, a worn purse, and yesterday's newspaper, may be half stuffed out of sight behind a bright blue glass cake dish.

At the other end of the continuum were the wealthy business-class families who lived in "fine old places," spacious brick or fieldstone houses with manicured lawns and a pair of stone lions at the driveway entrance. In between were the modest yet comfortable houses of the more prosperous working-class families, and the less prosperous business-class families.

Only 34 percent of the working-class families in the 1924 survey had achieved the single-family two-story house that was then the local ideal, compared with 80 per-

cent of the business-class families. By 1978 the single-family two-story house had ceased to be the predominant type for either class and most new dwellings in Middletown were one-story "ranch houses," but it is notable nevertheless that the class difference in the proportion of families occupying single-family two-story houses is now not significant.

Although it is not readily translated into numbers, the equalization of upkeep, furnishing, and decoration between the homes of the two classes has come a long way since 1924. Direct observation indicated the vast majority of working-class homes in 1978 were clean and well-kept and had tidy yards.

The marital relationship. The typical working-class marriage in the Middletown of the 1920s, as described by the Lynds, was depressing and frustrating. Husbands experienced difficulty and frequent failure in the effort to support their families; the fear of pregnancy cast a pall over sexual relationships; more children were born than were wanted and their support and care left both parents "weary." But in one of our 1978 surveys (not the replicative survey of housewives reported here), 92 percent of working-class respondents, as compared to 94 percent of business-class respondents, reported that their marriages were either "pretty happy" or "very happy." The large difference in marital satisfaction between working-class and business-class marriages observed by the Lynds in 1923–24 is no longer discernible.

Patterns of housework. Both working-class and business-class wives spent much less time doing housework in 1978 than in 1924. A majority of both classes reported more than four hours of daily housework in 1924 and fewer than four hours in 1978 (Table 14–6). The difference reported in 1924, when working-class housewives spent relatively more time at housework, still persisted in 1978, but the picture changes as we examine particular tasks. In 1924, 98 percent of working-class wives

TABLE 14-6
Daily housework time reported by Middletown housewives, by social class, 1924 and 1978

		Daily hours				
	Number	Under four hours (percent)	Four to seven hours (percent)	More than seven hours (percent)	X^2	P
1924:*						
Working class†	(112)	7	69	24		
Business class‡	(40)	23	55	23	7.11	.05
1978:						
Working class	(141)	53	38	10		
Business class	(192)	60	35	5	4.3	NS

* Lynd and Lynd, 1929:168.
† The difference between the working class in 1924 and in 1978 is significant at the .001 level, $X^2 = 59.7$.
‡ The difference between the business class in 1924 and in 1978 is significant at the .001 level, $X^2 = 24.1$.

spent two or more hours per week washing and ironing while the majority of business-class wives spent less than two hours. By 1978, nearly all working-class wives were still reporting more than two hours of laundry work per week, but so were 98 percent of the business-class wives, having lost their former immunity. The median number of laundry hours shifted *upward* for both groups from 1924 to 1978, but very much more for business-class wives (Table 14-7).

Another surprising trend appears with regard to sewing and mending. In 1924, most of the men's clothing worn in Middletown was store-bought, but much of the women's and children's clothing was made at home, especially by working-class wives, only 22 percent of whom reported two or less hours a week of sewing and mending compared to 51 percent of business-class wives. In 1978, about four fifths of *all* respondents reported two or less hours per week of sewing and mending, so that both groups had significantly decreased their commitment to this activity, but the working class decreased so much more that no class difference remained (Table 14-8).

An opposite evolution occurred with regard to home baking. In 1924, working-class wives were much more likely to bake bread than business-class wives, but the majority of women in both classes did not bake at all. In 1978, the great majority of respondents were involved in home baking, and there was no appreciable difference between working-class and business-class wives in this respect (Table 14-9).

One important difference between business-class families and working-class families in 1924 was the presence or absence of

TABLE 14-7
Daily washing and ironing time reported by Middletown housewives, by social class, 1924 and 1978

		Time					
	Number	Less than two hours (percent)	Two to four hours (percent)	Five to eight hours (percent)	Nine or more hours (percent)	X^2	P
1924:							
Working class*	(120)	2	20	54	24		
Business class†	(70)	60	15	20	5	75.87	.001
1978:							
Working class	(141)	1	21	41	37		
Business class	(92)	2	31	41	36	6.5	NS

* The difference between the working class in 1924 and in 1978 is not significant, $X^2 = 6.3$.
† The difference between the business class in 1924 and in 1978 is significant at .001, $X^2 = 106.2$.

TABLE 14–8
Weekly sewing and mending time reported by Middletown housewives, by social class, 1924 and 1978

		Weekly time				
	Number	Two or less hours (percent)	Three to six hours (percent)	Over six hours (percent)	X^2	P
1924*						
Working class† ...... (112)		22	42	36		
Business class‡ ...... (39)		51	23	26	10.3	.01
1978						
Working class .... (141)		78	14	8		
Business class .... (192)		80	10	9	1.2	NS

* Lynd and Lynd, 1929:165.
† The difference between the working class in 1924 and in 1978 is significant at the .001 level, $X^2 = 74.0$.
‡ The difference between the business class in 1924 and in 1978 is significant at the .001 level, $X^2 = 14.8$.

hired help. Ninety percent of the business-class families responding to the Lynds' survey had some paid help, typically part-time, while paid help was virtually unknown in working-class households. In 1978, the majority of business-class families had no hired help at all while the incidence of hired help in working-class families had increased, leaving very little difference between the classes (Table 14–10).

The parental role. Three questions in the 1924 survey, repeated in 1978, tell us something about trends in parental activities and attitudes in Middletown's families. The first of these asked respondents how much time they and their husbands spent with the children who lived with them. (It will be remembered that the sur-

vey sample was limited to intact families with children between the ages of 6 and 18.) Both mothers and fathers, in both working-class and business-class families, spent much more time with their children in 1978 than in 1924. In 1924, about one fourth of working-class mothers spent less than an hour per day with their children, and about one tenth of all fathers spent no time at all with them—or so their wives reported. By 1978, the incidence of parental neglect had much diminished. Only 7 percent of the mothers reported less than an hour per day with their children and fewer than 2 percent of the fathers were said to spend no time at all with them. At the other end of the scale, the proportion of mothers spending more than 16 hours

TABLE 14–9
Middletown housewives who baked bread at home, by social class, 1924 and 1978

		Baked bread			
	Number	Yes (percent)	No (percent)	X^2	P
1924:*					
Working class† ...... (119)		32	68		
Business class‡ ...... (39)		13	87	5.42	.05
1978:					
Working class .... (141)		82	18		
Business class .... (192)		81	19	.00	NS

*Lynd and Lynd, 1929:155.
†The difference between the working class in 1924 and in 1978 is significant at the .001 level, $X^2 = 67.8$.
‡The difference between the business class in 1924 and in 1978 is significant at the .001 level, $X^2 = 71.9$.

TABLE 14–10
Paid help in Middletown households, by social class, 1924 and 1978

	Number	Full-time servant* (percent)	One or more days per week† (percent)	No paid help (percent)
1924:‡				
Working class	(118)	0	1	95
Business class	(39)	33	64	10
1978:				
Working class	(141)	1	7	91
Business class	(192)	1	17	83

* The difference between working class and business class full-time servants in 1924 is significant at the .001 level, $X^2 = 167.3$, using Yates correction for continuity.

The difference between working class and business class full-time servants in 1978 is not significant, $X^2 = 0.5$.

† The difference between working class and business class part-time hired help in 1924 is significant at the .001 leve, $X^2 = 89.5$, using Yates correction for continuity.

The difference between working class and business part-time help in 1978 is significant at the .01 level, $X^2 = 7.4$.

‡ Lynd and Lynd, 1929:169–170.

per week with their children increased from fewer than half to nearly two thirds, and the percentage of fathers spending more than an hour per day with their children increased significantly also. What is more interesting for our present purpose is that the relatively greater neglect of their children by working-class mothers, observed in 1924, had disappeared without a trace by 1978.

Table 14–11 shows the educational aspirations of mothers for their children, in 1924 and 1978, separately by social class. In 1924, the class difference was dramatic. Nearly all business-class mothers wanted their children to go to college, and many of them looked forward to graduate education for them as well, while only 23 percent of working-class mothers aspired to college for their children and none anticipated graduate education for them. By 1978, this large difference was gone. The overwhelming majority of respondents in both classes want and expect higher education for their children and the slight remaining difference between classes is not significant.

Table 14–12 tells a somewhat more intricate story. The six characteristics listed in this table were those most desired in

TABLE 14–11
Middletown mothers' educational aspirations for their children, by social class, 1924 and 1978

	Number	Percent wanting			X^2	P
		High school	College	Graduate school		
1924*						
Working class† ...	(124)	31	23	0		
Business class‡ ...	(40)	100	93	20	22.4	.001
1978						
Working class	(141)	100	83	4		
Business class	(192)	100	90	7	1.1	NS

* Lynd and Lynd, 1929:186–187.

† The difference between working class responses in 1924 and in 1978 is significant at the .01 level, $X^2 = 14.5$.

‡ The difference between business class responses in 1924 and in 1978 is not significant, $X^2 = 4.3$.

TABLE 14–12
Traits Middletown parents desired in their children, by social class, 1924 and 1978

	1924 (percent)*			1978 (percent)		
	Working class parents	Business class parents	Class difference	Working class parents	Business class parents	Class difference
Strict obedience	46	43	3	11	15	4
Loyalty to the church	56	35	21†	23	23	0
Frankness in dealing with others	21	43	22‡	32	22	10
Tolerance	4	11	7	44	49	5
Independence	17	46	29‡	68	82	14†
Good manners	35	19	16‡	32	18	14†

* Lynd and Lynd.
† Significant at the .01 level.
‡ Significant at the .001 level.

children by at least a third of the survey respondents in either social class at either date. In 1924, the rank order of desired traits mentioned by working-class mothers was loyalty to the church, strict obedience, and good manners, while business-class mothers placed about equal weight on independence, strict obedience, and frankness. By 1978, independence and tolerance were the traits preferred by mothers in both classes, although other traits still received appreciable mention. The 1978 list shows a definite pattern of class differences, but the differences are consistently smaller and less significant than those of 1924.

SUMMARY AND DISCUSSION

In this paper, we have examined two sets of interwoven facts, the one having to do with the distribution of occupations and occupational prestige in Middletown from 1920 to 1970, the other with certain aspects of the lifestyles of Middletown's working-class and business-class families in 1924 and 1978. The first set of facts seems to tell us that the average occupational level of Middletown's families improved in a gratifying way during the past two generations. Middletown people in 1970 were better off than Middletown peo-

ple had been in 1920 in this respect—and in many others, such as income, education, health, and available leisure—that we have not discussed in this paper.[5] This general improvement in the level of social reward was not accompanied, however, by any significant equalization. Indeed, the distribution of occupations appeared somewhat more unequal at the end of the period than at the beginning.

The second set of facts, obtained by replicating in 1978 the survey of business-class and working-class housewives in Middletown conducted by Robert and Helen Lynd in 1924, tells us that most of the differences in lifestyle between business-class families and working-class families that were reported in 1924 had diminished or disappeared by 1978. In 1924, working-class families rose much earlier in the morning than business-class families and their breadwinners left for work about two hours earlier on the average. Unemployment was a dire threat to nearly every working-class family and not threatening

---

[5] But have examined elsewhere: Theodore Caplow, "The Gradual Progress of Equality in Middletown: A Tocquevillean Theme Reexamined." *Tocqueville Review*, vol. 1, no. 1, 1979; Bruce A. Chadwick and C. Bradford Chappell, "Inequality: 1920–1976," Center for Program Effectiveness Studies, Middletown III Project, Working Paper, 1977.

at all to business-class families. A substantial minority of working-class wives with children worked full-time at outside jobs when forced to do so by the unemployment of their husbands. Business-class wives with children at home did not look for jobs, but confined their outside activities to voluntary associations, recreation, and good works. Business-class families were comfortably housed and enjoyed the benefits of indoor plumbing, running hot water, central heating, telephones, and refrigerators as a matter of course. Some working-class families had some of these things but few had all, and some had none.[6] Their homes were often dirty, crowded, and uncomfortable, and their marital and parental relationships were often uncomfortable also. Women of both classes put in long hours doing housework every day, but working-class women did much more of the harder work—washing and ironing, sewing and mending, and baking bread. Hard-pressed as they were, working-class women were much more likely to neglect their children and had much lower aspirations for them.

On none of these items did we find working-class and business-class respondents further apart in 1978 than in 1924; on most of them, they had come much closer together. On some items, like housing quality, marital adjustment, and educational aspirations, the working-class re-

spondents of 1978 moved toward the business-class norms of 1924, which remained relatively unchanged for the business class. On one important item, the employment of women, the business class of 1978 had reached the norm of the working class of 1924, which the working class still retained. With respect to early rising, working-class and business-class families of 1978 had found a common norm close to the business-class norms of 1924. With respect to patterns of housework, the common norms of 1978 were closer to the working-class norms of 1924. The one difference that persisted from 1924 to 1978 was the much greater risk of unemployment for working-class husbands, but the social and psychological consequences of this difference had been considerably lessened by 1978.

We cannot, it seems to us, describe this complex pattern of shifts as the cultural absorption of Middletown's working class; that would require us to disregard the movement of the business class toward working-class norms with respect to the unemployment of married women, patterns of housework, and daily schedules, none of which are trivial components of lifestyle. The working-class families of 1978 resemble the business-class families of 1924 to some extent, but the business-class housewives of 1978 allocate their energies much more like the working-class housewives of 1924 than like their business-class "grandmothers." There has been a real convergence of lifestyles, and if the watershed between the two major classes in Middletown still exists, it is so eroded by now that its eventual disappearance does not seem unlikely.

---

[6] As late as 1935, 47 percent of Middletown's dwelling units lacked hot running water, 38 percent had no bathtub or shower, 19 percent did not have access to an indoor toilet, and 55 percent lacked central heating (Lynd and Lynd, 1937: Tables 25, 28, 29, and 31 in Appendix 3).

The community's vertical and horizontal patterns

SECTION THREE

INTRODUCTION

Two sets of relationships are particularly central in understanding the various parts or units of the local community. One is the ties which such units—be they churches, business establishments, governmental offices, or voluntary associations—have to organizations outside of the community. In many cases these relationships are strong, and the location of the unit in the community seems almost coincidental, as in the case of a military base. The major decisions regarding the unit are made outside the community, perhaps thousands of miles away; the principal activities of the units may have little special relevance to the community in which they are geographically located. Their whole focus of orientation may be elsewhere. Yet they are located within the community's confines, and certain symbiotic interrelationships with the local community may be clearly apparent, as well as other types of significant relationships and behavior.

Although few community units are oriented outward to the extent of a military base, nevertheless they all have some relationships to various organizations in the surrounding society, relationships which may be marked in some cases, extremely weak in others. This set of relationships of various community units to social systems outside the community may be described as the community's vertical pattern.

But there is another set of important relationships; those of various units—such as churches, schools, governmental offices, and business establishments within the community—to each other. Indeed, the presence and interrelationship of such institutions are widely considered one of the principal characteristics of the community, as distinguished from other social groupings such as formal organizations or small groups. These relationships of community units to each other constitute the community's horizontal pattern.

This section begins with selections from Roland Warren's *The Community in America*. In the two chapters excerpted here, Warren explains the basic distinctions between the community's vertical and horizontal patterns in light of the "great change." This "great change" is similar to the urbanization-industrialization-bureaucratization effects described in Section II by Maurice Stein. Specifically, the change has been a gradual but substantial strengthening of the vertical patterns in American communities. This has proceeded to such an extent that Warren asks, "What holds the whole thing together on the local level?" The answer to that question lies in the horizontal patterns, and ultimately determines whether or not the community, in any meaning which would emphasize a vital interrelation of local units, has disappeared as a significant social group.

Not only organizations, but also individuals can be considered in their relationship to extracommunity systems, on the one hand, and to other individuals within the community, on the other. The selection from Robert K. Merton's study of "influentials" in Rovere discusses this relationship. The selection is part of a much larger report of his findings.

In a section which precedes the present excerpt, Merton explains that it was only inadvertently, or "serendipitously," that the important contrast in the orientation of two types of influentials was found.

The distinction is between the localite and the cosmopolitan. The localite is oriented toward the local community as his primary focus of reference. "Devoting little thought or energy to the Great Society, he is preoccupied with local problems, to the virtual exclusion of the national and international scene." The cosmopolitan, though maintaining a modicum of relations within the community, "is also oriented significantly to the world outside Rovere, and regards himself as an integral part of the world. He resides in Rovere but lives in the Great Society. If the local type is parochial, the cosmopolitan is ecumenical." In the excerpt reprinted here, Merton explores the difference between these two types with regard to the strength or weakness of their roots in the community, the nature and number of their personal relationships in the community, the types of voluntary associations in which they participate and the nature of their participation, and the nature of the interpersonal influence which they exercise.

Merton is careful to note the smallness of the sample on which his generalizations are based, as well as the preliminary nature of his inquiry. Nevertheless, his initial conceptualization has proved useful as a frame of reference and as a basis for subsequent research. It has indicated the importance, on the individual as well as on the organizational level, of considering relationships within the community and relationships across community lines, as these affect community participation.

If the "mass society" has standarized communities in America, it follows that community stratification patterns should closely reflect national patterns. The relationship between local and national stratification is examined in this selection from Richard F. Curtis and Elton F. Jackson's *Inequality in American Communities*. Curtis and Jackson selected six communities of various sizes and locations and interviewed a sample of male heads of households in each. After comparing social class measures with life satisfaction, informal and formal participation, political ideology and identification, anomie, and intolerance, they report findings very similar to previous research based on national samples. Although some minor variation is found between communities, their general conclusion is that "local communities, although perhaps unique in many respects, are in their stratification systems mainly local manifestations of a national pattern."

This empirical support for the dominance of the vertical ties to the larger society over the unique horizontal patterning within the community, must be tempered, however. The variables selected by Curtis and Jackson are the same as those used in many national studies. Local factors such as the distribution of power and the ecological patterning of classes, races, residences, and businesses are not measured. There is, of course, a considerable body of literature that indicates the potential importance of local variation in such community variables (see also Caplow and Chadwick in Section Two). Still, until research appears that includes more local measures, Curtis and Jackson's study places the burden of proof on those who maintain that different communities do indeed possess significantly different stratification systems.

Abstract formulations of vertical and horizontal patterns and of status relationships may tend to obscure the processes through which people relate to each other in complex networks of social relationships. The intricate patterning of local relationships—so different in its vitality and variety from the allegations of individuals being lost in mass society—has recently been given renewed attention in network analysis and by the investigation of what Martin D. Lowenthal calls "the social economy."

Lowenthal points out that the usual meaning of the word *economy* as used by economists is "the sphere in which goods and services are produced for sale, are sold, and are purchased." But much activity of an economic nature is carried on outside the market economy, through a series of processes which Lowenthal investigates. "I call this economic system 'the social economy,'" he writes, "since the economic transactions which are being considered are imbedded in and based on the network of social relationships which people maintain over time." He proceeds to analyze some leading principles on which this social economy operates. In doing so, he describes and analyzes some of the important informal relationships which hold people together as part of the horizontal pattern of local communities.

The next selection is more a contribution to the study of the community than a substantive report of findings. Irwin T. Sanders, who over a period of decades had been engaged in conducting community studies, outlines a relatively brief method for conducting community studies for specific purposes. For various reasons, governmental agencies or business organizations or voluntary associations are concerned with gathering data about the social organization of a particular community for quite practical purposes. In this article, Sanders gives a practical procedure, which he himself has tried out on numerous occasions, for such a reconnaissance study of a particular community. Four or five workers can carry out such a study in less than a week's time, even in communities as large as 100,000 or so. The description of the kinds of data which are gathered and the way they are analyzed is suggestive both of the practical importance of community structure and function and of the way in which the necessary information can be obtained.

The final article in this section, by Albert Hunter, begins by tracing the theoretical development of the vertical versus horizontal issue through many of the writings included in this reader. It concludes by distinguishing between two developing perspectives on the relation between community and society: the *minimal-community view* which emphasizes the overwhelming dominance of the vertical pattern, and the *emergent-community view* which sees a new and important horizontal pattern developing in response to the mass society. Hunter's support for the emergent view is based on the proposition that the mass society produces homogeneous communities (or more specifically, neighborhoods) based on propinquity and mechanical solidarity.

In any case, it should be clear from these selections that (1) the relationship between the vertical and horizontal patterns of the community is at the very core of community analysis, and (2) a thorough understanding of the "great change" in these patterns is a necessary prerequisite to meaningful analysis of the current community issues.

— 15 —
The community in America
Roland L. Warren

At this point, our analysis of the systemic aspects of American communities may provide us with a set of useful conceptual tools. In that analysis, the concepts of vertical pattern and horizontal pattern were developed. A community's vertical pattern was defined as the structural and functional relation of its various social units and subsystems to extracommunity systems. Its horizontal pattern was defined as the structural and functional relation of the community's various social units and subsystems to each other. These terms were then shown to be related to, but not identical with, Homans' concepts of the external and internal systems, and to the task functions and maintenance functions (or instrumental and expressive functions) of small-group theory.

* * * * *

It is true that some types of units have a stronger vertical component (the branch plant of a national manufacturing company) and that others have a stronger horizontal component (a community welfare council). It may likewise be true that some individuals (Merton's "cosmopolitan influentials") are more strongly oriented vertically in their community participation, while other individuals ("local influ-

entials") are more strongly oriented horizontally.[1] But the attempt to identify a community's vertical units and its horizontal units is misleading. It is not the units which constitute the vertical or horizontal pattern; it is the vertical or horizontal aspects of the units—their relation, respectively, to extracommunity systems and to each other.

Thus, we can say that the clubs, unions, businesses, governmental units, churches, and other institutions of the local community have two sets of relationships which can be separately analyzed and whose characteristics are rather different. As we shall see, these two orders of relationships not only permeate community institutions but also characterize the established social roles within the community's organizational structure.

Most models of the community's relation to a larger region consider communities as units, relating them in their entirety to other communities in the region. Whether or not this type of analysis was adequate for preindustrial communities, it offers little help in analyzing contemporary American communities, for the relatively differentiated parts which constitute

---

Reprinted from Roland L. Warren, *The Community in America* (Chicago: Rand McNally, 1963) pp. 240–44, 267–71. Footnotes have been renumbered.

[1] See Robert K. Merton, "Patterns of Influence: A Study of Interpersonal Influence and of Communications Behavior in a Local Community," in Paul F. Lazarsfeld and Frank N. Stanton, *Communications Research 1948–1949* (New York: Harper & Brothers, 1949).

the contemporary American community are related increasingly to the outside world not so much as parts of the local community but as parts of a specialized extracommunity system to which they belong. Putting this another way, the important contemporary link between the community and the outside world is not an undifferentiated link between the community as such and other communities of the surrounding region, but rather it is the link between the highly differentiated parts of the community and their respective extracommunity systems. These systemic links relate the different parts of the community to many extracommunity units covering widely divergent geographic regions and often with widely diverse location of system headquarters.

What gives this highly varied pattern of extracommunity relationships particular cogency are two related facts. One is that, generally speaking, these vertical ties are stronger than the horizontal ties among units of any single community. The second fact is that the "great change" continuously operates to strengthen these vertical ties and to establish new ties between community units and extracommunity systems.

An important characteristic of the vertical pattern is the rational, planned, bureaucratically structured nature of the extracommunity ties. The ties between chain store and regional headquarters, between branch plant and national office, between school and state education department, between municipal government and state government, between the local office and the main office of a state or federal governmental unit, between voluntary association and state or national headquarters, between union local and union national, between church and denominational board—such ties are clearly defined through contract, charter, legislation, or administrative promulgations. They are structured along bureaucratic administra-tive lines, and the relation of the local unit to the extracommunity system is usually clearly prescribed in terms of the overall objectives and operating procedures of that system. The particular form of the relationship to the larger system is not left to chance—in Sumner's terms not "crescive" but "enacted." Consequently, the local community unit is an integral part of a rationally ordered, bureaucratically administered extracommunity system. Having said this, let us acknowledge that this description is not absolute, but relative, and that some types of extracommunity systemic ties are less deliberate, planned, and bureaucratic than others. Nevertheless, by contrast with the horizontal ties *among* diverse local community units, the vertical ties are far over toward the opposite extreme.

Thus, the "great change" brings with it a situation in which increasingly differentiated community units are coming to be related more integrally to extracommunity systems in ways which set up quite different norms, behavior patterns, and role expectations than those involved in the interrelation of these diverse units on the local level. Their interrelation on the local level, the community's horizontal pattern, is characterized not so much by bureaucratic structure and administration as by the symbiotic relationships associated with their geographic propinquity, not so much by "administered" decisions within a rationally organized structure as by the "market" decisions of individual units operating on the community level. Under these circumstances, the informal "power structures," within which mutual convergences of interest among community-based units can be recognized and points of possible friction can be worked out with some sense of their local relevance, perform a useful function. These and other aspects of the community's horizontal pattern will be considered in the following chapter.

There is a clear—though not perfect—correspondence between the community's vertical pattern and the performance of task functions and the horizontal pattern and the performance of maintenance functions. It will be recalled that both types of functions are essential to a social system, the one having to do with getting the things done which have to be done for the system to survive, the other having to do with maintaining the system itself as a viable entity.

A review of these locality-relevant task functions will indicate their strong vertical relevance, for the matter of economic production, distribution, and consumption and the performance of the various tasks associated with socialization, social control, social participation, and mutual support all involve working through such units as business companies, schools, governments, churches, and voluntary associations, usually with strong ties to extracommunity systems of which they are an integral part. In all these types of institutions the function of the headquarters "field staff" or its counterpart is characteristically that of working with the respective local units in a relationship within which the local units are encouraged or admonished or coerced to adapt themselves structurally and functionally to the tasks whose performance is the goal of the larger system. This relationship may vary from autocratic and coercive to democratic and permissive. No matter which, it is part of the role expectations of the field staff that they will be able to show a reasonable measure of success in achieving the conformity of the local unit to the purposes and procedural patterns of the larger system, again whether this is a church, a school, a welfare department, a voluntary association, a chain store, a union, a factory, or some other.

At the same time, there is a growing appreciation among widely varied types of extracommunity systems that the relationship of the local unit to the rest of the local community is important. The development of community relations departments and community relations consultants in various fields is indicative of this stress placed on local community relationships by extracommunity systems of different types.

Yet anyone familiar with the field and with community consultants in health, welfare, industrial, religious, or other areas will agree that these large systems, on their part, are caught up in the same dilemma as the local community units: The values, goals, norms, and behavior patterns of the vertical pattern and of the horizontal pattern do not coincide, and where they differ, a decision must be made which to follow. Many individuals in linkage positions are caught up in this dilemma, and we shall consider such positions shortly. Most extracommunity systems known to the author have resolved this problem in some combination of the following two ways (both of which opt in favor of the extracommunity system): Either the community-focused interest and activity are fairly deliberately a "public relations" attempt to achieve good will in the community while still keeping the local unit's program closely related to national program goals, or the community consultant staff find themselves a rather diffuse and peripheral part of the national system, occasionally able to accomplish a minor program accommodation but seldom having a strong voice in the administrative bureaucracy, which in contrast to them is deliberately and rationally task-oriented in terms of the larger system's objectives.

* * * * *

The strong ties linking many local units to extracommunity systems and orienting them structurally and functionally toward them form the basis for an important question to which the present chapter is addressed: With such a strong vertical pattern, how do the community units relate to each other on the local level in anything approaching a systemic manner? Put more simply, What holds the whole thing together on the local level?

The question is of great practical and theoretical importance. Theoretically, the answer will enable us to consider the apprehension shared by a number of specialists in community studies as to whether there is really any basis for using the concept of community to denote locality groups in American society. Might it not be better simply to study the various social organizations with their local units which we have been calling extracommunity systems? . . . Having done so, what remains to be considered?

Practically, the question has implications for many types of local action. Exactly what is involved in a "community relations" program of a national company, and why is it important? If national associations are to gear their programs more flexibly to suit the needs of the local community, what is meant here by "community"? And what is meant by the word community in the term "community development"? What is the community that is being developed?

In Chapter 5 the question was raised of whether and to what extent it is possible to identify a community—defined as that combination of social units and systems which perform the major social functions having locality relevance—as a social system with the attributes there described. It was pointed out that there exist on the locality level identifiable combinations of social units and systems which manifest the characteristics of a social system in varying degrees, but that generally speaking these characteristics, particularly as regards boundary maintenance and the strengths of the structural interrelationships, are weak in contrast to other types of social systems. A notable example of stronger, more clearly ascertainable systems are the extracommunity systems treated in the preceding chapter.

Nevertheless, a set of interrelationships does exist—even among the most diverse units—based on common locality, for the operation of one type of local unit presupposes the presence and operation of others. If a manufacturing plant needs employees, these employees in turn will need to have access in their daily lives and at the locality level to other types of function and facility—for providing food, offering possibilities for voluntary association, providing for the formal and informal enforcement of social norms, training the young, helping out in time of trouble, and so on. In turn, each of the units involved in the performance of these functions presupposes the others.

Despite their strong ties to extracommunity systems, the functioning of such local units characteristically involves at least a minimum of local interaction—sometimes more than a minimum. From the theoretical standpoint, the behavior of these units cannot all be explained without reference to such interaction on the locality level. From the practical standpoint, no local unit, no matter how strongly integrated in an extracommunity system, can function long in complete disregard of the impact which its own behavior makes on other units in the locality. Our present task is to explore and delineate the nature of the relations among units on the locality level. Included in the concept of local operating units are individual persons, insofar as their behavior has locality relevance, as well as combinations of individuals organized into functioning groups, whether formal or informal.

One might well question whether the nature of these relationships among local units does not constitute the "real" community—in the sense of the "community system"—in distinction from the relations of local units to their respective extracommunity systems. These latter by definition are not confined to the community but lead us out of the community into systems whose basic operating dynamics are only remotely related to any particular community. Perhaps the vertical pattern of organization on the locality level is not appropriate to an analysis of the nature of communities as we have defined them.

But this is overstating the case. We have acknowledged, even insisted on, the great influence of extracommunity systems on local units. But we have likewise emphasized that the presence of such highly vertically oriented units at the locality level has relevance to what happens there. No analysis of the local behavior of such units can account for what occurs without major reference to these extracommunity ties. Were this not so, there would be more justification for ignoring them in an analysis of community phenomena. Further, we have maintained that the ties to extracommunity systems are inherent in the structure and function of local units. One need not go "outside" the community to find the larger society. The larger society inheres in the local community in ways enumerated and described in the preceding chapter.

Thus, our conceptual platform for analyzing the ties existing between diverse units at the locality level is as follows: At the locality level, it is possible to locate a structured interaction which displays in minimal degree, at least, the characteristics usually thought of as constituting a social system. The units of such interaction, particularly as they engage in performing the enumerated locality-relevant functions, are often strongly related to extracommunity systems in a whole combination of relationship aspects which we have called the vertical pattern of social organization. These same functioning units, however, interact with each other on the local scene in a somewhat different combination of relationship aspects which we have called the horizontal pattern of

social organization. The behavior of local units at the community level consists of the dynamic interplay of these two patterns, an interplay which at one time may bring the vertical relationships into sharp focus, at another time the horizontal relationships, but an interplay from which neither type of relationship pattern is ever completely absent. The fluctuation between the two, analyzable in terms of input-output from one pattern to another, and the tendency for the confining pressures of one set of relationships to grow rapidly as the contrary set begins to move beyond a certain point, constitute the equilibrium-maintenance behavior of the community as a social system. Having considered the vertical pattern in the previous chapter, we now turn to the horizontal pattern.

Let us begin by reminding ourselves that the horizontal pattern, although not identical with the maintenance function of the task-maintenance dichotomy, closely approaches it. The horizontal pattern has to do with the formal and informal structures and processes through which the local units maintain a systemic relationship to one another. These include both the "internal system" described by Homans, the "group behavior that is an expression of the sentiments towards one another developed by the members of the group in the course of their life together,"[2] and that part of Homans' "external system" which has to do with the formal organization of relationships among units for task accomplishment as dictated by the conditions of the system's survival in its environment. For those interested in further cross-referencing, the horizontal pattern would correspond to the integrative function and the pattern-maintenance and tension-management function which Parsons subsumed under the internal category in a

---

[2] George C. Homans, *The Human Group* (New York: Harcourt, Brace, 1950), p. 110.

recent codification.[3] There is also an important sense in which the horizontal pattern corresponds to Redfield's concept of the "folk" society, as opposed to the urban society.

While the vertical pattern, as we have seen, is characterized by such *Gesellschaft*-like qualities as deliberate and rational planning and bureaucratic structure, the horizontal pattern is characterized by sentiment, informality, lack of planning, and diffuse, informal, and ad hoc structuring of an essentially nonbureaucratic nature. The bureaucratization of social organizations which forms an important aspect of the "great change" has had much greater impact on the task-oriented vertical organization of the community's units than it has had on the nature of their relationships to each other.

Nevertheless, some degree of formalization and bureaucratization has become evident in the community's horizontal pattern in the later stages of the "great change." This is apparent in the development of such institutions as the community chest, the community planning council, the chamber of commerce, the federation of churches, and the community development council. All of these represent attempts to structure in a rational and deliberate fashion the relationship of diverse community units to each other. Such rationalized, bureaucratic structures are perhaps best understood as adaptations of the community system to the increasing orientation of units to extracommunity systems. Community coherence which could earlier be achieved through market behavior involving custom, sentiment, and a high component of primary-group interaction must now be deliberately "administered" through express provision for its formal channeling. It is thus possible to offset strong centrifugal forces generated by the increase in strength of extracommunity ties and thus maintain the equilibrium of the system. Even so, the formal and rational ties which such organizations seek to structure are usually far weaker than the ties of the individual member units to their respective extracommunity systems.

---

[3] Talcott Parsons, "General Theory in Sociology," in *Sociology Today: Problems and Prospects*, ed. Robert K. Merton, Leonard Broom, and Leonard S. Cottrell, Jr. (New York: Basic Books, 1959), p. 7.

16

Local and cosmopolitan influentials

Robert K. Merton

The terms *local* and *cosmopolitan*[1] do not refer, of course, to the regions in which interpersonal influence is exercised. Both types of influentials are effective almost exclusively within the local community. Rovere has few residents who command a following outside that community.[2]

The chief criterion for distinguishing the two is found in their *orientation* toward Rovere. The localite largely confines his interests to this community. Rovere is essentially his world. Devoting little thought or energy to the Great Society, he is preoccupied with local problems, to the virtual exclusion of the national and international scene. He is, strictly speaking, parochial.

Contrariwise with the cosmopolitan type. He has some interest in Rovere and must of course maintain a minimum of relations within the community since he, too, exerts influence there. But he is also oriented significantly to the world outside Rovere, and regards himself as an integral part of that world. He resides in Rovere but lives in the Great Society. If the local type is parochial, the cosmopolitan is ecumenical.

Of the 30 influentials interviewed at length, 14 were independently assessed by three analysts[3] as "cosmopolitan" on the basis of case materials exhibiting their orientation toward the Rovere community, and 16 as "local."

These orientations found characteristic expression in a variety of contexts. For example, influentials were launched upon a statement of their outlook by the quasi-protective question: "Do you worry much about the news?" (This was the autumn of 1943, when "the news" was, for most, equivalent to news about the war.) The responses, typically quite lengthy, readily

Reprinted from Robert K. Merton, "Types of Influentials: The Local and the Cosmopolitan," in *Communications Research, 1948–1949*, ed. Paul F. Lazarsfeld and Frank N. Stanton. Copyright 1949 by Harper & Row, Publishers, Inc. Footnotes have been renumbered and those added in the version of the article printed in the author's *Social Theory and Social Structure* (Glencoe, Ill.: The Free Press, 1957) have been included.

[1] Upon identification of the two types of influentials, these terms were adopted from Carle C. Zimmerman, who uses them as translations of Tönnies' well-known distinction between *Gemeinschaft* (localistic) and *Gesellschaft* (cosmopolitan). The sociologically informed reader will recognize essentially the same distinction, though with different terminologies, in the writings of Simmel, Cooley, Weber, Durkheim, among many others. Although these terms have commonly been used to refer to types of social organization and of social relationships, they are here applied to empirical materials on types of influential persons. Cf. Ferdinand Tönnies, *Fundamental Concepts of Sociology* (New York, 1940), a translation by C. P. Loomis of his classic book *Gemeinschaft und Gesellschaft* and, more importantly, a later article bearing the same title. See also Carle C. Zimmerman, *The Changing Community*, (New York and London: Harper & Brothers, 1938), especially 80 ff. For a compact summary of similar concepts in the sociological literature, see Leopold von Wiese and Howard Becker, *Systematic Sociology* (New York: John Wiley & Sons, 1932), especially 223–26n.

[2] The concept of influentials has been taken up in a study of the influence-structure of a suburb which houses men of national reputation and influence. As the authors say, "It is hardly surprising then that the personal characteristics of these 'influentials' differ from those of the lower-ranking cosmopolitan influential in Rovere." Kenneth P. Adler and Davis Bobrow, "Interest and influence in foreign affairs," *Public Opinion Quarterly*, 1956, 20, 89–101. See also Floyd Hunter, *Power Structure: A Study of Decision-Makers* (Chapel Hill: University of North Carolina Press, 1953).

[3] This complete coincidence of assessments is scarcely to be expected in a larger sample. But the cosmopolitan and local syndromes were so clearly defined for this handful of cases that there was little doubt concerning the "diagnoses." A full-fledged investigation would evolve more formal criteria, along the lines implied in the following discussion, and would, accordingly, evolve an intermediate type which approaches neither the local nor the cosmopolitan pole.

lent themselves to classification in terms of the chief foci of interest of the influentials. One set of comments was focused on problems of a national and international order. They expressed concern with the difficulties which would attend the emergence of a stable postwar world; they talked at length about the problems of building an international organization to secure the peace; and the like. The second set of comments referred to the war news almost wholly in terms of what it implied for interviewees personally or for their associates in Rovere. They seized upon a question about "the news" as an occasion for reviewing the immediate flow of problems which the war had introduced into the town.

Classifying influentials into these two categories, we find that 12 of the 14[4] cosmopolitans typically replied within the framework of international and national problems, whereas only 4 of the 16 locals spoke in this vein. Each type of influential singled out distinctively different elements from the flow of events. A vaguely formulated question enabled each to project his basic orientations into his replies.

All other differences between the local and cosmopolitan influentials seem to stem from their difference in basic orientation.[5] The group profiles indicate the tendency of local influentials to be devoted to

localism: they are more likely to have lived in Rovere for a long period, are profoundly interested in meeting many townspeople, do not wish to move from the town, are more likely to be interested in local politics, etc. Such items, which suggest great disparity between the two types of influentials, are our main concern in the following sections. There we will find the difference in basic orientation is bound up with a variety of other differences: (1) in the structures of social relations in which each type is implicated; (2) in the roads they have traveled to their present positions in the influence structure; (3) in the utilization of their present status for the exercise of interpersonal influence; and (4) in their communications behavior.

STRUCTURES OF SOCIAL RELATIONS

Roots in the community

Local and cosmopolitan influentials differ rather markedly in their attachment to Rovere. The local influentials are great local patriots and the thought of leaving Rovere seems seldom to come in mind. As one of them gropingly expressed it:

Rovere is the greatest town in the world. It has something that is nowhere else in the world, though I can't quite say what it is.

When asked directly if they had "ever thought of leaving Rovere," 13 of the 16 local influentials replied emphatically that they would never consider it, and the other 3 expressed a strong preference to remain, although they believed they would leave under certain conditions. None felt that they would be equally satisfied with life in any other community. Not so with the cosmopolitans. Only three of these claim to be wedded to Rovere for life. Four express their present willingness to live elsewhere, and the remaining seven would be willing to leave under cer-

---

[4] It should be repeated that the figures cited at this point, as throughout the study, should not be taken as representative of a parent population. They are cited only to illustrate the heuristic purpose they served in suggesting clues to the operation of diverse patterns of interpersonal influence. As is so often the fact with quantitative summaries of case studies, these figures do not confirm interpretations, but merely suggest interpretations. The tentative interpretations in turn provide a point of departure for designing quantitative studies based upon adequate samples, as in Katz and Lazarsfeld [Elihu Katz and P. F. Lazarsfeld, *Personal Influence* (Glencoe: Free Press, 1955)].

[5] Nothing is said here of the objective *determinants* of these differences in orientation. To ascertain these determinants is an additional and distinctly important task, not essayed in the present study.

tain conditions. Cosmopolitans' responses such as these do not turn up at all among the locals:

I've been on the verge of leaving for other jobs several times.

I am only waiting for my son to take over my practice, before I go out to California.

These basic differences in attitude toward Rovere are linked with the different runs of experience of local and cosmopolitan influentials. The cosmopolitans have been more mobile. The locals were typically born in Rovere or in its immediate vicinity. Whereas 14 of the 16 locals have lived in Rovere for over 25 years, this is true for fewer than half of the cosmopolitans. The cosmopolitans are typically recent arrivals who have lived in a succession of communities in different parts of the country.

Nor does this appear to be a result of differences in the age-composition of the local and cosmopolitan groups. True, the cosmopolitans are more likely to be younger than the local influentials. But for those over 45, the cosmopolitans seem to be comparative newcomers and the locals Rovere-born-and-bred.

From the case materials, we can infer the bases of the marked attachment to Rovere characteristic of the local influentials. In the process of making their mark, these influentials have become thoroughly *adapted to the community* and dubious of the possiblity of doing as well elsewhere. From the vantage point of his 70 years, a local judge reports his sense of full incorporation in the community:

I wouldn't think of leaving Rovere. The people here are very good, very responsive. They like me and I'm grateful to God for the feeling that the people in Rovere trust me and look up to me as their guide and leader.

Thus, the strong sense of identification with Rovere among local influentials is linked with their typically local origins and career patterns in this community. Eco-

nomically and sentimentally, they are deeply rooted in Rovere.

So far as attachment to Rovere is concerned, the cosmopolitans differ from the locals in virtually every respect. Not only are they relative newcomers; they do not feel themselves rooted in the town. Having characteristically lived elsewhere, they feel that Rovere, "a pleasant enough town," is only one of many. They are also aware, through actual experience, that they can advance their careers in other communities. They do not, consequently, look upon Rovere as comprising the outermost limits of a secure and satisfactory existence. Their wider range of experience has modified their orientation toward their present community.

Sociability: Networks of personal relations

In the course of the interview, influentials were given an occasion to voice their attitudes toward "knowing many people" in the community. Attitudes differed sharply between the two types. Thirteen of the 16 local influentials in contrast to 4 of the 14 cosmopolitans expressed marked interest in establishing frequent contacts with many people.

This difference becomes more instructive when examined in qualitative terms. The local influential is typically concerned with knowing *as many* people as possible. He is a quantitativist in the sphere of social contacts. Numbers count. In the words of an influential police officer (who thus echoes the sentiments of another "local," the Mayor):

I have lots of friends in Rovere, if I do say so myself. I like to know everybody. If I stand on a corner, I can speak to 500 people in two hours. Knowing people helps when a promotion comes up, for instance. Everybody mentions you for the job. Influential people who know you talk to other people. Jack Flye (the Mayor) said to me one day, "Bill," he said, "you have more friends in town than I do. I wish I had all the friends you have that you don't even know of." It made me feel good. . . .

This typical attitude fits into what we know of the local type of influential. What is more, it suggests that the career function of personal contacts and personal relations is recognized by local influentials themselves. Nor is this concern with personal contact merely a consequence of the occupations of local influentials. Businessmen, professionals, and local government officials among them all join in the same paeans on the desirability of many and varied contacts. A bank president recapitulates the same story in terms of his experience and outlook:

I have always been glad to meet people. . . . It really started when I became a teller. The teller is the most important position in a bank as far as meeting people goes. As teller, you must meet everyone. You learn to know everybody by his first name. You don't have the same opportunity again to meet people. Right now we have a teller who is very capable but two or three people have come to me complaining about him. He is unfriendly with them. I told him, you've got to have a kind word for everyone. It's a personal and a business matter.

This keynote brings out the decisive interest of local influentials in all manner of personal contacts which enable them to establish themselves when they need political, business, or other support. Influentials in this group act on the explicit assumption that they can be locally prominent and influential by lining up enough people who know them and are hence willing to help them as well as be helped by them.

The cosmopolitan influentials, on the other hand, have notably little interest in meeting *as many* people as possible.[6] They are more selective in their choice of friends and acquaintances. They typically stress the importance of confining themselves to friends with whom "they can really talk," with whom they can "exchange ideas." If the local influentials are quantitativists, the cosmopolitans are qualitativists in this regard. It is not *how many* people they know but the *kind of people* they know that counts.[7]

The contrast with the prevailing attitudes of local influentials is brought out in these remarks by cosmopolitan influentials:

I don't care to know people unless there is something to the person.

I am not interested in quantity. I like to know about other people; it broadens your own education. I enjoy meeting people with knowledge and standing. Masses of humanity I don't go into. I like to meet people of equal mentality, learning, and experience.

Just as with the local influentials, so here the basic attitude cuts across occupational and educational lines. Professional men among the cosmopolitans, for example, do not emphasize the importance of a wide and extensive acquaintanceship, if one is to build up a practice. In contrast to a "local" attorney who speaks of the "advantage to me to know as many people as possible," a "cosmopolitan" attorney waxes poetic and exclusive all in one, saying:

I have never gone out and sought people. I have no pleasure in just going around and calling. As Polonius advised Laertes,

"Those friends thou hast, and their adoption tried,
Grapple them to thy soul with hoops of steel,
But do not dull the palm with entertainment
Of each new-hatch'd unfledged
    comrade. . . ."

---

[6] This was interestingly confirmed in the following fashion. Our informants were confronted with a random list of names of Rovere residents and were asked to identify each. Local influentials recognized more names than any other group of informants, and cosmopolitans, in turn, knew more persons than the noninfluential informants.

[7] In this pilot study, we have confined ourselves to the expression of attitudes toward personal contacts and relations. A detailed inquiry would examine the quantum and quality of *actual* personal relations characteristic of the local and cosmopolitan influentials.

In a later section of this study, we shall see that these diverse orientations of locals and cosmopolitans toward personal relations can be interpreted as a function of their distinctive modes of achieving influence. At the moment, it is sufficient to note that locals seek to enter into manifold networks of personal relations, whereas the cosmopolitans, *on the same status level,* explicitly limit the range of these relations.

Participation in voluntary organizations

In considering the sociability of locals and cosmopolitans, we examined their attitudes toward informal, personal relationships. But what of their roles in the more formal agencies for social contact: the voluntary organizations?

As might be anticipated, both types of influentials are affiliated with more organizations than rank-and-file members of the population. Cosmopolitan influentials belong to an average of eight organizations per individual, and the local influentials, to an average of six. This suggests the possibility that cosmopolitans make greater use of organizational channels to influence than of personal contacts, whereas locals, on the whole, operate contrariwise.

But as with sociability, so with organizations: the more instructive facts are qualitative rather than quantitative. It is not so much that the cosmopolitans belong to *more* organizations than the locals. Should a rigorous inquiry bear out this impression, it would still not locate the strategic organizational differences between the two. It is, rather, that they belong to different types of organizations. And once again, these differences reinforce what we have learned about the two kinds of influentials.

The local influentials evidently crowd into those organizations which are largely designed for "making contacts," for establishing personal ties. Thus, they are found largely in the secret societies (Masons), fraternal organizations (Elks), and local service clubs—the Rotary, Lions, and the Kiwanis, the most powerful organization of this type in Rovere. Their participation appears to be less a matter of furthering the nominal objectives of these organizations than of using them as *contact centers.* In the forthright words of one local influential, a businessman:

I get to know people through the service clubs; Kiwanis, Rotary, Lions. I now belong only to the Kiwanis. Kiwanis is different from any other service club. You have to be asked to join. They pick you out first, check you first. Quite a few influential people are there and I get to meet them at lunch every week.

The cosmopolitans, on the other hand, tend to belong to those organizations in which they can exercise their special skills and knowledge. They are found in professional societies and in hobby groups. At the time of the inquiry, in 1943, they were more often involved in Civilian Defense organizations where again they were presumably more concerned with furthering the objectives of the organization than with establishing personal ties.

Much the same contrast appears in the array of public offices held by the two types of influentials. Seven of each type hold some public office, although the locals have an average somewhat under one office. The primary difference is in the *type* of office held. The locals tend to hold political posts—street commissioner, mayor, township board, etc.—ordinarily obtained through political and personal relationships. The cosmopolitans, on the other hand, more often appear in public positions which involve not merely political operations but the utilization of special skills and knowledge (*e.g.,* Board of Health, Housing Committee, Board of Education).

From all this we can set out the hypothesis that participation in voluntary associations[8] has somewhat different functions

---

[8] For types and functions of participation in such organizations, see Bernard Barber, "Participation and Mass apathy in Associations," in *Studies in Leadership,* ed. Alvin W. Gouldner (New York: Harper & Brothers, 1950), 477–504.

for cosmopolitan and local influentials. Cosmopolitans are concerned with associations primarily because of the activities of these organizations. They are means for extending or exhibiting their skills and knowledge. Locals are primarily interested in associations not for their activities, but because these provide a means for extending personal relationships. The basic orientations of locals and cosmopolitan influentials are thus diversely expressed in organizational behavior as in other respects.

AVENUES TO INTERPERSONAL INFLUENCE

The foregoing differences in attachment to Rovere, sociability and organizational behavior, help direct us to the different avenues to influence traveled by the locals and the cosmopolitans. And in mapping these avenues we shall fill in the background needed to interpret the differences in communications behavior characteristic of the two types of influentials.

The locals have largely grown up in and with the town. For the most part, they have gone to school there, leaving only temporarily for their college and professional studies. They held their first jobs in Rovere and earned their first dollars from Rovere people. When they came to work out their career-pattern, Rovere was obviously the place in which to do so. It was the only town with which they were thoroughly familiar, in which they knew the ins and outs of politics, business, and social life. It was the only community which they knew and, equally important, which knew them. Here they had developed numerous personal relationships.

And this leads to the decisive attribute of the local influentials' path to success: far more than with the cosmopolitans, *their influence rests on an elaborate network of personal relationships.* In a formula which at once simplifies and highlights the essential fact, we can say: *the influence of local influentials rests not so much on what they know but on whom they know.*

Thus, the concern of the local influential with personal relations is in part the product and in part the instrument of his particular type of influence. The "local boy who makes good," it seems, is likely to make it through good personal relations. Since he is involved in personal relations long before he has entered seriously upon his career, it is the path of less resistance for him to continue to rely upon these relations as far as possible in his later career.

With the cosmopolitan influential, all this changes. Typically a newcomer to the community, he does not and cannot utilize personal ties as his chief claim to attention. He usually comes into the town fully equipped with the prestige and skills associated with his business or profession and his "worldly" experience. He begins his climb in the prestige structure at a relatively high level. It is the prestige of his previous achievements and previously acquired skills which make him eligible for a place in the local influence structure. Personal relations are much more the product than the instrumentality of his influence.

These differences in the location of career patterns have some interesting consequences for the problems confronting the two types of influentials. First of all, there is some evidence, though far from conclusive, that the rise of the locals to influentiality is slow compared with that of the cosmopolitans. Dr. A, a minister, cosmopolitan, and reader of newsmagazines, remarked upon the ease with which he had made his mark locally:

The advantage of being a minister is that *you don't have to* prove yourself. You are immediately accepted and received in all homes, including the best ones. [Emphasis supplied.]

However sanguine this observation may be, it reflects the essential point that the newcomer who has "arrived" in the outside world, sooner takes his place among those with some measure of influence in the local community. In contrast, the local influentials *do* "have to prove" themselves. Thus, the local bank president, who required some 40 years to rise from his job as messenger boy, speaks feelingly of the slow, long road on which "I worked my way up."

The age-composition of the local and cosmopolitan influentials is also a straw in the wind with regard to the rate of rise to influence. All but 2 of the 16 locals are over 45 years of age, whereas fewer than two thirds of the cosmopolitans are in this older age group.

Not only may the rate of ascent to influence be slower for the local than for the cosmopolitan, but the ascent involves some special difficulties deriving from the local's personal relations. It appears that these relations may hinder as well as help the local boy to "make good." He must overcome the obstacle of being intimately known to the community when he was "just a kid." He must somehow enable others to recognize his consistent change in status. Most importantly, people to whom he was once subordinate must be brought to the point of now recognizing him as, in some sense, superordinate. Recognition of this problem is not new. Kipling follows Matthew 13 in observing that "prophets have honor all over the Earth, except in the village where they were born." The problem of ascent in the influence structure for the home-town individual may be precisely located in sociological terms: the revamping of attitudes toward the mobile individual and the remaking of relations with him. The preexistent structure of personal relations for a time thus restrains the ascent of the local influential. Only when he has broken through these established conceptions of him, will others accept the reversal of roles entailed in the rise of the local man to influence. A Rovere attorney, numbered among the local influentials, described the pattern concisely:

When I first opened up, people knew me so well in town that they treated me as if I still were a kid. It was hard to overcome. But after I took interest in various public and civic affairs, and became chairman of the Democratic organization and ran for the State legislature—knowing full well I wouldn't be elected—they started to take me seriously.

The cosmopolitan does not face the necessity for breaking down local preconceptions of himself before it is possible to have his status as an influential "taken seriously." As we have seen, his credentials are found in the prestige and authority of his attainments elsewhere. He thus manifests less interest in a wide range of personal contacts for two reasons. First, his influence stems from prestige rather than from reciprocities with others in the community. Secondly, the problem of disengaging himself from obsolete images of him as "a boy" does not exist for him, and consequently does not focus his attention upon personal relations as it does for the local influential.

The separate roads to influence traveled by the locals and cosmopolitans thus help account for their diverging orientations toward the local community, with all that these orientations entail.

SOCIAL STATUS IN ACTION: INTERPERSONAL INFLUENCE

At this point, it may occur to the reader that the distinction between the local and cosmopolitan influentials is merely a reflection of differences in education or occupation. This does not appear to be the case.

It is true that the cosmopolitans among our interviewees have received more formal education than the locals. All but one of the cosmopolitans as compared with half of the locals are at least graduates of high school. It is also true that half of the locals are in "big business," as gauged by Rovere standards, whereas only 2 of the 14 cosmopolitans fall in this group; and furthermore, that half of the cosmopolitan influentials are professional people as compared with fewer than a third of the locals.

But these differences in occupational or educational status do not appear to determine the diverse types of influentials.

When we compare the behavior and orientations of professionals among the locals and cosmopolitans, their characteristic differences persist, even though they have the same types of occupation and have received the same type of education. Educational and occupational differences may *contribute* to the differences between the two types of influentials but they are not the *source* of these differences. Even as a professional, the local influential is more of a businessman and politician in his behavior and outlook than is the cosmopolitan. He utilizes personal relationships as an avenue to influence conspicuously more than does his cosmopolitan counterpart. In short, *it is the pattern of utilizing social status and not the formal contours of the status itself which is decisive.*[9]

While occupational status may be a major support for the cosmopolitan's rise to influence, it is merely an adjunct for the local. Whereas all five of the local professionals actively pursue local politics, the cosmopolitan professionals practically ignore organized political activity in Rovere. (Their offices tend to be honorary appointments.) Far from occupation serving to explain the differences between them, it appears that the same occupation has a different role in interpersonal influence according to whether it is pursued by a local or a cosmopolitan. This bears out our earlier impression that "objective attributes" (education, occupation, etc.) do not suffice as indices of people exercising interpersonal influence.

The influential businessman, who among our small number of interviewees is found almost exclusively among the locals, typically utilizes his personal relations to enhance his influence. It is altogether likely that a larger sample would include businessmen who are cosmopolitan influentials and whose behavior differs significantly in this respect. Thus, Mr. H., regarded as exerting great influence in Rovere, illustrates the cosmopolitan big-business type. He arrived in Rovere as a top executive in a local manufacturing plant. He has established few personal ties. But he is sought out for advice precisely because he has "been around" and has the aura of a man familiar with the outside world of affairs. His influence rests upon an imputed expertness rather than upon sympathetic understanding of others.

This adds another dimension to the distinction between the two types of influential. It appears that the cosmopolitan influential has a following because *he knows;* the local influential, because *he understands.* The one is sought out for his specialized skills and experience; the other, for his intimate appreciation of intangible but affectively significant details. The two patterns are reflected in prevalent conceptions of the difference between "the extremely competent but impersonal medical specialist" and the "old family doctor." Or again, it is not unlike the difference between the "impersonal social welfare worker" and the "friendly precinct captain,". . . It is not merely that the local political captain provides food-baskets and jobs, legal and extralegal advice, that he sets to rights minor scrapes with the law, helps the bright poor boy to a political scholarship in a local college, looks after the bereaved—that he helps in a whole series of crises when a fellow needs a friend, and, above all, a friend who "knows the score" and can do something about it. It is not merely that he provides aid which gives him interpersonal influence. It is *the manner in which the aid is provided.* After all, specialized agencies do exist for dispensing this assistance. Wel-

---

[9] The importance of actively seeking influence is evident from an analysis of "the upward mobile type," set forth in the monograph upon which this report is based. See also Granville Hicks, *Small Town* (New York: Macmillan, 1946), 154, who describes a man who is evidently a local influential in these terms: "He is a typical politician, a born manipulator, a man who worships influence, *works hard to acquire it,* and does his best to convince other people that he has it." (Italics supplied.)

fare agencies, settlement houses, legal aid clinics, hospital clinics, public relief departments—these and many other organizations are available. But in contrast to the professional techniques of the welfare worker which often represent in the mind of the recipient the cold, bureaucratic dispensation of limited aid following upon detailed investigation, are the unprofessional techniques of the precinct captain who asks no questions, exacts no compliance with legal rules of eligibility, and does not "snoop" into private affairs. The precinct captain is a prototype of the "local" influential.

Interpersonal influence stemming from specialized expertness typically involves some social distance between the advice-giver and the advice-seeker, whereas influence stemming from sympathetic understanding typically entails close personal relations. The first is the pattern of the cosmopolitan influential; the second, of the local influential. Thus, the operation of these patterns of influence gives a clue to the distinctive orientations of the two types of influentials.[10]

---

[10] All this still leaves open the problem of working out the patterns of social interaction and of influence-relations *between* local and cosmopolitan influentials. This problem has been explored in a current study of high schools in relation to the value-structure of the environing community, a study by Paul F. Lazarsfeld in collaboration with Richard Christie, Frank A. Pinner, Arnold Rogow, Louis Schneider, and Arthur Brodbeck.

In the course of this study, Frank A. Pinner found that school boards and school superintendents evidently varied in their orientation: some were distinctly "local," others "cosmopolitan" in orientation. Nor is this, it appears, simply a matter of historical "accident." Pinner suggests that communities of different types tend to elect people of differing orientation to the high school board. This, in turn, creates special circumstances affecting the interaction of the school board and the school superintendent, depending on the primary orientation of both. The orientations of school boards are also, it seems, linked up with the degree of control exercised over educational policies. The influentials in one community "being profoundly interested in local affairs, were bound to subject all community functions to constant scrutiny and to accept or reject policies as they seemed to be in agreement with or contradictory to commonly accepted standards [in the local community]. By the

same token, the [other] district was a 'loosely' organized area in more than the sheer geographical sense. Interest in local affairs was not equally shared by those who, in view of their social and economic position, were capable of exerting some influence. As a result, the policies controlling the operation of the high school need not represent the consensus of the influential groups in the community; rather, a large number of potentially influential people could, by default, leave the running of high school affairs to some group of citizens who happened to take an interest in high school affairs.

"Degrees of 'looseness' and 'tightness' of a community structure are perhaps best measured in terms of the administration's opportunity for maneuvering."

The study of the *interaction* between groups having differing composition in terms of local and cosmopolitan influentials represents a definite advance upon the ideas set forth in this paper. The concept of "tight" and "loose" community structures, as connected with the prevailingly local or cosmopolitan orientations of those in strategically placed positions, represents another advance. It is of more than passing interest that this conception of "loose" and "tight" social structures has been independently *developed* by those engaged in the afore-mentioned study and, at a far remove, by Bryce F. Ryan and Murray A. Straus, "The Integration of Sinhalese Society," *Research Studies of the State College of Washington*, 1954, 22, 179–227, esp. 198 ff and 219 ff. It is important to emphasize that these conceptions are being *developed* in the course of systematic empirical inquiry; else one becomes the professional adumbrationist who makes it his business to show that there is literally nothing new under the sun, but the simple expedient of excising all that is new and reducing it only to the old. It is only in this limited sense that one will find the "same" central idea of "rigid" and "flexible" social structures in the writings of that man of innumerable seminal ideas, Georg Simmel. See his essay, translated a half-century ago by Albion W. Small and published in the *American Journal of Sociology* during its early and impoverished years when American sociologists of intellectual taste were compelled to draw upon the intellectual capital of European sociologists: "The Persistence of Social Groups," *American Journal of Sociology*, 3 (1898), pp. 662–98; 829–36; 4 (1898), pp. 35–50. The most compact formulation of the ideas in question is this one: "The group may be preserved (1) by conserving with the utmost tenacity its firmness and rigidity of form, so that the group may meet approaching dangers with substantial resistance, and may preserve the relation of its elements through all change of external conditions; (2) by the highest possible variability of its form, so that adaptation of form may be quickly accomplished in response to change of external conditions, so that the form of the group may adjust itself to any demand of circumstance" (831).

Evidently, the more it changes, the less it is the same thing. The re-emerging concepts of loose and tight social structures resemble the Simmelian observations; they are nevertheless significantly different in their implications.

There is reason to believe that further inquiry will find differing proportions of local and cosmopolitan influentials in different types of community structures. At least this implication can be provisionally drawn from the ongoing studies of technological and social change in a Pennsylvania city during the past 50 years being conducted by Dorothy S. Thomas, Thomas C. Cochran, and their colleagues.[11] Their detailed historical and sociological analysis yields the finding that the city comprised two distinct types of population: "fairly permanent residents, many of whom had been born there, and a migrating group that continually came and went." On the basis of crude statistics of turnover of population in other American cities, the investigators conclude further that this condition is fairly widespread. It may well be that the first, more nearly permanent group includes the local type of influential and the second, relatively transient group, the cosmopolitan. Diverse types of communities presumably have differing proportions of the two kinds of population and the two kinds of influentials.

Other recent studies have found more directly that the proportions and social situations of the two types of influentials vary as the social structure of the community varies. Eisenstadt reports, for example, that a traditional Yemenite community almost entirely lacks the cosmopolitan type, whereas both cosmopolitans and locals play their distinctive roles in several other communities under observation.[12]

On the basis of Stouffer's study of civil liberties, David Riesman suggests ways in which the roles of local and cosmopolitan influentials may differ in different social structures. Cosmopolitans who take on positions of formal leadership in the community, he suggests, may be obliged to become middlemen of tolerance, and they are caught between the upper millstone of the tolerant elite and the nether one of the intolerant majority, and thus become shaped into being less tolerant than their former associates and more so than their constituency. As a result of differing structural context, also, cosmopolitans among the community leaders, themselves more "tolerant" of civil liberties than others, may be in more vulnerable situations in the South than in the East and West. For Stouffer has found that among all but the college-educated, Southerners are far less tolerant of civil liberties than Northerners of like education; "This means," Riesman points out, "that the college graduate in the South is, in these repects, quite sharply cut off from the rest of the community, including even those with some college attendance, for although education is everywhere associated with tolerance, the gradations are much less steep in the North. Moreover, much the same is true in the South for metropolitan communities against smaller cities, though in this dimension there are substantial differences in the East as well.[13]

From this evidence which is only now being accumulated, it would seem that the emergence of the two types of influentials depends upon characteristic forms of environing social structure with their distinctive functional requirements.

---

[11] As reported by Thomas C. Cochran, "History and the Social Sciences," in *Relazioni del X Congresso Internazionale di Scienze Storiche* (Rome, 4–11 September 1955), 1, 481–504, at 487–88 on the basis of Sidney Goldstein, *Patterns of Internal Migration in Norristown, Pennsylvania, 1900–1950*, 2 vol. (Ph.D. thesis, multigraphed, University of Pennsylvania, 1953).

[12] S. N. Eisenstadt, "Communication Systems and Social Structure: An Exploratory Comparative Study," *Public Opinion Quarterly* 19 (1955), pp. 54–67. A study of a small Southern town reports that the two types of influentials cannot be distinguished there; the present suggestion holds that, with the accumulation of research, it is no longer enough to report the presence or absence of the types of influentials. Rather, it is sociologically pertinent to search

out the attributes of the social structure which make for varying proportions of these identifiable types of influentials. See A. Alexander Fanelli, "A Typology of Community Leadership Based on Influence and Interaction within the Leader Subsystem," *Social Forces* 34 (1956), pp. 332–38.

[13] Samuel A. Stouffer, *Communism, Conformity, and Civil Liberties* (New York: Doubleday, 1955) provides the findings under review by David Riesman in his article, "Orbits of Tolerance, Interviewers, and Elites," *Public Opinion Quarterly* 20 (1956), pp. 49–73.

—————————————— 17 ——————————————
Inequality in American communities
Richard F. Curtis and Elton F. Jackson

The six-community design of this research was set up to compare communities which contrasted in ways that we thought might shape local systems of social stratification. The cities differed first in size and region, second in a number of known characteristics such as degree of industrialization, age distribution, and religious history and distribution, and third in a potentially infinite set of unknown and unmeasured characteristics. The question posed in this design was, do American communities represent distinct systems of stratification and contexts for the effects of social rank or do they represent local replications of the stratification of American society?

COMMUNITY DIFFERENCES IN STRATIFICATION

In terms of distributions along the major rank dimensions, our communities differed markedly only with respect to racial-ethnic rank. Although the larger and more industrialized cities were somewhat higher than other cities in achieved characteristics such as income and occupation, the city distributions on the achieved dimensions were basically similar, probably because of the general economic requirements of a community division of labor and corresponding differences in power and influence. The existence of a local economy of course places no necessary limits on the shape of the racial-ethnic distribution. The proportion of any given racial-ethnic group *could* conceivably vary all the way from 0 percent to 100 percent and the amount of actual variation, though less

than that, is nonetheless substantial. Two of our communities had very few members of what we have called minority racial-ethnic groups and the composition of the minorities in the other four cities were quite different.

The processes of rank attainment were basically similar in our six communities. The effects of origin on early attainment and early attainment on later attainment varied little across communities, with two exceptions: There were some differences, unpatterned by region or size, in the determination of income, and the handicaps imposed by minority rank appeared much more consistently in the two larger cities. The basic similarity across cities in process also appeared in the makeup of a principal component extracted from the relationships between all possible pairs of rank dimensions. Nor did the communities differ in the rigidity of the stratification system: All cities exhibited similar, rather high, rates of social mobility and status inconsistency.

We should emphasize the exact meaning of this finding: The *present inhabitants* of each community exhibited, in their life histories, the same process of attainment as the present inhabitants of the other communities. This does not imply that economic conditions are identical in the different communities, but that after migration has sorted people out, communities consist of individuals who have been subject to the same attainment process. If the conditions for rank attainment differ markedly by community, these differences are felt in the selective moving and staying of individuals, rather than in producing populations whose aggregated work histories indicate different processes. For example, when the economic base of a community declines, the result a generation

Reprinted with permission of the authors and publishers from Richard F. Curtis and Elton F. Jackson, *Inequality in American Communities* (New York: Academic Press, 1977), pp. 331–42. Footnotes have been renumbered.

later is not a community of family heads whose educations were not appropriately converted into occupations or incomes, but rather an older population: The "excess" youths have moved to other communities. Hence, the processes exhibited by present populations appear to be more or less similar.

In some aspects of the perceptions of rank and attitudes about the rank system, the communities were similar; with respect to other aspects they differed somewhat. First of all, respondents tended to place themselves in a prelisted set of class titles in much the same way across communities, both in terms of the resulting frequency distribution and in terms of the way in which self-placement was affected by other rank dimensions. However, there were several respects in which the small towns tended to differ from the other cities. Class self-placement was determined less strongly (although in the same fashion) by objective ranks in the small towns. Working-class respondents were less likely to see community dissensus in the small towns. And finally, the generally weak relationship between social rank and attributing legitimacy to the system of attaining success dropped to zero in the small towns, meaning that in this setting the disadvantaged were no more likely than the advantaged to attribute illegitimacy to the system. All these differences were more of degree than of kind.

Also, the statistical results are consistent with (but cannot prove) the proposition that self-placement is determined more by national than by local standards of ranking. That is, it does not appear that the poor attribute much higher status to themselves if they live in a relatively poor community.

In sum, our communities are surprisingly similar in many respects, especially those pertaining to the distribution on various dimensions of achieved rank, the processes for attaining achieved rank, and the processes determining subjective self-placement in a class category. It appears that even sharply different local conditions (size, region, industrial composition, etc.) do not produce sharply contrasting local systems of stratification. For example, stratification is not more rigid and success does not depend more on family background in the small towns. We will suggest below some of the reasons why local communities seem mainly to reflect national stratification patterns in these respects.

Some features of the local setting do appear, however, to have at least mild effects on some aspects of stratification. First, within limits, the distribution on occupation as well as income or education can differ across communities depending on the configuration of the local economy and the extent to which the local economy is totally self-contained. Second, substantial variations are possible with respect to racial-ethnic composition. Third, cleavages and conflict on the basis of rank may be somewhat more severe in the larger communities. In the cities, individuals of low achieved rank are more likely to place themselves in a relatively lower class category, and are more likely to deny legitimacy to the system and perceive political dissensus between businessmen and workers. Conflict between majority and minority also seems more likely, since in the large cities minority handicaps were larger and found at nearly every step of the process.

Finally, there are some trace suggestions in the data that local prestige may influence self-placement more in small towns than in larger cities. Perhaps objective rank explains less of the variance in small towns because local prestige is an important additional factor in those settings. Since our study included no direct measurement of local prestige, these must remain as strictly speculative notions. If local prestige is an important factor in small town stratification systems, it does not act to alter or disrupt the rank attainment processes found in other settings. These processes are found to be more or less similar from setting to setting. The importance of local prestige must be as an additional rank dimension affecting, possibly, perceived status and a variety of attitudes and behavior in addition to the effects of the variables measured in this study.

THE COMMUNITY AS CONTEXT FOR RANK EFFECTS: FORM

The question of this section is whether rank dimensions affect individual behavior in different ways in different community settings. That is, do cities which differ in size or region or other characteristics act as different contexts for the effects of social rank? In the section on rank effects earlier in this chapter, we concentrated on those effects which tended to be found across most communities. In this section, however, we are especially interested in those rank effects which did *not* replicate across our six community samples.

Let us consider hypothetical extremes. The communities could have been so similar as to resemble six samples drawn from the same population. If so, the pattern of rank effects should have been very similar from community to community, differing only due to random fluctuation. The rank effects on anomie came close to this hypothetical extreme. At the other extreme, the direct effects of various social ranks would have to reverse, or otherwise vary widely, from city to city, indicating no general regularities in rank effects. In fact, it would be impossible or the next thing to it to talk about rank effects at all, since every such discussion would have to be with reference to a specific community. In one city, poverty might produce dissatisfaction and anomie, while education reduced anomie, but in the next city in the sample we might see opposite patterns.

Our results for most other dependent variables fell between these two extremes: There was clear evidence that some rank effects occurred more or less consistently from community to community, accompanied by some cross-community fluctuations in the size of these replicable effects. Also, there were some relatively weak effects which fluctuated considerably from city to city. The variations across cities tended to occur within a moderate range. That is, we might observe standardized coefficients for education varying from about .25 to .10 or effects of, let us say, father's education varying from $+.07$ through 0 to $-.07$, but only very rarely would we find a very strong positive effect on a given rank dimension in one city and zero or a strong negative effect of that same dimension in other cities. It is this degree of replication that allowed us to reach the general conclusions on rank effects which were discussed above. For dependent variables strongly affected by social rank, the common effects across cities tended to swamp the variations between cities. Indeed, in many cases the between city variations were fragmentary and virtually uninterpretable. Our analyses of visiting preferences, political orientations, and the forms of intolerance tended to exhibit these consistencies coupled with minor variations. Our analysis of number of associational memberships provides a rare example of a variable powerfully affected by social rank but also exhibiting considerable variations in patterns of effects from community to community.

Cross-community variations in effects showed up principally with respect to those variables that were not powerfully affected by social rank. Our analysis of some aspects of informal and formal social participation tended to show this pattern. The additional variation explainable by taking cross-city differences into account ranged usually between 2 percent and 4 percent. Put differently, there were only infrequent instances where rank explained a considerable amount of variation in a given dependent variable within each city, coupled with substantial differences between cities in patterns of rank effects. In sum, the effects of social rank on individual behavior do tend to vary somewhat depending on the community context, but these variations are usually small relative to the replicable rank effects.

However, the findings fail to explain why the patterns vary the way they do from city to city. We had built size and regional differences into the sample, yet we almost never obtained clear differences in the form of rank effects by size or region. We had also expected that the shape of rank effects might vary depending on the social rigidity (for example, rates of mobility and status inconsistency) in the communities. This hypothesis also failed to work out, because the cities turned out to be more or less similar in their degrees of status rigidity.

The composition of the cities in terms of racial-ethnic status did have clear consequences for these effects. Columbus and Linton, with no measured minority exhibited no important racial-ethnic effects. In addition, for several dependent variables, we observed that racial-ethnic effects were stronger in Indianapolis than in the three Arizona cities, probably reflecting the fact that the minority in Indianapolis was composed almost entirely of blacks while in Arizona the minorities were either Mexican-American or Mexican-Americans combined with blacks. For some dependent variables (such as associational memberships) memberships in the different minorities had opposite consequences.

The effects of father's education, father's occupation and mother's education on many dependent variables tended to vary quite considerably across communities. In part, this was because these effects were relatively weak. However, with respect to some dependent variables the data suggested that the origin ranks had somewhat more effect in the small towns

than in the medium or larger size cities. The effects of father's occupation seemed especially pronounced in the city of Safford.[1] We also had an occasional glimpse of a consistent regional effect; with respect to a few dependent variables such as the forms of formal social participation, the effects of occupation tended to be stronger in Indiana than in Arizona, while the effects of education tended to be stronger in Arizona. None of our analyses, however, have provided a clear reason for this regional effect which in any case only appeared in a few of our regressions.

Those dependent variables which were strongly affected by education tended to show relatively consistent patterns of effects from community to community. Since these tended to be attitudinal rather than behavioral variables, this may account in part for the greater consistency of effects on the attitudinal dependent variables. It would appear that in contemporary American society public education institutions promote greater cultural uniformity (within a given educational level) than do the institutions involved in the other rank systems (such as corporations, ethnic associations, etc.).

As an overall conclusion it appears that the effects of social rank on individual attitudes and behavior within a community are local variations on a basic societal theme. Although the community context does make some nonnegligible differences in the effects of social rank, these contemporary American communities do not represent fundamentally different conditions of life. The patterns of rank effects on individual behavior do, however, vary more from community to community than the patterns of effects of one rank dimension on another. The system of status attain-

---

[1] In comparing the magnitude of the b's associated with various independent variables in the regressions of 25 dependent variables on 17 rank dimensions, the effects of father's occupation were strongest in Safford for a majority of these dependent variables.

ment appears to be more constant across cities than the ways in which social ranks affect other aspects of life. Also, we do not imply that if one picks two communities he can necessarily expect similar multidimensional patterns of rank effects in both. In fact, two extreme communities may differ quite substantially from one another. But neither will differ too greatly from the pattern of the societal average.

THE COMMUNITY AS CONTEXT FOR RANK EFFECTS: STRENGTH

Does social rank constrain behavior in general more in some communities than in others? In this section, we will investigate the strength with which social rank explains attitudes and behavior, regardless of whether the patterns of such rank effects are the same from community to community. Our original, tentative, hypotheses were that positions in the stratification system would be more constraining in Midwestern as compared to Southwestern cities, in small towns as compared to larger cities, and in those communities in which status rigidity was highest, that is, which exhibited lowest rates of social mobility and status inconsistency.

Such questions about the impact of rank in general can only be approached by comparing communities across a range of dependent variables. Our index of constraint is the proportion of variation in a given dependent variable explained by the 17 rank variables within each of the cities. We

have seen in previous chapters some differences among cities with respect to certain dependent variables, for example, that the R^2's yielded by regressing intolerance measures on rank dimensions were generally higher in Arizona than in Indiana cities. In this analysis, we want to ask if any pattern of city differences shows up generally for a large number of dependent variables. From an initial set of 50 dependent variables, we chose the 30 variables for which the 17-variable prediction equation was significant at the .05 level in four or more of the six cities. The other 20 dependent variables were discarded on the grounds that they were essentially not influenced by social rank.

We begin, then, with 180 R^2's, representing the strength of association between a collection of rank variables on the one hand and 30 dependent variables on the other, within each of six cities. With respect to each dependent variable, we ranked the six cities by the size of their R^2's. Each city can be characterized by a distribution of its 30 ranks, by the mean rank of its 30 R^2's, and by the absolute mean of its R^2's. These data are shown in Table 17–1.

If the structure and process of inequality in a given community are clearly more constraining or coercive than in other communities, we would expect that community to have a relatively high mean R^2, but also that many of its 30 R^2's would rank first or second, yielding a mean rank somewhere between 1 and 2. To what ex-

TABLE 17–1
City ranks by amount of variation explained in 30 dependent variables by dimensions of social rank

Rank of R^2	Indianapolis	Columbus	Linton	Phoenix	Yuma	Safford	Total
1 (largest)	11*	5	3	0	3	8	30
2	3	7	7	2	6	5	30
3	4	5	2	4	7	8	30
4	4	5	1	7	8	5	30
5	4	6	12	4	1	3	30
6 (smallest)	4	2	5	13	5	1	30
Mean rank	3.0	3.2	3.9	4.7	3.4	2.8	
Mean R^2	.149	.144	.121	.108	.135	.156	

tent do the results in Table 17–1 allow us to identify several communities as having highly constraining (or, conversely, relatively noncoercive) status systems?

The status system seems to constrain behavior somewhat more in Indianapolis and Safford and somewhat less in Linton and, especially, in Phoenix, as revealed by the mean R^2's and the mean ranks of the R^2's in Table 17–1. Closer inspection of the data, however, indicates that these differences are not so strong nor so regular as to dispel a basic impression that the cities are much alike in the general impact of social status. In the first place, the mean R^2's vary only within a relatively restricted range, from about .11 to about .16. More importantly, the ordering of the cities with respect to the size of the R^2's varies considerably from dependent variable to dependent variable. Rank may have especially strong or weak effects on some given dependent variable in some given city, that is, but the ordering of the cities varies so much by dependent variable that there is no compelling general sense in which the effects of ranks are notably stronger in one city than another. As Table 17–1 makes clear, each city ranked in every possible position with respect to some dependent variable (except for Phoenix, which never yielded the highest R^2)

In this sense, there is little consistency or regularity that gives an authoritative meaning to the way in which cities are ranked according to the average R^2. The variability is so great as to call into question the notion that any city is notable for a strong or weak impact of social stratification in general. At best, we can see some mild city differences in central tendency, but these differences are relatively unstable and relatively weak.[2]

These results disconfirm all the hypotheses which we had tentatively advanced. In the first place, the irregularities in the data incline us not to take the average orders of the cities very seriously. But even in these tentative orderings no clear patterns emerge. Constraint increases with city size in Indiana, but decreases with city size in Arizona. Therefore, there is no clear effect either of size or of region, and we are not inclined to take the interaction of size by region very seriously given both the small number of cases and the lack of any theoretical explanation for such a result. Nor does our hypothesis that social rank exercises more constraint in communities with rigid status systems fare much better. To the limited degree that we were able to order the cities by rigidity, Indianapolis was the most rigid and Yuma was the least. Constraint does appear to be relatively high in Indianapolis, but not as high as it is in Safford, a less status-rigid community. And Yuma, the least rigid community, tends to have a middling position with respect to the degree of average status constraint. In sum, the ordering of the cities with respect to constraint of status on attitudes and behavior is far from regular across dependent variables, shows only mild differences between cities, and does not appear to be due to city differences in size, region, or community rates of mobility and status inconsistency.

IMPLICATIONS OF THE RESULTS ON COMMUNITY DIFFERENCES

The basic question we have been asking is whether a community level of social stratification is important or irrelevant in the U.S. today. We took the importance of a community level to mean that the characteristics of the community would have important effects on the patterns or processes of inequality in the community which in turn might influence the effects of social rank on individual behavior within the community.

American cities are undeniably different

[2] Was this ordering due to the effect of a single rank dimension? The data indicate the answer is no. When we consider, for example, the regressions for the 11 dependent variables that yielded the highest R^2 in Indianapolis, we find that the set of 11 best predictors in these 11 regressions included 7 different rank dimensions.

in many ways; we chose our cities deliberately to contrast strongly in size and region. They also turned out to differ in many other respects. We thought it plausible that differences in many of these community characteristics might well produce differences in social stratification and its workings in the city. First of all, we thought systems of community stratification must vary with community size, for several reasons. Small towns might well have less extended ranges in occupation and income. This might mean that the processes of rank attainment might be different in such places, and also that relative deprivation might be less extreme. In smaller communities, each person should possess more information about other people and therefore a person's present and past social ranks are likely to be widely known in detail. Informal social controls might also be more effective. These factors suggest that a small town resident should find it more difficult to attain a position "inappropriate" to his background or other current ranks. This greater rigidity might also be matched by greater social constraint in a small town, that is, insistence that people's styles of life match their social ranks.

We also expected that community differences in region might be crucial, partly because of regional economies and partly because of regional differences in subculture. It seemed possible that status differences would be more salient in the older regions of the country than in the others. Regional differences in the definition and salience of racial-ethnic rank also seemed potentially important. The extent to which racial-ethnic rank is related to status achievement might well vary from community to community because of the degree of prejudice and discrimination organized into the normative system of the region.

Community differences in economic base might also have important effects on stratification systems. The nature of the major economic activities in the commu-

nity (the importance of manufacturing, for example) should affect the occupation and income distributions in the community. In addition, the prosperity of the community's economy should affect the degree of in-migration which in turn should be related to the extent of social mobility. Since our communities differed deliberately in size and region and turned out to differ substantially in economic activities and in rates of in-migration, as well as in many other respects, we were prepared to find that they differed substantially in their systems of social stratification.

What city differences we found, as summarized above, were not as striking as we might have expected. Indeed, the similarities between the communities were usually so marked as to lead us to think of the cities as local developments of a single underlying pattern, rather than as unique systems of stratification. Our results do not prove that various aspects of rank may not be manufactured within each community, nor that local conditions might not have some influence on social stratification. However, they do suggest that such local phenomena do not seriously alter the process of rank attainment nor the relationships between individual social ranks and individual social behavior.

The differences which we did observe between communities were not clearly patterned by either city size or region. Small towns usually did not differ in any predictable way from the other cities nor were Southwestern cities regularly different from Midwestern cities. We had also thought that stratification systems might operate differently in communities with high as opposed to low rates of mobility and status inconsistency, but this hypothesis was not supported either. (Although our test of this generalization was weak, since our communities did not turn out to differ greatly in these respects.) The only community characteristic which did seem effective was racial-ethnic composition, which, logically enough, did affect the way in which the minority-majority distinction influenced individual behavior within the cities. We concluded that the stratification system of each community seems mainly to be a particular embodiment of a national system of stratification. In most respects, it seems more reasonable to think of the communities as fluctuating around a central process which holds throughout the society, rather than as qualitatively different community systems.

Why are the regularities between communities more marked than the differences? Why should stratification at the level of the society-nation apparently dominate stratification at the community level? We seek here for society-wide processes strong enough to override importance differences in local conditions.

Consider first the "rules" which state how much education is needed for a job, the kinds of job and job performance required for a certain salary, etc., in other words, the rules which translate rank on one dimension into the appropriate rank on another. For several reasons, these rules of translation may well be the same in all communities within this society. Some of these rules may reflect technological requirements of an occupation position which in any community must be met for the successful performance of that job. The culture of the society may also reinforce some of these rules or prescribe others, for example, that doctors require more education than bricklayers. Some rules of translation may take their place in the general culture because of the success of an occupational group in raising standards for entrance to reduce competition, increase prestige, and increase income.

The rules of translation will also tend to be similar throughout the country because they are often administered by business corporation or by labor unions which operate on a national level and hence bring more or less uniform rules into any community they enter. As more of the economy comes to be handled by these national bureaucracies, their standards and practices come to overshadow those of any local community.

Uniformities in the relationships between education, occupation, and income (that is, in the process of rank attainment) may also be encouraged by the operation of national or regional labor markets. Such markets require both widespread communication and migration. Suppose, for example, that a given job in a particular community requires more education or pays less money than the same job elsewhere. If communication (through the mass media or by word of mouth from fellow employees or relatives) is easy and migration is feasible, individuals will seek that same job in that elsewhere. Under these conditions, that is, people who are locally disadvantaged have the right if not the duty to move to another locality where better opportunities exist. Thus, communication and the feasibility of out-migration should press local communities toward rules of translation as favorable (or as unfavorable) as they are elsewhere. This argument is underlined by the fact that a majority of the respondents in all six of our communities were in-migrants.

If migration were not present, each community would have to place in its local occupational structure all persons growing up there. If educational attainment rose while occupations were stable, some relatively well-educated people would have to take medium-prestige jobs, thus changing the education-occupation relationship. But if migration is possible, such persons seek appropriate employment anywhere in the region or in the nation. With the process of rank exchange thus not restricted to local environments, the same pattern of equilibration can appear at all places in the country; the market place for rank exchange thus becomes the whole nation rather than separate markets existing in each community. Communication and migration thus allow and encourage uniform processes of rank attainment throughout the society.

We might expect also that these same

conditions would encourage or at least permit the styles of life of persons of the same rank levels to be rather similar regardless of where they happen to live. Uniform rank effects should also be encouraged if the societal system of distribution is efficient. If the same kinds of goods are available everywhere, then wealth can be converted into the same sorts of consumption in all communities. The distribution of information by the mass media naturally encourages and strengthens this unifying process. Indeed, the mass media are the major system of distribution for many ideas and attitudes, so that as individuals of somewhat different educational levels partake of somewhat different sorts of mass media information throughout the country, attitudinal differences between educational levels tend to become uniform nationwide. The end result is that not only are ranks translated into other ranks in a

similar fashion across the society, but rank levels are also more or less uniformly translated into styles of life.

For these reasons, American communities tend to be similar rather than unique arenas for rank attainment and status display. If people, goods, and information flow more or less freely throughout the society and if the rules of rank translation are more or less uniform, then a picture emerges in which each community contributes its share of the population to the nation's labor force and draws from the national labor force workers for its local occupational structure, but only to a limited degree imposes special conditions on these processes. Hence, local communities, although perhaps unique in many respects, are in their stratification systems mainly local manifestations of a national pattern.

— 18 —
The social economy in urban working-class communities
Martin D. Lowenthal

The struggle for survival by working-class families in America has always been a difficult one. The problems of inadequate income from employment have been noted by many commentators on the American political economic scene. The estimates of the number of persons with incomes below the poverty line range between 25 million and 40 million people, depending upon the standard which is used. For urban working-class families, the more realistic measure of poverty is probably the

one developed by the Bureau of Labor Statistics, which looks at the actual living cost for an urban family of four living under specified conditions. The bureau computes three levels or standards of living— lower, intermediate, and higher—and the lowest standard for a family of four is now in excess of $7,000 per year. This would indicate that approximately 20 percent of the population of the country is near or below the governmental income measures for economic survival. . . .

These excerpts from "The Social Economy in Urban Working-Class Communities," by Martin D. Lowenthal are reprinted from *The Social Economy of Cities*, UAAR, vol. 9 (Gary Gappert and Harold Rose, eds.) © 1975, pp. 447–69 by permission of the Publisher, Sage Publications, Inc.

ECONOMIC FORMULATIONS

In searching for theories and models to assist in an understanding of helping and support networks, the field of economics, as it is articulated at this time, offers very little. When referring to the "economy," economists usually mean the sphere in which goods and services are produced for sale, are sold, and are purchased. This formulation derives out of the basic characteristics of the market economy. A market economy is based on the exchange of goods and services in the market for equivalent value, usually based upon a standardized monetary system. Market exchange depends upon measured payments in the buying and selling of goods and services, and is the organizing principle for transactions involving material products, labor, and natural resources. This means that, in general, people derive their livelihood and meet their needs from selling something in the market; for most people this is their labor.

It has been recognized by most economists that the payment of wages as an essential aspect of the organization of the productive process is a comparatively recent development. In almost every period of recorded history there existed transactions which could be described as the hiring of labor for a contractual payment. However, such transactions were only typical for a small sector of the economic process. Generally work was done and livelihoods gained through systems of social relationships which defined the rewards and responsibilities of the participants. It is only with the breakdown of the feudal restrictions and the replacement of the domestic worker by the factory system that the basis for a general wage system arises. In addition, the gradual monetization of an increasing number of economic transactions provides a further basis. Under these conditions, the "free" but propertyless worker must offer his only possession, his labor power, in order to maintain himself and his family, while the owner of the tools or land, the employer, can obtain the necessary labor force only by inducing people to work for him by offering them a wage.

Labor is thus considered a particular kind of commodity subject to the forces of supply and demand in the marketplace. This formulation of labor power in the industrialized societies of the West has become the sole preoccupation of most economists to the exclusion of other perspectives.

The concern of economists since the 19th century has been the development of economic models which attempt to deal with the question: what are the factors which determine the prices of labor, natural resources, and products in a national, market economy? Activities and transactions not subject to pricing mechanisms have generally been excluded from formal analysis, and thus social scientists and social planners at all levels, by accepting this traditional understanding of the economy, have tended to disregard the significance of women, the family, and the community from their economic analyses and their economic policies.

Other social scientists have also tended to accept these formulations of the nature of the modern economy. For example, Smelser (1963) examines only those activities in the market place as they are affected by or affect sociological variables in terms of status, political position, attitudes, and the family. The discussions of roles, function, authority, status, and change focus on wage labor and business within the context of a market economic system. While recognizing the importance of social dimensions and noneconomic elements in the market system and the impact of the market system on social arrangements, Smelser ignores the economic dimensions of social arrangements which are not necessarily in the market economy.

Within the classical and neoclassical framework of economic thought, a housewife cooking a meal is not performing economic activity, whereas if she were hired to cook a similar meal in a restaurant she would be. A so-called retired person who looks after grandchildren during the day is not performing apparent economic activity, although if the same person were hired to care for children by a day-care center it would be economic activity. If a daughter nurses and cares for a disabled or ill parent, she is not considered to be engaged in economic activity; however, the same work performed in a nursing home or in a hospital would be considered as part of the economic sphere. This conception of "economic" excludes activities within the family and the community, and an anlaysis of the economic dynamics of society based on this conception tends to exclude many economic actors, particularly women, except in their roles as wage earners.

To the extent that households are mentioned by traditional economic theory, they are treated as a collection of individuals who are engaged in the process of production or consumption of goods in the market place. There is no account taken of goods which are produced by a family for its own use—what the Greeks call "householding"—or of those transactions which transpire as part of the social and kinship relationships which make up major portions of people's lives.

This exclusion is most readily seen in the case of women's work, which for a variety of reasons has generally been excluded from the market economy. The responsibilies of women in relation to household management include the jobs of cleaning, maintenance, purchasing of household and family goods and supplies, cooking, laundering, and household planning. In addition to these tasks, the woman is generally responsible for the care, early education, and protection of children, not to mention the labor of bearing children.

Most of these services and goods can be purchased in the market; however, most families are not in financial positions to do so. In addition, the role of the woman, the family, and social relations in times of crisis—during illness of a member of the family or the sudden absence of a wage earner, for example—is crucial to the survival of the family and the maintenance of stability in communities.

If the origins of the term "economics" are traced back to its Greek roots, a basic concern becomes evident. The Greeks gave us the term "oikonomos" which is a compound of the word "oikos," meaning house, and a derivative of "nemein," meaning to distribute or to manage. Thus the word meant household management. The Latin word "oeconomis" meant specifically household management. When economics is approached from the question of how households are managed and maintained, the limitations of the market economy in our modern industrial society become obvious. For example, the poor know that the market system provides them with limited amounts of income through their wages and that this is often insufficient to meet their normal needs for goods and services and provides little protection in times of crisis. They know that only high-income persons can purchase many of the services they provide for themselves in the maintenance of their households, such as child care and household management. They know the importance of relatives, friends, and neighbors in time of illness, family problems, and loss of the job, for the survival of the people in the family and the maintenance of the household over time.

In searching for alternative economic theories to explain the nature, the extent, and the significance of nonmarket, nongovernmental economic transactions, a clue is suggested by Karl Marx. Marx at one point made reference to a larger conception of the economy in the preface to the *Critique of Political Economy*. The economic structure, he wrote, was "the total ensemble of social relations entered into in the social production of existence." However, from this broad starting point, Marx narrows his concern to the study and critique of market capitalist economies. The bulk of his theory and concerns revolves around the class structure as it is derived from the operations of capitalism.

This same limitation appears to apply to a lesser extent to the work of Engels (1942). In his *Origin of the Family, Private Property, and the State*, Engels attempted to write a history of the family from a materialist and economic viewpoint. He saw production and reproduction of "immediate life" as the determining factor in history. By this he meant the production of the goods and services by which people subsist as well as the production of "human beings themselves." By reproduction he meant not only simply physical reproduction but also socialization and care and protection. Social institutions are in turn conditioned by both these kinds of production—by the stage of development and organization of labor for subsistence and by the organization of the family for reproduction. Engels described the family as being an important determinant of the historical development of societies in that it determined much of what occurred in the process of reproduction.

For Engels, the ties of sex within the family play a more important role in the division of labor in societies in early stages of development; however, as production processes are developed, the family system becomes dominated by the forces of the property system in which class distinctions evolve around the ownership of the means of production and class conflict develops. According to Engels, the role of women was always domestic. In early hunting societies the domestic role of the woman is strong and primary vis-à-vis the male hunter and warrior. With the development of cultivation and domestication of animals, the pastoral shepherd and the farmer with their own property become the dominant force, and the claims of property dominate the social relations between the sexes and within the family. Later anthropologists have questioned the view that the social relations within the family were and are always consistent with particular property relations and that the stages of development of production and reproduction have followed universal patterns.

ANTHROPOLOGICAL FORMULATIONS

The field which has contributed most to the description of nonmarket exchange systems is anthropology. Anthropologists tend to examine the economic significance of all forms of social relationships. They also describe the units of social relations in terms of the factors which make them cohesive and in terms of how the units themselves are bound economically, socially, and politically into larger systems.

One of the few community studies that examines the mechanisms and significance of nonmarket economic activities is the investigation by Arensberg and Kimball (1968) of rural communities in Ireland in the 1930s. Production activities in these rural communities are limited to the production of farm goods and goods produced in the home for use by the family. The family is the primary economic unit with labor divided on the basis of sex and age. The work done by women is considered essential and an integral component of the total production scheme. The mother in the family is responsible for the management of the household, all work done within the home, the care of the children, the care of chickens and smaller farm animals, and lighter farm work. The father is in charge of the farm as a whole and does all of the heavy farm labor. The children are required to begin working early in life and assist the parent of their own sex in work on the farm.

The economic nature of the family is apparent in all aspects of daily life. A major criterion for the choice of a marriage partner is the potential economic contribution of the individual. Arensberg and Kimball note that the immediate family of husband, wife, and children carry on a kind of "corporate economy" in which the economic aspects are part and parcel of life of the basic social unit.

The secondary economic unit in the social economic system in rural Ireland is the community. The "community" refers to the families whose homes and farms are in the vicinity surrounding any particular farm. The communities will often consist of one or more extended families which are bound by an intricate network of kinship ties. The ties between community members were reported to have strong economic dimensions. The word "cooring" is used by people in these communities to describe all types of nonmonetary economic cooperation among neighbors. The word is derived from the Irish "comhair" which is used similarly. The authors observed that this nonmonetary cooperation betwen families takes the following forms: lending tools, assisting with labor, lending a member of the family to assist in farm work, pooling goods such as butter, lending a girl when extra help is needed in the household, helping in times of distress or crisis, communal harvesting, and obligations surrounding rites of passage and ceremonies.

Other anthropological works, particularly those concerned with tribal societies, contain many observations and descriptions about the operation of social economic systems which are primarily nonmonetized. The works of Richards (1932), Watson (1958), Epstein (1962), Ishwaran (1966), and Bohannan and Dalton (1962) are examples of such studies. However, there have been few attempts to treat the economies of these societies outside the framework of classical Western economics. Polanyi (1968) and Dalton (1971) have noted the limitations of the analytic power of traditional economic theory in anthropology and have suggested some alternative categories for a better comparative analysis of economic systems. On the basis of empirical studies, Polanyi suggests that economic activities fall into three main patterns. The first he calls "reciprocity" which

is illustrated by the ritualized gift-giving among families, clans, and tribes—as can be seen in the works of Malinowski and Mauss, for example. Another illustration of reciprocity is the cooperation among farming families to assist each other in the building of barns, known as "barn raising," and the mutual assistance they lend to each other at harvest times. In patterns of reciprocity, goods and services are given because of bonds which mutually obligate the parties involved. The rights and obligations of each party are usually determined according to some traditional concept of how they are supposed to relate socially.

The second pattern noted by Polanyi was "redistribution." This involves the gathering of economic goods and services to some form of central place—usually controlled by governmental or religious agents—and then redistributing the goods and services throughout the populace. Polanyi notes that many Asian societies and African tribes utilize this economic pattern of behavior and that, like reciprocity, redistributive patterns are characterized by the absence of equivalency calculations and price mechanisms. The principle of calculation in redistribution patterns seems to be one of a kind of "justice"—namely, determining what each class in the population traditionally deserves.

The third pattern noted by Polanyi is that of "exchange," by which he means the exchange of economic goods and services within some form of market context. Under exchange, prices and distribution are not determined on the basis of tradition but are the result of bargaining mechanisms which adjust and match supply and demand.

Although Polanyi and his associates and followers applied these categories to the study of primitive and nonindustrial systems, this type of analysis was not extended into the investigation of modern industrial society. Polanyi argues, particularly in his work *The Great Transformation* (1957), that the nonmarket patterns of economic intergration which prevailed in archaic economies were supplanted in the 19th century by the growth of the market economy under capitalism. Polanyi argues that the market economy transformed the whole of society and harnessed the economic and productive dimensions entirely to the institutional mechanism of the market. "The rise of the market to a ruling force in the economy can be traced by noting the extent by which land and food were mobilized through (market) exchange, and labor was turned into a commodity free to be purchased in the market." Polanyi argues that in the 19th century the organization of production under a market economy—when needs for food, clothing, and shelter had to be met through the purchase of commodities—hunger and gain became purely "economic." Thus, the meeting of basic needs was linked with the production system through the need of "earning an income." In order to get an income, a person needed to sell some goods in the market. For workers this meant that unless they had land to rent or ownership of a capital means of production, they had to convert their labor power into a commodity and sell it in the market place for wages. "No propertyless person could satisfy his craving for food without first selling his labor in the market." For Polanyi the rise of capitalism in the market economy transformed all resources, goods, services, and labor into commodities which were bought and sold in the market place, and thus the whole of society was transformed.

Polanyi, like Marx, overstated the extent to which the dynamics of the capitalist market organized the economic activities of Western societies. There is growing historical, sociological, and anthropological evidence that a large portion of goods and services are produced and distributed through mechanisms other than the market and governmental intervention. It has become clear that low-wage working-class populations are particularly dependent upon nonmonetized, nonmarket systems of production and exchange. The operations of these systems permit working-class families to survive and to reproduce, and in this sense they have also played a crucial historical role in the development of industrial capitalist societies. If survival had in fact been totally dependent upon the income derived from selling of labor in the market place, many workers would have perished or would have had to receive significantly higher wages than they did. In either case, the growth and development of large-scale capitalist enterprises would have been severely limited. In this way, the organization of production and the development of capitalism in Western society has depended upon the existence of other economic units such as the family and the community, and the economic functions which they perform. For example, the wage-labor system is sustained by the economically and socially necessary labor of housewives and mothers as they perform such functions as child rearing, cleaning, food preparation, property maintenance, health care, household purchasing, and reproduction; these are all necessary to maintaining life.

TOWARD A THEORY OF THE SOCIAL ECONOMY

The thesis of this paper is that many goods and services are provided through an economic system which is based on the network of social relationships. I call this economic system "the social economy," since the economic transactions which are being considered are imbedded in and based on the network of social relationships which people maintain over time.[1] These transactions have characteristics which suggest that they be treated as a system. They are a structured set of ar-

---

[1] For analytical purposes those systems in which economic transactions are primarily based in social relationships are social economies. It should also be noted that there are social economic dimensions in all economies and that the study of these dimensions is the study of the field of "social economy."

rangements for providing material goods and services. In addition, they are governed by certain rules which integrate the transactions and interdependencies and assure the continued cooperation of those involved in the provision of goods and services.[2]

The economic aspects of social relationships in the social economy are usually not primary; the relationships are based on other principles of organization which give them their primary significance and meaning, such as kinship, tradition, religion, friendship, community, or neighborhood. This is not to say that the economic dimension is not important, for it may play a vital role in maintaining the ties between the participants. The rules for the initiation and maintenance of relationships in the social economy derive out of the cultural values and social norms for the relationship in which the participant is engaged. For example, among some ethnic groups it is expected that grandparents will assist in the care and socialization of grandchildren. In many communities neighbors who are friendly with the corner grocer or pharmacist may purchase items on credit without interest or collateral and without a credit check. Neighbors may borrow food or share appliances. Parents may provide a newlywed couple with some funds to begin a household, and sons and daughters may provide money to help their parents in their old age.

One of the operating principles of the social economy is that of reciprocity. Reciprocity is the mutual recognition of rights, responsibilities, and privileges. This means that a party in a relationship has certain rights to goods and services from others in meeting his/her needs. The others in the relationship have the responsibility to respond to that need. In return the party is obligated to respond to certain needs of the others in the relationship.

In complex situations, the patterns of reciprocity may not be so obviously two-way. For example, members of a particular kin group need not reciprocate with one another but may do so with the corresponding members of a third kin group toward which they stand in an analogous relationship. Among the Trobriand islanders, the man's responsibility is toward his sister's family, but he himself is not necessarily assisted by his sister's husband. If he is married, he is assisted by his own wife's brother—a member of a third family. The point is that the rights and the corresponding responsibilities apply to all participants in the network of social relationships according to mutually accepted criteria.

In communities in which resources and commodities are very scarce, reciprocal arrangements tend to operate as a redistribution mechanism. Scarce goods are thereby spread among members and to those in need. One of the important reasons for this sharing and giving is that those who are poor realize how dependent they are upon familial, neighborhood, and community networks for their day-to-day survival and for assistance in times of crisis. Realizing this dependency, a family will tend to share its resources and services with those in need, with the expectation of having its own needs met at the appropriate time by others within the network.

The principle of reciprocity involves another principle for effective operation—the principle of adequacy of response. Unlike market-exchange transactions in which mathematical equivalencies are computed and in which the value of the good or service you give in an exchange is theoretically equivalent to the good or service you receive and is standardized in money terms, the principle of adequacy of response requires that those responding to a need do so as fully as they are able even though the person in need may not have responded to others to the same extent, owing to his own limitations. For example, a family may pass on outgrown children's

---

[2] The literature on social networks is useful in tracing the social economic arrangements and activities discussed in this paper. Of particular value is Mitchell (1969).

clothing to relatives with a newly born baby and the recipient family, in responding to the donor's needs during a time of illness of the mother for a few days, may do the cooking for the donor family. In another instance a grandmother may care for the children of her daughter during the day while the daughter works, and in turn may be able to turn to the daughter for extra cash when the rent is due, or utility bills must be paid, or when medical bills arise.

Cohesive, stable working-class communities have generally developed intricate and complex systems of reciprocal arrangements which can be effective as redistribution mechanisms within the community. These reciprocal arrangements are also important for the survival and integration of the community itself over time and help cement the social relationships themselves. The redistributional aspect of the social economy is particularly important in integrating groups in communities and assuring the permanence of the arrangement. The participants in the relationships are able to derive a measure of security within a larger society in which they are considered marginal by wage-market standards.

Another allocation principle which operates in the social economy in many communities can be called "command-subordinate." This allocation mechanism is based on hierarchical relationships in which a person in a superordinate position can command another person in a subordinate position to produce and deliver goods and services to him. The superordinate person usually has some form of recognized authority within the relationship or has the coercive resources to insure the hierarchical direction of transactions. This kind of relationship must be distinguished from those legal and governmental relationships where a person is acting as an agent of a legally constituted and recognized government.

Within command-subordinate relations and transactions there may be elements of reciprocity involved. A subordinate, in return for certain services, may be entitled to expect protection and sometimes assistance in times of need. However, the subordinate is not an equal partner is the relationship and does not have the authority or power to determine when and how much the person in command will deliver. These forms of relationships can be seen within certain family structures, within hierarchical kinship systems, within gangs, and within communities which have hierarchically organized patronage systems.

In many cases the superordinate in a command-subordinate set of relationships has many functions. If the person is a political boss of some sort, he may serve as the broker between his community constituency and the larger society. In this instance he is an advocate for the community in obtaining resources from the larger society and an advocate for the larger society in obtaining the community support for outside interests. In some instances the superordinate has the role of keeping order within the society and of maintaining certain community structures. The superordinate may also be an important mechanism by which redistribution of resources within the community takes place. By being able to command goods and services from people, he can also distribute them to others within a social network or community. This form of redistribution resembles the kind of central redistribution principles discussed by Polanyi.

Another allocation principle which operates in many traditional working-class communities is what might be called "ascriptive-prescription." In this case people with certain ascribed characteristics or statuses receive goods and services from others in the network according to certain prescribed rules. Gifts and various forms of assistance when a person has reached a certain age often fall within this category. A person who is considered incapable either physically or mentally may often be entitled to assistance from members of his social network because of his incapacity according to certain customs and traditions. An elder in a community may receive goods and services from people because of his age and status. A widow may be entitled to certain forms of assistance from kin and from people in the community until she remarries. A person who works within a religious order, such as a rabbi, a minister, or a priest, may be entitled to services from the community because of his religious calling and status.

This allocation mechanism can play an important role in the redistribution of resources within a community. In many instances it serves to provide goods and services to those who are considered to be legitimately incapacitated or exempt from having to engage in wage labor because of some highly valued calling or purpose. The rules which govern this form of allocation are usually established by custom and tradition, and these are exhibited most strongly in kin networks, communities, and societies which have resisted many of the values and orientations of modern industrial society.

REFERENCES

Arensberg, C., and S. Kimball (1968) *Family and Community in Ireland.* Cambridge: Harvard University Press.

Bohannan, P., and G. Dalton, eds. (1962) *Markets in Africa.* Evanston: Northwestern University Press.

Dalton, G. (1971) *Economic Anthropology and Development.* New York: Basic Books.

Engels, F. (1942) *The Origin of the Family, Private Property, and the State.* New York: International.

Epstein, S. (1962) *Economic Development and Social Change in South India.* Manchester: Manchester University Press.

Fried, M. (1965) "Transitional Functions of Working-Class Communities," in M. Kantor, ed. *Mobility and Mental Health.* Springfield, Ill.: Charles C. Thomas.

Ishwaran, K. (1966) *Tradition and Economy in Village India.* London: Routledge & Kegan Paul.

Komarovsky, M. (1967) *Blue-Collar Marriage.* New York: Random House.

Marris, P. (1958) *Widows and Their Families.* London: Routledge & Kegan Paul.

Marx, K. (1967) *Critique of Political Economy.* New York: International.

Mitchell, J. C. (1969) *Social Networks in Urban Situations.* Manchester: Manchester University Press.

Polanyi, K. (1968) *Primitive, Archaic and Modern Economics: Essays of Karl Polanyi.* G. Dalton, ed. Boston: Beacon.

Richards, A. (1932) *Hunger and Work in a Savage Tribe.* New York: Meridian.

Smelser, N.J. (1963) *The Sociology of Economic Life.* Englewood Cliffs, N.J.: Prentice-Hall.

Stack, C. B. (1974) *All Our Kin: Strategies for Survival in a Black Community.* New York: Harper & Row.

Townsend, P. (1957) *Family Life of Old People.* London: Routledge & Kegan Paul.

Watson, W. (1958) *Tribal Cohesion in a Money Economy.* Manchester: Manchester University Press.

Young, M., and P. Willmott (1957) *Family and Kinship in East London.* London: Penguin.

19
The community social profile
Irwin T. Sanders

Sociologists, who for a long time have been subjecting the community to intensive study, are frequently asked by action-oriented professional persons to assist in the preparation of the studies they undertake or to review the results they have obtained. Such assistance, which includes the careful analysis of all available statistical data, must go beyond these figures to community characteristics not already quantified. What is called for in many cases is a short-run, easily administered method which, though lacking in completeness of detail, nevertheless is accurate as far as it goes and at the same time penetrating enough to be helpful in program planning. This is a report of one such method which, through a clearly-formulated reconnaissance, makes possible the preparation of a community social profile essentially sociological in content. Its utility has been tested over a 20-year period in states as widely diverse as New York, Alabama, Kentucky, and Massachusetts.

THE FEATURES OF THE METHOD

The research team

In any short-cut approach there must be relatively little waste motion. Thus, research assistants must already have some skill in interviewing, some knowledge of how the data are to be processed, and some understanding of the community as a sociological concept. The tasks confronting such a research team are the interviewing of from 25 to 40 people in a local community, pulling together pertinent statisti-

Reprinted with permission of the author and the American Sociological Association from Irwin T. Sanders, "The Community Social Profile," *American Sociological Review* 25, no. 1 (February 1960), pp. 75–77.

cal support, and collecting available maps, documents, and newspapers which have some bearing upon the community situation. It is important to stress that this is essentially a sociological and not a social action undertaking. Its purpose is to describe competently and economically the chief social traits of the community; it is not designed to train the untrained citizen in community survey techniques.

Where possible, four or five people are formed into a team in preference to the more extended labors of a lesser number. This builds more cross-checking into the operation because more trained people are reacting to the community and interacting with each other. Ordinarily, each interviewer averages from two to three interviews per day, that is, 10 to 15 man-days in the cases of communities where 30 interviews suffice. Four or five workers can carry out the necessary data collection in less than a week's time.

Data collection

As already indicated, the chief schedule is one designed for administration to community leaders who, as experience has shown, have more knowledge about the community since they are accustomed to think of problems in a broader context than those whose major interests center almost exclusively around their jobs and their own homesteads. Experience also shows that, far from presenting a united and closed front, these leaders reveal in their responses the existence of the major groupings and social divisions one must investigate.

The "Community Leader Schedule" has undergone some modifications through the years but it remains essentially open-ended. It calls for data about the informant, social organizations and their leaders, and the "institutional" areas of church, school, economy, recreation, and local government. It asks what the informant likes best about the community and what he considers to be its chief problems, about social issues over the past five years, and major changes underway; and it asks the informant to list eight people whom he considers to be important community leaders and to give the reasons for their selection. Many of these questions, such as the one requesting the listing of community leaders, are carefully phrased and presented to each informant in a standardized way. But usually the main purpose of the questions is to prompt the informant to talk about his community with respect to certain topics set forth on the schedule. When these comments are fully recorded it turns out that what some people have called a "deceptively simple" schedule has elicited a wealth of valuable information.

But who are these key leaders to be interviewed? How are they determined? Before beginning a community study an effort is made to identify some of them, with whom appointments are arranged by telephone. When this is not possible the first three or four schedules are "wasted," that is, people are contacted who occupy positions which would seem to give them some knowledge of the community and

who, in addition to answering other questions, are asked to name the eight most important leaders.[1] After two or three interviews the tabulation of the names mentioned may be initiated and subsequent interviews held with the "most frequently mentioned." Communities vary, of course, in the extent to which the leadership is concentrated and the frequency with which the same people are mentioned. Nevertheless the leadership structure begins to emerge quite clearly after only a few interviews with well-informed citizens. In some studies, even of cities of 100,000 inhabitants, 20 interviews cover all of the leaders mentioned as many as three times, illustrated by the actual distribution for such a city shown in Table 19–1.

It is assumed that completing the total universe of those named as leaders, which is the crucial aspect of this method, would not have changed the rank order materially, nor would it have brought to light more than five or six other individuals not previously named. Long before all of those listed have been interviewed one is able to predict many of the answers an informant

---

[1] This approach may be compared with the approaches followed by Floyd Hunter, Delbert C. Miller, Peter H. Rossi, Robert O. Schulze, and others who have studied "power structure," "influentials," "economic dominants," and other types of local elites.

TABLE 19–1
Frequency distribution of mentions as key community leaders, New Bedford, Massachusetts, 1958

Number of times listed (out of 23 possibilities)	Number of persons listed this number of times	Total mentions (col. 1 × col. 2)
18	1	18
16	1	16
15	1	15
12	1	12
11	1	11
10	1	10
8	2	16
5	6	30
4	2	8
3	4	12
2	8	16
1	34	34
	62 people	198 mentions

will give, but the interviewing is continued in the hope that exceptions to the rule will be uncovered and thus reveal facets of community life that might not otherwise emerge. The team members find little difficulty in deciding where to "cut-off" the interviewing for they agree that they have gone well beyond the point of diminishing returns.

The leaders, however, do not necessarily represent all of the important social divisions which have been identified in the community. In this case, interviews are conducted with the spokesmen for these other groupings, starting with those suggested by the community leaders when they were asked to describe the community's significant social divisions. The interviews with these subleaders seek to determine how the divisions they represent fit into the overall community framework and only incidentally delve into the psychological problems of those involved.

Another aspect of the collection of data deals with contradictions in perceptions on the part of the informants. It is assumed from the beginning that these differential perceptions will be encountered, but it is expected that in some measure they will be consistent with socioeconomic characteristics and other social traits uncovered. When these perceptions run counter to previous experience or to theoretical expectations, further interviewing is required to account for the variation. In such cases, some leader already interviewed who has demonstrated a capacity to analyze such matters objectively may be revisited and asked to clear up the seeming difficulty.

The interview materials are checked with data collected from other sources. These include local histories, promotional literature prepared by the chamber of commerce, surveys and studies in such applied fields as health and education, statistical series of various kinds, and local newspapers. All of this material not only serves to cross-check what informants say but provides a depth of detail which proves most useful in preparing the community profile.

Analysis and preparation of the social profile

As soon as the field work has been completed the research team meets to decide on those social traits[2] which require stress if a useful picture of the community is to be obtained. This selection is necessary on two counts: description of all traits would not be in order even if there were data available since the purpose of the social profile is to highlight rather than to catalog the characteristics of the community; there are some traits not central to the inquiry about which the team believes that insufficient data have been collected for an adequate treatment. Both the research team and the reader need to keep in mind what can be stated with confidence and what should be set forth as mere conjecture.

By using practically the same schedule in every community almost the same ground is covered in each study, permitting some comparability between communities. This very comparability allows the selection of a special combination of traits for a particular community as the pattern best describing its social features. This is why tables of contents of social profiles will read differently. Yet these variations grow out of what is essentially a comparative approach.

The traits to be described form the working outline in terms of which the analysis of the data proceeds. The data relating to each trait are excerpted on cards so that the person writing up that section will have before him all pertinent comments. Different team members are as-

---

[2] These traits include those that sociologists would conventionally look into: social divisions and other evidences of stratification; institutional behavior (religion, local government, economy, education, family, recreation); major organizations and their interaction; evidences of major current changes; leadership structure; issues or major community problems as defined locally; indications of competing or conflicting value systems.

signed different topics in keeping with their training and with the types of informants they had encountered as the interviewing appointments were made.

Needless to say, any differences in points of view among the team members about a particular trait are ironed out by reexamination of the data, by a telephone call to some competent local informant, or by another field trip to the community. In preparing the study, budget provision is always made for a final "clean-up trip" when the report itself is nearing completion. But such a trip is seldom necessary if the methods outlined above have been carefully followed.

UTILITY AND APPLICATION OF THE APPROACH

This approach, of course, has a serious limitation: it is idiosyncratic, being designed to gather information about one community to serve some particular purpose. Those who engage in several successive studies of this sort gain a general understanding of community structure and processes although the methods used are not designed to demonstrate its validity. Therefore this approach does not have the cumulative value that other types of research may possess.[3] Granting this limita-

tion, it in no way reduces the utility of a well-executed reconnaissance report for those professionally interested in local social action programs.

In New England recently some of its possible applications have proven very interesting. An industrial firm wanted to know which of two New England towns was a better location for a new industrial facility on the basis of social traits alone. Another concern was interested in the connection between the controversy over industrial zoning and the general community traits; a third wished to learn whether or not a given community was a place to which engineers would be attracted.[4] In each of these cases the point was accepted that the easiest way to answer the central question was to use the reconnaissance method described here. Only after the overall social profile had been completed could a special "peel-off" report be prepared concerning the specific questions which had initiated the larger study. This same approach is adapted for use by local health departments, planning boards, school boards, library boards, and united community services, the representatives of which see their groups' activities in a new perspective when confronted with the overall picture provided by the community social profile.

---

[3] Samuel A. Stouffer is directing a project, in which the present writer is also engaged, designed to break through the idiosyncratic limitation of this approach. Through the use of special schedules and predetermined types of informants, an effort is being made to standardize information gained about cleavages, issues, and key leadership structure so that many communities can be studied simultaneously and generalizations can be derived. Field tests of the instruments are still underway.

[4] These queries and the resulting studies have been channeled through the Community Analysis Division of Associates for International Research, Inc., a private applied social science research company located in Cambridge, Massachusetts, of which the writer has been serving as part-time Research Director.

20

Persistance of local sentiments in mass society

Albert Hunter

A specter is haunting the rise of modern mass society, the specter of the isolated, alienated urbanite, uprooted, roaming un-attached through the streets of the city, a perpetual stranger, fearful but free. The purpose of this chapter is to trace this illusion and to assess its validity in the light of recent research. In the process we will see that the specter may be likened to a cloud: in part it is a wispy light entity full of holes through which rays of sunlight and blue sky pour through, while in part it is what the observer chooses to make of it, an imaginary beast of a benevolent or malev-olent mein. We must be careful in observ-ing and interpreting this specter, however, for it carries some of the more emotional concepts in the sociological literature—sentiment and attachment, community and kinship, neighbor and friend. We will have to be careful to maintain the eye of the sociological skeptic, being as neutral as possible, so that we more clearly under-stand and predict its fate.

Therefore, we must first establish the value positions that too often underlie dis-cussions of this topic. The first centers around a nostalgic yearning for the small community that many feel has been lost in today's world. Intertwined with this yearning is a nostalgia not only of place but also of time, as Kevin Lynch has noted in his book *What Time Is This Place?* (1972). The positive sentiments of past time and place are often juxtaposed with negative

sentiments toward the present, and polar-ities abound contrasting the simple with the complex, the innocent with the worldly, and the known with the un-known. The filtered past comes to us as known pattern, but the raw present pre-sents daily confusions that seem to def understanding.

A second bias centers around the con-notations of the word *community*. Ther exists an inherent bias not only in the la conception but more nefariously withi social science itself toward viewing con-munity as an unqualified good. The posi-tive connotations of friendliness, warmtł and support are seldom countered wit the accompanying characteristics of coi straint and conformity, and the loss of pr vacy, individualism, and freedom. We wi not debate these points except insofar a they have assumed a central position i sociological theories or have been explore empirically as variables in sociological re search. Instead, we will attempt to de scribe and define community and to ur derstand more clearly the sentiments assc ciated with it.

Finally, we must not confuse sentimer with sentimentalism. I will paint no ro mantic or romanticized pictures but rathe will treat sentiments as legitimate indivic ual and collective variables in the study communal life. In short, to study sent ments, we must take care not to be sent mental ourselves.

Reprinted with permission from the author and publisher from Albert Hunter "Persistance of Local Sentiments in Mass Society," in *Handbook of Contemporary Urban Life*, ed. David Street and Associates (San Francisco: Jossey-Bass, 1978), pp. 134–56.

THEORETICAL LEGACY

The initial visions of the specter I hav just alluded to are to be found in the majo writings of the classical social theorists, such as Marx, Weber, Durkheim, and Simmel. Their theories have been propagated elsewhere, as in Stein's *The Eclipse of Community* (1960), Nisbet's *The Quest for Community* (1953), and most trenchantly in the often cited article "Urbanism as a Way of Life" by Wirth (1938). To use Stein's categories, the argument simply put is that the major social transformations of the 18th and 19th centuries, urbanization, industrialization, and bureaucratization, produced a social structure that destroyed the previous local affinities such as kinship and community. It is as if these parochial sentiments and attachments were lost in the sheer size and density of cities, clouded over by the smog and smoke from factories and crushed lifeless under the bulk of the bureaucratic forms.

Although each of the classical statements may vary slightly in the specific characteristics emphasized in the emerging "mass society," the effect on local sentiments and attachments is generally interpreted in the same way—they will either be destroyed or lost. However, . . . the eclipse is partial, the destruction incomplete, and the loss limited.

. . . [W]e will begin our discussion with the 19th-century social theorists who described the transformation of Western society. To Stein's three global processes of urbanization, industrialization, and bureaucratization, we should add the massive immigrations that accompanied these, and the rise of nationalism and the modern nation-state.

For Marx (1956), the rise of capitalism out of and in opposition to the feudal order, based on tradition, land, the estates, and subinfeudation, presented a new social order based on a growing distinction between social classes. The bonds of community were being replaced by market relations just as the market itself became the organizing unit replacing the feudal estate. The growing density of the factors of production in cities during the later stages of industrial capitalism was seen to be a critical factor in the emergence of a new social bond, the bond of the working class with class consciousness that would replace the social bond of the traditional community. The community of land, epitomized in the agricultural peasantry, was seen to be at best a conservative, if not reactionary, force.

For Durkheim (1964), the increasing division of labor in society was seen to be an outcome of the increasing ecological density that in turn arose from the human propensity to aggregate. Out of the ecological density arose a dynamic "moral density," resulting in a diversity of interests and an organic social order based on difference and interdependence. The old mechanical order of similarity and shared interest gave way to diversity exemplified in the increasing division of labor. As in Marx's interpretation, however, the fall of the local community as a basis of social order would not long leave a vacuum, for in its stead one would find the rapid rise of work-related associations of interest. Defining these in occupational rather than in class terms, Durkheim emphasized the job-related homogeneity of interest, which implied a greater number and diversity of social solidarities than did Marx's classes. However, this new solidarity was not totally devoid of communal sentiments, for underlying the diversity of interests expressed in the organic social order would always remain some communal sentiments. However, these would be directed not toward parochial places as in the past but toward the overarching, emerging nation-state, which laid claim to monopolizing (among other things) personal allegiance and collective sentiments. The old local community was replaced by the new community of the nation-state.

For Weber (1958), the central process was one of an increasing rationalization or "demystification" of modern life. Rationality became formally embodied in the bureaucratic structure of organized social life.

Like Marx's industrial, capitalistic classes and Durkheim's urbanized, occupational groups, the ideal bureaucracy for Weber became the object of new allegiance that would supersede parochial sentiments. Efficiency and rationality became central values within the new social organization, which viewed the irrationality of sentiments in general and sentiments of community in particular as anathema.

Where Durkheim stressed the *nation* as the communal underpinning of the new nation-state, Weber stressed the *state* as the efficient structure that would maintain social order through its exclusive right to use violence.

A more vivid description of the developing specter of modern urban life was presented by Simmel (1950) in his essay "The Metropolis and Mental Life." Considering the market, the money economy, and the division of labor from the previous theories as key structural characteristics of the modern metropolis, Simmel then spelled out their sociopsychological consequences for individuals. The size, density, and heterogeneity that Wirth (1938) was later to emphasize were seen to lead to a cognitive and psychic overload that required the urbanite to blur distinctions and to become more categorical and less discriminating as well as more objective and less subjective—in short, to develop the aloof, blasé urban attitude. What some might have seen as tolerance for diversity, others saw as indifference. The demands for efficiency, punctuality, and specialization occasioned by the division of labor resulted in a narrowing of personality, a uniqueness that was rightly linked to individualism and freedom but that was objectively and not subjectively defined. People were different, given the diversity and division of labor, but at the price of not developing full personalities or interacting with and experiencing others as full personalities. People become things as their relationships become defined through the money economy and the market: "By

being the equivalent to all the manifold things in one and the same way, money becomes the most frightful leveler. . . . All things float with equal specific gravity in the constantly moving stream of money" (Simmel, 1950, p. 414). The result, according to Simmel, is that "the individual has become a mere cog in an enormous organization of things and powers which tear from his hands all progress, spirituality and value" (p. 422).

In summary, the historical legacy presented a picture in which the rise of modern mass society destroyed more parochial communal forms of association. Community was superseded by the overarching, industrial, bureaucratized nation-state, propelling every person toward individualism and freedom with the accompanying isolation, alienation, and anomie. New forms of association developed but did not rest on the broad-based, personal, and territorial sentiments of community; rather, they resulted from the narrow, specific, rational interests of individuals. The world was no longer one of people in communities but rather one of people against society.

COMMUNITY LOST— THE EMPIRICAL LEGACY

The study of the loss of local community sentiments in mass society is most clearly exemplified by two general empirical traditions: the research of the Chicago School of the 1920s and 1930s, which focused on the disorganization of primary kinship and ethnic bases of solidarity within Chicago's neighborhoods; and research on the transformation of small-town life as a result of the increasing scale of social organization at both the metropolitan and national levels. Exemplary studies of this transformation include Warner's *Yankee City* (1963), the Lynds' *Middletown* (1929) and *Middletown in Transition* (1937), and Vidich and Bensman's *Small Town in Mass Society* (1968).

The Chicago School. The research of the Chicago School has often been interpreted, somewhat inaccurately, as positing a ubiquitous disorganization of urban primary ties of neighbors and kin. This misreading stems largely from the emphasis placed on Wirth's "Urbanism as a Way of Life" (1938), which was considered to be a summary statement of the empirical research of the Chicago School. To be sure, much of the Chicago research did focus on the social problems of the day, such as family disorganization (Mowrer, 1927), mental illness (Faris and Dunham, 1939), crime and delinquency (Thrasher, 1926), transient marginal populations like *The Hobo* (Anderson, 1923) and *The Unadjusted Girl* (Thomas, 1927), and institutions that catered to these populations, such as *The Taxi Dance Hall* (Cressey, 1932). However, one must remember that these researchers had a specific social-problem orientation often coupled with an ameliorative policy perspective. These studies were, in fact, deviant case analyses and are often inaccurately interpreted as representing the full picture of urban life during this period.

A second series of studies on the ethnic groups that migrated to Chicago and settled in segregated "natural areas" also resulted in declining ethnic and neighborhood sentiments. The invasion-competition-succession sequence that resulted as wave after wave of ethnic groups passed through Chicago's neighborhoods was seen to lead to a decline of such sentiments, either positively as a result of the processes of acculturation and assimilation (Thomas and Znaniecki, 1958; Wirth, 1938) or negatively as a result of the previously mentioned social problems.

Wirth's (1938) essay, which drew on the related theoretical essay by Simmel (1950), failed to document persisting bases of social order and local sentiment that were also a part of the Chicago findings. Especially in the work of Burgess and his students (Burgess, 1972), one finds a careful documenting of the "natural areas" of the city that persist as "symbolic communities" to the present day (Hunter, 1974). Also, the "melting pot" hypothesis of acculturation and assimilation that was largely the basis for the expected decline of ethnic neighborhoods has proven to be questionable, as Glazer and Moynihan (1963) have shown in *Beyond the Melting Pot*. The need to maintain local ethnic and neighborhood sentiments was seen to be critical, for example, to the political processes of aggregating demands and establishing power bases (Gosnell, 1939) and to the governmental process of providing a manageable delivery of urban services (Lineberry, 1977).

Thus, although many of the Chicago School's empirical findings did focus on personal and social disorganization that were linked to a demise of local sentiments toward neighbor, kin, and fellow ethnic, the overemphasis on this perspective was partly a function of a social-problem orientation and a selective summary and one-sided interpretation of the Chicago School's empirical work.

Transformation of small town life. The second empirical tradition documenting the decline of local community sentiments focused not on the urban neighborhood but rather on the small towns of America as they were increasingly absorbed by the emerging metropolitan and national scale of modern social organization. Greer, in *The Emerging City* (1962a), described a process that explained this transformation: Technological changes in transportation and communication resulted in a shrinking space/time ratio that increased the geographical mobility of goods, people, and ideas. Socially, this resulted in the rise of nonspatial, large-scale organizations of interest, which replaced the parochial, spatially and temporally bounded social world of the local community. In short, modern man, as Webber (1963) suggested, was able to have "community without propinquity." This general thesis of an "increase in scale" may be seen to summarize the three studies we will briefly examine below.

Warner, in his *Yankee City* study (1963), pointed to the loss of local community sentiments as a function of the increasing metropolitan scale of industrial organization, which turned local, family-owned firms into branch plants of regional and national corporations. Power and control over industry shifted to ever larger corporations located in metropolitan centers, while management of local plants shifted to transient, professional managers. The new managers' interests lay with careers in the corporations. This was in contrast to the previous old-family owner/managers who maintained a major interest in the well-being of the social and political life of the community and its residents. This produced a distinction that Merton (1968) described as "locals" versus "cosmopolitans" and that a number of writers documented as a major shift in the nature of political power and control in local communities (Schulze, 1969; Dahl, 1961). As a result of this transformation of industry and shift in power, class interests, both of workers and managers, crosscut and undermined the existing common interests found within the community. Community died, according to Warner, in the violent strikes that ultimately erupted; class conflict replaced common community sentiments.

In their Middletown studies, the Lynds (1929, 1937) also documented a similar loss of local community sentiment and solidarity. The earlier Middletown study documented the degree to which a single extended family dominated the economic, political, and social life of their community, which was relatively stable, parochial, and seemingly self-sufficient and which maintained a set of institutions to satisfy its routine needs. This stability and self-sufficiency were shattered by the Depression, prompting the Lynds to return for their second study. As in Warner's *Yankee City*, Middletown was now comprised of fighting factions of workers versus the commercial and industrial elite. The communal harmony and complacency of the earlier period were replaced by class conflict. However, in contrast to Yankee City, this transformation was brought about not by the displacement of locally owned industry by national corporations but rather by the growing recognition of different groups and classes that the fate of Middletown was inextricably linked to national economic and governmental structures. Middletown, in short, had discovered that it was not an isolated, autonomous, self-sufficient community; the Depression had destroyed this illusion. Rather, it was a community that was a small part of a much larger whole over which Middletowners had relatively little influence. Collective interests assumed a class rather than a community base, and the new scale was national, not local.

A similar loss of small-town autonomy in the face of the large-scale institutions of mass society was studied by Vidich and Bensman (1968) in "Springdale," a farming community in upstate New York. In contrast to the harsh reality thrust upon Middletowners by the Depression, these authors documented the way in which Springdalers clung to the persisting myths about small-town life, which masked the prevailing and at times oppressive reality. For example, the myth of local autonomy was maintained in spite of the fact that farmers' complaints about crop prices did not acknowledge that these prices were set hundreds of miles away in the trading pits of the Chicago Board of Trade. Also, their myth of self-sufficiency prevented them from clearly seeing that for many services, such as highways and schools, they were dependent on the resources and expertise of higher levels of government. Although Springdale, like Middletown and Yankee City, had lost functions and lost control over its own destiny, its residents clung to a set of anachronistic beliefs about the friendly virtues of small-town life in contrast to the wicked ways of the big city. At times the reality crept through and the big city was seen to be awesome as well as awful, which resulted in a debilitating and profound ambivalence on the part of the Springdale residents. As the Whites noted in their little volume *The Intellectual Versus the City* (1962), such attitudes have long been a central part of American social thought. It is ironic, as Vidich and Bensman note, that one of the major sources for perpetuating these contrasting images of rural virtue and urban immorality is the mass media, itself emanating from the metropolitan centers of the mass society.

Thus, the studies of small-town life tended to reinforce the picture of a looming specter that was painted by the Chicago School, namely, that throughout America—in big-city neighborhoods and in small rural towns—the social structure and sentiments of local community were dissolving.

COMMUNITY FOUND: URBAN RESIDUES AND SUBURBAN SELECTIVITY

The rediscovery of local community sentiments in mass society occurred in a series of case studies that have become minor classics within contemporary American sociology. It is noteworthy that most of these were either case studies of ethnic communities in older urban areas or of the emerging post-World War II suburbs. These two empirical traditions were critical in causing a rethinking of the hypothesized loss of local community sentiments. These traditions differed not so much in their findings as in their interpretations. The urban ethnic studies tended to find isolated pockets of residual local sentiments, which were considered carryovers from a previous era. The suburban studies tended to emphasize a more conscious search for community that was a selective merger of the small-town life of the past with the modern requirements of metropolitan America.

Urban residues. Whyte's *Street Corner Society* (1943) was significant precisely because it documented the degree of social organization and social solidarity that existed in what followers of the Chicago School were more apt to refer to as the disorganized "slum." Although Whyte gave relatively little documentation for a full understanding of the institutional structure of Boston's North End, he presented a very clear picture of the strength of primary ties that existed in Doc's gang "the Nortons" and in Chick's club of upwardly mobile college men. The sentiments and loyalties engendered in these groups served to organize the routine day-to-day life of the community's residents. The one institution that Whyte analyzed in some detail for its linkage to these primary ties was the political machine. Doc's ill-fated political campaign for a local office allowed Whyte to study the almost feudal aggregation of personal loyalty that existed in the ethnic neighborhoods and that constituted the power base of local politicians.

A more comprehensive study by Gans (1962b) in another of Boston's Italian communities, the West End, came to essentially the same conclusions as Whyte's. The persistence of local community sentiments was rooted in the existence of a pervasive "peer group culture." The "urban villagers" were able to exist in this seemingly contradictory role because the primary groups (exemplified by the extended family and such male peer groups as childhood gangs and adult social athletic clubs) served to isolate the "villagers" from the larger urban world. Ironically, it was this insularity that rendered the West Enders incapable of dealing with the larger political and economic forces that threatened the destruction of their community through urban renewal.

A more recent study by Suttles (1968) in Chicago's multiethnic Taylor Street neighborhood also emphasized how the sentiments and loyalties of primary relationships formed a basis of social order. Going beyond Whyte and Gans, however, Suttles showed how the primary ties based on the status distinctions of age, sex, and ethnicity, coupled with territorial segregation of specific groups, provided a "segmental social order." This was a social order in which groups that otherwise would have been in frequent conflict instead negotiated a spatial and social ordering that provided a degree of tolerance and acceptance in a generally hostile and untrustworthy environment. By extending primary ties across these age, sex, and ethnic divisions, a network of knowledge about other persons provided a system of personal accountability, acceptance, and social control.

These are but a few of the studies that have attested to the persistence of residual elements of primary ties and local sentiments in urban neighborhoods within mass society. For the most part, these studies analyzed lower-class, ethnic communities in older urban neighborhoods.

These studies emphasized the strength of primary and peer relationships—often linked to extended kin and ethnic loyalties—as the basis for local community sentiments. It should be noted that just as the Chicago School had concentrated its efforts on the social-problem area and discovered social disorganization, so too may these studies be criticized as having focused on a somewhat unusual collection of communities. Their representativeness was questioned, and indeed the authors themselves seem not to have fully recognized that the areas they studied were more than anachronistic residues from an earlier era. Local community sentiments, in short, were seen to exhibit a selective persistence—they were surprisingly alive in a world that had earlier considered them extinct.

Suburban selectivity. At the same time that the researchers were busy discovering the urban residues of local community sentiments, other researchers were leaving the central city to follow their fellow urbanites to the emerging communities of single-family homes and green lawns in suburbia. The size, density, and heterogeneity of the city, with its negative personal and social consequences, were being replaced by this new merger of what was hoped would be the best of both urban and rural worlds. A central motivation in this movement was seen by some to be a conscious search for the personal relations and sentiments of local communities. However, as Rossi (1955) and Abu-Lughod and Foley (1970) have noted, the primary motive for the suburban movement was the linkage of family and child-centered interests with the single-family home.

Whyte (1956), in his study of the new suburban community of Park Forest, a suburb of Chicago; Gans (1967), in his study of Levittown, a suburb of Philadelphia; and Seeley, Sims, and Loosly (1956), in their study of Crestwood Heights, a suburb of Toronto, all documented the emergence of informal and formal associations of neighbors, which often centered on the joint interests of children and home. This family and child centeredness led Whyte to describe the suburban setting as a "filiarchy."

These writers saw the suburban community as a consumption unit, a homogeneous, residential, "bedroom" community linked to the larger metropolitan world primarily through the careers of commuting husbands and fathers. In contrast, then, to the effects of bureaucratization, urbanization, and industrialization that Warner and the Lynds had described earlier, the suburban setting was seen as a partial solution to the maintenance of selective sentiments of local community through a spatial segregation of home and work. As later writers such as Farley (1976) and Wirt and others (1972) began to show, suburbia did not constitute a new spatial and political phenomenon; rather, it was a selective migration—an extension of family- and locality-centered interests that had simply spilled beyond the city's rim as metropolitan areas increased in size and scale. These analysts of the suburban scene were careful to note that this social world did not represent a return to the idyllic small-town life of the past. The relationships with neighbors were more transient and less binding than those of friends and kin, and as Keller (1968) noted, . . . the neighbor emerged as a differentiated role. What Gans called the "quasi-primary" relationships of suburbia were still significant, however, in generating local sentiments of community.

In summary, both the older urban villagers and the newer suburbanites represented an important corrective to the earlier empirical studies of the loss of local community sentiments in mass society. In both, the family and the primary relationships existing in the residential neighborhood formed the basis for the persisting residues and selective sentiments of community.

MINIMAL VERSUS EMERGENT PERSPECTIVES

In the previous section we saw that in the 1950s American sociologists rediscovered the sentiments of community in urban residues and selective suburban developments. Ensuing research has generally accepted the presence of local sentiments but diverged into two perspectives. The first, or *minimal*, perspective sees local sentiments as persisting residuals that are real but of limited significance in modern social life. By contrast, the second, or *emergent*, perspective sees local sentiments as new social constructions of reality that are not simply holdovers from a previous era. It also sees the significance of local sentiments as varying across space and time.

The minimal view. The minimal perspective is exemplified in Keller's summary book *The Urban Neighborhood* (1968). The role of neighbor is seen as a limited and sharply circumscribed relationship providing a few residual functions, for example, mutual assistance and emergency

aid in times of need. Similarly, the work of Wellman (1976) on "urban networks" suggests that for the most part urbanites engage in social relationships based on interests that transcend the limited scope of the local urban community; instead, contemporary urbanites are seen to operate on a broader metropolitan-wide scale. However, Wellman found that certain functions, such as "helping relationships," are maintained at the scale of the local neighborhood. These include borrowing the proverbial "cup of sugar," watching a neighboring home while the family is on vacation, and providing emergency aid when needed.

A similar minimal argument is presented by Fischer (1976) when he distinguishes between "just neighbors" (people who live nearby) and "real neighbors" (an intimate personal group). The conversion of the former into the latter occurs, according to Fischer, under conditions of functional necessity (such as mutual assistance), prior relationships (as with the ethnic enclaves studied by Whyte, Gans, and Suttles), or lack of alternatives (especially for those with limited mobility, such as carless housewives, children, and the elderly). He concludes that in modern mass society these three factors are of decreasing significance and therefore the neighborhood is reduced from a meaningful social group to a mere happenstance of physical proximity.

The emergent view. Researchers taking the emergent perspective either see local community sentiments as the product of new and emerging reconstructions or see neighborhoods as occasionally playing a critical role in the organization of modern urban life. It is as if Adam Smith's "small good offices" were small in number but loomed large in their import, or as if Emile Durkheim's persisting neighborly needs were not trivial matters.

One of the earlier versions of this emergent perspective was the "community of limited liability" first proposed by Janowitz (1967) and more fully elaborated in Greer's *The Emerging City* (1962a). The community of limited liability holds that individuals' orientations and attachments to their communities are limited and variable across individuals, communities, and time. Communities, or more specifically local community sentiments, are variables that differ according to a resident's age, sex, social class, family characteristics, and, perhaps most importantly, length of residency. The question becomes not simply whether local sentiments are still significant, but for whom and for what reasons. This limited, variable orientation to community is seen in a sense to be an exchange relationship (Blau, 1967). An individual's investments in the community (emotional, social, and, economic) depend on the degree to which the community provides commensurate rewards. When the local community fails to meet an individual's needs, because of changes in either the individual or the community, the individual will withdraw—if not physically, then socially and emotionally. Conversely, if the local community is seen as an important social unit from which an individual feels he or she derives benefits, then the individual is likely to become involved socially, emotionally, and economically. Community organizers are acutely aware that such involvement may lead to a positive spiral of community development. The effectiveness of the local community in meeting residents' needs will attract new residents and entice fellow residents to become involved, thereby leading to increased resources and increased effectiveness.

Other examples of emergent community sentiments are outlined by Suttles (1972) in his volume *The Social Construction of Communities*. One of the communities that he identifies is the "defended neighborhood," which is basically a local area threatened by external social or ecological change. Such communities tend to become mobilized over issues that threaten the central values of the residents. It is be-cause proximity means a shared or common fate that such mobilization of action and sentiment occurs. The often hostile response to urban renewal programs by local residents (Wilson, 1966) exemplifies the defended community's spontaneous quality, while the Alinsky (1946) "conflict model" of community organizing represents a more conscious manifestation.

A more persistent and stable example of an emergent community is defined by Suttles as the "contrived community." However, this term has a pejorative connotation of being more artificial and more manipulative than what are often assumed to be unplanned, natural, grass-roots communities. Therefore, I suggest an alternative, more neutral category of "conscious community" that highlights several critical distinctions. First, conscious communities are positively assertive rather than negatively reactive; second, they are consciously defined and articulated in belief systems that may range from being relatively vague "images" (Lynch, 1960) to highly integrated, utopian world views (Kanter, 1972); and third, conscious communities exhibit a greater temporal/spatial stability.

The primary structural ingredient of the conscious community is the development of a more formal community organization that provides critical internal and external functions for maintaining local solidarity and sentiments. Internally, such groups provide a structure within which primary bonds of neighboring may be developed and within which the common community interests may become expressed and translated into specific organizational goals. Externally, the organization becomes the "legitimate" respresentative of the community, an identifiable vehicle or corporate body that may more easily interact with outside agencies and institutions (Hunter, 1974). It may even be that such organized local groups are fostered by external agencies and institutions that find it difficult to interact or deal with such a diffuse entity as a community (Taub and others, 1977). An example of the development of a conscious community is seen in the study of an urban neighborhood in Rochester, New York (Hunter, 1975). Responding first as a conflict community to external threats from the local airport and to the "blockbusting" tactics of local realtors, the residents developed a local organization that survived by broadening the scope of its activities and developing a conscious ideological position on the community's central values (specifically, commitment to urban living in a racially integrated community). This ideological community may be seen to lie between communities with a vague self-image and utopian communities with a totally encompassing belief system.

A final category of emergent communities that has been identified is what I will call "vicarious communities." Above all others, these exemplify the degree to which people, individually and collectively, may develop parochial sentiments and attachments independently of what are usually considered to be the functional and social bases of such sentiments. In a study of shopping behavior, Stone (1954) found that residents who lacked objective social ties to their local communities, such as formal and informal relationships with local residents, were more likely than those with such ties to transform typical shopping encounters into more personalized relationships. This vicarious primary tie is exemplified by the elderly person holding up the checkout line at the grocery store by engaging in friendly, personal gossip with the cashiers. This may occur much to the consternation of those waiting in line, who may feel that this should be nothing more than an efficient market transaction so that they may return to their families and friends more quickly. In short, what Weber (1958) and Simmel (1950) saw as the epitome of the rational urban relationship, the market encounter, is transformed into a more intimate personal relationship. In another study, Stone (1968) found that subjective identification

with a community by being a fan at spectator sports was more likely to occur among those people who had the fewest objective social ties to the community. Janowitz (1967) found that avid readers of the local community press in Chicago were often using it as a substitute for personal, first-hand involvement in the local social world.

Finally, in *Symbolic Communities* (Hunter, 1974), I documented the way in which people quite often maintain symbolic attachments to places in which they formerly lived or to the place in which they presently live but as it existed at a previous time in their lives. It should be noted that these vicarious communities are not simply individual aberrations. They may exist within a collective local culture often referring back to a significant historical event or period in the life of the community. This historical symbolism was precisely what Firey (1945) found to be a critical factor in preserving Beacon Hill and the Commons as distinct areas of collective sentiment in downtown Boston. In short, the vicarious community epitomizes the fact that local sentiments are emergent and socially constructed realities—at times existing without any clear referent to current objective reality.

In summary, the minimal and the emergent perspectives begin from the same point—local neighborhoods continue to exist, almost by definition, as social units based on physical proximity. These views differ most profoundly, however, in the significance attributed to local sentiments in the conduct of social life in modern mass society.

A DYNAMIC MODEL OF EMERGENT COMMUNITY SENTIMENTS

The preceding discussion of different approaches and interpretations to parochial sentiments in modern mass society may be used to organize a set of sequential stages in their development. It should be noted that I am referring to the process of community development in a broader sense than that currently in vogue. The current attempts at conscious institution building in urban neighborhoods represent but one possible stage in the general sequence that I am proposing. Furthermore, this model may be likened to Smelser's (1963) "value added" model of collective behavior, in that a community will not necessarily pass from one stage to the next unless critical structural preconditions exist.

The first stage is that of *residual neighborhoods*—Fischer's (1976) "just neighbors" and Wellman's (1976) "networks of necessity"—in short, minimal local collective sentiments based primarily on physical proximity. All successive stages presume the residual neighborhood or proximity. The second stage, which I term *emergent communities*, involves a more conscious and variable conception of parochial sentiments. Communities in this stage are often conflict communities that are responding to a real or perceived external threat to the existing state of the neighborhood that mobilizes an attempt to conserve or preserve threatened values. Such external threats may come from a population transition, such as blacks moving into previously all-white neighborhoods, but increasingly such opposition arises in response to governmentally planned actions, such as school busing or the building of expressways. This stage represents an inherently conservative force geared to preservation. The homogeneity of interest that arises in conflict communities is specific to the external threat, which may be seen as the galvanizing vehicle or catalyst for transforming residual communities into reactive communities. The discussion by Suttles of defended neighborhoods constitutes an excellent example.

The third stage is what I refer to as *conscious communities*. The critical distinction between these and emergent communities is the development of a rather clearly articulated set of central values that are positively advanced as defining characteristics of the community and their embodiment in a more formally structured community organization. Represented here are the wide range of activities usually included within the concept of community development. Such positive assertions may involve outside support such as federal funds for model cities or community action programs; but as a general principle, the transition from the second to the third stage requires at least a partial solution to external threats such that the community is not simply defending itself but instead has taken the offensive in promoting central values within the community. The transition also requires the ability to mobilize resources, internally and externally, to generate an enduring structure that becomes a legitimate representation of the community's interests in relationships with larger external institutions of mass society. The general range we are proposing here runs the continuum from partial "ideological communities" (Hunter, 1975) to the more extreme and encompassing "utopian communities" (Kanter, 1972).

The final and fourth stage I refer to as *vicarious* or *symbolic communities*. This stage epitomizes the notion of the consciously constructed community, for it may in fact be found even among those who do not overtly and behaviorally participate in the local organized social life of an area but nonetheless symbolically transform their local world into a meaningful unit of personal identification. Examples of this type of community are to be found in the research of Stone (1954) and Janowitz (1967), who found that individuals objectively unintegrated into the social life of a community maintained a vicarious identification through other symbolic activities. Another example is the many elderly residents symbolically identifying with an area because their past was spent within the locale and its institutions. This is perhaps most poignantly noted in Fried's (1969) study of "Grieving for a Lost Home." Such symbolic identification may extend beyond the individual's memory into the "cultural memory" of an area. Vicarious and symbolic identification with an area may stem from historical events and meanings. The sentiments and symbolism of Beacon Hill in Boston as studied by Firey (1945) exemplify this form of vicarious community. This stage of community sentiment requires at a minimum that some supporting institutions from the third stage either currently operate or at one time have operated in the area to provide an objective basis for this symbolic transformation.

In summary, the above stages of residual community, conflict community, conscious community, and vicarious community exemplify a progression in local sentiments that depend primarily on the external structural preconditions existing within the mass society and the relationship of the local community to that mass society, rather than simply the inherent characteristics and composition of the local community itself. Such propositions require that we rethink the nature of mass society and its linkage to local community sentiments.

RETHINKING MASS SOCIETY AND LOCAL SENTIMENTS

Mass society is usually viewed negatively. Kornhauser (1959) has summarized these negative conceptions under two general categories: the aristocratic critique and the democratic critique. The former sees the debasement of central values and institutions to the lowest common denominator; the latter sees a centralization of power and prestige that renders the isolated individual powerless and alienated. Kornhauser sees each of these as partial truths, with the true mass society represented by both high accessibility of elites to the masses (aristocratic critique) and

high manipulation of masses by the elite (democratic critique).

Most negative conceptions of mass society have been revised or qualified in the light of subsequent research. For example, the "two-step flow of communication" documented by Katz and Lazarsfeld (1955) in their study of the mass media emphasized the degree to which the media did not impinge directly on isolated individuals but rather was filtered both through "opinion leaders" and the natural social groups to which individuals belonged. In a similar vein, one may view much of the research that has "rediscovered" the existence of local community solidarities within urban society as representing a revision of mass society theories as they apply to urban life. In an important article, "Community Attachments in Mass Society," Kasarda and Janowitz (1974) have shown the degree to which what they call the "linear perspective" (derived from Wirth)—that size, density, and heterogeneity will lead to a disappearance of local attachments in mass society—is not supported. Instead, they found that local attachments are likely to persist as a function of such variables as family status, personal ties, and length of residence in the local community. This "systemic perspective," they argue, requires a reconception of mass society and local attachments that does not necessarily see the two as antithetical, but as coexisting in a more complex structure of institutions and interests than the previous simplified theories hypothesized. However, little has been done in developing a more systemic revision of mass society and local sentiments that incorporates these new findings. In this section, we will attempt this task, and in the next section we will present some exemplary data.

We will begin by rethinking mass society from the perspective of Shils (1975), one of the few theorists to give a positive interpretation to the social changes covered by the general rubric "mass society." Taking a comparative approach in contrasting modern society with traditional society and using the metaphor of "center and periphery," Shils maintained that "the novelty of 'mass society' lies in the relationship of the mass of the population to the center of the society. The relationship is a closer integration into the central institutional and value systems of the society" (p. 93). Echoing Marx, Durkheim, and Weber, he added that mass society "is vertically integrated in a hierarchy of power and authority and a status order" (p. 93). A society-wide, shared set of values that defines a status order are exemplified empirically in contemporary American society by the two status variables of occupation, or more generally class, and race. A generally shared value system of status ranking implies that within mass society a relatively common set of evaluations will be applied to the social positions and communal contexts within which individuals are located. Shared values, however, do not imply similarity in the outcome of evaluations, especially when comparisons are made between commonly shared standards and the more varied objective realities of given situations. Objective inequalities exist, and evaluations of situations will vary directly as the inequality varies. As Shils said, "Inequalities exist in mass society and they call forth at least as much resentment, if not more, than they ever did. Indeed, there is perhaps more awareness of the diversity of situation and the conflict of sectional aspirations in this society than in most societies of the past" (p. 96).

The "diversity of situation" when applied to the arena of local communities in modern urban societies has been one of the major research concerns of human ecology since its inception. The study of the spatial segregation of populations into different neighborhoods and local communities stems from the early Chicago School through research by the Duncans (1955) and Schnore (1965a) and more recent work by Guest (1971), Hunter (1974), and Berry

and Rees (1969). As recent research in "social area analysis" (Shevky and Bell, 1955), or "factorial ecology," has shown, socioeconomic status, racial-ethnic status, and family or life-cycle status have repeatedly emerged as the three most important dimensions of social differentiation and spatial segregation within modern industrial cities. It appears that these dimensions selectively distribute the population among homogeneous local communities. Viewing this as a "locational decision process" in which individuals attempt to maximize a complex set of values, Berry and Rees (1969, pp. 460–61) said:

The inhabitants of the city are faced with a fundamental decision: where to live. The principal determinants of such a housing choice are three in number—the price of the dwelling unit (either in rental or in purchase value terms); its type; and its location both within a neighborhood environment and relative to place of work. These determinants have parallels in the attributes of the individual making the housing choice: the amount he is prepared to pay for housing, which depends on his income; his housing needs, which depend on his marital status and family size, that is, his stage-in-life cycle; his life-style preferences, which will affect the type of neighbor he will want; and, finally, the location of his job. When the values of the two sets of characteristics match, a decision to purchase housing will be made.

In short, as Form (1954) and more recently Harvey (1973) have suggested, the various economic, governmental, and status-ranking institutions of mass society operate to determine the spatial distribution of scarce values in local residential communities. The result is a differentiated territorial matrix into which individuals will locate, by choice and by constraint, and which they will differentially evaluate. Mass society, then, has produced a constellation of local communities that exhibits *relative* homogeneity internally. However, externally among communities there is relative heterogeneity and diversity. The result, in Durkheim's terms, is to produce a micro local scale of mechanical solidarity based on similarity and a macro metropolitan-wide scale of organic solidarity based on diversity and interdependence. Given the presence of the mass media and the mobility of the population that are characteristic of mass society, it is likely that individuals, as Shils (1975) suggested, will be very aware of these differential evaluations of local areas and be able to make such judgments independently of actual residence.

As we have seen, many theorists and contemporary investigators of local community sentiments see them minimally as persisting residues of limited significance in modern mass society. However, contrasted with this view is what I refer to as the emergent perspective, which sees such local sentiments not only as a persistent and variable *condition* of mass society, but also in important ways as a unique *product* of mass society.

One may see local sentiments as a condition of mass society from the revisionist research and theories, which suggest that all social action requires some motivational element, some cathexis or sentiment that is rooted in personal relationships. For example, the importance of primary groups in the urban social structure has its parallel in the study of formal organizations (what to Weber constituted the epitome of rationality in mass society). From the research of Mayo (1945), Blau (1955), and Dalton (1959), one sees that formal organizations work not in spite of such primary relationships and sentiments but because of them. Similarly, as Stouffer and others (1949), Janowitz and Shils (1948), and more recently Moskos (1969) have shown, nationalism and patriotism, although significant realities of mass society, are insufficient to explain the behavior and motivations of soldiers in combat. Instead, one must look to the informal relationships and sentiments that inhere within primary groups as they operate within the larger structure.

In countering the view of the alienated individual in mass society, Shils (1975) said that personal attachment and sentiment were not simply residues or conditions of mass society, and more significantly that in mass society "there has been a transcendence of the primordially and authoritatively given, a movement outward toward . . . the experience of other minds and personalities. It gives rise to and lives in personal attachment" (p. 101). From this perspective, mass society has unfettered the growth of volitional personal attachments. Therefore, once located within the ecological matrix of mass society (that is, the *relatively* homogeneous local communities that are differentiated from one another by the central values of mass society), personal primary relationships will then emerge as a *product* of mass society. These in turn will foster personal sentiments that will be generalized to the setting in which they occur, the collective unit of the local community. It is not simply that local sentiment based on shared space is a residue, but rather that mass society has permitted propinquity itself to become an important basis for defining relationships. Within mass society the relatively autonomous, functionally and institutionally integrated local community may be lost, but the local sentiments of neighborhood persist and flourish. It is as if in Homans' (1950) model of the human group mass society provides the external *evaluative* system within which the internal *affective* system will emerge.

Thus, I am suggesting not only that local sentiments persist within mass society but that there are unique structural characteristics of mass society that when translated onto the urban landscape permit local community sentiments to develop. They emerge not simply as partial and archaic residues, but in new forms and with new functions that mass society has permitted and perhaps requires. These new forms are only hinted at above, but to be significant such sentiments must be translated into collective social action. The middle-class, suburban movement of the 1950s, the inner-city riots of the 1960s, and the ethnic, working-class neighborhood movement of the 1970s, along with various ideological and utopian communities that emerged throughout this period, attest to the uneven, faltering, but inexorable attempts to translate local community sentiments into collective political action. The emergence of metropolitan and national federations of local community groups throughout urban America (such as National Neighbors, National Alliance of Neighborhoods, and National People's Action) suggests a new social and political structure based on local community sentiments.

Furthermore, it should be noted that such federations imply that a zero-sum conception of community sentiments often assumed implicitly is questionable. Echoing Durkheim, Martindale (1958), for example, suggested that in modern mass society the community of the nation-state grows at the expense of the local community. I would suggest rather an additive or multiplicative system in which collective sentiments and attachments, up and down the vertical scale of integration (Warren, 1971; Walton, 1971), serve to reinforce one another. In Shil's (1975) words, mass society is characterized by a closer integration of the periphery with the center, and it appears that local community sentiments may operate as a new critical link in that integration.

Finally, I would caution against a simplification that would see local community sentiments persisting only as the territorial manifestation of class interests. To be sure, these are often of primary importance, but to ignore the other critical dimensions of race, ethnicity, religion, lifestyle, and life cycle would underrepresent the varied forms that community-based interests may take. It is at the level of the local community that mass society uniquely converges in its myriad forms and from which rises, in the shared fate of propinquity, the multiple and varying forms of community interests and local sentiments.

REFERENCES

Abu-Lughod, and Foley, M. "The Consumer Votes by Moving." In R. Gutman and D. Popenoe, eds., *Neighborhood, City, and Metropolis*. New York: Random House, 1970.

Alinsky, S. *Reville for Radicals*. Chicago: University of Chicago Press, 1946.

Anderson, N. *The Hobo*. Chicago: University of Chicago Press, 1923.

Berry, B. J. L., and Rees, P. "The Factorial Ecology of Calcutta." *American Journal of Sociology* 74 (1969), pp. 445–91.

Blau, P. *Exchange and Power in Social Life*. New York: John Wiley & Sons, 1967.

Burgess, E. W. *On Community, Family, and Delinquency*. Ed. L. S. Cottrell, A. Hunter, and J. F. Short. Chicago: University of Chicago Press, 1972.

Cressy, D. *The Taxi Dance Hall*. Chicago: University of Chicago Press, 1932.

Dahl, R. *Who Governs?* New Haven, Conn.: Yale University Press, 1961.

Dalton, M. *Men Who Manage*. New York: John Wiley & Sons, 1959.

Duncan, O. D., and Duncan, B. "Residential Distribution and Occupational Stratification." *American Journal of Sociology* 60 (1955), pp. 493–503.

Durkheim, E. *The Division of Labor in Society*. New York: Free Press, 1964.

Faris, R., and Dunham, H. W. *Mental Disorders in Urban Areas*. Chicago: University of Chicago Press, 1939.

Farley, R. "Components of Suburban Population Growth." In *The Changing Face of the Suburbs*, ed. B. Schwartz. Chicago: University of Chicago Press, 1976.

Firey, W. "Sentiment and Symbolism as Ecological Variables." *American Sociological Review* 10 (1945), pp. 140–48.

Fischer, C. S. *The Urban Experience*. New York: Harcourt Brace Jovanovich, 1976.

Form, W. H. "The Place of Social Structure in the Determination of Land Use." *Social Forces* 32 (1954), pp. 317–22.

Gans, H. J. "Urbanism and Suburbanism as Ways of Life: A Reevaluation of Definitions." In *Human Behavior and Social Processes*, ed. A. M. Rose. Boston: Houghton Mifflin, 1962a.

————. *The Urban Villagers: Group and Class in the Life of Italian-Americans*. New York: Free Press, 1962b.

————. *The Levittowners*. New York: Random House, 1967.

Glazer, N., and Moynihan, D. P. *Beyond the Melting Pot*. Rev. ed. Cambridge, Mass.: MIT Press, 1970.

Gosnell, H. F. *Machine Politics*. Chicago: University of Chicago Press, 1939.

Greer, S. *The Emerging City*. New York: Free Press, 1962a.

————. *Governing the Metropolis*. New York: John Wiley & Sons, 1962b.

Guest, A. M. "Patterns of Family Location." *Demography* 9 (1972), pp. 159–72.

Harvey, D. *Social Justice and the City*. London: Edward Arnold, 1973.

Homans, G. C. *The Human Group*. New York: Harcourt Brace Jovanovich, 1950.

Hunter, A. *Symbolic Communities: The Persistence and Change of Chicago's Local Communities*. Chicago: University of Chicago Press, 1974.

————. "The Loss of Community: An Empirical Test Through Replication." *American Sociological Review* 40 (1975), pp. 537–52.

Janowitz, M. *The Community Press in an Urban Setting*. 2d ed. Chicago: University of Chicago Press, 1967.

Janowitz, M., and Shils, E. A. "The Cohesion and Disintegration of the Wehrmacht in World War II." *Public Opinion Quarterly* 12 (1948), pp. 280–315.

Kanter, R. M. *Commitment and Community*. Cambridge, Mass.: Harvard University Press, 1972.

Kasarda, J. D., and Janowitz, M. "Community Attachment in Mass Society." *American Sociological Review* 39 (1974), pp. 328–39.

Katz, E., and Lazarsfeld, P. F. *Personal Influence*. New York: Free Press, 1955.

Keller, S. *The Urban Neighborhood: A Sociological Perspective*. New York: Random House, 1968.

Kornhauser, W. *The Politics of Mass Society*. New York: Free Press, 1959.

Lineberry, R., ed. "The Politics and Economics of Urban Services." *Urban Affairs Quarterly* 12 (1977), entire issue.

Lynch, K. *The Image of the City*. Cambridge, Mass.: MIT Press, 1960.

————. *What Time is This Place?* Cambridge, Mass.: MIT Press, 1972.

Lynd, R. S., and Lynd, H. M. *Middletown*. New York: Harcourt Brace Jovanovich, 1929.

Lynd, R. S., and Lynd, H. M. *Middletown in Transition*. New York: Harcourt Brace Jovanovich, 1937.

Martindale, D. "Prefatory Remarks: The Theory of the City." In M. Weber, *The City*, ed. and trans. D. Martindale and G. Neuwirth. New York: Free Press, 1958.

Marx, K. *Karl Marx: Selected Writings in Sociology and Social Philosophy*, trans. T. B. Bottomore. New York: McGraw-Hill, 1956.

Mayo, E. *The Social Problems of an Industrial Civilization*. Boston: Harvard Graduate School of Business Administration, 1945.

Merton, R. K. *Social Theory and Social Structure*. New York: Free Press, 1968.

Moskos, C. "Why Men Fight: American Combat Soldiers in Vietnam." *Trans-Action* 1 (1969), pp. 13–23.

Mowrer, E. *Family Disorganization*. Chicago: University of Chicago Press, 1927.

Nisbet, R. *The Quest for Community*. New York: Oxford University Press, 1953.

Rossi, P. H. *Why Families Move*. New York: Free Press, 1955.

Schnore, L. F. "On the Spatial Structure of Cities in the Two Americas." In *The Study of Urbanization*, ed. P. M. Hauser and L. F. Schnore. New York: John Wiley & Sons, 1965a.

————. *The Urban Scene*. New York: Free Press, 1965b.

Schulze, R. O. "Economic Dominants in Community Power Structure." In *The Community*, ed. R. French. Itasca, Ill.: Peacock, 1969.

Seeley, J. R., Sims, R. A., and Loosly, E. W. *Crestwood Heights*. New York: Basic Books, 1956.

Shils, E. A. *Center and Periphery: Essays in Macrosociology.* Chicago: University of Chicago Press, 1975.

Simmel, G. "The Metropolis and Mental Life." In *The Sociology of Georg Simmel,* trans. K. H. Wolff. New York: Free Press, 1950.

Smelser, N. *Theory of Collective Behavior.* New York: Free Press, 1963.

Stein, M. *The Eclipse of Community.* New York: Harper & Row, 1960.

Stone, G. "City Shoppers and Urban Identification." *American Journal of Sociology* 60 (1954), pp. 276–84.

Stone, G. "Urban Identification and the Sociology of Sport." Paper presented at the annual meeting of the American Association for the Advancement of Science, 1968.

Stouffer, S., and others. *The American Soldier.* Princeton, N.J.: Princeton University Press, 1949.

Suttles, G. D. *The Social Order of the Slum: Ethnicity and Territory in the Inner City.* Chicago: University of Chicago Press, 1968.

————. *The Social Construction of Communities.* Chicago: University of Chicago Press, 1972.

Taub, R., and others. "Urban Voluntary Associations, Locality Based and Externally Induced." *American Journal of Sociology* 83 (1977), pp. 425–42.

Thomas, W. I. *The Unadjusted Girl.* Chicago: University of Chicago Press, 1927.

————., and Znaniecki, F. *The Polish Peasant in Europe and America.* New York: Dover, 1958. (Originally published in five volumes, 1918–20).

Thrasher, F. M. *The Gang: A Study of 1,313 Gangs in Chicago.* Chicago: University of Chicago Press, 1926.

Vidich, A. J., and Bensman, J. *Small Town in Mass Society.* New York: Doubleday, 1958.

Walton, J. "The Vertical Axis of Community Organization and the Structure of Power." In *Community Politics,* ed. C. Bonjean and others. New York: Free Press, 1971.

Warner, W. L. *Yankee City.* New Haven, Conn.: Yale University Press, 1963.

Warren, R. L. "A Note on Walton's Analysis of Power Structure and Vertical Ties." In *Community Politics,* ed. C. Bonjean and others. New York: Free Press, 1971.

Webber, M. M. "Order in Divsity: Community without Propinquity." In *Cities and Space: The Future Use of Urban Land,* ed. L. Wingo. Baltimore: Johns Hopkins University Press, 1963.

Weber, M. *The City.* Ed. and trans. D. Martindale and G. Neuwirth. New York: Free Press, 1958.

Wellman, B. "Urban Connections." Research Paper no. 84. Toronto: Center for Urban and Community Studies, University of Toronto, 1976.

White, M., and White, L. *The Intellectual Versus the City.* New York: Mentor Books, 1962.

Whyte, W. F. *Street Corner Society.* Chicago: University of Chicago Press, 1943.

Whyte, Jr., W. W. *The Organization Man.* New York: Simon & Schuster, 1956.

Wilson, J. Q., Ed. *Urban Renewal.* Cambridge, Mass.: MIT Press, 1966.

Wirt, F., and others. *On the City's Rim: Politics and Policy in Suburbia.* Lexington, Mass.: Heath, 1972.

Wirth, L. "Urbanism as a Way of Life." *American Journal of Sociology* 44 (1938), pp. 1–24.

*Metropolis, city, suburb,
neighborhood, and village*

SECTION FOUR

INTRODUCTION

In recent decades, changes in the structure and function of American communities have been characterized in large measure by a reduction in contrasts between urban and rural social organization and by a rapid growth of communities surrounding the central cities. Associated with these and other factors have been a number of different kinds of change which have tended to blur the contrast between the metropolis and the village or small city.

The small community's Main Street increasingly embraces types of activity which resemble "city ways." One need only mention the chain stores, branch banks, supermarkets, and parking meters to indicate the changed social relationships which underlie these tangible symbols of change. They symbolize changes in other aspects of village and small-city life as well.

But in numerous instances, Main Street itself has grown from its earlier status as a smalltown shopping center to become the "downtown" section of a growing city in its own right. Perhaps even more significant, Main Street has in many cases come clearly within the orbit of the nearest largest city, becoming in a very real sense a suburb of that city.

Looked at from a different perspective, the development of large metropolitan complexes has come to characterize whole sections of the country, and although there may be some fields and woods and smaller communities within these large agglomerations, the network of their symbiotic interconnections grows ever stronger, and the character of their institutions changes.

Delbert C. Miller has examined the complexities of interconnection among cities along a large stretch of the American eastern seaboard, extending from north of Boston to south of Washington, a region which Jean Gottman, in an earlier and much publicized work, had called Megalopolis. This region is characterized by high population density and numerous urban centers with various types of overlapping relationships. Miller's impressive book is a study of the networks of leadership and power that extend beyond the community level and that link various leaders in important ways.

In the present selection, Miller describes briefly the geographic and demographic characteristics of Megalopolis, and presents data indicating both the networks of interconnection of various leaders across this region and the important positions of power they occupy in national economic organizations.

As one views the growing agglomerations of groups of central cities and suburbs into metropolitan areas and into megalopolitan regions, one characteristic becomes startlingly clear. This is the multiplicity of municipal general-purpose governments and special districts which fragment the larger areas and regions into thousands of political units. The advantages of this fragmented governmental system have been often repeated and are well known. But there is a high cost associated with such fragmentation. The advantages and disadvantages have been variously argued by sociologists, political scientists, geographers, and others. Kenneth Newton, a British observer, makes a strong case in the article included here for the disadvantages of governmental fragmentation in metropolitan areas. Not only does it present problems of efficiency, he contends, but it operates systematically to favor the well-to-do and to place the less well-to-do at even greater disadvantage.

How is the persistence of municipal fragmentation to be explained? One way to approach this question is to note that the presence of fragmentation and the absence of metropolitan government—that is, a governmental structure that would include an inner city and its surrounding suburbs—serves certain ends which would be jeopardized by reducing the fragmentation. Oliver P. Williams and his associates made an intensive study of the situation with regard to Philadelphia and its surrounding suburbs. They diagnosed the situation in Philadelphia and elsewhere as reflecting "the basic dualism characteristic of metropolitan areas: the existence of specialization and the need for integrative mechanisms."

An important reason for the existence of areal specialization—that is, the use of land areas for different purposes and by different people—is that many people want it that way. They have moved to the suburbs precisely because—among other reasons—they wish to escape the inner city environment and the inner city problems. To have their present suburban governments consolidate with the city is the farthest thing from their minds.

The result, as this study points out, is that a process takes place in which metropolitan problems such as water and sewage disposal are handled piece-meal through setting up special-purpose districts, thus proliferating the governmental maze but making it possible for the system of areal specialization to persist. The authors show the importance of discriminating between three kinds of metropolitan problems, which are surrounded by different sets of political dynamics: the problem of maintaining the system of areal specialization, the problem of unequal distribution of resources and services among the municipalities of the metropolitan area, and the problem of border relationships between contiguous municipalities.

Again, looking at the growth of megalopolitan regions, developments are taking place which make earlier conceptions of central cities—surrounded by suburbs populated largely by people who have recently moved out from those central cities and who find work in those central cities—inadequate. Important changes taking place are the development of exurbia, the increase in population of nonmetropolitan counties, and the fact that increasing numbers of suburbanites were born and brought up in the suburbs.

Sylvia Fava, who has spent many years studying the suburbs, gives a colorful depiction of the rapidly changing trends which are transforming the nature of suburban life and tipping the scales of dominant living patterns for the entire nation.

Gerald D. Suttles has developed a conceptualization of the local residential area as "the defended neighborhood." He develops this in the passage included here. He does not define the concept rigorously, and one derives the impression that he uses it in a rather broad sense, as exemplified by his mention of delinquent gangs, restrictive covenants, and sharp boundaries. Perhaps more useful than the term, which has enjoyed wide circulation, is Suttles' identification of several important social-psychological characteristics of neighborhood definition, including its volatility or fluidity, changing with different contexts and functions. His emphasis on children as the population group most highly restricted to the local neighborhood area, and mothers with young children as the next most restricted group, underlines his point that the local neighborhood means different things to different types of people, a meaning which is related to his concept of "cognitive mapping."

A neighborhood is typically thought of as a residential group within a larger community. Sometimes, however, neighborhoods are thought to be the ideal representation of a community—or at least the ideal representation of the *Gemeinschaft*-like qualities of the community. The relationships between neighborhoods, community and society are explored in the insightful article by Barry Wellman and Barry Leighton. Their use of a network perspective allows the investigation of both spatially based communities (the "saved" community) and nonterritorial communities of interest (the "liberated" community) similar to those discussed in Section One by Israel Rubin.

This entire section documents the great fluidity and intermingling of different community forms extending from the neighborhood to the metropolitan area and megalopolitan region. The major impression is one of flux and change, of somewhat determinate centers but highly vague peripheries, of shifting fields, of wheels within wheels. The final selection is included by way of contrast.

How much simpler things appeared to be in the days when one could be fairly confident about locating and delineating the small rural community, with its trade center and surrounding service area! Within the boundaries so drawn, people lived out the major roles of their lives, being thrown together in meaningful interaction on the basis of their common residence and identification with the locality. Building on an earlier tradition of community studies, Dwight Sanderson arrived at what was perhaps the classic formulation of the concept and major social characteristics of the rural community. He also was instrumental in perfecting a methodology for locating and delineating it in quite practical fashion. His procedure is presented here for two reasons. First, its simple method for delineating the community exemplifies, perhaps better than any other approach, the classic conception of the rural community as a largely self-contained unit with definite boundaries. Second, the very consideration of such a concept and method under today's conditions dramatizes the enormous changes which have taken place in recent decades, changes which have led to the increasing lack of relevance of this model of community living for most American communities. For better or worse, it becomes more and more meaningless to mark a series of mutually exclusive geometric figures on a map to purport to represent any meaningful units called communities. The structures of social interaction which are closely related to propinquity have become much more complex than that, and the prospects of their becoming simpler in the foreseeable future are virtually nonexistent.

----------------------------- 21 -----------------------------

System characteristics of megalopolis

Delbert C. Miller

WHAT IS MEGALOPOLIS?

Megalopolis ("large city") as a term was first applied by Jean Gottman in his study of the urbanized Northeastern Seaboard of the United States (1961)[1] in which he gave new identity to what has often been called the "East Coast" or just "the East." He describes a region stretching north of Boston to south of Washington and points out that 38 million persons (1960) populate the central cities, suburbs, and satellite areas lying along an axis about 600 miles long and 30 to 100 miles deep—more the size of a nation than a metropolis. A close look at the area shows that the axis of Megalopolis crosses the boundaries of 10 states and the District of Columbia. Thus Megalopolis is administered by 10 state governments plus the committees of the Congress which control the District of Columbia. On the local level the administrative map includes 117 counties and 32 major cities of more than 50,000 population,

and the counties are subdivided into many more townships and boroughs.[2] . . .

Gottman stresses the economic integration of Megalopolis as the major index of regionalism. He describes Megalopolis as a grouping of the main seaports, commercial and financial centers, and manufacturing activities in the United States. He points also to the function of cultural leadership expressed in its universities, laboratories, and libraries, periodicals and publishing houses, theater, music, and art.

Speaking of Megalopolis as a community, Gottman concludes that

even though we do not feel justified in considering this region as one community, much less, of course, as one city, we have found enough integration in the whole and enough interplay between its various parts to indicate strongly that all those 37 million inhabitants counted in Megalopolis by the 1960 Census are close neighbors.[3]

_____

Reprinted with permission from pp. 8–29 of Delbert C. Miller, *Leadership and Power in the Bos-Wash Megalopolis: Environment, Ecology and Urban Organization.* Copyright © 1975 by John Wiley & Sons, Inc., Publishers. Footnotes have been renumbered.

[1] Jean Gottman, *Megalopolis, The Urbanized Northeastern Seaboard of the United States* (New York: The Twentieth Century Fund, 1961).

_____

[2] Ibid., p. 740. The U.S. Department of Commerce, commenting on the 450 miles of seacoast extending immediately from Boston to Washington, D.C., reports an overall population increase of 11.2 percent between 1960 and 1970. Less than 1 percent of the nation's land is occupied by Megalopolis, but 18 percent of all residents of the United States are now found in this region. *Washington Post,* September 29, 1970.

[3] Ibid., p. 692.

200

Lewis M. Alexander, the geographer, divides the Boston-Washington axis into four subregions: Southern New England, Metropolitan New York, the Delaware Valley, and the Baltimore-Washington conurbation.[4] In each of the four subregions the urbanized areas focus on the principal cities: Boston, New York, Philadelphia, Baltimore-Washington. The proximity of Baltimore and Washington brings them into a tight regional configuration. In contrast, Southern New England is focused on Boston and its satellite cities of Brookline, Cambridge, and Somerville. Its subregion includes such metropolitan districts as Worcester, Providence-Pawtucket, Fall River, and Lawrence-Haverhill. In Southwestern New England there is not one large urban center but rather a series of cities in the Connecticut River Valley and along the shore of Long Island Sound. Starting with Springfield, Massachusetts, this area contains Hartford, New Haven, Bridgeport, and Stamford.

The New York and Philadelphia metropolitan areas sit in the center of the Bos-Wash axis. With 15 million people in the New York subregion and close to 5 million in the combined Philadelphia-Wilmington region, or 20 million all told, these two subgroups contain almost half the population of Megalopolis.

The Regional Plan Association examined Megalopolis and chose to call it the Atlantic Urban Region.[5] It found that a number of issues, especially high-speed ground transportation, air travel and airport location, water supply, major parks for day-long and weekend recreation, and freeway location, were pulling the region together. They found little evidence, however, that Megalopolis could be considered a single community. In a recent report they say that even with continuous urbanization between Boston and Washington

"this whole urban belt would consist of somewhat self-contained communities, both local and metropolitan—strung together one by one like beads."[6] They base the probability that communities can remain separate and self-contained on a mapping of commuter-sheds for each of the metropolitan areas of more than 250,000. . . . The map shows that even today's older cities in the Atlantic Urban Seaboard have distinct commuter areas with little overlapping. The Regional Plan Association recommends that new metropolitan centers be encouraged to grow around older regional centers—New York, Philadelphia, Boston, Washington, Baltimore, Hartford, and Providence. "Organizing the population into metropolitan communities by strengthening urban centers should clarify and strengthen the sense of community and the process of self-government even as population increases along the Atlantic Urban Seaboard."

In the face of this evidence of differentiated communities there is also a strong case for an underlying integration of Megalopolis. The economic integration has been noted, the social intercourse has been documented. Gottman has done both and he points out that

the emphasis on flow especially of people, demonstrates graphically the vast web of variegated and often abstract relationships that unite the different cities and counties of megalopolis in one regional system. Beyond the limits we have outlined for this region the intensity of all these flows slackens, the density of interconnections weakens.[7]

The five major cities lie close to one another: Washington to Baltimore is 39 miles, Baltimore to Philadelphia, 98 miles, Philadelphia to New York, 87 miles, and New York to Boston, 231 miles, a total of 455

[4] Lewis M. Alexander, *The Northeastern United States*, (Princeton, N.J.: Van Nostrand, 1967), p. 15.
[5] Regional Plan Association, *The Region's Growth*, Bulletin No. 105, New York, May 1967.
[6] The Regional Plan Association, *The Second Regional Plan, A Draft for Discussion*, Bulletin No. 100, New York, November, 1968, p. 30.
[7] Gottman, *Megalopolis*, pp. 691–92.

miles. By automobile the most distant of the cities can be reached in one day's drive over high-speed freeways. The four cities, New York, Philadelphia, Baltimore, and Washington, are situated within a maximum of 224 miles. By train, New York and Philadelphia are 1 hour and 36 minutes apart; New York and Baltimore, 3 hours and 50 minutes.

* * * * *

IS MEGALOPOLIS A COMMUNITY?

There are five possible answers to this question:

1. Megalopolis is a regional community united by common sentiments and identity. It is a psychosocial concept that exists in the thinking of the inhabitants and leaders as the community to which they belong.
2. Large subregions (such as Southern New England, Metropolitan New York, the Delaware Valley, and the Baltimore-Washington conurbation) are unified communities but Megalopolis is not.
3. Megalopolis is a regional system of interrelated metropolitan areas that contains a network of leaders and organizations who interact with concerns that are local, state, interstate, regional, and national in character. This network indicates the presence of an incipient power base for a regional unit but does not provide its inhabitants with a full sense of community.
4. Distinct regional groups organized around specific functions (such as water supply and highways) have communal significance in Megalopolis, but a regional subcommunity does not function as a meaningful sociological unit.
5. Megalopolis exists as a congeries of metropolitan centers. No evidence of an overall communal base can be found.

OPERATING DEFINITIONS OF MEGALOPOLIS FOR RESEARCH STUDY

An examination of the five possibilities of community in Megalopolis shows that in one sense all are useful definitions. For different functions they are all literally true because Megalopolis is a macroscopic concept within whose boundaries are numerous overlapping subcommunities. Our research tasks have led us to employ differing concepts. For the study of urban-oriented leaders and organizations the concept of best fit seems to be that which conceives of Megalopolis as interrelated major metropolitan areas with a network of leaders and organizations interacting across the region (option 3).[8]

It is known that business and professional leaders assemble in their own associations and that the Eastern regional component in all national associations is large and vigorous. Some national organizations have leaders from many walks of life, and Eastern leaders active in business, politics, and religious, labor, and civic groups are often reported meeting together. Meanwhile the movement of people and the flow of telephone calls and letters indicates that a tremendous web of contacts binds the residents of Megalopolis.[9]

Faced with this evidence, we turned to the concept of linkage. Charles P. Loomis

---

[8] For our studies of environmental quality leaders and organizations we chose options 3 and 4 and examined the interaction in Megalopolis and regional interest groups. For tests of decision-making processes, studies were designed for the specific subregion, the Delaware River Basin, and issues involving water quality and trust of leaders were examined.

[9] Gottman concluded that, "As the vast region of Megalopolis grows, regional integration into one interwoven system is bound to progress. The first evolution must be achieved in the minds of the people, and many signs indicate it is already occurring. . . . The people of Megalopolis must first realize fully the implications of the region's present structure and the assets and liabilities involved in the present tighter neighborhood on a large scale." Gottman, *Megalopolis*, 738.

defines systemic linkage as "the process whereby the elements of at least two social systems come to be articulated so that in some ways and on some occasions they may be viewed as a single system."[10] In Megalopolis the major problem is how systemic linkage relates members of the five principal metropolitan areas to one another. The research problem is to discover the kinds of activity and the degree of interaction between leaders and organizations of the major cities.

SYSTEMIC LINKAGE IN MEGALOPOLIS

Linkage of eastern leaders to national associations in Megalopolis

Many national associations establish bases from and to which residents and leaders of Megalopolis move or communicate in pursuit of their professional or civic duties. There are 13,600 national associations of trade, professional, labor, fraternal, and patriotic affiliation in the United States. . . . The national headquarters of 5,606 of them (42 percent) are located in Magalopolis. . . .

New York with more than 67 percent has the largest share. Washington is second with about one-fourth (23.2 percent), Boston and Philadelphia can muster only 4.5 and 3.4 percent, respectively, and Baltimore has less than 1 percent. A study of national associations most influential in urban problems is a part of this research and is described in detail in Chapter 7. It is important here to report that among the 37 national associations identified as most powerful in dealing with urban problems 29 (80 percent) are located in Washington, 7 (19 percent) are located in New York, and only 2, the U.S. Junior Chamber of Commerce and the Council of State Governments, are located outside Megalopolis.[11]

At these national headquarters people can meet and discuss their common problems. The most influential organizations are active communication centers that keep in constant touch with members and government and other association officials by telephone, letter, or literature, in an effort to persuade them to support their goals. Some also operate government lobbies. Washington is a major hub of political action, and many strong New York-based business, professional, labor, and civil rights associations maintain large Washington offices.

A matrix of major organizations which shows the interaction of members in and between national and regional organizations would reveal a large part of the policy participation network in Megalopolis. It is this network that weaves the growing fabric of regional ties and it is this network that is so little known.

The locus of leadership participation can be identified. It is known, for example, that powerful business leaders can be found in the Business Council, on the National Industrial Conference Board and the Committee on Economic Development, in the National Alliance of Businessmen, and in the National Urban Coalition. . . .

The Business Council is one of the most prestigious bodies of businessmen in the United States. It is composed of men in private industry, chosen as broadly representative of a geographical as well as a product point of view and for their own characters, ability, and sense of public responsibility. The Council stands ready on request to provide advice to all departments of government. The Council's active membership is limited under the bylaws to 65. A small number may be reappointed to

---

[10] Charles P. Loomis and Zona K. Loomis, *Modern Social Theories*, Van Nostrand, New York, 1961, p. 16.

[11] The Council of State Governments has a sizable Washington office and an Eastern regional office in New York in addition to its national headquarters in Chicago.

graduate or honorary membership after completing service as active members. All members are appointed by the Council's nominating committee and are given final approval by the Executive Committee. In April 1968 there were 191 active, graduate, and honorary members, 72 of whom lived in Megalopolis. . . . This distribution is an indication of the concentration of top business leaders in the New York area. Two out of three are found there. Washington has eight, Boston seven, Philadelphia five, Hartford two, Wilmington one, and Baltimore one. These leaders of Megalopolis are able to communicate with one another through this organization. Note that Megalopolis provides 38 percent of the Business Council members of the nation.

The National Industrial Conference Board was founded in 1916 to provide information on the experience of companies in the management of their enterprises. It brings leaders together in committees and councils and in seminars, conferences, and training sessions. A group of 250 regular members are distinguished business leaders who are officers or directors of firms that support the Conference Board. New York has 67, Boston eight, Wilmington five, Philadelphia and Camden six, Hartford and Bridgeport four, Newark two, and Washington one. Megalopolis claims 37 percent of the leaders in the NICB.

The Committee on Economic Development was formed in 1942 to bring businessmen and industrialists into a close working alliance with outstanding economists and social scientists for the development of new ideas. In the World War II years the Committee worked on postwar planning. Today 183 members from all over the United States are on the Board of Trustees. The Research and Policy Group, which provides major direction, has 49 members, 26, or 53 percent, of whom come from the cities of Megalopolis. Megalopolis also supplies 53 percent of the steering committee members.

The National Alliance of Businessmen received its charter following President Lyndon B. Johnson's manpower message to the Congress on January 23, 1968. The president asked business to find jobs for the hard-core unemployed. The Department of Labor was enjoined to work closely with the Alliance, whose chairmanship was assumed by Henry Ford II, Chairman of the Ford Motor Company, and who appointed a vice chairman, an executive vice chairman, and five members-at-large. A national office was opened in Washington. The United States was divided into eight regions and major cities were designated. Top businessmen were recruited to serve without compensation as a public responsibility. A regional chairman was appointed and appointees were named in 49 cities. Boston, New York, Philadelphia, Jersey City, Newark, Baltimore, and Washington, D.C., were named in Eastern Megalopolis. Various top posts were filled by Roger P. Sonnabend and Louis W. Cabot of Boston; G. William Miller of Providence; Harold S. Geneen, A. L. Nickerson and Floyd D. Hall of New York; Thomas J. Stanton of Jersey City; Orville E. Beal of Newark; Stuart T. Sanders of Philadelphia; Jerold C. Hoffberger of Baltimore; and Stephen Ailes of Washington. By their membership, often multiple, in such organizations business leaders in Megalopolis maintain a network of contacts.

All of these links stress the ties of business leaders. The National Association of Manufacturers, the U.S. Chamber of Commerce, the American Management Association, and numerous trade associations based in Megalopolis multiply the opportunities for communication. It would be of interest to know how top business leaders interact with labor, political, religious, civic, and civil rights leaders in Megalopolis. If one seeks organizational contexts, it is necessary to examine those private associations and governmental commissions and committees that bring leaders together from different walks of life.

Some government commissions and private associations demand wide representation. The National Urban Coalition was born in the midst of the violent urban crisis of 1967. National leaders in business, labor, religion, government, and civic rights were assembled and organization plans were developed. The Urban Coalition became a nonprofit corporation with John Gardner as its chairman and chief executive officer. A steering committee of 38 members was selected, 20, or 53 percent, of whom were residents of Megalopolis. Powerful business leaders, such as David Rockefeller (Chase Manhattan Bank), James F. Oates (Equitable Life Insurance Co.), Theodore Schlesinger (Allied Stores Corp.), Joseph H. Allen (McGraw-Hill Book Co.), and James Rouse (The Rouse Co.), met with powerful leaders from government, labor, religion, and civil rights—men like John V. Lindsay, Roy Wilkins, James H. J. Tate, George Meany, Rabbi Jacob P. Rudin, Dr. Ellen G. Hawkins, A. Philip Randolph, John F. Collins, Andrew Heiskell, I. W. Abel, the Reverend George H. Guilfoyle, and others.[12]

This kind of interoccupational communication is encouraged for many more leaders of Megalopolis in the Boston, New York, Philadelphia, Baltimore, and Washington urban coalitions.[13] It is difficult to estimate how many have been brought together.

---

[12] The late Whitney Young was a member of the Steering Committee.

[13] A roster of Urban Coalitions in the five major cities shows the following: Boston, Small Organizing and Development Committee. New York, 33 on Board of Directors; 22 on Economic Development Task Force; 27 on Education Task Force; 23 on Housing Task Force; 44 on Education Task Force. Philadelphia, 21 on Board of Directors and numerous persons on various task forces to study economic development, education, housing, and manpower. Baltimore, three major committees: Business in the Ghetto Committee, 12 members; Committee on Racism, 7 members; Legislative Committee, 8 members; Washington, 84 members of which 22 are blacks and 62 are white.

The examination of this overlapping, multiple participation became an important part of the process of identifying influential leaders of Megalopolis active in urban problems. Patterns of multiple participation are presented in Chapter 10. At this point it is our purpose to sketch the bases of leadership linkage by occupational groupings. We want to know if leaders in Megalopolis make contacts and establish working relations. We could determine the intensity of interaction as Megalopolis labor leaders interact with national labor officals in Washington, where the AFL–CIO and other major labor organizations have headquarters. Washington is the labor center for making national policy and initiating programs for exerting influence on Congress. Political and government leaders of Megalopolis come to Washington to engage in the activities of such organizations as the National League of Cities, National League of Counties, the U. S. Conference of Mayors, the National Council of State Governments, and the U.S. Governor's Conference. Religious leaders meet in New York at the National Council of Churches, the Catholic Federations, and the American Jewish Congress. As the home of the National Association for the Advancement of Colored People, the Urban League, and the Congress of Racial Equality, New York is also the civic rights center of the nation.

Professionals go to New York and Washington to visit their national and regional organizations. Teachers, lawyers, doctors, professors, architects, bankers, planners, broadcasters—all are drawn into common contact in one of these two centers. Boston, Philadelphia, and Baltimore serve as important regional centers and hold many annual meetings of the numerous national organizations.

Civic leaders belong to myriad organizations. Politically active women gather at the national headquarters for the League of Women Voters or the National Federation of Business and Professional Women's Clubs. Civic leaders active in environmental problems may be found at the Conservation Foundation, the Sierra Club, the National Parks Association, the Izaak Walton League of America, the Wildlife Management Institute, the National Audubon Society, and the National Wildlife Federation.

The channels in which leaders of different institutional segments of the region can meet have special interest because interoccupational contacts widen the scope of relationships. Government commissions and government advisory or fact-finding committees provide outlets for such acquaintance.

The roster of boards, committees, and commissions attached to the executive and legislative branches of government is long. The executive branch calls largely on lay personnel outside the federal government. In 1968 there were 68 bodies variously called board, committee, advisory committee, study commission, commission, council, or conference, three of which were especially important to the study of urban problems—the National Commission on Urban Problems, the National Advisory Commission on Civil Disorders, and the National Advisory Council on Economic Opportunity. All provide examples of an effort to represent business, labor, government, religion, and civil rights.

The National Commission on Urban Problems was appointed by President Johnson on January 12, 1967, and charged with seeking ways to increase the supply of decent housing for low-income families. Among the 16 members appointed 7 were residents of Megalopolis: Mrs. Cloethiel W. Smith and Paul H. Douglas, Washington, D.C.; Lewis Davis, Richard O'Neil, and Richard Ravitch, New York; Alex Feinberg, Camden, New Jersey; and Jeh V. Johnson, Poughkeepsie, New York.

Leaders of Megalopolis were brought together in the National Advisory Commission on Civil Disorders which was formed in 1967 to make a full investigation of the large-scale riots in Detroit, Washington, and many other American cities in that year. A national crisis was recognized and the Commission was asked to get the facts and make recommendations with all haste. Governor Otto Kerner of Illinois was appointed chairman and ten other members represented business, labor, government, and civil rights groups. Megalopolis provided Edward W. Brooke, U.S. Senator from Massachusetts, John V. Lindsay, Mayor of New York, and Roy Wilkins, Executive Director of NAACP, all of whom were powerful and influential leaders and were well known in Megalopolis and the nation.

The National Advisory Council on Economic Opportunity was established on March 31, 1968, to deal with the problems of employment and opportunity. In this 19-member council were five lawyers, two physicians, two religious leaders, two educators, three government officials (one federal, one state, and one city), one television official, one civic leader, one labor leader, one civil rights leader, and one American Indian leader. All the major metropolitan sections of Megalopolis except Philadelphia had one or more members. The Washington area was represented by Mrs. Robert McNamara, civic leader, George R. Davis, Sr., religious leader, James A. Suffridge, labor leader, and Horace Busby, governmental aide to President Johnson. Theodore McKeldin, attorney and former governor of Maryland and former Mayor of Baltimore, was a member, as were New York's Morris Abram, attorney, Donald H. McGannon, broadcasting official, and the late Whitney Young, civic rights leader. Otto Eckstein, professor at Harvard, represented the Boston area.

Other sources of interoccupational communication are the boards of the various foundations. Generally the stress is on wide leadership representation. Because most of the large foundations and many associations are headquartered in Megalopolis, many Eastern leaders meet at such intersections.

American urban politics: Social class, political structure, and public goods

Kenneth Newton

FRAGMENTATION AS A STRUCTURAL ATTRIBUTE OF U.S. URBAN GOVERNMENT

The careful attention paid to individuals has led to one of the most notable structural properties of the political system of the United States being largely overlooked, namely, that it is splintered and fragmented into an extraordinary complex mosaic of over 80,000 separate units. First, it is divided between federal, state, and local levels, and then within each level it is divided, according to the principle of the separation of powers, into executive and legislative branches. Third, and most important from the present point of view, it is divided geographically at the local level into over 80,000 units of government—in 1967 the 227 SMSAs had 20,703 units of government (Maxwell, 1969: 71), and in 1960 there were approximately four times as many governments in the St. Louis SMSA as there were nation states in the world (Lineberry and Sharkansky, 1971: 25). It is often pointed out that the number of school districts in the U.S.A. is rapidly decreasing, but it is less widely known that the number of special districts is actually increasing, especially in urban areas.

"American Urban Politics: Social Class, Political Structure and Public Goods," by Kenneth Newton is reprinted from *Urban Affairs Quarterly* 11, no. 2 (December 1975), pp. 243–64 by permission of the Publisher, Sage Publications, Inc. Footnotes have been renumbered.

Author's note: This paper was prepared while the author held an American Council of Learned Societies' Fellowship at the Sociology Department of the University of Wisconsin, Madison. Michael Aiken at Madison and James Sharpe at Oxford helped with useful comments on the first draft.

In 1957 the 174 SMSAs had 3,180 special districts, but by 1962 the numbers had risen to 5,411 in 212 SMSAs, and by 1967 the figures were 7,049 in 227 SMSAs. Part of this increase was more apparent than real and due only to the Census of Government's changes in definition, but the actual increase was also substantial (Smith, 1969: 22–27).

As if this degree of fragmentation were not enough, these units of local government overlap and are superimposed on top of each other in such a way that even a short journey to work may take a commuter across several boundary lines dividing counties, municipalities, townships, and school and special districts. Small wonder that Robert Wood (1961: 1) calls the governmental arrangements of the New York Metropolitan Region "one of the great unnatural wonders of the world." The degree of local government fragmentation in the United States as a whole is probably unique among the urban-industrial societies of the world and the question which begs to be asked is, very simply, what are the social and political causes and consequences of such an extraordinary pattern?

APOLOGISTS OF FRAGMENTATION

The fragmented nature of the system has not, of course, been overlooked. On the contrary. But liberal individualism has caused many American social scientists to overlook some of its most important consequences and to systematically misinterpret others. Many sociologists, economists, and political scientists have explained and justified fragmentation in terms of two highly prized values—efficiency and democracy. Among the economists, Charles M. Tiebout is notable for arguing that fragmentation is efficient because a large number of local political units, each with its own special package of private and public goods and services, gives each and every citizen a chance to maximize his or her own particular set of preferences (Tiebout, 1972: 513–523; see also Ostrom et al., 1961: 831–842). Fragmentation is also efficient, it is said, because it produces competition between jurisdictions in exactly the same way that market mechanisms produce competition between firms. Writers who argue the efficiency and competition case often draw upon classical economic theory in drawing parallels between the supposed behavior of rational, self-interested, individual consumers in the market place, and the supposed behavior of rational, self-interested individual voters in the political market place. In fact, methodological individualism is to be found in a relatively pure form in much of this literature, although only rarely are the full range of assumptions laid out in such a naked form as they are by the economist Robert Bish (1971: 3) when he writes:

Four basic assumptions of economic analysis are common in the recent applications of economics to political phenomena. They will be discussed in detail at this point, being essential throughout this study. They are the assumptions of scarcity, methodological individualism, self-interest, and individual rationality in the use of scarce resources.

A little later the same author (Bish, 1971: 10) hints at a fifth assumption of perfect competition.

The overwhelming difficulties of the Tiebout-Bish approach to urban political economy have been pointed out by economists themselves (see, for example, Brazer, 1964: 132–133; Bradford and Oates, 1974: 43–90; Buchanan and Goetz, 1972) and few political scientists or sociologists have been sufficiently naive about the realities of social behavior to use the model or its assumptions in their simplest form. Nevertheless, the perspectives which one typically finds among many economists have tinted and guided much of the theorising and empirical research on urban politics in the United States. This is true of pluralist theory, in particular, insofar as it has a tendency to borrow from economic theory and to view the political arena as if it were an economic market place, marked by competition, knowledge of the market, and individual rationality in the pursuit of self-interest. Pluralist theory is also individualistic (see Anton, 1963: 425–457), as I have already argued, in that the question "Who governs?" has led, almost invariably, to studying the power of individuals rather than the power of groups, rules, institutions, or a consideration of the ways in which certain sorts of structures shape the very nature and distribution of power.

Pluralist theory provides the other main defense of fragmentation on the grounds that it is democratic. Dahl, for example, has grave doubts about the efficiency of the 80,000 units of local government in the United States, but he argues that fragmentation creates a multiplicity of political arenas each with a variety of access points, so that any individual or group which loses out in one can turn to another where they have a good chance of achieving at least some of their goals (Dahl, 1972: 211–239). He goes on to say that by partitioning power, fragmentation creates a number of centers of power and influence which, in turn, act as a system of checks and balances, help protect individual freedom, defuse some of the more intractable national political conflicts by generating cross-cutting allegiances, offer a diverse range of solutions to problems, provide many different training grounds for political leaders and many different ladders to the top of the political system, and give citizens small enough political units to foster a sense of belonging and control.

A STRUCTURAL APPROACH TO FRAGMENTATION

All this has become quite commonplace in the literature on American urban politics and, given liberal individualistic assumptions, it may well have the ring of eternal truth about it. The point of this paper is to challenge these assumptions and to argue that while fragmentation may produce an efficient form of government for some, it is grossly inadequate and inefficient for others, and that far from contributing to an open, pluralist, and democratic system, fragmentation contributes towards a closed, elitist, and undemocratic one. These conclusions are reached by avoiding a discussion of individuals and turning instead to a discussion of certain characteristics of a fragmented system which, by design, default, or accident, structure certain sorts of outcomes in the field of urban public policy. It is the fragmented structure which sets, in the short run at least, immutable limits around the range of options open to individuals or groups within the system.

The point of departure is a distinction between two different dimensions of a political system.

1. The power of public authorities. Any political system with a legitimate government has a number of centers of formal, public authority. The totalitarian dictatorship, in its ideal-typical form, has just one center of authority, but real political systems range from a relatively small number to, in the case of the United States, the other extreme of a relatively large number. The number of public authorities is important, as the pluralists well recognize and as this paper will show a little later, since this has a strong influence on their power and their capacity to generate public goods and services. However, American theorists have a strong tendency to concentrate unduly on the dangers of the concentration of governmental power in a political system, a tendency which

goes hand-in-hand with a finely tuned fear of the threat to democracy posed by governments which are too strong and powerful, and a somewhat underdeveloped fear of the threat to democracy posed by the possibility of weak public bodies being captured by strong and powerful private interests. Therefore, the second dimension of the political system which must be examined is the strength of private interests.

2. The power of private interests. Social and political theorists have long argued that democracy requires many different centers of private power, each of which should be capable of mobilizing its defenses against other interests and government itself. Totalitarianism begins with the destruction of all private centers of power—churches, trade unions, political parties, professional associations, and so on. While many independent centers of private power are a sine qua non of a pluralist democracy, it is just as true that the public interest will be perverted if it is captured by these private interests. Democracy, pluralist or otherwise, rests on a fine balance of public authority and private power.

In many ways the central theoretical thrust of this paper is that it is crucial to separate out these two dimensions of public authority and private power and to recognize that different combinations of the two will produce political systems with different properties. Figure 22–1 lays this out in a rudimentary form.

At one extreme a system with only a few centers of strong formal authority and only weakly developed private interests is bound to lean toward a form of totalitarianism, while at the other extreme a society with both weak formal authorities and private interests is likely to be a preindustrial and parochial system. On the other hand, a society with strong formal authorities capable of producing the public goods and services needed in any urban-industrial society, yet with a fairly complete range of

FIGURE 22–1
Public authority and private power

		Public authorities are:	
		Strong	Weak
Private interests are:	Strong	Liberal democracies, e.g., Scandinavian countries	Free enterprise systems, U.S.
	Weak	Totalitarian systems, e.g., East European block, Spain	Parochial and developing systems

strong and independent centers of private power which cannot be cowed and dominated by government in the totalitarian mold, is likely to approximate the liberal democratic ideal. The fourth permutation which, I argue, is typified by the United States, has a relatively weak set of public political institutions but a strong set of private interests which causes it to be crucially different from a fully fledged liberal democracy. In the remainder of the article I shall examine the case of the United States, the social basis of its fragmented local government structure, and the economic and political consequences of fragmentation, in an attempt to show why the system fails to live up to the requirements of liberal democracy.[1]

THE SOCIAL BASES OF FRAGMENTATION

When the development of cheap and quick forms of private transport in the late part of the 19th and the early part of the 20th century allowed those who could af-

ford it to leave the danger and discomforts of living in the city, they invariably made sure that the old communities they moved into retained their political independence, or else they created new political units out of the suburbs they built. Up until about 1900, cities were able to keep up with their over-expanding perimeters, but after 1900 annexation was made more difficult and there started, instead, a wave of incorporation of new local governments which scarcely abated even into the 1950s (Wood, 1958: 69). It was no accident that the suburbs created their own independent governments for most of the new suburbanites were wealthy and it was, and still is, very much in their interests to cut themselves off politically, legally, socially, and financially from the poorer, inner-city areas. The result of this wave of incorporation of middle- and upper-class suburbs is that the political units of local government with the most resources and the fewest problems are cut off from those with the fewest resources and the most problems.

Of course, not all the suburbs are affluent middle- and upper-class enclaves, any more than all core cities are dominated exclusively by poverty, crime, ignorance, disease, slums, and ghettos. There are some suburbs which are of no more than average wealth, some which are decidedly working class in composition, and even a sprinkling of poor and black ones too (Wirt et al., 1972: 25–48; Dobriner, 1963: 13;

---

[1] It is not just the overall number of local government units which is important but also the fact that they are relatively independent and autonomous. The French system also has a very large number of municipalities although they are fairly closely controlled by higher governments. Even so the large number and small size of French communes contributes to the immobilism of the total system and to the inability of units within it to provide important public goods and services (Becquart, 1975).

Berger, 1960). Nevertheless, practically all the very considerable body of research shows that the suburbs are appreciably and significantly wealthier than their inner city cores (Wirt et al., 1972: 13; Campbell and Sacks, 1967: 237; Cox, 1973: 27–69). The fact that this conclusion can be drawn from studies which invariably include the poor and averagely wealthy suburbs, suggests that the aggregate figures conceal the existence of a few extraordinarily wealthy suburbs.

There may be only a few fabulously rich suburbs compared with a fairly large number of modestly affluent ones, but it takes only a few super-rich and politically autonomous suburbs to throw the whole fiscal system of the metropolis off balance. The logic is very simple: if the mean income of the whole metropolitan area is, say, $10,000, then it takes only one suburb with a mean income of $30,000 to leave another four of equal size with half the mean. This magnitude of variation is well within the norm. From the point of view of local tax capacity, the property base is most important, and it is reported that one New Jersey community had an assessed valuation of $5.5 million per pupil (Sharkansky, 1972: 138). Another source reports per capita property values 18 or 19 times higher in some jurisdictions than in others within the same state, and points out that ratios of four or five to one are not at all unusual (hearings before the Select Committee on Equal Educational Opportunities of the United States Senate, 1971: 3–4). The average assessed value in the Cleveland metropolitan area was $3,000 but in one area it was $1,307 and in another it was over $122,000 (Wirt et al., 1972: 137).

What is important, in this part of the argument, is not just the fact of fragmentation but also the fact that political lines tend to follow socioeconomic lines fairly closely. For the larger urban areas the whole situation is exacerbated still further. The evidence is not at all clear or conclusive but the general picture seems to be as follows. The larger the metropolitan area, the greater the economic disparities between the city centers and their suburbs (Dye, 1970: 363–373; Schnore, 1963: 76–85; Campbell and Sacks, 1967: 237). This one might expect from the fact that the largest metropolitan areas tend to be centers of both very great wealth and great poverty. Second, the larger the metropolitan area the more fragmented it is likely to be (Hawkins and Dye, 1970: 17–24; Danielson, 1966: 57).[2] Third, the greater the disparity between city and suburb the greater the fragmentation of government is likely to be (Schnore, 1963: 76–85). And fourth, the higher the socioeconomic status of the local government unit, the smaller the population is likely to be (Masotti and Bowen, 1965: 39–58; Downes, 1968: 264). The overall picture, therefore, is one in which the largest urban areas tend to be the most fragmented, to have the greatest disparities in wealth, and to have small pockets of extraordinarily dense wealth. The great suburban movement between 1920 and 1960 did very little, if anything, to dilute these concentrations of wealth (Farley, 1964: 38–47). On the contrary, the evidence is that the disparity between the city and its suburbs is increasing steadily and remorselessly (Cox, 1973: 31; Riew, 1970: 145).

SOME ECONOMIC CONSEQUENCES OF FRAGMENTATION

There is a vicious economic circle entailed in urban fragmentation in that to keep taxes and expenditures down, the wealthiest suburbs must use their powers to keep in their own money and to keep other people's problems out. The result is that "the very cities that can most easily afford to carry the burdens of inexpensive homes are the ones which most vigorously

---

[2] There are variations in the degree of fragmentation according to region, age, and size of city, but even regions with the fewest local government units have added to them in the past 50 years.

resist such homes and are the most successful in avoiding them" (Fagin quoted in Wood, 1958: 217). Because of this imperative to protect the purity of its local gold, the wealthiest suburb must protect itself against the slightly less wealthy, which is forced to defend its borders from invasion by the still less wealthy, and so on down the line until the working-class suburb is forced to use its powers against the block-busting tactics of nonwhites or white ethnics. At each boundary, the more affluent have better weapons than the less affluent to protect their interests (Wood, 1958: 212–221). One consequence of the economic tightrope that all but the super-rich suburbs must walk, is that they must prop themselves up on the suburbs of slightly lower socioeconomic standing, so that the chain of exploitation passes from the top to the bottom of the suburban system, and from there it spills over into the yet poorer city center. The logic of the economic situation means that dog must eat dog *within* the suburban network, as well as between the suburbs and the city.

Although competition between the suburbs may drive some of them precipitously close to the brink of bankruptcy or over, it is still the suburban-city relationship which presents the most dire problems in the short run, and probably in the long run also. Some economists and geographers describe the relationship in terms of such words as exploitation, parasitism, and even imperialism (see, for example, Heilbrun, 1972: 538; Brazer, 1964: 144; Cox, 1973: 69; O'Connor, 1972: 592). The older central cities are

neatly impaled on the horns of a dilemma; if they spend more on the poor, they increase the fiscal pressure that encourages the rich to move out, thus eroding the tax base and undermining the future prospects for those who remain; if they attempt to defend the tax base by choosing policies that are less distributive, they fail in their obligation to join in the war on poverty, and incidently increase the likelihood of riot and bloodshed (Heilbrun, 1972: 532).

In a similar vein, Harvey Brazer has written

The inefficiencies, in terms of underallocation of resources to the public sector, and the accompanying inequities, go a long way toward providing some understanding, if not explanation, of the major problems confronting metropolitan America (Brazer, 1964: 145).

Curiously enough, one article which tries to point out the great political and economic advantages of a "polycentric" (fragmented) metropolitan government, finds an important weakness of this sort of system as an effective political framework for the provision of public services.

More difficult problems for polycentric political systems are created when the provision of public goods cannot be confined to the boundaries of the existing units of government. . . . No community on its own initiative, has much incentive to assume the full costs of controlling adverse consequences which are shared by a wider public. . . .
Concerted action by various units of government in a metropolitan area is easier to organize when costs and benefits are fairly uniformly distributed throughout the area (Ostrom et al., 1961: 839).

In a system in which different socioeconomic groups were randomly distributed over the metropolitan area, the costs and benefits of public services would indeed be fairly uniformly distributed throughout the area, and one might well have a high quality of public services. But the sad and indisputable fact about the metropolitan area is that this is not the case, that socioeconomic groups with their characteristic interests tend to be clustered together, and hence concerted action is difficult or simply impossible. The authors of the quotation above have picked out a highly significant cause of metropolitan government's inability to deliver certain sorts of public goals and services, except at a very high cost.

This brief treatment by no means exhausts the financial implications of city-suburban fragmentation. There is also the problem of the regressiveness of local taxes (Fitch, 1964: 117; Netzer, 1970: 459–479), the unwillingness of governments in fragmented areas to provide services with positive externality effects for nearby municipalities (Adams, 1972: 504–513), the effect of increasing housing costs (Downs, 1973: 48–53), and limiting urban space for cheaper-cost housing (Wood, 1958: 214–216), and a host of other major and minor considerations.

From the point of view of the present argument, however, the most important economic consequence of fragmentation is that each jurisdiction is forced by the logic of the situation in which it finds itself to use the full array of zoning regulations, subdivision controls, building regulations, tax and service differentials, and a good measure of old fashioned social prejudice, in order to protect its tax base, which enables it to aim for that combination of public and private goods that enables it to maintain its quality of life at the highest possible level. In other words fragmentation, and its concomitant zoning, building, and tax laws, helps to create a rigid social structure which prevents the free mobility of different social strata and ethnic groups. Only the wealthiest are in a position to survey the full range of packages of goods and services produced in different jurisdictions and to choose freely the combination they prefer. By then deploying the powers of their chosen local government unit in order to protect this combination of goods and services, they automatically limit the choices available to the not-so-wealthy who, in their turn, use their power to limit the choice of lower social strata, and so on down to the bottom of the social pile where there is virtually no choice whatsoever.

This, of course, is contrary to the whole thrust of Tiebout's "pure theory of local expenditures." Tiebout concludes his article by saying "if consumer-voters are fully mobile, the appropriate local govern-ments, whose revenue-expenditure patterns are set, are adopted by the consumer-voters. While the solution may not be perfect because of institutional rigidities, this does not invalidate its importance" (1972: 522–523). The free mobility of the consumer-voter is at the very heart of the Tiebout argument, and yet if the fragmented structure on which he bases his model is to survive at all, it must create a massive array of institutional rigidities which block the free mobility of all but a small number of consumer-voters. Seen from the individualist's point of view, the Tiebout argument may make sense, although this is doubtful; a rudimentary look at the workings of the total system is enough to kill the argument stone dead, and the irony is that the argument contains within itself the seeds of its own destruction. In the words of Harvey Brazer (1964: 133) "Tiebout's model cannot be said to be even a rough first approximation of the real world."

SOME POLITICAL CONSEQUENCES OF FRAGMENTATION

The fiscal disparity between city and suburbs, and within different suburbs, combined with the political fragmentation of local government upon which it is built, is a fact of the utmost importance for an understanding of contemporary urban politics in the United States, and, indeed, for an understanding of national politics as well. From what has already been said it seems quite clear that the economic and political autonomy of the middle-class suburbs is a device which helps maintain the unhappy equilibrium between private affluence and public squalor, and which helps to keep the other America out of sight and out of mind. Far from creating a whole set of political arenas with many different access points to them, as in the pluralist model, they create political arenas which are promptly sealed off to any form of potential political opposition. By making themselves politically independent, middle-class suburbs use their powers to deal with the wider environment in the simplest possible way—by keeping it out. For example, it has been calculated that over half the whites in metropolitan areas live outside the central city, but that the black percentage of suburban population has declined for every decade since 1900 and was about 4.5 percent in the mid-1960s (Strange, 1966: 46; see also Cottingham, 1975: 276). In Amos Hawley's words (1963: 422–423), "the community constitutes a mobilization of power—the capacity to produce results for dealing with the environment, whether physical or social," or, to use the evocative phrase of Gamson, political fragmentation is a mechanism which helps maintain a system of "stable unrepresentation."

In the same way that the adoption of a form of city government may represent the victory of one social group over another (Alford and Scoble, 1970: 395), so the very drawing of political boundary lines may represent the victory of one social group over another, and it may be that different forms of city government and the structure of government within political units are much less important as basic determinants of the patterns of urban politics in the United States than is the drawing of political boundaries around and between different communities. Simply giving a middle-class suburb its autonomy as a unit of local government affects the total system of the metropolis, since money, the life blood of public services, is redirected along different arteries to different bodies politic. Sociologists and political scientists cannot afford to take this form of political and economic division of labor for granted.[3] As a structural attribute of the metropolis it

has a basic and profound influence on the whole network of social, economic, and political relationships in the area.

Sociologists with an interest in community politics did start to examine the process of what has been called "the governmentalization of discrimination" (Rosenbaum, 1974), when they took an interest in the withdrawal of big businessmen from community politics. Usually the explanations were cast in terms of the shift from locals to cosmopolitans, the growing size and increasingly national and multinational focus of corporations, and the competitive pressure on businessmen to devote themselves full-time to the pursuit of profit. To these we might add a further explanation. In the same way that economic push and pull factors caused the migration to the cities, so push and pull factors helped the suburban exodus. The economic elite may have been pulled to the suburbs by the prospects of green and pleasant surroundings, but they may also have been helped on their way by the increasingly unpleasant political environment of the city. One way to deal with the rapidly increasing urban working class, which was beginning to engage in a degree of socialist activity before World War I (Weinstein, 1967: ch. 2), was to take power away from it by reforming city government. Another way was to flee the city and build a new political system outside it. Both tactics were used, and ultimately the second proved the most popular.

Besides isolating the financial resources necessary to solve metropolitan problems, political fragmentation also depletes the political resources needed to solve these problems. In the first place, fragmentation means political units which are too small to produce a whole range of public goods. As Schmandt and Stephens's study of Milwaukee shows (1960: 369–375), smaller units provide a smaller range of public goods and services than larger ones (see also Bradford and Oates, 1974: 43–90 and Beequart, 1975). In the second place, hun-

---

[3] With the notable and eloquent exception of Gans (1969: 163–174), few sociologists have systematically discussed the effects of fragmentation on urban social patterns in the United States. Political scientists have not ignored it, but, as I argue in this paper, they have usually misinterpreted its effects.

dreds of overlapping, competing, and duplicating political units make it virtually impossible to reach any commonly agreed solution to a metropolitan problem, and even more impossible to implement the solution in a sensible and efficient manner. Fragmentation makes for immobilism and nondecision making (Stedman, 1972: 167).[4] It is important to note that this is the consequence of structural attributes and not of the motives of people or groups who happen to operate the structures. In fact, the original formulation of the nondecision-making argument was a structural and organizational one of this kind. "All forms of political organization have a bias in favor of the exploitation of some kinds of conflict and the suppression of others, because organization is the mobilization of bias" (Schattschneider, 1960: 71). It is significant, in the context of the opening remarks of this paper about liberal individualism, that the contemporary discussion of nondecision making is almost wholly in terms of the motives and powers of individuals and groups to suppress issues, and very rarely in terms of the impersonal workings of structural or institutional relations.

The costs of this sort of nondecision-making system are not distributed randomly across socioeconomic groups, or across different political units which contain clusters of socioeconomic types. For those with few private resources who depend upon a large measure of public action to solve public problems, nondecision making in the political arena means they are left with the burden of the problems. For those with private resources, nondecision making may be a minor, or even, perhaps, a major aggravation which lowers the quality of urban life, but they at least have the option of using their own private resources to solve the problem. If the system is unable to reach a decision about adding fluoride to the water supply, those who care enough and have money enough, can buy a private machine or fluoride tablets. If the system fails to provide good schools, then there are private ones, if you can afford them. If the system fails to produce a decent fire service, then one can opt for the second best and take out more home insurance. These all cost money and there is a limit to what even the super-rich can buy, but the costs of failing to make a collective decision to solve a collective problem fall most heavily upon those with the fewest private resources. In a phrase, the poor cannot buy their way out of trouble.

It has been said over and over again that metropolitan fragmentation creates an extremely wasteful and inefficient form of government, that it is ineffective, and leads mainly to immobilism, stagnation, and an inability to solve the most pressing problems of the cities. Yet the fact is that fragmentation *is* a solution to problems— the middle-class solution which tries to ensure that other people's problems do not encroach on their suburbs. This is the intent of local zoning, house building, and tax laws.

Land-use planning in any comprehensive sense really does not exist in our large urban areas. What does exist is a complex game of chess among localities, each attempting to palm off the undesirable applicants for urban space upon their neighbors. . . . This is warfare, not planning [Vernon, 1964: 101].

One is tempted to add that it is indeed warfare. Class warfare. At any rate, the social and economic costs of "treating" problems in this way may be much lower to those with ample private resources, than would be any attempt to tackle the problems at their root causes. Fragmented government amounts to nondecision making, nonplanning, and the separation of resources from problems. The result is too many governments and not enough gov-

---

[4] Luther Gulick (1966: 124) sums up this much-discussed aspect of metropolitan misgovernment in one crisp sentence—"Once an indivisible problem is divided, nothing effective can be done about it."

ernment. As Lowi puts it (1969: 193), "Cities are well run but badly governed." Consequently American city governments are weak in some areas of urban public policy and virtually impotent in others.

In short, fragmented government is nongovernment, and nongovernment is good government, at least for those with the capacity to solve their own immediate problems with their own private resources. Oliver Williams (1971: 51) points out that "there is a relationship between the distribution of social benefits derived from urbanism and the decentralization of urban control. Decentralization of political control favors those who can most easily achieve social access through mobility, and penalizes the least mobile" (see also Orbell and Uno, 1972; and Shepard, 1975). The more liberal members of the social science professions who complain bitterly about the inadequacies of fragmented metropolitan government neglect the fact that it is an extremely efficient and adequate political solution to middle-class problems.

It is an efficient solution both in the sense that it helps shut out nonmiddle-class problems, and hence minimize the cost to the middle-class taxpayer of solving these problems, and also in a more positive sense that fragmented government is highly likely to leave private economic interests relatively uncontrolled and unregulated. Ross Stephens (1971: 135) makes the point plainly, and is worth quoting at some length.

In every community and metropolitan area there are groups and individuals who have a stake in the nonexistence of an effective decision-making structure. That is, they have a stake in the maintenance of the status quo of limited and impotent local government in core cities, fragmented and easily influenced politics for suburban governments and the manager-governed "non-political" policies of medium sized towns.

Land development, rapidly assuming critical importance in most urban areas, exemplifies the kind of issue that involves important interests. If urban government should deal effectively with questions of development, the results would threaten realtors, land speculators, and bankers.

Fragmentation also sets the horizons of the possible. If government is weak and ineffective, and if attempts at metropolitan reform are usually unsuccessful, then citizens and politicians will scale down their expectations of what governments could and should be able to accomplish (see Long, 1962: 156–160). Certain sorts of solutions to public problems will be ruled out as utopian—often with the explanation that they run against the grain of human nature! Certain sorts of public policies will not even be considered, and a whole range of solutions to problems will not begin to permeate public thinking. This is the mobilization of bias in its most powerful, structural form. It operates on elites and masses alike: it is not simply a matter of the elite using its power to suppress forms of political action. Moreover, this sort of system contains the seeds of its own preservation. If the local political system is unable to deliver public goods, then there is little point in political participation. A more rational strategy is to try to make enough money to move to the suburbs, but the "exit" alternative simply makes the whole situation worse. The question which remains is whether those who are forced to stay in the city and use the "voice" strategy will find adequate financial and political resources to solve some of their more acute problems (see Orbell and Uno, 1972: 487). The argument developed in this paper suggests that solutions of any kind are unlikely without some fairly major structural changes, but that the very nature of the structure makes it exceedingly difficult to change.

CONCLUSION

Without too much stretching of the imagination, one can stand Robert Dahl's

(1972: 238–239) defense of "the other 80,000 governments" on its head, and summarise the effects of fragmentation in the following way.

1. Fragmentation does not create a pluralist multiplicity of political arenas, each with many access points, but rather it creates a large number of political arenas, each of which uses its powers to seal off its access points to those it does not want.

2. Fragmentation does not so much allow for the possibility of diverse solutions to problems as it prevents the possibility of any solutions to these problems.

3. Fragmentation does not so much create the conditions for the partitioning of power as it helps to create powerless forms of government.

4. Fragmentation does not so much permit some potential conflict to be taken out of the arena of national politics to be handled at local levels as it obstructs the placing of conflictual issues in any political arena.

5. Fragmentation does not so much provide oppositions with a base when they are defeated elsewhere as it ensures that the defeated have no powerful base anywhere.

6. Fragmentation does not so much make citizen access to officials easier as it creates a gulf between officials with resources and the citizens who most need those resources.

7. Fragmentation does not so much give citizens the feeling that they can grasp local issues better and be more effective in dealing with them as it gives those with the most urgent issues to raise a very good reason to feel powerless and hopeless.

REFERENCES

Adams, R. F. (1972) "On the variations in consumption of public services," pp. 504–513 in M. Edel and J. Rothenberg (eds.) *Readings in Urban Economics.* New York: Macmillan.

Alford, R. R., and H. Scoble (1970) "Political and socioeconomic characteristics of American cities," pp. 393–413 reprinted in J. S. Goodman, ed. *Perspectives on Urban Politics.* Boston: Allyn and Bacon.

Anton, T. J. (1963) "Power, pluralism, and local politics." *Admin. Science Quarterly.* 7 (March), pp. 448–57.

Becquart, J. L. (1975) "French mayors and communal policy outputs: the case of small cities." Paper presented to the annual meeting of the European Consortium for Political Research, Urban Politics Workshop, London, England, April 7–13.

Berger, B. M. (1960) *Working Class Suburb: A Study of Auto Workers in Suburbia.* Berkeley and Los Angeles: University of California Press.

Bish, R. L. (1971) *The Public Economy of Metropolitan Areas.* Chicago: Markham.

Bradford, D. E., and W. E. Oates (1974) "Suburban exploitation of central cities and governmental structure," pp. 43–90 in H. M. Hochman and G. E. Peterson, eds. *Redistribution through Public Choice.* New York: Columbia University Press.

Brazer, H. E. (1964) "Some fiscal implications of metropolitanism," pp. 127–150 reprinted in B. Chinitz, ed., *City and Suburb: The Economics of Metropolitan Growth.* Englewood Cliffs, N.J.: Prentice-Hall.

Buchanan, J. M., and G. J. Goetz (1972) "Efficiency limits of fiscal mobility: An assessment of the Tiebout model." *Journal of Public Economics* 1 (April), pp. 25–43.

Campbell, A. K., and S. Sacks (1967) *Metropolitan America: Fiscal Patterns and Governmental Systems.* New York: Free Press.

Castells, M. (1974) "Urban sociology and urban politics: from a critique to new trends in research." Paper delivered to the annual meeting of the American Sociological Association. Montreal, Canada, August 28.

Cottingham, P. H. (1975) "Black income and metropolitan residential dispersion." *Urban Affairs Quarterly* 10 (March), pp. 273–96.

Cox, K. R. (1973) *Conflict, Power and Politics in the City: A Geographic View.* New York: McGraw-Hill.

Dahl, R. A. (1972) *Democracy in the United States: Promises and Performance*. Chicago: Rand McNally.

Danielson, M. N. (1966) *Metropolitan Politics: A Reader*. Boston: Little, Brown.

Dobriner, W. M (1963) *Class in Suburbia*. Englewood Cliffs, N.J.: Prentice-Hall.

Downes, B. T. (1968) "Suburban differentiation and municipal policy choices," pp. 243–267 in T. N. Clark, ed., *Community Structure and Decision Making: Comparative Analyses*. San Francisco: Chandler.

Downs, A. (1973) *Opening Up the Suburbs*. Yale: Yale University Press.

Dye, T. R. (1970) "City-suburban social distance and public policy." *Social Forces* 43 (September), pp. 363–73.

Farley, R. (1964) "Suburban persistence." *American Sociological Review* 29 (February), pp. 38–47.

Fitch, L. C. (1964) "Metropolitan financial problems," pp. 113–126 in B. Chinitz, ed., *City and Suburb: The Economics of Metropolitan Growth*. Englewood Cliffs, N.J.: Prentice-Hall.

Gans, H. J. (1969) "The white exodus to suburbia steps up," pp. 163–174, reprinted in H. R. Mahood and E. L. Angus, eds., *Urban Politics and Problems: A Reader*. New York: Charles Scribners' Sons.

Gulick, L. H. (1966) "The rationale for metropolitan government," reprinted in M. N. Danielson, ed., *Metropolitan Politics: A Reader*. Boston: Little, Brown.

Hawkins, B. W., and T. R. Dye (1970) "Metropolitan fragmentation: a research note." *Midwest Review of Public Administration* 4 (February), pp. 17–24.

Hawley, A. (1963) "Community power and urban renewal success." *American Sociological Review* 68 (January), pp. 422–31.

Hearings before the select committee on equal educational opportunities of the United States Senate (1971) *Inequality in School Finances: General Appendix*, Part 16D-1 Washington D.C.: Government Printing Office.

Heilbrun, J. (1972) "Poverty and public finance in the older central cities," pp. 523–45 in M. Edel and J. Rothenberg, eds., *Readings in Urban Economics*. New York: Macmillan.

Laumann, E. O., L. Verbrugge, and F. U. Pappi (1974) "A causal modelling approach to the study of a community elite's influence structure." *American Sociological Review* 39 (April), pp. 162–74.

Lineberry, R. L., and I. Sharkansky (1971) *Urban Politics and Public Policy*. New York: Harper & Row.

Long, N. E. (1962) *The Polity*. Chicago: Rand McNally.

Lowi, T. J. (1969) *The End of Liberalism*. New York: W. W. Norton.

McKay, D. H. (1974) "Political science and urbanism in Europe: some lessons from the American experience." Paper delivered at the annual meeting of the European Consortium for Political Research, Workshops on Urban Politics, Strasbourg, France, March 28–April 4.

Masotti, L. H., and D. Bowen (1965) "Communities and budgets; the sociology of municipal expenditures." *Urban Affairs Quarterly* 1 (December), pp. 38–58.

Maxwell, J. A. (1969) *Financing State and Local Government*. Washington, D.C.: Brookings Institution.

Netzi, R. D. (1970) "Tax structures and their impact on the poor," pp. 459–479 in J. P. Crecine, ed., *Financing the Metropolis*. Beverly Hills, Calif.: Sage Publications.

O'Connor, J. (1972) "The fiscal crisis of the state," pp. 590–602 in M. Edel and J. Rothenberg, eds., *Readings in Urban Economics*. New York: Macmillan.

Orbell, J. M., and T. Uno (1972) "A theory of neighborhood problem solving: political action vs. residential mobility." *American Political Science Review* 66 (June), pp. 471–89.

Ostrom, V., C. M. Tiebout, and R. Warren (1961) "The organization of government in metropolitan areas: a theoretical enquiry." *American Political Science Review* 60 (December), pp. 831–42.

Riew, J. (1970) "Metropolitan disparities and fiscal federalism," pp. 137–161 in J. P. Crecine, ed., *Financing the Metropolis*. Beverly Hills, Calif.: Sage Publications.

Rosenbaum, A. (1974) State Power, Political Power, and Public Policy: The Case of Illi-

218

nois. Phd.D. dissertation. Political Science Department, University of Chicago.

Schattschneider, E. E. (1960) *The Semi-Sovereign People*. New York: Holt, Rinehart & Winston.

Schmandt, H., and G. Stephens (1960) "Measuring municipal output." *National Tax Journal* 6 (December), pp. 369–75.

Schnore, L. (1963) "The socioeconomic status of cities and suburbs." *American Sociological Review* 28 (February), pp. 76–85.

Sharkansky, I. (1972) *The Maligned States*. New York: McGraw-Hill.

Shepard, W. B. (1975) "Metropolitan decentralization: a test of the life-style values models." *Urban Affairs Quarterly* 10 (March), pp. 297–313.

Silverman, L. (1974) "A plea for more structural analysis in urban political studies." Paper delivered to the annual meeting of the European Consortium for Political Research, Workshop on Urban Politics, Strasbourg, France, March 28–April 4.

Smith, R. G. (1969) *Public Authorities in Urban Areas*. Washington, D.C.: National Association of Counties Research Foundation.

Stedman, M. (1972) *Urban Politics*. Cambridge, Mass.: Winthrop.

Stehr, N., and L. E. Larson (1972) "The rise and decline of areas of specialisation." *The American Sociologist* 7 (August), pp. 3–6.

Stephens, G. R. (1971) "The power grid of the metropolis," pp. 125–45 in F. M. Wirt, ed., *Future Directions in Community Power Research: A Colloquium*. Berkeley, Calif.: Institute of Governmental Studies.

Strange, J. H. (1966) "Racial segregation in the metropolis," in M. N. Danielson, ed., *Metropolitan Politics: A Reader*. Boston: Little, Brown.

Tiebout, C. M. (1972) "A pure theory of local expenditures," pp. 513–23 reprinted in M. Edel and J. Rothenberg, eds., *Readings in Urban Economics*. New York: Macmillan.

Vernon, R. (1964) "The myth and reality of our urban problems," pp. 97–112 reprinted in B. Chinitz, ed., *City and Suburb: The Economics of Metropolitan Growth*. Englewood Cliffs, N.J.: Prentice-Hall.

Walton, J. (1971) "A methodology for the comparative study of power: some conceptual and procedural applications." *Social Science Quarterly* 52 (June).

Weinstein, J. (1967) *The Decline of Socialism in America*. New York: Vintage.

Williams, O. P. (1971) *Metropolitan Political Analysis*. New York: Free Press.

Wirt, F. M., B. Walter, F. F. Rabinowitz, and D. R. Hensler (1972) *On the City's Rim: Politics and Policy in Suburbia*. Lexington, Mass.: D. C. Heath.

Wood, R. (1958) *Suburbia: Its People and Their Politics*. Boston: Houghton Mifflin.

———— (1961) *1400 Governments*. Cambridge, Mass.: Harvard University Press.

23

Suburban differences and metropolitan policies

Oliver P. Williams, Harold Herman,
Charles S. Liebman, and Thomas R. Dye

The term "metropolitan problem" has often been affixed to any situation requiring cooperation or interaction between adjacent units of government in urban areas. Problems are usually identified on a service basis, and there is hardly any governmental activity which has not been identified as constituting a metropolitan problem.[1] The advocacy of metropolitan government is, for some, based merely on the belief that almost every activity has an intergovernmental aspect.

Some writers have distinguished between *metropolitan problems* and *problems in a metropolitan area*.[2] This observation contains a very sound insight, but it lacks specificity. The following classification attempts to make explicit the crucial distinction between the two. The distinction is based on the recognition that the major characteristic of metropolitan areas is the coincidence of spatial specialization and autonomous local governing units. A metropolitan problem is one that, unlike other intergovernmental problems, results from this coincidence.

Problem one: Maintaining the system. If people want to work in one community, sleep in another, shop in a third, and play

in a fourth; if high-status persons want to reside apart from those of low status; if smoky factories are to be separated from homes; in short, if spatial specialization is to exist within a metropolitan economy— then basic services necessary for the development of each subarea and means through which they may be accessible to one another, must be provided.

Transportation and communication are the primary avenues of maintaining accessibility. The latter is provided primarily through the private sector of our economy, the former is shared by private and public management, with government playing an increasingly important role. But transportation is not the only service through which government makes the system feasible. Certain basic utilities, such as water and sewage disposal, are often requisites for urban development. If they cannot be locally provided, and if a larger service area is a technical or financial necessity for continued development, then autonomy in policy formulation must give way to integrated mechanisms if the component units are to survive. Thus we characterize as a truly metropolitan problem the *maintenance of services providing the supports necessary for the continued existence of areal specialization.*

Problem two: Unequal distribution of resources and services. In every metropolitan area, thers are "have" and "have not" communities, with the core city often being the most advertised of the "have nots." Such disparities are largely a byproduct of the system of areal specialization. Of course there always have been, and probably always will be, differences in individial and community wealth. In a metropolitan context, such differences are

---

Reprinted with permission of the authors and the University of Pennsylvania Press from Oliver P. Williams, Harold Herman, Charles S. Liebman, Thomas R. Dye, *Suburban Differences and Metropolitan Policies: A Philadelphia Story* (Philadelphia: University of Pennsylvania Press, 1965), pp. 299–312.

[1] In a recent national study, even the universal governmental function of personnel management has been given the metropolitan label. See: *Governmental Manpower for Tomorrow's Cities*, a report of the Municipal Manpower Commission (New York: McGraw-Hill, 1962).

[2] Edward C. Banfield and Morton Grodzins, *Government and Housing in Metropolitan Areas* (New York: McGraw-Hill, 1958).

aggravated by the efficiency with which the system of differentiation is maintained. Moreover, the multiplicity of local governing units, when imposed upon specialized populations, affects their ability to reconcile differences between groups. It is in this sense that we take exception to views such as that of Banfield and Grodzins who argue that housing is not a metropolitan problem. We agree that the structure of metropolitan government is not the *cause* of slums or blight; we agree that the mere existence of different housing standards does not constitute a problem; but we disagree with their belief that alterations in governmental structure will not alter housing policies. Such alteration can distribute the burden of housing costs over wider areas, it can impose higher minimum standards, it can organize leadership that is lacking in those areas where housing is poorest, it can attack the roots of the social and economic differences that segregate the poor and dictate their housing. It can do all this if one recognizes the extent to which urban differentiation affects the distribution of the supply of housing and the costs of remedying its inadequacies, and if one holds government responsible for producing change.

Our disagreement with Banfield and Grodzins is similar to that between the professionals and local politicians. As we have seen, some suburbs may choose to deemphasize or do without some services. Although we did not specifically probe this question, we suspect that some working-class suburbs would willingly forgo basic health services, for example, if commensurate tax savings would accrue. Thus the existence of different service standards reflect both differences in burdens associated with supplying financial support and differences in the preferences of specialized populations. Whether or not the local people approve of the differentials, disparities in services result. Professionals will identify such disparities as metropolitan problems when local officials and residents will not.

There is still another basis for labelling inequities in resources and services a metropolitan problem. When upper-middle-class suburbs draw off leadership and, more particularly, wealth from the rest of the system, the remaining areas are impoverished thereby. As a result the cost and burden of providing services vary throughout the metropolitan area. The attainment of a recognized minimum standard becomes excessively costly to some communities and so an acceptable standard of service is not always provided throughout the area.

Thus we characterize as a metropolitan problem *the unequal distribution of resources and services that result from the process of specialization.*

Problem three: Border relationships. Contiguous units of government must engage in many reciprocal relations merely as a result of their proximity to one another. This is as true for rural as urban areas. The fleeing criminal crossing municipal boundaries is a clear example. Such fugitive pursuit problems are common to all governments; yet we frequently refer to this situation as metropolitan when it occurs in an urban environment, but not when it occurs in rural areas. River pollution evokes upstream-downstream conflicts regardless of whether the jurisdictions involved are urban or rural. Factories in rural areas may poison animals and plants with discharges of noxious fluids or fumes. That such discharges affect more than one political jurisdiction does not make the problem metropolitan.

The politics of mere propinquity does not constitute a truly metropolitan problem, since it is unrelated to the fundamental metropolitan characteristic—areal specialization. For this reason, cooperative demands that emanate simply from border relationships represent pseudometropolitan issues. Success in initiating and maintaining cooperation on matters such as fugitive-search systems, police-radio networks, common streets, minor utility exchanges, etc., should not be viewed as symbols of metropolitan fraternalism which are precursors of true union.

It should be added, however, that the density and greater activity of urban governments increases the number of border contacts between municipalities in metropolitan areas. While urbanism may thus generate a high level of municipal interaction, the qualitative nature of border policies is not thereby changed. These policies deal with problems that are distinct from those of system maintainance and resource and service inequities. Generally, border problems are easily solved until money is required. At that time, the nature of the problem changes, as questions of the proration of costs and obligations arise.

The three classes of problems described above are not mutually exclusive. It is difficult to conceive of any governmental policy or service without some overtones that would qualify it for inclusion in all three categories. Moreover, the importance of the three, and the degree to which they are popularly recognized at any one time, differ. Proposals offered as solutions to metropolitan problems are received and judged in accordance with how problems are perceived and what interest they evoke. A proposal for a joint sewer authority may at the same time be perceived as relating to (1) maintenance of the system, (2) service and resource inequities, or (3) a border problem of contiguous urbanized communities. How individual municipalities will react to the proposal is conditioned largely by what problem they view it as solving and what problems they feel may result from the proposal. Nevertheless, some policy areas tend to fall in one category more frequently than in another.

Transportation would undoubtedly head any list of policies related to the maintenance of the system of metropolitan specialization. While some integrated means of planning and managing transportation systems are increasingly being employed, their consequences are such as to profoundly influence the manner in which communities specialize their relationships to other communities and area-wide distributions of wealth. Thus, while municipalities depend upon a more-or-less integrated transportation system for their accessibility to complementary municipalities, it is with the greatest reluctance that they relinquished control over transportation policy. But they have relinquished it.

In nearly every metropolitan area, state highway departments have always supplied a modicum of coordination over the highway network. In the Philadelphia area, transportation planning and operation is sufficiently recognized as metropolitan in character that the county and state governments have assumed jurisdiction over it. The creation of a regional transportation-planning agency sustained mostly by federal funds, and the signing of intercounty and interstate agreements on transit development, reflect recognition of the essential integrative role of transportation. Municipal activity is becoming confined to lobbying before these higher units of government.

Water and sewage disposal systems are second only to transportation in providing support to the metropolitan system. It has been possible to secure cooperation from very diverse suburbs for the provision of both these utilities. Cooperative arrangements between Philadelphia and the suburbs are also common. Indeed, the only firm cooperative arrangements involving financial obligations between the suburbs and the central city have concerned transportation, sewage disposal, or water.

In considering metropolitan problems which result from inequities, it must be recognized that the seeking of specialized areas by homeowners or businesses is the very cause of the "problem." To attempt to redress inequities on a voluntary basis is largely unrealistic. Wealth-sharing plans have never achieved great popularity among those who enjoy favored positions. Furthermore, in most areas, resolving inequities is not essential to maintaining the system. The fact that older industrial centers may, in the process of social segregation, end up with indigent populations for whom they cannot provide is, if of any interest to Main Line residents, perhaps welcomed by them. The very existence of inequities testifies to the success of specialization. Redistributions of resources and services are the most difficult area in which to achieve metropolitan agreement, in part because they are closely related to social inequalities.

The redistribution achieved by the state's school-subsidy program is the result of pressures applied from the outside. Hard-pressed suburbs can find many other hard-pressed districts with which to ally in the state legislature, and the resulting redistribution encompasses not only metropolitan areas but the entire state. Service inequities peculiar to urban areas have found less favorable reception in state capitols; hence grants-in-aid for municipal services are a rarity in comparison with school grants.

THE BASIC CONFLICT OF METROPOLITAN GOVERNMENT

The question of structuring metropolitan government reflects the basic dualism characteristic of metropolitan areas: the existence of specialization and the need for integrative mechanisms. Most metropolitan proposals are caught between these centrifugal and centripetal elements of the system. The fact that one cannot have specialization without integration does not furnish a basis for agreement. It only assures that questions touching on these two facets of the system will continually be raised and not permanently ignored. Thus the metropolis furnishes an inexhaustible political agenda for discussion by political leaders, political scientists, and urbanists.

The underlying normative question implicit in any proposal for structuring government in a metropolitan area is whether the proposed government is designed to maintain or to modify the system. In the past, those who have advocated consolidation as the ultimate "solution to the metropolitan problem" have, in effect, sought a comprehensive modification of the existing system of areal specialization. So, too, have some of the "Garden City" planners, who, although they would not consolidate, would decentralize the metropolis into economically, though not socially, specialized subareas. On the other hand, the narrowly designed, single-purpose special district or authority and the intermunicipal contract concepts have been conceived so as to have as small a disturbing effect on the status quo as possible.

Of the two extreme suggestions for structuring government in metropolitan areas, proposals closer to the latter have been most successful. Metropolitan politics in the United States, as well as in Philadelphia, have never really encompassed a radical revamping of the metropolis as a system of specialization. Why should it? It is unrealistic to expect citizens to acquiesce voluntarily in giving up the prized values of urban differentiation. Thus, while the general-purpose, consolidated metropolitan government has had little acceptance, the special-purpose government has been used frequently. The criticism directed toward this latter development has been that we are in danger of assembling such a complex of special-purpose governments that the problem of policy coordination will be intensified rather than reduced. Such fears are well grounded.

Frequently, the quest for a solution to metropolitan problems is a quest for a governmental structure as politically acceptable as the special district and yet as comprehensive as consolidation. Such solutions do not exist. Moreover, the quest is perhaps misguided. While centralization or decentralization do affect such questions as economy, efficiency, and speed of action, the true test of the adequacy of a metropolitan governmental system is whether it can so structure the political process of negotiation and compromise as to deal effectively and adequately with metropolitan problems.

In the absence of a local political arena in which the demands for integrative services and the claims for greater equities can be arbitrated, such issues are often taken to the state capital and increasingly to Washington. The integrative demands take the form of requests for special regional agencies. Redressing inequities occurs through grants-in-aid. To achieve either goal, parties in the metropolitan area must gain allies or at least still opposition from parties outside the immediate region. The strategy with regard to state capitol or Washington is much the same— the use of political party organizations to form a coalition of urban interests with their nominally affiliated partisan colleagues from nonurban territories. While the procedure varies from state to state, most of the essential metropolitan decisions are made outside the metropolitan area.

In part, this locus for decision making is an outgrowth of the legal foundations upon which our federal system rests. In part, it is the inevitable outcome of the search for outside coalitions that has been fostered by the inability to gain consensus within the area.

PROSPECTS FOR METROPOLITAN GOVERNMENT

Metropolitan problems are not being overlooked entirely. Yet there are cogent arguments to suggest that the most effective and perhaps the only way to handle these problems adequately is to create *one* forum within the area to which *all* problems can be brought for negotiation and compromise—in short, to create *one metropolitan government*. But to posit metropolitan government as a desirable goal and to view it as attainable are separate matters. Our analysis offers little encouragement to

those who are working for metropolitan government. Our outlook is pessimistic, not because of the record of failures, but because of the underlying bases for the failure of metropolitan government proposals.

The attainment of metropolitan government is unlikely either through direct approaches or through the expansion of single-purpose agencies into general-purpose units. Single-purpose metropolitan agencies, whether special districts or new county departments, tend to concentrate on those activities that supply the integrative supports for subarea specialization. These are the services most widely recognized as essential to the well-being of the entire area and each of its parts. It is unrealistic to expect officials and supporters of such programs to endanger their agencies by expanding operations to include issues over which there is less agreement. Although county and regional planners often speak as if they would like to have it, would there be county planning agencies if it were seriously proposed that they be given zoning authority?

The creation of single-purpose agencies to provide integrative supports has an additional and even more important effect on the prospects for metropolitan government. By isolating these services in separate agencies, the political incentives for a general forum are removed; for the "piecemeal" approach to governing the metropolis first siphons off those issues for which there is little choice but cooperation between have and have nots, suburbs and core cities. Left are those problems for which there is least incentive to negotiate and the least amount of flexibility in bargaining—those which most divide the metropolis. Will the stimulus for metropolitan government come from these?

Most metropolitan areas have developed governmental mechanisms for providing some integrative services. In so doing, the thornier problems of regional agreement on minimum service standards and equitable distributions of costs have been left in the cold. Denied the ability to attach their issues to the bargaining around integrative services, those who are concerned with problems of resource and service inequities have little leverage in their favor. No metropolitan area is likely to obtain voluntary cooperation among all its municipalities in pooling resources to furnish hospital care for the indigent. Such an issue will not even be accepted as a "legitimate" metropolitan responsibility. Dozens of other unevenly distributed services will be similarly dismissed. These questions cannot be raised as metropolitan problems if there is no metropolitan government to appeal to. There can be no metropolitan government if those activities which bind the region are handled on an item by item basis.

A pattern of government for metropolitan areas is emerging. Those services which maintain the system are increasingly being supplied by area-wide agencies of one type or another. Problems of inequities are ignored or shunted to the state and federal level. Border incidents are left to an intermunicipal ambassadorial system.

Thus ways are found to handle metropolitan problems. They are often slow, uneven, awkward, uncoordinated, and incomplete, but there are ways. The case for a metropolitan government is not based on the lack of alternatives, but in the belief that the alternatives do not work well enough. Does the pattern of government we have described provide a process of negotiation and compromise that deals effectively and adequately with metropolitan problems?

The question may be moot; for by now we may have built in so many provisional remedies that it may be too late to try to restructure the process. In most major metropolitan areas, regional organizations which are not limited to single purposes but which also have no operating responsibility are being superimposed on the pattern of metropolitan government. The RCEO in Philadelphia, the MRC in New York, the COG in Washington, the ABAG in San Francisco, are examples of general-purpose metropolitan forums. Most are straining to keep going. Not the least of their difficulties is finding an agenda with which to occupy themselves; for existing single-purpose agencies have skimmed off those issues for which there is agreement on the necessity for regional action. The new metropolitan councils do not promise to alter the emerging governmental pattern. In those jurisdictions where activities necessary to maintenance of the system have not yet been organized, the councils may fix their agenda on one or more such issues and sponsor or become themselves single-purpose agencies. Elsewhere they will become fraternal, no-purpose organizations.

A change in the pattern of government coming from within the metropolitan area is hard to imagine. An alternative is the vision of pressure from outside the region producing change, and the possibility of federal and/or state action seems the more probable. Federal programs in urban areas have, for some time, been stressing regional planning and cooperation. Indeed, federal stimulus can be blamed for some of the single-purpose agencies that now exist. If the federal government can tie its programs together, a more comprehensive approach to metropolitan areas might be reflected in local reorganization of thought and action. An even greater "if" in the prospects for change is the actions of state governments. As yet, state governments have been reticent to use grants as enticements toward regional compromises. Will the stimulus to change federal and state policy be forthcoming?

An even greater "if" in the metropolitan future is the impact of technological change. So important is this "if" that it may remove the conditions relevant to discussion of metropolitan government. Earlier, we described the automobile's effect on the structure of the metropolis. There is every reason to believe that new technology will have even more radical effects. Already there are indications that transportation and communication technology are reshaping the urban structure into a new mold. The automobile ended the rail-centered form. The perfected auto and improved communications may be ending the early automotive form. Improved highways and truck transport are enabling industrial plants to sever their connections with metropolitan centers. Increased automation will undoubtedly affect both the process of production and the nature and location of labor markets. Air transport and closed circuit television have already diminished the need for proximity in communications and supervision.

We do not wish to draw a picture of a completely automated society in which each person manipulates electronic impulses from a cell that can be located anywhere. Nevertheless, one should recognize that we are entering an era in which a new type of national system whose economic, social, and political consequences have yet to be felt, is being superimposed on the metropolitan system.

New forms of specialization are beginning to emerge. We already have national recreation and retirement towns, socially graded and related to the entire nation. More important, specific industrial activities that promise to represent a greater proportion of total economic activity in the future are already showing their independence from the urban complex. Some large research institutions can locate practically anywhere that their prized employees want to live.

The new interstate highway system raises the prospect of industrial centers scattered in small or large clusters around the intersections of major routes. The increased household and industrial appetite for space encourages a new form of development utilizing low-cost land in order to maintain a reasonable balance of land to total development costs. Conceivably, now widely scattered employment centers may separate into high- and low-wage places fostering a new form of areal specialization.

While we might speculate further on the specific possibilities of a new urban form, it would serve little useful purpose to do so here. We must emphasize, however, that there is no present indication that technology will be a servant helping to reknit the urban society into an integrated unit. Instead, all the forces of technology will enable high- and low-social-status communities to have even greater physical distances between them. Whether this in fact happens will depend upon national policies affecting the distribution of income and opportunities as well as on compromise in metropolitan and regional bargaining agencies. But those who are concerned about metropolitan government as a form of local control over local problems should not look to technology for any comfort. If we confine our discussion to present conditions and technology, then we must reiterate that the governing of the metropolitan area is a matter of living with differences. The premise for action can never be leveling those differences, but only one of trading advantages or disadvantages.

24

Beyond suburbia

Sylvia F. Fava

Beyond suburbia lie paradoxes: suburbs dominating an increasingly urban society; the emergence of major changes among blacks and women whose potential impact on suburban housing demand and activity patterns is largely ignored; and megalopolis as the new urban-suburban "reality" which exists neither as a political unit nor as a focus of governmental policy and which does not even serve as a viable analytic unit of social science theory. This article explores these and other paradoxes in the future of suburbia in terms of the changing shape of the metropolitan region; the problems of incorporating suburban dominance into social science theory; and the restructuring of governmental programs and agencies to take account of the new distribution of people and problems.

THE SHAPE OF SUBURBAN AMERICA

Numerically the United States is already suburban. Since the 1960s suburbanites have comprised the largest share, although not the majority, of the American population. Defining suburban as the territory within the census Standard Metropolitan Statistical Area (SMSAs) but outside the central cities, the 1970 census counted more than 75 million Americans as suburbanites, comprising 37.6 percent of the total American population; only 31.4 percent of Americans lived in the central cities of metropolitan areas, and the small-est percentage, 31.0, did not live within metropolitan areas at all. This distribution represents a complete reversal of the situation in 1900, when the nonmetropolitan population was by far the most numerous, accounting for 57 percent of the population, while the central city population was a distant second with 27 percent, and the suburban population accounted for only 15 percent of all Americans.[1] The shift to suburbia occurred throughout the 20th century, but with a dramatic spurt after 1940. After World War II the so-called age of suburbia reached popular awareness, although the systemic changes affecting American life—locational flexibility based on new forms of transportation, communication, and information handling; affluence arising from advanced post-industrial productivity; and a highly differentiated, albeit large scale, mass society—had been accumulating for decades.[2]

Suburban growth of the kind we have been accustomed to has passed its peak. It represented one stage of urban decentralization, occurring when there were still large tracts of undeveloped land relatively close to large cities and when there was also a substantial reservoir of nonmetropolitan population migrating to metropolitan areas, especially to their central cities. Suburbanites—that is, people residing in metropolitan areas but outside the central cities—will undoubtedly become a majority of the American population in the

---

[1] Based on data from U.S. Bureau of the Census, *Selected Area Reports, Standard Metropolitan Statistical Areas*, 1960, Final Report PC(3)-1D, Table 1, and *Statistical Abstract of the United States*, 1972, Table 15.

[2] *See*, for example, Noel P. Gist and Sylvia F. Fava, "The Urban Transformation of the United States," *Urban Society*, 6th ed. (New York: T. Y. Crowell, 1974), pp. 55–81.

near future, but these suburbanites will represent a new stage of metropolitan expansion. American cities, established in a virgin land and experiencing most of their growth under the conditions of industrial technology, expanded outward, with the highest growth rates at the outer edges. This suburbanizing pattern has been linked with an upward thrust in the highrise "downtown" of the central city, concentrating the bureaucracies which coordinate the complex metropolitan economic network.

As the ripples of growth expand outward, however, especially around the larger metropolitan areas, they not only encounter the expanding suburban edges of other, typically smaller and newer metropolitan areas, but they also eddy around both the man-made environment of the nonurban past—such as retirement communities, resorts, and truck farms—and the natural environment of parks and wildlife preserves. In addition, a wider range of activities is decentralizing from the old central cities, either into "strip" development along major highways or into lesser "downtowns" serving the increasing population of "suburbia."

SUBURBIA IN MEGALOPOLIS

These coalescing metropolises are megalopolis, the name being as unwielding as the form. This is the new suburban America,

Grow[ing] amidst an irregularly colloidal mixture of rural and suburban landscape; it melts on broad fronts with other mixtures, of somewhat similar though different texture, belonging to the suburban neighborhoods of other cities. . . . This region serves thus as a laboratory in which we may study the new evolution reshaping both the meaning of our traditional vocabulary and the whole material structure of our way of life.[3]

[3] Jean Gottmann, *Megalopolis: The Urbanized Northeastern Seaboard of the United States* (New York: Twentieth Century Fund, 1961), pp. 5, 9.

Megalopolitan development was first described by Jean Gottmann, the French geographer, for the area of the Northeastern seabord extending from north of Boston to south of Washingtn, D.C. Early megalopolitan development has also been analyzed for the California coastal strip extending from north of San Francisco through Los Angeles and south to San Diego.[4]

Using the term *urban region*, Jerome Pickard has indicated how general megalopolitan development has become.[5] In 1920 there were 10 urban regions, making up a third of the United States population; all but 1 of the regions were in the Northeast. By 1960 there were 16 urban regions comprising more than half (56 percent) of the nation's population; important new regions had emerged in the South, the West, and the Middle West, although the Northeast still contained the largest regions. By the year 2000, based on an average of two children per family, continued horizontal growth, and the linking together of regions, Pickard estimates that more than 80 percent of the American people will be living in at least 25 urban regions.[6] These urban regions are veritable metropolitan galaxies. Pickard's projections indicate that, by the year 2000, the six largest re-

[4] Staff, University of California, Los Angeles, Population Research Laboratory, "California's Urban Population: Patterns and Trends," in *California's Twenty Million*, ed. Kingsley Davis and Frederick Styles (University of California, Berkeley, Institute of International Studies, 1972), pp. 259–96.

[5] "An Urban Region is a coterminous area within which urban population predominates. By definition, it must contain a total population of at least 1 million. It is composed of one or more contiguous Metropolitan Areas and adjacent or intervening counties with relatively high population density or single counties of lower density which contain a major transportation corridor linking two or more Metropolitan Areas." Jerome Pickard, "U.S. Metropolitan Growth and Expansion, 1970–2000," in U.S. Commission on Population Growth and the American Future, *Population, Distribution, and Policy,* ed. Sara Mills Mazie, vol. 5 of the Commission Research Reports (Washington, D.C.: Government Printing Office, 1972), p. 142.

[6] Ibid., pp. 142–47.

gions will contain 116 metropolitan areas, and most of the remaining urban regions will have an average of more than 3 metropolitan areas each.

Data on actual settlement patterns since the 1970 census cover too brief a period to be definitive, but they suggest that the major focus of growth has shifted from the census-defined metropolitan areas to the adjacent exurban counties. This shift is not only compatible with megalopolitan development, but even expected, despite reports in the popular press about the reversal of historic trends. Specifically, the census estimated that between March 1970 and March 1974 more than 5.9 million people moved out of metropolitan areas, while only 4.1 million moved in, resulting in a net migration from metropolitan to nonmetropolitan counties of 1.8 million.[7] As the report points out, this does not indicate a total population loss to metropolitan areas, but rather a decline in the metropolitan growth rate.

Since 1970, nonmetropolitan counties— that is, those not in metropolitan areas— have apparently been growing at a faster rate than metropolitan counties.[8] Most nonmetropolitan growth represents spillover from metropolitan areas, however;

[7] U.S. Bureau of the Census, *Current Population Reports*, Series P-20, no. 273, "Mobility of the Population of the U.S., March 1970–March 1974" (Washington, D.C.: Government Printing Office, December 1974), p. 1.

[8] There is now evidence that nonmetropolitan counties adjacent to large metropolitan areas had begun significant growth before 1970. The differences in growth rates and socioeconomic characteristics among the six types of nonmetropolitan counties (ranging from "Urbanized Adjacent" to "Totally Rural Not Adjacent") described by the census are also another indication of the extensive influence of the metropolis. Regional Plan Association, *Growth and Settlement in the U.S.: Past Trends and Further Issues* (New York City: Regional Plan Association, June 1975), p. 44; and "Social and Economic Characteristics of the Population in Metro and Nonmetro Counties, 1970" (Washington, D.C.: Economic Research Service, U.S. Department of Agriculture, Agricultural Economic Report no. 272, March 1975), pp. 7–8.

Calvin Beale, a demographer with the Economic Research Service of the Department of Agriculture, has calculated that five eighths of the new nonmetropolitan population growth has been in counties adjacent to metropolitan counties.[9] The specific factors facilitating growth in these counties are currently being debated, but they probably include the decentralization of manufacturing, construction of major highways in outlying areas, more flexible working hours, early retirement, and longer life expectancy. The energy crisis and the recession would presumably operate against metropolitan expansion, but their effects are either unimportant or not yet apparent. In any event, the dispersed pattern of megalopolis already exists.

SUBURBAN BORN AND SUBURBAN BRED

The most important implication of current and projected settlement patterns is that soon the majority of Americans will have only suburban experience. The central cities of metropolitan areas have been losing population in absolute numbers since the 1960s or, at best, barely holding their own. Virtually all recent metropolitan growth has been in their suburban areas, and by the early 1970s almost all of the 33 metropolitan areas of more than 1 million had the majority of their populations in the suburbs. Since 1970, as already indicated, major growth may already have shifted to the adjacent, currently nonmetropolitan, counties.

The redistribution of population into megalopolitan patterns mean that proportionately fewer people will experience urban densities and related life styles: highrise housing, public transportation, pedestrian access, and the concentration of ac-

[9] Cited in Roy Reed, "Rural Areas' Population Gains Now Outpacing Urban Regions," *New York Times* (May 18, 1975), pp. 1, 32 BL.

tivities and diverse people. In 1950 about 15 percent of the United States population lived at genuinely urban densities of more than 10,000 persons per square mile, but by 1970 this had dropped to only 10 percent of the nation's population.[10] Below the 10,000 level, major clustering into centers cannot occur, although densities of 1,000 or more people per square mile are considered urban since they signify that the land is built up and no longer available for agriculture or open space. Yet the lower densities are precisely the point at which recent metropolitan expansion has taken place; between 1950 and 1970 the population living in counties with average densities of more than 1,000 persons per square mile rose from 29 to 37 percent of the total national population. These "urban" densities are suburban sprawl.

Translated into personal terms, these population trends mean the reality of megalopolis in suburban America will be distant. Although the suburban majority will live within the complex economic web of these enormous urban regions, their daily social, civic, and often their work lives will be spent in relatively small communities. Elazar has pointed out that within the context of metropolitan development, most Americans actually live in small towns.[11] The 1970 census shows, for example, that 21 percent of all Americans live in places of 2,500 to 25,000 people; 17 percent in places of 25,000 to 100,000; and only 28 percent in places above 100,000, with the remaining one third of the population living in other urban areas or in rural places.

Megalopolis, then, does not portend big city living. On the contrary, it portends a generation of Americans most of whom are suburban born and suburban bred. Their experience of high density, central city living will be limited to visits and perhaps educational training, work, and residence in early adulthood. The emergence of a suburban-reared suburban majority is of particular significance because of the suburban population composition. Despite the "suburbanization of everyone" and the increasingly broad mix of lifestyles and classes in the suburbs,[12] suburbanites still represent a disproportionate share of those who are "better off," highly participatory, and influential.

SUBURBAN DOMINANCE AND SOCIAL THEORY

The suburban theory which emerged during the 1950s dealt essentially with a population that had *become* suburban, that is, which had decentralized from central city to suburb. Thus, such now-classic studies as *The Levittowners, Working Class Suburb,* and *Crestwood Heights,*[13] covering various socioeconomic segments, examined the changes taking place as former urban dwellers settled into suburban homes. The theory governing suburban study has been essentially an extension of the urban theory of the 1920s and 1930s. For example, Louis Wirth's classic summary of the effects of size, density, and heterogeneity, which reflects the approach developed at the University of Chicago during the period of very rapid central city growth and concentration in the United States, has been widely applied to the sub-

---

[10] Regional Plan Association, *Growth and Settlement,* p. 11.

[11] Daniel Elazar, "Smaller Cities in Metropolitan Society: The New American 'Towns'," Temple University Center for the Study of Federalism, Working Paper no. 9 (c. 1969).

[12] *See,* for example, Louis H. Masotti, "Prologue—Suburbia Reconsidered—Myth and Countermyth," in *The Urbanization of the Suburbs,* ed. L. H. Masotti and J. K. Hadden (Beverly Hills, California: Sage Publications 1973).

[13] Herbert Gans, *The Levittowners* (New York: Pantheon, 1967); Bennett Berger, *Working-Class Suburb* (Berkeley and Los Angeles: University of California Press, 1960); John Seeley, R. Alexander Sim, E. W. Loosley, *Crestwood Heights* (New York: Basic Books, 1969).

urban setting.[14] There is, of course, every reason why such theories as Wirth's should be tested in suburbia. However, since the theories include the explicit or implicit assumption that suburbanites will have considerable urban life experience, the applicability of that assumption in the "postsuburban" period must also be tested. New research questions must be formulated to take account of the emerging suburban majority which will be suburban by birth and life history and whose moves will be from suburb to suburb or from suburb to exurb.

In the virtual absence of such studies, I take a quantum leap and offer the following suggestions about some aspects of the suburb-dominated society. These suggestions, based on fragmentary evidence, should be regarded as hypotheses: (1) being suburban born and reared will exert a strong influence toward preferring suburban residence in the future; (2) suburbanites are more locally-oriented in their contacts, a characteristic which is likely to intensify as there are more suburbanites whose life history is suburban; and (3) suburban attitudes toward blacks and toward big-city problems can best be described as tolerant aloofness and noninvolvement, based on the few case studies of suburban communities settled by those who moved from other suburbs.

The effect of suburban community of origin was examined by Zelan in a secondary analysis of data from a National Opinion Research Center (NORC) survey of the June 1961 graduating class of American colleges, totaling more than 33,000 ques-tionnaires received from students in 135 colleges.[15] Zelan was primarily interested in whether those raised in suburbia (suburbs of metropolitan areas of 100,000 or more) differed in antiintellectualism from those raised in large cities (central cities of those metropolitan areas). Simple correlation showed no differences in intellectual attitudes between the groups. However, when antiintellectualism responses were correlated with where the graduates *wished* to live, rather than by community of origin, the group preferring to live in suburbs had higher levels of antiintellectual responses than those preferring urban living. Being married was also strongly associated with preferring suburban residence.

For our purposes, Zelan's important finding is that the factor most predictive of choosing suburban residence is one's community of origin—"those who have lived in the suburbs are most likely to be oriented toward suburbs."[16] Thus, even the suburban-reared graduates who manifested low antiintellectualism and who were single said they would choose to live in suburbs. This study suggests that, although other factors are also influential in determining whether one will choose suburban residence, on the whole a suburban childhood apparently prepares one to choose a suburban adulthood. The generation now growing up in suburbs will probably wish to live in them as adults. Suburbanism is not a self-destructive phenomenon.

Suburbanites are local; that is, their social circles and interests are more concentrated in their immediate residential localities than are those of urban dwellers. Fisher and Jackson's comprehensive review of existing literature, as well as their secondary analysis of two large-scale surveys, amply documents that suburbanites engage in more neighboring, that more of

---

[14] *See,* for example, Sylvia F. Fava, "Suburbanism as a Way of Life," *American Sociological Review* 21 (February 1956), pp. 34–38; Herbert J. Gans, "Urbanism and Suburbanism as Ways of Life: A Re-evaluation of Definitions," in *Human Behavior and Social Processes,* ed. Arnold Rose (Boston: Houghton Mifflin, 1962), pp. 625–48; for a summary of the many suburban applications of Wirth's thesis, *see,* the suburban portion of Claude S. Fischer, "Urbanism as a Way of Life: A Review and an Agenda," *Sociological Methods and Research* 1 (November 1972), pp. 187–242.

[15] Joseph Zelan, "Does Suburbia Make a Difference?" in *Urbanism in World Perspective,* ed. Sylvia F. Fava (New York: T. Y. Crowell, 1968), pp. 401–8.
[16] Ibid., p. 408.

their individual ties and friendships are within short distances, and that their interest in the involvement with local concerns are greater than urbanites.[17] After examining various possible theories to account for these differences, Fischer and Jackson conclude that there are three sources of suburban localism.

The two most important explanations are nonecological. First, the individual characteristics of suburbanites—age, ethnicity, home ownership, and family cycle—are those associated with high levels of localism. For example, home owners are more locally-oriented than renters, no matter where they live. Thus, the most important reasons suburbanites behave as locally as they do are personal and not related to suburbanism per se. However, the second most important level of explanation of suburban localism is that of contextual effects, that is, consequences of the concentration in suburbs of certain population types. The suburban whole is more than the sum of the individuals residing in it. According to Fischer and Jackson:

> While it may be that the average suburban individual is "localized" only to a minute degree . . . the suburban community as a whole is composed of such individuals. The cumulation of small individual effects in one place can have larger consequences at the aggregate level; e.g., the election of representatives hostile to metropolitan government.

The third and least important explanation for suburban localism is ecological and related to the outlying location of suburbs and to their low population density, both of which increase time/cost when engaging in nonlocal activities. Thus, the friction of space contributes to localism in suburbia.

Fischer and Jackson conclude that the localism effect in suburbia of each level of causation—individual, contextual, and locational—is quite small, but this should not, they say, mislead us about potentially significant community effects. As American society continues to suburbanize, a larger proportion of its population shifts from a city to suburban location and social context. Slight as the effects might be on each person, the balance moves increasingly, for better or for worse, from urban ways of life to suburban ones. . . . In neighboring and localism, as well as in other ways, small towns and suburbs are alike. In that sense, the increasing suburbanization of America may mean, in part, the de-urbanization of America.[18]

WESTLAKE: LIFESTYLE BEYOND SUBURBIA

The phrase "de-urbanization of America" seems almost prophetic when viewing the attitudes and lifestyle of the suburbanites' suburbs—that is, the communities attracting those who have already experienced suburbia and want something better. These suburbanites are not so much opposed to cities as they are detached and aloof. They do not seem to find cities real enough to be concerned about them. At least these are judgments which may be made on the basis of Rabinovitz and Lamare's study of Westlake Village, a "new community" in the San Fernando valley outside Los Angeles and populated largely by former suburbanites.[19] Only 4 percent of the residents of Westlake Village came there from central cities; almost three quarters of the residents moved to Westlake from the suburbs of Los Angeles or other large cities. New communities like Westlake are springing up in California and in the suburban periphery of other

---

[17] Claude S. Fischer and Robert Max Jackson, "Suburbs, Networks, and Attitudes," in *The Changing Face of the Suburbs,* ed. Barry Schwartz (Chicago: University of Chicago Press, 1975).

[18] Ibid.

[19] Francine F. Rabinovitz and James Lamare, "After Suburbia, What?—The New Communities Movement in Los Angeles," in *Los Angeles: Viability and Prospects for Metropolitan Leadership,* ed. Werner Z. Hirsch (New York: Praeger, 1971), pp. 169–206.

large American areas, providing an opportunity "to predict what will come after suburbia in metropolitan America."[20]

Westlakers are white upper-middle class persons (professional and managerial occupations, average yearly family income $21,979 in 1969, college-educated) whose reasons for moving to Westlake contrast markedly with those listed by people of a similar socioeconomic level who make an initial move from central city to suburb. The suburban "new community" to which they have moved is likewise different. Westlake Village is not a suburban subdivision, but a "new community" in that it is large (12,000 acres, ultimate population goal 70,000, current population 6,000) and has a master plan aiming at some controlled variety and self-sufficiency by providing a range of commercial establishments and services, a town center, employment opportunities, a variety of single-family and apartment housing (but no low-income housing), and extensive recreational facilities (pools, bridle paths, golf course), as well as the preservation of the natural environment in areas designated as permanent open space.

Westlakers rarely mention moving to the new community for the sake of their children or for the quality of the schools— the prime reasons of the earlier generation of city-to-suburb movers. Westlakers appear to take these amenities for granted. Neither did they move to achieve greater participation in local neighboring or community affairs (although most actually had high local political and civic participation), nor to find social protection in a homogeneous group, although as Rabinovitz and Lamare indicate, this protection is "built in" because of the limited range of housing in the master plan.

The main attraction of Westlake in drawing and retaining its population is the natural environment—location, preservation of natural ecology, and air quality;

"85.6 percent of the respondents mention environment as primary in at least one dimension of their orientation to Westlake."[21] Of the total environment produced by new communities such as Westlake, it appears that the natural environment and its protection are the main drawing cards—not the social features, the opportunities for community interaction, or even the recreation facilities (Westlakers use them relatively rarely). Old-style suburbs have "delivered" on all of these features to a large extent, but not on natural environmental features. Among other things, this indicates the new suburbanites will be even greater consumers of space, a finding reflected in our earlier discussion of the trends in megalopolitan form.

Westlakers are neither overtly racist nor anti-city. They believe in integration, seemingly practice it at work, and probably would accept residential integration with minorities of their own class level. On a scale of negative feelings about Los Angeles, only 9 percent were highly negative, 39 percent were somewhat negative, and the largest percentage, 45, had low negativism scores. On the other hand, although they frequently visit downtown Los Angeles, Hollywood, and West Los Angeles, they seldom or never visit South Central Los Angeles (two thirds had been there never or only once) or East Los Angeles (one half had been there never or only once), which are the areas of minority and poverty concentration in Los Angeles.[22] Westlakers do not consciously reject the city, its problems, and the problems of the minorities concentrated there; rather, these problems are simply not part of their experience or awareness.

The findings of the Westlake study have been presented at some length because they constitute one of the very few case studies consciously directed at examining

---

[20] Ibid., p. 171.

[21] Ibid., p. 191.
[22] Ibid., p. 189.

lifestyles and attitudes in the suburbs of lifelong suburbanites. The results make it clear that we cannot assume that suburb to suburb or suburb to exurb migration will simply produce more of the same social consequences as central city to suburban migration. This creates a problem for social theory, but also for social justice, as Rabinovitz and Lamare indicate:

Our most striking finding is the degree to which environmental qualities are rated as important by Westlake residents, and the social community as less significant. Westlake responses suggest that environmental problems may now be the ultimate middle-class issue. We guess that rurality is sought rather than community, not necessarily because community is not desired, but because it is achieved already within acceptable limits. The success of the commitment of the native white majority to homogeneity in Los Angeles seems to have so undermined the visibility of the foreign and colored minorities that homogeneity is not an objective goal. And a half-life spent in suburban neighborhoods, in the companionship of one's family, in commuting and in working among others distinguishable by personal but not by group characteristics, has been not lonely or isolating but really quite satisfying, so seeking out "community" also loses salience. . . .

How one evaluates this depends on how one rates the issue of environment in importance as against the solution of inner-city problems. We think the two are separable, and that middle-class America is beginning to rank the environment first.[23]

ECOLOGICAL THEORY BEYOND SUBURBIA

Urban theory faces problems in approaching suburban America not only in terms of lifestyle but also in terms of formulating an adequate ecological theory to explain the form and dynamics of the megalopolis in which the suburban majority is imbedded. Social scientists have approached even the metropolis with the

ecological concepts of an earlier day. The Park-Burgess concentric zonal theory of urban growth and structure, for example, has been expanded to include a suburban "zone."[24] This approach has yielded some valuable insights, as in Schnore's work indicating the variety of central city-suburban contrasts and their evolutionary aspects.[25]

While these approaches are defensible as applied to the metropolis—which, despite its complexity, has one clearly dominant center—they are unsuited to the megalopolis which is not only truly multi-centered, but whose centers are often in competition. Commuting and reverse commuting to and from the dominant center are characteristic only of the metropolis. The patterns of ecological interdependence, and consequently of individual movement and contact, have shifted to a qualitatively different level of complexity in megalopolis. As a result there can be no relatively simple typology of suburbs in megalopolis, a fact which already is becoming apparent as metropolitan expansion continues.[26]

The United States Bureau of the Census (the basic source of descriptive data on suburbs) has, under metropolitan conditions, treated suburbs as a residual category, that is, as the part of the metropolis outside the central city. Census suburban concepts suffer from the same difficulty as formal theoretical approaches in that they were predicated on a concentrated city,

---

[23] *Ibid.*, pp. 202, 204.

[24] There are some derivations from earlier ecological theory which are more suitable to megalopolitan ecological analysis. Factorial ecology, for example, makes no assumptions about a *single* ecological distributive pattern radiating from a center.

[25] Leo F. Schnore, "The Socioeconomic Status of Cities and Suburbs," *American Sociological Review* 28 (February 1963), pp. 76–86; Schnore, "Urban Structure and Suburban Selectivity," *Demography* 1 (1964), pp. 164–76; Schnore and Joy K. O. Jones, "The Evolution of City-Suburban Types in the Course of a Decade," *Urban Affairs Quarterly* 4 (June 1969), pp. 421–43.

[26] *See*, for example, the discussion in Gist and Fava, "Urban Transformation," pp. 306ff.

expanding from a single center, to which diverse population groups were oriented, as were all the major economic, social, and cultural affairs of the city. The census has retooled slowly to meet the problems of urban-suburban definition raised by megalopolis.

With the 1970 census, data are available which permit a fine-grained analysis of the structure of megalopolis. The census has gathered both residential and work addresses for individuals. Geographer Brian J. L. Berry emphasizes the importance of tabulation of this data in depicting the network of daily urban systems in the United States.[27] On the basis of his earlier work with 1960 census data, Berry contends "20th century metropolises have so burst their 19th century boundaries that . . . a network of DUS's [Daily Urban Systems], each with a radius of 75–80 miles, now blankets all except the most sparsely settled parts of the country, embracing daily activities and travel of 90 percent of the nation's population."[28]

Berry also contends that the DUS is an accurate predictor of future megalopolitan growth because the DUS is based on the delineation of actual job and housing markets rather than being restricted to the somewhat arbitrary inclusion or exclusion of whole counties. In this kind of assessment the hinterland plays a dynamic role in the establishment of distinguishing characteristics of the megalopolis rather than representing, as it does in the metropolitan concept, a mere petering out at the margins of central-city influence.

---

[27] Brian J. L. Berry, "Urban Definitions Beyond Megalopolis," in *Research and the 1970 Census*, ed. Abbott Ferriss (Oak Ridge, Tenn.: Southern Regional Demographic Group, Oak Ridge Associated Universities, Inc., 1971), pp. 151–57.

[28] Brian J. L. Berry. "Population Growth in the Daily Urban Systems of the United States, 1980–2000," in U.S. Commission on Population Growth and the American Future, *Population, Distribution, and Policy*, p. 240 (see footnote 5).

RACISM AND SEXISM IN MEGALOPOLIS

Two groups are "invisible" in the theory of megalopolis—blacks and women. Although there is much research and discussion on blacks, the findings are from housing and locational decisions of major constraint and limited choice. Recent studies of black population movement indicate that the dual housing market has now extended to suburbia: since the late 1960s there appears to be a stream of "true" suburban migration of blacks, that is, the decentralization of middle-class blacks rather than the engulfing by expanding urban growth of peripherally located, lower-status blacks. However, the newly suburban blacks remain residentially segregated, often by racial succession in the "inner ring" of aging suburbs, by tokenism in white suburbs, and sometimes by living in new suburban developments designated, unofficially, for blacks. Black suburbanization has not decreased residential segregation.

New communities, especially those designated to receive federal financial guarantees under the 1968 (Title IV) and the 1970 (Title VII) Housing Acts, were widely heralded as ways to widen residential choice for blacks, including the poor black; in fact, one of the express goals of Titles IV and VII was to lessen the movement toward "two societies." However, both federally and privately sponsored new communities have only small percentages of blacks. Except for Soul City, North Carolina, blacks have not participated as organized groups in the planning and promoting of new communities. In January 1975 the Department of Housing and Urban Development (HUD) announced that no additional federally sponsored new communities would be designated; they and the privately sponsored new communities, too, are suffering from the combined effects of inflation in interest rates and building costs and recession in family purchasing power.

New communities have not extended black residential choice to any significant degree, in part because they lack knowledge of (and willingness to implement) the full range of black residential choice. What institutions and amenities would attract and retain specific groups of black residents? Piecing together the available evidence suggests, not surprisingly, that in terms of residential choice (degree of racial integration, central city versus suburban location, and the like) there are several major subgroups among blacks.[29] No one type of community can satisfy all these subgroups. Megalopolis should provide for true freedom of residential choice among blacks rather than having black suburbanization represent merely the black "inheritance" of out-dated suburbs, as blacks earlier "inherited" deteriorating central city areas. The evidence so far is that the new patterns of megalopolitan development have shown no new basis for wide racial integration and the old urban patterns are found to be repeated in the suburban environment. The problems of racial discrimination seem to be abating only for some of the well educated and prosperous blacks.

Although distinctions must be drawn in entirely different ways for women and for racial minorities, in terms of megalopolitan structure women are also a deprived group. The trends toward an ever more dispersed suburbia and the separation of work and residence are founded on deep-seated sexist assumptions about the role of women. Sociologist and planner Janet Abu-Lughod, having attended a recent major urban conference where she was the only woman, relates a discussion of the city of the future as follows:

Discussion moved to the issue of increased leisure and its implications for projected alteration in the workday and workweek and, hence, for anticipated changes in the physical arrangement of the metropolis. Great interest and indeed excitement began to generate, revolving around the prospect of the four-day week. This, one after another concurred, would be an absolutely marvellous design for living. It would permit even *more complete separation of work from residence! "A man* could go into the city to work, spend three nights there, and then *return to his family* out in the country for the other four nights."

. . . the vision of the future city they were so enthusiastic about was one which . . . was designed for men only. Married females with children presumably were to remain on rural "breeding farms." The status of single women was indeterminate; perhaps they were to be kept in the city for those other three nights? Sex roles were to be totally differentiated for, obviously, both women with children *and* their husbands could hardly expect to desert the children in the exurbs for four days and three nights, even given the existence of TV dinners!

. . . No woman I have told this story to has felt that it was a matter to joke about. We are frightened by this handwriting on the wall[30] (emphasis in the original).

PLANNING FOR WOMEN

Planning for women in the expanding megalopolis occurs rarely, but when it does, according to a recent literature review by Goldstein, it focuses very much on the "typical" young mother, and it rests on the rigid separation of home (women) from work (men) described

---

[29] For extended discussion on this point, *see*, Sylvia F. Fava, "Blacks in American New Towns: Problems and Prospects," *Sociological Symposium* 12 (Fall 1974), pp. 111–29.

[30] Janet Abu-Lughod, "Designing a City for All," in *Planning, Women, and Change*, ed. Karen Hapgood and Judith Getzels (Chicago: American Society of Planning Officials, proceedings of the Workshop on Planning for Women, December 3–4, 1974, sponsored by U.S. Department of Housing and Urban Development), p. 37.

above by Abu-Lughod.[31] Thus, in his recommendations to James Rouse, the builder of Columbia, Maryland—the large, privately developed new community between Baltimore and Washington, D.C.—Gans said, "For the man: job, job satisfaction, and job security are most important, as is freedom from financial pressure. He wants his wife and children to be happy. . . . For the wife: welfare and happiness of husband and especially children are most important. . . ."[32]

It is fitting that we are able to "return" to Columbia six years after its founding to examine the results of the planning recommended by Gans and others. A survey using a stratified random sample of households in Columbia found a much more diverse range of expressed needs, interests, and problems of Columbia's women and led to the following recommendations: guidance counseling; educational opportunities, particularly at the graduate level; social and other activities to serve women who differ from the typical married woman with children (for example, women under 24, childless women, divorced women and black women), counseling in the areas of mental health, marital problems and dealing with one's children; childcare facilities; public transportation for women and also to relieve them of the need for transporting children; information services; and low-cost group meals so cooking would not always have to be done at home.[33] The women of Columbia display a much wider range of needs and interests than are met by stereo-typed planning. Another illustration is the failure in Columbia of the neighborhood centers to serve as gathering places and information centers.[34]

The suburb, old and new, is geared to the married woman with children and, furthermore, allows for little change in her role or goals. The single woman, the divorcee or widow, the parent without a partner, and the woman who works or wishes to work are poorly served by suburb or exurb. Low density and its resultant lack of public transportation limit the accessibility of nonlocal associates, activities, and jobs.

Michelson, in an interim report of new residents' experience a little more than a year after their move, compares the reaction of married couples in four different residential environments—apartments downtown, single-family homes downtown, suburban apartments, and suburban single-family homes. On a scale rating from 1 to 10 the degree of satisfaction with how they spend their time, women in suburban houses had by far the lowest scores among all four residential groups, while the husbands in suburban homes had the highest scores![35] Few of these wives in single-family homes had a job, while most of the wives in the other three residential settings were employed.

The data show . . . that suburban housewives are *increasingly satisfied* with the social characteristics of their neighbourhood and *increasingly dissatisfied* with the locational aspects of the very same neighbourhood over time. In contrast, their husbands, who expect to be out of the neighbourhood every day, and who have the added social benefits of their family's extensive contact pattern within the neighbourhood

---

[31] Joan Goldstein, "Planning for Women in the New Towns: New Concepts and Dated Roles" (Paper delivered at the Annual Meeting of the American Sociological Association, San Francisco, August 1975).

[32] Herbert J. Gans, "Planning for the Everyday Life and Problems of Suburban and New Towns Residents," in *People and Plans*, ed. H. J. Gans (New York: Basic Books, 1968), p. 188.

[33] Mary Stuart, "A Study of Women's Needs in Columbia" (Columbia, Md.: Columbia Association, April 1974).

[34] Charlotte Temple, "Planning and the Married Woman with Children—a New Town Perspective," in *Planning, Women, and Change*, pp. 45–46 (see footnote 31).

[35] William Michelson, "Environmental Change," Centre for Urban and Community Studies, Research Paper no. 60 (University of Toronto, October 1973), p. 38.

when they return, remain very pleased with their location.[36] (emphasis in the original).

Michelson's study is longitudinal and will cover a five-year period. His final results, when available, should be most revealing for the long-range assessment of suburban (and urban) locational effects on men and women.

The physical structure of suburbia limits the horizons and opportunities of women, often forcing them to choose between fulfilling their family roles and developing as persons in their own right. The limited career ladder open to suburban women is a case in point. Local jobs are typically dead-end service jobs in stores or schools; other jobs require heavy commuting or further training—which also involves heavy commuting. Yet, as noted above, the low density which inhibits the growth of clustered facilities widely accessible by public transportation is becoming even lower. The expanding megalopolis is not facilitating the expansion of the roles of women.

Nevertheless, women's roles are changing, as indicated by several recent trends: the marriage rate in 1973 was down for the first time since World War II, and more women are staying single until their mid-20s; the birth rate is only slightly above the 1973 record low of 15 per 1,000; the divorce rate continues to rise as it has every year since 1962; the proportion of women with paying jobs continues to increase, even among those with young children (in 1970, 43 percent of all women worked, as did 30 percent of those with children under six years of age).

The consequences of these trends beyond suburbia can now only be speculated. Future developments might include families' remaining in dispersed locations but with much more sharing of household and childcare tasks; declining marketability of large homes; and further decentralization of factory and office jobs as firms move closer to their labor pool. Changes such as these might be involved in the development of a megalopolitan structure flexible enough to permit women a wide choice of roles.

MEGALOPOLIS—REAL OR UNREAL?

Megalopolis is real as a highly complex entity, but not now as a social or political entity. This analysis has indicated how the new suburbanization has removed an increasing proportion of the American population from the immediate experience of inner-city problems and high-density living. The social problems of racism and sexism have been major concerns of the postwar period. Expectations have been high that the new physical developments and the lifestyles that have emerged would provide a way out of the old dilemmas. But the changes that have occurred have not altered, for the most part, the underlying patterns of discrimination which remain to trouble future generations.

The recent focus of public policy has shifted away from the central city and problems popularly associated with it. Federal expenditures favor small metropolitan areas and those with lower densities.[37] The federal government has declared that the "urban crisis is over."[38] These are only straws in the wind, however, and may not indicate the direction of future policy.[39] Various public needs exist in the component parts of megalopolis; how and through what political structures these needs will be expressed and met remains a major question.

---

[36] Ibid., p. 42.

[37] Regional Plan Association, *Growth and Settlement*, p. 12.

[38] Ernest Holsendolph, "Urban Crisis of the 1960s is Over, Ford Aides Say," *New York Times* (March 23, 1975), pp. 1, 46.

[39] A recent analysis of some issues of leadership and power in our largest megalopolis concluded that although "megalopolis as a meaningful sociological community has not arrived . . . a power base exists." Delbert Miller, *Leadership and Power in the Bos-Wash Megalopolis* (New York: Wiley-Interscience, 1975), p. 357.

25

The defended neighborhood

Gerald D. Suttles

The residential group which seals itself off through the efforts of delinquent gangs, by restrictive covenants, by sharp boundaries, or by a forbidding reputation—what I will call the defended neighborhood— was for a time a major category in sociological analysis. In their efforts to analyze the territorial configuration of the city, Park and Burgess and their followers left a wealth of descriptive and analytical material on this sort of residential group.[1] Most of this analysis, however, attempted to resolve the defended neighborhood into a manifestation of other social categories thought to be of prior importance: ethnicity, income, race, and the like.[2] In due course the defended neighborhood was frequently dismissed as a sort of epiphenomenon because it was thought only to reflect more substantive social differences.

It is my intent to resurrect the concept of the defended neighborhood and show that it may still be usefully applied to urban areas if we keep in mind two different levels of analysis.

First, there is the physical structure of the city; the location of its facilities, residential groups, transportation, and communication lines; and its specialized activ-

ities. These are the items which urban ecologists have discussed in greatest detail and which have formed the empirical basis on which theories of urban structure have risen or fallen.[3]

Second, there is the cognitive map which residents have for describing, not only what their city is like, but what they think it ought to be like. This cognitive map of the city need not necessarily correspond closely with the actual physical structure.[4] The discrepancy is often quite apparent when residents give very discrete boundaries for a neighborhood or area of usage despite there being no sharp disparities between such adjacent spaces. Similar departures are even more apparent when we compare the actual physical structure of the city with the structure its residents think it ought to have.

These two levels for analyzing urban structure are not wholly independent, for people do seize upon actual markers in the physical makeup of the city to draw up their cognitive maps no matter how unrealistic they are otherwise. Also, within broad and shifting limits, the ideas that people have about where things belong do carry some weight. The problem, however, is not simply to correlate or draw some causal chain between the city's physical structure and the cognitive maps which residents use to describe urban areas. It is of equal or greater importance to find what function these cognitive maps of the city serve and why people should

Reprinted with permission of the author and publisher from Gerald D. Suttles, *The Social Construction of Communities* (Chicago: University of Chicago Press, 1972), pp. 21–43. © 1972 by The University of Chicago. Footnotes have been renumbered.

[1] Robert E. Park, Ernest W. Burgess, and Roderick D. McKenzie, *The City*, 4th ed. (Chicago: University of Chicago Press, 1967), provides the classical essays on this topic and a bibliography tracing much of the subsequent work.

[2] David Riesman, *The Lonely Crowd* (New Haven: Yale University Press, 1950); and Donald L. Foley, "Neighbors or Urbanites," in *The University of Rochester Studies of Metropolitan Rochester* (Rochester: University of Rochester Press, 1952).

[3] See Beverly Duncan, "Variables in Urban Morphology," in *Contributions in Urban Sociology*, ed. Ernest W. Burgess and Donald J. Bogue (Chicago: University of Chicago Press, 1963), pp. 17–30.

[4] For a discussion of this issue see Morris Janowitz, *The Community Press in an Urban Setting: The Social Elements of Urbanism*, 2d ed. (Chicago: University of Chicago Press, 1967).

bother with such reifications in the first place.

The principal point of view expressed here is that these cognitive maps are part of the social control apparatus of urban areas and are of special importance in regulating spatial movement to avoid conflict between antagonistic groups. In this respect, such cognitive maps provide a set of social categories for differentiating between those people with whom one can or cannot safely associate and for defining the concrete groupings within which certain levels of social contact and social cohesion obtain. These cognitive maps, then, are a creative imposition on the city and useful because they provide a final solution to decision making where there are often no other clear cutoff points for determining how far social contacts should go. The actual structure of most cities is best described as a series of gradients, and there are very few clear boundaries or sharp junctures which cannot be crossed by a simple decision to do so. In order to regulate one's spatial movement and locational possibilities, then, one needs a simpler model, because in the final analysis most decisions must be answered "yes" or "no". The utility of a more qualitative map of the city is that it permits this type of decision making, whereas the physical structure of the city leaves one in an eternal state of ambiguity.[5] . . .

---

[5] The same observation is made by Milla Aissa Alihan, *Social Ecology: A Critical Analysis* (New York: Columbia University Press, 1938). James A. Quinn has attempted to reply to this criticism by saying: "The contention by Alihan that a gradual gradient makes impossible the existence of zones does not seem valid. In the field of physics, for example, the gradual change in the length of light rays throughout a rainbow spectrum may be taken as an example of a gradient. Nevertheless, distinct zones of red, yellow, and blue appear in the rainbow even though no sharp line of demarcation can be drawn between them. It seems possible, therefore, for distinct zones to appear even when gradients unquestionably exist." What Quinn fails to point out, however, is that the distinct zones of the rainbow are imposed by the viewer rather than being self-evident in the light spectrum itself. ("The Burgess Zonal Hypothesis and Its Critics," *American Sociological Review* 5 [April 1940], pp. 210–18.)

DISTRIBUTION OF DEFENDED NEIGHBORHOODS

The imperative for a set of rules to govern one's spatial movement does not fall equally on all people or on all areas of the city. The inadequacies of formal procedures of social control are most striking where there are sharp cleavages between people, where anonymity is great, and where people have little assurance that everyone will observe legal or customary norms. Historically in the United States these sources of deviance and conflict have tended to be concentrated in the inner city. This is where ethnic and racial cleavages are still most apparent, undiluted, and irreconcilable. It is also that part of the city where population density and transiency are highest and together promote high levels of anonymity.

In addition to containing these cleavages and anonymity, the inner city is typically the residential area relegated to people with little or no income. In the United States financial insecurity and failure in the job market have always been taken as signs of an individual's character indicating that he is shiftless in the first place or desperate in the second. In either case the poor, and thus the majority of the residents in the inner city, are expected to be rather unruly, predatory, and unprincipled.

These apprehensions about the poor, of course, are shared by the poor themselves. Indeed, there is at least some evidence that the poor are the most likely to assume a simple connection between poverty and unprincipled greed.[6] Since the poor generally live near one another, it is among them that there is the greatest need for a set of rules by which people can safely navigate within their own residential areas.

---

[6] Edward A. Shills, "Primary Groups in the American Army," in *Continuities in Social Research: Studies in the Scope and Method of The American Soldier*, ed. R. Merton and P. Lazarsfeld (Glencoe, Ill.: Free Press, 1950), pp. 16–39.

The coincidence of poverty, anonymity, and social cleavages compounded within the inner city, then, dictate a highly differentiated cognitive map among its residents. It is here that the defended neighborhood should have its greatest appeal and serve best to mollify the imagined or real dangers which exist in the inner city.

Judging from the fragmentary evidence available, the empirical pattern, at least in Chicago, seems to support this conclusion. Zorbaugh's study, *The Gold Coast and the Slum* as well as practically all similar studies done under Park and Burgess,[7] shows the inner city to be finely differentiated into many relatively small defended neighborhoods. My own study of the Near West Side and Thrasher's more extensive account of gangland report a similar pattern with a high incidence of defended neighborhoods toward the inner city and many fewer toward the periphery of the city.[8] Even Park and Burgess's classic mapping of the gross outlines of Chicago show the zone in transition to be divided into a greater number of small defended areas than the zones farther out.[9] In at least one recent study of the outer city there is a striking lack of spatial differentiation, boundaries, and defensive arrangements.[10]

The inner city is also the area where one finds most of the other obvious earmarks of the defended neighborhood. It is here that street-corner gangs claim a "turf" and ward off strangers or anyone else not a proper member of the neighborhood. It is here that one finds vigilante community groups, militant conservation groups, a high incidence of uniformed doormen, and frequent use of door buzzers and TV monitors. Not all of these defensive tactics are equally available to all residents of the inner city, and in many instances one may replace the other. What they indicate is the general apprehensiveness of inner city dwellers, rich and poor alike, and the necessity for each of them to bound off discrete areas within which he can feel safe and secure.

SOCIAL COHESION OF DEFENDED NEIGHBORHOODS

Although the defended neighborhood does not always seem to arise from preexisting cohesive groupings, it may itself create cohesive groupings. The defensive measures of these neighborhoods, of course, generally call for some level of concerted action and thus a certain degree of cohesion. This cohesion is most apparent in street-corner gangs, vigilantelike citizens' groups, and restrictive covenants. All of these measures require joint action and produce at least traces of cohesion that endure for purposes other than defense.

By far the most common type of cohesion said to exist in all types of neighborhoods is a positive and sentimental attachment to neighbors, local establishments, and local traditions to the exclusion of other persons, establishments, and traditions. No doubt such warm attachments to neighborhoods do exist, but they are too narrow and special a case to characterize fully the range and forms which neighborhood cohesion can take. Indeed, it is because of such a narrow focus on positive and exclusive sentimental attachments to the neighborhood that some researchers may have simply discounted the very existence of the neighborhood. Similar reasoning, however, would discount the existence of the family since there also not all members are always firmly and positively attached to one another.

Like the family, the neighborhood is

[7] Harvey Warren Zorbaugh, *The Gold Coast and the Slum* (Chicago: University of Chicago Press, 1929); Roderick D. McKenzie, *The Neighborhood: A Study of Neighborhood Life in the City of Columbus, Ohio* (Chicago: University of Chicago Press, 1923); and Burgess and Bogue, *Urban Sociology.*

[8] Gerald D. Suttles, *The Social Order of the Slum* (Chicago: University of Chicago Press, 1968); and Frederick Thrasher, *The Gang* (Chicago: University of Chicago Press, 1927).

[9] Park, Burgess, and McKenzie, *City.*

[10] Harvey Molotch, "Intervention for Integration: A Community Competes for Whites," (Ph.D. dissertation, University of Chicago, 1967.

largely an ascribed grouping and its members are joined in a common plight whether or not they like it. The preeminent characteristics of the defended neighborhood, then, are structural rather than sentimental or associational. Perhaps the most important of these structural elements is the identity of the neighborhood itself. A neighborhood may be known as snobbish, trashy, tough, exclusive, dangerous, mixed, or any number of other things. Some neighborhoods may simply be unknown, and reference to one's residence may arouse only puzzlement and necessitate one's explaining one's guilt or virtue by residential association. In any case, neighborhood identity remains a stable judgmental reference against which people are assessed, and although some may be able to evade the allegations thrown their way, they nonetheless find such evasions necessary.

A second structural characteristic of the defended neighborhood is that its coresidents often share a common fate at the hands of city planners, realtors, politicians, and industry. Like the residents of the city itself, these initiators of change often must selectively apply their resources to distinct areas of the city rather than distribute their impact generally over a metropolitan region. In the end, a factory or high school must be placed somewhere, political jurisdictions must be drawn, and social welfare programs must have distinct target areas. The boundaries drawn by these intrusive and exogenous institutions may or may not coincide with those already accepted by coresidents. The net result is a continuous shifting of boundaries of foci of concern by residential groupings. Protest groups, conservation committees, landowners' groups, and realty associations spring into existence, thrive, and then decline, as the issue which brought them into existence waxes and wanes. All this tends to give the defended neighborhood an ephemeral and transient appearance, as if it were a social artifact. But these social forms are real enough, and

they leave at least a residue of a formula for subsequent cohesion.

Perhaps the most subtle structural feature of the defended neighborhood is its shared knowledge or what might be called its underlife. People who share a residential identity are privy to a variety of secrets which range from the assured truths of gossip to the collective myths of rumor. These bits and pieces of knowledge touch intimately on the lives of those who share a residential area because they add to the collective guilt or pride of coresidents. But they are also some of the surest markers which separate insiders from outsiders. And at the same time these local half-truths are much valued because they provide at least an omen of what one's neighbors are really like. Thus, while persons who share a common residential identity may collude at impression management, they are also apt to pry into one another's business and jointly move farther and farther away from an official version of what people are supposed to be like. Taken to their full extreme, these local truths may add up to a sort of subculture where a private existential world takes hold and overshadows that provided by an equally undependable version of truth available through official sources.[11] More often the subterranean bits and pieces of information available to coresidents are received as gossip pure and simple. Persons who share a residential identity, however, have a special right to such knowledge, and this inside "dope" may lead them to what seem aberrant or provincial ways of behaving.

Yet another structural characteristic of the defended neighborhood is the fact that it may be divided into levels or orbits which radiate from an egocentric to a sociocentric frame of reference. When a person speaks of "my neighborhood," he may be referring to a small area which

---

[11] Lee Rainwater, "The Problems of Lower Class Culture," Paper prepared for the Department of Sociology Colloquium, University of Wisconsin, September 23, 1966.

242

centers on himself and is different for any
two individuals. "Our neighborhood," on
the other hand, tends to refer to some localized group which can also be identified
by other structural boundaries such as ethnicity or income. "The neighborhood,"
however, has a more fixed referent and
usually possesses a name and some sort of
reputation known to persons other than
the residents.

All of these structural characteristics
give the defended neighborhood an amorphous and indistinct appearance so long
as we look for only a single bounded unit
persisting through time. The defended
neighborhood can expand or contract
boundaries; its activation is episodic; and
the cohesion of its members is always
qualified by alternative loyalties. This does
not mean that the defended neighborhood
is unimportant but it calls for a specification of that realm of life over which it exercises its special influence.

SPECIALIZATION OF
NEIGHBORHOOD FUNCTIONS

The segmental character of urban life
leaves only some people free some of the
time to invest their energy and interests in
the defended neighborhood. This introduces into the maintenance of neighborhood life a qualified involvement and a
certain specialization.

The extent to which persons can or
must concern themselves with the defended neighborhood is especially likely to
vary with the life cycle. Of all those who
reside in a neighborhood, children seem to
be most nearly contained in its boundaries. Most of the groups to which they
can belong—school groups, church
groups, athletic teams, and the scouts—
remain territorially defined. These groups
may not coincide very closely in the
boundaries they select, but together they
greatly narrow the range of childhood
movement and association. Children
must, more often than adults, walk to

most of the places they frequent, and this
gives them a rather obvious interest in
their personal safety and the routes and
places where they are welcome or unwel-
come. Age restrictions on certain places of
entertainment, the child labor laws, and
curfews sharply delimit their participation
in the wider society.

The dangers of the city are especially
relevant to children because they are generally thought rather defenseless. One major reason for selecting a particular residential area, in fact, is that it is a safe or
agreeable place to raise children.[12] Indeed,
perhaps the best way to discern the spatial
orbits which make up a neighborhood is to
listen to how parents allow or restrict the
movements of their children.

Because they are so restricted to their
neighborhood or its immediate vicinity,
children may be the major producers and
carriers of neighborhood life: its local
stereotypes, its named boundaries, its
known hangouts, its assumed dangers,
and its informal groupings. Certainly there
are a number of studies and observations
which suggest as much.[13] In many inner-
city areas, the adults may remain rather
atomized while their children quickly
coalesce into local street-corner gangs.
Seemingly it is only children—or teenagers—who persistently organize to defend a local turf, name themselves after
some shabby street corner, and regard
their betters elsewhere with contempt.
Adults, in turn, complaining about their
present neighborhood, frequently engage
in a good deal of nostalgia that mixes ref-

---

[12] Peter Rossi, *Why Families Move: A Study in the Social Psychology of Urban Residential Mobility*, conducted under the joint sponsorship of the Bureau of
Applied Social Research and the Institute for Urban
Land Use and Housing Studies of Columbia University (Glencoe, Ill.: Free Press, 1955).
[13] Roger G. Barker and Herbert F. Wright, *The Midwest and Its Children: The Psychological Ecology of an American Town* (Evanston, Ill.: Row, Peterson, 1954);
and William Foote Whyte, *Street Corner Society* (Chi-
cago: University of Chicago Press, 1943), pp. 5–6,
104–8.

erences to their youth and "the old neighborhood."

Perhaps the most telling index to the connection between children and the defended neighborhood is the continuing importance of residential segregation compared with segregation in most other areas of life. A long line of research shows that Americans are less willing to desegregate their residential areas than almost any other public realm of life.[14] This resistance to residential desegregation seems to grow directly from the fears which surround childhood contacts and the basic safeguards which the defended neighborhood erects in the first place. The defended neighborhood is largely, although not entirely, a way of assuming that children will have "safe associates."

There may be good reason for this resistance to residential integration so long as equalitarian or casual interracial relations are seen as a source of conflict and danger. Within the workplace and most public establishments, formal procedures of social control can be fairly adequate. On the streets, on playgrounds, and in alleys, formal procedures of social control are, at best, imperfect. These, however, are often the avenues that children take to enjoy their most personal moments.

Morever, there is at least some reason to think that this sort of territorial configuration is essential to the personality development of children. Full access to all areas of the city permits a highly segmentalized style of life where role playing need not go beyond impression management. To avoid this sort of chameleonlike behavior and personal development, individuals must be encompassed in a smaller and more nearly closed framework of social relations where they have to "keep their stories straight." Presumably, this type of closed informational system is especially crucial

to the development of children who are still in the process of acquiring a holistic personality.[15] By allowing for close proximity among those who handle youth (parents, schoolteachers, store owners, youth officers, the parents of peers), the defended neighborhood acts as a sort of container which helps keep together an informational network surrounding each child.

Next to children, mothers with young children are probably the most confined and involved in the defended neighborhood. At minimum, they have an interest in knowing enough of the neighborhood to advise and direct the movement and associations of their children. Like children and like other women, mothers are likely to have to walk to various local facilities and to be concerned especially with their personal safety. The defended neighborhood, then, is particularly relevant to these women, and they are apt to have a considerable investment in its defenses and a clear view of its internal structure.

One can extend this analysis to other age groups, income groups, and various stages in the family life-cycle. The point, however, is that neighborhood participation and the maintenance of neighborhood life may be rather specialized responsibilities.[16] Children and their mothers may continue the more traditional forms of neighborhood life: primary relations, information exchange, and affective attachments. Old people may unwittingly provide a certain measure of surveillance and social control. Formal neighborhood associations and other means of competing for municipal services may fall largely into the hands of those who have political connections, an ideological commitment to neighborhood work, or some reputation for

---

[14] Herbert H. Hyman and Paul B. Sheatsley, "Attitudes toward Desegregation," *Scientific American* 211 (July 1964): 14.

[15] James S. Plant, *The Envelope: A Study of the Impact of the World upon the Child* (New York: Commonwealth Fund, 1950).

[16] Frank L. Sweetser, Jr., *Neighborhood Acquaintance and Association: A Study of Personal Neighborhoods* (New York, 1941).

expertise in this area. The remaining residents, particularly those who are young and single, may cooperate only to the extent that they remain detached from neighborhood affairs and do not impose their cosmopolitan interests on the locals.

Such a differentiated and specialized participation in the defended neighborhood means that its content and structure must be obtained by a selective inquiry from those segments of the population which transmit and defend its traditions, informal relations, and distinct identity. To evaluate the viability and vigor of a neighborhood, then, it is not enough to find out the proportion of all residents who are appreciably involved in "neighboring" or local voluntary organizations. A far more pressing problem is the extent to which certain select groups, no matter how few in number, are able to keep intact neighborhood boundaries, to provide a general knowledge of its internal structure, and to keep alive their myth of unity and cohesion.

EMERGING "ARTIFICIAL" NEIGHBORHOODS

In the past, the physical structure of most American cities and the cognitive maps which people imposed on these cities have tended to follow rather independent courses. The physical structure was determined largely by an economic process with locational possibilities being worked out through an unplanned market system. The cognitive maps which people imposed on the city were largely retrospective and a way of coping with a reality out of their control. These cognitive maps and the defended neighborhood had their own consequences, but these did not include much influence on the city's physical structure.

Now, with the advent of urban planning, the physical structure of the city is no longer subject only to an economic process but involves politics and some cultural image of what the city ought to be like. Many of the new, planned residential areas, particularly those in the inner city, seem to be incorporating at least three elements of the defended neighborhood into the physical structure of the city itself. First, each new residential development seems to have extremely distinct boundaries laid out by through streets but also reinforced by a unified architectural design and a single source of ownership.

Second, each of these new developments possesses a ready-made name and an image or identity even before it is occupied. For private developments this identity is usually manufactured by owners and advertising men. Nonetheless, the residents seem to fully accept their somewhat contrived identity, and it is as much a source of pride or shame as one homegrown. For public-housing developments, governmental bodies provide a name and at least enough of an official line to allow people to elaborate a rather obvious stereotype since most of the eligible residents are black or poor or both. The ready-made identity provided the residents in public housing is probably not very agreeable to them, but nonetheless it is a social fact with which they must contend.

The cultural homogeneity of these new residential developments is a third characteristic of the defended neighborhood which is being incorporated into their physical structure. The old defended neighborhood attempted to maintain its ethnic, racial, and economic purity, and although this attempt was not very successful, its residents often pretended they were alike and created their own cultural unity. The cultural unity of most of these new residential developments seems to be in better hands because the screening of new residents is centralized in the hands of a single realtor.

In many of these recent residential developments, traditional indices to cultural unity seem to be observed, and in Chicago, at least, some of these new residential enclaves are far more segregated than any defended neighborhood. In some of the private developments, however, ethnic and racial considerations have been subordinated to more subtle indices of cultural uniformity. Sometimes the size of the dwelling unit is the determining factor, and in some developments the two-bedroom rental assures that only young couples with one or two young children, old people, and singles will live there. More often the policy of realtors intervenes to assure that the people in these residential aggregates will get along. In Chicago, for example, one can find entire developments which are reserved primarily for family types, for young singles, or for retired couples. There is even one new development which aims to appeal to people who want the maximum mix in terms of income, sex, age, familialism, and ethnicity so long as they can pay the rent.

These new residential developments may seem scarcely comparable to what I have called the defended neighborhood. Despite many structural alterations, however, they continue many of the same functions as the defended neighborhood. Their boundaries are in most cases more sharply drawn and as closely guarded as those of any ethnic neighborhood. The identity of each development is well cultivated and well publicized by central management and advertising men. Even the myth of cultural unity in the defended neighborhood is perpetuated through screening policies and the selection of compatible residents.

Judged against our image of the defended neighborhood as an emergent and sentimental union of similar people, these new residential developments may seem rather foreign. This image of the defended neighborhood, however, was always partial. Its cultural unity and the sentimental attachment of coresidents was sometimes a myth and sometimes a secondary development. The basic functions of defense, the segregation of conflicting populations, and the provision of a residential identity were always somewhat specialized activities. The new and inclusive urban residential developments take this specialization to an extreme. This specialization may eliminate from many new residential areas those characteristics we thought most commonly associated with the defended neighborhood.

This, however, does not mean that the local residential group is going to lose all importance. What is happening to the defended neighborhood seems analogous to what happened to the nuclear family during the early part of this century when the domestic group lost most of its economic functions and became more exclusively a child-rearing group. A parallel pattern of specialization and differentiation may be appearing in the defended neighborhood. The new residential development with physically distinct boundaries and a single source of management does not imply the decline of the defended neighborhood but brings into greater relief its basic functions.

--------------------------------- 26 ---------------------------------

Networks, neighborhoods, and communities: Approaches to the study of the community question

Barry Wellman and Barry Leighton

NEIGHBORHOOD OR COMMUNITY?

Urban sociology has tended to be *neighborhood sociology*. This has meant that analyses of large-scale urban phenomena (such as the fiscal crisis of the state) have been neglected in favor of small-scale studies of communities. It has also meant that the study of such communities has been firmly rooted in the study of neighborhoods, be they the "symbiotic" communities of Park (1936) or the "street corners" of Liebow (1967). It is to the sorting out of this second tendency, the merger of "neighborhood" with "community" that we address this paper.

There are a number of reasons why the concept of "neighborhood" has come to be substituted for that of "community":

First, urban researchers have to start somewhere. The neighborhood is an easily identifiable research site, while the street corner is an obvious and visible place for mapping small-scale interaction.

Second, many scholars have interpreted the neighborhood as the microcosm of the city and the city as an aggregate of neighborhoods. They have emphasized the local rather than the cosmopolitan in a building-block approach to analysis which has given scant attention to large-scale urban structure.

Third, administrative officials have imposed their own definitions of neighborhood boundaries upon urban maps in attempts to create bureaucratic units. Spatial areas, labeled and treated as coherent neighborhoods, have come to be regarded as natural phenomena.

Fourth, urban sociology's particular concern with spatial distributions has tended to be translated into local area concerns. Territory has come to be seen as the inherently most important organizing factor in urban social relations rather than just one potentially important factor.

Fifth, and most importantly, many analysts have been preoccupied with the conditions under which solidary sentiments can be maintained. Their preoccupation reflects a persistent overarching sociological concern with normative integration and consensus. The neighborhood has been studied as an apparently obvious container of normative solidarity.

For these reasons, at least, the concentration on the neighborhood has had a strong impact on definitions of, research on, and theorizing about community. Neighborhood studies have produced hundreds of finely wrought depictions of urban life, and they have given us powerful ideas about how small-scale social systems operate in a variety of social contexts. But does the concept of "neighborhood" equal the concept of "community"? Are the two really one and the same?

Definitions of community tend to include three ingredients: *networks of interpersonal ties* (outside of the household) which *provide sociability and support* to members, residence in a *common locality*, and *solidarity sentiments and activities* (see Hillery, 1955). It is principally the emphasis on common locality, and to a lesser

Reprinted with permission of the authors and Sage Publications from Barry Wellman and Barry Leighton, "Networks, Neighborhoods, and Communities: Approaches to the Study of the Community Question" in *Urban Affairs Quarterly* 14, no. 3 (March 1979), pp. 363–90.

extent the emphasis on solidarity, which has encouraged the identification of "community" with "neighborhood."

Yet the paramount concern of sociologists is social structure, and concerns about the spatial location of social structures and their normative integration must necessarily occupy secondary positions. To sociologists, unlike geographers, spatial distributions are not inherently important variables, but assume importance only as they affect such social structural questions as the formation of interpersonal networks and the flow of resources through such networks.

The community question

With its manifest concerns for the activities of populations in territories (Tilly, 1974), urban sociology has often seemed to stand apart from broader theoretical concerns. Yet its concentration on the study of the neighborhood-as-community is very much a part of a fundamental sociological issue. This fundamental issue, which has occupied much sociological thinking, is the *community question*: the study of how large-scale divisions of labor in social systems affect the organization and content of interpersonal ties.

Sociologists have been particularly concerned with that form of the community question which investigates the impact the massive industrial bureaucratic transformations of North America and Europe during the past 200 years have had on a variety of primary ties: in the home, the neighborhood, the workplace, with kin and friends, and among interest groups. Have such ties attenuated or flourished in contemporary societies? In what sort of networks are they organized? Have the contents of such ties remained as holistic as alleged to be in preindustrial societies or have they become narrowly specialized and instrumental?

The community question thus forms a crucial nexus between macroscopic and microscopic analysis. It directly addresses the structural integration of a social system and the interpersonal means by which its members can gain access to scarce resources. We urge, therefore, that the study of the community question be freed from its identification with the study of neighborhoods.

Neighborhood/Community

The entangling of the study of community ties with the study of the neighborhood has created a number of problems for the analysis of the community question.

First, the identification of a neighborhood as a container for communal ties assumes the a priori organizing power of space. This is spatial determinism. Even if we grant that space-time costs encourage some relationships to be local, it does not necessarily follow that all communal ties are organized into solidary neighborhood communities. These neighborhood ties may exist because of the attraction of ready accessibility to a few people and not because of a tangible neighborhood social organization.

Second, even the presence of many local relationships does not necessarily create discrete neighborhoods. There may well be overlapping sets of local ties, the range of these ties being affected by the needs and physical mobility of the participants.

Third, the identification of neighborhood studies with community studies can omit major spheres of interaction. There are important ties outside of the neighborhood even in the most "institutionally complete community" (Breton, 1964). Perhaps work relationships are the most serious and prevalent omission from community studies: residents tend to disappear from view in the morning and mysteriously reappear at dusk.

Fourth, the focus on the neighborhood may give undue importance to spatial characteristics as causal variables. Are cities just concrete and concentrated manifestations of larger structural forces? For instance, Castells (1976) argues that most Western urban sociology can be explained by studying capitalist modes of production.

Fifth, many analyses of neighborhoods have been preoccupied with the conditions under which solidary sentiments can be maintained. Consequently, when there has been an observed lack of locally organized behavior and sentiments, the assumption has easily been made that community has decayed. When not found in the neighborhood, community is assumed not to exist.

THE NETWORK PERSPECTIVE

We suggest that the *network analytic perspective* is a more appropriate response to the community question in urban studies than the traditional focus on the neighborhood.[1] A network analysis of community takes as its starting point the search for social linkages and flows of resources. Only then does it enquire into the spatial distribution and solidary sentiments associated with the observed linkages. Such an approach largely frees the study of community from spatial and normative bases. It makes possible the discovery of network-based communities which are nei-

ther linked to a particular neighborhood nor to a set of solidary sentiments.

However, the network perspective is not inherently antineighborhood. By leaving the matter of spatial distributions initially open, this perspective makes it equally as possible to discover an "urban village" (Gans, 1962) as it is to discover a "community without propinquity" (Webber, 1963). A network analysis might also tell us that strong ties remain abundant and important, but that they are rarely located in the neighborhood. With this approach we are then better able to assess the position of neighborhood ties within the context of overall structures of social relationships.

The community question has been extensively debated by urban scholars. In this paper, we evaluate three competing scholarly arguments about the community question from a network perspective. The first two arguments to be discussed both focus on the neighborhood: the *community lost*, asserting the absence of local solidarities, and the *community saved* argument, asserting their persistence. The *community liberated* argument, in contrast, denies any neighborhood basis to community. General tendencies in each argument are summarized, although not every article making each argument neatly fits into the analytic categories we have imposed on them. We review each argument's development, portrayal of urban networks, underlying normative imagery, policy implications, and current scholarly status. We conclude the paper by suggesting different circumstances in which saved and liberated network structures might be more prevalent and more useful.

COMMUNITY LOST

Development

The community lost argument contends that the transformation of Western societies to centralized, industrial bureau-

---

[1] Network analysis is essentially a perspective which focuses on structured relationships between individuals and collectivities. As yet there is no commonly agreed definition. We believe that network anlaysis's salient characteristics are that it gives attention to: (a) structured patterns of relationships and not the aggregated characteristics of individual units, analyzed without reference to their interrelationships; (b) complex network structures and not just dyadic ties; (c) the allocation of scarce resources through concrete systems of power, dependency, and coordination; (d) questions of network boundaries, clusters, and cross-linkages; (e) structures of reciprocal relationships and not just simple hierarchies. For summaries of the network perspective, see White (1965); Mitchell (1969, 1974); Barnes (1972); White, Boorman, and Breiger (1976). See also the bibliographies of Wellman and Whitaker (1974); Freeman (1976); Klovdahl (1977).

cratic structures has gravely weakened primary ties and communities, making the individual more dependent on formal organizational resources for sustenance (see the reviews in Stein, 1960; Nisbet, 1962; Gusfield, 1975; Castells, 1976; Mellor, 1977). The first attempts to deal with the community question (e.g., Tönnies, 1887) were, at the turn of the century, closely associated with broader sociological concerns about the impact of the Industrial Revolution on communal ties and normative integration (e.g., Durkheim, 1893; Simmel, 1908).

Scholars working in the lost tradition have initiated the analysis of the impact of large-scale social changes upon community structures. A number of such significant changes have been suggested, although not all analysts proposing them would necessarily agree that the loss of community was the ultimate outcome:

a. An increase in the scale of the nation-state's activities, with a concomitant decrease in local community autonomy and solidarity.
b. The development of bureaucratic institutions for production and reproduction, which have taken over many family, neighborhood, and friendship activities.
c. The large size of cities, which provides a basis for the population and organizational potential for more, and diverse, interest groups.
d. The high social density of interactions among segments of the population (even where spatial density is decreasing), with the ensuing complexities of ecological sorting and social arrangements.
e. The diversity of people with whom city dwellers can come into contact under conditions of heightened physical mobility.
f. The proliferation of cheap, efficient, and widespread transportation and communication facilities, increasing the ease with which contact can be made and enabling urbanites to be less tied to the neighborhood. The increased velocity of transactions fosters interactional density, and links to multiple social circles are even more readily maintained.

The lost argument has had continuing academic attention. It underlay much of the 1920s–1930s theoretical writing of the dominant "Chicago school" of urban studies (although the Chicago scholars found much evidence of communal organization in their empirical work). Robert Park's early programmatic statement asserted that "the growth of cities has been accomplished by the substitution of indirect 'secondary' for direct, face-to-face 'primary relations'" (Park, 1925a: 23). Over a decade later, Louis Wirth (1938) summarized the lost argument well in his now classic statement of "urbanism as a way of life." Primary ties are recognized as still existing, but in a weaker, more narrowly instrumental fashion than those which had flourished in traditional solidary communities. More recent statements making the lost argument have not been as closely associated with empirical research but have been primarily concerned with normative theorizing and moralizing (e.g., Kornhauser, 1959; Nisbet, 1962; Banfield, 1968; Slater, 1970).

Lost scholars have seen modern urbanites as alienated isolates who bear the brunt of the transformed society on their own. Many research procedures have reinforced this perspective by using survey techniques which lump together individuals *qua* individuals in analytically imposed categories which do not take into consideration their structural connectedness (i.e., the statistical assumption of independence elevated to a world view). Such individual-as-unit-oriented research techniques have been particularly suited to social psychologistic explanations which see internalized attitudes as determining social activity; they have not been nearly as well-suited towards the direct study of social-structural effects.

Lost networks

The community lost argument makes a number of specific assertions about the kinds of primary ties, social networks, and community structures that will tend to be present under its assumptions. By casting the lost argument in network analytic terms, we shall be better able to evaluate it in comparison with the community saved and community liberated arguments:

a.   Rather than being a full member of a solidary community, urbanites are now *limited members* (in terms of amount, intensity, and commitment of interaction) of *several social networks*.
b.   Primary ties are *narrowly defined;* there are *fewer strands* in the relationship.
c.   The narrowly defined ties tend to be *weak in intensity*.
d.   Ties tend to be *fragmented* into isolated *two-person* relationships rather than being parts of extensive networks.
e.   Those networks that do exist tend to be *sparsely knit* (a low proportion of all potential links between members actually exists) rather than being densely knit (a high proportion of potential links exists).
f.   The networks are *loosely bounded;* there are few discrete clusters or primary groups.
g.   Sparse density, loose boundaries, and narrowly defined ties provide *little* structural basis for *solidary activities or sentiments*.
h.   The narrowly defined ties dispersed among a number of networks create *difficulties in mobilizing assistance* from network members.

Imagery

Community lost imagery has had a good deal of scholarly impact, appealing to radical (e.g., Engels, 1845; Castells, 1976), liberal (e.g., Kornhauser, 1959; Stein, 1960; Slater, 1970), and conservative (e.g., Nisbet, 1962; Banfield, 1968; Grant, 1969) concerns. Lost scholars of all political persuasions have been concerned about the upheavals caused by the large-scale transformation of industrial bureaucratic societies and the social disorganization and depravity allegedly let loose by the weakening of traditional communal bonds. Running through many lost analyses has been the implicit assumption that human beings are fundamentally evil (or easily capable of being driven to evil by industrialism, bureaucraticism, or capitalism), and that where restraining communal structures have been destroyed by the Industrial Revolution, riot, robbery, and rape have swept the city.

The social disorganization theme has remained a popular one in North American thought (for reviews, see White and White, 1962; Marx, 1964; Bender, 1978). Nostalgia for "the myth of the lost paradise" (Gusfield, 1975) has mingled with the identification of the contemporary city as the home of rootless masses in a continuing tradition from Jeffersonian pastoralism through Progressive reformism (e.g., Woodsworth, 1911) to such recent urban panic movies as "Death Wish" (1974). Affluent suburbs (see the review in Popenoe, 1977) as well as poor inner cities are despaired of as privatized, isolated, and alienated.

Policy implications

The community lost argument has significantly affected urban policy in North America and Western Europe. There have been extensive "community development" programs designed to end alienation and to grow urban roots, such as the putative War on Poverty. The desired community ideal in such programs has been the regeneration of the densely knit, tightly bounded, solidary neighborhood community. When, despite the programs, a return to the pastoral ideal has not seemed achievable, then despair about social disorganization has led to elaborate social control policies, designed to keep in check the supposedly alienated, irrational, violence-prone masses. When even the achievement of social control has not seemed feasible, policies of neglect—benign or otherwise—have developed. Administrators have removed services from inner-city neighborhoods, asserting their inability to cope with socially disorganized behavior and leaving the remaining inhabitants to fend for themselves. The residents of such inner-city American areas as Pruitt-Igoe and the South Bronx have come to be regarded as unredeemably "sinful" as they suffer the supposed war of all against all.

Current status

The principal scholarly value of the community lost argument has been the attention it has focused on some important theoretical issues. First, it has sharpened perceptions of the ways in which industrial bureaucratic social systems can affect the nature of traditional communities. Second, it has raised the problem of the impact of residential and social mobility on the maintenance of community ties. Because it has seen community as only existing in neighborhoods, the lost argument has interpreted such mobility as a loss of community. However, if community becomes redefined in nonspatial terms, then the lost argument has served as an important precursor of the more recent community liberated argument (see below).

Despite its tenacity, the lost argument has received little empirical confirmation. Indeed, much of the impetus behind the saved and liberated arguments since World War II has been to disprove the loss of community contention (see the reviews in Craven and Wellman, 1973; Feagin, 1973; Hunter, 1975; Fischer, 1976). A modified version of the lost argument has recently emerged, taking into account the

extensive documentation of primary ties that has been performed by saved and liberated scholars (see below). This modified lost version acknowledges the persistence of primary ties but contends that they are now markedly narrower in scope: the former wide range of content in kinship, neighborhood, and friendship ties has been reduced to sociability and emotional support, with formal institutions and the nuclear family now taking over much of the former content of such relationships (e.g., Sennett, 1970; Lasch, 1977). While this new version of the lost argument offers its scholars an opportunity to move from normative ideologizing to systematic investigations, extensive empirical confirmation of its contentions has not yet appeared.

COMMUNITY SAVED

Development

The community saved argument maintains that neighborhood communities have persisted in industrial bureaucratic social systems as important sources of support and sociability. It argues that the very formal, centralizing tendencies of bureaucratic institutions have paradoxically encouraged the maintenance of primary ties as more flexible sources of sociability and support. The saved argument contends that urbanites continue to organize safe communal havens, with neighborhood, kinship, and work solidarities mediating and coping with bureaucratic institutions.

The saved argument shares with the lost argument the identification of "community" with "neighborhood." However, saved scholars have reacted against the tendency of some lost scholars to write secondary analyses *about* the neighborhood community rather than primary analyses *of* neighborhood communities.

In marked contrast to the lost argument scholar's proclivity for armchair theorizing, much of the saved argument's case has rested on the sheer empirical demonstration of the continued vitality of those urban primary ties which had been pronounced lost. Since World War II, hordes of scholars have presented carefully documented community studies, using systematic survey and field-work techniques, to make the saved argument. These studies have concentrated on delineating the social structure of neighborhood communities and have not just presented urbanites as aggregates of unconnected individuals. They have shown that urbanites still neighbor, still have a sense of local community, and still use neighborhood ties for sociability and support (see the reviews in Keller, 1968; Wellman and Whitaker, 1974; Warren and Warren, 1976; Fischer, 1976; Warren, 1978).

Saved networks

The saved argument, cast into network analytic terms, is quite different from the lost argument:

a. Urbanites tend to be *heavily involved members* of a *single neighborhood community*, although they may combine this with membership in other social networks.

b. There are *multiple strands* of relationships between the members of these neighborhood communities.

c. While network ties vary in intensity, many of them are *strong*.

d. Neighborhood ties tend to be organized into *extensive networks*.

e. Networks tend to be *densely knit*.

f. Neighborhood networks are *tightly bounded*, with few external linkages. Ties tend to loop back into the same cluster of network members.

g. High density, tight boundaries, and multistranded ties provide a structural basis for a good deal of *solidary activities and sentiments*.

h. The multistranded strong ties clustered in densely knit networks *facilitate* the *mobilization* of assistance for dealing with routine and emergency matters.

Imagery

Saved scholars have tended to regard human beings as fundamentally good and inherently gregarious. They are viewed as apt to organize self-regulating communities under all circumstances, even extreme conditions of poverty, oppression, or catastrophe.

Hence the saved argument has shared the neighborhood community ideal with the lost argument, but it has seen this ideal as attainable and often already existing. Neighborhood communities are valued precisely because they can provide small-scale loci of interaction and can effectively mediate urbanites' dealings with large-scale institutions. Densely knit, tightly bounded communities are valued as structures particularly suited to the tenacious conservation of its internal resources, the maintenance of local autonomy, and the social control of members (and intruders) in the face of powerful impinging external forces (e.g., Jacobs, 1961; Newman, 1972).

Policy implications

Public acceptance of the saved argument has greatly increased during the past two decades. Active neighborhood communities are now valued as antidotes to industrial bureaucratic societies' alleged impersonality, specialized relationships, and loss of comprehensible scale. "Streetcorner society" (Whyte, 1955), "the urban village" (Gans, 1962), and "Tally's Corner" (Liebow, 1967) have become exemplars of saved communities.

The neighborhood unit has been the 20th-century planning ideal for new housing. Saved ideologues have also argued the necessity for preserving existing neighborhoods against the predations of ignorant and rapacious institutions. The saved argument has been the ideological foundation of the neighborhood movement which seeks to stop expressways, demolish developers, and renovate old areas (e.g., Powell, 1972). Some neighborhoods have been successfully rescued from "urban renewal," although Gans' West End in Boston (1962) and Clairmont and Magill's Africville in Halifax (1974) have been lost.

In political analyses, rioters, far from being socially disorganized, are now seen to be rooted, well-connected community members (see Feagin and Hahn, 1973; Tilly, 1973, 1978). Their motivations tend to be in defense of existing communal interests or claims to new ones, rather than the irrational, individualistic, psychologistic responses claimed by the lost argument. Indeed, the means by which urbanites get involved in a riot are very much associated with the competitions, coalitions, and solidary ties of their social networks.

Many saved social pathologists have encouraged the nurturance of densely knit, bounded communities as a structural salve for the stresses of poverty, ethnic segregation, and physical and mental diseases (see the review in Caplan and Killilea, 1976; Ratcliffe, 1978). Getting help informally through neighborhood communities is alleged to be more sensitive to peculiar local needs and protective of the individual against bureaucratic claims. Furthermore, such programs have been welcomed by administrators as most cost-effective (or, as some critics allege, merely cheaper to operate) than the formal institutional intervention implied by the lost argument.[2]

Current status

In the early 1960s the saved argument became the new orthodoxy in community studies with the publication of such works as Gans' *The Urban Villagers* (1962), Greer's (1962) synthesis of postwar survey research, and Jacob's (1961) assertion of the vitality of dense, diverse central cities. Such case studies as Young and Willmott's (1957) study of a working-class London neighborhood, Gans's (1967) account of middle-class, new suburban networks, and Liebow's (1967) portrayal of inner-city blacks' heavy reliance on network ties helped clinch the case.

The rebuttal of the lost argument's assertion of urban social disorganization has therefore been accomplished, theoretically and empirically, by studies emphasizing the persistence of neighborhood communities. In the process, though, the lost argument's useful starting point may have come to be neglected: that the industrial bureaucratic division of labor has strongly affected the structure of primary ties. Saved scholars have tended to look only for—and at—the persistence of functioning neighborhood communities.[3] Consequently we now know that neighborhood communities persist and often flourish, but we do not know the position of neighborhood-based ties within overall social networks.

Many recent saved analyses have recognized this difficulty by introducing the "community of limited liability" concept, which treats the neighborhood as just one of a series of communities among which urbanites divide their membership (see Janowitz, 1952; Greer, 1962; Suttles, 1972; Kasarda and Janowitz, 1974; Hunter, 1975; Warren, 1978). Hunter and Suttles (1972: 61), for example, portray such communities as a set of concentric zones radiating out from the block to "entire sectors of the city." However, while such analyses recognize the possibilities for urbanites to be members of diverse networks with limited involvement in each network, the "limited liability community" formulation is still

---

[2] One mental health technique, questionably labeled "network therapy," has as a principal goal the "retribalization" of those with whom the patient is in close contact (see Speck and Attneave, 1973).

[3] Perhaps only Banfield (1958) and Vidich and Bensman (1958) have set forth in search of solidary communities and not found them.

predicated on the neighborhood concept, seeing urban ties as radiating out from a local, spatially defined base.

COMMUNITY LIBERATED

Development

The third response to the community question, the liberated argument, agrees with the lost argument's contention that the industrial bureaucratic nature of social systems has caused the weakening of neighborhood communities. But the liberated argument also agrees with the saved argument's contention that primary ties have remained viable, useful, and important. It shares the saved argument's contention that communities still flourish in the city, but it maintains that such communities are rarely organized within neighborhoods.

The liberated argument contends that a variety of structural and technological developments have liberated communities from the confines of neighborhoods and dispersed network ties from all-embracing solidary communities to more narrowly based ones: *(a)* cheap, effective transportation and communication facilities; *(b)* the separation of workplace and kinship ties into nonlocal, nonsolidary networks; *(c)* high rates of social and residential mobility (e.g., Crump, 1977).

The liberated argument, like the other two arguments, begins with the concept of space. Yet where the other arguments see communities as resident in neighborhoods, the liberated argument confronts spatial restrictions only in order to transcend them. Although harkening back to some of the more optimistic writings of Simmel about the liberating effect of urban life (e.g., 1902–1903; last portion; 1908; 121) and Park (e.g., 1925b: 65ff.), the argument has become prominent only in the past two decades following the proliferation of personal automotive and airplane travel and telecommunications in the Western world. It contends that there is now the possibility of "community without propinquity" (Webber, 1964) in which distance and travel time are minimal constraints (e.g., Hiltz and Turoff, forthcoming).

Liberated networks

With its emphasis on aspatial communities, the liberated argument has been methodologically associated with network analytic techniques (e.g., Kadushin, 1966; Walker, 1977; Wellman, 1979). However, it must be emphasized that network analysis does not necessarily share the liberated argument's ideological bias and can be used to evaluate the existence of *all three* community patterns: lost, saved, and liberated.

In network terms, the liberated argument contends that:

a. Urbanites now tend to be *limited members* of *several social networks*, possibly including one located in their neighborhood.

b. There is *variation in the breadth of the strands* of relationships between network members; there are multi-stranded ties with some, single-stranded ties with many others, and relationships of intermediate breadth with the rest.

c. The ties range in intensity: *some* of them are *strong*, while others are weak but nonetheless useful.

d. An individual's ties tend to be organized into a *series of networks with few connections* between them.

e. Networks tend to be *sparsely knit* although certain portions of the networks, such as those based on kinship, may be more densely knit.

f. The networks are *loosely bounded*, *ramifying* structures, branching out extensively to form linkages to additional people and resources.

g. Sparse density, loose boundaries, and narrowly defined ties provide *little structural basis for solidary activities and sentiments* in the overall networks of urbanites, although some solidary clusters of ties are often present.

h. *Some network ties can be mobilized* for general-purpose or specific assistance in dealing with routine or emergency matters. The likelihood of mobilization depends more on the quality of the two-person tie than on the nature of the larger network structure.

Imagery

The liberated argument is fundamentally optimistic about urban life. It is appreciative of urban diversity; imputations of social disorganization and pathology find little place within it. The argument's view of human behavior emphasizes its entrepreneurial and manipulative aspects. People are seen as having a propensity to form primary ties, not out of inherent good or evil, but in order to accomplish specific, utilitarian ends.

The liberated argument, as does the lost argument, minimizes the importance of neighborhood communities. But where the lost argument sees this as throwing the urbanite upon the resources of formal organizations, the liberated argument contends that sufficient primary ties are available in nonneighborhood networks to provide crucial social support and sociability. Furthermore, it argues that the diverse links between these networks organize the city as a "network of networks" (Craven and Wellman, 1973) to provide a flexible coordinating structure not possible through a lost formal bureaucratic hierarchy or a saved agglomeration of neighborhoods.

The liberated argument recoils from the lost and saved arguments' village-like community norm. The argument celebrates the structural autonomy of being able to move among various social networks (e.g., Cox, 1966; Burt, 1976). It perceives solidary communities as fostering stifling social control and of causing isolation from outside contact and resources. Multiple social networks are valued because the cross-cutting commitments and alternative escape routes limit the claims that any one community can make upon its members.

Policy implications

Liberated analysts have called for the reinforcement of other social networks in addition to the traditional ones of the neighborhood and the family. Whereas industrial power considerations have worked against the development of solidary networks in the workplace, much attention has been paid recently to fostering "helping networks" that would prevent or heal the stress of physical and mental diseases (e.g., Caplan and Killilea, 1976; Hirsch, 1977; Ratcliffe, 1978). No longer is the neighborhood community seen as the safe, supportive haven; no longer are formal institutions to be relied on for all healing attempts. Instead, networks are to be mobilized, and where they do not exist they can be constructed so that urbanites may find supportive places. However, the efficacy of such deliberately constructed "natural support systems" (to use current jargon) has not yet been adequately demonstrated.

The liberated argument has had an important impact on thinking about political phenomena, especially that related to collective disorders. Research by Charles Tilly (e.g., 1975, 1978) and associates, in particular, has shown such collective disorders to be integral parts of broader contentions for power by competing interest groups. In addition to the internal solidarity emphasized by the saved argument, a contending group's chances for success have been shown to be strongly associated with the capacity for making linkages in external coalitions that crosscutting ties between networks can provide (e.g., Gans, 1974a, 1974b; Granovetter, 1974b).

Recent British New Town planning (e.g., Milton Keynes) has been predicated on the high rates of personal automotive mobility foreseen by the liberated argument. However, the argument's contention that there are minimal costs to spatial separation has come up against the increase in the monetary costs of such separation associated with the significant rise in the price of oil within the last decade. One response has been to advocate increased reliance on telecommunications to maintain community ties over large distances. New developments in computer technology foreshadow major increases in telecommunications capabilities, such as "electronic mail" and "computer conferencing" (see Hiltz and Turoff, forthcoming). Yet the strength of the liberated argument does not necessarily depend on technological innovations. Recent research in preindustrial social systems has indicated that long-distance ties can be maintained without benefit of telephone or private automobiles, as long as such ties are structurally embedded in kinships systems or common local origins (e.g., Belshaw, 1965; Cohen, 1969; Laslett, 1971; Jacobson, 1973; Howard, 1974; Mayer and Mayer, 1974; Ross and Weisner, 1977; Bender, 1978).

Current status

Contemporary studies making the liberated argument have proliferated in the past decade. They have examined the nature of membership in multiple social networks (e.g., Kadushin, 1966; Laumann, 1973; Boissevain, 1974; Breiger, 1976; Bell and Newby, 1976; Shulman, 1976), the use of network ties to obtain needed resources (e.g., Cohen, 1969; Lee, 1969; Granovetter, 1974a; Jacobson, 1975), and the ways in which links between social networks can structure social systems (e.g., Granovetter, 1973; Wireman, 1978; Laumann, Galaskiewicz, and Marsden, forthcoming).

The strength of the liberated argument is that it can account for, and at the same time propose, socially close communities which stretch over large distances. "Community" need no longer necessarily be tied to "neighborhood." However, in propounding the virtues of nonlocal communities the liberated argument may have unduly neglected the usefulness of quick local accessibility and the advantages of the solidary behavior that can come with densely knit, tightly bounded, multistranded ties. To assert that one should not set out initially to search for solidarities, as the network perspective does, may be quite a different matter than the liberated argument's assertion of the nonexistence of such solidarities.

COMMUNITIES: LOST, SAVED, OR LIBERATED?

Are communities lost, saved, or liberated? Too often, the three arguments have been presented as (a) competing alternative depictions of the "true" nature of Western industrial bureaucratic social systems, or (b) evolutionary successors, with preindustrial saved communities giving way to industrial lost, only to be superseded by postindustrial liberated.

In contrast, we believe that all three arguments have validity when stripped of their ideological paraphernalia down to basic network structures.[4] Indeed their

---

[4] Our review of the saved literature has already indicated the abundant evidence for the presence of densely knit, tightly bounded communities in contemporary Western social systems (e.g., Whyte, 1955; Young and Willmott, 1957; Gans, 1962; Liebow, 1967). While only Bender (1978) has explicitly attempted to argue the prevalence of liberated patterns in preindustrial social systems, historians have begun reporting nonsolidary aspects of preindustrial Western Europe (e.g., Laslett, 1971; Scott and Tilly, 1975; Shorter, 1975; Tilly, 1975). We can look to studies of peer groups, interest groups, travel out of the local area, and complex households (masters, servants, laborers; multiple generations, with nonlocal marriages) having a variety of external ties as providing some basis for the existence of liberated patterns. The prevalence of long-distance, liberated ties in contemporary non-Western social systems has been more extensively documented (see review of the liberated literature).

structural character might be highlighted by thinking of them as sparse, dense, and ramified network patterns. Different network patterns tend to have different consequences for the acquisition and control of resources (see the discussion of kinship systems in Wolf, 1966). We might then expect to find the prevalence of lost, saved, and liberated communities to vary according to the kinds of societal circumstances in which they are located.

Saved communities/Defense networks

In saved networks, densely knit ties and tight boundaries tend to occur together. This may be because network members have a finite lump of sociability, so that if they devote most of their energies to within-network ties, they do not have much scope for maintaining external linkages. Conversely, tight boundaries may also foster the creation of new ties within the community, as internal links become the individual's principal hope of gaining access to resources.

Such dense, bounded saved networks, be they neighborhood, kinship, or otherwise based, are apt to be solidary in sentiments and activities. They are well-structured for maintaining informal social control over members and intruders. The dense ties and communal solidarity should facilitate the ready mobilization of the community's resources for the aid of members in good standing. But because solidarity does not necessarily mean egalitarianism, not all of the community's resources may be gathered or distributed equally.

Community studies have shown the saved pattern to be quite prevalent in situations in which community members do not have many individual personal resources and where there are unfavorable conditions for forming external ties. Certain ethnic minority and working-class neighborhoods clearly follow this pattern (e.g., Liebow, 1967). In such situations, concerns about conserving, controlling,

and efficiently pooling those resources the beleaguered community possesses also resonate with its members' inability to acquire additional resources elsewhere. A heavy load consequently is placed on ties within the saved community.

Liberated communities/Ramified networks

If saved network patterns are particularly suited to conditions of resource scarcity and conservation, liberated network patterns are particularly suited to conditions of resource abundance and acquisition. Such sparsely knit, loosely bounded networks are not structurally well-equipped for internal social control. Implicit assurance in the security of one's home base is necessary before one can reach out into new areas.

Loose boundaries and sparse density foster networks that extensively branch out to link up with new members. These ramifying liberated networks are well-structured for acquiring additional resources through a larger number of direct and indirect external connections. Their structure is apt to connect liberated network members with a more diverse array of resources than saved networks are apt to encounter, although the relative lack of solidarity in such liberated networks may well mean that a lower proportion of resources will be available to other network members.

It may well be that the liberated pattern is peculiarly suited to affluent sectors of contemporary Western societies. It places a premium on a base of individual security, entrepreneurial skills in moving between networks, and the ability to function without the security of membership in a solidary community. However, its appearance in other social contexts indicates that it reflects a more fundamental alternative to the saved community pattern.

Both the saved or liberated community patterns can appear as desirable alternatives to those enmeshed in the other pattern. To those unsatisfied with the uncertain multiplicities of liberated networks, holistic, solidary saved communities can appear as a welcome retreat. To those who feel trapped in all-embracing saved networks, the availability of alternative liberated primary networks may offer a welcome escape route. Much migration from rural areas may follow this tendency.

Lost communities/Sparse networks

What of circumstances where no alternative network sources of escape or retreat are possible? It is in such situations that the lost pattern of direct affiliation with formal institutions can become attractive: the army, the church, the firm, and the university (see Shorter, 1973). However, the lost pattern may always be unstable for individuals and communities as formal institutional ties devolve into complex primary network webs. Therefore, as primary ties develop between or within organizations, we may expect to find networks taking on the patterns of saved or liberated communities.

Personal communities

When studying neighborhoods and communities, we are likely to find diversity rather than a universal pattern to either local or personal networks. We have proposed that dense saved network patterns are better suited for internal control of resources while ramified liberated patterns are better suited for obtaining access to external resources. Although we have suggested that each of these patterns should be more prevalent in one sort of a society than another, it is quite likely that the total network of a community will comprise a mixture of these two patterns in varying proportions. That is, some of the ties within a network will be densely knit and tightly bounded, while others will be sparsely knit and ramified. The different patterns are useful for different things.

As Merton (1957) early pointed out, most communities have some network members for exchanging resources with the outside world ("cosmopolitans") and some for allocating them internally ("locals").

Our own research in the Borough of East York, Toronto, has revealed that individuals, too, may be simultaneously members of both saved and liberated pattern networks.[5] Some of an urbanite's ties tend to be clustered into densely knit, tightly bounded networks, their solidarity often reinforced by either kinship structures or residential or work-place propinquity. Such saved networks are better able to mobilize help in emergencies through efficient communication and structurally enforced norms. Their density and boundedness tend to give these clusters more of a tangible collective image, so that network members have a sense of solidary attachment.

Yet we have found (Wellman, 1979) that such clusters are likely to comprise only a minority of one's important network ties. The other ties tend to be much less densely connected Instead of looping back into one another within boundaries, they tend to be ramified, branching out to encounter new members to whom the original network members are not directly connected. These sparsely knit, loosely bounded liberated networks are structurally not as efficient in mobilizing collective assistance for their members, but their branching character allows additional resources to be reached. Furthermore, the liberated ties,

---

[5] The data collected in 1968 random-sample, closed-ended survey of 845 adult East Yorkers, directed by Donald B. Coates, with Barry Wellman as coordinator. East York (1971 population = 104,646) is an upper working-class, lower middle-class, predominantly British-Canadian inner-city suburb of Toronto. It has the reputation of being one of the most solidary areas of the city. Respondents were asked about "persons outside your home who you feel closest to" up to a maximum of six. See Wayne (1971), Shulman (1972, 1976), Crump (1977), Wellman (1979), and Wellman, Shulman, Wayne, and Crump (forthcoming) for the findings.

while not as conducive to internal solidarity as the saved clusters, better facilitate coalition building between networks.

Neighborhood and community

Almost all of the people we studied have many strong ties and they are able to obtain assistance through a number of close relationships. Yet only a small proportion of these "intimate" ties are located in the same neighborhood (Wellman, 1979). While neighboring ties are still prevalent and important in East York, they rarely achieve the intensity of intimacy (see Gates, Stevens, and Wellman, 1973).

Neighborhood relationships persist but only as specialized components of the overall primary networks. The variety of ties in which an urbanite can be involved —with distant parents, intimate friends, less intimate friends, co-workers, and so on—and the variety of networks in which these are organized can provide flexible structural bases for dealing with routine and emergency matters.

In sum, we must be concerned with neighborhood *and* community rather than neighborhood *or* community. We have suggested that the two are separate concepts which may or may not be closely associated. In some situations we can observe the saved pattern of community as solidary neighborhood. In many other situations, if we go out and look for neighborhood-based networks, we are apt to find them. They can be heavily used for the advantages of quick accessibility. But if we broaden our field of view to include other primary relations, then the apparent neighborhood solidarities may now be seen as clusters in a rather sparse, loosely bounded structures of urbanites' total networks.

REFERENCES

Banfield, E. (1968) The Unheavenly City. Boston: Little, Brown.

————. (1958) The Moral Basis of a Backward Society. New York: Free Press.

Barnes, J. A. (1972) Social Networks. Reading, Mass.: Addison-Wesley.

Bell, C., and H. Newby (1976) "Community, communion, class and community action," pp. 189–207 in D. T. Herbert and R. J. Johnson (eds.) Social Areas in Cities II: Spatial Perspectives on Problems and Policies. London: John Wiley.

Belshaw, C. (1965) Traditional Exchange and Modern Markets. Englewood Cliffs, N.J.: Prentice-Hall.

Bender, T. (1978) Community and Social Change in America. New Brunswick, N.J.: Rutgers University Press.

Boissevain, J. (1974) Friends of Friends, Oxford: Basil Blackwell.

Breiger, R. L. (1976) "Career attributes and network structure: A blockmodel study of a biomedical research specialty." *American Sociological Review* 41 (February), pp. 117–135.

Breton, R. (1964) "Institutional completeness of communities and the personal relations of immigrants." *American Journal of Sociology* 70 (September), pp. 193–205.

Burt, R. (1976) "Autonomy in a social topology." Unpublished paper. Chicago: National Opinion Research Center, University of Chicago.

Caplan, G., and M. Killilea (1976) Support Systems and Mutual Aid. New York: Grune & Stratton.

Castells, M. (1976) The Urban Question. London: Edward Arnold.

Clairmont, D., and D. Magill (1974) Africville, Toronto: McClelland & Stewart.

Cohen, A. (1969) Custom and Politics in Urban Africa. Berkeley: University of California Press.

Cox, H. (1966) The Secular City. New York: Macmillan.

Craven, P., and B. Wellman (1973) "The network city." *Social Inquiry* 43 (December), pp. 57–8.

Crump, B. (1977) "The portability of urban ties." Paper presented at the Annual Meetings of the American Sociological Association, September, Chicago.

Death Wish (1974) Directed and Coproduced by Michael Winner. Written by Wendell Mayes. Produced by Hal Landers and Bobby Roberts. Starring Charles Bronson. A Dino DeLaurentis Production. From the novel by Brian Garfield.

Durkheim, E. (1893, 1933) The Division of Labor in Society. New York: Macmillan.

Engels, F. (1845, 1969) The Condition of the Working Class in England. St. Albans, Herts.: Panther Books.

Feagin, J. R. (1973) "Community disorganization: some critical notes." *Social Inquiry* 43 (December), pp. 123–46.

————, and H. Hahn (1973) Ghetto Revolt: The Politics of Violence in American Cities. New York: Macmillan.

Fischer, C. S. (1976) The Urban Experience. New York: Harcourt Brace Jovanovich.

Freeman, L. C. (1976) A Bibliography of Social Networks. Monticello, Ill.: Council of Planning Librarians, Exchange Bibliographies nos. 1170–1171.

Gans, H. J. (1974a) "Gans on Granovetter's 'Strength of Weak Ties.'" *American Journal of Sociology* 80 (September), pp. 524–27.

————. (1974b) "Gans' response to Granovetter." *American Journal of Sociology* 80 (September), pp. 529–31.

————. (1967) The Levittowners. New York: Pantheon.

————. (1962) The Urban Villagers. New York: Free Press.

Gates, A. S., H. Stevens, and B. Wellman (1973) "What makes a good neighbour?" Paper presented to the Annual Meeting of the American Sociological Association, August, New York.

Granovetter, M. (1974a) Getting a Job. Cambridge, Mass.: Harvard University Press.

————. (1974b) "Granovetter replies to Gans." *American Journal of Sociology* 80 (September), pp. 527–29.

————. (1973) "The strength of weak ties." *American Journal of Sociology* 78 (May), pp. 1360–80.

Grant, G. (1969) "In defence of North America," pp. 15–40 in Technology and Empire. Toronto: Anansi.

Greer, S. (1962) The Emerging City. New York: Free Press.

Gusfield, J. R. (1975) Community: A Critical Response. New York: Harper & Row.

Hillery, G. A., Jr. (1955) "Definitions of community: areas of agreement." *Rural Sociology* 20 (June), pp. 111–23.

Hiltz, R. S., and M. Turoff (forthcoming) The Network Nation: Human Communication via Computer. Reading, Mass.: Addison-Wesley.

Hirsch, B. (1977) "The social network as a natural support system." Paper read at the Annual Meetings of the American Psychological Association, August, San Francisco.

Howard, L. (1974) "Industrialization and community in Chotanagpur." Ph.D. disseration. Cambridge: Harvard University.

Hunter, A. (1975) "The loss of community: an empirical test through replication." *American Sociological Review* 40 (October), pp. 537–52.

————, and G. Suttles (1972) "The expanding community of limited liability," pp. 44–81 in G. Suttles (ed.) The Social Construction of Communities. Chicago: University of Chicago Press.

Jacobs, J. (1961) The Death and Life of Great American Cities. New York: Random House.

Jacobson, D. (1975) "Fair-weather friend: label and context in middle-class friendships." *Journal of Anthropological Research* 31 (Autumn), pp. 225–34.

————. (1973) Itinerant Townsmen: Friendship and Social Order in Urban Uganda. Menlo Park, Calif.: Cummings.

Janowitz, M. (1952) The Community Press in an Urban Setting. New York: Free Press.

Kadushin, C. (1966) "The friends and supporters of psychotherapy: on social circles in urban life. *American Sociological Review* 31 (December), pp. 786–802.

Kasarda, J. D., and M. Janowitz (1974) "Community attachment in mass society." *American Sociological Review* 39 (June), pp. 328–39.

Keller, S. (1968) The Urban Neighborhood. New York: Random House.

Klovdahl, A. S. (1977) "Social networks: selected references for course design and research planning." Mimeographed. Canberra: Department of Sociology, Australian National University.

Kornhauser, W. (1959) The Politics of Mass Society. New York: Free Press.

Lasch, C. (1977) Haven in a Heartless World: The Family Besieged. New York: Basic Books.

Laslett, P. (1971) The World We Have Lost. London: Methuen.

Laumann, E. O. (1973) Bonds of Pluralism. New York: John Wiley & Sons.

————. J. Galaskiewicz, and P. Marsden (forthcoming) "Community structures as interorganizational linkages." *Annual Review of Sociology.*

Lee, N. H. (1969) The Search for an Abortionist. Chicago: University of Chicago Press.

Liebow, E. (1967) Tally's Corner. Boston: Little, Brown.

Marx, L. (1964) The Machine in the Garden. New York: Oxford University Press.

Mayer, P., and I. Mayer (1974) Townsmen or Tribesmen. Capetown: Oxford University Press.

Mellor, J. R. (1977) Urban Sociology in an Urbanized Society. London: Routledge & Kegan Paul.

Merton, R. K. (1957) "Patterns of influence: local and cosmopolitan influentials," pp. 387–420 in Social Theory and Social Structure. New York: Free Press.

Mitchell, J. C. (1974) "Social networks." *Annual Review of Anthropology* 3: 279–299.

————. (1969) "The concept and use of social networks," pp. 1–50 in J. C. Mitchell (ed.) Social Networks in Urban Situations. Manchester: University of Manchester Press.

Newman, O. (1972) Defensible Space. New York: Macmillan.

Nisbet, R. (1962) Community and Power. New York: Oxford University Press.

Park, R. E. (1936) "Human ecology." *American Journal of Sociology* 42 (July), pp. 1–15.

————. (1925a) "The city: suggestions for the investigation of human behavior in the urban environment," pp. 1–46 in R. E.

Park, E. W. Burgess, and R. D. McKenzie (eds.) The City. Chicago: University of Chicago Press.

————. (1925b) "The urban community as a spatial pattern and a moral order," pp. 55–68 in R. H. Turner (ed.) Robert E. Park on Social Control and Collective Behavior. Chicago: University of Chicago Press.

Popenoe, D. (1977) The Suburban Environment. Chicago: University of Chicago Press.

Powell, A., ed. (1972) The City: Attacking Modern Myths. Toronto: McClelland & Stewart.

Ratcliffe, W. (1978) "Social networks and health." Connections 1 (Summer), pp. 25–37.

Ross, M. H., and T. S. Weisner (1977) "The rural-urban migrant network in Kenya." *American Ethnologist* 4 (May), pp. 359–75.

Scott, J., and L. Tilly (1975) "Women's work and the family in nineteenth century Europe." *Comparative Studies in Society and History* 17 (January), pp. 36–64.

Sennett, R (1970) Families Against the City. Cambridge, Mass.: Harvard University Press.

Shorter, E. (1975) The Making of the Modern Family. New York: Basic Books.

————. (1973) "Female emancipation, birth control, and fertility in European history." *American Historical Review* 78 (June), pp. 605–640.

Shulman, N. (1976) "Network analysis: A new addition to an old bag of tricks." *Acta Sociologica* 19 (March), pp. 307–323.

————. (1972) "Urban social networks." Unpublished Ph.D. dissertation, Department of Sociology. University of Toronto.

Simmel, G. (1908, 1971) "Group expansion and the development of individuality," pp. 251–293 in D. N. Levine (ed.) Georg Simmel: On Individuality and Social Forms. Chicago: University of Chicago Press.

————. (1902–1903, 1950) "The metropolis and mental life," pp. 409–424 in K. Wolff (ed.) The Sociology of Georg Simmel. Glencoe, Ill.: Free Press.

Slater, P. E. (1970) The Pursuit of Loneliness. Boston: Beacon.

Speck, R. V., and C. Attneave (1973) Family Networks. New York: Pantheon.

Stein, N. (1960) The Eclipse of Community. Princeton, N.J.: Princeton University Press.

Suttles, G.D. (1972) The Social Construction of Communities. Chicago: University of Chicago Press.

Tilly, C. (1978) From Mobilization to Revolution. Reading, Mass.: Addison-Wesley.

––––––. (1975) "Food supply and public order in Modern Europe," pp. 380–455 in C. Tilly (ed.) The Formation of National States in Western Europe. Princeton, N.J.: Princeton University Press.

––––––. (1974) "Introduction," pp. 1–35 in C. Tilly (ed.) An Urban World. Boston: Little, Brown.

––––––. (1973) "Do communities act?" Sociological Inquiry 43 (December), pp. 209–240.

Tönnies, F. (1887, 1955) Community and Association. London: Routledge & Kegan Paul.

Vidich, A. J., and J. Bensman (1958) Small Town in Mass Society. Princeton, N.J.: Princeton University Press.

Walker, G. (1977) "Social networks and territory in a commuter village, Bond Head, Ontario." Canadian Geographer 21 (Winter), pp. 329–350.

Warren, D. I., and R. B. Warren (1976) "The helping role of neighbors: Some empirical findings." Unpublished paper, Department of Sociology, Oakland University, December.

Warren, R. (1978) The Community in America. Chicago: Rand McNally.

Wayne, J. (1971) "Networks of informal participation in a suburban context." Unpublished Ph.D. dissertation, Department of Sociology, University of Toronto.

Webber, M. (1964) "The urban place and the nonplace urban realm," in M. Webber et al. (eds.) Exploration into Urban Structure. Philadelphia: University of Pennsylvania Press.

––––––. (1963) "Order in diversity: Community without propinquity," pp. 23–54 in L. Wingo, Jr. (ed.) Cities and Space: The Future Use of Urban Land. Baltimore: Johns Hopkins.

Wellman, B. (1979) "The community question." American Journal of Sociology (forthcoming).

––––––, N. Shulman, J. Wayne, and B. Crump (forthcoming) Personal Communities in the City. New York: Oxford University Press.

––––––, and M. Whitaker (1974) Community—Network—Communication: An Annotated Bibliography. Toronto: Centre for Urban and Community Studies, Bibliographic Paper no. 4 (University of Toronto.

White, H. (1965) "Notes on the constituents of social structure." Cambridge: Department of Social Relations, Harvard University (mimeographed).

White, H. C., S. A. Boorman, and R. L. Breiger (1976) "Social structure from multiple networks I: Blockmodels of roles and positions." American Journal of Sociology 81 (January), pp. 730–80.

White, M., and L. White (1962) The Intellectual Versus the City. Cambridge: Harvard University Press.

Whyte, W. F. (1955) Street Corner Society. Chicago: University of Chicago Press.

Wireman, P. (1978) "Intimate secondary relations." Paper presented at the Ninth World Congress of Sociology, August, Uppsala, Sweden.

Wirth, L. (1938) "Urbanism as a way of life." American Journal of Sociology 44 (July), pp. 3–24.

Wolf, E. R. (1966) "Kinship, friendship, and patron-client relations in complex societies," pp. 1–22 in M. Banton (ed.) The Social Anthropology of Complex Societies. London: Tavistock.

Woodsworth, J. S. (1911, 1972) My Neighbour. Toronto: University of Toronto Press.

Young, M., and P. Willmott (1957) Family and Kinship in East London. London: Routledge & Kegan Paul.

27

Locating the rural community

Dwight Sanderson

Altho the real community is a relationship, a "form of association," it is necessary to recognize that, because farm people have to have certain services which can be obtained only at centers where there is sufficient patronage to support them, they inevitably associate themselves more or less definitely with one or more village centers. The area within which this association occurs between farms and village forms the geographical basis of the rural community.

Thus, while recognizing the psychological and sociological aspects of the rural community, for practical purposes one wishes to locate the areas within which these common associations exist. One may, then, define the geographical basis of the rural community as *a rural area within which the people have a common center of interest, usually a village, and within which they have a sense of common obligations and responsibilities.* The rural community is the smallest geographical unit of organized association of the chief human activities.

Professor C. J. Galpin,[1] formerly in charge of The Division of Farm Population and Rural Life of the United States Department of Agriculture, originated a method of determining the community area. He starts from the business center and marks on a map the most distant farm homes which do most of their business at that center. This information is obtained from the village merchants and is then checked by personal inquiry from the people on the edge or boundary of the community. The same procedure is followed with the surrounding communities. When this information is mapped, usually the trade areas overlap those of adjoining communities. People near the common boundary of two communities possibly trade more or less at both centers. This overlapping territory has been termed the *neutral zone.* The same method of mapping, is also used to determine the areas served by the village church, the school, the bank, the milk station, the grange, and like institutions. The boundaries of these areas do not coincide, as may be seen in Figure 27–1, which shows several of these areas for the rural communities in Genesee County, New York. However, when the service areas of the chief institutions of the adjacent communities are so located, it will be found that a composite of their boundaries will give a fairly clear line of demarcation between the areas serviced by the respective centers. A line which divides adjacent community areas so that most of the families either side of this line go most frequently to the center of which it is the boundary, or whose chief interests are at that center, will be the boundary of the respective communities. Thus, from the standpoint of location, a community is the local area tributary to the center of the common interests of its people.

In determining the boundaries of the community area it will be well to study the land-use maps of those counties for which they have been published. . . . Small communities with a large proportion of marginal land have declined and will probably become parts of larger communities that have enough good farm land to

Reprinted from Dwight Sanderson, *Locating the Rural Community*, Cornell Extension Bulletin 413 (Ithaca: New York State College of Agriculture at Cornell University, 1939), pp. 6–8, 11–12. The footnote has been renumbered.

[1] C. J. Galpin, *The Social Anatomy of an Agricultural Community.* (Agricultural Experiment Station of the University of Wisconsin, Research Bulletin 34, 1915); and, *Rural Life* (New York: Century Company, 1918).

FIGURE 27-1
Seven representative service areas of Leroy, Oakfield, Bergen, and Corfu, Genesee County

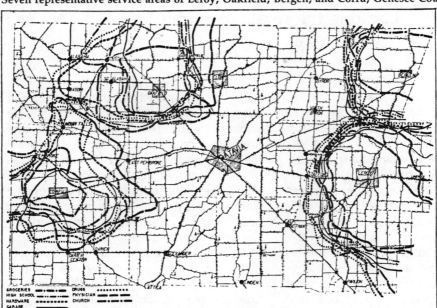

THE COMMUNITY CENTER

The community "center" is essential to the individuality of any community. It need not necessarily be at the geographical center of the community; indeed in many communities it is not; tho in an open, level country it will tend to approximate the center. The community center, in this sense, is that point in the community where the interests and activities of its people focus. Dr. Galpin uses the business center, where the people trade, as the base point, or community center, from which to determine the boundaries of the community. Usually a village is the community center, altho exceptional communities may have more than one village.

give an economic basis for the support of their institutions. The location of the community centers that will be most important in the future and of the boundaries of their areas, will be determined very largely by the geography of the different classes of land.

However, in some small communities, particularly in the older parts of the country or in hilly or mountainous regions, the trade or business center is not always the same as the center of the chief social activities of the people, and hence may not be the community center. Not infrequently a church, a school, and possibly a grange or lodge hall close together may form the nucleus of an open-country community which does its business at a railroad-station village some distance away, possibly over a range of hills. Some of these small open-country communities seem to have no real center, for the store, the church, and the school may be at some distance from each other in different parts of the community; but if these, or other, institutions draw their constituency from practically the same area, then the community boundary may be determined by a composite of the boundaries of the areas of these institutions.

The term *community center* as here used should be distinguished from the *community-center idea*, which refers to a building, whether it be a community house, a school, a church, or a grange hall, as a community center. Such a building in which the activities of the community are largely centered may be a community center in a very real sense, but usually these activities will be divided between church, school, grange hall, and the like. Not one of them can then be a center for the whole community, but taken together they constitute the center in which the chief interests of the community focus. Every community must necessarily have a more or less well-defined community center; it may or may not have some one building in which the chief activities of the community have their headquarters. But if such buildings exist, they may well be called *community houses* or *social centers*.

In the larger rural communities, the village where most of the people trade and where their children go to high school is the community center. It is these larger rural communities which will be important in the social organization of the country in the future and to whose location one needs to give attention.

MAPPING THE RURAL COMMUNITY

To locate the rural community, it is necessary to draw its boundaries on a map. For this map of the area and adjoining areas showing the roads is needed. . . .

To map the community, first determine the "community center" . . . and the centers of the surrounding communities, and mark each of these on the map.

Next, determine the trade, or business, area of the community. Ask the leading merchants to locate on each of the roads radiating from the community center their regular customers who are farthest from the center on each road. On the map make a mark at each of the houses so located; then connect these points by straight lines. This will give the approximate trade area of the community. It will be found that the trade areas for groceries, hardware, and

clothing differ considerably in size and shape.

In the same way locate on the map the areas of the different churches, of the high school or consolidated school, the bank, and of the grange and lodges, and draw their boundaries. Draw the boundary line of each area with a different color or use a different kind of line, as shown in Figure 27–1. Use the same color or kind of line for the boundaries of the trade areas, church areas, or school areas, respectively, of each community. Usually these areas will be sufficient to determine the community area, altho it may be desirable to locate the area from which farm produce is drawn to this center.

After having determined the principal areas for each of the surrounding communities, it will now be possible to draw a boundary line for the community, which will be a composite of the boundary lines of the various areas previously located, and which will include all homes whose major interests are clearly connected with this community. The community boundary line should be a heavy black line, which will stand out from the other area boundaries.

The interest and the value of the map will be increased by mapping the state and hard-surfaced highways, with heavier lines than the unimproved dirt roads. In mapping the various areas of the community, it will be desirable to have each farm house marked by a dot, and each school or church in the open country with a uniform symbol. If the map is large enough, it will be well to number the farm homes, and make a list of the families corresponding to these numbers. . . .

This method of determining the social and economic area of the community brings out many points of value concerning the area served by its different institutions and agencies. However, a simpler method, which is sufficiently accurate for most purposes, is to mark each farm home toward the edge of the community with a

FIGURE 27–2
Composite service areas of Wayne County

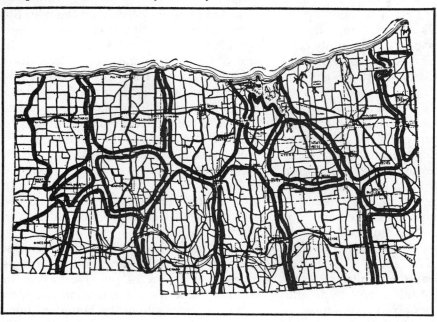

colored dot or symbol indicating the village which its members visit most frequently and with which it is most closely identified. A boundary line can then be drawn around the area within which a majority of the families patronize the village center for economic and social services more frequently than any other. In most cases this is a quicker and more practicable method than that discussed in the preceding paragraphs.

It will now be necessary to pursue the same process in locating the areas for each of the surrounding communities, for it will be found that many of the areas overlap and will be claimed by two, or sometimes three, communities. In such areas, it is best to see the people living in this "neutral zone," and to learn from them to which center they go most frequently or at which center are their chief interests. Not infrequently families between two communities trade at one center and go to church or school at another. It may not be possible to make one boundary that will separate the two communities, and the boundary of each should be so drawn as to include those homes which clearly belong to it, leaving a strip of neutral territory between them (Figure 27–2). . . .

Community politics and economics

SECTION FIVE

INTRODUCTION

In the previous edition, this section was entitled "Power in the Community," reflecting the most prodigious output of articles and books the field of community sociology has ever witnessed. Community power research, spurred on by the elitist versus pluralist polemic initially engaged by Floyd Hunter's *Community Power Structure* in 1953, produced descriptions of local power structures by the hundreds. So many, in fact, that summarizing conclusions are necessarily difficult. The few that can be drawn are, on the whole, somewhat disappointing. For example, while it appears that inequality in the distribution of power varies significantly by the definition of power and the community considered, these variations in power remain still largely inexplicable. Further, more recent research indicates that the local distribution of power (or at least our measures of power) often seems to have little demonstrable effect on local phenomena.

While community power research was moving away from the elitist-pluralist concerns in the 1970s, another local issue that seemed potentially related to community politics was growing in visibility: the deteriorating financial condition of many urban centers. Thus the current title of this section reflects a new and broader focus toward the relationships between politics and economics at the local level, including the increasingly important issue of urban fiscal stability.

Before examining some of the economic issues that have appeared recently in this field, it is instructive to briefly review the earlier developments in community power research. The critical, retrospective article by John Walton provides such an overview. Walton, who has been a major contributor to the field, traces the evolution of community power from its controversial "discovery" by Floyd Hunter. He points out that Hunter was interested in the distribution of power not as an academic exercise but in relation to the strengthening of democratic processes. His research was conducted in an area with important policy implications— "not descriptive generalities such as elitism (a term he never used) or pluralism, not stratification or interest-group theory, but reformed and efficacious democracy." But studies following Hunter became embroiled in problems of alternative methodologies and conceptualizations. Multicommunity research was conducted largely on the basis of available secondary statistical data which lent themselves to statistical analysis of the relation between community characteristics, power structure configurations, and community outputs, but without a cue as to the dynamics of the process, which could be obtained only through direct study at the local level. The studies did not pursue the question of the implications of power configurations for distributive justice or even for the quality of local life. But Walton cites more recent works which begin to show a different, more promising, more socially relevant approach.

A recent and serious problem has surfaced in many American cities: fiscal instability. Increasingly, cities are finding it difficult to pay for the services provided to their citizens. As the political debate continues on whether additional services now provided by the federal government might be transferred to state or local governments, the importance of understanding the causes of our urban fiscal problems grows.

Included in this section are two very different explanations of the origins of our current financial difficulties. The first article by Roger Friedland, Frances Fox Piven, and Robert Alford, points to the inherent, long-term, contradictions within a capitalistic society as the basis for the fiscal crises experienced by many of the population centers in the Northeast. Specifically, they argue that urban fiscal strain is the product of attempts to redirect potential class conflict between business and consumers into escalating demands for municipal services. This redirection eventually produces financial instability which in turn is labeled a fiscal crisis beyond the community's control. This "crisis" allows capitalists to regain control of the cities and place them back on "sound" financial ground by cutting services and taxes.

Friedland, Piven, and Alford are critical of "trivial" research efforts that focus on "such idiosyncratic aspects of contemporary American cities as the quality of municipal leadership, or the functional responsibilities of particular municipal governments, or the irrationalities in revenue collection and service delivery resulting from fragmented local government jurisdictions." However, some American cities *do* appear to be in much worse fiscal condition than others, and the reason for this significant difference in fiscal strain may lie, at least in part, in their "trivial idiosyncracies." Additionally, the policy implications from the Friedland, Piven, and Alford selection are not encouraging. Barring the development of "not yet visible" political changes, we can expect the urban fiscal crises to continue. Thus the article by Terry N. Clark can provide a very different and useful view of this issue.

This summary of Clark and his associates' analysis provides several interesting findings. First, popular explanations of fiscal strain based on population size, population decline, age of the city, and region of the county are *not* supported in their research. While it is true that cities with weak tax bases and large numbers of poor residents are more likely to encounter financial difficulties, there are also some local characteristics affecting fiscal strain that are more amenable to local control. Clark suggests that "competitive" taxes and reduced payroll and capital expenditures are important in reducing fiscal strain. Finally, he argues that a more centralized local leadership will be less susceptible to increased expenditures for "separable" goods like housing or jobs. These suggestions, of course, resemble the capitalist solutions mentioned earlier by Friedland et al. Drawing on the distinction made in Section Three, we see that Friedland et al. focus on the *vertical* dimensions of the urban fiscal crisis while Clark focuses primarily on the *horizontal* dimensions. A clear understanding of both perspectives is essential for a complete picture of the economic problems facing our cities.

The abbreviated chapter included from Joseph Galaskiewicz's *Exchange Networks and Community Politics* is concerned with the distribution and effects of local power, much like the numerous research efforts following Floyd Hunter's now-classic study of Atlanta. However, Galaskiewicz's theoretical conception of community power structure and his measurement strategies present a new and promising direction for community power research. Theoretically, organizational linkages are his key area of concern. For example, it is hypothesized that: "The greater the amount of money that an organization's interorganizational contacts control, the more successful it will be in different community decision-making situations."

Empirically, this and similar hypotheses are tested through the "network analysis" technique developed by Edward O. Laumann and his students at the University of Chicago.[1] Unfortunately, the explained variance levels of approximately 30 percent (Table 31–2) are not substantially higher than many of the earlier community power studies that we labeled as "disappointing" in their explanatory power. Nevertheless, the focus on networks of interacting organizations is so compatible with the popular conception of the community as an interorganizational field (much like the approaches of Long and Wilkinson in Section One), and the network analysis technique is so technical as to be still emerging (i.e., with the potential for new variations to produce new and more powerfully supported conclusions) that this is clearly becoming one of the most popular new approaches to community power.[2]

Another new approach is based on a neo-Marxian, conflict model of the community. Larry Lyon, Lawrence Felice, Ray Perryman, and Stephen Parker have tested an indirectly Marxian explanation of community power developed by Harvey Molotch and found much of it to be supported, especially the causal link between business power and population growth. Specifically, they find that those communities dominated by business interests are the most likely to grow. This business-growth linkage has implications for community development strategies that try to influence local growth. Additionally, it implies new directions for community power studies that may increase the theoretical relevance and statistical significance of the field. Still, the degree to which other community phenomena lend themselves to a political-economy explanation such as this by Lyon et al. is yet to be empirically demonstrated.

In fact both the network and the neo-Marxist approaches to the community in general, and community power in particular, are still too emergent to fully assess. It appears, however, that they may be moving in opposite directions. The network approach, as it becomes more empirically sophisticated, risks the chance that it will become increasingly separated from interorganizational theory. Conversely, the article by Lyon and his associates notwithstanding, political economists appear more committed to the type of theorizing found in Tabb and Sawers in Section One or Friedland et al. in this section. They have been generally reluctant to develop the necessary empirical support for their assertions. Certainly a more balanced development of theory and methods will be

---

[1] As an early example, see Laumann and Pappi (1973).

[2] It is unclear at this stage whether network analysis is a theoretical approach (see Wellman and Leighton in Section Four) or a statistical technique, or both. Theoretically, it is similar to the interorganizational conceptions of Warren (1967) or Turk (1970) or those in Section One by Long and Wilkinson. Statistically, it is a powerful computer-aided refinement of early community sociograms, but with organizations as the unit of analysis. In any event, its potential for aiding our understanding of the community is considerable.

beneficial for both approaches. Otherwise, the goal of accounting for "who gets what and why?" in the community surely will remain as elusive for these new approaches as it proved to be for their predecessors.

REFERENCES

Laumann, Edward O., Franz Pappi (1973) "New Directions in the Study of Community Elites." *American Sociological Review* 38, pp. 212–230.

Turk, Herman (1970) "Interorganizational networks in urban society: Initial perspectives and comparative research." *American Sociological Review* 35 pp. 1–18.

Warren, Roland (1967) "The interorganizational field as a focus for investigation." *Administrative Science Quarterly* 12, pp. 396–419.

------------------ **28** ------------------

Community power and the retreat from politics: Full circle after twenty years?

John Walton

After 20 years of research, commentary, and debate since the appearance of Hunter's classic work *Community Power Structure*, I expect many of you share with me the feeling that little remains to be said. Few specialities in the social sciences have been the subject of such close scrutiny. Books and papers on the topic run into many hundreds of titles. For more than ten years bibliographies of this literature have been compiled numbering nearly a dozen including annotated bibliographies and bibliographies of other bibliographies.[1] Similarly, anthologies on the sub-ject have proliferated, often duplicating one another.[2] As if this were not enough, we have also been treated to repeated studies of other studies.[3] A disinterested observer might regard this outpouring of activity as evidence of increasing scientific maturity, the incremental and cumulative growth from crude to more exacting measurement and understanding of the dy-

Reprinted with permission of the author and publisher from John Walton, "Community Power and the Retreat from Politics," *Social Problems* 23, no. 3 (February 1976), pp. 292–303. Copyright © 1976 by the Society for the Study of Social Problems. The footnotes have been renumbered.

[1] Some of the more complete bibliographies are Roland J. Pellegrin, "Selected Bibliography on Community Power Structure," (Southwestern) *Social Science Quarterly* 48 (December 1967), pp. 451–65, and Michael Aiken and Paul E. Mott, *The Structure of Community Power* (New York: Random House, 1970), pp. 527–38. Recent annotated bibliographies include Willis D. Hawley and James H. Svara, *The Study of Community Power —A Bibliographie Review* (Santa Barbara: ABC-Clio, 1972) and Irving P. Leif, *Community, Power and Decision Making: An International Handbook* (Metchen, N.J.: Scarecrow Press, 1974). A bibliography of other bibliographies is found in Willis D. Hawley and Frederick M. Wirt (eds.), *The Search for Community Power*, 2d ed. (Englewood Cliffs, N.J.: Prentice Hall, 1974), p. 390.

[2] Cf. Aiken and Mott, ibid., Hawley and Wirt, ibid. Terry N. Clark, ed., *Community Structure and Decision Making* (San Francisco: Chandler, 1968); Charles M. Bonjean, Terry N. Clark, and Robert L. Lineberry, *Community Politics: A Behavioral Approach* (New York: Free Press, 1971).

[3] Five such efforts by myself, Gilbert, Clark, Aiken, and Grimes and Bonjean, and Lineberry are summarized in my article, "The Structural Bases of Political Change in Urban Communities," *Sociological Inquiry* 43 (1973), pp. 174–206.

namics of power. Indeed, authors identified with the field have described these developments in terms of "stages" (e.g., from case study to broad comparative approaches) with the evolutionary implication that the field has progressed scientifically. While I would not question the fact that the last 20 years have witnessed a number of imaginative and useful innovations in technique, I am dubious about whether we have progressed intellectually. As the title for these remarks suggests, I believe that a cogent interpretation for developments over the last 20 years may be found in a regression from the original purpose and promise that once animated this research. On the occasion of this meeting it may be worthwhile to return to the wellsprings of community power work: the way we were, where we have gone and gone wrong, where credit and responsibility lie. Such an undertaking may appear to have only a narrowly historical interest to those who believe, as I do, that community power and decision making as a special field is *passé*. Yet, I shall attempt to demonstrate the irony that while the field and the well-known controversies that characterized it are dead, the basic questions that started it all live on in contemporary research. By locating an explanation for this circumstance we may discover some clues to the solution of continuing problems.

In order to develop this argument it is necessary to return briefly to the fundamentals of Hunter's study *Community Power Structure*. On this belated, if appropriate, occasion I want to indicate the heavy debt that students of social problems owe to Floyd Hunter. Like his contemporary, C. Wright Mills, Hunter did radical sociology long before it became faddish. Also like Mills, Hunter personified the "new sociology" that openly confronts the relationships between moral and intellectual values and research on major political issues. Unlike Mills, however, Hunter seldom received proper credit for his pioneering work (the SSSP gives no Floyd Hunter award), perhaps because he devoted his efforts to serious empirical research and scrupulously avoided academic polemics. . . .

Whether or not you will agree that Hunter's study is a "classic" is, of course, a matter of opinion. What I think we should all be concerned about, however, is why these features of the work, and some I will go on to indicate, were so totally overlooked or perverted in subsequent expositions and criticisms. This has long been a matter of profound puzzlement for me, never adequately explained with the glib observation that people simply did not read the book. I believe now that I have an answer of sorts, one that helps explain *"Where have we been since Community Power Structure?"*

Simply stated, the answer seems to me to lie in the fact that the social science of the 1950s and early 60s was not prepared ideologically or methodologically to deal with the kinds of questions Hunter raised.

What were these questions? Here again we encounter gross misunderstandings that portray Hunter, paradoxically, as a muckraker *and* a "stratification theorist." Parenthetically, let me comment that Hunter's principal shortcoming—one he admits to freely and shares with most students of the field—was the failure to explicitly develop a theory of community power. Nevertheless, returning to the original text, Hunter's purpose appears emminently clear. The opening paragraph states:

It has been evident to the writer for some years that policies on vital matters affecting community life seem to appear suddenly. They are acted upon; but with no precise knowledge on the part of the majority of citizens as to how these policies originated or by whom they are really sponsored. Much is done, but much is left undone. Some of the things done appear to be manipulated to the advantage of relatively few.[4]

---

[4] Floyd Hunter, *Community Power Structure: A Study of Decision Makers* (Chapel Hill: University of North Carolina Press, 1953), p. 1.

The purpose, then, was to identify the origins of these policies, the interests they served, and the process in which they were formulated and implemented. But, equally important, Hunter was concerned as a citizen and social scientist with what the analysis of policy making implied for the democratic process. Like the pluralists who followed, he was deeply concerned for the viability of local democracy. Where he differed was in holding a less sanguine view of its workings in contemporary urban society. Indeed, he begins and ends his book on these fundamental themes.

The line of communication between the leaders and the people needs to be broadened and strengthened—and by more than a series of public relations and propaganda campaigns—else our concept of democracy is in danger of losing vitality in dealing with problems that affect all in common.[5]

The task of social reconstruction may never be finished once and for all. It is a recurring task confronting each generation, which somehow manages to find courage to meet social issues as they arise. In spite of the limitations that confront the individual in relation to community participation on the level of policy decision, there is still room for him in this area. He may not find himself at the top; but with proper attention given to structural arrangements of power in the community, he may find ways of having a voice in determining who should be at the top.[6]

Given these sympathies it can be asked (and it should have been) what does this study imply for those interested in institutional reform. Once again the answers are clearly drawn in the concluding chapter, which provides the real key to Hunter's purpose. Here he engages in a debate with Saul Alinsky and the strategy for change set out in *Reveille For Radicals*. Hunter argues that while Alinsky's characterization of the cooptation and impotency of citizens groups is largely correct, the strategy of creating people's organizations *de' novo*

and out of whole cloth is "politically utopian." He explains,

Working outside of functional groupings and organizations or attempting to cut across their organizational lines has proved in practice to be an unfruitful experience for many community organizers who feel the need of getting mass support for particular projects. Organizational structures usually do not allow for such fluidity. It is also a vain hope, perhaps, to expect to organize unorganized individuals on anything like a community-wide basis. Some early experiences along these lines have led to disappointing results.[7]

These reservations about Alinsky's approach did not, however, lead Hunter to recommend "working within the system." His own sense of realism led him to believe that,

The leaders in the policy-making realm are not going to open the doors of participation with charitable graciousness. It has been noted that they may even use police power and the power of governmental machinery to keep back criticism and threatening political elements.[8]

Between each of these unrealistic options there was a third alternative illuminated by the study of community power. This entailed mapping the influence structure, identifying policy making groups and others, such as the black community, that were becoming organized, thereby determining strategic access points and "finding strength through perfecting social organizations along interest lines."[9]

Now clearly we have here a difference in theoretical and practical politics reminiscent of the issues that separated Lenin and Trotsky or Madison and Jefferson. On these we can disagree, and obviously the evidence is variable. What I wish to state most emphatically is that these are the issues that concerned Floyd Hunter—not descriptive generalities such as elitism (a term he never used, or pluralism, not stratification or interest-group theory, but

---

[5] Ibid.
[6] Ibid., p. 253.

[7] Ibid., pp. 248–49.
[8] Ibid., p. 253.
[9] Ibid., p. 250.

reformed and efficacious democracy. Obviously, there are other things that social scientists justifiably worry about and other ways of approaching this question. But I do not see how such legitimate interests are served by obfuscating the questions Hunter posed.

Returning to the question "where have we been?," I have suggested that the social science of the 1950s and early 60s was prepared neither ideologically nor methodologically to pursue the kinds of questions raised by *Community Power Structure.* Ideologically this was a period dominated by conservative structural-functional theories, general acceptance of the end of ideology thesis, and emphasis on status politics. It was also a period in which social scientists still held to a belief in the separation of fact and value, failing to recognize the normative premises of the foregoing theories while attributing value biases to alternative positions. Methodologically it was a period of (pre-computer) limited applied skills and a good deal of anxious concern for scientific rigor presumably embodied in quantitative or at least behaviorally oriented research.

The combination of these two circumstances, I believe, explain what happened next. Hunter's questions were set aside (assuming they were even understood in this climate) as ideologically malevolent in favor of rather mechanical replications of that part of his general method amenable to easy application yielding quantitative results: the reputational technique. Stated differently, the first generation of researchers in this field changed the nature of the questions and narrowed the scope of inquiry. No longer concerned with the origins of public policy and strategic points of access, research shifted to serial descriptions of leadership groups produced by sociometric techniques. Of course there were some interesting exceptions that focused on special topics such as absentee-ownership, civic welfare, and small towns in mass society. But, in the main, between

1953 and 1961 most research told us simply that community x, y, or z looked somewhat different from Regional City. This would have been a more worthwhile pursuit had the studies attempted to answer the new question they were posing, that is, had they provided a general, even theoretical, explanation for the differences. But, initially, they did not, prefering "fact gathering" and descriptive research which, ironically, would later be put to largely different uses.

Given this state of the art, it is little wonder that Robert Dahl's 1961 book *Who Governs?* chose a new direction, combining historical and case-study methods for the analysis of participation in public issues. Dahl's methods were not especially novel; analyses of the social backgrounds of public officials (as in Matthews' early work) and case studies of issues (as in Hunter) were standard and useful approaches. Indeed, the much celebrated "decisional method" was never systematically developed beyond the injunction of doing thorough detective work. That is, it was not distinguished in principle from unconstrained case study. The method did produce pools of issue participants, but it was never clear among a conceivable variety of forms and degrees of participation what criteria were used to determine inclusion or exclusion from the pool. Obviously some criteria were used, but this raised the question of whether these were not essentially "reputational," that is, relied on someone's perception (an informant, newspaper reporter, minutes-taker, etc) of who participated.

Remaining consistent with our argument here, these methodological differences are far less important than tracing the evolution of ideas. There was nothing unreasonable about Dahl's methods and the long debate over the "right" method yielded two rather paltry results. First, it told us what we should have known anyway, that different methods are sensitive to different features of the environment necessarily producing different results. And second, it obscured fundamental differences in the questions being asked about local politics. . . .

Marking developments in the field, as we have, with changes in questions or ideas, the next step involved a shift to the study of cities. That is, the important new ingredient of research in the late 1960s was not, as it usually supposed, that it was focused on comparative studies. In principle, comparative (case study) work had been done all along. But that was comparative work based on the premises of Hunter, Dahl, or some combination of the two. This new work put forth by Aiken and Alford, Clark, Turk, and others was qualitatively distinct. It depended little if at all on first-hand research at the local level, focusing instead on archival data on a large number of cities. In the inevitable tradeoffs any research must make, these studies chose to sacrifice depth and measurement validity as regards the local political process in favor of comparative breadth and a wide assortment of variables relating to community structure and policy "outputs."

This strategy stemmed from, or itself required, a new kind of question that can be phrased as "what are the structural characteristics of cities associated with some facet of the local political system (e.g., decentralization) and how, in turn, are these related to certain policy outcomes—notably public expenditures and program adoptions." Again, these are valid questions, but their answers have little direct bearing on the concerns of earlier approaches. They scantly address such matters as origins, access, and consequences of policy. Indeed, a major criticism of this line has been that dependent variables like expenditures on urban renewal or welfare tells nothing about "who benefits" or the distributional consequences of such programs, except on the assumption that greater spending or program innovation benefits more people, an assumption that is very likely wrong given what we know from case studies about the inequalities perpetuated by these programs (urban renewal being the choicest example). Similarly, these studies do not address matters of political participation and changing patterns across time and issues. They do tell us about the relationship between certain city characteristics and governmental activity, although some of these associations may be spurious according to recent work on the wide variability in the "functional scope" of U.S. cities (i.e., what cities are legally chartered to do).[10] Nevertheless, these studies do represent imaginative efforts at dealing with measurement problems and the multivariate analysis of political questions using large samples.

By carrying the study of community power to its broadest comparative and most abstract measurement levels, this work, in my judgment, brought an end to the field as a special area of research. It exhausted the range of methodological alternatives prescribed by conventional approaches to community power, showing the process a steady retreat from the substance of the concepts of power and politics. Just as case studies emphasizing validity through firsthand observations of the political process soon confronted limitations of generalizability, so too did these broad comparisons based on archival data and/or very limited encounters with local informants soon reach limitations of valid measurement. As Alford has candidly recognized about his own work, this approach did not address distributional questions of the relationship between policy and the quality of life.[11] More fundamentally, it did not really address political

---

[10] Roland J. Liebert, "Municipal Functions, Structure, and Expenditures: A Reanalysis of Recent Research," *Social Science Quarterly* 54 (March 1974), pp. 765–83.

[11] Robert R. Alford, "Quantitative Indicators of the Quality of Life: A Critique," *Comparative Urban Research* 3 (Summer 1973), pp. 5–8.

questions in the Laswellian sense of "who gets what, when, where, and how." Correlations between structural or demographic characteristics of cities and the sheer quantitative resultant of tangled bureaucratic processes represented by levels of spending or program adoption are abstractions far removed from the stuff of politics. I believe it is for this reason that many have become dissatisfied with the directions the field has taken. As research became more technically sophisticated, it drifted further from its conceptual moorings to the notions of power, inequality, and the workings of the political process. Somewhere along the line the baby went out with the bath.

Now, in a few concluding remarks, let me suggest that there are some new and encouraging trends which were set in motion by a variety of inquiries focused on the tumultuous events taking place in U.S. cities beginning in the late 1960s and on policy responses to these events. Faced with a set of problems that had become alien to community power work, researchers began developing new approaches that drew selectively on available ideas but forged ahead where others had been reluctant. Characteristically this work was inspired by problems akin to those of Hunter and Dahl, but it sought less stereotyped solutions. Central to the research were problems of inequality, access, participation, and redistribution, but these were cast in a relational context. That is, various groups or contestants, whether the disadvantaged or the powerful, were viewed as engaged in a competitive struggle. In contrast to community power work, this approach focused simultaneously on the relatively powerful and powerless just as it moved beyond a concern for individual actors to structural processes. In brief, an enlarged analytic framework was incipient in this work that incorporated the study of politics in a systemic or structural perspective.

It is convenient to suggest three general topical areas that incorporate much of the work reflecting these characteristics. First are those studies which continue in many respects with older traditions, but distinguish themselves by viewing urban political systems as parts of broader regional and national structures. Delbert Miller's new book on the "Bos-Wash Megalopolis" treats the urban agglomeration consisting of 32 major cities between Boston and Washington, D.C., as a single regional community linked by common interaction and environmental problems.[12] Frederick Wirt's lively study of decision making in San Francisco systematically traces out "extramural forces" (i.e., state and federal) affecting local autonomy.[13]

A second exciting style of work is concerned with the distributional consequences or costs and benefits of public policy. Edward Hayes' study of Oakland maps the local power structure but goes on to analyze how poverty programs created by local authorities variously (and regressively) benefit social classes.[14] Matthew Crenson's comparative study of "non-decision-making" on air pollution provides a thoughtful critique of pluralism and analysis of the politics of collective versus specific benefits of policies.[15] Closely related to these is the work of Richard Cloward and Frances Fox Piven on who benefited from the urban crisis and political response strategies of Great Society programs.[16] Robert Alford's recent work on health care[17] and many more reflect this approach, recently termed "political economy."

Third is the extensive literature on participation, power, and urban unrest. Ralph

---

[12] Delbert C. Miller, *Leadership and Power in the Bos-Wash Megalopolis* (New York: John Wiley & Sons, 1975).

[13] Frederick M. Wirt, *Power in the City* (Berkeley: University of California Press, 1974).

[14] Edward C. Hayes, *Power Structure and Urban Policy* (New York: McGraw-Hill, 1972).

[15] Matthew A. Crenson, *The Un-Politics of Air Pollution* (Baltimore: Johns Hopkins Press, 1971).

[16] Richard A. Cloward and Frances Fox Piven, *The Politics of Turmoil* (New York: Pantheon Books, 1974).

[17] Robert R. Alford, *The Political Economy of Health Care* (Chicago: University of Chicago Press, 1974).

Kramer's comparative study of poverty programs within the Bay Area[18] parallels neatly the work of J. David Greenstone and Paul Peterson analyzing participation in these programs across four major cities.[19] Here, as before, what is distinctive about the research is a relational focus on power struggles between program participants and local bureaucracies. Beyond these particular programs the organizational efforts of the urban underclass bidding for power have been studied in black neighborhoods by Donald Warren[20] and across minority group political movements by Norman and Susan Fainstein.[21] Finally, the work of Peter Rossi, Richard Berk, and Bettye Edison[22] illustrates several of the characteristics of these newer approaches. In a comparative study of 15 cities with different experiences of severity in urban disorders, Rossi and his colleagues attempted to explain sources of discontent by obtaining data on several systemic levels. Consequently, they interviewed political and civic elites as spokespersons for the power structure, but moved on to related interviews with a variety of institutional agents (e.g., police, merchants, welfare workers, etc.) responsible for delivering services to ghetto residents, and to a survey of black and white residents in each of the cities. While notable in its own right, this work is also in many ways typical of new efforts to pursue the fundamental questions that once inspired and later escaped students of community power.

These three lines of research activity are neither mutually exclusive nor jointly exhaustive and, of course, the representative studies cited are only a small fraction of many commendable efforts to move in new directions. What I am stressing here is the idea of a metamorphic change at the frontiers of research on urban politics, a shift that has superseded the community power and decision making tradition by, ironically, returning to its own fundamental intellectual concerns. In its broadest outlines the new "field"—call it political economy if you like—is defined by a concern for the origins and distributional features of social policy, and responses to such policy as these are determined by collective action across levels of urban hierarchies. As yet this work is diverse and incohate, scarcely recognizable as a "field" or new perspective. Like its predecessor, its principal failing is the lack of a theory that would integrate diversity and foster critical research. Nascent in this approach there seems to be a theory of social inequality based on race, class, and power that would challenge interest group pluralism, but this needs to be worked out. Indeed, my expectation is that the next major development in U.S. urban social science will be the development of new theory implied in recent urban research. This is neither an idle guess nor a genuine prediction since the effort is already well underway by our colleagues in England, France, and Latin America.[23] As North American social scientists begin to confront the twin challenge of constructing theories that account for their own new fund of urban research and engage new comparative perspectives, I believe a major chapter in the history of our understanding of social problems will be written.

[18] Ralph M. Kramer, *Participation of the Poor* (Englewood Cliffs, N.J.: Prentice-Hall, 1969).

[19] J. David Greenstone and Paul E. Peterson, *Race and Authority in Urban Politics* (New York: Russell Sage, 1973).

[20] Donald I. Warren, *Black Neighborhoods: An Assessment of Community Power* (Ann Arbor: University of Michigan Press, 1975).

[21] Norman I. Fainstein and Susan S. Fainstein, *Urban Political Movements: The Search for Power by Minority Groups in American Cities* (Englewood Cliffs, N.J.: Prentice Hall, 1974).

[22] Peter H. Rossi, Richard A. Berk, and Bettye K. Edison, *The Roots of Urban Discontent* (New York: John Wiley & Sons, 1974).

[23] See for example David Harvey, *Social Justice and the City* (Baltimore: Johns Hopkins Press, 1973); Manuel Castells, *La Question Urbaine* (Paris: Librairie Francois Maspero, 1972); Manuel Castells, ed., *Imperialismo y Urbanizacion en America Latino* (Barcelona: Gustavo Gili, 1973); Christopher Pickvance, *Critical Essays on Urban Sociology* (London: Methuen, forthcoming, 1976).

29

Political conflict, urban structure, and the fiscal crisis

Roger Friedland, Frances Fox Piven,
and Robert Alford

During the last few years, many of the older cities in the United States have experienced in intense form a series of stresses that are sometimes treated as and called "the urban fiscal crisis." Current dramatics notwithstanding, the so-called fiscal crisis is a familiar feature of urban life. Its classic symptoms are widening disparities between revenues and expenditures on the one hand, and rising demands for municipal services on the other. These symptoms are not only a recurrent fact of American urban history, but also, if often in less intense form, a feature of many other cities in advanced capitalist nations. Juxtaposed to the scope of these symptoms, the explanations that have dominated discussion of the so-called crisis in the United States have been remarkably trivial, emphasizing as they do such idiosyncratic aspects of contemporary. American cities as the quality of municipal leadership, or the particular functional responsibilities of particular municipal governments, or the irrationalities in revenue collection and service delivery resulting from fragmented local government jurisdictions. Even the somewhat more plausible explanations that have recently come to the fore, emphasizing changing in trametropolitan and interregional patterns of capital investment with the resulting erosion of the municipal tax base (e.g., Sternlieb and Hughes, 1976;

Reprinted with permission of the publisher from Roger Friedland, Frances Fox Piven, and Robert Alford," Political Conflict, Urban Structure, and the Fiscal Crisis," in *Comparing Public Policies*, Douglas E. Ashford, ed. (Beverly Hills: Sage Publications, 1978) pp. 197–201, 218–20.

Perry and Watkins, 1977; Starr, 1976; Baer, 1976), fail to consider these developments in appropriate historical and comparative perspective. American cities have experienced fiscal strains at earlier historical junctures, at periods when capital was concentrating in the cities, not deserting them. And not all cities, either in the United States or in Western Europe, that are suffering fiscal strains are the victims of territorial shifts in capital investment. In short, while some empirical verification can be found for all of these assertions, they do not propose an explanation of urban fiscal strains commensurate with their perennial and widespread occurrence.

A potentially more illuminating perspective from which to view these urban troubles is suggested by a growing body of work by neo-Marxists on the theory of the state. Perhaps the best known exemplar of this new tradition is James O'Connor. Stated simply, O'Connor (1973) and others postulate that the capitalist state must provide the infrastructure and subsidies which will ensure the profits of monopoly capital; it must subsidize and protect the accumulation process, while continuing to permit the private appropriation of profits. At the same time, the state must absorb popular discontent generated by the social costs of the accumulation process. The theory of the state argued that the fiscal crisis is the result of the increasing demands on government arising from these dualistic functions. This is a provocative perspective, but also has certain flaws. The theory asserts a structural and inherent tendency to crisis, although the visible manifestations of the crisis are in fact variable. Also, the theory of the state remains very general and does not deal with variations in symptoms of fiscal stress from one historical period to another, from one city and nation to another, and even from one function or level of the state to another.

In this paper, we begin our argument with the premise that urban areas are critically important sites at which both economic growth and political integration are organized. Government structures in urban areas must therefore perform key functions both to support urban economic processes and to promote the political integration of the urban population. On the one hand, urban governments must be responsive to the infrastructural and service requirements of capital accumulation, and to changes in these requirements generated by economic growth. On the other hand, they must also manage political participation among the masses of the urban population who do not control capital accumulation and may not benefit from it either. Whether or not these dual functions of urban government are, as the theory of the state argues, inherently and consistently contradictory, they are clearly contradictory at certain junctures in the process of capitalist economic development—for example, during extreme downturns in the business cycle when large numbers of people become unemployed and real wages fall, or during periods of rapid economic concentration and modernization that displace workers and uproot or undermine communities.

Considered apart from specific structural arrangements, such periods might be expected to generate extraordinary convulsions in municipal politics. The electoral-representative arrangements which underpin municipal governments make them vulnerable to popular discontent, and also limit their ability to employ extraordinary strategies of collective mobilization or repression to cope with discontent. At the same time, municipal authorities are helpless to intervene in the economic developments which may have triggered discontent and, indeed, find it difficult to resist even new demands arising from the private sector on which they are fiscally dependent. During such periods, the responses required of city government to successfully accomplish political integration and support economic growth might be expected to intensify, and to become antagonistic or contradictory.

However, such convulsions are not frequent. The reason, we will argue, is that specific structural arrangements are developed on the municipal level that mediate these potentially antagonistic functions posited by the theory of the state, and allow urban governments to cope with both the requirements of economic growth and the requirements of political integration, even during periods of potentially intense conflict. Among the structural arrangements that we think are important in mediating economic and popular pressures are (1) the degree of decentralization or centralization of government functions and (2) the degree of segregation of economic and political functions within urban governments.

All Western nations provide for some degree of decentralization in the governance of cities, but the degree of decentralization varies from nation to nation and from city to city, as does the specific forms of governmental authority which are decentralized or centralized. Similarly, all Western nations provide for some degree of structural segregation between those governmental activities that further economic growth and those that facilitate the political integration of the urban population. And there is also a widespread but varying tendency for these functions to be fragmented among different agencies and programs. These variations in the scope and substance of decentralization of government authority, and in the segregation and fragmentation of government activities, may help to account for differences among nations and cities in the capacity to cope with periodic eruptions of political conflict.

But while these structural arrangements help to diffuse and manage conflict, they also lead to the proliferation of government activities and costs and the contraction of government revenues. The tensions which might otherwise take form in direct struggles between business, industry, and finance on the one hand, and workers and consumers on the other hand, take form instead in escalating demands on municipal agencies—for jobs, services, contracts, tax concessions—with the result that municipal activities and budgets expand while municipal revenues are reduced. As a consequence, periods of potential social and class conflict become instead periods of fiscal strains.

Finally, the fiscal problems of municipal governments tend to be cumulative as a result of the institutionalization of past concessions. Municipal agencies and activities become a repository of historical demands, and this accumulation of commitments obviously aggravates fiscal strains. Moreover, these existing patterns may inhibit responses to new and emerging requirements of economic growth and political integration. Hence periodic reform efforts to solve the fiscal crisis often concentrate on restructuring of local government in order to purge it of obsolete concessions. These efforts may succeed, at least for a time, in managing the recurrent urban fiscal strains.

Before we go on to elaborate these points, we want to frankly acknowledge that our speculations are based primarily on our knowledge of urban processes and structures in the United States. We have tried to distill from this experience the propositions which might form the basis for more intensive comparative examination of the nature of urban fiscal strains and the institutional arrangements which we think help to explain them. And, although we refer to empirical studies to illustrate our argument, our main object is

to suggest theoretical perspective which at this stage remains largely untested.

* * * * *

FISCAL CRISIS AS AN OCCASION AND STRATEGY FOR COPING WITH FISCAL STRAINS

The post-World War II experience of major metropolitan centers in the West seems to us to reveal the effects of these structural arrangements. The postwar period saw the concentration and expansion of economic activity in many major cities, with accompanying investments in infrastructure and business-oriented services by municipalities. At the same time, the displacement of many people from agriculture, and the need for labor generated by expansion in the cities, led to the concentration in the cities of large new populations, usually distinguished by race or ethnicity from the older populations. The conflicts that erupted during this period of dislocation, however, were mainly conflicts between working- and lower-class-groups fractured by neighborhood, race, and ethnicity, and focused on competition over the provision of public services and, in some places, the traditional patronage of public employment. To cope with rising conflicts and rising demands, municipal services and patronage expanded.

In response to these different pressures, public expenditure for urban capital projects, social services, and public employment grew by leaps and bounds. By the late 1960s, municipal and regional governments began to suffer budget deficits, rising debt, and increasing dependence on state (or provincial) and national government fiscal aid. "In all of the Western democracies the costs of social programs have grown considerably in the post-war period. In the United States and western Europe, government spending tended to rise faster than gross domestic product of the economies between 1961 and 1972, with social transfer payments rising even faster than general government spending" (Heidenheimer et al., 1975: 275).

Economic decline only exacerbated these fiscal strains, and the political tensions underlying them. In the late 1960s and 1970s, serious recessions in many countries exacerbated the discrepancy between urban revenues and expenditures. Revenues shrank, but popular political demands did not, and in fact were heightened by unemployment, reduced real wages, and inflation. As urban expenditure, taxation, and debt increased together, many cities were thrown into a politically intractable fiscal crisis. Municipal workers were increasingly organized and resisted cutbacks with paralyzing strikes. City residents tried to hold onto existing services, or even to press for improved services, confronting urban bureaucracies with rent strikes, fare reduction campaigns, and housing occupations. Many corporations resisted any threatened service reduction or tax increase that would cut into their profitability with threats of relocation to other cities, and even to other countries.

The dilemma of cities in capitalist societies is how to maintain a structure of expenditure and taxation that can stimulate stable economic growth, while at the same time maintaining the popular legitimacy of governmental institutions, even when the potential for political conflict becomes intense. The series of structural arrangements described above tend to convert political conflict between groups and classes into demands on the state which force state expansion. But this process also tends to create fiscal strains. Public expenditures increase faster than the state's ability to finance them from its own revenues. Thus fiscal strains are a recurrent feature of capitalist cities.

These fiscal strains result in increased pressures for higher taxes on business and industry, indirectly push up wage costs, and potentially constrain the expansion of public services and infrastructure upon which corporate profitability is dependent. Under these conditions, fiscal strains provide capitalist groups with an occasion and a strategy to increase their control over the city's budget.

The process by which capitalist groups politically manage fiscal strains seems to follow a natural historical sequence, if New York City may be taken as a prototype, although perhaps an extreme one. First, financial and other capitalist interests declare an emergency, publicly redefining fiscal strains as a "fiscal crisis." Second, the fiscal crisis is attributed to natural economic laws beyond the control of political parties, governmental units, corporations, and banks themselves. Capitalist arguments that urban governments must balance their budgets, that there simply is not enough money, are elaborated by explanations of the inevitable erosion of the economic base of the cities as a mobile capital responds to the "natural laws" of profit maximization.

Third, capitalist interests assert control. Bankers refuse to finance the urban debt. Industrialists and developers make their investments conditional upon expanded subsidies and services, and reduced taxes. Business-backed reform groups push for policy changes to increase public sector productivity and reduce waste and duplication.

Depending on the level of indebtedness, the locational dependency of investors, and the political power of the reform groups, the parameters of urban policy are reorganized. On the one hand, structural changes may be introduced which remove even formal policy and budgetary authority from electoral control, as when an Emergency Finance Control Board was created in 1975 in New York City with the authority to supersede the budgetary decisions of city officials. On the other hand, expenditures and revenues are selectively reorganized to favor business through reduced taxes, enlarged subsidies and a relaxation of public regulation in matters such as environmental pollution. Public employment and neighborhood services which are less necessary to private profitability are cut back. In New York City, for example, half of the Hispanics and two fifths of the blacks on municipal employment have been fired (Piven and Cloward, 1977: 13), most of whom were located in public agencies created to absorb the political protest of the 1960s. Finally, policy proposals for more progressive revenues are suppressed. For example, in the Banker's Agreement of 1932, loans were extended to the city of New York on condition that proposals for taxes on stocks, savings banks, and life insurance companies would be dropped (Darnton, 1977: 226).

In conclusion, we believe that municipal expenditures tend to expand, fueled by the dynamism of group and class conflict. Given the structural arrangements we have described, when popular discontent intensifies, expenditures escalate more rapidly than revenues, producing the various symptoms we have called fiscal strains. At these junctures, capital mobilizes within the framework of these urban structures to declare a fiscal crisis and subdue popular demands. Whether this strategy is viable in the long run seems doubtful, but this conclusion rests on a faith in the possibility of an emergence of political challenges which, at least in the United States, are not yet visible.

REFERENCES

Alcaly, R. E., and Mermelstein, D., eds. (1977) The fiscal crisis of American cities. New York: Vintage.

Alford, R. R. (1975a) Health care politics. Chicago: University of Chicago Press.

————. (1975b) "Ideological filters and bureaucratic responses in interpreting research: Community planning and poverty." In N. J. Demerath III, O. Larsen, and K. F. Schuessler, eds., Social Policy and sociology. New York: Academic Press.

Alford, R. R., and Friedland, R. (1975) "Political participation and public policy." Annual Review of Sociology 1 pp. 429–79.

Andersen, G., Friedland, R., and Wright, E. O. (1976) "Modes of class struggle and the capitalist state." Kapitalistate, 4–5 (Summer), pp. 186–220.

Apilado, V. (1971) "Corporate-government interplay: The era of industrial aid finance." Urban Affairs Quarterly (December), pp. 219–41.

Baer, W. C. (1976) "On the death of cities." Public Interest 45 (Fall), pp. 3–19.

Bell, D. (1974) "The public household." Public Interest 37 (Fall), pp. 29–68.

Caro, R. A. (1974) The power broker. New York: Vintage.

Castells, M. (1972) "Urban renewal and social conflict in Paris." Social Science Information 2(2), pp. 93–124.

————. (1976) "Urban sociology and urban politics: From a critique to new trends of research." In J. Walton and L. H. Masotti, eds. The city in comparative perspective. Beverly Hills: Sage Publications.

Castells, M., Cherki, E., Godard, F., and Mehl, D. (1974) Sociologie des Mouvements Sociaux Urbains, Enquete sur la Region Parisienne (vols. 1 and 2). Paris: Ecole Des Hautes Etudes en Sciences Sociales, Centre d'Etude des Mouvements Sociaux.

Cloward, R. A., and Piven, F. F. (1974) The politics of turmoil: Essays on poverty, race and the urban crisis. New York: Vintage.

Congressional Budget Office, United States Congress (1975) "New York City's fiscal problem: Its origin, potential repercussions, and some alternative policy responses." Washington, D.C.: U.S. Government Printing Office.

Darnton, J. (1977) "Banks rescued the city in a similar plight in '33." In R. Alcaly and D. Mermelstein, eds. The fiscal crisis of American cities. New York: Vintage.

Edelman, M. (1964) The symbolic uses of politics. Urbana: University of Illinois Press.

Edwards, R., Reich, M., and Gordon, D. (1975) Labor market segmentation. Lexington, Mass.: D. C. Heath.

Epstein, J. (1976) "The last days of New

York." New York Review of Books (February 16).

Eyestone, R. (1971) The threads of public policy: A study in policy leadership. Indianapolis, Ind.: Bobbs-Merrill.

Fried, R. C. (1975) "Comparative urban performance." In F. I. Greenstein and N. W. Polsby, eds. Handbook of political science (vol. 6). Reading, Mass.: Addison-Wesley.

Friedland, R. (1977) Class power and the central city: The contradictions of urban growth. Unpublished Ph.D. dissertation, University of Wisconsin–Madison.

Friedman, L. (1968) Government and slum housing. Chicago: Rand McNally.

Hartman, C. (1974) Yerba Buena: Land grab and community resistance in San Francisco. San Francisco: Glide Publications.

Harvey, D. (1975) "The political economy of urbanization in advanced capitalist societies: The case of the United States." Pp. 119–163 in G. Gappert and H. M. Rose, eds. The social economy of cities. Beverly Hills: Sage Publications.

Heidenheimer, A. J., Heclo, H., and Adams, C. T. (1975) Comparative public policy: The politics of social choice in Europe and America. New York: St. Martin's Press.

Huntington, S. P. (1975) "The democratic distemper." Public Interest, 41 (Fall), pp. 9–38.

Jones, V. (1972) "Bay Area regionalism." Quoted in F. W. Wirth, Power in the city: Decision making in San Francisco. Berkeley: University of California Press.

Katznelson, I. (forthcoming) City trenches. New York: Pantheon.

Lupsha, P. (1975) "New federalism: Centralization and local control." Paper delivered at the Annual Meeting of the American Political Science Association, San Francisco.

Marmor, T. R., Wittman, D. A., and Heagy, T. C. (1975) "The politics of medical inflation." Journal of Health Politics, Policy and Law, 1:69–84.

McConnell, G. (1966) Private power and American democracy. New York: Knopf.

Meltsner, A. J. (1971) The politics of city revenue. Berkeley: University of California Press.

Mollenkopf, J. (1977) "Untangling the logics

of urban service bureaucracies: The strange case of the San Francisco Municipal Railway." Paper presented at the Conference on Urban Political Economy, American Sociological Association and International Sociological Association, Santa Cruz, Calif.

O'Connor, J. (1973) The fiscal crisis of the state. New York: St. Martin's Press.

Offe, C. (1975) Stress and contradiction in modern capitalism: Public policy and the theory of the state (associate editor with Colin Crouch and Robert Alford. Principal Editor, Leon N. Lindberg). Lexington, Mass.: Lexington Books.

Perry, D., and Watkins, A. (1977) "Contract federalism and the socioeconomic realignment of yankee and cowboy cities: Two stages of urban decay." Paper presented at the Conference on Urban Political Economy, American Sociological Association and International Sociological Association, Santa Cruz, Calif.

Piven, F. F., and Cloward, R. (1977a) "The urban crisis as an arena for class mobilization." Radical America 11 (January–February), pp. 9–17.

———. (1977b) Poor people's movements: Why they succeed, how they fail. New York: Pantheon.

Pressman, J. L., and Wildavsky, A. B. (1973) Implementation. Berkeley: University of California Press.

Reich, M., Gordon, D., and Edwards, R. (1973) "The theory of labor market segmentation." American Economic Review (May), pp. 359–65.

Sbragia, A. (1976) "Public housing and private profit: Some inferences for comparative policy studies from an Italian case." Paper delivered at the Annual Meeting of the American Political Science Association, Chicago.

Scarrow, H. A. (1971) "Policy pressures by British local government." Comparative Politics 4 (October), pp. 1–28.

Starr, R. (1976) "Making New York smaller." New York Times Magazine (November 14).

Sternlieb, G., and Hughes, J. W. (1976) "New York: Future without a future?" Society 13 (May/June), pp. 1–23.

Tarrow, S. (1974) "Local constraints on regional reform: A comparison of Italy and France." *Comparative Politics* 7 (October), pp. 1–36.

U.S. Senate, Subcommittee on Housing and Urban Affairs (1973) The central city problem and urban renewal policy. 93rd Congress, 1st Session. Washington, D.C.: U.S. Government Printing Office.

Weber, M. (1968) Economy and society: An outline of interpretive sociology (vol. 1, edited by G. Roth and C. Wittich). New York: Bedminster Press.

Wildavsky, A. (1964) The politics of the budgetary process. Boston: Little, Brown.

30

How many more New Yorks?

Terry Nichols Clark

Is New York the "bellwether" city for America in its financial difficulties? If others follow New York's path, their futures will certainly be bleak. Many observers, especially those based in Manhattan, have suggested that other cities must be close behind. But, what is the evidence?

This was the first question my associates and I posed a few months ago. To answer we used the Permanent Community Sample, 51 cities (municipalities) chosen as representative of the places of residence of the American urban population. About half are central cities and half suburbs, with populations as low as 50,000. We have monitored these sample cities for eight years, conducting interviews with local leaders using the staff of the National Opinion Research Center, and continually updating socioeconomic and fiscal data. For our work on fiscal strain in American cities, data for New York, Chicago, and Los Angeles were added.

Reprinted from *New York Affairs*, vol. 3, no. 4, November 4, 1976. © 1976 by Institute for the Study of the City. Used with permission. Minor revisions in original article have been made by author for inclusion in this collection of readings.

There is no single thermometer to test for fiscal health. We therefore computed most measures used by municipal finance analysts, 29 in all. Since many are slightly different versions of the same thing, we isolated four basic indicators, each quite distinct: (1) per capita long-term debt; (2) per capita short-term debt; (3) per capita expenditures for nine functions common to most cities (police, fire, highways, parks and recreation, sewerage, sanitation, financial administration, courts, and city buildings); and (4) the ratio of total revenue from local sources to sales value of all local taxable property. The four indicators were simply standardized and summed for each city to form our Municipal Fiscal Strain Index, shown in column one of Table 30–1. New York is indeed at the top, although Boston and San Francisco are not far behind.

One common argument is that New York is in fiscal difficulty because the city is forced to provide certain services, like public education and welfare, which in other cities are the responsibility of school districts, special districts, county or state governments. To deal with this issue, we created the County Area Fiscal Strain Index, shown in the second column of Table

TABLE 30–1

	Municipal fiscal strain index	County area fiscal strain index		Municipal fiscal strain index	County area fiscal strain index
New York	165.03	122.91	Tampa, Fla.	44.27	49.80
Boston	128.82	100.16	Phoenix, Ariz.	42.38	30.30
Newark, N.J.	105.91	97.79	Tyler, Texas	40.89	39.87
San Francisco	102.97	95.25	Charlotte, N.C.	39.95	33.65
Albany, N.Y.	102.88	115.99	South Bend, Ind.	39.24	35.47
Buffalo, N.Y.	89.00	71.59	Waco, Texas	38.67	18.24
Atlanta, Ga.	87.29	64.45	Indianapolis	38.65	36.65
Cambridge, Mass.	81.44	40.08	Fort Worth	38.65	38.23
Malden, Mass.	81.13	55.15	Euclid, O.	36.64	41.54
Seattle	79.34	59.09	Santa Monica, Cal.	35.39	39.24
Waterbury, Conn.	78.88	60.21	Schenectady, N.Y.	32.68	40.35
Jacksonville, Fla.	73.69	22.89	Bloomington, Minn.	32.33	61.02
Utica, N.Y.	72.41	74.66	Irvington, N.J.	32.04	75.21
Los Angeles	68.27	46.05	St. Petersburg, Fla.	32.03	16.69
Akron, O.	63.57	41.69	Hamilton, O.	30.80	51.82
Memphis, Tenn.	60.28	40.48	Hammond, Ind.	30.60	35.83
Birmingham, Ala.	60.08	15.59	Berkeley, Cal.	29.81	52.25
St. Louis, Mo.	58.76	54.76	Clifton, N.J.	27.85	26.83
Manchester, N.H.	58.20	42.63	San Jose, Cal.	25.95	56.56
Palo Alto, Cal.	55.67	42.49	Duluth, Minn.	25.32	55.05
Chicago	55.33	56.55	Gary, Ind.	21.21	31.38
Pasadena, Cal.	54.47	44.26	Waukegan, Ill.	20.70	28.05
St. Paul, Minn.	54.16	96.86	Warren, Mich.	20.43	43.51
Minneapolis	51.35	63.95	Salt Lake City	18.99	19.74
Long Beach, Cal.	49.67	44.43	Amarillo, Texas	18.05	21.46
Pittsburgh	48.35	55.06	Fullerton, Cal.	13.25	35.90
Milwaukee	45.38	58.46	Santa Ana. Cal.	10.53	39.73

Note: Both indexes, as described in the text, sum the z scores for four separate indicators of fiscal strain. Five was then added to make all scores positive, and the result multiplied by 10. Consequently, if a city was precisely at the mean on all eight fiscal strain indicators, it would receive a score of 50 on both of the indexes.

The four indicators summed to create the County Area Index were (1) per capita overlapping long-term debt; (2) per capita overlapping short-term debt (both for the municipality, school district, special district, and county governments): (3) overlapping revenues (for these county area governments plus the per capita share of total state revenues): (4) tax effort (county area total revenues/municipal taxable property value).

The Municipal Index data were for 1973–74, County Area data for 1971–72. Both were the most recent comparable figures available in April 1976 from the U.S. Census (*Finances of Municipalities* 1973–74 and the U.S. *Census of Governments*, 1972, vol. 4, no. 5). Some municipalities, school districts, and special districts are coterminous with a county, others are not. Measurement error is thus introduced into the County Area Fiscal Strain Index which indicates the average level of fiscal strain for the entire county area.

30–1. It includes four measures analogous to those for the Municipal Fiscal Strain Index, but is computed by summing the debt or expenditure for all "overlapping" local governments serving the county (or counties) within which each municipality is located. This County Area Index thus shows the total debt or tax burden falling on residents and firms of the county area. New York again scores first on the County Area Index, but stands out much less than on

the Municipal Index. The New York figures in both columns include the five boroughs.

WHY DO CITIES DIFFER IN FISCAL STRAIN?

Many interpretations have been offered for New York's fiscal difficulties. Numerous statistical analyses are included in our technical report; these are mentioned here only to indicate that multivariate analysis, especially regression analysis, was used. These procedures permit us to isolate the amount of fiscal strain added, for example, by a 1 percent change in the tax base compared to a 1 percent change in population size, controlling for the effects of several other variables. The results come from comparing the 51 cities to one another; any single city may thus be an exception for certain findings. Data are taken from fiscal 1973–74 or the closest years for which comparable data were available. A number of unexpected results emerged. Consider four.

Population size. Population size, despite the stereotype, has almost no relation to fiscal strain. Although New York and other large cities in Table 30–1 do show more fiscal strain than the smaller cities, population size is a "spurious" explanation—size becomes insignificant when we take into account other variables associated with size, like the percentage of poor residents.

Population growth (or decline). The percentage population change from 1960 to 1974 was practically unrelated to fiscal strain.

Older cities. City age (years since population exceeded 20,000) and old housing (percentage of structures built prior to 1950) were also unrelated to fiscal strain.

Region. Cities in the Northeast and Midwest were not distinctly high in fiscal strain.

These four results initially surprised us as they directly contradict the common wisdom that large, declining, older cities of the Northeast and Midwest suffer most fiscal strain while the "Sunbelt" cities are fiscally sound. New York, Boston, Newark, and Albany are, in fact, under great fiscal strain, but Waukegan, Hammond, Schenectady, and Pittsburgh are fiscally sound. More important than these first four characteristics are others, which do make significant, independent contributions to fiscal strain when the above four (and others) are controlled.

The tax base. Cities with lower taxable property values suffer greater fiscal strain. This time the folk wisdom is sustained.

Poor residents. Cities with higher percentages of families with annual incomes below the federal government's definition of "low" (3,721 in 1969) suffered greater fiscal strain. However, New York is not unusual in having 11.5 percent of its residents classified as "low-income"—Chicago had 10.6 percent below the line, Memphis 15.7 percent, Birmingham 17.4 percent, and Newark 18.4 percent. We note in passing that New York also does not have an exceptionally high percentage of welfare recipients (12.4 percent compared to 11.1 percent in Chicago, 16.9 percent in Boston and 14.4 percent in Newark —data for county areas in 1974).

Are all New Yorkers "poorer" because of a higher cost of living? Only a little. The Bureau of Labor Statistics provides an Intermediate Family Budget Index on which New York ranks 116, above Chicago (103) and San Francisco (106), but similar to Boston (117) and Newark (116).

THE IRISH FACTOR

A few years ago, it was discovered, almost by chance, that the percentage of city residents born in Ireland, or with one or more parents born in Ireland, was highly related to municipal spending. We initially thought it was spurious and contemplated dropping it out of the study after controlling for elements like having a strong Democratic party or population size or city age. But although we introduced 26 such variables to the study and checked the same pattern in 1880, 1930, and 1968, it held strong.

Why? To construct a meaningful answer, we analyzed several surveys of the American population.[1] For example we classified the places of birth and names of

[1] See Terry Nichols Clark, "The Irish Ethnic and the Spirit of Patronage," *Ethnicity* 2 (1975), pp. 305–59.

all municipal employees in Albany by decade—from 1870 to 1970. The percentage
Irish dipped dramatically about 1900 when
the Republicans came to power, but from
1920 to the present the figure rises continually to about 50 percent. Dan O'Con-
nell has astutely led Albany's Democratic
party for the post-1920 period. Using another approach, a survey asked four questions of 3,095 Americans: if they had ever
worked for a party or candidate in elections, attended political meetings, contributed money, or tried to persuade others
about a candidate or party. The four items
were combined in a campaigning index on
which Irish Catholics scored 37, Slavic
Catholics 15; most other groups were under 5.

Although they comprise only 4 percent
of the American population, Irish Catholics have exerted an impact on municipal
politics and finance that far transcends
their numbers. It has been a style distinguished not by abstract ideology, but by
a dense network of friendship and social
relations. On several surveys, Irish Americans report they are unusually *sociable*
("like to do things with others"), trusting
("think most people can be trusted"), *localistic* (prefer a local man), *practicing Catholics* (over 90 percent attended weekly
Mass and sent their children to parochial
schools in the 1960s, compared to about a
third of Italian Americans) and *socially conservative* (in favor of compromise and moderate solutions). Together these five sets of
beliefs comprise what we have called "the
Irish ethnic." Reinforced by such organizations as the Democratic Party and Roman Catholic Church, it helps support a
distinctive style of politics. Patronage is
central. Most important, the emphasis on
friendship and enduring social contacts
(the Irish ethic) makes patronage politics
legitimate. For example, when Mayor
Daley was recently criticized by the press
for awarding insurance contracts to his
son's firm, he replied "What's wrong with
a father helping his sons?" Imagine the
same response from Mayor Lindsay! The

important point here is that Mayor Daley
was not being hypocritical, but essentially
reflecting the Irish ethic. The ethical consistency of Richard Daley far transcends
that imagined by many of his critics.

Personal networks, and rewards for
party work and campaigning activities,
have increased municipal payrolls for
Irishmen and their political allies. The pattern is familiar in Chicago; more striking
was to learn how important it was nationally. Indeed, although previous discussions of municipal finance have generally ignored the Irish, we found that the
percentage of Irish residents in the municipality was often the most powerful single
variable predicting fiscal strain. Certainly
the Irish ethic is not unique to the Irish,
but along with some knowledge of English
and slightly earlier arrivals in the U.S., it
helped the Irish in urban politics. If Italian-
Americans, blacks, and others are succeeding the Irish in many American cities,
they often seek to follow similar patterns
of governance.

THE LEADERSHIP FACTOR

Chicago may be unique with its highly
organized Democratic Party, but other cities still use related leadership and decision-making patterns. These significantly
affect fiscal strain.

Strong mayors and weak businessmen.
In interviews conducted with local leaders
in each of the 51 cities, we asked about the
importance of different actors for such decisions as mayoral elections, floating municipal bonds, antipoverty and urban renewal programs. Two major actors were
mayors and local businessmen. They were
assigned scores for their importance in
these decisions. Cities with moderately
strong mayors and weak businessmen suffered greater fiscal strain.

Union contracts. About half the cities
had signed collective-bargaining contracts
with the American Federation of State,
County, and Municipal Employees. Those
that had scored higher on fiscal strain.

Numerous municipal employees. The (per capita) number of municipal employees in each city working in the nine common functions discussed above was computed. It was adjusted for basic socioeconomic characteristics of the city (taxable property base, percentage poor, etc.). The result was a standardized score indicating the number of municipal employees above or below what one would expect in the city based on its socioeconomic characteristics. Albany scored highest (+2.58), San Jose and Santa Ana lowest (−1.2, −1.4), zero was average. This Index of Overstaffing also correlated positively, as expected, with the percentage of Irish residents and with fiscal strain.

Tax collection rates. We sought a measure of sound fiscal management that could be used across cities, and found that cities vary substantially in the percentage of levied taxes collected. Boston was lowest, collecting only 85 percent of all taxes levied, whereas many cities collect 99 percent or more. (New York collects 94 percent.[2])

These five dimensions of local leadership are generally interrelated; that is, cities with strong mayors also tend to have weak businessmen, union contracts, numerous municipal employees, and low tax collection rates. We thus combined the five dimensions in a single Index of Political Leadership. It was one of our strongest predictors of fiscal strain. The basic pattern looked like this:

Numerous Irish residents → High index of political leadership → High capital outlays → Fiscal strain

CAPITAL OUTLAYS

The distinction between municipal operating expenditures (salaries, etc.) and capital outlays (normally for highways, public buildings, and so forth) is important. Cities can issue bonds to finance capital outlays, whereas operating expenditures must be funded from taxes and revenues for the same fiscal year (according to most state laws). In 1960, Chicago's capital outlays were $42 per capita; in 1974 they were still $42 per capita. By contrast, New York's capital outlays were $54 in 1960, but they jumped to $153 in 1973 and to $195 in 1974. The average for our 51 cities in 1974 was $60. Cities were often high on capital outlays if (as in the diagram) they had numerous Irish residents and a high score on the Index of Political Leadership. High capital outlays, in turn, lead to fiscal strain.

This is perhaps obvious—if you build new capital facilities and pay for them by borrowing, eventually interest payments on the debt can strain the budget. The story is familiar for New York, where the problem was compounded by supporting certain operating expenditures using the capital budget. What deserves emphasis is that in New York as elsewhere, one of the most important and direct causes of fiscal strain is high capital spending in earlier years. Supporting projects like the reconstruction of Yankee Stadium can cause more fiscal strain than supporting the poor.

PREDICTING FISCAL STRAIN

The most consistent message of these findings is that local leadership can make a substantial difference. Fiscal strain is greater on local officials in cities with weak tax bases and large numbers of poor residents. But some cities are fiscally healthy (like Pittsburgh, Schenectady, and St. Louis) even though they share many socioeconomic problems with Boston and New York. If the leadership characteristics we have isolated are crucial in explaining fiscal strain, and some cities are fiscally sound, one might conclude that at least some cities can solve their own problems

---

[2] However, this ratio is affected by the tendency in some, like New York City, to knowingly extend property tax levies against nontaxable property which is then fictitiously shown as delinquent. The purpose of this is to permit a greater volume of seasonal borrowing in the form of tax anticipation notes.

without major assistance from higher levels of government. This is not to argue against more federal and state assistance, especially for programs like higher education, which affect the entire society as students migrate, or income transfer programs which people can migrate from to avoid supporting.[3] But as far as the fiscal well-being of American cities is concerned, the evidence suggests that much can be done at the local level.

In many cities in the past, only the financial officials paid close attention to fiscal difficulties. The major elected officials are now focusing more attention on such matters with support from the press and local citizens. Comparisons with past fiscal performance for the individual city are useful; so are comparative rankings. Increasingly, officials will have to try to spot fiscal overburden before the situation becomes critical.

If this is to be done, fiscal reporting will have to be improved. Even many elected officials, not to mention municipal employees and citizens, have only a cloudy picture of their local finances. Current reporting of fringe benefits for municipal employees, pension provisions, and short-term debt is also poor (although improving). City workers might appreciate their jobs more if they knew just how much they received in fringe benefits and pensions. The municipal bond market could charge cities less interest if it were clear that their finances were sound.

The city tax burden must be kept competitive if fiscal strain is to be avoided. If local leaders do not compare their tax burdens to those elsewhere, citizens and firms do. Newer towns and suburbs in the "Sunbelt" are growing for many reasons, but one seems to be their low tax rates.

Given free migration, if any city deviates too far from the others, it is likely to lose residents and firms. This has been happening to Boston, New York, and many cities in the Northeast and Midwest for some time. But, not to all of them. From 1970 to 1974, Chicago's Cook County lost about 2 percent of its population, as did Los Angeles County, while New York's, five boroughs lost 4 percents.[4] If the sunny California weather is more pleasant than wintry breezes off Lake Michigan, the taxes are still lower in Chicago. The average per capita taxes and charges paid to all local and state governments for residents in the three county areas were approximately $765 in Chicago, $849 in Los Angeles and $1,064 in New York. They were less in Jacksonville, Fla. ($536), and Fort Worth ($439) and Tyler ($474), Texas.

City officials must watch particularly closely the municipal payroll as well as capital expenditures. These are the two largest items in most city budgets. And, unlike welfare or Medicare, cities must rely primarily on local taxes and charges to support their employees. Capital expenditures can be eased through borrowing, but interest payments can obviously become burdens. Even if local officials are largely autonomous in payroll and capital expenditure decisions, some cities always seem to spend more, despite the wishes of leaders and citizens. What can be done?

CENTRALIZATION AND "PUBLIC-GOODS"

Until recently, New York represented an extreme but not unique case of decentralized decision-making. "Decentralized" is here used to refer not to neighborhood participation, but to the involvement of numerous organizations and individuals in basic municipal decisions. The

---

[3] There is a misconception which should be corrected—that is, most welfare costs have already been taken over by federal or state governments. Nationally, local governments pay only about 6 percent; of public welfare from locally raised funds: New York City, because of its peculiar method of handling Medicaid, pays about 8 percent (1973–74).

[4] "Estimates of the Population of Metropolitan Areas, 1973 and 1974, and Components of Change since 1970," *Current Population Reports*, P-25, no. 618 (January 1976). Population data here and fiscal data below are for county areas.

mayor of New York generally was only one of many participants in decisions. If LaGuardia built up a substantial following, Lindsay never succeeded. He, like many other actors in a decentralized context, had to provide a continual flow of benefits to piece together one fragile coalition after the next—which is expensive.

The situation was similar in turn-of-the-century Chicago. Construction firms and others complained that aldermen could not be "bought" for more than one vote at a time. A political organization gradually developed that coordinated the votes of aldermen. Today, unlike New York and other more decentralized cities, in Chicago both the mayor and the voters know that Richard Daley is responsible for major decisions. He can and does say no to demands for spending, because he is strong enough to say no. Few mayors are, and Chicago, as Table 30–1 indicates, is fiscally sound.

If few Americans would welcome back political machines of the Tammany variety, they might nevertheless consider some of the advantages derived from giving mayors—or someone—enough legal authority to govern effectively.[5] This has happened by political if not literal fiscal default in New York. Creating the Municipal Assistance Corporation and Emergency Financial Control Board centralized power. They stand behind the mayor and help govern without having to respond to the demands of all interest groups in the city.

Goods provided by government may be classified along a continuum from "pub-lic goods" to "separable goods." Public goods, or, in this case, "bads" like air pollution or municipal bankruptcy, are shared by citizens throughout a city. By contrast, separable goods, like jobs or housing, are allocable to distinct individuals or interest groups.

Thus, the comparison of Chicago and New York may be restated more abstractly: centralization encourages public goods, but decentralization generates separable goods. To achieve the public good of fiscal health, centralization helps. It obviously is not sufficient. But, unless enough authority is given to someone to confront the big issues, no one will. Instead, local officials usually become so caught up in resonding to day-to-day demands that thinking beyond next week seems utopian. Yet it is hard for most local leaders to survive otherwise.

Centralization also helps to hold down costs because leaders can be less responsive to immediate demands. Over the last decade, some people have held that "democracy" is defined by immediate response to forceful citizen demands, especially from the poor. By now the short-sightedness of this view should be apparent: fiscal strain often follows.

Many American cities are declining; their economies are stagnant and their populations are migrating. The New York fiscal crisis may have the salutary effect of frightening people enough to consider new modes of urban governance. To effect the sorts of dramatic changes that are taking place in New York, someone, most likely the mayor of a MAC-style committee, must be given more authority. There are many well-known legal alternatives: a longer term of office as well as broader veto, spending, and appointment powers. The civil service structures have been citicized by several commissions; they now largely tie the hands of chief executives. Centralization need not imply a larger budget or staff. Indeed, given the leveling

---

[5] Although we reported above that cities spent more if the mayor was stronger, strong was only relative to other cities. In virtually all major cities except Chicago, the mayor is relatively weak—at least by comparison with a president of a private firm. Mayors are thus much less able to choose a desirable level of spending and stick to it. See John P. Kotter and Paul R. Lawrence, *Mayors in Action* (New York: Wiley-Interscience, 1974) for documentation.

of population, in the next decade mayors are likely to distinguish themselves by creatively doing more with less. But unless mayors have sufficient authority to implement such productivity improvements, they are unlikely to consider them seriously.

31

Exchange networks and community politics

Joseph Galaskiewicz

So far we have described the positioning of organizations within three resource networks in Towertown. We have also identified the participants in different community issues and described the positions that they occupied in these networks. In this chapter we are more concerned with explaining just how organizations' positions in these networks affect their overall influence in community affairs and their chances of winning and losing in specific community decision-making situations. We suspect that an organization's success in community decision making is a function of the direct linkages which it has with other actors in the respective networks of money, information, and support as well as the resources which it controls.

RESOURCES, RESOURCE MOBILIZATION, AND COMMUNITY POWER

In most any decision-making situation there will be different opinions on the way that a particular problem should be solved. The simple fact that actors become involved in a particular issue, either because

of their interest in the problem or because others in the community expect them to be responsible for the maintenance of certain institutional sectors of the community, does not mean that they will all be of one mind in addressing the problem. As we suggested . . . an action set emerges in response to certain demands in the environment; yet parties in the action set may very well have different points of view. In this chapter we will analyze the relative success and failure of the organizations which became involved in each of the five issues as well as the overall influence in community affairs of all organizations in the community.

Several factors might explain why some actors are more influential than others. Both pluralists and elitists have commented extensively on the relationship between resources and political influence (see French and Raven, 1959; Dahl, 1961; Gamson, 1966b; Clark, 1968; Coleman, 1971; and Laumann and Pappi, 1976). Both schools agree that the actor or actors who control highly valued resources are more likely to "get what they want" in the community. The difference between the two perspectives is in their description of how resources are distributed among actors in the American community. The pluralists see resources as widely dispersed throughout the system; the elitists

Reprinted with permission of the author and publisher from Joseph Galaskiewicz, *Exchange Networks and Community Politics* (Beverly Hills, Calif.: Sage Publications, 1979), pp. 129–40, 143–52.

argue that resources are more concentrated. However, there seems to be little disagreement that resources are important for the exercise of power.

An actor's influence, however, usually does not rest solely on his own resources. Often an actor must be able to mobilize the resources of other actors as well. This is typically done through coalition formation. Two general types of coalitions are found in the literature: the *issue specific coalition* which comes out of the pluralist tradition and the *institutional coalition* which comes out of the elitist tradition.

Issue specific coalitions are formed by independent actors who rationally decide to "deal" some of their resources for support on a particular issue. They may pool resources with other actors to get a single measure passed, or they may engage in logrolling where they promise future support to other actors in return for support on a decision which they have a greatest interest in. Whether the coalition is for one issue or across a series of issues, actors are expected to act in their own self-interest at all times and to construct their coalitions through a bargaining process.[1]

Institutional coalitions are much different. Rather than being loosely structured, special purpose social arrangements which actors freely negotiate among themselves in the face of different decisions, these coalitions are usually permanent community fixtures. This type of coalition is made up of actors who are dependent upon one another for a wide range of goods and services and thus are obligated to support one another's position on issues (e.g., Hunter, 1953). These dependency relations are often quite complex, covert, and

hierarchially structured. At times they take on the character of "conspiracies." In the spirit of Bachrach and Baratz (1962, 1963), we would argue that the coalitions which develop around specific issues (or across a series of issues) are almost totally irrelevant, for the networks among certain actors are often so tightly structured that they can even determine the sorts of issues that emerge in the first place. The distribution of resources among actors and the ongoing, structural linkages which exist among actors prior to any single issue affect the overall course of community decision making to a much greater extent than the ad hoc coalitions which develop after an issue has emerged in the public arena. Perrucci and Pilisuk (1970) argue that these networks constitute the community's power structure.

Although these two models purport to explain who "wins" and "loses" in community decision making, we are still skeptical. On the one hand, the pluralist position seems incredibly naive, for it virtually ignores the presence of informal, institutionalized, dependency relations among actors in the community (see Marsden and Laumann, 1977). On the other hand, the elitist position is almost paranoid; systems are just too complex for tightly integrated, omnipotent conspiracies to prevail. Consequently, an alternative model is needed which can explain more realistically how coalitions are used to mobilize resources and, in turn, explain the power of actors in a community political system. We think that a model which is more sensitive to actors' position is institutional resource networks will help to remedy the situation, drawing on the strengths of both perspectives while avoiding their weaknesses.

A LATENT STRUCTURAL MODEL OF COMMUNITY DECISION/MAKING PROCESSES

A quick survey of the literature indicates that issues seldom develop to the

---

[1] Political scientists have been in the forefront of analyzing these types of coalitions (see, e.g., Niemi and Weisberg, 1972; deSwann, 1973; Riker, 1962). Sophisticated mathematical models of coalition formation have been constructed which take into account not only the types and amounts of resources which actors control but also actors' rankings of goals, their alternative sources of goal satisfaction, and the constraints which decision rules impose upon them.

point where all interested actors are brought into a controversy and all available resources are mobilized (see Banfield, 1961; Dahl, 1961; Coleman, 1957). For numerous reasons complete mobilization would be disastrous for almost all parties involved.[2] More often we find that elected officials, bureaucrats, and committees responsible for making certain political decisions take into account the opinions of various groups in the community that do become active, assess these actors' potential to form coalitions with other actors in the community, and then make decisions accordingly so as to minimize the level of conflict over the issue. This process is described narratively in several accounts of decision making in large metropolitan areas (see Caro, 1974; Hayes, 1972; and Rakove, 1976). Proposals which would threaten potentially powerful interests are regarded by decision makers simply as "absurd" or "irresponsible" and are thus ignored. The successful politician is one who is sensitive to the potential coalitional partners that different groups may recruit without ever having to actually "test the waters." We would argue that it is in this way that actors are successful in different decision-making situations and not through the actual activation of allies.

Needless to say, this model certainly differs from the pluralist and elitist models. In our model an actor really never mobilizes his own resources or the resources of others. His success is a function of the probability that he could form a coalition with resourceful actors in the community if he wanted to. Decision makers only peruse the situation and make decisions so as to minimize conflict. Actors neither mobilize other actors' resources by bargaining their way into issue specific coalitions nor do they mobilize others' resources by "calling in their notes" and activating an institutional coalition. Rather, once their opinions are made known, they just wait and see what decision makers will do (see Banfield, 1961).

Our model differs from the pluralist and elitist models in other ways as well. For example, interested parties are not the ones who decide the issues. All too often pluralists give the erroneous impression that any actor in the private sector can get together with other private sector actors, strike a bargain among themselves and lay their decision before the appropriate governmental officials, who readily rubber-stamp their "deal." Our model rejects this point of view entirely. It also rejects the idea that public decision makers are the pawns of business or party interests. Our perspective sees public decision makers as taking an active role in the political process anticipating the needs, wishes, and potential coalitional strength of different actors in the community. Public officials are not simply "window dressing" that elites use to disguise their own control over community institutions.

Evaluating the coalitional potential of actors

Although it is relatively easy to assess an actor's resources, it is not all that easy to judge an actor's potential to form political coalitions. We will argue that the probability of an organization mobilizing the resources of other organizations is a function of how proximate it is to other corporate actors in community institutions. Laumann and Pappi (1976) found this to be true for organizations in the communities they studied. In Altneustadt coalitions of organizations reflected the proximity of organizations in the networks of overlapping memberships. In effect, the "closer" organizations were to one another, the more likely they were to take the same position on an issue.

Although reduced social distance may increase the probability that two actors will

---

[2] For an interesting treatment of this phenomenon from the point of view of purposive action theory, see Gamson's (1961) discussion of minimum winning coalitions.

form a coalition, it is not clear just why this should be. Two very different models might explain this phenomenon. The first we will call the *support model.* Here organizations would support other organizations politically because of loyalty. Organizations which interact with one another regularly are likely to develop common interests and to trust one another. If an actor becomes politically involved, those actors which routinely provide goods and services to it will likely support it in times of political crisis as well. There may be some pay-offs in the long run; however, actors are motivated primarily out of loyalty to those which they already support. The second model will be called the *dependency model.* Here actors would come to the aid of other actors because they are obligated to them for some reason or another (see Emerson, 1962; Blau, 1964). Organizations may be dependent upon some actor for goods and services; consequently, when that actor gets politically involved, they may very well give him their political support. Here motives are more selfish. Dependent actors fear that their supplier will cut off their resources if they refuse to support him. In all likelihood, dependent organizations will welcome the opportunity to support more dominant actors because this would help to equalize their relationship.

Whether one model or the other is more appropriate for any given community will probably be affected by the size, composition, and history of the community. In terms of our general argument it makes little difference. The important point is that the growth of elaborate resource exchange systems could put some actors in very strong bargaining positions vis-a-vis authorities. To the extent that actors develop extensive working ties with one another, a power structure of sorts does evolve. Even though these networks linkages may never actually be used to mobilize resources to support a political position, the potential coalitional strength of some actors could be so formidible that political decision makers would always think twice before challenging these actors' interests.

Why does it work?

This "politics by default" works so well because it benefits a number of actors in the community. On the one hand, it gives authorities and public decision makers at least the appearance of autonomy and control over the community. Authorities are still perceived by the public as taking the initiative in public matters and providing "leadership." In the eyes of their constituents they are very influential and respected, and this deference is not completely unfounded. Authorities do make decisions autonomously, and they may very well have no ties or obligations to special interests in the community. So long as authorities make the "right" decisions, there is no need on the part of potentially powerful interests to react and create a disturbance. Authorities are simply doing "a good job" and preserving social order.

Even if authorities make the "wrong" decisions, they will probably still escape retribution. Interest groups, though offended, are not likely to engage in conflict strategies hastily. Actors must first carefully weigh the consequences of activating a coalition, for activation would entail transforming their day-to-day contacts into real-life political activists. Such a course of action is very risky. Actors are often unsure if they can convert their business and personal contacts into political allies because these contacts also have "contacts" and obligations to others in the community. Even more importantly, actors are never really sure who their true antagonists are. Authorities are usually the immediate opponents; however, there is often a vague feeling that there are other actors in the community who are in favor of the decision and that they will mount a counteroffensive if anyone challenges the decision. Often this feeling is found among out-groups (e.g., racial and ethnic minorities) where there is a belief that the "system" is out to get them. Although both decision makers and academics scoff at this paranoia, these groups' anxieties may not be all that unreasonable. If our model is correct, powerful interest groups will "lay back" to see what happens, and they may become active given a disappointing turn of events. If marginal groups become politically active at all, it is perhaps more a testimony to their naivete or despair than to the openness of the political system.

Many actors in the private sector should find the situation advantageous as well. In our model more resourceful and well-connected actors need not expend their resources or activate their contacts to exercise political influence. An actor can "get what he wants" politically simply by pursuing its own day-to-day business.

For example, this is often the situation for large economic actors who can insure their influence in the community simply by establishing overlapping board memberships among themselves. The actual recruitment of board personnel may have little to do with political considerations (Allen, 1974; Pfeffer, 1972; Aldrich and Pfeffer, 1976); however, we suspect that the political impact of board interlocks is far reaching. Extensive board interlocks can effectively intimidate potential adversaries and decision makers alike. Although the organizations represented on the boards are not political allies per se, they are potential coalition partners.

Another advantage to special interest groups is that if conflict does break out, either because authorities are insensitive to the political realities in their environment or simply are unable to avoid offending one interest or another, the "fallout" will likely remain in the public sector. Because interest groups do not exercise influence directly, authorities alone are held accountable and blamed for their lack of "judgment" or "leadership." Subsequently, the most influential actors in the community will likely come through any community controversy virtually unscathed.

RESOURCE NETWORKS AND THE GENERATION OF POLITICAL INFLUENCE

Given our model, how can we apply it to the study of decision making in Towertown or any other community? In this section we will argue that examination of organizations' positions within the resource networks of money, information, and support may be of great use to us.

Traditionally, network analysis has been more useful for describing social structures (see Leinhardt, 1977). This is how we have used network analysis in this study so far. There is, however, another tradition in the social sciences which takes a more process-oriented approach toward social networks. Social networks have been used to help explain the spread of innovations (e.g., Coleman, Katz, and Menzel, 1966; Aldrich, 1976), the integration of a job market (e.g., Granovetter, 1974), political mobilization (e.g., Perrucci and Pilisuk, 1970; Turk, 1973a; Marsden and Laumann, 1977), and economic stabilization (e.g., Allen, 1974; Pfeffer, 1972; Zald, 1967). In each of these contexts, networks have been interpreted as avenues through which information or resources flow so as to bring about greater coordination or integration among a set of actors in a group or social organization. The various social processes alluded to above are facilitated or retarded by the network ties that exist among actors.

Our intention in this section is to demonstrate how networks are important in transforming economic resources in a community into political resources. The crux of our argument above was that an actor's day-to-day transactions with other actors in his environment constitute a set of bonds which can be utilized to further the actor's political interests. That is, an actor's network ties are the avenues through which other actors' resources can be transformed into political influence for that actor. We will call these resources an actor's *interorganizational resources*. Since we argued that public decision makers decide issues on the basis of each actor's potential capacity to create political coalitions, an actor's day-to-day contacts in the community become all important in determining just what this potential is.

One way to think about this is to argue that an organization's influence in community affairs is a function of his contacts via money, information, and support multiplied by the monetary resources of these contacts. In other words, one could estimate an actor's potential coalition strength by merely summing up the resources of those actors which he has routinized, continuous relations with. If one believes that the most important interorganizational contacts are an actor's "support" linkages, then one needs to sum across those actors who give money, information, and moral support to him. If one believes that the most important interorganizational contacts are an actor's "dependency" linkages, then one needs to sum across those who receive money, information, and moral support from the actor. Algebraically, for a given population of actors and a given network of resources the relationship between resources, influence, and network inflows can be expressed as follows:

$$\bar{A}_{n \times n}(R_n) = P_n$$

and the relationship between resources, influence, and network outflows:

$$A_{n \times n}(R_n) = P_n$$

where A is the asymmetric $n \times n$ adjacency matrix of a given type of linkage, R is the vector of resources for all actors n in the population, and P is the vector of influence scores for all actors n.

Algebraically, we could argue that the matrix representation of the digraph describing the network that exists among a set of actors is equivalent to the coordinates of a matrix representation of some linear transformation of the original resource vector. To think of this matrix/vector product in this way is theoretically very appealing. One can easily conceive of some function (e.g., a set of social relationships) as transforming a vector in one social space (e.g., a set of economic resources —money) into a vector in another social space (e.g., a set of political resources— influence). Phrasing this a little differently, we can think of a set of social relations as the effective means by which resources in one area of community life (e.g., the economy) are transformed into resources useful in another (e.g., the polity). In this way we can talk about how resources in a social system are mobilized for power.[3] Needless to say, the manner in which resources are mobilized or transformed will differ considerably across communities depending upon the patterns within relational systems. Also it will differ if one focuses on inflow or outflow vectors. Our argument simply states that if we are going to determine the capacity of a social organization to translate resources into collective action, then we must pay attention to the existing set of relationships among community actors as well.

HYPOTHESES

H14: The greater the amount of money controlled and the greater the number of people affiliated with an organization, the more others in the community will view it as influential in community affairs.

H15: The greater the amount of money controlled and the greater the number of people affiliated with an or-

---

[3] Our panel of experts also indicated the positions that organizations took on the issues in which they became activated.

ganization, the more successful it will be in different community decision-making situations.

H16: Organizations which are involved in community problem solving will be perceived by other actors to be very influential in community affairs.

H17: Organizations which are involved in community problem solving will be more successful in different community decision-making situations.

As we argued above, the resources of an actor are going to contribute to its overall influence in community affairs and to its success in different issues. Organizations that control resources which others value (e.g., money and "people") are going to get their way in community affairs more often than not. As decision makers evaluate the political arena, they obviously are going to respect organizations which control resources that can be used against them.

The importance of organizational activities/function is based on a somewhat different argument. In our model, decision-making bodies are autonomous actors in the community who reserve the right to pursue one public policy or another as they see fit. That they are sensitive to the political realities enhances rather than detracts from their influence. As long as these actors make decisions which do not offend powerful interest groups, they should be very influential in community affairs and successful in various issues.

H18: The greater the amount of money that an organization's interorganizational contacts control, the more others in the community will view it as influential in community affairs.

H19: The greater the amount of money that an organization's interorganizational contacts control, the more

successful it will be in different community decision-making situations.

These hypotheses simply summarize our arguments in the section above. The resources of organizations with which an actor has routine contact should greatly affect how other actors perceive him. If an actor's interorganizational partners have a great deal of money, then the actor will be viewed as potentially very influential in the community because he has the potential to mobilize very powerful coalitions. This view of the organization will be reflected in other actors perceiving him as very influential in community affairs and decision makers pursuing policies which are in line with his positions on various issues.

Either mode of resource conversion may be effective in our case community. Therefore, we will test both the "support" and "dependency" models with our data. Because of the small size of the community and its homogeneity, we suspect that organizations with more resourceful support linkages will tend to be more influential and successful than organizations with more resourceful dependency linkages. Because of the *gemeinschaft* quality of social relations in a community of this sort, the coalitional potential of actors will likely depend more upon the loyalty of their current supporters than upon the fears and anxieties of those who they support.

* * * * *

ANALYSIS

Our analysis will be presented in two parts. First, we will analyze the reputed influence of organizations (Influence) and organizations' overall success rate (Success). We will examine zero-order correlations and perform regression analyses to determine the relative effects of the different organizational and interorganizational variables on Influence and Success. Special attention will be given to the effects of

Money-funds, Infor-funds, and Support-funds. The second part of the analysis will identify just who was successful on each of the four issues. We will describe "winners," "losers," and "neutrals" by examining the mean values of each of our different variables for each category of actors.

General community influence

Table 31–1 presents the zero-order correlations between the organizational variables, the interorganizational resource variables, and our measures of organizational influence.[4] To begin with, we see that Influence and Success are weakly correlated. That is, there is no significant relationship between an actor's reputed influence and his actual successes and failures. There has been debate in the decision-making literature for years over the advantages and disadvantages of various measures of influence (Aiken and Mott, 1970). Our findings suggest that each indicator is measuring something quite different and call into question the argument that an actor's reputation is simply based on his "track record."

Looking at the correlations of the six interorganizational resource variables with Influence, we find strong positive associations. Organizations which are perceived as being very influential in the community have interorganizational linkages (both inflows and outflows) to very wealthy actors. A skeptic might argue that more extensive network contacts increase the visibility of an organization and thus artificially increase its reputation as being very influential. In response, one might say that these networks are important community structures, and that it is position in these structures which make actors influential. Regardless of the interpretation, there is clearly a strong association

---

[4] Once again we have not reported the levels of statistical significance for our analysis because we are still analyzing a population and not a sample of organizations.

between interorganizational resources and organizations' reputed influence. The zero-order correlations between the six interorganizational resources and actors' success rates (Success) are not that impressive. From these results, the resources of actors' interorganizational contacts do not seem to affect actors' chances of winning and losing in actual decision-making situations.

The simple correlations between our influence variables and organizational resource and activities variables follow a somewhat different pattern. The correlations of Success and Influence with Funds are high while the correlations with Pers are low. Problem-solving organizations have a slight tendency to be viewed as more influential in community affairs, but to its success an organization's activities are unrelated in community issues.

Finally, the correlations between the interorganizational resource variables and Funds are high while the correlations of these network variables with Pers and Problem are low. Not surprisingly, organizations with more economic resources tend to have interorganizational linkages to other wealthy actors.

Table 31–2 presents four step-wise regression models.[5] The first two test the effects of actors' inflow and outflow linkages on their reputed influence; the second two test the effects of inflow and outflow linkages on their success rate. In these models Funds, Pers, and Problem are entered first, and the respective sets of interorganizational resource variables are entered in turn.[6] The object of this analysis is to see how much of the variance in Influence and Success can be explained by entering sets of interorganizational resource variables. Also, we hope to compare the

---

[5] List-wise deletion was used for each regression analysis. This means that only 68 cases were analyzed for Influence and 35 for success.

[6] Interorganizational resource variables were entered according to the amount of variance they could explain in the dependent variable.

TABLE 31-1

Correlation matrix, means, ranges, and standard deviations for selected organizational variables, interorganizational resource variables, and measures of organizational influence

	Influence	Success	Funds	Pers	Problem	Mean	S.D.	Range	N
Organizational influence:									
Influence	1.000					24.48	18.53	2–67	73
Success	.081	1.000				.56	.76	–1–2	37
Organizational resources:									
Funds	.322	.277	1.000			4.19	2.41	1–8	73
Pers	.143	–.099	.255	1.000		4.60	2.46	1–8	73
Organizational activities:									
Problem	.263	–.056	–.527	–.145	1.000	.52	.50	0–1	73
Interorganizational resources (inflows only):									
Money-funds	.411	.087	.343	–.141	–.118	3.57	1.12	1–6	73
Infor-funds	.433	–.123	.271	–.013	–.029	3.53	1.20	1–6	73
Support-funds	.332	.041	.370	–.017	–.144	3.53	1.20	1–6	73
Interorganizational resources (outflows only):									
Money-funds	.533	.048	.513	.256	–.089	3.54	1.17	1–6	73
Infor-funds	.506	.012	.290	–.134	–.052	3.53	1.20	1–6	73
Support-funds	.547	.024	.326	.075	.016	3.53	1.20	1–6	73

TABLE 31–2
Regression analysis for organizations, reputed influence (Influence) and success on four community issues (Success)

	Influence			Success		
	$N=68$	Inflow variable effects	Outflow variable effects	$N=35$	Inflow variable effects	Outflow variable effects
Organizational resources:						
Funds	.594	.398	.276	.468	.551	.663
Pers	.074	.143	.099	−.398	−.514	−.367
Organizational activities:						
Problem	.552	.520	.446	.051	−.006	.074
Interorganizational resources:						
Money-funds	—	.155	.212	—	−.376	−.343
Infor-funds	—	.238	.301	—	−.047	−.064
Support-funds	—	.114	.183	—	.196	.090
R^2	.327	.454	.557	.202	.305	.277

relative effects of all the variables in the model on our dependent variables.

We see that the addition of the interorganizational outflow variables is more important in explaining Influence than the introduction of the interorganizational inflow variables. We should note, however, that both significantly increase the R^2 for Influence. Substantively, these are important findings. They indicate that the resources of the actors that are dependent upon an organization for money, information, and support affect the reputed influence of that organization more than the resources of the actors that give that organization money, information, and support. Our respondents seem to believe that organizations on which a number of wealthy actors depend are more influential in community affairs. We might add that the effect of funds is much less after each set of interorganizational variables is added.[7] This suggests that having linkages to actors with money, rather than simply having money, may be an important re-

source, which observers have overlooked. This, of course, would explain why organizations, such as banks and savings and loan associations, are typically respected in a community.

One variable, however, proves resistant to the effects of our interorganizational resource variables. This is the dummy variable designating whether an organization was a community problem solver (Problem). The strong effect of Problem is evidence that certain organizations, simply because of their role as community decision-making organizations, are regarded as being more influential. This strengthens Field's (1970) argument that a division of labor exists among community actors. It also strengthens Levine and White's (1961) argument that organizational domains are operative in community interorganizational fields.

The addition of the interorganizational resource variables has a much different effect on the model explaining Success. With the addition of interorganizational inflow variables, R^2 increases from .202 to .305; however, the effects of Funds and Pers become stronger, and the effect of Money-funds is negative. The only anticipated effect is that Support-funds is positively as-

---

[7] The Beta weight for Funds dropped most when Infor-funds was added. For both inflows and outflows this interorganizational variable came first into the model, followed by Money-funds and Support-funds.

sociated with Success. The "winners" here are then wealthier and smaller organizations which receive moral support from other wealthy organizations. This, of course, is in contrast to the profile of actors who are perceived as being very influential.

When the interorganizational outflow variables are added, the effect of Funds once again becomes stronger; however, the effect of Pers stays about the same. The only interorganizational variable that has any effect is Money-funds, but this effect is unexpectedly negative.

Winning and losing on four community issues

Analyzing the difference among winners, losers, and neutrals on individual issues is more complicated than analyzing actors' reputed influence in community affairs on their overall success rate. In Table 31–3 we present the mean values of selected organizational and interorganizational resource variables for the three types of actors.[8] In our discussion we will try to assess the relative impact of each variable by contrasting the characteristics of those who won with those who lost.[9]

As expected, in the two more expressive issues the winners tended to control more resources than the losers. In the school issue, the activists who favored closing the Garvey school controlled, on the average, more money and more "bodies" than those who opposed the closing of the school. In the curfew issue, we find a slightly different pattern. Those that were in favor of the curfew had more

people available than those who opposed it. We also see that in both issues, community decision-making organizations favored the outcomes.

Also, as we had hypothesized, the interorganizational contacts of the actors that were winners had more money than the interorganizational contacts of those who lost. Since resource inflows were more important than outflows in explaining Success, we present only the average funds of organizations' "supporters." Linkages via moral support seemed to be especially important for winners. In both cases the supporters of the winners tended to have considerably more money than supporters of the losers. On the other hand, linkages via money and information exchanges do not seem to be that effective in influencing the decision-making process. While the winners of the school issue had access, via information contacts, to more money than the losers, the winners of the curfew issue had access, via information contacts, to less funds than losers. Looking at the available interorganizational resources via money linkages, there is no appreciable difference between winners and losers on either issue.

Our hypotheses are not so clearly supported in the cases of the two more instrumental issues. To begin with, neither resources nor the activities of organizations had a consistently positive effect on either issue. In both cases, poorer rather than wealthier organizations got their way, and only on the hospital issue did larger organizations prevail over smaller ones. Similarly, the activities of organizations did not have a consistent effect. While the winners of the post office issue tended to be problem-solving organizations, the winners of the hospital issue were not.

Looking at the interorganizational resources of actors, we again find only scant support for our hypotheses. In fact, only on the hospital issue did the resources of organizations' supporters seem to make a

---

[8] For the sake of simplicity, we used the raw data for Funds and Pers as well as for Support-funds, Infor-funds and Mon-funds.

[9] Needless to say, it would have been much more desirable to use multivariate statistical techniques (e.g., discriminant function analysis) to determine the independent effects of the organizational and interorganizational resource variables. The small number of "winners" and "losers" made such an analysis unfeasible.

TABLE 31–3
Average values of selected organizational and interorganizational variables for "winners," "losers," and "neutrals" on four community issues

	School issue			Curfew issue			Hospital issue			Post office issue		
	Winners	Neutrals	Losers	Winners	Neutrals	Losers	Winners	Neutrals	Losers	Winners	Neutrals	Losers
Organizational resources:												
Funds*	5.40	1.22	3.76	1.83	1.58	2.40	3.05	.39	5.01	2.51	1.02	5.56
Pers	680.00	403.14	601.25	122.28	476.25	14.00	433.21	443.70	61.00	33.25	445.74	509.28
Organizational activities:												
Prob	1.00	.47	.87	.85	.48	.50	.46	.53	1.00	.75	.52	.43
Interorganizational resources (inflows):												
Mon-funds*	15.04	16.19	14.31	16.02	16.12	11.15	22.17	12.38	6.33	8.64	13.18	44.90
Infor-funds*	57.02	36.02	39.13	64.54	32.16	82.76	43.21	31.46	56.25	49.77	33.25	59.23
Support-funds*	52.21	21.98	29.07	29.70	23.03	4.55	29.95	19.07	16.26	20.80	21.99	34.98

* The figures for Funds, Mon-funds, Infor-funds, and Support-funds are in millions.

difference. Actors that gave winners moral support and money tended to be wealthier than the moral and financial supporters of the losers. However, on the post office issue it is clear in every instance that the losers had access to more interorganizational money than the winners. That losers tended to have more money and access to more interorganizational money than winners obviously goes against our hypotheses. It also is in contrast to our findings for the two more expressive issues.

When we try to figure out just why different actors won and lost on these two issues, it seems that very few things counted. In a way, our hypotheses are strengthened considering that the only thing which might have enabled the proponents of the hospital to get their project through was that they had routinized money and support flows from some of the wealthiest actors in the community. Going back to our journalistic description of the issue, this seems like a plausible explanation. Throughout its history, the project was the pet of the business community and thus a strong impact of Money-funds and Support-funds on the issue's resolution would not be surprising.

The explanation of who won and lost in the case of the post office is more straightforward, and again in a way supports our hypotheses. It is clear that the only reason the proponents of the east-end location won is that they tended to be local community decision makers. Rather than reacting to the different interest groups that became active on the issue as we expected, decision makers took the initiative. From our fieldnotes we learned that city officials were directly drawn into this issue because of their responsibility for administering federal dollars. The fact that proponents had only the authority of their role as an advantage over the opposition gives evidence that certain problem-solving roles are operative in community decision-making systems. Furthermore, it suggests that these culturally defined "positions" have a certain clout independently of the organizational and interorganizational resources of the actors that occupy them.

DISCUSSION

It is clear that systems of community influence are quite complex. An actor's influence, whether it be measured in terms of reputation or success in community decisions, cannot be predicted simply on the basis of his own resources and activities. Organizations' funds and functional role in the community were important in almost all our analyses. Only in the hospital issue were they unimportant. However, we found that the resources of actors' interorganizational contacts might also be critical in explaining the influence of organizations. More specifically, actors on whom wealthier organizations depended for money, information, and support tended to be seen as more influential in community affairs while organizations that had the moral support of wealthier actors tended to be more successful in various issues. Particularly in the more expressive issues, linkages of moral support may have been very important in mobilizing the resources of other actors.

These findings certainly are not conclusive, but they do provide some support for our theory. The strength of the interorganizational resource variables in our analyses suggests that decision makers and other actors in the community respect the potential of well-connected actors to establish powerful political coalitions. The fact that the resources of an actor's outflow and inflow partners might be transformed into a reputation for being influential and successful on issues was evidence of this. Needless to say, our analysis is quite rudimentary, and more sophisticated modeling is certainly needed to draw out the more subtle complexities of resource transformative processes.

Some implications of these findings, however, are quite interesting. . . . [W]e

304

see that the stratification of actors in a community setting cannot be determined simply by inspecting the distribution of resources among individual actors. The resources that one controls certainly contribute to one's influence, but the researcher must also take into account the set of resources that actors can mobilize through their existing set of social relationships. This seems critical even though these network ties may appear to have little to do with political action. Needless to say, our analysis of organizations can be extended to an analysis of individuals and population subgroups. Although this demands a more thorough documentation of all three types of resource networks, the reward of such an effort seems well worth it.

REFERENCES

Aldrich, H. (1975) "An organization-environment perspective on cooperation and conflict between organizations in the manpower training system." Pp. 49–70 in *Interorganization Theory*, ed. by A. Negandhi. Kent, Ohio: Kent State University Press.

Aldrich, H., and Pfeffer, J. (1976) "Environments of organizations." Pp. 79–105 in *Annual Review of Sociology*, 2, ed. by A. Inkeles. Palo Alto: Annual Reviews Inc.

Allen, M. (1974) "The structure of interorganizational elite cooptation: Interlocking corporate directorates." *American Sociological Review* 39, pp. 393–406.

Banfield, E. (1961) *Political Influence*. New York: Free Press.

Blau, P. (1964) *Exchange and Power in Social Life*. New York: John Wiley & Sons.

Caro, R. (1974) *The Power Broker: Robert Moses and the Fall of New York*. New York: Knopf.

Clark, T. (1968) *Community Structure and Decision-making: Comparative Analyses*. San Francisco: Chandler.

Coleman, J. (1957) *Community Conflict*. New York: Free Press.

Dahl, R. (1961) *Who Governs? Democracy and Power in an American City*. New Haven, Conn.: Yale University Press.

deSwann, A. (1973) *Coalitions Theories and Cabinet Formation*. The Hague: Elsevier.

Emerson, R. (1962) "Power dependence relations." *American Sociological Review* 27, pp. 31–41.

Field, A. (1970) *Urban Power Structures: Problems in Theory and Research*. Troy, New York: Schenkman.

French, J., and Raven, B. (1959) "The basis of social power." Pp. 150–57 in *Studies in Social Power*, ed. by D. Cartwright. Ann Arbor: Institute for Social Research.

Gamson, W. (1961) "A Theory of coalition formation." *American Sociological Review* 26, pp. 373–82.

Granovetter, M. (1974) *Getting a Job: A Study of Contacts and Careers*. Cambridge: Harvard University Press.

Hayes, E. (1972) *Power Structure and Urban Policy: Who Rules in Oakland?* New York: McGraw-Hill.

Laumann, E. O., and Pappi, F. (1976) *Networks of Collective Action: A Perspective on Community Influence Systems*. New York: Academic Press.

Leinhardt, S. (1977) *Social Networks: A Developing Paradigm*. New York: Academic Press.

Levine, S., and White, P. (1961) "Exchange as a conceptual framework for the study of interorganizational relationships." *Administrative Science Quarterly* 5, pp. 583–601.

Marsden, P., and Laumann, E. O. (1977) "Collective action in a community elite: Exchange, influence resources, and issue resolution." Pp. 199–250 in *Power, Paradigms, and Community Research*, ed. by R. Liebert and A. Imershein. Beverly Hills: Sage Publications.

Niemi, R., and Weisberg, H. (1972) *Probability Models of Collective Decision-Making*. Columbus, Ohio: Bobs-Merrill.

Perrucci, R., and Pilisuk, M. (1970) "Leaders and ruling elites: The interorganizational bases of community power." *American Sociological Review* 35, pp. 1040–57.

Pfeffer, J. (1972) "Size and composition of corporate boards of directors: The organization and its environment." *Administrative Science Quarterly* 17, pp. 218–28.

Rakove, M. (1976) *Don't Make No Waves . . . Don't Back No Losers.* Bloomington: Indiana University Press.

Riker, W. (1962) *The Theory of Political Coalitions.* New Haven, Conn.: Yale University Press.

Turk, H. (1969) "Comparative urban studies

in interorganizational relations." *Sociological Inquiry* 38, pp. 108–10.

Zald, M. (1967) "Urban differentiation, characteristics of boards of directors, and organizational effectiveness." *American Journal of Sociology* 73, pp. 261–72.

32

Community power and population increase: An empirical test of the growth machine model

Larry Lyon, Lawrence G. Felice, M. Ray Perryman, and E. Stephen Parker

Early community power research has produced hundreds of descriptions of the nature and distribution of local power. For most of these studies the description was an end in itself, but more recently it has been felt that the differences themselves must also make a difference (Warren 1977). That is, variations in community power should help account for variations in local policy outputs. Numerous attempts have been made to link power with policy, but the theoretical base often seems devoid of implications for political change and the statistical relationships usually range from weak to nonexistent. These twin problems of theoretical relevance and statistical significance represent major difficulties in the development and perhaps even the continuance of the subfield of community power as a major avenue of academic inquiry.

As an example, note Roland Warren's (1977, p. 368) gloomy summation of com-

munity power research: "The exciting study of community power structures opened up in the 1950s has run a rather full course, and the ratio of firm conclusions to energy expended leaves the burden of proof on its proponents as to its explanatory value for local community phenomena." In a similar vein, John Walton's (1976, p. 299) dismal assessment of the field emphasizes the lack of concern with practical politics: "Correlations between structural or demographic characteristics of cities and the sheer quantitative resultant of tangled bureaucratic processes represented by levels of spending or program adoption are abstractions far removed from the stuff of politics. I believe it is for this reason that many have become dissatisfied with the directions the field has taken. As research became more technically sophisticated, it drifted further from its conceptual mooring to the notions of power, inequality, and the workings of the political process." Even those who have produced the correlations Walton criticizes are less than satisfied with the results. Surveying the weak statistical associations he found between community power and policy outputs, Aiken (1970, p. 516) concludes: "It seems apparent from

Reprinted with permission from "Community Power and Population Increase: An Empirical Test of the Growth Machine Model," *American Journal of Sociology* 86, no. 6 (May 1981), pp. 1387–1400. © The University of Chicago, Appendix with operational definitions of variables has been omitted and footnotes have been renumbered.

the results here that the community power perspective, as it now exists, is simply not the most appropriate model to use." As a final example, Lyon (1977*a*, p. 429) asks, "Aren't we really saying that the direct measurement of community power is not worth the effort and that community power can contribute little toward explaining and predicting local policy outputs?"

The remarks above should suffice to illustrate that traditional community power research appears to many to be in need of new directions. Specifically, they suggest that what is needed is a theoretical model that is politically based and change oriented and that addresses the question of "who benefits" from community policies (Walton 1976, 1979). Furthermore, this theory or model should be able to produce a measurable power-policy relationship that is statistically significant and relatively important when compared with competing explanatory variables (Aiken 1970, Lyon 1977*a*). This paper attempts to employ such a theory of community power in order to build an empirical power-policy model that meets these requirements.

THE GROWTH MACHINE AS A THEORETICAL BASE FOR COMMUNITY POWER

In a provocative article on the structure and dynamics of community power, Harvey Molotch (1976, p. 313) argues that the key to understanding local politics is to conceptualize the city as a growth machine: "I aim to make the extreme statement that this organized effort to affect the outcome of growth distribution is the essence of local government as a dynamic political force. It is not the only function of government, but it is the key one and, ironically, the one most ignored. . . . This is the politics which determines who, *in material terms*, gets what, where, and how."

Briefly, it is Molotch's (1976, pp. 314–15) position that community elites such as local businessmen form a coalition devoted to promoting growth because it provides them with a number of tangible economic advantages (e.g., increased markets and property values). Although these elites may disagree on other issues, the desire for growth finds wide support so that civic "boosterism" becomes institutionalized through chambers of commerce, newspapers, athletic teams, and so forth. It is maintained that the basic purpose of these local phenomena is to allow the community to compete with other communities for increased growth. However, in a departure from conventional wisdom, Molotch (1976, p. 318) claims that beyond the local elite, very few residents benefit from their community's growth. Tax burdens rise during growth periods; and the commonly expected benefit, a decrease in unemployment rates, does not occur. Thus, the local elite has convinced residents that the quality of life improves with growth when, actually, it deteriorates.

In this description of local growth, Molotch has developed an explanation of community power that meets the requirements specified by Walton. It is based in a political economy framework (Walton 1979) and answers the "who gets what" question. Furthermore, it has potential for change: Molotch (1976, p. 327) argues for antigrowth movements to wrest control from the business elites and describes the improved quality of life that can be expected from such a change. Such characteristics as a political economy framework or a potential for change do not, of course, guarantee the validity of conceptualizing the community as a growth machine. They do, however, indicate that the concept is potentially useful and important for our understanding of community power and, hence, should be subjected to further analytical and empirical investigation.

Since the explanation developed by Molotch is largely of a logical-deductive form, with little supporting empirical evidence, this paper constructs an empirical model to test the key relationship between elites and growth as well as other aspects of the growth machine explanation of community phenomena. If this model provides evidence of a strong statistical relationship between the power of local businessmen and community growth, it will respond positively to the two common criticisms of community power research mentioned above: (1) a lack of theoretical relevance and (2) a relatively weak statistical relationship.

THE GROWTH MACHINE MODEL

The growth machine model will be evaluated with data based on 48 communities from the Permanent Community Sample (PCS).[1] Clark's (e.g., 1971) intensive study of these communities provides direct measurement of many of the variables in the model. Other, more demographic variables are available from traditional sources such as the U.S. Bureau of the Census.

The model in Figure 32–1 represents much of Molotch's theory with variables for which there is full operationalization for the PCS. The key variables for our purposes is the power of the business elite. It is directly measured in the PCS by questions asked of knowledgeable informants to gauge the power of businessmen and business organizations in the community (Clark et al. 1977). While Molotch specifies other elites also as promoters of growth,

businessmen are clearly viewed as the most important group (Molotch 1976, p. 314), and the PCS represents the only large community sample with such a direct measure of business power. If the Molotch thesis is correct, there should be a strong, positive relationship between this variable and population growth. This relationship is a pivotal one for answering the question, Does it make a difference "who governs"? According to the model, it should make a substantial difference: The greater the power held by business in the community, the greater the local growth.[2]

There are other relationships specified in the model. It is predicted that business strength will reduce the tax rate and the power of unions.[3] The tax rate (or effort, or burden, depending on one's ideology and definition) is a ratio of local governmental revenues to local property values. The higher the revenues and the lower the property values, the higher the tax rate. Union power is measured by an index that estimates the perceived influence of unions in local decision making. In addition, it is expected that population growth will have effects on policy outputs rarely mentioned by growth proponents. As the growth rate increases, the model predicts increases in tax rates and per capita expenditures, a decrease in net revenues (Molotch 1976, p. 319), and no change in unemployment (Molotch 1976, pp. 320–25). Finally, it is expected that growth will in-

[2] While there are obviously other types of growth that could be considered besides population growth, e.g., various types of economic growth, Molotch clearly sees population growth as the key variable in the growth machine model.

[3] Tax rate is measured for 1960 in order to construct a change measure for 1970. However, the surveys that determine business and union strength were conducted in 1967. Thus the model is forced to reverse the causal and temporal order in this one instance. While it would be possible to construct that model with the 1960 tax rate as a cause of business power, the growth machine theory views business power as a cause rather than an effect. In addition, Molotch (1976, p. 312) sees the progrowth "business climate" as characterized by "good" labor relations and "reasonable" taxes. To operationalize them as *weak* unions and *low* taxes seem appropriate.

FIGURE 32–1
The growth machine model

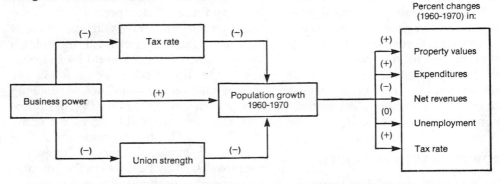

The arrows graph predicted causal links and the signs (+, −, and 0) indicate hypothesized positive, negative, and absent relationships that are based on Molotch's growth machine model and are evaluated in Table 32–1. Other possible causal relationships between these variables that are not explicitly predicted by the model are also evaluated in Table 32–1.

crease property values and thereby benefit the elites who promoted it originally (Molotch 1976, p. 311).

There is, of course, a possibility that some of the relationships in the model are spurious and merely reflect basic historical, political, or geographic causes. Thus, the model needs a series of control variables. Unfortunately, with a limited sample size, the number of explanatory variables must necessarily be small in order to conserve degrees of freedom. Thus, ten potential control variables suggested in the literature are utilized in a principle component analysis (Jöreskog and Sörbom 1979) which results in the creation of two vectors that combine to account for approximately half of the intervariable variance among the ten control variables. These ten variables include two measures of informal community power, *political decentralization* (Clark 1971) and *decision-making structure* (Vanecko 1967; Brick 1975), and one measure of formal political structure, an *index of municipal reform* (Lineberry and Fowler 1967). In addition, five largely demographic variables measured at the county level are utilized: *population, percentage nonwhite, median age, median income, and median education.* Finally, a dummy variable of *city/suburb status* and the *age of the city* (Liebert 1976) are employed. Vector I is

interpreted as a demographic measure that loads highest on city age and city/suburb status. It appears to reflect many of the basic regional and historical differences among communities described by Liebert (1976) as being associated with "functional scope," by distinguishing between the older, central cities and the newer, suburban cities. Vector II is a political construct that loads on the three formal and informal political variables and separates communities with reformed municipal governments and more elitist power structures from those with less reformed governments and a more pluralistic distribution of power (Lineberry and Fowler 1967; Clark 1971; Lyon 1977*b*). The exact interpretation of the vectors is not crucial to the present analysis in that they serve mainly to create a *ceteris paribus* situation in which the growth machine explanation can be more adequately assessed.[4] To the extent that these vectors are important as causal

---

[4] This is not to suggest that only two vectors can account for "community structure." We cannot even claim that they represent totally the 10 control variables. However, the independence of business power from these 10 variables and the effect of business power on growth still hold when the 10 variables are entered separately as individual controls. More detailed information about the creation and interpretation of these vectors can be found in Lyon et al. (1979).

TABLE 32–1
Standardized coefficients of the growth machine model

Dependent variables	N*	Vector I	Vector II	BusPow	Union	TaxRate	PopGrow	R² (Adj.)
		Independent variables						
Business power	48	A	A	...	...	...	...	.00
Union strength	48	A	A	A	...	...	...	.00
Tax rate 1960	45	.306	A	.432	A	...	...	.21
Population growth	45	−.520	A	.400	A	A	...	.47
Property values change	43	A	A	A	A	.231	.192	.05
Unemployment change	45	−.252	−.227	.237	A	A	A	.11
Tax rate change	43	A	−.233	A	−.244	−.480	A	.29
Expenditures change	44	A	A	A	A	A	−.394	.14
Net revenues change	43	A	A	A	.309	.425	.362	.30

Note: A = The empirical absence of a theoretically possible causal relationship. All standardized coefficients shown are significant at .05 level with the exception of four betas that allow measurable increase in adjusted R^2 by their inclusion even though they are not statistically significant (Vector II and BusPow on Unemployment change; and TaxRate and PopGrow on Property values change).

* N's are total number of communities with full information for the relevant variables and therefore available for that segment of the model.

factors in the model, it is predicted that the power of the business elite will compare favorably with them in statistical strength. Otherwise, the aforementioned difficulty of easily measured control variables being more important than measures of community power reasserts itself. It is necessary, then, that the power of the business elite have a significant effect on growth after the control vectors are introduced and that the business elite variable have a causal impact of similar or even greater magnitude than the two control vectors.

TESTING THE MODEL

The relative causal effects of the variables in the growth machine model are exhibited in Table 32–1. The initial relationship in Table 32–1 essentially shows the independence of business and union power from the two community vectors. The R^2 values of zero strongly suggest the absence of significant covariance between these measures of community structure and the power of business and unions.

For the two proposed concomitances of local business power, there is little initial support for the model. It is expected that business will seek weak labor unions and low taxes in order to develop an overall economic climate conducive to profit and growth. As indicated in Table 32–1, business power is not empirically related to the measure of labor, perhaps because the union variable is a measure of local union influence rather than unionization.[5] Business strength shows a strong positive relationship with local tax levels. A possible explanation of this disparate finding focuses on the aggregate nature of the tax measure used. It represents the total tax burden of the community, and to the degree that business is able to secure special advantages through lower or delayed taxation, investment tax credits, and so forth, the measure may be inappropriate for an accurate test. In any event, the lack of a measurable relationship between business and labor and the positive association for business and taxation are not as predicted by the model.

---

[5] In fact, when business power is correlated with the presence of municipal labor unions, there is the expected negative relationship (Lyon et al. 1979).

For the key dependent variable in the model, population growth, the observed relationship conforms closely to the Molotch predictions, that is, the greater the power of business in the community, the higher the levels of local growth. Moreover, this relationship is a strong one that compares favorably in explanatory power with the community structure vectors. Thus, it appears that the level of business strength within the local elite is a substantial force in creating community growth and that this relationship is largely independent of many other elements of community structure.

The consequences of growth and business power on subsequent community phenomena are generally as predicted. For increase in property values, population growth exercises a weak but positive effect. According to the theoretical explanation of the model, this is an expected relationship because increased property values are one of the primary benefits the business elite receives from growth.

Another local output important to the model is the unemployment level. Molotch maintains that elites will attempt to convince the citizenry that lower unemployment levels result from growth; but as Molotch (1976, pp. 320–25) demonstrated, there appears to be no relationship between growth an unemployment. There is, however, a moderate link between business power and increases in unemployment.

The relationships between growth, taxation, and other financial outputs are complex and not always as predicted in the model. There is no relationship between increases in population and increases in the local tax burden. And while growth may not reduce the tax effort or burden, it appears to reduce expenditures significantly in that, for per capita expenditures, the relationship with growth is strong and negative. This suggests that population increases more rapidly than expenditures during growth periods. Furthermore,

when the net revenues (total revenues less local expenditures) are considered, the effect of growth is positive. This contradicts Molotch's contentions of higher taxes, higher expenditures, and a net revenue loss for growing communities and implies generally favorable consequences for population growth.[6]

In sum, however, this analysis of the PCS still supports the major tenets of the growth machine model: As business elites gain local power, they are able to promote population growth which appears to provide them with greater profits through higher property values; but the most widely cited common good for growth, lower unemployment, does not accrue.

IMPLICATIONS

The foregoing test of the growth machine model has significant implications for (1) understanding the dynamics of local growth, (2) using a political economy framework to account for community phenomena, and (3) assessing the current state of community power research. With respect to local growth, it seems clear that Molotch's description and explanation of the growth process merit serious consideration. To the degree that the parts of the theory that were testable are supported in this analysis, portions less suited to empirical evaluation (e.g., the economic motivation for elite control and manipulation of

---

[6] A concept as broad as "net revenues" is admittedly difficult to operationalize. However, we feel relatively confident in the positive relationship between growth and net revenues because six different measures were initially constructed using various combinations of several revenue and expenditure variables, and the five not shown in the text supported the positive association more strongly than the one used here (which seems best to represent the concept as used by Molotch). The relationship is weakened by the method used here because that revenue measure includes intergovernmental revenues, and rapidly growing communities received proportionately smaller funds from the federal government. Measures based only on local revenues show a stronger relationship.

community events) can be given at least some indirect support. And if local growth can be seen as a phenomenon that is promoted and caused by a special elite, this elite influence must be considered in order to understand or control the growth process.

There are some growth dynamics in this empirical model that are not anticipated by Molotch's theoretical model. The relationshp between business power and taxation seems to be considerably different from the Molotch explanation. It may be that business requires high levels of government services and thereby requires high local taxes. In any event, this relationship needs further investigation and refinement. Similarly, the effects of growth require considerably more investigation and analysis than exist to date. While many of the consequences of growth are as Molotch predicts, others, such as the change in taxation and net revenues, are not. These differences do not necessarily invalidate the growth machine model because they are not as crucial to it as the business-growth relationship. In addition, these output factors can be more adequately analyzed with samples larger than the PCS.[7] To assess the effects of local growth, it is not necessary to measure or control for community power. Thus, analysis based on larger samples is possible and desirable (e.g., Greenwood 1975; Appelbaum 1976). It is only for un-

derstanding the causes of growth that community surveys of elite characteristics appear necessary; hence, samples must be limited in size.

The empirical model developed in this paper gives support to Molotch's and Walton's (and others', e.g., Harvey 1973; Castells 1977) position that a political economy approach is appropriate for understanding community phenomena. In this case, the contention is predicated on the proposition that the desire to increase the profit potential of local property is sufficient to unify the elite and that fostering community growth is a common and effective technique for increasing property value. Although this proposition is not completely addressed by the empirical model developed in this paper, the basic relationship of business, growth, and increased property values suggests the appropriateness of the model for community sociology. In other words, it appears that much can be gained by conceiving of a community "as the areal expression of the interests of some land-based elite" (Molotch 1976, p. 309). And in a more general context, this model shows support for Walton's (1979, pp. 141, 142) contentions that class control "predict[s] or explain[s] in some considerable part the pattern of urban development" and that "the [political economy] perspective does offer theoretical explanations amenable to empirical evaluation."

Finally, the model tested here says much about the current state of community power research. The findings reported in this analysis suggest that attempts to correlate the distribution of power with traditional policy outputs such as local expenditures may be ill conceived for two reasons. First, in many major comparative efforts the measure of community power is based on the distribution of power rather than on who has the power and what they can be expected to do with it. Although distribution is of immense theoretical importance, in terms of prag-

---

[7] E.g., there is some intercorrelation in the output variables. The strongest intercorrelations occur when change in net revenues is correlated with change in tax revenues ($r = -.47$) and in expenditures ($r = -.53$). Individually controlling for these correlated output variables would produce two substantive changes in our conclusions, both of which would provide greater support for Molotch's model. Specifically, (1) the positive relationship between population growth and net revenues disappears, and (2) population growth is shown to increase the tax rate. Such controls are questionable, however, because the correct causal ordering is difficult to specify, and they use up degrees of freedom and sometimes reduce sample size. More rigorous specification and elaboration of the effects of growth can be made best with significantly larger samples.

matic import, the characteristics of the power holders seem more crucial. In this case, who holds the power (i.e., businessmen) has a much greater effect on growth than does the distribution of power (i.e., decentralization).[8] The characteristics of power holders have been measured in other comparative community research (e.g., Clark et al. 1977); and from this analysis, it now appears that for explaining important community phenomena such as growth, the characteristics of power holders are more crucial than the distribution of power.

The idea that some community phenomena are more important than others suggests a second reason for the difficult position in which community power research currently finds itself. It is probably incorrect to think that the typical community output variables, such as expenditures for one function or another, are closely tied to elite interests. For example, Molotch maintains that growth is the most important community output and the only one that unites local elites. Thus, it is an output that should be affected by elite characteristics, and the model shows this to be the case. However, if an output is not an important concern of the elite, there is no necessary relationship between power and policy.

The idea that local elites are interested in only a small number of community issues is not a new one (e.g., Hunter 1953). Clearly, growth is an issue that concerns local elites, as shown by Molotch's theory and this empirical test. An important question is whether there are other issues that are equally important to local elites, and that will unify these elites in pursuit of a common local output. We believe only issues that are both extremely important and virtually consensual can be theoreti-

cally justified and empirically supported in a power-policy model to the same degree as population growth is here. It is unclear whether there are such issues, but it is now clear what is necessary to demonstrate their existence. The issue and output should be suggested by a well-developed theory (e.g., Molotch's growth machine explanation) and be supported as significant in an empirical model. The growth machine model defines the key leadership characteristics, the important issue and output, and explicitly specifies the relationships between them. It is not surprising, then, that this is one of the few empirical studies to show community power as an important cause of community phenomena.[9] The implication for community power research, finally, is much like Walton's earlier prescription. There should be less initial emphasis on qualification and more on the development of sound qualitative theory. Given powerful theories to build on, more powerful statistical relationships can be expected to follow; and this much-maligned subfield may finally achieve the potential it held in the 1950s and 1960s.

REFERENCES

Aiken, Michael. (1970) "The Distribution of Community Power: Structural Bases and Social Consequences." Pp. 487–525 in *The Structure of Community Power*, ed. by Michael Aiken and Paul Mott. New York: Random House.

Appelbaum, Richard. (1976) "City Size and Urban Life: A Preliminary Inquiry into Some Consequences of Growth in Ameri-

---

[8] Although it is not shown in the text, Clark's (1971) decentralization measure has no relationship with business power ($r = -.06$) and never develops a significant beta with growth under a number of different specifications in the model.

[9] Because community power has so rarely been found to be causally important, the exceptions are notable. An important exception is Clark et al.'s (1977) finding that cities with strong mayors and weak businessmen are more likely to have fiscal difficulties. Another type of analysis that may prove to be an exception by raising the explanatory levels of power-policy models is the increasingly popular policy typology approach (Aiken 1970; Clark 1972; Ostrum 1974; Smith 1976; Peterson 1979).

can Cities." *Urban Affairs Quarterly* 12, pp. 139–70.

Brick, Yitzchak. (1975) "The Relation of Vertical Ties to Community Competence." Ph.D. dissertation, Brandeis University.

Castells, Manuel. (1977) *The Urban Question: A Marxist Approach.* Cambridge, Mass.: MIT Press.

Clark, Terry N. (1971) "Community Structure and Decision-Making, Budget Expenditures, and Urban Renewal in 51 American Communities." Pp. 293–313 in *Community Politics*, ed. by Charles M. Bonjean, Terry N. Clark, and Robert Lineberry. New York: Free Press.

————. (1972) "Centralization Encourages Public Goods, But Decentralization Generates Separate Goods." Research Report no. 39, Comparative Study of Community Decision Making, University of Chicago.

Clark, Terry N., Irene S. Rubin, Lynne C. Pettler, and Erwin Zimmerman, 1977. "How Many New Yorks? The New York Fiscal Crisis in Comparative Perspective." Research Report no. 72, rev., Comparative Study of Community Decision Making, University of Chicago.

Greenwood, Michael J. (1975) "A Simultaneous-Equations Model of Urban Growth and Migration." *Journal of the American Statistical Association* 70 (December), pp. 797–810.

Harvey, David. (1973) *Social Justice and the City.* Baltimore: Johns Hopkins Press.

Hunter, Floyd. (1953) *Community Power Structure.* Chapel Hill: University of North Carolina Press.

Jöreskog, Karl G., and Dag Sörbom (1979) *Advances in Factor Analysis and Structural Equation Models.* Cambridge, Mass.: Abt Books.

Liebert, Roland J. (1976) *Disintegration and Political Action: The Changing Functions of City Government in America.* New York: Academic Press.

Lineberry, Robert, and Edmund Fowler (1967) "Reformism and Public Politics in Ameri-

can Cities." *American Political Science Review* 61 (September), pp. 701–16.

Lyon, Larry (1977a) "Community Power and Policy Outputs: A Question of Relevance." In Warren 1977.

————. (1977b) "A Re-examination of the Reform Index and Community Power." *Journal of the Community Development Society* 8 (Spring): 86–97.

Lyon, Larry, Lawrence G. Felice, M. Ray Perryman, and E. Stephen Parker (1979) "Evaluating the Causes and Effects of Local Growth." Working paper no. IA-1, Studies in Interdisciplinary Areas, Center for the Advancement of Economic Analysis, Baylor University.

Molotch, Harvey (1976) "The City as a Growth Machine: Toward a Political Economy of Place." *American Journal of Sociology* 82 (September), pp. 309–32.

Ostrom, Elinor (1974) "Exclusion, Choice and Divisibility: Factors Affecting the Measurement of Urban Agency Output and Impact." *Social Science Quarterly* 54 (March), pp. 691–99.

Peterson, Paul E. (1979) "Inter-City Competition and the Politics of Development." Paper presented at the annual meeting of the American Political Science Association, Washington, D.C.

Smith, Richard (1976) "Community Power and Decision: A Replication and Extension of Hawley." *American Sociological Review* 41 (August), pp. 691–705.

Vanecko, James J. (1967) "Resources, Influence, and Issue Resolution in Large Urban Political Systems: The Case of Urban Renewal." Ph.D. dissertation, University of Chicago.

Walton, John (1976) "Community Power and the Retreat from Politics." *Social Problems* 23 (February), pp. 292–303.

————. (1979) "Phoenix in New Haven?" *Social Science Quarterly* 60 (June), pp. 136–43.

Warren, Roland (1977) *New Perspectives on the American Community.* Chicago: Rand McNally.

Social change at the community level

SECTION SIX

INTRODUCTION

One of the most interesting aspects of social behavior in American communities is the attempt, through concerted action, to bring about change. Many changes occur within communities on the basis of un-planned modifications in the structure of the population, the gradual growth or decline of industries, the constant competition for land use, the gradual development or infusion of new ideas or usages, and the discarding of old ones. But some kinds of change are deliberately brought about. The development of a new pattern of health services or of a program of low-cost housing, the adoption of a new plan of land use, the mounting of a campaign for industrial expansion, a concerted attempt to reduce juvenile delinquency or poverty—are all examples. How is it possible to organize efforts for community change, and what are some of the conditions of effectiveness of such efforts?

One of the dynamic processes frequently in operation at the commu-nity level is controversy. Typically, such controversy centers on specific issues, the resolution of which occasions a contest between those taking opposing sides. Numerous studies of controversies in communities have been recorded and analyzed. Most often, however, these are reported as single episodes without an attempt being made to group a number of them for comparative study in order to make general state-ments about such uniformities as may be observable. In a brilliant work, James S. Coleman gathered together for systematic analysis the reports of a large number of such controversies. Using these as data, he devel-oped a theory of the general nature and dynamics of such episodes of controversy.

The selection presented here is devoted to analyzing the dynamics of the process of controversy. Put in another way, it seeks to illuminate the factors which operate to move a controversy along from one stage to another, usually toward greater intensity. For one thing, the controver-sial issue itself often is redefined, frequently in the direction of expand-ing the area of controversy. Specific differences become generalized into larger, more inclusive ones. At the same time, disagreement on the issues becomes transformed into antagonism toward the opposite side. During the process, changes in the social organization of the community occur, as individuals and organizations gradually range themselves on one side or the other of the controversy. It becomes difficult to remain uncommitted. Partisan organizations emerge, as do new leaders. These latter often do not have a strong sense of identification with the commu-nity and the sense of constraint which such identification implies. Word-of-mouth communication, often in the form of unverified rumors, helps to intensify the controversy. The actions of each side become the stimulus for more decisive action by the other, and thus the process gathers momentum as it goes along. Coleman notes a relationship which might be called a "Gresham's Law of Conflict," in that often the harmful and dangerous elements drive out the more moderate groups who might otherwise keep the conflict within bounds.

While Coleman's analysis continues to be the classic *theoretical* statement on community conflict, the classic *application* of community conflict lies in the community organization efforts of Saul Alinsky. In this review of Alinsky's contributions by Donald C. and Dietrich C. Reitzes, we see that while Alinsky's career was avowedly nonacademic and atheoretical, his ideas were often predecessors of more recent theoretical views of the community. Using Gerald Suttles and Albert Hunter's concept of the "community of limited liability" (communities that result from the strengthening of the vertical patterns described in Section Three), the Reitzeses are able to synthesize many of Alinsky's organizing principles into a broader theoretical base for community development. They maintain that tactics such as inducing conflict with a common enemy to build solidarity, or focusing simultaneously on several local issues in order to appeal to diverse interests, are particularly well suited for communities of limited liability.

The Alinsky approach to neighborhood organizations (along with several others) is critiqued in the selection from David J. O'Brien's *Neighborhood Organization and Interest-Group Process.* In the summary chapter excerpted here, O'Brien outlines the set of organizing principles he has developed in response to the difficulties encountered by Alinsky and other "traditional" advocates of collective action. The key assumption made by O'Brien is that the poor must be conceptualized as rational seekers of individual self-interest. This means that they will be reluctant to organize in pursuit of *nonindividual* public goods. Such goods, however, typically constitute the total set of goals for community organizers. Thus, O'Brien concludes that the organization strategies of labor unions and professional groups can provide more useful guides for community development than most reform efforts of the 1960s.

One of the long-standing methods of seeking community change in presumably desirable directions is that of comprehensive planning. Virtually every American city of any considerable size has a planning commission or department which, through controlling the direction of physical growth, seeks to assure that land use, zoning, and other aspects will contribute to community well-being. Walter W. Stafford and Joyce Ladner present a critical review of the relation between comprehensive urban planning and racism. They point out that this relationship has been neglected by blacks and whites alike, and offer reasons why this has been the case. They assert the importance of defining racism and its two aspects, individualized and institutionalized racism, and they give their own definitions. They then proceed to document the manner in which city planning procedures result in decisions which are racist, falling heavily on the black population. They argue that more attention should be given to the racist aspect of such measures, and they note that "if there is any area in which social scientists have failed politicians, planners, and social agencies, it has been their lack of attention to institutional aspects of racism." But more knowledge on the subject will probably not be sufficient to bring about nonracist city planning. One possible means of bringing about such change is through the use of advocacy organizations.

In an important book (*The Structure of Scientific Revolutions,* Chicago:

University of Chicago Press, 1962, 1970), Thomas S. Kuhn asserts that natural science does not develop in incremental fashion, but rather through a series of "revolutions" in which one scientific paradigm, or unifying principle, supplants another. Such paradigms help explain certain problem areas; but since no explanation is capable of accounting for all the data in equally satisfactory fashion, alternative explanations or paradigms arise which themselves are fragmentary.

Although Kuhn confined his analysis to the natural sciences, Roland L. Warren, in the selection included in this section, applies it likewise to the area of social problems. Here, as Valentine, Rose, and others had pointed out, there are alternative "paradigms" for explaining poverty and for addressing it as a social problem. The paradigm which explains poverty in terms of individual deficiency quite understandably takes as its intervention strategy a program of social services to remedy the deficiencies in those who are poor.

The main point of the selection quoted here is that the definition of poverty in terms of individual deficiency and the seeking of a remedy in terms of expanded and better coordinated social services are in turn related to a supporting belief-value system, the specific rationales of the comunity decision organizations involved, their legitimation and power within the community, the characteristics of the interorganizational field within which they interact, and the nature of social research and evaluation. These components comprise an institutionalized thought structure with components of beliefs, organizational structures, technical practices, and social power. The operation of this institutionalized thought structure helps make understandable a number of findings from a nine-city study of the development of Model Cities programs. As an analytical framework, it also provides perspective for assessing programs of social change through coordination of agencies and citizen participation.

In the past three decades, community development has been widely accepted and employed as an effective and desirable method of bringing about community change. It has been variously defined. In the critically evaluative article included here, Shanti K. Khinduka describes it as "a composite of process and program objectives." As a process, it is directed at helping people become more competent, become aware of their potentialities, and work together to achieve them. As a set of program objectives, it is multipurpose, intersectoral in nature. That is, it does not confine itself to one sphere of community interest, such as housing, education, or social services, but rather extends across the whole range of community concern. But its primary emphasis, in the eyes of many experts, including Khinduka, is on process.

Khinduka examines the various aspects of this emphasis on process, thus giving a broad, though critical, overview of the method. It seeks to change attitudes and values of local residents; it avoids overly hasty change, preferring slow growth; it emphasizes decisions and actions based on consensus; it is committed to the broadest possible citizen participation in the change process; it promotes individual identification with the local community. In each of these points of emphasis lie grave defects in community development as a method for bringing about structural social change. At the same time, each of these aspects has its advantages. Khinduka prefers to see these positive aspects as a method of social service rather than of social change. For the latter requires much more attention to the economic factors, to inequities in the local social system, to national institutions, and to the need for bringing about changes even where consensus cannot be achieved.

In their article on "Community Development and Social Justice," William L. Blizek and Jerry Cederblom address a crucial problem. Is the community development worker simply to put himself or herself at the disposal of the local community, to help it carry out its goals whatever these may be? This is the usual assumption, justified by the commitments to local self-determination—that the social change agent should not impose his or her values and goals on the community, but help it develop its own and then carry out a program to implement them. This is the conventional position of the community developer.

Blizek and Cederblom challenge this position. They examine its justification, which is usually based either on the idea of value-neutrality, or on the idea that the community developer should help develop a "healthy" community—surely a noncontroversial objective. The authors examine each of these justifications and find them untenable.

The implication is clear. The community development worker must take a stand on values. The authors point out that since this position has not been widely accepted, there are few guidelines for the value stand which the community development worker should take. By way of opening the issue further, they give as a possible guideline the principles which John Rawls laid down in his book *A Theory of Justice*.

33

The dynamics of community controversy

James S. Coleman

The most striking fact about the development and growth of community controversies is the similarity they exhibit despite diverse underlying sources and different kinds of precipitating incidents. Once the controversies have begun, they resemble each other remarkably. Were it not for these similarities, Machiavelli could never

have written his guide to warfare, and none of the other numerous works on conflict, dispute, and controversy would have been possible.[1] It is the peculiarity of social controversy that it sets in motion its own

Reprinted with permission of Macmillan Publishing Co., Inc., from *Community Conflict*, by James S. Coleman, pp. 9–14. Copyright © 1957 by The Free Press, a Corporation. Some footnotes have been renumbered.

[1] The one man who emphasized particularly the possibility of abstracting principles of conflict from particular situations of conflict is Georg Simmel, who wrote several essays on the subject. Unfortunately, Simmel never got around to writing a comprehensive theory of conflict, though he did set down a number of insights into particular aspects. See Simmel (1955). Lewis Coser has brought together the best of Simmel's insights and elaborated on them (Coser, 1956).

dynamics; these tend to carry it forward in a path which bears little relation to its beginnings. An examination of these dynamics will occupy the attention of this chapter.

One caution is necessary: we do not mean to suggest that nothing can be done about community controversy once it begins. To the contrary, the dynamics of controversy *can* be interrupted and diverted— either by conscious action or by existing conditions in the community. As a result, although the same dynamic tendencies of controversy are found in every case, the actual development in particular cases may differ widely. In the discussion below, the unrestrained dynamic tendencies will be discussed. . . .

CHANGES IN ISSUES

The issues which provide the initial basis of response in a controversy undergo great transformations as the controversy develops. Three fundamental transformations appear to take place.

Specific to general

First, specific issues give way to *general* ones. In Scarsdale, the school's critics began by attacking books in the school library; soon they focused on the whole educational philosophy. In Mason City, Iowa, where a city-manager plan was abandoned, the campaign against the plan started with a letter to the newspaper from a local carpenter complaining that the creek overflowed into his home. This soon snowballed, gathering other specific complaints, and then gave way to the general charge that the council and manager were dominated by local business interests and had no concern for the workingman.

Most of the controversies examined show a similar pattern. (Even those that do not are helpful, for they suggest just why the pattern *does* exist in so many cases. Political controversies, for example, ex-

hibit the pattern much less than do disputes based primarily on differing values or economic interests. The Athens, Tennessee, political fight began with the same basic issue it ended with—political control of the community (Key, 1950). Other political struggles in which there is little popular involvement show a similar restriction to the initial issue.)

It seems that movement from specific to general issues occurs whenever there are deep cleavages of values or interests in the community which require a spark to set them off—usually a specific incident representing only a small part of the underlying difference. In contrast, those disputes which appear not to be generated by deep cleavages running through the community as a whole, but are rather power struggles within the community, do not show the shift from specific to general. To be sure, they may come to involve the entire community, but no profound fundamental difference comes out.

This first shift in the nature of the issues, then, uncovers the fundamental differences which set the stage for a precipitating incident in the first place.

New and different issues

Another frequent change in the issues of the dispute is the emergence of quite *new and different* issues, unrelated to the original ones. In the Pasadena school controversy, the initial issue was an increased school budget and a consequent increased tax rate. This soon became only one issue of many; ideological issues concerning "progressive education," and other issues, specific as well as general, arose. In another case, a controversy which began as a personal power struggle between a school superintendent and a principal shifted to a conflict involving general educational principles when the community as a whole entered in (Warner et al., 1949, pp. 201–204). A study of the adoption of the city-manager plan in 50 cities (Stone, Price, and Stone, 1940, pp. 34–38) shows that in one group of cities, designated by the authors "machine-ridden," the controversy grew to include ethnic, religious, political, and ideological differences. Political campaigns generally, in fact, show this tendency: issues multiply rapidly as the campaign increases in intensity.

There are two different sources for this diversification of issues. One is in a sense "involuntary"; issues which could not have been raised before the controversy spring suddenly to the fore as relationships between groups and individuals change. We see how this operates in an argument between two people, e.g., in the common phrases used to introduce new issues: "I hesitated to mention this before but now . . . ." or, "While I'm at it, I might as well say this too. . . ." As long as functioning relations exist between individuals or groups, there are strong inhibitions upon introducing any issue which might impair the functioning. In a sense the stable relation suppresses topics which might upset it. But once the stability of the relation *is* upset, the suppressed topics can come to the surface uninhibitedly. We suggest that exactly the same mechanisms are at work in the community as a whole; networks of relations, however complex, act in the same fashion.

But in many other cases, illustrated best by political disputes, the diversification of issues is more a purposive move on the part of the antagonists, and serves quite a different function: to solidify opinion and bring in new participants by providing new bases of reponse. Again, this is evident in the two-person argument: each antagonist brings to bear all the *different* arguments he can to rationalize his position to himself and to convince his opponent. Just the same thing occurs in community conflict: each side attempts to increase solidarity and win new adherents from the still uncommitted neutrals by introducing as many diverse issues as will benefit its cause. Both these functions—

increasing solidarity among present members, and gaining new members—are vital; the first aids in the important task of "girding for action" by disposing of all doubts and hesitancies; the second gains allies, always an important aim in community conflict.

The issues introduced must be very special ones with little potential for disrupting the group that initiates them. They are almost always "one-sided" in the sense that they provide a basis for response only in one direction, and they gain their value by monopolizing the attention of community members. In controversies where a challenge is offered to an incumbent administration, the issue of "maladministration" is, typically, a one-sided issue; the administration can only offer defense and hope that attention soon shifts elsewhere. In school controversies, the issue of Communist subversion in the schools is one-sided; as long as it occupies the attention of the community, it is to the advantage of school critics. In contrast, the issue "progressive education versus traditional education" offers no differential advantage to either side (unless, of course, progressive education can be identified by its opponents as "Communistic") until one group can prove to the majority of the community that one approach is better from all points of view. Analysis of the different functions of different kinds of issues can be found in Berelson, Lazarsfeld, and McPhee (1954), and in Coleman (1955, p. 253).

Disagreement to antagonism

A third change in the nature of issues as a controversy develops is the shift from *disagreement* to *antagonism*. A dispute which began dispassionately, in a disagreement over issues, is characterized suddenly by personal slander, by rumor, by the focusing of direct hostility. This is one of the most important aspects in the self-generation of conflict: Once set in mo-

322

FIGURE 33-1

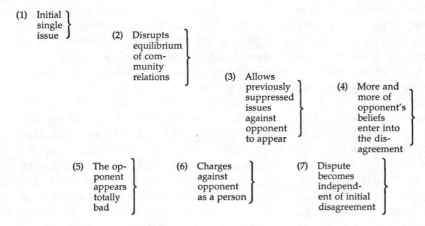

tion, hostility can sustain conflict unaided by disagreement about particular issues. The original issues may be settled, yet the controversy continues unabated. The antagonistic relationship has become direct: it no longer draws sustenance from an outside element—an issue. As in an argument between friends, a discussion which begins with *disagreement* on a point in question often ends with each *disliking* the other.[2] The dynamics which account for the shift from disagreement to antagonism are two: "involuntary," and deliberate. Simmel explains the involuntary process by saying that it is "expedient" and "appropriate" to hate one's opponent just as it is "appropriate" to like someone who agrees with you (1955, p. 34). But perhaps there is a stronger explanation: we associ-

ate with every person we know certain beliefs, interests, traits, attributes, etc. So long as we disagree with only one or a few of his beliefs, we are "divided" in our feelings toward him. He is not wholly black or white in our eyes. But when we quarrel, the process of argument itself generates new issues; we disagree with more and more of our opponent's beliefs. Since these beliefs constitute *him* in our eyes, rather than isolated aspects of him, his image grows blacker. Our hostility is directed toward him personally. Thus the two processes—the first leading from a single issue to new and different ones, and the second leading from disagreement to direct antagonism—fit together perfectly and help carry the controversy along its course.[3] Once direct antagonism is felt toward an opponent, one is led to make public attacks on him.

Perhaps it would be fruitful to set down a little more precisely the "involuntary" processes which we suggest operate to shift issues from one disagreement to a multitude, ultimately to antagonism. In a

---

[2] Conversely, a relationship which begins with two people *agreeing* in tastes and interests often ends with both *liking one another*. For a discussion of the process through which this occurs, see Merton and Lazarsfeld (1954).

Georg Simmel notes the formal similarities between relations of positive and negative attachments, contrasting these with the *absence* of relationship. He suggests that the psychological processes generating antagonism are just as fundamental as those generating linking. Simmel also notes the difference between a negative relationship based on disagreement over an outside object, and one which needs no such object, but is directly antagonistic. See Simmel (1955, p. 34, 36, passim), and Coser (1956).

---

[3] It should be emphasized that these suggestions for processes are highly tentative; systematic research into the psychological dynamics involved in these changing relations would contribute greatly to our knowledge about the development of controversy.

diagram it might look something like Figure 33–1.

Men have a strong need for *consistency.* If I disagree violently with someone, then it becomes psychologically more comfortable to see him as totally black rather than gray.[4] This drive for consistency may provide the fuel for the generalization processes in Steps 3 and 4 of Figure 33.1.

Apart from these "involuntary" or "natural" processes, the use of personal charges by the antagonists is a common device to bypass disagreement and go directly to antagonism. Sometimes consciously, often unconsciously, the opposing nuclei attempt to reach new people through this means, drawing more and more of the community to their side by creating personal hostility to the opponent.[5] In political disputes the degeneration to personal charges is particularly frequent. V. O. Key notes that in the South, state political campaigns are often marked by candidates' personal attacks on each other. He suggests that such attacks grow in the absence of "real" issues (1950,

pp. 194–200). This seems reasonable since the use of personal attacks may be an attempt to incite antagonism in cases where there is not enough disagreement for the natural processes of conflict to operate. In other words, the attacks constitute an attempt to stimulate controversy artificially —a "shortcut"—by bypassing a stage in the process which might otherwise let the conflict falter. Such actions would seem to occur only when community leaders need to gain the support of an otherwise apathetic community which has no real issues dividing it.

In another group of controversies, focused around certain value differences, the shift to personal attacks is sometimes immediate, and seems to be a result of real disagreement and incipient antagonism. School controversies often begin with personal charges against teachers or principals of moral impropriety or, more frequently in recent days, subversion. Why is it that personal attacks in these instances succeed in creating immediate hostility within the community, while other kinds of personal attacks are viewed with disfavor by the community, that is, until the late, intense stages of controversy when all inhibiting norms and constraints are forgotten? The reason may be this: When a personal accusation refers to behavior viewed as extremely illegitimate by community members, it outweighs the norm against personal attacks. Presumably the community members put themselves in the place of the attacker and say, in effect, "If I knew these things to be true, would I feel right about speaking out publicly?" When the charges concern sexual immorality or political subversion, many persons can answer "yes" to such a question,[6] thus

---

[4] One might speculate that this tendency would be stronger among those who tend to personalize easily; they move more quickly perhaps from specific disagreement to hostility toward the opponent as a whole. Feuds among hill people (who are highly "person-oriented"), for example, seem to bear this out. Thus the course of controversy may vary greatly in two communities, simply as a result of differences in "person-orientation."

[5] The general process by which new people respond to such appeals is discussed more fully later under the heading "Social relations as a basis of response."

Whether or not persons previously neutral can be brought into the controversy seems to depend greatly upon the time at which they are confronted with the alternative. If the antagonists are too involved too early they are viewed with puzzlement and distaste and detachment by neutrals. The situation is much the same as confronts a man arriving sober in the middle of a drunken party: he cannot join in because these people are "too far gone" for him to experience the events of the party as they do. The similarity between an orgy of community controversy and a drunken orgy is more than superficial in this and other respects. People collectively "forget themselves" in ways they may be ashamed of later. One of the major questions of community conflict concerns the processes through which this "forgetting" occurs.

[6] It is a matter of the relative strengths of different values: some, like those against immorality and subversion, override the values against personal slander. If we knew the relative strength of certain social values among various segments of the population, we would be far better able to judge the course of controversy ranged around a certain issue. But we lack even methods for measurement.

they feel unconcerned about making the kind of attacks that they would ordinarily never allow except in the heat of dispute.[7] These attacks, in turn, quickly create the heat that might otherwise be slow in coming.

Changes in content and character of issues constitutes only one kind of change going on in the development of a controversy; at the same time, the whole structure of organizations and associations in the community is undergoing change as well. The nature of these changes is examined below.

CHANGES IN THE SOCIAL ORGANIZATION OF THE COMMUNITY

Polarization of social relations

As controversy develops, associations flourish *within* each group but wither *between* persons on opposing sides. People break off long-standing relationships, stop speaking to former friends who have been drawn to the opposition, but proliferate their associations with fellow-partisans. Again, this is part of the process of stripping for action: getting rid of all social encumbrances which impede the action necessary to win the conflict. Polarization is perhaps less pronounced in short-term conflicts, and in those in which the issues cut across existing organizational ties and informal relations. But in all conflicts, it tends to alter the social geography of the community, to separate it into two clusters, breaking apart along the line of least attachment. . . .

---

[7] In contrast to "putting oneself in the place of the attacker," those who hold civil liberties to be of great importance evidently put themselves in the place of the attacked, and ask themselves how it would feel to be unjustly charged in this fashion. It appears that the *variations in relative values* between these two groups cause them to identify with opposing parties in a case of such charges. Thus they are immediately brought in on one side or the other in such a dispute.

The formation of partisan organizations

In many types of community conflict, there are no existing organizations to form the nuclei of the two sides. But as the controversy develops, organizations form. In a recent controversy in Cincinnati over the left-wing political history of the city planning director (Hessler, 1953), supporters of the director and of the councilman who hired him formed a "Committee of 150 for Political Morality." This Committee used considerable sophistication in the selection of a name and in their whole campaign. Rather than remain on the defensive, and let the opposition blanket the community with charges of subversion, this committee invoked an equally strong value—of morality in politics—and took the offensive against the use of personal attack by their opponents. This technique constitutes a way in which controversy can be held on a relatively high plane: by involving community norms against smears, using these very norms as an issue of controversy. If the norm is strong, it may keep the controversy "within bounds."

In general, as a dispute intensifies the partisans form ad hoc groups, which have numerous functions while the controversy lasts: they serve as communication centers, as communication becomes more and more important within each side and attenuates between groups; they serve as centers for planning and organizing partisan meetings and other activities; and especially they can meet quickly—in a situation where speed is of utmost importance —any threat or challenge posed by the opposition.

The most common variation upon this theme is the union; in industrial disputes, the union is a defense organization *already* in existence; in a real controversy, it takes on all the aspects of the usual partisan organizations: secrecy, spirited meetings, pamphleteering, [and] fundraising.[8]

---

[8] See Pope's (1942) graphic account of union operations in Gastonia, North Carolina, and Jones's (1941) discussion of union activity in Akron.

The Emergence of new leaders

As partisan organizations are formed and a real nucleus develops around each of the opposing centers, new leaders tend to take over the dispute; often they are men who have not been community leaders in the past, men who face none of the constraints of maintaining a previous community position, and feel none of the cross-pressures felt by members of community organizations. In addition, these leaders rarely have real identification with the community. In the literature they often emerge as marginal men who have never held a position of leadership before. A study of the fight against city-manager plans pictures the leaders of the opposition as men personally frustrated and maladjusted (Stene and Floro, 1953, pp. 21–39). The current desegregation fights have produced numerous such leaders, often young, one a former convict, usually from the outside. (*Life*, 1954; *Southern School News*, 1956.)

The new leaders, at any rate, are seldom moderates; the situation itself calls for extremists. And such men have not been conditioned, through experience in handling past community problems, to the prevailing norms concerning tactics of dispute.

One counter-tendency appears in the development of these organizations and the emergence of their leaders. In certain conflicts, e.g., in Cincinnati, one side will be composed primarily of community leaders, men of prestige and responsibility in the community. Though such groups carry on the functions of a partisan organization, they act not to lower the level of controversy but to *maintain* or raise it. As did the Committee of 150 (and the ADA in Norwalk, Connecticut, and other groups in other controversies), they attempt to invoke the community's norms against personal attacks and unrestrained conflict. Sometimes (as in Cincinnati) they are successful, sometimes not.

In the face of all the pressures toward increasing intensity and freedom from normal constraint this last development is puzzling. The source of the reversal seems to be this: in certain controversies (particularly those having to do with the accusation of subversion), one side derives much of its strength from personal attacks and derogation, that is, from techniques which, were they not legitimated by patriotism or sex codes or similar strong values, would be outlawed by the community. Thus, to the degree that such methods are permitted, the attackers gain; and to the degree that community norms are upheld against these methods, the advantage is to the attacked. The more the attacked side can invoke the norms defining legitimate controversy, the more likely it is to win.

Invocation of community constraints is almost the sole force *generated by the conflict itself* which acts in a restraining direction. It is a very special force, which appears to operate *only* under the conditions discussed above. Even so, it represents one means by which some controversies may be contained within bounds of normal community decision making.

Community organizations as the controversy develops

As conflict develops, the community's organizations tend to be drawn in, just as individual members are. It may be the American Legion, the PTA, the church, the local businessmen's association; if its members are drawn into the controversy, or if it can lend useful support, the organization will be under pressure from one or both sides to enter the controversy. This varies, of course, with the nature of the organization and the nature of the dispute.

At the same time there are often strong pressures, both within the organization and without, to remain neutral. From within: if its members hold opposing sentiments, then their disharmony forces the organization itself to remain neutral. And from without: the organization must maintain a public position in the community which might be endangered by taking sides in a partisan battle threatening to split the community.

Examples of internal and external constraints on community organizations and leaders are not hard to find. In the Denver school controversy a few years ago, the County PTA felt constrained to dissociate itself publicly from the criticisms of the school system made by their retiring president (Martin, 1951). In Hastings, New York, the positions were reversed: the school administration and teachers remained neutral while a battle raged over the PTA election (McPhee, 1954). Similarly, in the strike in Gastonia, North Carolina, local ministers felt constrained not to take a public position (Pope, 1942, p. 283). If they had done so, the course of the strike might have been quite different as religious matters entered in explicitly. In some fights over the city-manager plan, businessmen's associations tried to keep out because the plan was already under attack for its alliance with business interests (Stene and Floro, 1953, p. 60); and in at least one fluoridation controversy, doctors and dentists were reluctant to actively support the fluoridation plan, singly or as a group, because of possible community disfavor affecting business (Mausner, 1955).[9] In another case, union leaders who had originally helped elect a school board could not bring their organizations to support a superintendent the board had ap-

pointed when he was accused of "progressivism" and favoritism to ethnic minorities. Their own members were too strongly split on the issue (McKee, 1953, p. 244). Ministers who were in favor of allowing Negro children to use the community house were influenced by the beliefs of influential members of their churches not to take a stand (Inquiry, 1929, pp. 58–59). Even in Scarsdale, which was united behind its school board, the Town Club incurred disfavor with a minority of its members, who supported the school's critics, for taking as strong a stand as it did.

In sum, both community organizations and community leaders are faced with constraints when a dispute arises; the formation of a combat group to carry on the controversy and the emergence of a previous unknown as the combat leader are in part results of the immobility of responsible organizations and leaders. Both the new leader and the new organization are freed from some of the usual shackles of community norms and internal cross-pressures which make pre-existing organizations and leaders tend to soften the dispute.

The immobility of organizations resulting from a lack of internal (or sometimes external) consensus is one element which varies according to the kind of issue involved. This is best exemplified by different issues in national politics: when the issue is an economic one, e.g., Taft-Hartley legislation, groups mobilize on each side of the economic fence; labor unions and allied organizations versus the National Association of Manufacturers, trade associations, and businesses themselves. When the issue has to do with tariffs, the composition of each side is different,[10] but there is still a mobilization of

---

[9] There is some evidence that men in certain occupations are more sensitive than others to public opinion and thus less willing to commit themselves to either side and less able to hold on to a position of principle. On the Pasadena school board, the two members most sensitive to the mass mood were a retail merchant and an undertaker (both, it should be noted, like doctors and dentists, have a retail product to sell) (Hurlburd, 1950, p. 31 ff.). This and other evidence leads to the hypothesis that persons who have a clientele or set of retail customers in town cannot generally be trusted to stand up against a majority though they believe in the cause. Or even more generally, it seems that such men cannot *start* a controversy, since the initiator is always in a minority; neither can they continue against the initiator once he has gained the majority.

[10] Sometimes labor unions and trade associations find themselves on the same side of the fence. The issue over an increase in watch tariffs saw the watchmakers' union and the manufacturers on the same side: both opposed a principle laid down by a tariff commission headed by the president of a steel company.

organizations on both sides. Sometimes the issue cuts directly across the organizations and institutions in society, thus immobilizing them, e.g., "McCarthyism," which blossomed such a short time ago. Labor unions never opposed McCarthy—their members were split. The Democratic party never opposed him—its constituency was split. Few of the powerful institutions in the country had enough internal consensus to oppose McCarthy. As it was, he drew his followers from all walks of life and from all levels of society. The cross-pressures resulting from lack of internal group consensus were reinforced by external pressures against opposing McCarthy, for all the values of patriotism were invoked by his forces. Almost the only organizations with neither internal nor external pressure against taking sides were the professionally patriotic groups like the American Legion and the DAR. If the issue had not immobilized labor unions and the Democratic party, then opposition to McCarthy would have been much more effective.[11]

The increasing use of word-of-mouth communication

As the controversy proceeds, the formal media of communication—radio, television, and newspapers—become less and less able to tell people *as much* as they want to know about the controversy, or the *kinds of things* they want to know. These media are simply not flexible enough to fill the insatiable need for news which develops as people become more and more involved. At the same time, the media are restricted by normative and legal constraints against carrying the kind of rumor which abounds as controversy proceeds. Word-of-mouth communication gradually fills the gaps, both in volume and in content, left by the mass media. Street-corner discussion amplifies, elaborates, and usually distorts the news that it picks up from the papers or the radio. This interpersonal communication offers no restraints against slander and personal charges; rather, it helps make the rhetoric of controversy consistent with the intensity.

SUMMARY

Several characteristic events carry the controversy toward its climax. The most important changes in *issues* are: *(a)* from specific disagreements to more general ones, *(b)* elaboration into new and different disagreements, and *(c)* a final shift from disagreement to direct antagonism. The changes in the *social organization* of the community are as follows: the polarization of social relations as the controversy intensifies, as the participants cut off relations with those who are not on their side, and elaborate relations with those who are; the formation of partisan organizations and the emergence of new, often extremist partisan leaders to wage the war more efficiently; and the mobilization of existing community organizations on one side or the other. Finally, as the pace quickens and the issues become personal, word-of-mouth communication replaces the more formal media. It now remains to examine some of the reciprocal causations constituting the "vicious circles" or "runaway processes" so evident in conflict. These should give somewhat more insight into the mechanisms responsible for the growth of conflict.

RECIPROCAL CAUSATION AND THE DEVELOPING DISPUTE

The inner dynamics of controversy derive from a number of mutually reinforcing relations; one element is enhanced by another, and, in turn, enhances the first,

---

[11] Interestingly, what is at one time an aid is at another time a hindrance: a movement with little organizational opposition also has little organizational support, and finds it difficult to become institutionalized without a coup.

creating an endless spiral.[12] Some of the most important relations depend heavily upon this reciprocal reinforcement; if one or more of these cycles can be *broken*, then a disagreement already on the way to real conflict can be diverted into normal channels.

Mutual reinforcement of response

Relations between people contain a built-in reciprocity. I smile at you; if you smile back, I speak to you; you respond, and a relationship has begun. At each step, my reaction is contingent upon yours, and yours, in turn, contingent upon mine.[13] If you fail to smile, but scowl instead; I may say a harsh word; you respond in kind, and another chain of mutual reinforcement builds up—this time toward antagonism. It is such chains which constitute not only the fundamental character of interpersonal relations, but also the fundamental cycle of mutual effects in controversy. Breaking that cycle requires much effort. The admonition to "turn the other cheek" is not easily obeyed.

The direct reinforcement of response, however, is but one—the most obvious—of the mutually reinforcing relations which constitute the dynamics of controversy. Others, more tenuous, are more easily broken.

The mutual effects of social and psychological polarization

As participants in a dispute become psychologically "consistent," shedding doubts and hesitancies, they shun friends who are uncommitted and elaborated their associations with those who feel the way they do. In effect, the psychological polarization leads to social polarization. The latter, in turn, leads to mutual reinforcement of opinions, that is, to further psychological polarization. One agrees more and more with his associates (and disagrees more and more with those he *doesn't* talk to), and comes to associate more and more with those who agree with him. Increasingly, his opponents' position seems preposterous—and, in fact, it *is* preposterous, as is his own; neither position feeds on anything but reinforcing opinions.

The outcome, of course, is the division of the community into two socially and attitudinally separate camps, each convinced it is absolutely right. The lengths to which this continually reinforcing cycle will go in any particular case depends on the characteristics of the people and the community involved. . . . It is these characteristics which provide one "handle" for reducing the intensity of community conflict.

Polarization and intensity: Within the individual and within each side

As the participants become psychologically polarized, all their attitudes mutually reinforcing, the *intensity* of their feeling increases. One of the consequences is that inconsistencies within the individual are driven out; thus he becomes even more psychologically polarized, in turn developing a greater intensity.

This chain of mutual enforcement lies completely *within* the individual. But there is an analogous chain of reinforcement on the social level. As social polarization occurs (that is, the proliferation of associations among those who feel one way, and the attenuation of association between those who feel differently), one's statements meet more and more with a positive response; one is more and more free to

---

[12] The dynamics of controversy is a topic for the theoretician in sociology: it comes as close as any area of social life to constituting a closed system, in which all the effects are from variables within the system. When a theory of controversy does exist, the sets of mutually reinforcing relations like those examined in this section will constitute the heart of the theory.

[13] Talcott Parsons (1951, p. 36) who studies this characteristic of interpersonal relations in detail, speaks of it as the "double-contingency of interpersonal relations." Parsons has a full discussion of this aspect of relations between persons.

express the full intensity of his feeling. The "atmosphere" of the group is open for the kind of intensity of feeling that previously had to remain unexpressed. This atmosphere of intensity, in turn, further refines the group; it becomes intolerable that anyone who believes differently maintain association within the group.

These are examples of reciprocal causation in community conflict, as they appear in the literature of these controversies. They constitute the chains which carry controversy from beginning to end as long as they remain unbroken, but which also provide the means of softening the conflict if methods can be found to break them. It is important to note that these reciprocal relations, once set in motion by outside forces, become independent of them and continue on their own. The one continuing force at work is the drive of each side to win, which sets in motion the processes described above; it carries the conflict forward "under its own steam," so to speak. But reciprocal relations also affect the initial drive, amplifying it, changing it; no longer is it simply a drive to win, but an urge to ruin the opponents, strip them of their power, in effect, annihilate them. This shift in goals, itself a part of a final chain of reciprocal causation, drives these processes onward with ever more intensity.

Gresham's law of conflict

The processes may be said to create a "Gresham's Law of Conflict": the harmful and dangerous elements drive out those which would keep the conflict within bounds. Reckless, unrestrained leaders head the attack; combat organizations arise to replace the milder, more constrained preexisting organizations; derogatory and scurrilous charges replace dispassionate issues; antagonism replaces disagreement; and a drive to ruin the opponent takes the place of the initial will to win. In other words, all the forces put into effect by the initiation of conflict act to drive out the conciliatory elements and replace them with those better equipped for combat.

In only one kind of case—exemplified best by the Cincinnati fight in which one side formed the "Committee of 150 for Political Morality"—"Gresham's Law of Conflict" did not hold. As we have said, it was to the *advantage* of that side—not altruism—to invoke against the opponents the community norms which ordinarily regulate a disagreement.

Yet a rather insistent question remains to be answered: if all these forces work in the direction of increasing intensity, how is it that community conflicts stop short of annihilation? After all, community conflicts *are* inhibited, yet the processes above give no indication how. Forces *do* exist which can counteract these processes and bring the dispute into orderly channels— forces which are for the most part products of preexisting community characteristics, and may be thought of here as constituting a third side in the struggle.[14] Primarily this "third force" preserves the community from division and acts as a "governor" to keep all controversies below a certain intensity.

In part the variations in these forces in the community are responsible for the wide variation in the intensity of community conflicts. Thus, a conflict which reaches extreme proportions in one community would be easily guided into quieter channels in another.

Certain attributes of the community's leadership, techniques which are used— or not used—at crucial points to guide the dispute into more reasonable channels, also affect the development of conflict. These methods, along with the pre-existing community attributes, constitute the means by which a disagreement which threatens to disrupt the community can be kept within bounds. . . .

---

[14]This is not to say that some of these forces are not *within* the partisans themselves. Insofar as this is true, it leads to one of the important mechanisms by which conflict can be restrained.

REFERENCES

Berelson, Bernard, Lazarsfeld, Paul F., and McPhee, William. *Voting*. Chicago: University of Chicago Press, 1954.

Coleman, James. "Political Cleavage within the International Typographical Union." Ph.D. dissertation, Columbia University, 1955.

Coser, Lewis. *The Functions of Social Conflict*. Glencoe, Ill.: The Free Press, 1956.

Hessler, William H. "It Didn't Work in Cincinnati." *The Reporter* 9 (December 22, 1953), pp. 13–17.

Hurlburd, David. *This Happened in Pasadena*. New York: Macmillan, 1950.

Inquiry. *Community Conflict*. New York: The Inquiry, 1929.

Jones, Alfred W. *Life, Liberty, and Property*. Philadelphia: Lippincott, 1941.

Key, V. O., Jr. *Southern Politics*. New York: Knopf, 1950.

"Outsider Stirs Up Small Town Trouble." *Life* 36 (October 11, 1954), pp. 45–46.

Martin, Lawrence. "Denver, Colorado." *Saturday Review* ("The Public School Crisis") 34 (September 8, 1951), pp. 6–20.

Mausner, Bernard and Judith. "A Study of the Anti-Scientific Attitude." *Scientific American* 192 (February 1955), pp. 35–39.

McKee, James B. "Organized Labor and Community Decision-making: A Study in the Sociology of Power." Ph.D. dissertation, University of Wisconsin, 1953.

McPhee, William. "Community Controversies Affecting Personal Liberties and Institutional Freedoms in Education." Unpublished memorandum, Columbia University, Bureau of Applied Social Research, July 1954.

Merton, Robert K., and Lazarsfeld, Paul F. "Friendship as a Social Process." In *Freedom and Control in Modern Society*, ed. Monroe Berger, Theodore Abel, and Charles Page. New York: Van Nostrand, 1954.

Parsons, Talcott. *The Social System*. Glencoe: The Free Press, 1951.

Pope, Liston. *Millhands and Preachers*. New Haven: Yale University Press, 1942.

Simmel, Georg. *Conflict and The Web of Intergroup Affiliations*. Glencoe, Ill.: The Free Press, 1955.

Southern School News 3 (October 1956), p. 15.

Stene, Edwin K., and Floro, George K. *Abandonment of the Manager Plan*. Lawrence, Kansas: University of Kansas, 1953.

Stone, Harold S. Price, Don K., and Stone, Kathryn H. *City Manager Government in the United States*. Chicago: Public Administration Service, 1940.

Warner, W. Lloyd and Associates. *Democracy in Jonesville*. New York: Harper, 1949.

34

Alinsky reconsidered: A reluctant community theorist

Donald C. Reitzes and Dietrich C. Reitzes

A recent review of the treatment of the works of Saul D. Alinsky in the social sciences (Reitzes and Reitzes, 1980) suggests

Reprinted with permission from the authors and The University of Texas Press from "Alinsky Reconsidered: A Reluctant Community Theorist" *Social Science Quarterly* 63, no. 2 (June 1982), pp. 256–79.

that he was widely known and frequently cited: (1) as a social and academic critic, for comments such as his description of the War on Poverty as political pornography (Alinsky, 1965) or his observation that, "Asking a sociologist to solve a problem is like prescribing an enema for diarrhea (Alinsky, 1972: 64);" (2) for the notoriety and actions of his community organizations; and, (3) as an advocate for urban social change and the use of nonviolent conflict. There have also been in-depth studies of the activities and assessments of Alinsky organizations (Haggstrom, 1964; Silberman, 1964; Sherrard and Murray, 1965; Irvine, 1967; Bailey, 1972; Fish, 1973). What appears less well recognized and often masked by Alinsky's flamboyance is the theoretical orientation which underlies his specific organizational strategies and community actions.

While Alinsky probably would have scoffed at the label of theorist, his analysis of community demonstrates an implicit grasp of urban processes and structures. An awareness of Alinsky, beyond the recognition of his masterful use of tactics and strategies, broadens the appreciation of his diverse contribution to urban social science. A community of limited liability perspective (Janowitz, 1952; Suttles, 1968; Hunter and Suttles, 1972; Hunter, 1974) will be used to highlight and organize Alinsky's theoretical insights. Embedded in Alinsky's rhetoric, observations, and rules for organizers is the recognition of: (1) the complex and multifaceted character of urban social structure; (2) the need to purposively generate and continuously support community-wide ties and attachments; and (3) the use of conflict to heighten cohesiveness within the community and to create an organization capable of effectively defending local interests in bargaining with external institutions. Alinsky community organizations provide a broad and diverse set of cases which may be used to assess some of the central features of a community of limited liability perspective as well as extending its practical implications.

One of the negative implications of Alinsky's alienation from academic social science was a "frozen" picture of urban political science and sociology, more appropriate to the 1930s and 1940s than to the present. The use of current concepts, such as a community of limited liability perspective, to clarify Alinsky's underlying approach may aid in the training of organizers and in the evaluation of community organizations (Irvine, 1967; Bailey, 1972; Lancourt, 1979). In one of his last works, Alinsky (1971: 68) noted that he probably failed more times than he succeeded in training organizers. A possible source of his difficulty was that he failed to link his understanding of community with his organizational strategies. A community of limited liability provides a model of local community which is compatible with Alinsky's insights and may aid in the clarification and interpretation of his strategies to community organizers. In the sections to follow, Alinsky's community theory will be developed around the issues of local community social structure, the construction of local attachments, and community power.

COMMUNITY SOCIAL STRUCTURE

Community of limited liability

A community of limited liability approach states that local communities are neither complete local social systems, based on an ever-expanding set of complementary and supporting social ties, nor that local communities have been completely replaced by city-wide or national ties (Janowitz, 1952). Instead, advocates of the perspective maintained that community is a "uniquely linked unit of social/spatial organization between the forces and institutions of the larger society and localized routines of individuals in their everyday lives" (Hunter, 1979: 269). Hunter and Suttles (1972: 47–48) argue that the advantage of Janowitz's conception of community of limited liability is two-fold. On the one hand, it points "to the importance of local voluntary associations as a response to issues broader than those particular to an isolated area. . . .

On the other hand, the community of limited liability provides a way of understanding the partial or incomplete involvement of people in their individual areas."

Suttles and Hunter (1972) extend earlier analyses (Greer, 1962; Suttles, 1968) to form four partial and overlapping levels of social participation and involvement. *Faceblocks* range from children's peer groups to adult block clubs and comprise networks of acquaintances known through the sharing of residence and common usage of local facilities. *Defended neighborhoods* reflect the fear of invasion from adjacent community areas, such as vigilante citizen groups, street-corner gangs, conservation committees, and local consumer groups. *Communities of limited liability* reflect service and district boundaries of city-wide and large-scale extracommunity organizations. The overlapping boundaries of police districts, school districts, and church parishes form the distinctive characteristic of communities of limited liability. Since there are often two or more such districts, residents frequently find their interests divided. Action on behalf of the community of limited liability becomes specialized and self-consciously oriented towards limited issues (Hunter and Suttles, 1972: 59). *Expanded communities* of limited liability are larger areas composed of multiple communities whose boundaries are imposed by external organizations and institutions. While local residents' initial identification here is weak, these areas become increasingly important due to the centralization of decision making. The community of limited liability approach provides a general scheme for the analysis of local structure. However, it does not provide guidelines for the analysis of the process by which a community can deal effectively with outside forces.

Alinsky

While Alinsky never developed a typology of community social structure, his observations complement and foreshadow a community of limited liability perspective. Alinsky saw that local community reflects larger social processes and that the internal organization contains multiple, partial, and fragmented networks of organizations and groups. As early as 1941, Alinsky criticized traditional community organizations and neighborhood councils for assuming that local communities are social, political, and economic entities which are more or less insulated from the general social scene. Alinsky (1941: 807) pointed out that unlike other community organizations, his Back of the Yards Neighborhood Council made residents aware that "many of their problems stem from sources far removed from their own community" and that the council itself became concerned with national issues. Underlying the criticism of traditional community organizations was Alinsky's recognition that local communities are not autonomous social units but are directly related to larger social structures and reflect local responses to the external social environment.

Alinsky's understanding of the complex character of local community social structure was revealed in his advice to organizers. Alinsky cautioned organizers to dismiss a simplistic and inaccurate assumption that slums are disorganized or without patterns of social interaction. Such an assumption would lead to the expectations that residents of a local community may be merely indifferent to community-wide organization and that once isolated individuals are aroused and enlightened, that community organization may be expected to proceed smoothly and without local opposition. Instead he suggested an alternative initial assumption:

The ghetto or slum in which the organizer is organizing is not a disorganized community. It is a contradiction in terms to use the two words "disorganization" and "community" together: the word community itself means an organized, communal life; people living in an organized fashion. The people in the community may have experienced successive frustrations to the point that their will to participate has seemed to atrophy. . . . Call it organized apathy or organized nonparticipation, but that is their community pattern. They are living under a certain set of arrangements, standards, way of life (Alinsky, 1971:115–16).

Organized apathy reflects Alinsky's awareness that local communities may contain traditions and interaction patterns which are not only indifferent but potentially are antagonistic to community-wide organization.

The implications of organized apathy and local social patterns influence community organization in a number of ways. First, Alinsky (1946: 66) noted that social service agencies and traditional community organizations tend to apply conventional standards of status in their selection of local representatives which overlook the more personalistic and local standards of status used by neighborhood residents in their selection of leaders. While local professionals may possess a legitimate claim to being native to the community, they may not have valid claims to local leadership. These professionals may not be viewed as sharing the hopes, desires, and aspirations of local residents. Alinsky cited Whyte's (1943) study of Cornerville as a case where residents prefer local leaders, whose expectations and behaviors are consistent with their own custom, even if the local leaders cannot offer services provided by external agencies. Along the same lines, an outside organizer may antagonize residents by failing to be aware of local standards of proper behavior. As examples, Alinsky (1946: 78–79) pointed to the "tolerance" of drinking and gambling in a Catholic neighborhood, and the "strict" moral standards in a Protestant neighborhood. Thus, indifference and opposition to an organizer or organization may not be due to the absence of local involvement but to the presence of community traditions and customs. Alinsky's

advice to organizers implied an awareness of potential provincialism.

Alinsky's (1946:64–75) discussion of local leadership highlights his recognition that the existence of multiple, fragmented, and possibly competing group ties may exist creating a large number of partial leaders or leaders of small groups reflecting specialized interests. Relationships among these groups and leaders may often be hostile reflecting their competition for the economic resources and the social commitments of the same set of residents. Similarly, hostilities may arise between heterogeneous segments of a local population over the control and dominance of the local area. Local groups with external affiliations, such as unions and churches, may also vie for influence among members with overlapping affiliations. Thus, the absence of unified action on the community-wide level may be due less to isolation than to a pattern of fragmented social participation. Alinsky was arguing that defended neighborhood or community of limited liability groups may resist and weaken attempts to organize an expanded community of limited liability.

Assessment

Alinsky and advocates of a community of limited liability perspective note that local community is not a complete local social system but powerfully influenced by external organizations and institutions. Second, both recognize that urban communities tend to be differentiated, fragmented, and to have multiple potentially competing levels of social participation. Third, both recognize that among the multiple levels of community social structure, participation on the community-wide level may be weak, short-termed, and centered on particular issues.

Alinsky deserves recognition for his understanding of the interdependence of community and larger institutions and the complexity of local social structure. His community analysis parallels and foreshadows the main themes of a community of limited liability perspective. Yet community of limited liability advocates have paid little attention to Alinsky's community analysis: Janowitz (1952) did not cite Alinsky; Hunter (1974:79) included a passing reference to Alinsky's Back of the Yard organization; and Hunter and Suttles (1972:63) used Alinsky organizations as an example of expanded communities of limited liability. Alinsky's focus on community organization rather than the question of defining community may be partially responsible for the failure of urban social scientists to recognize the significance of his interpretation of local community power and social structure.

Further, Alinsky's awareness of the difficulty of establishing a community organization and the need for a careful analysis of existing structural patterns suggests a direct application of urban social science to the task of community organization. Hunter and Suttles' typology provides an excellent framework for synthesizing Alinsky's community analysis. A community of limited liability perspective may provide a better foundation for sensitizing organizers and activists to the particular character of social ties within a locality and between a community and outside institutions than Alinsky's own method of stating rules for community organization.

THE SOCIAL CONSTRUCTION OF LOCAL COMMUNITY AND COMMUNITY ATTACHMENTS

Community of limited liability

Hunter and Suttles (1972:45) noted that most models of local community have failed to realistically describe the sources of local cohesiveness. One of the interesting trends in recent social science theory and research has been the challenge mounted against the assumption that communities are *Gemeinschaft*-like, closed social systems. Warren (1978) argues for the full recognition of vertical patterns of coordination which may complement and/or replace horizontal integration. Similarly, recent research has stressed the importance of external forces on the shape and form of local community power structures (Long, 1958; Banfield, 1961; Walton, 1974; Domhoff, 1978).

Hunter and Suttles (1972:65), recognizing the importance of external organizations in the definition of the boundary and identity of local communities, suggest that cooperation and cohesiveness on each level of local community social structure needed the presence and reactions of outside adversaries and advocates. The pattern and strength of face-block and defended neighborhoods depended in part on the perceived threat and common distrust of neighboring or adjacent residential groups. A common enemy rather than ties based on mechanical solidarity often provided the impetus for group formation and identification. Similarly, both the community of limited liability and expanded community of limited liability tended to define their scope and activity in response to extraterritorial organizations and issues. The pattern of partial and multiple communities of limited liability reflected the overlapping service districts of city-wide police, school, and electoral districts, while the few examples of expanded communities of limited liability suggested that they were organized in response to larger external organizations and issues. However, unlike face-block and defended neighborhood groups, where an organization on one block or neighborhood served as a stimulus and antagonist for similar organizations in other parts of the community, external organizations were less aware of their role and less reliable as adversaries and advocates of communities of limited liability.

Alinsky

Hunter and Suttles used conflict and competition with both internal and external groups to explain the pattern of fragmented, partial, and multiple levels of local community social structure. They did not, however, suggest a strategy for the conscious "building" or development of community-wide organizations. Alinsky offered a general scheme for purposive action which suggests three key stages in the development of community organization.

It's the kind of thing we see in play writing; the first act introduces the characters and the plot, in the second act the plot and characters are developed as the play strives to hold the audience's attention. In the final act good and evil have their dramatic confrontation and resolution (Alinsky, 1971:115–116).

The purpose of the first stage is to win local acceptance of the organizer and to generate an awareness of the need for a community organization. If community organization is viewed as a play, the first act contains three possible scenes with flexible sequences. An Alinsky trademark was a formal invitation extended by local leaders to the organizer. In some cases, the invitation marked the beginning of Alinsky's contact with the local community. Thus, in Rochester, New York, race riots in 1964 led the City Council of Churches to ask Alinsky to organize the city's black community. When the council agreed to fund the community organization, Alinsky further insisted that a representative of the black community must also formally invite him into the community. In Chicago's Woodlawn, a group of local leaders offered the initial invitation. The strategy in each case was to encourage local acceptance and generate interest in community-wide participation (either to stimulate an invitation or to broaden local support after the invitation) by provoking a public, hostile reaction to Alinsky by some external, city-wide leader or spokesman.

Upon arrival in Rochester, Alinsky called a press conference and responded to a question with, "Maybe I am innocent and uninformed of what has been happening here, but as far as I know the only

thing Eastman Kodak has done on the race issue in America has been to introduce color film" (Alinsky, 1971:137). He proceeded to "confuse" W. Allen Wallis, president of the University of Rochester with George Wallace. Alinsky claimed the resulting negative reaction of city officials was sufficient to arouse local black leaders to invite him into their community.

The strategy parallels Hunter and Suttles' (1972) argument that community of limited liability and extended community of limited liability are mobilized in response to the policies and organizational units of external adversaries. The negative welcome by external adversaries not only aids in establishing the legitimacy and credibility of the organizer within the local community, but also heightens a community-wide identification. Further, in Rochester, external advocates were also identified and organized through the establishment of "Friends of Fight," an associated group of some 400 due-paying white liberals, which provided funds, moral support, legal advice, and instruction for community training projects (Alinsky, 1972:176).

A second scene or part of the initial stage of community organization consists of a listening, observing, and learning period. As noted before, Alinsky cautions organizers that no community is disorganized and to stay within the experiences of local residents. The task of the organizer, during this facet of the organization venture, is similar to that of a social scientist doing field research and includes the identification of existing patterns of local social structure, community customs, and potential leaders.

A third scene, or part of the initial stage of community organization stems from the assumption that no community is disorganized, but in many cases is organized for apathy. The existing network of fragmented and partial social groups may work against the acceptance of a unified organization. Therefore Alinsky called for disorganization, or reorganization of the local community structure.

The organizer dedicated to changing the life of a particular community must first rub raw the resentments of the people of the community; fan the latent hostilities of many of the people to the point of overt expression (Alinsky, 1971:116).

An organizer must stir up dissatisfaction and discontent; provide a channel into which the people can angrily pour their frustration. He must create a mechanism that can drain off the underlying guilt for having accepted the previous situation for so long. Out of this mechanism, a new community organization arises (Alinsky, 1971:117).

Given the fragmented and partial loyalties of local groups, community-wide participation required the mobilization of community-wide sentiment. The identification of external adversaries accomplished in the "listening" stage was now reintroduced and used as a means to bridge competition and hostilities among local groups. The strategy suggests Alinsky's use of external adversaries in defining the boundaries, identity, and issues pertinent to the creation of communities of limited liability.

The purpose of the organization should be interpreted as proposing to deal with those major issues which no single agency is—or can be—big enough or strong enough to cope with. Then each agency will continue to carry out its own program, but all are being banded together to achieve sufficient strength to cope with issues that are so vast and deep that no one or two community agencies would ever consider tackling them (Alinsky, 1946:87).

Alinsky recognized that community is not a self-contained, complete social system, but a response to issues which define sets of common interests.

Thus, Alinsky's first stage of community organization contained an introduction to the organizer, identification of external adversaries and the development of shared community issues. When an invitation to organize was not initially offered, the sequence of activities changed. It became the organizers' task to create the situation which would generate an invita-

tion. The sequence began with scene two, the listening stage, then came scene three, the heightening of issues directed at external adversaries, followed by scene one, the provoking of a negative reaction from external adversaries to generate the invitation and initiate community acceptance.

The second major stage in Alinsky's community development process was the establishment of a community-wide organization. In his analogy the task of the second act was to hold the audience's attention. Alinsky used three types of activities to maintain residents' interest and participation in community-wide activities. First, as in Austin, the Alinsky organizer spent his first year establishing a network of block clubs (Bailey, 1972:66). In addition to continuing the process of introducing local residents to community action and a shared approach to individual troubles, the network of block clubs provided a foundation for organization on the community-wide level. Whenever possible, Alinsky used existing groups, particularly church groups (in Woodlawn) and unions (in Back of the Yards) to demonstrate that community organization is compatible with local interests. Second was a call for a community congress. Its main purpose was to transform the coalition of groups into a broad-based, multiple-issue, permanent community organization. After the first congress has ratified the constitution, approved the budget, and elected representatives and executive officers, succeeding annual congresses were to keep the community up-to-date on the activities of the organization. An important aspect of the structure was the multiple standing committees dealing with salient local issues. This permitted the organization to pursue multiple issues simultaneously and thus to mobilize the interests of the majority of the residents.

The third activity geared to maintaining interest in community-wide participation was the demonstration of the organization's capacity to win confrontations and to deliver improved services to the community. Alinsky urged that initial issues should be highly visible and concrete, salient to local residents but not divisive or antagonistic to other local groups, and easy to win (Alinsky, 1971:114–59). He consistently argued that the first set of issues are particularly important when organizations and leaders are inexperienced, members are tentative in their commitment, and acceptance of the organization and organizer is still in question. A series of successful specific and localized confrontations built confidence among leaders and members and demonstrated the organization's ability to improve the quality of neighborhood life. The focus on confrontations was on outside agencies, which defined their service and market areas within the local community. Thus, outside merchants, realtors, landlords, hospitals, social service agencies, and municipal services with local branches were frequent targets, in part, because they were dependent on the local community for clients, customers, employees, and constituents. However, unlike a play, Alinsky noted that in order to maintain local interest, these confrontations must be a continual part of community organization (Alinsky 1946:151–54).

Assessment

Alinsky shares with the community of limited liability perspective the position that community identification is not the product of mechanical solidarity but a conscious response to a perceived adversary or common enemy. Alinsky extends the position by formulating a set of strategies to actively build local attachments. The first two of his three stages deal directly with the process of community development. Alinsky used negative response from external groups to heighten local awareness that individual troubles may be shared and stem from a common enemy. Alinsky approached the second task of maintaining interest and involvement in community-wide affairs by: (1) focusing

organization on multiple issues which appeal to diverse interests in the community; (2) using the structure of the organization and its annual meetings to remind residents of the activities of the community organization; and (3) pointing to a series of conflicts usually with external groups to demonstrate the capacity of the organization to service the needs of residents and improve the quality of the community.

One of the important contributions of social science to community organization is the expanded analysis of factors which may facilitate or retard attempts to actively strengthen community-wide ties. Alinsky, in his zeal to present the accomplishments of community organization, never fully developed the social background characteristics or neighborhood contextual factors which influence the creation and maintainance of community ties. Bailey (1972) notes that in Austin, commitment to cooperative approaches to social problems contributed to the success of Alinsky's community organization. Further, Bailey found that the Alinsky organization was more successful in attracting the residents who: (1) were more socially integrated into the area and were more committed to the local community; (2) were more dissatisfied with local governmental programs and services; and (3) were relatively better educated and had higher incomes. Irvine (1967) noted that hostilities among the heterogeneous residents of Chelsea (New York City) weakened a shared local identity. External antagonists and common advocates were needed to create an effective community organization capable of managing relations among local residents and across territorial boundaries.

COMMUNITY POWER AND PARTICIPATORY DEMOCRACY

Community of limited liability

Hunter and Suttles (1972:64) noted that the task of the extended community of limited liability is to "get high administrators together with the community representatives at the bargaining table to acknowledge the legitimacy of the organization's presence." Beyond the mobilization of community-wide participation, the task of community organization was to handle the "foreign policy" of the local community which is to protect and define the interests of the community in its relationships with external organizations whose policies and programs directly influence the local residents. The difficulty in establishing and maintaining extended communities of limited liability capable of representing local residents in external affairs stems from two sources. First, Hunter and Suttles (1972:67) noted that at present neither public nor private agencies regularly consulted with interested local parties in policy making nor have there been attempts to coordinate serving the same community. Second, both external and internal groups persisted in defining local communities as grass-roots, self-initiated, and sustaining collectivities (Hunter and Suttles, 1972:66). Such a model implied that it was the responsibility of the residents to pull themselves up by their bootstraps and to enter into interest groups politics as independent parties. Given the difficulty of the task, Hunter and Suttles (1972:64) suggested that it was not the record of limited success of community organizations which was remarkable but the resistance and opposition they had encountered.

Hunter and Suttles acknowledged that extended communities of limited liability have no established procedures for either winning recognition as legitimate representatives of the local community nor for pressuring external adversaries to include them in their policy and decision-making processes. They proposed that the goals of a strong and viable community organization may best be achieved by federal regulations and guidelines which would create a framework for regular consultation between the local community and federal, state, and municipal agencies (Hunter and Suttles, 1972:79). Sponsored communities represented an alternative to both the myth of autonomous, independent entities and to the reality of powerless communities by formally establishing a structure or administrative procedure for direct negotiations between local representatives and external organizations.

Alinsky

Alinsky proposed a comparable role for community organizations. Following the analogy of the play, the third stage of community development contained "the dramatic confrontation and resolution of good and evil." The brilliance of Alinsky as a strategist lay in his conceptual or theoretical recognition of the role of power and conflict. During the 1950s and 1960s when social scientists were debating the theoretical, methodological, and empirical shape of community politics (Wirt and Hawley, 1968; Aiken and Mott, 1970; Bonjean, Clark, and Lineberry, 1971) Alinsky was focusing on the related issue of expanding the scope of community power and using locally controlled community organizations to achieve social and political change.

Nonviolent conflict is central to Alinsky's goal of broadening local political participation. Conflict was used in the first two stages of community organization to win local acceptance of the community organization and to create interest in community-wide participation. In the final stage of community organization, conflict with external adversaries was further used to win external acceptance of the community organization as a bargaining agent to press the claims of the local community for participation in external decision making. Alinsky used confrontation with a large national department store in Back of the Yards (Alinsky, 1946:135–46), with the University of Chicago and the City of Chicago in Woodlawn (Alinsky, 1972:169–

73), and Kodak in Rochester (Alinsky, 1972:173–77) to force external organizations to recognize their responsibility to the community and to negotiate with community organizations.

Critics have tended to confuse Alinsky's radical strategies with his popularist and pluralist political goals (Owens, 1975). The purpose of nonviolent conflict with external adversaries has been further obscured by Alinsky's own description of himself as a radical. However, as Alinsky repeatedly stated, his goal was not a fundamental altering of existing values or revolutionary political change but rather participatory democracy and the broadening of political participation in institutional decision making (Alinsky 1946:217–18).

Conflict with external groups did not become a goal itself but a means of extending participatory democracy. The key to the use of conflict was to create a situation where external adversaries perceived that it was less costly to their own self-interest and goals to recognize the demands of the community organization than to continue the conflict. Boycotts, sit-ins, mass demonstrations, and an assortment of other strategies became the means of pressuring external groups and demonstrating the power of the community organization. Yet, as important as the specific issues are, Alinsky suggested that the success of the conflict lay in the establishment of a process for implementing citizen participation and the creation of a "new" structural tie between the local community and external organizations (Alinsky, 1971:169–70).

Assessment

Advocates of a community of limited liability and Alinsky share the conviction that the task of community-wide organization was to represent the community in its external affairs. However, they differ on the means to maintain effective and viable community organizations. Hunter and Suttles (1972) argue that since de Tocqueville there has been a tendency to romanticize community self-initiative and the feasibility of local self-governance. Their critique of restoration and their proposed sponsored community suggest an unresolved dilemma in Alinsky's search for a means to maintain strong local communities. Alinsky, by refusing to consider a government-sponsored procedure to mediate conflict between local communities and external groups, was obligated to defend the position that such intervention was necessary. Thus, Alinsky persistently maintained that by skillfully defining issues, mobilizing community resources, and applying creative strategies, adversaries could be pressured into negotiation with community organization. Yet a review of his own examples suggests the tenuous and indirect character of Alinsky's strategies. Alinsky (1946:135–46) described a conflict with "Tycoon's Department Store" where it took the threat of court injunction restraining Tycoon's from "murdering Protestant ministers and Catholic priests" before the store would negotiate with the community organization. Similarly, to gain the recognition of a union in Back of the Yards, Alinsky had to rely on personal ties with John L. Lewis to appeal to Chicago's Mayor Kelly before stockyard owners would begin to seriously bargain with the union. Later in Woodlawn, Alinsky's inability to pressure Mayor Daley led to a threat to tie up toilets at O'Hare airport.

Alinsky recognized that the maintenance of a viable community organization required the mobilization of external advocates. However, the organization of external advocates remained a problem. Throughout his career Alinsky repeatedly proposed a national alliance of community organizations. Yet an alliance of Alinsky organizations never materialized, and as Lancourt (1979) noted, even existing Alinsky organizations in the same city did not readily aid each other in conflict with external groups. His second solution was the creation of a national organization to collect stock proxies to be used to pressure corporations on local and national issues (Alinsky, 1972:61). Yet, even by his own favorable account, the use of proxies only indirectly succeeded in pressuring Kodak (Alinsky, 1972:177).

While Alinsky did not solve the problem of creating organized external advocates, he did offer some observations which directly apply to Hunter and Suttles' sponsored communities. Alinsky (1965, 1968, 1970), in a series of articles, criticized the War on Poverty. One of his objections was that the responsibility for the identification of legitimate representatives of a local community was taken away from local residents. Under the guise of "consensus," Alinsky argued that city officials and political machines were able to bar community organizations which posed political threats and replace them with "paper" organizations which did not reflect the interests and concerns of local residents. The selected organizations did little to improve either the economic or political conditions of the community. Alinsky proposed that local authorities be bypassed and that the Woodlawn Organization serve as a model for the selection of legitimate community organization. A process for regulating the conflict between local community and external adversaries may work best when there is already present a strong community organization which reflects local interest but whose continued existence remains uncertain as long as the means of overt influence on external groups remain precarious. However, when extended communities of limited liability are not present, Alinsky tactics and strategies may be needed to generate local acceptance and a structure for a community organization.

CONCLUSION

Saul Alinsky would probably have resisted being praised as an applied urban theorist, yet his contribution to social science extends considerably beyond his masterful strategies and tactics. The underlying theoretical orientation contains a rich and innovative understanding of community social structure, sources of local attachment, and the role of the community organization as a representative of the local community. Alinsky had a sophisticated awareness of the multifaceted and fragmented composition of urban social structure and a realistic recognition of the impact of external social and political processes on the local community. He recognized that community ties are typically less salient than either primary group or city-wide associations, but that community participation is necessary to protect and defend local interests. His community analysis provides an independent verification of the main tenents of a community of limited liability perspective. On the other hand, Alinsky's difficulty in training organizers may have been the result of his failure to systematically organize and present his understanding of local community processes and structures. A community of limited liability provides an excellent framework for synthesizing Alinsky's community analysis and explaining the rationale for his tactics.

Alinsky's activities extend a community of limited liability perspective by focusing on purposive community development. He expands the theme that community attachments are not self-generating nor self-contained but often are the direct outcome of the actions of community advocates and in reaction to external adversaries. Alinsky's community organization ventures may be viewed as quasi experiments which demonstrate the utility of applying community theory to community development. He applied a perspective consistent with a community of limited liability when he used conflict with external antagonists to strengthen community cohesiveness. Similarly, he extends a community of limited liability perspective to a strategy for bolstering community-wide identification by advocating that organizations: (1) pursue multiple issues which appeal to diverse interests in the community; (2) use annual meetings to remind residents of their shared goals and interests; and (3) constantly demonstrate to local residents the instrumental and material benefits of community involvement. Finally, Alinsky applies and extends a community of limited liability perspective with his recognition that a strong local community requires an organization capable of bargaining with external organizations and representing local interests in city-wide politics. Thus, consideration of Alinsky's theoretical orientation sheds a new light on the broad scope of his contribution to urban social science and community theory.

REFERENCES

Aiken, Michael, and Paul E. Mott, eds. 1970 *The Structure of Community Power*. New York: Random House.

Alinsky, Saul D. 1941 "Community Analysis and Organization." *American Journal of Sociology* 46 (May), pp. 797–808.

_____. 1946 *Reveille for Radicals*. Chicago: University of Chicago Press, 1969.

_____. 1965 "The War on Poverty—Political Pornography," *The Journal of Social Issues* 21 (January), pp. 41–47.

_____. 1968 "What Is the Role of Community Organization in Bargaining with the Establishment for Health Care Services?" In *Medicine in the Ghetto*, ed. J. C. Norman. New York: Appleton-Century-Crofts, pp. 291–99.

_____. 1970 "Citizen Participation and Community Organization in Planning and Urban Renewal." In *Strategies in Community Organization*, ed. F. M. Cox, J. L. Erlich, J. Rothman, and J. E. Tropman. Itasca, Ill.: F. E. Peacock, pp. 216–66.

_____. 1971 *Rules for Radicals*. New York: Random House.

_____. 1972 "Interview with Saul Alinsky," *Playboy* (March), pp. 52–178.

Bailey, Robert. 1972. *Radicals in Urban Politics*. Chicago: University of Chicago Press.

Banfield, Edward C. 1961. *Political Influence*. New York: Free Press.

Bonjean, Charles M., Terry N. Clark, and Robert L. Lineberry, eds. 1971. *Community Politics: A Behavioral Approach*. New York: Random House.

Domhoff, William G. 1978. *Who Really Rules? New Haven and Community Power Reexamined*. Santa Monica, Calif.: Goodyear.

Fish, John H. 1973. *Black Power/White Control*. Princeton, N.J.: Princeton University Press.

Greer, Scott. 1962. *The Emerging City: Myth and Reality*. New York: Free Press.

Haggstrom, Warren C. 1964. "The Power of the Poor" in *Mental Health of the Poor*, ed. F. Riessman, J. Cohen, and A. Pearls. New York: Free Press, pp. 205–23.

Hunter, Albert. 1974. *Symbolic Communities: The Persistence and Change of Chicago's Local Communities*. Chicago: University of Chicago Press.

Hunter, Albert. 1979. "The Urban Neighborhood: Its Analytical and Social Contents." *Urban Affairs Quarterly* 14 (March), pp. 267–88.

Hunter, Albert, and Gerald Suttles. 1972. "The Expanding Community of Limited Liability." In *The Social Construction of Communities*, ed. G. Suttles. Chicago: The University of Chicago Press, pp. 44–81.

Irvine, Bruce K. 1967. "Saul Alinsky: A History of Chelsea Community Council, 1956–1960." Master's thesis, Columbia University.

Janowitz, Morris. 1952. *The Community Press in an Urban Setting*. Chicago: The University of Chicago Press.

Lancourt, Joan. 1979. *Confront or Concede: The Alinsky Citizen-Action Organizations*. Lexington, Mass.: D.C. Heath.

Long, Norton E. 1958. "The Local Community As an Ecology of Games." *American Journal of Sociology* 44 (November), pp. 251–61.

Owens, Raymond. 1975. "On Rubbing Raw the Sores of Discontent: Competing Theories and Data on the Effects of Participation in Black Protest Groups." *Sociological Focus* 8 (April), pp. 143–59.

Reitzes, Donald C., and Dietrich C. Reitzes. 1980. "Saul D. Alinsky: A Neglected

Source but Promising Resource." Paper presented at the Annual Meetings of the American Sociological Association.

Sherrard, Thomas D., and Richard C. Murray. 1965. "The Church and Neighborhood Community Organization." *Social Work* 10 (July), pp. 3–14.

Silberman, Charles E. 1964. *Crisis in Black and White.* New York: Random House.

Suttles, Gerald. 1968. *The Social Order of the Slum: Ethnicity and Territory in the Inner City.* Chicago: University of Chicago Press.

Walton, John. 1974. "The Structural Bases of Political Change in Urban Communities." In *The Community: Approaches and Applications,* ed. Marcia P. Effrat. New York: Free Press, pp. 174–201.

Warren, Roland. 1978. *The Community in America.* Chicago: Rand McNally.

Whyte, William F. 1943. *Street Corner Society.* Chicago: University of Chicago Press.

Wirt, Frederick, and Willis Hawley. 1968. *The Search for Community Power.* Englewood Cliffs, N.J.: Prentice-Hall.

35

Neighborhood organization and interest-group process

David J. O'Brien

In view of the complexity and interdependence of the problems and principles of neighborhood organization, I believe this brief outline will be helpful to the reader.

PRINCIPLES OF INTEREST-GROUP ORGANIZATION

I. The basic unit of analysis is the rational self-interested person. The central task of the organizer is to find incentives to induce this individual to pay for nondivisible collective goods (that is, public goods).

II. The size of an aggregate makes a qualitative difference in the way in which inducement problems are experienced. In the case of a small aggregate, support for collective goods can be accomplished through voluntary means; but in the case of a large

aggregate, the individual's voluntary contribution will not be significant and thus the aggregate must adopt one or some combination of the following alternatives:

A. A coercive device with which members can ensure that everyone will contribute toward the costs of collective goods (for example, the closed shop).

B. Or a by-product strategy in which the individual receives selective individual benefits in addition to collective benefits and pays for the latter as a means of receiving the former.

C. Or a federal-group strategy in which a number of small groups form a coalition to support a federated effort. The incentives for inducing individual support for this effort come from the respective small groups.

III. Once the public goods problem is recognized, the organizer's primary task is to find a strategy to obtain

Reprinted with permission of the author and publisher from David J. O'Brien, "Neighborhood Organization and Interest-Group Process" (Princeton, N.J.: Princeton University Press, 1975), pp. 175–87. Reference footnotes have been omitted.

organizational resources. This means that he must persuade other, existing interest groups to grant the organization either:

A. Legitimacy to guarantee the group's right to impose a coercive device upon its members (for example, the Wagner Act)

B. And/or the material resources necessary to provide individuals with selective benefits (for example, professional privileges).

IV. The interest-group process must be seen as a force operating within the broader parameters of its environmental milieu in which:

A. The interest group is competing for resources with other organizations and institutions, which may be adversely affected by the mobilization of the group and which may therefore resist efforts to grant it legitimacy or material resources.

B. Adversaries can learn to change their "counterstrategies" in response to the interest group's strategies.

V. The need to obtain resources in a changing environment means that organizational success will be contingent on the ability of the organizer to make adaptations in the form of *trade-offs* with other interest groups and accommodations in his own goals and means (as illustrated by the evolution of the American labor movement). The outcome of this process will be affected by:

A. The quality of information (including ideologies, scientific knowledge, and pragmatic action strategies) about the relationship between the interest group's goals and the position of other self-interested persons in the environment; especially with respect to persuading other institutional spheres and interest groups (for example, labor's efforts vis-a-vis Congress and the courts) of the need to recognize the interest group's claim to legitimacy or to prevent unfair competition with the group's provision of selective benefits.

B. The constraints imposed by organizational structures, each of which will impose different cost-benefit ratios on its group's goals (in both the short-term and the long-run). We can expect:

1. "Cooperative" structures to increase the probability of obtaining material resources but place constraints on the ability of the group to maintain an aggressive adversary posture vis-a-vis other interest groups.

2. "Autonomous" organizational structures to permit the group to maximize its aggressive adversary posture but reduce the probability that it can obtain resources.

C. The costs and benefits of different structural arrangements. Hence the adaptability of different structures will vary according to the parameters of the environmental milieu in which the group operates.

THE PROBLEMS WITH TRADITIONAL ORGANIZING APPROACHES OF THE 1960S

I. *The primary source of difficulty in neighborhood-organization theory is its failure to view the poor as rational self-interested people who must be induced to support collective action.* All of the approaches we have examined assume that the poor person must be changed, either as a prelude to participation or as a result of the involvement process. This is especially pronounced in conceptualizations of neighborhood organization as a "therapeutic process," either in terms of "community building" (that is, the community-development and community-action approaches) or in terms of using protest and confrontation (that is, social action-protest approaches) as a means for cutting through the "institutionalized apathy" of the poor. The poor person is called upon to lend support to nondivisible collective goals (that is, the "community" in community-development and community-action work and the "movement" in social action-protest efforts). In all of these instances, organizers have avoided asking the critical question: what payoffs exist for the *individual* to contribute to collective action?

II. *Neighborhood organizers assume, often implicitly, that the problem of organizing the large aggregate is analytically similar to that faced in dealing with the small group. Thus they fail to recognize the need to apply the exclusionary principle in order to solve the public goods dilemma.* None of the strategies adequately treat the relationship between group size and interest-group organization. The attempt to involve the poor in neighborhood organization on a purely *voluntary* basis has resulted in a disproportionate involvement of persons with higher socioeconomic status who already belong to associations in the neighborhood (that is, the "double filtration effect"), widespread indifference by the poor toward neighborhood organization efforts, and a lack of sustained strength of neighborhood organizations vis-a-vis adversaries (for example, the Community Action Program struggles over "maximum feasible participation").

A. The indifference of the poor to-ward supporting the Community Action Programs as opposed to the interest of workers in supporting unions is accounted for by the fact that the latter possess a coercive device (the closed shop) to mobilize collective action, whereas the "maximum feasible participation" clause did not provide such a device for the poor.

B. Community-development cooperatives failed because organizers attempted to transfer a model of organization based on the small rural village to the large urban aggregate. They did not understand that the by-product principle of organization in the large aggregate demands the exclusion of noncontributors from receiving the selective benefits.

C. The Alinsky model comes closest to solving the public goods problem insofar as it employs the federal-group principle; however, it possesses two weaknesses with respect to the neighborhood organization issue:

1. Utilization of existing organizational structures in the neighborhood results in the federated organization's attracting a disproportionate number of persons with higher socioeconomic status than the poor (e.g., only 2 percent of the Woodlawn residents were actually involved in TWO).

2. The Alinsky version of the federal-group model is geared toward dramaturgical conflict over specific issues and has not focused on the problem of inducing individuals to support long-term organizational efforts.

III. *By focusing on changing the poor person*

and upon immediate issue resolution instead of the public goods problem, neighborhood organizers have not seen their primary organizational objectives in terms of obtaining long-term legitimacy or material resources to produce selective benefits. The approaches we have examined treat the issue of long-term influence of neighborhood organizations in local decision-making processes as secondary to their primary concern with the therapeutic process or their success in winning victories over adversaries on specific issues. Thus, organizers have not anticipated either:

A. The problem of obtaining guarantees of the group's legitimacy vis-a-vis other interest groups *prior* to participation in social service programs (as shown by the Community Action Programs and community-development projects) or the difficulty of turning a "tactical victory" on a specific issue into permanent neighborhood residents (as shown by the Alinsky recognition of the group's right to bargain for the approach).

B. Or the fact that although some individuals may be induced to support collective efforts on a short-term basis because of the dramaturgical effects of conflict, they will not maintain that support over a long period unless they are able to obtain a coercive device or receive some selected individual benefits.

IV. *Above all, neighborhood organization theoreticians and practitioners tend to treat the organizing process as isolated from its environment. Thus they fail to anticipate how other rational self-interested men will react to their efforts to change the balance of power in local decision making.* One of the most striking features of neighborhood-organization theory and practice is the almost total absence of any kind of comprehensive view of urban political, social, and economic processes. Although references are often made to pluralism and democracy, little attention is paid to the costs and benefits accruing to different parties as a result of mobilization of a new interest group and of the types of strategies employed to block such an effort. Two opposing tendencies can be discerned here:

A. To deny conflict altogether and to treat neighborhood organization as a "technical problem" (as in the case of "maximum feasible participation") or as part of a process of social integration (as in the community-development perspective.) The effect of this view is to define what are essentially political problems as social problems and to create the conditions for a "winner-take-all" struggle between the neighborhood organization and other interest groups over whose view best represents what is in the "common interest."

B. To treat conflict (that is, the protest strategies) as a zero-sum condition and to fail to recognize that in a democratic society the flexibility of institutions permits adversaries to learn ways to handle conflict without granting legitimacy to a protesting group.

V. *By either pretending that conflict does not exist or treating it as a zero-sum situation, neighborhood organizers have been unable to establish bases for tradeoffs among rational self-interested men.* The difficulty here is that neighborhood organizers have not adequately recognized that the nature of the conflict situation in which they are engaged is analogous to conflict institutionalized by labor through the mechanism of collective bargaining (that is, they must accept the inevitability of conflict and the principles of the public goods dilemma). The Alinsky model goes much further than the community-development or community-action models in this regard, but it, along with the others, has not:

A. Provided a rationale for the *need* of residents of a neighborhood to organize (because they have a latent conflict relationship with other interest groups) and the kinds of benefits that might accrue to other interest groups by institutionalizing this conflict (in other than the zero-sum form) by granting the neighborhood organization either legitimacy or material resources.

B. Provided a mechanism for institutionalization of conflict. Thus the organizational structures that have been developed generate irreconcilable organizational maintenance dilemmas. The costs and benefits of specific structural arrangements are different, however, insofar as:

 1. The "cooperative," "community-wide" structure of the Community Action Programs permitted neighborhood organizations to gain material resources, but the organizational maintenance needs of the larger organization became more important to its director than the goals of neighborhood organization. The lack of specification of inputs of opposing interest groups into the programs led to the development of zero-sum games. The poor eventually lost because of restrictions on the ability of neighborhood organizations to assume an aggressive interest-group stance in relation to other interest groups.

 2. The autonomous organizational structure of social action-protest groups permitted them to achieve greater freedom of action vis-a-vis other interest groups, but created long-term problems in attaining legitimacy or material resources.

C. Although mayor-council governments are typically more responsive than reform governments to minority-group input into the *electoral process*, maximum feasible participation (because of the creation of parapolitical structures and competing patronage bases) posed a direct threat to the viability of the Democratic party coalition. Thus conflict over participation of the poor was more likely to manifest itself in rancorous forms in cities with a strong Democratic party organization than in reform cities.

REFOCUSING THE NEIGHBORHOOD ORGANIZATION PROBLEM

The demise of neighborhood-organization efforts cannot be attributed so much to the failure of organizers to find the right answers as to their inability to ask the right questions. The public goods dilemma was never identified as the source of the frustrations experienced by neighborhood organizers, even when traditional approaches had failed.

The appropriate questions cannot be asked until the paradigmatic[1] assumptions

---

[1] Here I am referring to the a priori assumptions from which theory is developed. In the case of neighborhood organization, the logical relationships of propositions and assertions to the assumptions from which they have been drawn are frequently explicated only vaguely.

underlying neighborhood-organization theory are reevaluated. Any chance of altering the initial assumptions about the nature of the poor depends upon the willingness of reformers to change their view of man in general.

Rationality, self-interest, and freedom

My description of the poor person is relevant *only* to the political problem at hand and in no way is applicable to his total human nature. Nonetheless, the concept of a rational self-interested man is often viewed with disdain by sociologists and reformers, partly because of its close association with classical economic thought, which provided the intellectual foundations for 19th-century capitalism. The dehumanizing consequences of political economy, which grew out of this system of thought, is well expressed by Benjamin Jowett's statement, "I have always felt a certain horror of political economists . . . since I heard one of them say that he feared the famine of 1848 in Ireland would not kill more than a million people and that would scarcely be enough to do much good." In our country, laissez-faire economics complemented by social darwinism employed the concepts of rationality and self-interest to block the efforts of reformers to obtain government intervention to prevent child-labor abuses and to allow workers the right of collective bargaining.

For reformers, one of the most disturbing aspects of the laissez-faire doctrine is its insistence that the rational self-interested man is ultimately responsible for his own fate. This position, of course, was used to justify the gross inequalities that existed in the 19th and early 20th centuries. Thus, it is not surprising that reformers have sought to demonstrate that conditions outside of the control of the individual are as much responsible as his own actions for the specific behaviors he might engage in. This effort has been greatly assisted by the growing sophistication of techniques in psychiatry, psychology, and the social sciences, so that today we do not ask whether environmental factors influence behavior. Instead we usually ask, what is the extent of their influence and what are the "relevant" independent variables? Consequently, we are more likely to look at the way in which individuals are *acted upon* (that is, by norms, values, childrearing, and so forth) than the manner in which they initiate action themselves.

This tendency to turn away from the individual as the basic unit of analysis is reinforced by the reformer's substitution of the notion of "common interest" for the classical economists' concept of self-interest. In turn, we find that the replacement of the idea of conflicting *individual preferences* with the idea of meeting *collective needs* invariably leads to the belief that the assessment of "needs" is essentially a scientific and technical matter, limited only by imperfections in the state of our knowledge and our willingness to use it. In turn, this belief generates the rationale for having professional classes of experts who are "trained" to define and meet human needs.

While the intent of reformers has been to provide a more humane approach to the poor, the mentally ill, criminals, and other disadvantaged parties, it sometimes results in the denial of basic existential human properties. Thomas Szasz, for example, points out that although the view that the "mentally ill" are sick and should not be punished for wrongdoing was introduced for humanitarian reasons, it has been used to justify the denial of rights willingly granted to other citizens. Moreover, the psychiatrist's definition of "normality" is imposed on modes of behavior which formerly were defined as matters of individual ethical and political consideration. The problem is not whether certain types of behavior are healthy or unhealthy, but whether such claims should be used to thwart debate and conflict between men over their differing individual preferences.

One of the most damaging effects of reform efforts to eliminate the concept of the rational self-interested man is that along with his culpability, the individual also loses his human dignity. He is pictured as lost in the midst of social forces over which he has no control and we are much less likely to see him in the "tragic" sense of a struggling, searching person trying to find meaning in his life. If we view the poor person from the perspective of his supposed culture of poverty, alienation, or anomie, we absolve him from moral condemnation for his condition, but, by the same token, we deny him qualities that we readily recognize and accept in other men. It strikes me as more than coincidental that sociologists are apt to see the executive decision maker as a rational, choosing individual *constrained* by information problems and environmental exigencies, while they look upon the poor person as a passive, robot-like creature who is merely *pushed along* by forces of which he is not even aware, much less having any control over how he might react to them.

Alternatively, I have proposed that the poor person *does* make rational calculations in order to survive within his environmental parameters. His lack of interest in voluntary collective action is not a result of apathy or "not caring," but rather is a very reasonable assessment of the costs and benefits of such action in the large "latent group" situation. Thus, we see that the real problem with the classical economist's model is not the assertion that persons are rational and self-interested but rather the failure to account for the *structure of choice*, which makes different options more or less reasonable for the individual phenomenologically experiencing it.

Consequently, neighborhood organizers face the key intellectual task of understanding why the poor person's freedom to elect collective action as a solution to his problems is limited so long as he does not have a reasonable chance to solve his public goods dilemma. To do this, they must first reconcile the exclusionary principle with the generalized goals of neighborhood organizations. Excluding noncontributors may seem to many idealistic organizers as precisely the kind of principle of organization that grassroots movements are committed to fight. Indeed, some of the most successful applications of this principle have been by organizations, such as the AMA and the farm-bureau cooperatives, which regularly support conservative or even reactionary causes. Thus, the neighborhood organizer is faced with the difficult choice between maintaining the "purity" of his ideology and accepting a principle that may be distasteful but that does offer some hope of truly giving power to the poor. In making this choice, the organizer will have to weigh the relative importance of involvement as an end in itself (for example, experience in democratic participation) on the one hand, and the goal of collective strength on the other. Obviously, the latter option does not preclude the issue of democratic participation and the *degree* of involvement and influence of various members in an organization—as discussions of the oligarchical tendencies in labor unions illustrate. However, this issue can only be dealt with after the primary task of finding a solution to the public goods problem is accomplished.

Accepting the public goods problem as the core concept in neighborhood-organization theory means, of course, that the primary organizational objective of neighborhood organization work will have to be redefined as a search for ways to acquire the resources to solve this problem. For many organizers this entails eschewing a collective behavior model of organization while for others it means giving up the emphasis upon the "therapeutic effects" of involvement in neighborhood organizations. Most importantly, neighborhood-organization theory will have to provide analytic definitions of the environmental milieus in which the organizing process takes place. In order to obtain either legitimacy or material resources, a neighborhood organization will have to state precisely what resource problem residents face and propose a rationale for obtaining the necessary resources in a competitive situation with other rational, self-interested men affected by the organizing process. These objectives demand that we develop a clearer perspective on the relationship between neighborhood-organization problems and the general problems of creating and maintaining a pluralistic society.

36

Comprehensive planning and racism

Walter W. Stafford and Joyce Ladner

Unless future comprehensive plans for major urban areas in the U.S. are developed around a solid understanding of the implications of racism, they will not only be ineffectual but they may also be agents of disaster. Future black population majorities in thirteen major central cities will make old assumptions of "colorless" planning totally untenable.

For those planners who accept this premise, the first task is attempting to understand racism. Such an understanding should be based on social science and should afford a workable connection with planning cities. It should provide a framework for the changes necessary in urban political institutions if the cities of the future are not to become racial battlefields.

Our objective here is to offer working definitions of the two basic types of racism—*individual* and *institutional*—and to use them to analyze (1) some of the recent programs and plans devised to counter various urban crises, and (2) some expected institutional alternatives such as black political majorities, metropolitan planning, and advocacy planning.

BACKGROUND

Unfortunately there is a real lack of systematic information on racism as related to urban planning. There have been many social science studies on race since the 40s, but the majority do not relate racism to planning cities. Moreover, planning journals have shown little interest in the problems of black communities. This omission can be partially explained by the physical design bias which dominated planning in the early stage of its development. Another contributing factor is the failure of blacks—not only lower income groups but black intellectuals and scholars as well—to assign significant priority to planning. Black intellectuals, in a somewhat obvious attempt to relate colonialism to the U.S. racial crisis, should note the impact that culturally biased American and British planners have had on the development of Indian and African cities in countries that have achieved their independence. Major journals developed to study blacks—frequently begun by blacks because of segre-

Reprinted by permission of the *Journal of the American Institute of Planners* 35, no. 2 (March 1969), pp. 68–74.

gation in scholarly circles—do not mention the impact of planning.

The divergence between planning and the black community is unfortunate, for their are interesting and important aspects in the history of both which are significant for the understanding of urban development in this country. Planners interested in utopian traditions should be interested in "organized Negro communities," such as Nashoba, founded by freed slaves during the period when utopian ideals were prevalent in American thought.[1] Blacks, on the other hand, should be aware of the history of urban form and transportation patterns that have limited their job accessibility.[2]

A history of exploitive political decisions in urban development has discouraged the black community. Blacks have not wished to build a body of knowledge upon former racist patterns, preferring to reject the decisions of white interest groups and decision makers on approaches to racial problems in urban areas and propose their own. Thus, the planner, responsible for even the simplest single function plans for black clients, faces a dilemma in what he can propose to crucial political decision makers.

Traditionally, planners have not been concerned with what blacks thought or how they perceived planning proposals. In our opinion, this occurred because of three basic factors:

1. Blacks have traditionally been excluded from decision-making roles;
2. As subunits of the pattern of political decision making, blacks have had few resources with which to bargain;
3. Until recently, blacks have failed to see the important role of technicians who advise politicians.

Lower income blacks in Chicago's Westside, Atlanta's "Bottom," or Pittsburgh's Homewood district are not likely to understand the technical proposals of planners, nor are they likely to be concerned. The exigencies of their day-to-day existence preclude concern with long-range comprehensive goals, but it does not follow that they are not concerned or interested in how planners and politicians manipulate their lives. The tendency toward inactivity in urban affairs within the black community stems from a lack of understanding of urban processes that resulted partially from migration of rural people to urban areas without an accompanying introduction to the complexities of urban administration. Rigid patterns of segregation maintained their lack of access to knowledge about important urban institutions.

One major change in this situation has been the recent emergence of new catalysts in the form of young black professionals loosely organized into coalitions—for example, the Afro-American Teachers Association. A major resource of these groups is the knowledge of urban culture and institutions their parents lacked. The new coalitions have been aided by: a decline of machine politics and the loss of power by old-line blacks who aligned themselves with the machine; increased security of status which is largely established within the black community; creation of lower-level management jobs and federal positions; and, most importantly, the inflexibility of large-scale organizations, such as school systems and welfare departments, which prevents them from meeting demands from the black community and from adjusting to their own internal frictions without decentralizing their decision-making apparatus. These factors have helped to create a class of young pro-

---

[1] Jane and William Pease, "Organized Negro Communities," *The Journal of Negro History*, 47, no. 1 (January 1962), pp. 19–34.

[2] John Kain, *Commuting and the Residential Decisions of Chicago and Detroit Central Business District Workers* (Santa Monica, Calif.: The Rand Corporation, April 1963).

fessional blacks in decision-making positions.

The growth of such coalitions among professional blacks is of crucial importance to planning. These groups generally see themselves as having cultural roots within the black community but are cosmopolitan enough in outlook to link urban and national politics to their local goals. *In the future it is important for planners to understand that they are more likely to deal with these loosely organized coalitions than with individual blacks accorded political status.* The coalitions are more interested in changing and controlling the administrative apparatus of local government than in attempting to persuade influential whites (usually by giving them status on boards of voluntary agencies such as the Urban League or NAACP) to act in proxy for them by manipulating key decision makers. Increasingly discontented with white policymakers in black affairs, the coalitions are interested in changing older political arrangements to become more responsive to black needs and demands.

What the planner will face is a complex set of black community strategies bearing on the administration and planning of central cities with racial problems. We contend that, because of the implications of these local strategies for national politics, federal requirements for comprehensive planning have already increased. Existing physical and social conditions in our cities determine the direction of the strategies. In racially tense urban areas there is usually little vacant land for residential expansion of the rapidly growing black population. Additionally, surrounding suburban communities with direct zoning and subdivision controls are maintaining segregated patterns which accentuate inner-city problems. Planning decisions in many cases are reduced to decisions of which race gets what.

Planning decision makers cannot afford a narrow view of the consequences of their decisions. They must relate planning proposals to the needs of the black community, and establish criteria for analyzing effects of planning programs. Twelve years ago Martin Myerson emphasized this approach to broader measures of comprehensive planning.[3] However, if it has been adopted within cities with large black ghettos, the effects have not been widely publicized. Moreover, and perhaps of equal importance, the *process* of comprehensive planning must become participatory in the broadest sense, especially where the black community is concerned.

WHAT IS RACISM?

The most serious problems that have confronted intellectuals and scholars attempting to study racism have sprung from ineffective and diverse definitions of the term. Unable to establish an operational definition of racism, students of race relations have been hampered in their efforts to formulate a viable methodology that would act to counter racism and its effects on the social system. Sociologists, psychologists, intergroup relationists, and race relations experts have assigned various meanings to racism, referring to it in the same vein as prejudice, discrimination, norm conflicts, and so on. No strong attempt was made to place it in the position of prominence it has recently been assigned: that of being our society's most destructive force, which continues to systematically destroy an abundance of this nation's human potential. One of the primary reasons students of race relations were not more effective in formulating a viable theory and methodology of racism was their inability (or unwillingness) to treat racism as a very serious problem. They were willing to simultaneously ac-

[3] Martin Myerson, "Building the Middle Range Bridge for Comprehensive Planning," *Journal of the American Institute of Planners* 22 (Winter 1956), p. 59.

cept the "reality" of the abstract equality set forth in the Constitution along with the "normality" of institutional subjugation.

The most popular meanings assigned to racism generally revolve around the consequences of being black in the United States and the solutions that should be adopted to end the negative effects that accrue from the inferior social status to which black people are relegated. A broad definition taken from interdisciplinary approaches would be that racism is *an adaptive system of subjugation and exploitation based on a set of norms, roles, and expectations assigned by or to individuals, groups, or organizations.* Theoretically, the system can be divided into two patterns: *individualized racism* and *institutional racism.* However, this division somewhat oversimplifies the concept of racism since it is frequently difficult to separate individual and/or group attitudes from the institutions in which racism is incorporated. Under careful examination, one observes that attitudinal and institutional racism are intricately related since each depends on the other for sustenance. The individual racist must have an institutional framework for his behavior—for instance, he successfully fights integrated housing in his neighborhood because the local open housing ordinances are not enforced.

The adaptive nature of the system adjusts to individual practices and institutional norms which delineate between subordinate and superordinate positions, thus making it extremely difficult to distinguish class and racial implications. For example, individual practices or institutional policies which delineate subordinate positions may easily be substituted for stereotyped ideas about minority groups. Equally important for planners is the fact that some of the tools of planning—such as zoning, urban renewal, and subdivision controls—are not racist per se but are utilized to separate socioeconomic groups and thus adapt easily into the local racist framework and become de facto exclusionary measures.

The majority of the literature on racism is concerned with individual and, to a lesser degree, group prejudices. Attitudinal studies by social scientists have provided foundations for race relations policies of many social agencies in the United States. However, if there is any area in which social scientists have failed politicians, planners, and social agencies, it has been their lack of attention to institutional aspects of racism. The insistent emphasis upon small group behavior and group attitudes has forced a narrow focus on the implications of racism. As Irving Horowitz noted:

My own belief is that the problem of sociology can be boiled down as follows: It has transformed the study of race into the study of small groups, hence moving sociology away from a wider appreciation of the socio-economic conditions of Negroes and toward a narrower psychological-introspective evaluation.[4]

Moreover, some of the assumptions utilized by planners have been based on early stereotyped views of such individuals as urban sociologist Robert E. Park:

The temperament of the Negro as I conceive it consists in a few elementary but distinctive characteristics, determined by physical organizations and transmitted biologically. These characteristics manifest themselves in a genial, sunny, and social disposition, in an interest and attachment to external, physical things rather than to subjective states and objects of introspection, in a disposition for expression rather than enterprise and action.[5]

More recently, the work of Nathan Glazer and Daniel P. Moynihan has been influential despite the fact that one of their major arguments is: "The Negro is only an

---

[4] Irving Horowitz, "Black Sociology," *Trans-action* 4, no. 9 (Summer 1967), p. 8.

[5] Robert Park and Ernest Burgess, *Introduction to the Science of Sociology* (Chicago: University of Chicago Press, 1924), pp. 138–39.

American and nothing else. *He has no values and culture to guard and protect*"[6] (emphasis supplied). A sensitive and controverial dispute is currently underway between social scientists who support this position and black intellectuals who disagree.

Although sociologists have been singled out and perhaps indicted for their failure in this area, they are not alone. Other students of race relations have been just as ineffective. They have generally ignored the broader institutional framework which would relate to political policies (for example, influencing abolition of racism in institutional and land use arrangements). The clearest rationale for the attitudinal approach has been concern with conflicts and hostilities of races as groups, and hope that by understanding and eventually changing attitudes a benign relationship between races would be created. In proper perspective, attitudinal racism falls in a separate category of intergroup relations, which does not as a rule emphasize structural changes but instead devises within the system strategies that are designed to implement a "human relations" approach.

Institutional racism, on the contrary, can be defined as the operating policies, priorities, and functions of an on-going system of normative patterns which serve to subjugate, oppress, and force dependence of individuals or groups by: (1) establishing and sanctioning unequal goals, objectives, and priorities for blacks and whites, and (2) sanctioning inequality in status as well as in access to goods and services.

A profound revelation of the impact of institutional racism resulted from the research by social psychologist Kenneth Clark on the effects and consequences of racism in Harlem. Clark maintains that the ghetto ". . . is institutionalized pathology; it is chronic, self-perpetuating pathology; and it is the futile attempt by those with power to confine that pathology so as to prevent the spread of its contagion to the 'larger' community."[7] Presently, variations of institutional racism ranging from sophisticated to naive are recurrent themes in "mainstream" America as well as in the black community. In some sense, it received an "official stamp of approval" as the root cause of urban disorders when the U.S. Commission on Civil Disorders assigned it top priority as an explanatory variable. Racism subsequently gained popular usage and, for the first time in American history, was placed in proper perspective.

In the black community, racism is considered to be the cause of the "powerlessness" of its residents. A strong emphasis is also placed on identifying and strengthening the culture of the black community, for it is here, its advocates maintain, that racism has taken a heavy toll by attempting to destroy the uniqueness of black culture. It is within this cultural context that the black community often attempts to relate to the broader urban institutional framework. Much of the impetus has arisen from the approach developed by Charles Hamilton and Stokely Carmichael in *Black Power: The Politics of Liberation*[8] and essays by Carmichael and other Black Power advocates. These authors assert that the powerlessness of black people is the primary reason for their inability to determine what course of action will be taken in their community on a given program, such as urban renewal. The theory of powerlessness can also be applied to a black community's inability to decentralize school boards and

---

[6] Nathan Glazer and Daniel Moynihan, *Beyond the Melting Pot* (Cambridge, Mass.: MIT Press, 1963), p. 53.

[7] Kenneth Clark, *Dark Ghetto* (New York: Harper & Row, 1965), p. 81.

[8] Charles Hamilton and Stokely Carmichael, *Black Power: The Politics of Liberation* (New York: Random House, 1967).

welfare assistance programs. An additional view draws analogies between American ghettos and colonial situations.[9] These analogies are espoused not only by black intellectuals but by many rank-and-file blacks. Finally, even white social scientists such as Banfield and Greer have so emphasized power relationships that seeking power among blacks has ceased to be viewed as abnormal and outside the range of their achievable goals.

This move toward themes of institutional racism, colonial analogies, and power relationships is important for planning, especially for supporters of an approach which purports to attack poverty of lower income blacks within the comprehensive planning framework. While the individual planner, professional, or technician responsible for the plan may or may not be prejudiced, the agencies and urban institutions which must implement the plan are under siege in the black community as being racist in how they define blacks and black community priorities. Today a proposed slum clearance program is prone to come under much more frequent attack by a wider range of black individuals and organizations than before the widespread acceptance of the racism concept.

CONFLICTS IN PROGRAMS

That large numbers of black people are rapidly becoming alienated from the dominant values of American society is attested to by the increasing emphasis that blacks place on: proving that the United States is a racist society; forming strong associational networks with other blacks to the exclusion of whites; and for many, Africanizing their cultural values. The alienation of the black community may also be witnessed in the manner in which the definitions of self, environment, and the goals of alleviating racism are used to define programs. The programs presently demanded in the black community are remarkably similar to those proposed in the emerging social welfare-physical planning approach. Most of the programmatic demands are not revolutionary but are closely aligned with the notion of democratic reformism. It is within this context that urban renewal plans can be assessed. For example, if the plans successfully accomplish the goal of providing standard low-income housing for poor people, then they are simply adhering to one of the premises of the welfare state—that every citizen is entitled to a decent standard of living. Beyond this premise is the most important issue of *which definitions of racism will be utilized in establishing guidelines for policy, personnel, utilization of skills, and goals of particular programs.*

A summary view of the most frequently used urban programs has been provided by Herbert Gans. The programs are typified as schemes for lower class *guided mobility,* or, since 1964, *antipoverty* programs. These schemes emphasize four major programmatic goals: "to extend the amount and quality of present social services to the hard-to-reach lower-class population; to offer new methods of education, especially in the area of job training; to reduce unemployment by training and creation of new jobs; and to encourage self-help both on an individual and group basis, notably through community organization. In addition, programs in recreation, public health, delinquency prevention, and housing are often included in the plan."[10] But as Gans notes, the plans are not intended to deal with social structures but with neighborhoods and their residents.[11] For example, the Chicago and Denver comprehensive plans, as well as the Model

---

[9] Frantz Fanon, *The Wretched of the Earth* (New York: Grove Press, 1963).

[10] Herbert Gans, "Urban Poverty and Social Planning," in Paul Lazarsfeld, ed., *Uses of Sociology* (New York: Basic Books, 1967), p. 441.

[11] Ibid., p. 440.

Cities approach, illustrate the conflicts inherent in such programs. This disparity between the *need* to change social institutions and *programs* of individual and neighborhood improvement threatens to stalemate most of the programs.

Given the definition of racism assumed by planners and social agencies, the guided mobility approach presents a specific danger. Both these comprehensive plans and the Model Cities program emphasize utilization of the existing (discriminatory) political framework to determine policy, and neither plan goes beyond broad abstract goals down to the level of program priorities. *Without programs to alter specific institutional frameworks, tensions will probably increase instead of decrease.* Moreover, the programs relay a false expectancy to the black community about citizen participation and decision making on all levels, but the reality is that they are not intended to give blacks any significant power in determining planning priorities in their communities or in the overall social and physical planning framework. They are programs which are designed to fulfill the cities' vested interests, not to solve the problems of poverty stricken communities. The mayors of large central cities have not been willing to compromise on this issue.

For example, the proposed Model Cities program in Chicago is dependent upon the Chicago Housing Authority's (conclusively racist) site selection policies and City Council decisions on racial balances among communities. Yet, organizations in the black community expect that utilization of the Model Cities program will enable them to shape policies and priorities of site selection for public housing. Specifically, many organizations are interested in low-rise walkups scattered throughout the city. However, the citizen participation arm of the Model Cities program is the local antipoverty program, which in Chicago affords political patronage leverage with limited benefits for low-income

blacks. In Atlanta, an acknowledged member of the Ku Klux Klan is a member of the Model Cities board of directors. It is difficult to see how the program will address itself to the needs of Atlanta's low-income black community when an acknowledged racist is voting on these programs.

Finally, the difficulties of structural changes in the black community are closely related to the established institutional network of urban social services—schools, hospitals, AFDC, and general assistance programs—of which many are racist in their structures and functions and can become meaningful only through a change in sociopolitical structure. Moreover, these programs are aimed only at aiding those individuals who are attracted to them. Many of the dispossessed never hear about the programs, and others have become so alienated through prior negative experiences with social service institutions that they no longer attempt to seek their services.

Thus, the social programs which would be the primary inputs in comprehensive plans for the black community remain basically a part of the larger institutional framework which maintains racism. The issues of racism have largely been defined as problems of attitudes, family disorganization, income, and so on, to give the programs local political feasibility and general acceptance. This is a dangerous game to play in angry black central cities . . . extremely dangerous.

CONFLICTS IN PLANS

The anger of blacks in the ghetto cannot be overemphasized. Given the oppressive political realities, the lack of systematic definitions of racism, and the realization that the professionals given responsibility for social and physical proposals are frequently either part of the oppressive structure or unconcerned with adequate definitions, blacks should be angry. Continuation of present trends in comprehensive planning and the social-welfare approach to ghettos will probably do little to alleviate this peculiar condition of urban bondage.

Many comprehensive plan proposals would only irritate problems in racially torn areas. The goals which offend influential whites are made abstract, without any programmatic means—perhaps indicating a lack of intention to carry out these goals. The goals which affect blacks are linked with specific means which have proven oppressive—such as urban renewal programs. These oppressive goals are supposedly legitimated by citations of citizen participation.

Some examples can be cited to document this serious criticism. *The Chicago Comprehensive Plan,*[12] faced with the possibility of a 41 percent black population and 900,000 or more blacks living in spatially restricted poverty areas by 1985, has placed the highest priority upon maintaining and attracting a white middle class, even though whites have been fleeing Chicago at a rate of 50,000 per year for the past five years. Urban renewal projects are proposed to accommodate middle-income whites remaining or returning to the city with public housing for lower-income blacks. Over a 15-year period, a total of 35,000 units of public housing will be built. Most of these units—unless blacks alter the established political pattern—will be built in the ghetto. Moreover, the public housing program combined with other clearance efforts will force the relocation of 7,500 persons a year, most of whom will be from the ghetto. This vicious cycle will only intensify welfare enclaves in other sections of the city, such as the Westside— where some of the worst of the nation's riots have occurred, and living conditions defy imagination. Yet the *Chicago Comprehensive Plan maintains that its policies and*

priorities were established by citizen participation and public discussion.

The General Plan of Boston,[13] with a smaller black population, utilized a similar approach to renewal within the overall policy framework. Yet both plans represent advances over other efforts. The Boston Plan is honest in its appraisal of the situation of blacks in the region, and the *Chicago Comprehensive Plan* is generally conceded to be a radical departure in its attempt to unify social, economic, and administrative factors with physical improvement programs.[14] Both go considerably further than the *Proposed Comprehensive Plan for the National Capital.*[15] This plan, released in 1967 when over 50 percent of the District of Columbia's population was black, fails to present a clear strategy or a coherent statement of policy and priorities related to the black majority population. The emphasis of the plan, like the Chicago plan, is to attract and retain more middle-income families. However, in fairness, one must note that some time ago integration ceased to be a relevant issue in Washington, and when the Chicago Plan was released, one criticism was that it did not give enough attention to integration.[16] The approach of the Washington Comprehensive Plan was "to produce a physical environment which will support the host of social activities which make up the life of a city. In other words, the physical plan serves social purposes. . . ."[17] Without

---

[12] Department of Development and Planning, *The Chicago Comprehensive Plan* (Chicago: DDP, 1966).

[13] Boston Redevelopment Authority, 1965/1985 *General Plan for the City of Boston* (Boston: BRA, 1964).

[14] Phillip Wallick, "Comment" on Louis B. Wetmore, "The Comprehensive Plan of Chicago," *Journal of the American Institute of Planners* 33, no. 5 (September 1967), pp. 354.

[15] National Capital Planning Commission, *The Proposed Comprehensive Plan for the National Capital* (Washington, DC: NCPC, 1967).

[16] Louis Wetmore, Stanley Hallet, Walter Stafford, Jerome Kaufman, et al., *The Racial Aspects of Comprehensive Planning* (Chicago: Chicago Urban League, 1968).

[17] *The Proposed Comprehensive Plan for the National Capital,* p. 12.

this stated purpose the plan could have manipulated abstract social goals to cover its physical purposes. However, the danger of the approach is that only the middle class (in this case black *and* white) will directly benefit from shaping a physical environment proposed by middle-class planners to support social activities. As we have previously indicated, many blacks consider their sociocultural outlook different from whites, and Washington, D.C., would certainly be an adequate example of our contention. Of equal importance, as other authors have pointed out, structuring physical goals to achieve social ends does not necessarily improve social ills and frequently has no positive effect.[18]

The overall social-physical effects cannot be taken lightly. Eunice and George Grier showed that in the *Policies Plan for the Year 2000*, developed in Washington in 1961 in anticipation of growth of the Washington region: three of the six proposed radial corridors would probably be segregated, and if "Negro expansion is cut off along the three corridors which are presently 'open,' the future population growth will be forced back into the city, thereby intensifying dangerous pressures which already exist."[19] The type of pressure that the Griers alluded to were evident in the April riots of 1968. While we do not propose that the Washington plan was a *direct* contribution to the riots, if our definition of "institutional racism" has any credence, the plan for the U.S. capital, with its unequal priorites for blacks and whites, represents an ideal type. It can be found in central cities all around the country. Integration is not the issue. Whether whites accept blacks is not nearly as relevant as the institutionalization of racism, either in the form of class or race biases, or

in the severe limitations placed on the upward mobility of blacks.

The crucial question then is how to devise comprehensive plans in the face of the problems of massive lower-income black populations. One answer is to obtain a greater knowledge of racism. It is clear that none of the plans previously mentioned adequately defined racism before proceeding to develop a comprehensive plan. The definition of racism was inadequate in approaches to both land use problems and program choices. *Another answer stems from the reality of the political process which confronts the planner. Once the planner adequately defines racism, will the city council, aldermen, or the interest groups who influence planning decisions accept the definition?* Or placed in a broader perspective, can planning, once it develops an approach to racism, equalize the priorities between blacks and whites without developing alternative approaches to the existing central city political situation? The answer to this question, as we perceive it, is *no*. New alternatives must be found and utilized.

SOME ALTERNATIVES

Black majorities

The task of equalizing priorities in central cities will not be simple even if blacks obtain political majorities. The available planning tools are simply not effective in the face of widespread racism. Comprehensive Plans of Chicago, Denver, Boston, and Washington propose that stronger areawide open occupancy laws for housing and zoning be adopted to allow freedom of area residence and increased job availability. Such laws would have limited effectiveness. Evidence shows that open occupancy laws fail to provide any reasonable solution. Usually the passage of fair housing ordinances at the local or state level (22 states have fair housing laws) have been innocuous to say the least, and

---

[18] Gans, p. 439.
[19] Eunice and George Grier, "Equality and Beyond: Housing Segregation in the Great Society," *Daedalus* 95, no. 1 (Winter 1966), p. 89.

only in rare instances have regulations been enforced. Additionally, where these ordinances exist there are usually zoning and subdivision controls which have so effectively boxed in lower income blacks that the ordinances are no more than moralistic gestures. An example of the great future effect of suburban zoning on central city problems has been presented by the Regional Plan Association. "Right now about 2 million persons are living in municipalities which control the zoning and building codes determining where some 13 million will live in the year 2000. . . ."[20]

Furthermore, whites fail to grasp the fact that no one knows how many blacks want to suburbanize. Even if this was the consensus, the fact remains that the sheer numbers required for dispersal of the ghetto through suburbanization make the occurrence unlikely. For example, achieving the population level of 350,000 blacks outside the central city of Chicago by 1980, as projected by the *Chicago Comprehensive Plan*, would require a net migration plus natural increase of over 15,000 blacks per year for the next 15 years.[21] This type of planning is not only politically unfeasible—it reflects wishful thinking!

Nor do the advocates of suburbanization specify the type of communities which would be advantageous for blacks, despite the fact that jobs are in the suburbs and blacks need employment. In the Chicago region, blacks in several suburban communities have been confronted with significant problems which planners have not been able to answer. For example, the black community in Joliet, Illinois, is having considerable difficulty because of an urban renewal project without an adequate relocation plan for the displaced persons. While this type of problem is also

found in the central city, the likelihood of blacks raising a cry and being heard in the suburbs is significantly lessened. Moreover, many of the older suburbs where blacks are likely to eventually find housing are ineffectual political bodies with outstanding land use problems which for a politically isolated black population would be insurmountable. Most central cities are surrounded by communities of this type.

Metropolitan planning

Another response to the problems of black central cities and exclusionary white suburbs has been the requirement of metropolitanwide planning as a condition of federal aid for metropolitan communities. Even if this requirement was strictly enforced, blacks would probably realize only minor gains. Officials in metropolitan planning ageniies are more likely to be persuaded by influential whites than by blacks, who are loosely organized on a metro basis. The effect of metropolitan planning would be to usurp many of the rising political strengths blacks are likely to gain in central cities. Furthermore, response to demands even by regional offices of HUD will not necessarily favor blacks, especially since various federal program requirements are not interlocked. For example, in East Chicago, Indiana, the black community had been demanding that lower income housing be placed outside the ghetto, and the local city council refused. Blacks approached the regional office of HUD. According to newspaper accounts, the officials were sympathetic; however, they could not condition other federal program grants on refusal to select housing sites outside the ghetto. Finally, as Alan Altshuler has pointed out, metropolitan planning eventually approximates metropolian government,[22] and blacks

---

[20] Regional Plan Association, *Basic Issues of the Second Regional Plan* (New York: RPA, 1967).

[21] Wetmore, et al., *The Racial Aspect of Comprehensive Planning*, p. 19.

[22] Alan Altshuler, *The City Planning Process* (Ithaca, N.Y.: Cornell University Press, 1965), p. 420.

have been reluctant to endorse this political arrangement.[23]

Advocacy planning

The limited alternatives that are available are forms of advocacy planning utilizing regional and national political alliances to further its causes. The political impetus in the black community closely approximates the format for advocacy planning. Both are basically concerned with *accountability* of political structure. For blacks, accountability concerns the relevance of organization or group definitions of racism, the layout of the decision-making apparatus, and what influence particular organizations have upon decisions which affect blacks. Planners seem to be concerned much more with the pluralistic democracy which advocacy planning affords. However, both approaches are concerned with the use of power, particularly how power is utilized to maintain and sanction oppressive patterns. Second, advocacy planning offers the possibility of analyzing the racial content of proposed planning programs and land use alternatives. Within this framework, advocacy planners would not only serve as technical advisors but would frequently become instigators of political reforms. Local leaders might even run for office on "technical" issues such as zoning or sewerage, thus bringing a new dimension to the political life of the ghetto while pinpointing the accountable elements in city government. A third possibility for advocacy planning is that blacks through increased political leverage will be able to secure demonstration grants from foundations and government sources to document the impact of social and physical planning proposals on racism. A fourth possibility for advocacy planning is suggesting institutional alternatives. Frieden has discussed the case of health service

planning being extended into already established areas of social policy.[24] In this case, advocate planners with knowledge of the potential impact that particular policies are likely to have on black communities could suggest alternatives or propose new approaches. This, however, would require a new type of social-scientist-planner who could not only *propose* but *predict* patterns of change. Fifth, advocacy planning, through its emphasis upon political conflict as a desirable end, appears to lean toward decentralization of authority. Finally, an intermediate group of semiprofessional advocates could be trained in basic design, analysis of census tract data, surveys, and other primary techniques to build a semiprofessional planning staff in local black communities. Many black communities will not be able to provide adequate salaries to hire competent planners in the near future. Rather than settling for well-meaning planners without knowledge of racism, comprehensive planning, and politics, it would be better to train young blacks (including dropouts) who wish to learn art, drafting, community organization, and the like.

PLANS AND BATTLES

We have not presented all the ramifications of comprehensive planning and racism. It would take a book—which incidentally needs to be written—to document a systematic theoretical approach to racism and planning. All we are sure of at this point is that the approach needs further development and that blacks are now waiting for planners to develop it. Planners have to realize that they are very close to the urban battlefield, and on the urban battlefield one recognizes only the relevant. For the planner, an irrelevant understanding and definition of racism is worse than no definition at all.

---

[23] Scott Greer, *Metropolitics* (New York: John Wiley & Sons, 1963).

[24] Bernard Frieden, "The Changing Prospects for Social Planning," *Journal of the American Institute of Planners* 33, no. 5 (September 1967), pp. 311–23.

37

The sociology of knowledge and the problems of the inner cities

Roland L. Warren

This paper examines the social structuring of knowledge concerned with the problems of the inner cities, particularly involving low-income residents in deteriorated neighborhoods. The analysis emerged from a series of perplexing problems encountered in a study of the participation of a number of community decision organizations in the Model Cities programs of nine cities. In the course of addressing these theoretical problems, relationships among various aspects of an institutionalized thought structure became apparent. Considered together, these aspects constitute an interlocking, mutually supporting, cognitive ordering of the "poverty problem" which is reflected not only in a knowledge and belief system but in the social structure of the interactional field of those organizations which are legitimated to address the problem. The bulk of this article analyzes the interrelationship between thought system and social structure in this segment of society.

As is well known, the examination of the relationship between knowledge and social structure raises the question as to whether the pointing out of such relationships invalidates the substantive aspects of the knowledge itself. In this, we take the

epistemologically conservative position (or actually, non-position), asserting, with Znaniecki, that the sociologist "is not entitled to make any judgments concerning the validity of any systems of knowledge except sociological systems."[1] Hence, the observation that a certain idea serves to perform a "function" in relation to some system or group is not to challenge its validity, any more than the *argumentum ad hominem* constitutes a logically acceptable refutation of a debated idea.

The "ordering" of experience into a conceptual framework related to the social position of the observer is approached by Kuhn in a special way which is particularly relevant to the present analysis. His central concept is that of the scientific paradigm. He explains his use of the concept of paradigms:

By choosing it, I mean to suggest that some accepted examples of actual scientific practice— examples which include law, theory, application, and instrumentation together—provide models from which spring particular coherent traditions of scientific research. These are the traditions which the historian describes under such rubrics as "Ptolemaic astronomy" (or "Copernican"), "Aristotelian dynamics" (or "Newtonian"), "corpuscular optics" (or "wave optics"), and so on.[2]

Although Kuhn does not deal with the sociology of knowledge (in terms of the social-relational aspects of scientific knowledge), his analysis is highly relevant to it, and compatible with it. For he main-

Reprinted with permission of the University of Texas Press from Roland L. Warren, "The Sociology of Knowledge and the Problems of the Inner Cities," *Social Science Quarterly*, 52, no. 3 (December, 1971): 468–85. Copyright © 1971 by the Southwestern Social Science Association. The footnotes have been renumbered.

The author's work is supported by a research scientist award (No. K3-MH-21, 869) from the National Institute of Mental Health. The research project on which this paper is based was supported by a grant from the National Institute of Mental Health. Special thanks are due Stephen M. Rose, who acted as stimulus for this paper and as critic of earlier drafts.

[1] Florian Znaniecki, *The Social Role of the Man of Knowledge* (New York: Columbia University Press, 1940), p. 5.

[2] Thomas S. Kuhn, *The Structure of Scientific Revolutions* (2d ed.; Chicago University of Chicago Press, 1970), p. 10.

tains that contrary to widely-held impressions, scientific knowledge does not advance through gradual accumulation of new knowledge and correction of previous error marked by particularly important discoveries. Rather, these important discoveries tend to mark discontinuities in the historical process; for a discovery is not merely a new addition to knowledge but characteristically brings with it a new definition of research problems and has reverberations throughout fairly large areas of scientific knowledge. Data which were formerly thought important are now regarded as inconsequential; problems which were recognized as unexplained but relatively unimportant now become critical. A new set of ways of conceptualizing, of relating data to each other, of ways of defining problems, of research techniques, usually accompanies such "scientific revolutions." These he defines simply as the supplanting of one scientific paradigm by another. He indicates that paradigm development is a symptom of the maturity of a science, and expresses doubt as to the status of the social sciences, saying that "it remains an open question what parts of social science have yet acquired such paradigms at all. History suggests that the road to a firm research consensus is extraordinarily arduous.[3]

The importance of Kuhn's analysis for the present paper lies in his emphasizing the characteristic discontinuities in scientific knowledge which exist between paradigms, and his explanation of the way in which the acceptance or rejection of an alternative paradigm involves a whole interrelated series of theoretical statements, problem formulations, testing methods, and data analyses. Once the structured paradigm is accepted, "normal science" can be pursued. It proceeds by "extending the knowledge of those facts that the paradigm displays as particularly revealing, by increasing the extent of the match between those facts and the paradigm's predic-

tions, and by further articulation of the paradigm itself."[4] He characterizes these procedures as "mopping-up operations" and asserts that such activities "engage most scientists throughout their careers."[5]

We need only add here that according to Kuhn such operations often lead to the uncovering of "anomalies," data which are not readily assimilable by the paradigm. As such anomalies increase, a crisis is reached which is accompanied on the one hand by increasing doubt in the adequacy of the paradigm and on the other by the emergence of one or more alternative paradigms which purport to account better for the anomalies. With the supplanting of the original paradigm by one of these new contenders, a scientific revolution has been affected.

In incorporating Kuhn's concept of the paradigm into the sociology of knowledge and applying it to the social structuring of the problems of the inner cities, we will make special use of his notion that a paradigm brings with in not only an "explanation" of a problem, but also a "reformulation" of the problem in conjunction with the explanation, a redefinition of what orders of data bear significantly on the problem, what orders of data are more or less irrelevant to it, and what methods of research validation are called for.

All of the above characteristics are present in the diagnosis of the social problems associated with poverty in the inner cities, and hence this complex of ideas will be referred to in this paper as the "diagnostic paradigm."

THE INTERORGANIZATIONAL STUDY PROJECT

The research project on which this paper is based was addressed primarily to theory, as distinguished from practice. Its goals were to provide exploratory generalizations regarding the behavior of a pur-

---

[3] Ibid., p. 15.

[4] Ibid., p. 24.
[5] Ibid.

posive sample of community decision organizations, to test a number of hypotheses concerning their interorganizational behavior, and to explore the nature of the interorganizational field in which this interaction occurs.

Community decision organizations are defined as organizations which are legitimated to make decisions on behalf of the community in a specified sector of interests.[6] Six such organizations were chosen for study, in nine different cities. The six organizations are: public school system, urban renewal agency, health and welfare council, community action agency (poverty program), model cities agency, and mental health planning agency. The cities were chosen as a purposive sample. Seven are middle-range cities with populations of 250,000 to 750,000, chosen to represent a broad distribution on 13 different variables, including such "hard" variables as "per capita income" and "percent nonwhite" and such "soft" variables as "degree of commitment to citizen participation in the Model Cities planning grant application." These cities are: Oakland, Denver, San Antonio, Columbus, Atlanta, Newark, and Boston. In addition, Detroit was chosen as a city of much larger population than the others, and Manchester, N.H., as a smaller city.

Field research associates were in these cities on a half-time basis for a period of 26 months from July 1968 through August 1970, gathering data in the form of schedules, questionnaires, structured interviews, and documents, as well as through observation at various meetings.

It was decided to give special emphasis to the Model Cities program (all these cities were deliberately chosen from the "first round" of Model Cities), since it was anticipated that this program by its very nature would generate interaction among these sample organizations. Extensive data were gathered regarding certain organizational variables as well as a number of interaction variables, at first before the Model Cities program, then during its planning stage, and again during the early part of the implementation stage.

Among the several variables of the study, three were given special attention and included in a number of preliminary hypotheses. These were: interaction on a cooperation/contest scale; agency responsiveness to the needs and wishes of slum area residents; and innovativeness in administration, program, or interaction patterns. Each of these concepts required painstaking conceptual clarification and became somewhat transformed in the process of clarification and operationalization, as will be indicated later. It was partly in relation to this transforming process that some of the interconnections between knowledge and social structure became apparent.

We turn now to a consideration of the component parts of the institutionalized thought structure referred to earlier.

THE DIAGNOSTIC PARADIGM

By diagnostic paradigm is meant that paradigm which carries the "explanation" for why certain people are poor or disadvantaged, and in so doing implies the way poverty will be conceptualized as a problem, what strategies will be utilized to deal with it, what technologies will be required, and what aspects of the total situation surrounding poverty will be singled out as highly significant, and what aspects will be left as unimportant or irrelevant.

Two alternative paradigms are available for diagnosing poverty as a basis for conceptualization, strategy, and technology.

---

[6] For an elaboration of the concept of community decision organizations, see Roland L. Warren, "The Interaction of Community Decision Organizations: Some Basic Concepts and Needed Research," *Social Service Review* 41 (September 1967), and "The Interorganizational Field as a Focus of Investigation," *Administrative Science Quarterly* 12 (December 1967). Both these articles are contained in the author's *Truth, Love, and Social Change—and Other Essays on Community Change* (Chicago: Rand McNally, 1971).

Although both are fairly familiar in the poverty literature, one is clearly preferred when it comes to the moment of strategy choice. These two paradigms can be called, respectively, the approach based on "individual deficiency" and the "dysfunctional social structure" approach. The one paradigm takes as its point of orientation the particular situation of the individual-in-poverty, emphasizing that his poverty, as well as other attendant problems, is associated with his inability to function adequately within the accepted norms of American society. We call this Diagnostic Paradigm I. The other paradigm takes as its point of orientation the aspects of the social system which purportedly produce poverty as a system-output. We call this Diagnostic Paradigm II. Looked at from the standpoint of action orientation, Diagnostic Paradigm I indicates the need for a change in the individual, while Diagnostic Paradigm II indicates the need for a change in the social structure. We need not burden the reader by repeating the contents of these two positions which are widely familiar. A recent work by Rose gives a lucid and systematic resumé of the two positions, in relation to a study of the anti-poverty program.[7]

The sophisticated reader may ask, "*Must* we choose? Isn't it perfectly plausible to consider poverty as an integral property of the social structure while at the same time acknowledging that on a different level, individual people may experience serious social handicaps because of their poverty, and may need individual help to overcome these deficiencies?" The logical answer would seem to be an unqualified affirmative. But the sociological answer must be more equivocal. For in actual practice, just as Kuhn indicates for the natural sciences, the choice of either paradigm presumes a different conceptual framework, steers attention to different variables, poses problems of a different order, and suggests different methods of approach to solve these problems.

Hence, there are at present two competing diagnostic paradigms, each of which calls attention to different components of the problems, each of which can be granted "face" validity. But as will be shown, only one of these diagnostic paradigms, the approach based on individual deficiency, is part of an institutionalized thought structure.

THE INTERVENTION STRATEGY

The intervention strategy associated with Diagnostic Paradigm I is that of "providing services," broadly speaking, to a disadvantaged population. By such means, they will be restored, equipped, rehabilitated, and helped to become more nearly adequate to cope as self-sustaining, norm-abiding members of the larger society. As this occurs, they will take positions in the social structure which are provided for all who have "normal" competence to perform as members of society.

Diagnostic Paradigm I thus leads to an array of services, broadly considered, which permeate the institutional structure. In education, these are illustrated by special classes for slow learners, remedial reading courses, special education courses, and an array of other remedial approaches. As regards the economy, there are the manpower training programs, including the more widespread programs designed to instill regular and acceptable work habits, dress and speech habits, and vocational training, as well as the programs to help minority group members learn how to become individual entrepreneurs—"black capitalists." In the political area, inarticulate groups are

---

[7] Stephen M. Rose, *Community Action Programs: The Relationship between Initial Conception of the Poverty Problem, Derived Intervention Strategy, and Program Implementation*, Doctoral Diss., Florence Heller Graduate School for Advanced Studies in Social Welfare, Brandeis University, 1970. Published in 1972 by Schenkman Publishing Co., Cambridge, with the title *The Betrayal of the Poor: The Transformation of Community Action*.

taught that the pluralistic democratic system of government leaves room for all groups to represent their interests and win the support of a majority. Hence, they must be taught the value of voting, and something about the official decision-making processes and the way citizens can influence them. In the area of family life, they are helped through casework and counseling to become more adequate as family members, to play their family roles more responsibly and more effectively. In the area of associational activity, they are helped through "social group work" to learn to participate more effectively in formal and informal groups. Many of the poor get into trouble with the law. Consequently, protective services are designed to assure that children will not be abused nor come under immoral home influences. Children or adults who have committed law violations are afforded probation services in lieu of being held in custody. For those who are incarcerated, there is a parole system to ease the transition to law-abiding behavior after release. Since health problems are often associated with inability to function adequately, special social services are afforded to the sick and their families. Finally (although this list does not exhaust the service field), many of the above deficiencies or handicaps are associated with personality difficulties which require the services of psychological counseling, psychotherapy, or casework, or some mixture thereof.

This partial list serves to illustrate the extent to which the "social services" strategy permeates the spectrum of problems associated with various parts of the institutional structure. There are one or more services to correspond to almost every type of deficiency in institutional participation.

Accepting the paradigm and implied social services strategy, then, what are the normal "mopping up" problems within the human services field, impeding prog-

ress toward solving the poverty problem?

These "mopping up" problems are subsumable under the rubric of "improving service delivery systems." Various factors are thought to impede the optimal application and utilization of the social services described above, with the result that they are and continue to be ineffective in their impact on poor people.

A major problem area is recognized to inhere in the agencies themselves. This is the widely acknowledged tendency for middle-class professional people to prefer to serve middle-class clients and patients, people with whom they feel comfortable, people who make "good patients," people who, whether or not they are poor, don't act that way. The middle-class "knows" how to manipulate the system, how to get its share, and so service programs as programs are systematically deflected to the more advantaged groups and do not reach those for whom they were intended.

In summary: within Diagnostic Paradigm I and its attendant service strategy, the professional "problems" lie in the structure of service delivery systems, and "progress" lies in their improvement. The Model Cities program represented an intervention strategy to solve these problems as a means of more effectively attacking poverty.

SUPPORTING BELIEF/VALUE SYSTEM

We shall here discuss briefly certain relevant aspects of the belief-value system of the larger American society, of which the community decision organizations, along with more numerous direct-service agencies, are a part and from which they derive support.

The first aspect of the relevant belief-value system of American society is closely related to Diagnostic Paradigm I. American society, though hardly perfect, is *essentially sound in its institutional composition*.

The social problems which attend it, including slums and poverty, are caused either by temporary periods of malfunctioning which are only transitory (business depressions or readjustments), by wickedness (dishonest politicians, occasional fraud and malfeasance among industrial leaders, and organized criminals), and by a residual problem-population comprising individuals who will not or cannot cope with the demands made for norm-abiding performance in various segments of the institutional structure.

Although such problems are serious, progress in solving them is being achieved. The two most important dynamics in such progress can be subsumed under the rubrics of democratic pluralism and science.

Democratic pluralism is a political and governmental system in which an equitable structure of governmental decision making, administration, and adjudication prevails and in which these governmental channels are appropriately responsive to the needs, wishes, and rights of the electorate. If a group is unorganized it is its own fault, for all citizens have the right to organize and press their interests.

The second major dynamic of progress is *science*. As science advances, not only is a basis provided for improved physical well-being, but various professions are able to draw on scientific knowledge to help solve the so-called human problems attendant upon technological progress.

Another dynamic of progress, perhaps less basic than the first two, is *organizational reform*. Problems of bureaucracy and unresponsiveness must be acknowledged. But there is a constant process of organizational reform taking place which inevitably improves organizational performance. The constant clamor for organizational improvement is reflected in most any professional journal in the various service fields mentioned earlier.

A final aspect of the belief-value system can be called the *principle of inducements*. In many cases, an agency must be given an inducement—often in the form of a financial grant—to "make it worth its while" to take on some new responsibility, function, program, or clientele group.

This selection of aspects of the supporting belief-value system is not exhaustive, but it includes some of the more relevant and important components: the basic soundness of the American institutional structure, democratic pluralism, science, organizational reform, and the principle of inducements. These major beliefs from the larger society sustain Diagnostic Paradigm I and the social services strategy. They also support the technical and administrative rationales of the community decision organizations engaged with problems of the inner cities.

TECHNICAL AND ADMINISTRATIVE RATIONALES

Direct service is based on a professional-client relationship. The professional has as the basis for his performance a practice theory presumably derived from "science." Although the professional may be "permissive" and "non-directive," he is this way because of his own professional conviction, and not because of an accountability to the client to be so. The professional person is responsible for serving the client, but is not directly accountable to the client.

Whether or not they provide such direct services, community decision organizations such as the six in this study are by definition legitimated to make decisions on behalf of the community in their respective sectors of interest. In this function they are concerned with the planning and coordination of the direct services which are administered by them or by others. This function can be conceptualized as the concerting of decisions at the community level. By concerted decision making is meant a process through which the decisions of a plurality of actors which would otherwise be made independently are made in direct relation to one another.[8] The objective of such concerted decision making is to optimize the benefits derived from the actions based on those decisions.

In the interorganizational field of community decision organizations, concerted decision making is usually called "planning" or "coordination of agency efforts." The principles of comprehensiveness and coordination are widely accepted as axiomatic.

Comprehensiveness constitutes a constant justification for striving toward a "full" battery of services, which in turn becomes a rationale for proliferation of varieties of service and expansion of agency budgets. But it is important in that it creates a need for "coordination." New and improved techniques such as psychological tests, teaching machines, and closed circuit television—to use the educational field as one example—constantly push out the borders of what constitutes "comprehensiveness." Operational coordination is facilitated by data banks and other data control systems assuring that service recipients will be referred to the proper facilities at the proper time. Allocational coordination is facilitated not only by advanced data control systems, but also by system analysis, PPBS, cost-benefits analysis, and a number of other new and complex technologies.

LEGITIMATION AND POWER

Legitimation is here taken to mean the acknowledged right of an organization to operate in a particular field. By definition, community decision organizations are legitimated to carry on decision-making activities in their respective fields of interest. The rationale for such legitimation has already been considered. American society has a certain residual problem population unable to function adequately without assistance; these people must therefore be helped through social services. These services must be comprehensive, and they must be coordinated. Such coordination is facilitated through technical efficiency. Community decision organizations fulfill this important function of coordination.

Although it cannot be adequately substantiated in this paper, it is pertinent to note the considerable power which lies in the ability of such community decision organizations to:

1. Define the "social problems" which they are addressing.
2. Define the nature of what "must be done" in order to solve them.
3. Control the intervention strategies that are brought to bear on them.
4. Evaluate the results of their interventions.
5. "Control" the communications media through which these listed aspects become the subject matter for public discussion—in newspapers, professional schools, and professional journals.

Needless to say, each of these power aspects is currently under challenge by various militant groups speaking for ghetto residents as well as by intellectual dissidents. We shall return to this challenge later for analysis from the standpoint of the sociology of knowledge.

SOCIAL RESEARCH AND EVALUATION

Organizational reform, science, and technical efficiency constitute strong related supports for research and evaluation. We refer here to the application of the methods and findings of social science in order both to develop more effective services to help those who need them and to

---

[8] For an elaboration of the concept, see Roland L. Warren, "Concerted Decision-making in the Community," in *The Social Welfare Forum, 1965* (New York: Columbia University Press, 1965). It is also included in *Truth, Love, and Social Change.*

evaluate the effectiveness of the services which are given. The ascendancy of social science and social research in relation to social service agencies in the last two decades hardly needs documenting. Its function in relation to Paradigm I will be considered later.

CHARACTERISTICS OF THE INTERORGANIZATIONAL FIELD

The Brandeis study was directed not only to the class of individual community decision organizations as units of analysis, but also to the field, or network of such organizations in each city, taken as a unit of analysis in its own right. Several characteristics of this interorganizational field in the various cities are pertinent to the present discourse.

First, the field was found to be surprisingly stable in its major dimensions over a period of years during which many impacts were being made both from national programs and from slum resident agitation. An earlier study by Rose documented substantially the same phenomenon for the poverty program as was found for the Model Cities program. Organizational domains remained substantially the same, and taken as a whole the organizations were able to absorb the impact from federal programs and local disadvantaged groups with a minimum of noticeable change either as individual organizations or in relationship to each other.

Surprisingly little interaction of any but the most routine type among these organizations was uncovered by the study. It had been anticipated—mistakenly—that the scramble for federal funds would engender much intense competitive interaction. Very little was found. The reason seems to be that the respective domains have emerged through time and through a process of competitive mutual adjustment, so that only rarely do these agencies struggle intensely over the question of which of them should do a particular thing. Likewise, since their respective technologies and administrative styles are geared to the same basic diagnostic paradigm and intervention strategy, they contest with each other only rarely about the substance of what should be done.

This ecological balance among and within CDOs, like Norton Long's owls and field mice in a five-acre woodlot, is well adapted to the technologies, administrative styles, and institutional positions of the individual CDOs. The ecological balance is based on reciprocal support. Putting this another way, given the existing balance, if any particular CDO did not exist, it would almost "have to be invented" —or at least its function would have to. This may be one reason why such CDOs appear so characteristically across the whole face of the United States, and why in this nine-city study, the entire *dramatis personae* of CDOs was there in each city.

As an interacting system, these CDOs and others like them do not often manifestly or dramatically "resist change." Rather, they manifestly "desire change" and attempt to bring it about on behalf of their clients. But they dominate the definition of where the problem lies, what has to be changed, and by whom and with what methods. As indicated above, the resulting "changes" constitute mutually compatible adaptive adjustments at the margins within a stable and controllable (even if not wholly predictable) environment.

"MODEL CITIES" AND THE INSTITUTIONALIZED THOUGHT STRUCTURE

The Model Cities program was a program to "improve the quality of urban life," especially in the slum areas of the 150 participating cities. This was to be accomplished through concentrating a comprehensive program in these slum areas. It was recognized that if the effort was to be successful, the agencies, public and private, concerned with these problems and operative in the slum areas would have to become increasingly responsive to the needs and wishes of the residents. An essential means for bringing this about was to be the participation of the residents in the planning of these programs. Final authority must rest with the municipal government. Although not mentioned in the 1966 legislation, the objective of strengthening the city government, particularly the mayor or chief executive, was considered highly desirable and essential for lasting progress. It was also recognized that new types of programs would have to be developed.

A specific list of objectives was given in the 1966 legislation and became the outline for the administrative guidelines to implement the program:

. . . to plan, develop, and carry out locally prepared and scheduled comprehensive city demonstration programs containing new and imaginative proposals to rebuild or revitalize large slum and blighted areas; to expand housing, job, and income opportunities; to reduce dependence on welfare payments; to improve educational facilities and programs; to combat disease and ill health; to reduce the incidence of crime and delinquency; to enhance recreational and cultural opportunities; to establish better access between homes and jobs; and generally to improve living conditions for the people who live in such areas, and to accomplish these objectives through the most effective and economical concentration and coordination of Federal, State, and local public and private efforts to improve the quality of urban life.

It should be noted that these objectives are compatible with the prevalent diagnostic paradigm of individual deficiency (Diagnostic Paradigm I) as well as the alternative paradigm of a dysfunctional social structure (Diagnostic Paradigm II).

In the Model Cities activity in the nine cities of the Brandeis study, two observations seem warranted:

1. Although the Model Cities objectives were amenable to either of the two diagnostic paradigms, Diagnostic Paradigm I prevailed in almost all situations. We believe that the explanation for this circumstance is available in the analysis of the operation of the institutionalized thought structure based on this paradigm.

2. A major difference between the two diagnostic paradigms is that Paradigm I is accompanied by other components of an institutionalized thought structure, but Paradigm II is not. The absence of, or severe deficiency in, other components of an institutionalized thought structure corresponding to Paradigm II helps account for the constantly observed "drift" of organizational behavior toward Paradigm I wherever an alternative is presented.

On the basis of the above, we state a third proposition:

3. Purposive change strategies such as the antipoverty program and the Model Cities program are bound to have extremely little effectiveness in changing social conditions so long as they do not help to create alternative institutionalized thought structures based on different diagnostic paradigms and containing components which are as integrally supportive of the alternative paradigms as are the components of Paradigm I.

These propositions are stated didactically here, so that the reader may keep them in mind as he considers the following analysis of the relation of the response to Model Cities in these nine cities to the existence of an institutionalized thought structure associated with Paradigm I. We shall try to show how the response, even on the part of residents who were hostile to the existing interorganizational structure, was such as to strengthen this existing structure rather than to weaken it or supplant it or modify it in major fashion.

SOME CONSEQUENCES OF THE INSTITUTIONALIZED THOUGHT STRUCTURE

Consider Diagnostic Paradigm I with its attendant institutionalized thought structure. It accepts the main outlines of the American social structure but sees individual deviants as problematic, the anomalies which still impede the optimal functioning of the system. It defines the intervention problem as treating these anomalies. Ineffectiveness in the application of such therapy is in turn diagnosed in terms of the system as a whole: the essentially therapeutic social services are not coordinated, they are not rationalized. The remedy lies in their being brought into more deliberate and purposive systemic relationship to each other. Hence: comprehensiveness, coordination, planning, and participation. There are all directed at making the system more effective as it controls the anomalies of individual deviance. Note that the remedy is not in changing the major structural aspects of the system, but rather in improving the coordination among those components of the system which treat anomalies. The anomalies, deficient individuals, constitute the fringe problems which supporters of the paradigm work on in system-maintaining activities corresponding to "normal science" in the explanatory mode—marginal "mopping-up" operations. By the same token, attention is upon the "public interest," rather than the interests of such marginal problematic individuals. They must be helped, but it may be in the public interest to put welfare mothers to work, to remove low-income homes for highway construction, to gather data banks for the more effective operation of agency programs, etc.

Again, participation of the poor in devising programs for improving living conditions (amenable to either Diagnostic Paradigm I or II) is desirable; but it must of course flow through regularized channels, must not become "disruptive," and must somehow blend into the notion of comprehensive planning in the public interest. If not, it is obstructionist, disruptive, irrational, ineffective, and rebellious.

Innovation, in turn, take on a particular meaning when associated with a thought structure which emphasizes system stability, which seeks to "contain" deviancy, and which looks for maximal "coordination" of parts (whether or not it finds it). Innovation is mightily constrained by such considerations. Innovation which is not so constrained is considered nonprofessional, irrational, unscientific, wasteful, and potentially destructive.

And, indeed, we have been impressed by the finding that innovation in Model Cities programs has been contained almost completely within the components and constraints of the institutionalized thought structure associated with Diagnostic Paradigm I. Further, in those very few instances in which innovation took the form of a program derived from Diagnostic Paradigm II, it was vigorously opposed by the existing organizations.

Likewise, responsiveness—sensitivity to the needs and wishes of the disadvantaged population—was considered an objective to be striven for in the Model Cities program in order that services might be made more effective in helping deficient individuals. Our findings indicated that the moves toward increasing responsiveness were almost all within the constraints of the control of the situation by the agencies, and under such constraints as those of scientific and professional expertise (technical rational) and of the need for continued convenience and viability of the organizations (administrative rationale) and within the mandate of these community decision organizations to provide needed services to a clientele who in the last analysis are laymen and not in a position to define their own needs, even though they may be highly articulate about their own wishes.

One can go right down the line indicating the manner in which the Model Cities program has been molded to fit the components of the prevalent institutionalized thought structure. The overwhelming preponderance of individual projects, in Model Cities as earlier in the poverty programs, was based on a services strategy rather than a structural change strategy.[9]

We have already indicated, in terms of comprehensiveness, concentration, coordination, participation, and central control (in the form of strengthening City Hall), how the intervention strategy of Model Cities was directed not at changing the social structure which generates poverty and "deviancy" but rather at changing (by making more effective through "planning") the organizations directly dealing with poor populations so that their services would be more effective.

We have indicated that a belief-value system which emphasizes the essential soundness of the institutional order, democratic pluralism, science, organizational reform, and the principle of inducements, is admirably suited to a response such as Model Cities to the increasing salience of inner cities problems.

We have also alluded to administrative and technical rationales which, as we shall show, operate to form constraints on change, particularly on change which would institute programs based on a different diagnostic paradigm.

Four developments have appeared frequently in the Model Cities activities in the nine cities and are related especially to the matter of the technologies associated with Paradigm I. We believe they all are accountable for by the apparent rejection of Paradigm I by disadvantaged groups but the absence of a technology which would implement programs based on an alternative paradigm, such as Paradigm II (dysfunctional social structure).

1. The first is the widely noted dissent behavior, involving protests, boycotts, and other kinds of veto activity. This activity we conceive as a rudimentary and elementary way of reacting against the institutionalized thought structure of Para-

digm I in the absence of a technology suited to a different paradigm. The criticism is often made that such resident groups are loud in their protest but have no viable alternatives to present. We believe this is quite true; but it is given an adequate assessment only if the relationship of the dissent to the entire institutionalized thought structure is properly understood. Yes, they only protest; and yes, they have no alternative technology to offer.

2. This being the case, the second development is highly relevant. There has been a growth of "advocacy planning" precisely in order to afford disadvantaged groups the technical competence which they need in order to formulate program proposals of their own. But the important—widely ignored—aspect of this situation is that advocacy planners, themselves, have technical competence only of the type which is applicable to operation within the prevalent institutionalized thought structure. They do not have an articulate technology and expertness regarding alternative strategies designed to change the institutional structure on the basis of Paradigm II. Hence, we come to a development which was seen at first as quite anomalous in terms of the study's original assumptions.

3. The third development has been that to the extent that resident groups have gained power in the program-planning process, they almost without exception have come up with substantially the same type of (Paradigm I) programs as have the more established agencies in cases where resident groups had little power. Decision-making power, often hard-fought and hard-won by resident groups,[10] seems to have made little difference in the actual programs. We had

---

[9] This statement is based on Rose's work cited earlier and on an analysis of the supplementary funded Model Cities programs in the nine cities of the present study.

[10] Roland L. Warren, "Model Cities First Round: Politics, Planning and Participation," *Journal of the American Institute of Planners*, 35 (July, 1969). This is also included in the author's *Truth, Love, and Social Change*.

anticipated that since such resident groups were highly critical of the existing programs, and since many of them expressed in one way or another an apparently clear grasp of and identification with Paradigm II (dysfunctional social structure), they would drastically alter the nature of the programs when they had power. Both they and their advocacy planners, where they had them, slipped inadvertently into modes of response based on Paradigm I, the only paradigm which offered explicit technologies for addressing the problems.

4. The fourth development overlaps the other somewhat, but deserves special treatment. Cooptation occurred, both of the usual types and of a type not yet treated in the literature.[11] We have seen in numerous instances the success which community decision organizations have had in confronting challenges by disadvantaged citizens who were rejecting the placing of the problem at their own door and who claimed to see it in the institutional structure. The interaction process characteristically worked out in such a manner that the organization could appeal to its administrative and technical constraints—to the exigencies of running an organization, to civil service requirements, to law or regulation, to the "facts of organizational life"—or to a set of professional standards or procedures—whether for curriculum building or for the administration of health care or the proper role of therapist and client—which in effect resulted in the problem's being defined in such a way that no matter how it was resolved, the organization could accommodate the resolution without major difficulty, and often with distinct advantage. This often was accompanied by an incipient redefinition of the problem from that of Paradigm II to that of Paradigm I.

Thus, the absence of a technology to correspond to Paradigm II was a distinct handicap in the citizens' attempt to challenge or repudiate Paradigm I, and eventuated in their inadvertently returning to Paradigm I either of their own accord, or in interaction with an agency, or through the mediation of advocacy planners.

But such cooptation is not the only resource available to existing agencies in encountering challenges to Paradigm I. The analysis by Berger and Luckmann is especially crucial at this point. They note that "the appearance of an alternative symbolic universe poses a threat because its very existence demonstrates empirically that one's own universe is less than inevitable."[12] They indicate that those who question the existing ideology are perceived as deviants, and they then point out that the expected strategy for the deviant is "therapy." They note the important function of such therapy from the standpoint of the sociology of knowledge: "Successful therapy establishes a symmetry between the conceptual machinery and its subjective appropriation in the individual's consciousness; it resocializes the deviant into the objective reality of the symbolic universe of the society."[13] Therapy, they point out, is a means of keeping everyone within the accepted thought structure. Nihilation, on the other hand, is a process used to "liquidate conceptually" everything *outside* the same thought structure.[14] They speculate further: "Whether one then proceeds from nihilation to therapy, or rather goes on to liquidate physically what one has liquidated conceptually, is a practical question of policy.[15] Such physical liquidation, in the current jargon, is the familiar "repression." The

[11]J. Wayne Newton, "Cooptation in the Interaction of Community Decision Organizations," Mimeographed, Florence Heller Graduate School for Advanced Studies in Social Welfare, Brandeis University, December 1970.

[12] Peter L. Berger and Thomas Luckmann, *The Social Construction of Reality: A Treatise in the Sociology of Knowledge* (Garden City, N.Y.: Anchor Books, 1967), p. 108.

[13] Ibid., p. 114.

[14] Ibid.

[15] Ibid., p. 115.

widespread use of the term, one might add, indicates that the possibility of physical liquidation as an alternative to therapy is not only an abstract, conceptual one, but one which plays a role in the struggle of competing ideologies.

But again, on what power base would new, competing ideologies rest? "How many troops do they have?" Many ideas that challenge the prevalent thought structure are entertained and considered with little apparent resistance so long as they are not linked to a power base, to a dynamic movement which threatens to "carry" the ideas in competition with the prevailing ones. It is at such a point of threat that power beyond the ordinary system-maintaining operations of the institutionalized thought structure will likely be employed. But such power is a second line of defense for an existing institutionalized thought structure, the first being its ability to redefine the challenge in its own terms, or, in our language, to translate it into the prevalent paradigm, where what "fits" can be dealt with within the institutionalized thought structure and what cannot be made to fit can be sloughed off as unimportant or as a temporary aberration —an anomaly. Berger and Luckmann's stern words about physical liquidation are therefore pertinent primarily in those situations where therapy and "translation" are ineffective in neutralizing the counter-paradigm, and where that paradigm has acquired the social dynamic of a supporting group with sufficient power to challenge the prevalent institutionalized thought structure.

These statements are didactic; we do not claim to have proved them. Rather, we merely assert that such statements help clarify our own findings, and our findings lend them strong circumstantial support. This is especially the case in regard to the central theme of "therapy" in Diagnostic Paradigm I and to the processes of administrative, technical, and personnel cooptation which were operative.

The power to define the problem, or, in our terms, to impose one's own diagnostic paradigm and its attendant institutionalized thought structure, is especially pertinent to the conducting of research. In considering the supportive role of social research, it is important to recognize that most of the prevalent research takes as its point of departure the prevalent diagnostic paradigm.

One can identify five principal types of social science research related to the attack on the problems of the inner city. The first is a general category of social science studies which were not designed specifically for the improvement of services, but which nevertheless describe conditions or circumstances in findings which have been picked up by the agencies and social scientists doing research for them. An excellent example of this is the work of Oscar Lewis on the culture of poverty, a conception which gives universal credibility to the notion of individual deficiency.[16] Other types of social science analysis, equally relevant, do not get "picked up" in such a manner. One is the Marxian studies, both in this country and abroad, which not only challenge the paradigm but have the most nearly complete set of component parts of an alternative institutionalized thought structure. The other is the writings in this field of the New Leaf "radical" sociologists who most explicitly challenge the paradigm but, like dissident resident groups in the inner city, do not have a set of component parts for an alternative institutionalized thought structure. Even in connection with their own special field, they tend to veer back toward existing paradigms, unable to establish a bridgehead to an alternative. As Gouldner observes, "Many radical sociologists, however, divorce their radicalism and their sociology and write a conventional sociology which is often

---

[16] See for example, Oscar Lewis, the Introduction to *La Vida: A Puerto Rican Family in the Culture of Poverty—San Juan and New York* (New York: Vintage Books, 1966).

scarcely distinguishable from that of their apolitical or conservative brethren."[17]

The second category is research having to do with client populations and their cultural and other resistances to social services.

The third is research on service delivery systems, with a view toward making them more effective.[18]

The fourth is evaluative research on "social action" projects.

A fifth pursuit has to do with evaluating the impact of service programs, a particularly crucial challenge, especially since many such studies have been so negative in their findings. But here again, the remarkable thing is that although such studies often reach conclusions which challenge Diagnostic Paradigm I, the conclusions are seldom picked up and implemented. The reason seems apparent: There is no other place to go with such conclusions than to cast them back against Diagnostic Paradigm I and formulate the new problem as: How to give services in a manner that *will* be effective in its impact. Indeed, the studies which report negative findings on the impact of services usually are strong in their support of the more inclusive intervention strategy of coordination. It is just such studies which provide the intellectual base for the Model Cities program, and which support its strategy of comprehensiveness, coordination, concentration, and the rest.

Viewed from the standpoint of their manifest or latent support of the prevalent institutionalized thought structure, the social research and evaluation are reminiscent of Znaniecki's social role of the "sage."

A distinct kind of social role develops which may be called by the old term "sage." . . . It is his duty to "prove" by "scientific" arguments that his party is right and its opponents are wrong. . . . The traditional order is thus normatively criticized, systematized, and perfected. This does not mean that the sage desires to innovate: the essence of the existing order is right; its defects are accidents due to the imperfection of human nature.[19]

The social researcher, in other words, performs the "mopping-up" operations of "normal science" within the assumption of the validity of the prevalent diagnostic paradigm.

---

[17] Alvin Gouldner, "Toward the Radical Reconstruction of Sociology," *Social Policy* 1 (May/June, 1970), p. 21.

[18] Edwin J. Thomas, ed., *Behavioral Science for Social Workers* (New York: Free Press, 1967) contains several examples.

---

[19] Znaniecki, *Social Role of the Man of Knowledge*, pp. 72, 73, 77.

38

Community development:
Potentials and limitations

Shanti K. Khinduka

Despite numerous definitions by conferences, international bodies, and writers, the concept of community development remains vague. This vagueness has evoked two entirely different reactions. Some social scientists tend to dismiss community development as a totally "knowledge-free" area, remarkable for "the murky banalities, half-truths, and sententious nonsense that abound" in its literature.[1] Other writers maintain that community development is the only key to the modernization of traditional societies.[2]

Community development includes a composite of process and program objectives. As a process, it aims to educate and motivate people for self-help; to develop responsible local leadership; to inculcate among the members of rural communities a sense of citizenship and among the residents of urban areas a spirit of civic consciousness; to introduce and strengthen democracy at the grass-roots level through the creation and/or revitalization of institutions designed to serve as instruments of local participation; to initiate a self-generative, self-sustaining, and enduring process of growth; to enable people to establish and maintain cooperative and harmonious relationships; and to bring about

gradual and self-chosen changes in the community's life with a minimum of stress and disruption.

The multipurpose, intersectoral character of its program is the other major feature of community development. In rural areas, agriculture, irrigation, rural industries, education, health, housing, social welfare, youth and women's programs, employment, cooperatives, and training of village leaders constitute important components of community development. In the urban areas, community development covers a wide array of similar activities.

It is inevitable that such a gigantic international movement, which has received official sanction and support from governments in Asia, Africa, and Latin America and which is viewed by many as a cure for the riot-torn cities of this country, should encounter difficulties in achieving its goals. Problems of manpower, training, and organization have proved formidable barriers to the realization of its objectives in some nations. Inadequate staff, indifference in national bureaucracies, and lack of coordination and communication among specialists at the local level have often combined to create bottlenecks in the implementation of programs. Some governments have paid lip service to community development, but have not earmarked adequate funds for the projects. In a number of instances, community development programs have created adverse side effects which were neither intended nor anticipated. Moreover, accentuation of intergroup tensions instead of a strengthened community solidarity, and the rise of an opportunistic type of party politics instead of a widespread consciousness of people's

Reprinted with permission of the author and publisher from Shanti K. Khinduka, "Community Development: Potentials and Limitations," in *Social Work Practice, 1969.* Copyright © 1969, National Conference on Social Welfare.

[1] David Brokensha, "Comments," *Human Organization* 27, no. 1 (1968), p. 78. See also Charles J. Erasmus, "Community Development and the *Encogido* Syndrome," ibid., pp. 65–74.

[2] See, for example, B. Mukerjee, *Community Development in India* (Calcutta: Orient Longmans, Ltd., 1961), p. vii.

rights and responsibilities, have not been altogether absent. In some situations, the equalitarian rhetoric of community development has infuriated the rich, while the unequal distribution of its benefits has frustrated the poor.

However serious these may be, neither the flaws in implementation nor the possibility of undesirable consequences reflects the real weakness of community development. With a better trained cadre of workers, a stronger commitment by governments, and a more efficient pooling of international experience, many of these deficiencies can be substantially rectified. What is more difficult—and more important—to change, is the basic ideology of community development; for, more than anything else, the ideology of community development has definite assumptions and biases in favor of citizen involvement, consensus, localism, and gradualism. In its extreme form, this ideology prefers nonmaterial goals to tangible ones. It holds the change in the individual's values, motivation, attitudes, and aspirations is a necessary precondition for any worthwhile alteration in the society. Although some theorists recognize the significance of accomplishing physical tasks,[3] the community development approach to social change, by and large, is still dominated by a process orientation which evaluates the actual outcome of a community project primarily in terms of what happens in the minds of men rather than in terms of its impact on the social structure.

It is the thesis of this paper that community development is a rather soft strategy for *social change*. As a method of *social service*, however, its contribution can be very significant.

Community development has a latent propensity for delaying structural changes in the basic institutions of a society. No-

where does this become clearer than in the familiar strain for precedence between its process and task-accomplishment goals.[4] In such a conflict, the community developer typically upholds the process aspect, which stresses citizen involvement, consensus, localism, and change in the attitudes and values of people as a necessary condition for effecting institutional changes.

There is no doubt a great deal to commend in community development's concern with human values and aspirations. As an antidote to some experts' penchant for explaining all industrial backwardness in purely economic terms, and to the equally unwise preoccupation of some governments with narrow models of economic growth, community development's wholesome attempt to underline the human factor and to plead for balanced social and economic progress has indeed had a salutary effect. No wonder that recent approaches to national development have turned away from exclusively economic models.[5] An increasing number of economists now appreciate the significance of noneconomic variables in economic development. "Economic development," two economists observe, "is much too serious a topic to be left to economists."[6]

While community development and social welfare workers have been among the first to recognize the lopsidedness of many prevailing models of economic growth, they have made the reverse error of overstressing the culturally and psychologically propitious preconditions for development. Ever since Max Weber suggested a positive correlation between a people's value system and their economic develop-

---

[3] Arthur Dunham, "Community Development—Whither Bound?" *Social Work Practice, 1968* (New York: Columbia University Press, 1968), pp. 48–61.

[4] Melvin M. Tumin, "Some Social Requirements for Effective Community Development," *Community Development Review*, no. 11 (1958), pp. 3–4.

[5] See, for example, Gunnar Myrdal, *An Asian Drama: An Inquiry into the Poverty of Nations* (New York: Twentieth Century Fund, 1968).

[6] G. M. Meier and R. E. Baldwin, *Economic Development* (New York: John Wiley & Sons, 1957), p. 119.

ment,[7] it has become commonplace in many circles to attribute the poverty of a people to their otherworldliness, fatalism, lack of thrift, industry, and entrepreneurial aptitude, and, more recently, to their low achievement motivation. Weber's thesis is now being used not only as a counterpoint to the Marxian theory of economic production and social classes, but also as spurious anthropology that overlooks internal and external exploitative economic relationships and explains economic backwardness as if its causative factors were located entirely within the individuals who suffer from it. In embracing this theory, community development, like much of professional social work, leaves itself vulnerable on scientific as well as on strategic grounds.

Attitudinal and value modifications do not necessarily precede behavioral or structural changes; they may often follow them. It is not necessary, for example, to wipe out prejudice (an attitude) in order to eradicate segregation (a behavioral practice). Modifications in individual and group behavior can be brought about by a change in the social situation in which people function.[8]

Festinger's theory of Cognitive Dissonance holds that, under certain conditions, behavior can produce cognitive and attitudinal realignments in the person. When a person commits an act which is contrary to his beliefs, he is in a state of dissonance, which is unpleasant to him. Reduction of this dissonance is achieved mainly by changing his beliefs, since the "discrepant behavior" has already taken place and cannot be undone.[9] Epstein's study of two Indian villages showed that it was economic development that led to behavioral changes, not vice versa. She reports:

Whenever there was . . . economic change we also found corresponding changes in political and ritual roles and relations as well as in the principles of social organization. Thus we have established a positive correlation between economic, political, ritual, and organizational change, with economic change being the determining variable.[10]

It is an oversimplification to attribute all or most of the difficulties in development to people's mental outlook. It will not do to invoke values to explain economic underdevelopment without referring back to the social structure and economic processes which permit some values to persist and others to change.

One might add that even if modification of attitudes and values is considered a necessary precondition for structural social change, community development has chosen an incomplete, if not an inappropriate, target group. Although it may be important to change the attitudes of the victims of social and economic injustice, it may be more useful to bring about a shift in the attitudes and values of those sections of the population who are its principal beneficiaries. That is why concentration of community development programs among blacks, Puerto Ricans, Mexicans, and Indians will not be enough unless they are accompanied by a similar educational effort to resocialize the privileged, affluent, and suburban segments of the society.

Once it is recognized that values, beliefs, and aspirations are not in every circumstance the optimum locus of professional intervention for social change, the strategic weakness of the community development approach becomes clear. The strategy of concentrating on a group's out-

[7] Max Weber, *The Protestant Ethic and the Spirit of Capitalism*, tr. Talcott Parsons (London: George Allen & Unwin, Ltd., 1930).

[8] Kenneth B. Clark, "Some Implications for a Theory of Social Change," *Journal of Social Issues* 9, no. 4 (1953), p. 72.

[9] Leon Festinger, *A Theory of Cognitive Dissonance* (Evanston, Ill.: Row, Peterson, 1957). See also Albert O. Hirschman, "Obstacles to Development: A Classification and a Quasi-vanishing Act," *Economic Development and Cultural Change*, 13 (1965), p. 391.

[10] T. Scarlett Epstein, *Economic Development and Social Change in South India* (Calcutta: Oxford University Press, 1962), p. 334.

moded attitudes which are assumed to constitute the principal obstacle to its growth does not recognize that there may be legitimate reasons for people not to take the initiative or the necessary risks in the adoption of new practices. Where benefits are apt to be absorbed by middlemen or moneylenders, for example, it would be unrealistic to expect the villagers to venture the investments or muster the enthusiasm for a new project.[11]

Since a change in value systems of tradition-haunted societies is a matter of generations, such an emphasis on changing the value system may have a pessimistic and despairing implication for the rapid socioeconomic development of the "third world." The assumption that a man's activities cannot be changed without altering his values may result in neglect of the appropriate targets of intervention. A psychologist observes:

An effective strategy for inducing social change would consist of bringing about change in the societal system—and its reinforcing mechanisms—and the development of the appropriate patterns of motivation—and expectancy— through suitable programs. For any social change, the primary condition is a change in the societal system, without which appropriate changes cannot be introduced or, if introduced, cannot be sustained.[12]

If the planners and policymakers wait for attitudes to change and do not intervene at the structural level with social policy and legislation, then achievement of economic development in the third world and of social justice in the "first world" is likely to take a hopelessly long time.

Another dimension of the inadequacy of community development as a strategy for large-scale social change is concerned

with the time and rate of change. In the belief that far-reaching social change produces tensions and maladjustments— which are to be avoided at all cost—community development has put great emphasis on moving at a slow pace. Time, it is suggested, should not be allowed to become a major factor in the process of community growth.[13] Here, again, community development has aligned itself with only one school of thought in the social sciences. Heilbroner, however, states that the world political situation enjoins the speediest possible timetable for development.[14] Under some circumstances, notes Margaret Mead, the least dislocating change is one which is introduced rapidly.[15] A social scientist from the third world, Guillermo Bonfil Batalla, of Mexico, makes another point clear:

Sometimes it looks as if those who work along the road of slow evolution intend to achieve only minimal changes, so that the situation continues to be substantially the same; this is, in other words, *to change what is necessary so that things remain the same.* Those who act according to such a point of view may honestly believe that their work is useful and transforming; however, they have in fact aligned themselves with the conservative elements who oppose the structural transformations that cannot be postponed in our (Latin American) countries.[16]

Community development's insistence on consensus as the only satisfactory basis for major community decisions provides another example of its limitations. It is, of course, more pleasant to work in an atmosphere of consensus than in one of contest, controversy, or conflict. However, it is easier to obtain near-unanimity on superficial and innocuous matters; issues of

---

[11] United Nations, Department of Economic and Social Affairs, *Local Participation in Development Planning: A Preliminary Study of the Relationship of Community Development to National Planning* (New York: United Nations, 1967), p. 27.

[12] Udai Pareek, "Motivational Patterns and Planned Social Change," *International Social Science Journal* 20 (1968), pp. 465–66.

[13] Murray G. Ross, *Community Organization: Theory and Practice* (New York: Harper & Brothers, 1955), p. 22.

[14] Robert L. Heilbroner, "Counterrevolutionary America," *Commentary* 43, no. 4 (1967), p. 33.

[15] Margaret Mead, *New Lives for Old* (New York: William Morrow, 1956), pp. 445–47.

[16] Quoted in Gerald D. Berreman, "The Peace Corps: A Dream Betrayed," *The Nation*, February 26, 1968, p. 266.

substance, which affect the diverse sub-groups of the community in different ways, often generate controversy as well as a clash of interests.

Major structural reforms have rarely been instituted with the enthusiastic consent of those who are most likely to lose as a result of those reforms. A certain modicum of legal coercion is a necessary component of any effective strategy of social change. Community development has been rather slow to appreciate this elementary principle. This may in part account for the more or less peripheral role that it has played in movements for rural land reform in most Asian nations.

Its fondness for consensus, however, is only an extension of community development's faith in the desirability and efficacy of citizen involvement. Here, it seems, an essentially instrumental value has been converted into an ultimate value. Citizen participation takes various forms; each form, in turn, rests upon certain assumptions and conditions peculiar to itself. It cannot be assumed that all types of citizen participation are appropriate for all occasions or for all organizations.[17] Excellent participation is not sufficient to introduce major changes into a community,[18] nor is voluntary participation always a prerequisite for rapid, extensive cultural change.[19] The principle of citizen participation has been advanced on ethical grounds: people are intrinsically good; given an opportunity, they will do the "right thing." As a technique, it is not backed up by unequivocal evidence that it is indeed as crucial a mechanism for the success of a community development project as has been so frequently suggested.[20]

A noteworthy feature of community development is that it seeks to promote an identification with, and a loyalty to, the local community. The locality is the key unit around which people are to be mobilized for community development projects, and a locality-centered strategy for social change has to face certain problems.

In the first place, the local community no longer exercises decisive control over the lives of an increasingly mobile population. Due largely to the population explosion, implosion, and diversification, and the accelerated tempo of social and technological change—factors which constitute the "morphological revolution"[21]— the local community does not offer any realistic possibilities of a genuine *Gemeinschaft* environment dictated by natural will and characterized by intimate, spontaneous, inclusive, and enduring personal relationships. Even if the morphological revolution could be halted, it would require all the power and resolution of a sovereign world organization; local communities are too feeble to effect such a reversal.

Local institutions can no longer remain unaffected by the extracommunity system. Local destinies, for the most part, cannot be decided locally. Nor can the major problems of a locality—poverty, unemployment, housing, and discrimination— be solved merely or mainly by mobilizing local efforts.

History is replete with examples showing that some of the most progressive policies have emanated from the legislative, executive, and judicial branches of a national government. Untouchability would never have been proscribed in India if each

[17] Edmund M. Burke, "Citizen Participation Strategies," *Journal of the American Institute of Planners* 34 (1968), p. 293.

[18] See Peter H. Rossi, "Theory, Research and Practice in Community Organization," in *Social Science and Community Action*, ed. Charles R. Adrian et al. (East Lansing: Michigan State University, 1960), pp. 9–24.

[19] Alex Weingrod, *Reluctant Pioneers: Village Development in Israel* (Ithaca, N.Y.: Cornell University Press, 1966), pp. 197–203.

[20] Gilbert Kushner, "Indians in Israel: Guided Change in a New-Immigrant Village," *Human Organization* 27 (1968), pp. 359–60.

[21] Philip M. Hauser, "The Chaotic Society: Product of the Social Morphological Revolution," *American Sociological Review* 34 (1969), pp. 1–19.

local community had been allowed to fashion its own rules. Nor would much progress be made in the United States in establishing racial equality if the decision-making power were vested entirely in the local political institutions. Paradoxically, an indiscriminate application of the seemingly sound principle of local self-determination is at times incompatible with the tenets on which a democracy rests. The fact that it is not possible today to preserve total local autonomy is thus a cause for optimism, not for alarm.

A complicating factor is that the idea of local autonomy is used for two quite conflicting purposes. On the one hand, there are champions of local rights who oppose federal interventions so that they can perpetuate the injustice of the local political and economic arrangement. The principle of local rights is thus invoked mainly to defeat, delay, or dilute national policies designed to correct the inequities of the local system. An entirely different and socially much more justifiable demand is also couched in the idiom of local self-determination. When the blacks in the ghettos ask for control over local institutions, they are, in effect, saying that they no longer want white domination of their lives and institutions. This is a demand for self-determination, *not* local self-determination. Despite their superficial and deceptive similarity, these demands represent two diametrically divergent objectives: the latter seeks to restore respect for a group often subjected to conscious and unconscious indignities; the former is calculated to deny precisely this egalitarian end.

It has often been assumed that local development and national development always proceed hand in hand. However, community development may inadvertently reinforce economically inefficient customs and practices which prolong the hold of growth-resisting tradition. The desire for local autonomy may create distrust of the national government, its central bureaucracy, and those federal laws which curb a locality's power to manage its own affairs. Recognition of this dilemma has led some community development advocates into an even less tenable position: they will have nothing to do with national development and focus all their efforts on the local community.[22]

The besetting limitation of community development as a strategy for social change is its psychological rather than socioeconomic approach to social problems. Community development programs aim at revolutionary change in the people's psychology without bringing about an actual revolution in their socioeconomic relations.[23] They are concerned with people's psychological capacity to make decisions, not with their economic power to do so. By encouraging them to participate in community activities, community development seeks to give them a feeling that they count and that they are competent, but it stops there. Community development will do practically everything to improve the psychological lives of the poor: it will create among them a sense of self-respect and confidence, of civic pride, an identification with their locality—which may be an uninhabitable slum; it will provide recreational programs; needs; it will even organize courses and encourage handicrafts to increase their earning capacity. But it will not usually question the economic system which permits the coexistence of poverty and plenty. And when poverty is at least as much a function of social injustice as it is of individual ineptitude, it is questionable if psychological repair of an individual can accomplish what requires a fundamental rearrangement of economic and social institutions.[24]

---

[22] William W. Biddle, "Deflating the Community Developer," *Community Development Journal* 3 (1968), pp. 191–94.

[23] Charles Madge, "A Sociologist Looks at Social Education," *Community Development Bulletin* 12, no. 1 (1960), p. 23.

[24] Simon Slavin, "Community Action and Institutional Change," in *The Social Welfare Forum, 1965* (New York: Columbia University Press, 1965), pp. 155–57.

Some community developers are really caseworkers practicing in a community setting. They use the community development method for expediting the personality growth of the members of the community. According to William and Loureide J. Biddle, personality growth, through responsibility for the local common good, is the focus of all community development.[25] No wonder economic improvement is dismissed as a "materialistic measure" not quite fit to become a community development goal. "If economic betterment is not an extravagant hope, it is an inappropriate one," writes William Biddle.[26] It is just this preoccupation with process and with personality that keeps community development from becoming an effective instrument for large-scale institutional change.

We do not deny the value of community development as a program of social service or its validity as a response to specific local situations. By stressing the crucial role of the human factor in national development, community development has done a great service to mankind. Its integrated and holistic concept of development is, similarly, a refreshing improvement over the narrow, sectoral approaches to national planning.

For certain types of goals and within a certain sphere, community development can be a very effective strategy. Community development is a gentleman's approach to the world. It brings people together; it helps them live and reason together. By involving them in the local decision-making process in the community, it aims to strengthen participatory democracy. If some values and attitudes are detrimental to social progress, it attempts to modify them gradually, with the least disruption and maximum voluntary cooperation, without conflict or contest, shunning bitter controversy, seeking better consensus. Perhaps it does not recognize the existence of classes; it sees only a community. Where this community has "eclipsed," it seeks to resuscitate it. Where it is disintegrated, it reorganizes it. When passions run high and factions grow intolerant of one another, it applies the healing touch of understanding and empathy. In this sense, community development is an extension of group work to the community setting: both processes are dedicated to helping people live harmoniously with fellow human beings.

Essentially, community development is a humanistic and humanizing method. The promise and potentials of such a method are almost self-evident in an age when much of what we call "progress" conceals widespread alienation, apathy, antagonism, cynicism, impersonal bureaucratization, and self-centered pursuit of purely hedonistic ends. The only problem is that community development's relative neglect of such equally humanizing principles as equality, justice, and material well-being are apt to create an uncomfortable gap between its intent and its effect.

Community development can be a potent program for mental health. Students of urban life have noted with dismay the strong feelings of anomie, dependency, and personal worthlessness among the residents of urban slums. Many of these people feel uprooted and marginal; they do not identify with, or belong to, communal organizations. Community development programs can meet the socialization needs of such people.[27] These programs can also be used, as they have been in many countries, to educate people in the art and intricacies of the democratic

[25] William W. Biddle and Loureide J. Biddle, *The Community Development Process: The Rediscovery of Local Initiative* (New York: Holt, Rinehart & Winston, 1965), p. 78.

[26] William W. Biddle, "Deflating the Community Developer," p. 192.

[27] Lloyd E. Ohlin and Martin Rein, "Social Planning for Institutional Change," in *The Social Welfare Forum, 1964* (New York: Columbia University Press, 1964), p. 87.

processes of participation and persuasion. Community projects can likewise strengthen the spirit of unity in a community. Community development activities, which create linkages between various communities, can, similarly, be helpful in improving intercommunity relations. By successfully completing even relatively inconsequential community projects, the participants may develop a sense of competence, a new faith in their ability to overcome forces of nature. This faith in their capacity may be very important for people who live in small, rural areas of traditional societies.

Community development stands for cooperation between public and private effort. Problems sometimes arise in working out arrangements between governmental and voluntary agencies. The idea of "maximum feasible participation" of the local people, for example, may at times result in "maximum feasible misunderstanding." Nevertheless, community development presents a fairly workable model for combining outside technical assistance with indigenous enterprise. As a strategy for mobilizing voluntary efforts at the local level, it is particularly applicable in those communities where people have become excessively dependent on government and community initiative has more or less atrophied.

Although community development is generally viewed as a program designed to strengthen the horizontal pattern of a community,[28] its great potential consists, especially for the third world, in its ability to help weld numerous small localities into a large national polity. Community development can make a significant contribution to the political development of the third-world nations if it puts greater emphasis on inculcating a sense of national purpose and national identification than on merely identifying with the local community. Equally valuable is its potential as a feedback mechanism. In many countries, community development programs have resulted in a better understanding of local problems by higher government officials.[29] Community development can thus provide two-way communication between the local community and the state or national government. Such channels are particularly important in newly independent countries where long periods of foreign rule have created a hiatus between the people and their governments.

Even at the local level, community development is capable of making a more significant contribution if it deemphasizes its earlier self-help orientation and boldly but discriminately incorporates in the mainstream of its ideology some of the features of recent attempts to organize the urban poor. The main objectives of the former model are: creation of community feeling, self-reliance, local leadership, and cooperation between the government and the people in the use of services.[30] The latter model extends the goals of community development to include economic and political objectives, such as the realignment of power resources in the community.[31] The community developer following this model does not fight shy of using negotiation, bargaining, advocacy, protest, noncooperation, and other forms of nonviolent social action[32] in order to help the community attain a composite of so-

---

[28] Roland L. Warren, *The Community in America* (Chicago: Rand McNally, 1963), p. 324.

[29] Irwin T. Sanders, "Community Development," in *International Encyclopedia of the Social Sciences,* ed. David L. Sills (New York: Macmillan Co. & Free Press, 1968), 3, 172.

[30] For an example of this model, see Marshall B. Clinard, *Slums and Community Development* (New York: Free Press, 1966).

[31] Charles Grosser, "Community Development Programs Serving the Urban Poor," *Social Work* 10, no. 3 (1965), pp. 15–21.

[32] See George Brager, "Organizing the Unaffiliated in a Low-Income Area," *Social Work* 8, no. 2 (1963), pp. 34–40; George Brager and Harry Specht, "Mobilizing the Poor for Social Action," in *The Social Welfare Forum, 1965* (New York: Columbia University Press, 1965), pp. 197–209.

cial, psychological, and political-economic objectives.

Community development is no substitute for centrally planned changes in the institutional structure of a society. However, one should not downgrade the services of the thousands of dedicated community development workers who quietly help bring about slow, incremental adaptations in the social system. Within this less ambitious sphere, community development is potentially quite a powerful social invention. Its effectiveness will perhaps increase if it modifies the locality-oriented, enabling model and recognizes the legitimacy of other nonviolent approaches to organizing people for redressing their grievances.

39

Community development and social justice
William L. Blizek and Jerry Cederblom

A survey of community development literature suggests that both theorists and practitioners are willing to accept such principles as (a) *communities have the right to determine their own goals*, or (b) *the goal of community development is a healthy community*. These appear to be harmless, if not outrightly commendable. We would argue, however, that these principles represent two views of community development which obscure the relation between community development and social justice.

The two principles are related in this way: by holding either one of them the community developer could be led to see his enterprise as social-scientific rather than normative. By holding that communities have the right to determine their own goals, community development could see itself as freed of any responsibility for determining how a community ought to perform and direct itself instead to determining how a community can best be organized and activated to carry out its goals, whatever they are. Or, by taking the healthy community to be the end toward which it is working, community development could see itself as modeled after the practice of medicine, except that it attends to larger organisms-communities instead of individual people.

The principle that communities have the right to determine their own goals is representative of a point of view from which community development is seen as normatively neutral. The "healthy community" principle is typical of the attitude that community development is normative, but in such a noncontroversial way that the consideration of normative principles is not a major problem for the discipline. In this paper we will sketch the views of normative neutrality and noncontroversiality, and argue that such views of community development are deficient because they ignore the possibility—or probability—of conflict within and among communities. Principles are needed for resolving these conflicts, and we would contend that such principles ought to be formulated so as to ensure a just community and a just society. If then, justice is one aspect of the good or healthy community, principles of justice are an important guide for the community devel-

Reprinted with permission of the authors and publisher from William L. Blizek and Jerry Cederblom, "Community Development and Social Justice," *Journal of the Community Development Society* 4, no. 2 (Fall 1973), pp. 45–52. The footnotes have been renumbered.

opment practitioner and an important subject for the community development theorist.

The first view, that community development is normatively neutral, is expressed by Albert Meister when he describes community development as ". . . essentially a set of actions based on local participation and initiative, the role of outside experts being only to foster and sustain them by specialized assistance."[1] The community developer, then, does not make normative decisions; rather, he supports the normative decisions of the community with his expertise. Malcolm J. Brown expresses this same view when he says, ". . . communities have the right to decide for themselves to which particular goal they will direct their efforts."[2] And J. D. Mezirow even goes so far as to rebuke those who ask for an ethical justification of community development by saying, ". . . systematically sharing insights with a villager which will enable him to become more competent to handle the problems of change with which he is already engaged or engulfed is helping him control his own destiny, not controlling it for him."[3] Such quotes suggest that it is commendable for the community developer to excuse himself from making value judgments and to remain normatively neutral.

The larger context in which the community developer finds himself operating and which he takes as a justification for his normative neutrality might be described as follows. In an enormous, complex, bureaucratic nation such as ours, it becomes increasingly difficult for citizens to make their interests known and receive due consideration. The result is that citizens who share common interests need to organize into effective communities, often politically effective communities. The role of the community developer, then, is to master the techniques of organization and politicization, and to provide his services to communities.

If the position of normative neutrality is to be accepted, it is important to note that it must be maintained either that any and all interests held by communities deserve to be activated, or that it is not the business of the community development agent to make judgments concerning the interests of the communities he serves. We will return to this point later in our criticism of normative neutrality.

The second view of community development is that it is a normatively oriented discipline, but that its normative orientation is noncontroversial in the way that the goal of medical science, for instance, is commonly seen as noncontroversial. The major underpinning of this view seems to be the analogy of the community to the individual. "There are great similarities between the social worker helping an individual client," writes Malcolm J. Brown, "and a community developer working with a community. Each recipient of help (whether an individual or community) must mobilize inner resources for growth, and each has the right to direct this power toward a self-determined goal."[4]

The analogy of community to individual is also made explicit by Louis M. Miniclier: "Community Development provides an approach to the problem of poverty through a new kind of public servant who is trained to see the village as a *whole*—as a social organism with all parts related."[5] In another context, Miniclier also contends

[1] Albert Meister, "Introduction—Training Local Leaders," *International Review of Community Development*, no. 3 (1959), p. 7.

[2] Malcolm J. Brown, "Community Development, the Non-Democratic State, and the Concept of Open-Endedness," *International Review of Community Development*, no. 21–22 (1966), p. 37.

[3] J. D. Mezirow, "Community Development as an Educational Process," *International Review of Community Development*, no. 5 (1960), p. 150.

[4] Brown, "Community Development."

[5] Louis M. Miniclier, "Introduction," *Community Development Review*, vol. 4, no. 2, June 1959, p. 1. Excerpted from an address by Louis M. Miniclier, U.S. National Conference of Social Welfare, San Francisco, Calif. (May 1959).

that "the acceptance of the community as a social organism with all parts interrelated where a change in part of the culture affects the whole has been accepted by important national community development leaders . . ."[6]

We do not, in general, question enterprises designed to help individuals. There is no cry for an investigation of the normative principles that guide the practices of education, law, or medicine, even in these troubled times. Why, then, can't community development find its niche among other noncontroversial disciplines? The reason, we will claim below, is that the analogy between individual and community breaks down.

What we have been calling the position of normative neutrality is one which typically stresses democratic participation, felt-needs, and community autonomy.[7] These elements suggest that what a community *ought* to do—and thus, what the community developer ought to support and encourage—is whatever the community *wants* to do or *feels* that it needs to do. The acceptance of substantive principles by the community developer, however, would require him to refrain from assisting some activities that may have been selected by the community and to encourage

others even though they may have been disfavored by the community. We believe that the position of value neutrality is unacceptable and that substantive principles are required of community developers and the community development profession.

There are at least three significant criticisms which are applicable to the normative-neutralist position. First, the community developer who seeks to remain normatively neutral may find himself called upon by a community to carry out or support, by means of his expertise, actions which may readily be seen to be wrong. A community developer might be asked by a segregated community, for example, to assist them in excluding people of other racial, ethnic, or religious backgrounds. Or, an emerging nation might seek help in developing weapons technology that would allow it to attack or harass those who dominated it in the past. The community developer who is committed to leaving the decisions of goals and priorities up to the community may be committed to supporting activities which are wrong.

A second criticism concerns the relations between communities. The community developer who does not decide which community to help or which community activities to support might find himself in the paradoxical position of negating the activity of one community through the actions of another community. For example, he might assist one community in cleaning its river for beautification and recreation, but also assist an upstream community in building a chemical plant that contributes to the very pollution he is seeking to eradicate by helping the downstream community. The economy of one community may damage the ecology of another, and the community developer who seeks normative neutrality may find himself acting in self-defeating ways.

The third criticism concerns the conflict of interests which arise within communities. Unless the community developer helps both sides (which would be self-de-

[6] Miniclier, "Values and Principles of Community Development," *International Review of Community Development*, no. 5 (1960).

[7] For discussions of participation and democracy, *see* Meister, "Training Local Leaders;" Murray G. Ross, "Community Participation," *International Review of Community Development*, no. 5 (1960): and Roland L. Warren, "The Good Community—What Would It Be?", *Journal of Community Development Society* 1, no. 1 (Spring), 1970. For discussions of felt needs, *see* Meister, Training Local Leaders"; Mezirow, "An Educational Process"; Miniclier, "Values and Principles of Community Development", and J. A. Ponsioen, "Community Development as a Process," *International Review of Community Development*, no. 6 (1960). For discussions of autonomy, *see* D. Solomon, "An Approach to Training for Community Development," *International Review of Community Development*, no. 3 (1959); Warren, "The Good Community"; and Philip Zealey, "Training Local Leaders for Community Development," *International Review of Community Development*, no. 3 (1959).

feating as in the case of intercommunity conflict), he is called upon to decide which of the competing interests he ought to assist. The question then arises: What principle should be used in choosing among interests? One might adopt, for example, the principle of majority rule, on the basis that the majority of the community best represents the whole community. But to adopt this principle is, first, to give up value neutrality, and second, to adopt a principle that is compatible with great injustice to minority interests. What is called for is a principle which results in the just resolution of conflicting interests.

The second position we are criticizing relies on normative principles which are considered noncontroversial; principles such as "helping the community," or "promoting the health of the community."[8] The underlying assumption which makes the principles appear nonproblematic is that a community is a single organism similar to an individual person. Since there is little controversy surrounding the idea of helping a man in need or promoting the health of an individual, there should be little controversy about those principles applied to communities, insofar as communities are seen as organisms like men.

But here again, it is the possibility of conflict that undercuts the position. If a community were like an individual organism, then promoting the welfare of the community (or promoting its "health," or helping it achieve its potential) would be an obviously worthy pursuit. But there is a crucial point at which the analogy between community and individual organism breaks down.

In the case of an individual organism (a man, for instance), well-being or ill-being is experienced by the whole individual, not by the parts. In the case of the community, on the other hand, well-being or ill-being can *not* be experienced by the whole. It can *only* be experienced by the parts (the individual persons within the community).

The importance of the disanalogy can be seen from the following example. Suppose a person has an infected limb which is causing him to suffer. And suppose that, correspondingly, a community has a particular segment within it (a racial or religious group, for instance) which is constantly at odds with the rest of the community. In the case of the individual person, the decision to amputate the infected limb is nonproblematic in a way in which the decision to annihilate the troublesome racial or religious group is not. In the case of the individual person, all that need to be considered is the well-being of the whole, not of the part. Or, to be more precise, it is only insofar as the condition of the part contributes to the well-being of the whole that the part is to be considered; the part itself does not experience well-being or ill-being. If the limb is amputated, we might be remorseful that it could not have been saved to aid the person in his life, but the remorse is for him, not his limb.

Contrast this case with the case of the community containing a troublesome group. It is *not* the well-being of the whole which is to be considered in a decision to "amputate" the part: unless one is willing to posit something like a "group mind" which experiences pain and pleasure, the whole community experiences neither well-being nor ill-being. It is *only* the parts which have such experience. And when it comes to weighing the ill fate of the "amputated" parts against the well-being of the remaining parts, we run straight into the problem of justice. In the case of the person with the infected limb, the problem of justice does not arise.

It is because of this disanalogy that seemingly noncontroversial principles like "promoting the health of the community"

---

[8] The terms *help* and *health* are noncontroversial in broad usage, although they may become problematic when the details and implications of helping or promoting health are exposed.

are simply not sufficient in determining what path a community should take in those all-too-common cases in which no alternative is maximally satisfactory to every person in a community.

If the positions of normative neutrality and noncontroversiality are deficient, as we have argued, it follows that the community development discipline must develop principles by which to resolve conflicts of interest. These would be principles of justice, insofar as community development seeks a just resolution of conflicting interests. What we are proposing, then, is that community development theorists engage in the philosophical investigation of the nature of justice and its implications for human conduct.

Our reference to "principles of justice" has so far relied upon the reader's common-sense understanding of that phrase. We must now indicate what is involved in the determination of principles of justice and their application. The notion of justice concerns problems which arise when individuals with differing interests enter cooperative arrangements for the sake of mutual advantage. Principles of justice dictate the distribution of benefits and burdens incurred as a result of cooperation.

As an example of the kind of principles we believe community development theorists should be considering, we wish to cite two examples of justice which have been proposed recently by Professor John Rawls and which are receiving considerable attention in philosophical circles.[9] Rawls argues that the principles of justice are those that would be derived by any rational self-interested person who did not know in advance what place he would occupy in the social system. The perspective from which these principles are chosen in what Rawls calls "the original position." The principles which Rawls argues would be selected by those in the original position are:

1. Each person is to have an equal right to the most extensive total system of equal basic liberties compatible with a similar system of liberty for all.
2. Social and economic inequalities are to be arranged so that they are both: *(a)* to the greatest benefit of the least advantaged . . . and *(b)* attached to offices and positions open to all under conditions of fair equality of opportunity.[10]

The first principle provides a basic equality of liberty and has priority over the second principle such that no sacrifice of liberties can be made in favor of, for example, an increase in the general economic prosperity of the community. Any diminution of liberty must strengthen the total system of liberties shared in equally by all. The second principle provides a maximization of the minimum. That is, the least advantaged—those with the minimum—are to be improved by whatever inequalities of economic or social good (other than liberty) are allowed. At the same time, everyone must have an opportunity to attain the offices and positions which receive unequal shares of economic or social goods.

There is no room here for a defense of these principles, but it is clear that their adoption requires conduct quite different from that required by other principles of justice. For example, the economic health of a community might be improved by increasing the number of unemployed. The impoverishment of a small minority would be justifiable, given utilitarian or majority-vote principles, but would be a violation of Rawls' second principle. Or, an equal distribution of wealth might be called for on egalitarian grounds, but would be rejected in accordance with Rawls' principles, because the incentive of additional benefits

---

[9] John Rawls, *A Theory of Justice* (Cambridge, Mass.: Harvard University Press, 1971).

[10] Ibid., p. 302.

to some might produce corresponding benefits to the least advantaged. Choosing one practice over another clearly requires justification by acceptable principles, and it is the development of such principles that we see as an important but neglected goal of community development theory.

Now, it might be objected that we have presented a mistaken or misleading picture of community development. That is, community developers might contend that they are quite in agreement with our position on the development of principles of justice and claim that the development of such principles has been a focal point of community development theory for many years. If this were the case, however, we would expect to find considerable evidence in the community development literature, i.e., the regular publication of articles dealing with principles of justice. Since that evidence is lacking, we believe that community development has not yet paid due consideration to the problems of social justice and we hope that this brief paper will encourage such consideration.

Alternative communities

SECTION SEVEN

INTRODUCTION

What can be done with American communities? Or perhaps the question should be: What can be done *instead of* American communities? In one form or another, both questions are being raised these days, as public concern mounts for a series of problems mainifested not only in large cities, where they are perhaps more dramatic, but also in smaller cities, suburban communities, and rural villages.

There are many ways of summing up the current disenchantment with conditions at the locality level, and the problems which occasion it. Two strains stand out among these. One is the old, familiar concern that the face-to-face community is dying out as people come to live in larger and more impersonal population aggregates. The "glue" which held together the rural communities of previous centuries was compounded of such components as shared values, face-to-face relationships among those who knew each other, shared facilities, and comparative isolation and self-sufficiency. As such characteristics become progressively less relevant to local community living, the more formal organizations and less personal relationships and great discrepancy in values, points of view, and life styles apparently do not provide for the same kind of solidarity and coherence which presumably characterized earlier times.

A related concern is the spectrum of social problems such as delinquency, crime, drug addiction, dependency, rising costs of health care, and on through a long list, which leads some public leaders to state that cities are rapidly becoming virtually ungovernable.

What are the alternatives to the troubled perplexities of contemporary American communities? Under current circumstances there is an extraordinary amount of casting about for such alternatives. The selections in this final section all relate in direct fashion to the alternatives to the existing configuration of most American communities. They are far from a complete "sampling," but they do illustrate four important directions of thought.

First, one may inquire, What kind of community do people really want? Two selections examine the "good" community and the "competent" community, respectively. A second line of inquiry is to follow the experience of people who have deliberately gone about setting up a new community, markedly different in values and social structure from the dominant community forms. Another selection examines this experience with communes. A third possibility is to try to apply the latest technical and planning technology to build new communities, or new towns, which represent not a rejection of modern urban society but rather a deliberate attempt to derive advantages from it for community living. One selection examines this experience with "new towns." A fourth line of investigation is to try to think imaginatively about how existing communities might be developed into more habitable places. A final selection attempts to sketch out this sort of development.

The first selection, entitled "The Good Community—What Would It Be?" by Roland L. Warren, challenges the assumption that people are largely in agreement on what a good community would be like. Indeed, it asserts that sometimes quite contradictory characteristics are sought for in a new or improved community, either by people with different preferences or even by the same people who express preferences which are inherently self-contradictory but do not realize it because they have not examined the possible interplay of different objectives. Sometimes in this interplay, two objectives may actually be mutually antagonistic, in the sense that progress towards one jeopardizes the other. Hence, "the good community is not a 'grab-bag of goodies' to satisfy every conceivable desire. It involves choices and rejections which we make either deliberately or by default."

One desirable characteristic of a community would presumably be competence—competence to confront its problems and deal with them effectively. Leonard S. Cottrell, Jr. has dealt extensively with the question of "personal competence." With this background and on the basis of his extensive experience as consultant to a number of federal programs, he examines the components of community competence and then proceeds to identify its "essential conditions." They are commitment, self-other awareness and clarity of situational definitions, articulateness, communication, conflict containment and accommodation, participation, management of relations with the larger society, and machinery for facilitating participant interaction and decision making.

But this list of conditions for the competent community seems bland in comparison with the incisive treatment he gives each of these topics. In connection with commitment, for example, he writes: "Commitment grows with realization that what one does makes a difference. People may be encouraged and helped to achieve what appear to be significant roles in the community, but if they do not find that they are actually making a significant impact on community processes and problems, the activity becomes meaningless." In another passage he writes of the need for clarification of real issues. "Such a development," he comments, "should aid greatly in reducing the bottless shouting, name calling, and obfuscating nondiscussion that so frequently passes for 'community action.'" While his discussion of each of the aspects of a competent community is derived from his extensive experience with community programs, it is deepened by an acute ability to seize important aspects of each component for penetrating analysis.

Those who foster alternatives to present community living have the alternative of striking out on their own to form communities of like-minded individuals, differing from the values and lifeways of conventional communities, or of building new communities ("new towns") along more conventional lines, but taking advantage of technical planning and the opportunity to "start from scratch." Or, they may seek to introduce changes into present communities so as to alter them in some drastic fashion.

Rosabeth Moss Kanter has concerned herself over a period of years with both the utopian communities of the 19th century and contemporary communes. For both, in her estimation, the greatest problem is that of securing commitment to the ideals and behavior patterns of the group. This task is made particularly crucial by the fact that these communities reject the behavior patterns of the surrounding society and in some ways, at least, go about striving to forge new, alternative ways of relating to each other.

Commitment arises at that point where the community's needs and the individual's desires converge. Full commitment is present when people voluntarily do the things which the community needs to get done in order to survive and prosper, and when they do them because they find them approvable and personally satisfying. There are three points at which this correspondence between community needs and individual wishes is especially important. These have to do with the retention of members, the cohesiveness of the communal group; and social control over member behavior. Kanter points out that these three major aspects are analytically distinct from each other, in that one may be present without the others.

On the personal side, there are likewise three aspects of commitment: instrumental, affective, and moral. They correspond to the communal needs for retention of members, for cohesiveness, and for social control.

It can therefore be asked of any intentional community, whether commune or utopian community, how it is organized to achieve sufficient commitment to provide that the necessary work get done and that individuals have the motivation to remain within it. A number of commitment mechanisms can be developed to generate strong commitment and thus ensure the viability of the group and the satisfaction of its members.

A more conventional, but still substantially innovative alternative to present-day communities is offered by the "new town" approach. Generally speaking, the new towns are characterized by unified planning from the outset and thus can utilize available design and planning technology to build attractive and desirable communities. One of the goals of new town development is to build stronger communities under contemporary conditions. Richard O. Brooks made an intensive study of one of the better-planned new communities, Columbia, Md., with the purpose of assessing the degree of its success in achieving communal values. Brooks came out with mixed findings and conclusions. In the final chapter of his book, however, he raised a more fundamental question, namely the extent to which the nature of the locality is still relevant to the realization of "communal" values. He asserts that "urban civilization is a form of civilization in which the nexus between proximity of living and the achievement of communal values is broken." Since this is the case, one should no longer seek to realize communal values through the exclusive preoccupation with spatial concentrations of people.

Brooks asserts that three steps are necessary: first, a more precise specification of the component values making up the community ideal; second, an assessment of their individual desirability; and third, a realization that these desirable components "will be achieved as the product of the workings of many institutions within society." He maintains the position that "rather than a study of local settlements, the study of the contribution of local and nonlocal institutions to the achievement of communal values becomes the central focus of inquiry."

The concluding selection is a vignette—an imaginative scenario of how life might be in a drastically altered urban community under today's conditions of advanced technology. The passage fleshes out the various aspects of daily living in a sort of Utopian setting in the heart of a large city. The neighborhood people grow as much of their own food as possible, using the most modern technological knowledge and using land formerly covered over with concrete, even using rooftops. They are organized into cooperatives or collectives, with decisions made from the bottom up in participatory fashion. Work is distributed as evenly as possible, and basic essentials are available to all. People pitch in cooperatively on various services such as day-care centers. Actually, the imaginary community combines the idea of neighborhood control with neighborhood efficiency based on advanced technology; with an equalitarian, noncompetitive ethic; and with participatory democracy.

The excerpt constitutes the final chapter of the book by David Morris and Karl Hess on *Neighborhood Power: The New Localism.* The preceding chapters in the book are more didactic, explanatory, describing new technologies, new urban forms, and in effect laying out systematically the kinds of constituent parts of the imaginary community which they construct.

It is interesting that Morris and Hess seek to decentralize the city, to build up local neighborhoods, and, in a sense, to recreate the *Gemeinschaft* largely destroyed by the great changes of the past few centuries. The continued interplay of *Gemeinschaft* and *Gesellschaft* as aspects of living which each generation must balance for itself, though dramatized in is final passage, is a theme which has run throughout the many selections in this book and will no doubt be with us for the predictable—or unpredictable—future.

40

The good community— What would it be?

Roland L. Warren

Although social scientists have been active in addressing themselves to community problems and in engaging in community development efforts, they have produced little systematic thinking regarding the characteristics of "good" community. Nine issues confront anyone who seeks to formulate a model of a good community under today's circumstances. These are:

primary group relationships, autonomy, viability, power distribution, participation, degree of commitment, degree of heterogeneity, extent of neighborhood control, and the extent of conflict.

Not only is there extensive disagreement on what resolution of these individual issues a "good" community would embody, but some research findings indicate that certain commonly-accepted characteristics of a good community—autonomy, viability, and broad distribution of power—may be incompatible. Research

Reprinted with permission of the publisher from Roland L. Warren, "The Good Community—What Would It Be?," *Journal of the Community Development Society* 1, no. 1 (Spring 1970), pp. 14–23.

regarding such interrelationships can illuminate political decision making, though it cannot replace it.

When I was writing *Studying Your Community* about 15 years ago, I came across a passage from Josiah Royce which had a great deal of meaning for me. So I included it on a separate page at the beginning of the book. It read: "I believe in the beloved community and in the spirit which makes it beloved, and in the communion of all who are, in will and in deed, its members. I see no such community as yet, but nonetheless my rule of life is: Act so as to hasten its coming."

The statement was appealing in its suggestion that there is a good way for us to live together; there is a regard for the whole and a compassion for the individual, a way in which we can treat each other as brothers, a sense of caring and being cared about. I found the image very moving; and I still do. I suppose it is another way of getting at what some of our young people are also seeking to express: that there must be a way to love and to care, but our local communities today fail miserably in measuring up to this simple image of what human life really might be, if we took it—and some of our other professed aspirations—seriously.

In these days when riots break out in our cities, when parents find it difficult to maintain a meaningful relationship with their children, when fluoridation creates violent controversy, when part of the people think that the local community is too conservative and another part think that the old values are being undermined by liberalism and the welfare state, when neither whites nor blacks can agree among themselves or with each other on desegregation or separatism, when the call is for greater federal involvement at the same time as more neighborhood control, and greater rationality and systems analysis for efficiency are demanded at the same time as increased citizen participation in policymaking—few people are thinking in any systematic fashion about what a good community would be if we had one.

How is it possible for citizens working to improve their own communities, or for professional community development workers, to operate effectively? How can they set realistic goals, and measure progress toward them, unless they have, even in general terms, a clear conception of what the community would be like that they are striving for? Let us examine the nine issues mentioned earlier.

1. PRIMARY GROUP RELATIONSHIPS

By way of illustrating the problems involved, let us take the question of the extent to which people may or really should know each other in the community, and should interact with each other on a personal basis. The very ambiguity of the term "community" allows us to sustain some extremely implausible images of what communities should be. For example, when we read in Baker Brownell's *The Human Community* that "A community is a group of people who know one another well," we nod our heads in agreement.[1] He goes on to point out that "knowing well" must mean "the full pattern of functional social relationships which people may have with one another." To put this another way, we must know the grocer or lawyer not only as such, but also as persons—whether or not they go to church, how they feel about politics, where they live, how they get along with their family, what they think about the local school, and so on.

At the same time we nod our heads in assent, however, we realize, when reminded, that such *personal acquaintance* among all community people is impossible in all but the very smallest communities.

---

[1] Baker, Brownell, *The Human Community: Its Philosophy and Practice for a Time of Crisis* (New York: Harper & Brothers, 1950), p. 198.

And since more than 70 percent of our people in this country live in large metropolitan areas, this component of the community—so important that Brownell makes it a criterion of community—becomes largely irrelevant. Brownell acknowledges this situation—but he doesn't have to like it. He writes:

The great city rises; the human community declines. The stability of little places and the ordered rhythm of rural life are lost. The intimate faith that this man belongs here in the little group of people known well calls only for a "wisecrack" or contemptuous indifference.[2]

Three questions may be useful as we examine Brownell's prescription, or prescriptions by others regarding desirable characteristics of a community.

To what extent is the desired characteristic possible under the circumstances of 20th century living?

How much of any particular good thing do we want?

What is its price in terms of other values?

Brownell's conception of a desirable community does not do well in answering our first criterion: To what extent is it possible under circumstances of 20th century living? But even if it did, there are those who question whether this small community, where everyone knows his own and everyone else's place, actually is or ever was quite so desirable as many people assume.

Yet the issue is more complex. If both advantages and disadvantages exist in the primary relationships of a tightly-knit neighborhood, this can be extremely important. For example, Zorbaugh pointed out four decades ago that in Chicago it was in the "World of Furnished Rooms," a neighborhood characterized by little primary group contact, where neighbor did not know neighbor, where one was truly anonymous, that there was the greatest freedom from the prying eyes of neigh-

bors, the greatest liberation from small town gossip and back-biting, the freedom to be oneself. At the same time, there was the highest suicide rate of any area in the city, and other social indicators suggested that a price was paid for this freedom. There was little gossip because people didn't care enough to gossip about each other. They also didn't care enough to help out a person if he got sick, or even to know who the neighbor was, let alone knowing or caring if he was sick.[3]

The question of how well people should be expected to know each other has relevance today to what may be called the revival of the neighborhood movement and increased emphasis on neighborhood self-determination. These neighborhoods are each comprised of many components, including the movement toward decentralization, emphasized by the present federal administration, the movement for participatory democracy, and the Black Power movement. The question of how well people should know each other not only illustrates the complexity of the problem of what sort of communities we want, but it illustrates the relevance of the three questions raised concerning any proposed characteristic of the good community.

2. AUTONOMY

The next issue to be considered is autonomy. It is often said that a community should, insofar as possible, be "master of its own fate." Decisions as to what goes on in the community should be made by local people. They should not be made by federal officials, or in the state house, or in the headquarters offices of a national corporation or voluntary association. Rather, local people should have the principal say about business, governmental, and voluntary associations operating in the local community.

---

[2] *Ibid.*, p. 289–90.

[3] Harvey W. Zorbaugh, *The Gold Coast and the Slum* (Chicago: University of Chicago Press, 1929).

Unless the talk about *local community autonomy* is to be empty rhetoric, we must be willing to follow some of its implications. A community which was serious about its own local autonomy would tend to be rather resistant to things which made definite encroachments on local autonomy. Since federal and state grant-in-aid programs often place considerable limitations on such local freedom of choice, a community that was serious about its autonomy would turn them down—at great financial expense to itself, incidentally.

It would also shy away from voluntary organizations such as some of the national health associations, whose local units are merely branches whose policies are determined at state or national headquarters. Likewise, it would hesitate to attrack branch plants of national industrial firms, since decisions as to whether the local plant is to be expanded or not, whether local workers will be hired or laid off, would likewise be made by absentee owners, not local people.

These may seem like extreme examples. But if we mean anything at all when we say that local communities should insofar as possible direct their own affairs, what do we mean? We may mean these things, and we may mean other things. My point is not which ones we should mean, but rather that we are not at all clear about this business of local autonomy, and if we want to be clear about what kind of community we really want, we have to think it through.

3. VIABILITY

A third important issue with which we have to grapple in conceiving of the good community is that of *viability*. By viability I refer to the capacity of local people to confront their problems effectively through some type of concerted action. Much of the community development movement, much of voluntary community work and professional community organization has been devoted to this goal of helping communities to assess their problems and take action with respect to them. I shall return to this matter of viability later.

4. POWER DISTRIBUTION

Another issue with which we must come to grips if we are serious about our communities is the issue of *power*. Although numerous studies of community power structure have followed upon Floyd Hunter's ground-breaking book published in 1953,[4] not a single study finds power over decision making to be equally distributed throughout the population. To the contrary. Although differing in degree, all the studies find that the power over community decisions is unevenly distributed, with a relatively small minority of people exercising inordinate power in decision making.

The numerous studies of community power distribution have been conducted by sociologists and political scientists. They have directed themselves at how power is actually distributed, rather than at how it should be distributed. Yet, in many of the study reports it is quite clear that the author has a frankly "democratic" bias in the sense of believing that community power should actually be distributed more broadly than it is. The concentration of power, in other words, is looked upon with diffidence—sometimes, as in Hunter, to the point of alleging that it constitutes a conspiracy to subvert democracy. The relative "powerlessness" of poor and black groups constitutes an important current issue. But I do not know of a study which attempts to answer the question of how power should be distributed in the good community, beyond the simple and unex-

---

[4] Floyd Hunter, *Community Power Structure: A Study of Decision Makers* (Chapel Hill: University of North Carolina Press, 1953).

amined admonition: "More broadly than now."

Should all people have equal power? Can they? And if they can, at what price in terms of other desirable values?

5. PARTICIPATION

The fifth issue raised is *participation*. Most people who concern themselves with the community believe that it would be better if more people participated in community affairs. This has been especially true of community development workers.

Two interrelated circumstances are pertinent. On the one hand, as indicated by various power structures studies, large groups of citizens are systematically excluded from the decision-making process governing some of the most important community decisions. On the other hand, there is often widespread apathy, and many citizens do not participate, even where the opportunity is there for them.

But how widespread should participation be? Should all community people actively pursue all the important decisions that are made in the community? This would be mathematically impossible, for there is not time enough in the day for citizens to keep themselves well informed and fully participating on all issues. Some of them they must leave to others. Where are the limits, here? And if not everyone can participate in everything, what would be a suitable arrangement?

6. DEGREE OF COMMITMENT

A sixth issue closely related to participation, is the matter of *commitment*. How important should my local community be to me? Should it be an overriding preoccupation, or is it purely secondary? Many community workers assume that the community should be an important focus for the individual's life. Lawrence Haworth, a philosopher who has come as close as any-

one I know of to writing a systematic work on the good community, writes:

If the city is to become a community, then, the inhabitants must identify the settlement itself as the focal point of their individual lives.[5]

But in today's differentiated world of continental and intercontinental communications and transportation, and of changes of residence as people move from place to place, how realistic is it to presume that the local community will be the identification of overriding importance? And should it be? Should we all be localities, rather than cosmopolitans, in Merton's terminology?[6] And what of the many people who are very happy being cosmopolitans, equally at home in any community? Is there something deficient about them? Clearly, many people would not want to live in a community where people expected them to make the community the most important focus of their lives. Yet, obviously, there must be some people who consider the local community most important. How many? What proportion? And, how much is too much?

7. DEGREE OF HETEROGENEITY

Let us turn now to a matter which is even more perplexing: the matter of *homogeneity or heterogeneity*. How much difference would you have among people in your good community—and how much likeness?

Consider just a few random aspects of this controversial question. In the city planning field, as well as in many other fields, the idea of heterogeneity has long

---

[5] Lawrence Haworth, *The Good City* (Bloomington: Indiana University Press, 1963), p. 87.
[6] Robert Merton, "Patterns of Influence: A Study of Interpersonal Influence and of Communications Behavior in a Local Community," in Paul F. Lazarsfeld and Frank N. Stanton, eds., *Communications Research 1948–1949* (New York: Harper & Brothers, 1949).

held moral sway. It has simply been accepted as a value that it is better for people to live in communities which are more or less a cross-section of the population than to live in economically or racially or ethnically segregated communities. Yet, interestingly, many of these same city planners show through their behavior that they themselves prefer to live in communities which are segregated, in the sense of being economically, racially, and ethnically homogeneous. They choose to live, according to the standard joke, where the man gets off the commuter train, gets into the wrong station wagon, goes home, spends the night, and gets back onto the train the next morning never having noticed the difference.

Note also the gradual breakdown in the constitutionality of ordinances or convenants which exclude poor people by acreage zoning, and exclude blacks and other minorities by collusion or covenant. At the same time, note the rise in separatism on the part of black and Chicano militants, as well as the more long-standing separatism practiced by whites in the form of segregation. Note the different decisions made in various cities in determining the borders of the Model Neighborhood in the Model Cities program, with some deliberately opting for a mixed neighborhood, others for a homogeneous neighborhood—in most instances, all black.

It is one thing to talk of the values of different life styles, the greater variety caused by a plurality of subcultures. But how much heterogeneity can a community stand and still retain some degree of coherence? If we really want a heterogeneous community, if we really want all kinds of people, from John Birchers to socialists, can we expect not to see the sparks fly once in a while? And, in a different vein, how acceptable is the notion, often voiced today in one form or another, of homogeneous neighborhoods within heterogeneous communities?

8. EXTENT OF NEIGHBORHOOD CONTROL

This brings us to the matter of *neighborhoods*, and their relation to the larger local community. Here we have an issue around which there is great controversy today. How much shall we invest in the neighborhood as an important social unit, as distinguished from investing in the community as a whole. Haworth concludes:

We would not want to decentralize urban institutions to such an extent that the city becomes a mere confederation of neighborhoods. But this danger appears so remote at least in American cities, that it seems insignificant.[7]

In recent years, however, there has been a tremendous acceleration in the movement toward decentralization and neighborhood control. There are many reasons for this, one being the simple one that the complex larger cities are proving themselves more and more difficult to manage from centralized offices. Another is the increasingly recognized need, in many fields, to have services distributed closer to the recipient in his own neighborhood. Still another is a growing sense, both within racial ghettos and outside them, that control centers are too remote and insensitive, that neighborhood institutions have too long been run by outsiders in the larger community, that neighborhood people must have a larger say in the decisions that govern their lives. In short: "community autonomy," but in this case at the neighborhood level.

An additional underlying reality is that many so-called city neighborhoods are larger than many entire cities, so that in one sense the autonomy that some people demand in the name of an entire community may be demanded with equal logic by the inhabitants of a neighborhood of similar size. If 60 thousand people in a small

---

[7] Haworth, *The Good City*, p. 72.

city can control their own schools through their own board of education, why shouldn't 60 thousand people in one of the many large neighborhoods of a metropolis have the same right? In any case, the question of the relative strength of the neighborhood versus that of the city has to be faced by anyone presuming to become specific about what he means by a good community.

9. EXTENT OF CONFLICT

Only one more knotty issue, last but not least: How much *conflict* will there be in your good community? Up until 10 years or so ago, the answer by most interested Americans would have been virtually: "None." For conflict was simply a dirty word. Conflict was something whose effect could only be destructive. Now, all that has changed, and each of these statements is questioned.

Probably the most identifiable intellectual influence in this change in viewpoint has been Coser's book on *The Functions of Social Conflict.*[8] Although this book has a deservedly high reputation, its great impact may be based in part upon a misunderstanding of its contents. Most of the book is devoted to the ways in which conflict is functional for a unit taken as one of the parties to a larger conflict, rather than a unit which is itself torn by conflict. Thus, conflict in Belfast between Catholics and Protestants may be functional for the solidarity of each conflicting group, but I don't think Coser would argue that it promotes solidarity in the city as such.

Another reason for the growing acceptance of conflict is the growing conviction in many quarters that strategies based on consensus play into the hands of the status quo, and permit the continuation of gross injustices. Hence, though conflict may be

less desirable as a method of change than collaborative change strategies based on consensus, it is considered by many to be preferable to its alternative, the seeking of consensus and hence the preservation of social injustices in substantially their current form.

It is no longer generally agreed that the good community is a community without conflict—which places conflict on the agenda as one of the issues we must face if we are to speak meaningfully about what a good community would be like.

One possible implication of this list of issues which must be addressed in considering the character of a good community is that there is no such thing as *the* good community. There are *many* good communities, all according to the specific combination of preferences which may be held regarding each of these issues, in an almost infinite variety of combinations. On so many of these issues, there is simply no way to demonstrate that one viewpoint is more valid or more moral than another.

It is perhaps for this reason that social scientists have avoided the pursuit of definitions of the good community. Nevertheless, a review of the issues raised here does substantiate their importance. Such issues must be faced, and unless we face them, we are working in the dark when we seek to build better communities.

Perhaps the most we can aspire to is to give sustained attention to such considerations as have been raised in this paper, especially in connection with the three questions raised:

How much of what we want is actually possible?

How much of what seems desirable do we actually want?

How much of a price are we willing to pay for it when other values are jeopardized by it?

In closing, this last question can be illustrated by examining the relation between the first three values mentioned:

[8] Lewis Coser, *The Functions of Social Conflict* (New York: Free Press of Glencoe, 1956).

Community autonomy, community viability, and a broad distribution of community power. There is some research which indicates that these three values, as desirable as they may be, do not always support each other. In a sense, what you gain in trying to pursue one of them may be paid for in a loss to the others. For example, a considerable number of studies are beginning to show that the broader the distribution of power and the more vigorous the public participation in a city, the less likely is a school integration campaign or a fluoridation campaign or an urban renewal proposal or other types of community improvement venture to be successful.[9]

Hence, those who accept such measures as indications of a community's viability and its ability to confront and resolve its own problems must recognize that in such cases, viability and broad power distribution are likely to work at cross-purposes.

Although other research findings offer almost contradictory conclusions,[10] the important point is that one is not justified in simply assuming that such values as these can be maximized simultaneously.

Likewise, there is much theory and research to support the statement that community autonomy and a broad distribution of power are mutually incompatible. In a review of the power structure literature, John Walton found that it was the cities which were the least autonomous which had the broadest distribution of power. Dependence on governmental, business, and political networks extending beyond the community tends to diffuse power, rather than concentrate it.[11]

By the same token, community autonomy, if pressed too far, apparently threatens viability, the ability of community people to confront their own problems. Obviously, to the extent that a community deliberately cuts itself off from sources of grant-in-aid programs, whether from state or federal government or from national foundations, it foregoes the access to important financial resources which might help to solve its problems. Likewise, to the extent that it discourages branch plants and other types of absentee-owned industrial activity, it takes on a self-imposed threat to its economic base.

How much of what kind of autonomy do communities want, and how much are they willing to sacrifice for this autonomy in terms of other things they want—like problem-solving ability and a broad distribution of power, rather than a concentrated power structure? These are the kinds of questions that seem relevant when we begin to dig underneath the surface of our conception of what a good community would be like.

I want to return to my earlier quotation from Royce. I believe in the beloved community. But unless this concept is to be a mere poetic expression, a sort of sentimental catharsis, we have to become serious with it and make some difficult choices.

Hence, the question: Do we really agree

---

[9] Amos H. Hawley, "Community Power and Urban Renewal Success," in Clark, "Community Structure," p. 405; Donald B. Rosenthal and Robert L. Crain, "Structure and Values in Local Political Systems: The Case of Fluoridation Decisions," in Clark, "Community Structure," pp. 241–242 et passim. See also Robert L. Crain, Elihu Katz, and Donald B. Rosenthal, *The Politics of Community Conflict: The Fluoridation Decision* (New York: The Bobbs-Merrill Company, 1969); and Herman Turk, *A Method of Predicting Certain Federal Program Potentials of Large American Cities* (Los Angeles: Laboratory for Organizational Research, University of Southern California, 1967).

[10] Terry N. Clark, "Community Structure, Decision-Making, Budget Expenditures, and Urban Renewal in 51 American Communities," *American Sociological Review* 33, no. 4 (August 1968): Michael Aiken and Robert R. Alford, "Community Structure and Innovation: The Case of Urban Renewal," Institute for Research on Poverty, University of Wisconsin, June, 1969, mimeographed, paper presented at the September 1969, annual meeting of the American Sociological Society; and Wayne Paulson, Edgar W. Butler, and Hallowell Pope, "Community Power and Public Welfare," *American Journal of Economics and Sociology* 28, no. 1 (January 1969).

[11] John Walton, "The Vertical Axis of Community Organization and the Structure of Power," *Southwestern Social Science Quarterly* 48, no. 3 (December 1967).

on what a good community would be like? When we become specific about its qualities, a number of crucial questions arise, about which there is much disagreement. The good community is not a "grab-bag of goodies" to satisfy every conceivable desire. It involves choices and rejections which we make either deliberately or by default.

These choices are worked out in the interplay of political forces, as different groups bring their different combinations of preferences to the arena of community decision making. A careful analysis of the implications of such choices can help illuminate the political decision-making process, though it cannot replace it.

41

The competent community

Leonard S. Cottrell, Jr.

One of the more obvious characteristics of the average American local community is the presence in it of a multiplicity of agencies and organizations directed to nourishing some interest, meeting some need, or rendering some service. Even in the most impoverished areas of the inner city there are usually an impressive array of so-called service agencies supported by outside sources, in addition to numerous indigenous organized groups.

A second pervasive condition becomes evident only when an attempt is made to mobilize and coordinate the resources of a community for a focused attack on some problem. Such an attempt quickly reveals such a welter of institutional rivalries, jurisdictional disputes, doctrinal differences, and lack of communication that effective joint action seems well beyond practical possibility. And the problem of original concern begins to appear relatively simple compared with that of rendering the community capable of coordinated collective action.

A less frequently noted but nevertheless equally real feature is that the majority of those organizations designed to render service or cope with particular problems are so constituted that the recipients of services or targets of problem-solving efforts—i.e., clients—have little or nothing to do or say about setting policy or making decisions concerning goals and operations of these institutions.

When the President's Committee on Juvenile Delinquency and Youth Crime undertook to organize programs to test the feasibility and utility of coordinated, comprehensive, community-based attacks on the problems of juvenile delinquency and youth crime, it made initial grants to a number of communities. The grants were intended to assist the communities in developing a coordinated plan based upon a careful diagnosis of the critical problems of their youth, and in projecting a new program of action in which the agencies and institutions would closely integrate their operations in such a way as to produce a coherent focused attack on all aspects of the youth problem. The effort to produce such a plan with the kinds of commitments, institutional changes, and accommodations it required was exhausting, frustrating, and sometimes exhilarating.

Reprinted from Chapter 11, The Competent Community," by Leonard S. Cottrell, Jr., in *Further Explorations in Social Psychiatry*, ed. by Berton H. Kaplan, Robert N. Wilson, and Alexander H. Leighton, © 1976 by Basic Books, Inc., Publishers, New York. The footnotes have been renumbered.

No community achieved the perfect plan. Most were only able to put together an uneasy and rather half-hearted accommodation that in several instances collapsed under the strain of actual operation.

As the planning efforts continued and action phases were initiated, it became increasingly evident to the staff and consultants of the president's committee that the impact of programs, regardless of how good their content, would be relatively minor unless the indigenous populations of the communities themselves were involved in all phases of their development and operation. It is hardly necessary to point out that for professional agency personnel, trained to provide services for clients and to operate programs for people, the requirement that they work with their clients in identifying what the problems are, deciding on priorities as to goals, and working out ways of implementing them, was an enormous complication. Some simply refused to attempt the task; others tried and failed. Most achieved at least some degree of participation of community members—sometimes with startling results, gratifying as well as painful.

This is not the place to recount the exciting history of the brief but highly significant and instructive experience of the president's committee. (Knapp and Polk[1] have written an excellent history and a highly illuminating analysis of this experience.) It is sufficient for purposes of this chapter to report that the staff and consultants early began to recognize that they were involved in much more than a program to control juvenile delinquency. What they found themselves doing was attempting to aid the demonstration communities in the novel and complicated task of upgrading their capabilities to function as communities in coping with a wide range of problems, including those of youth. It was in this broadening of perspective and through the rich empirical experience of trying to aid communities to evolve feasible and effective programs that the notion of a competent community emerged.[2]

The concept of a competent community is still far from precise definition. However, as communities were observed from

---

[1] D. Knapp, and K. Polk, *Scouting the War on Poverty* (Lexington, Mass.: D. C. Heath, 1971).

[2] The general concept of competence as applied to the interpretation and evaluation of human behavior has been used by various writers since it was first explicitly suggested by Harry Stack Sullivan in 1947. Foote and Cottrell proposed six component elements of what they defined as interpersonal competence. They elaborated hypotheses concerning the interaction processes in the family and other socializing agencies that determined the degree of development of the components of interpersonal competence. Later White used the term primarily as a motivational concept positing the presence in the organism of a drive toward effectiveness in interaction with the environment. Inkeles uses the concept with primary emphasis on the socialization of the person to meet the role requirements in a given social structure. M. Brewster Smith published a very useful review of the literature on competence and kindred concepts, with special reference to the problem of the socialization of the child for competent behavior. In this review he proposes his own conception of the core characteristics of "the competent self." Prior to the present chapter, Cottrell has used the term in describing the performance of communities. While there is no clear theoretical continuity between the concept of competence as applied to the behavior of the person and as applied to a collectivity such as the community, readers who have reviewed the six components of interpersonal competence proposed by Foote and Cottrell will detect a certain kinship between some of those components of interpersonal competence and certain of the proposed components of community competence, e.g., empathetic or role-taking ability of the person and communicative competence in the community, or autonomy of the person and self-other awareness in community relations. Furthermore, those familiar with the conceptualizations of the processes of interaction by George H. Mead, will see that both the concepts of personal and community competence are rooted in the Meadian tradition. Virginia Boardman has made the most explicit use of the concept of competence of a collectivity thus far reported. Adapting the proposed components of community competences, she constructed an index of family competence and found that this index correlated significantly in the negative direction with school attendance records of the children in the family.

the perspective of evaluating their competence and as further thought and discussion were devoted to the attempt to determine what appeared to differentiate the more competent from the less competent, some tentative defining characteristics and essential conditions were identified. These will be discussed later in this chapter. For our present discussion, a competent community is here conceived as one in which the various component parts of the community: (1) are able to collaborate effectively in identifying the problems and needs of the community; (2) can achieve a working consensus on goals and priorities; (3) can agree on ways and means to implement the agreed-upon goals; and (4) can collaborate effectively in the required actions. It is proposed here that a community that can provide the conditions and generate the capabilities required to meet the above performance tests will be competent to cope with the problems of its collective life.

It is recognized, of course, that conditions imposed by larger political, economic, and social contexts provide resources as well as intrude problems with which the local community cannot cope, regardless of how competent it may be. This we shall have to consider later in our discussion. But it should be noted here that a competent community in our terms can go a long way in coping with problems, even when they arise from larger external conditions.

When beginning to consider whether problems arise from conditions inside or outside the community, one immediately runs into the difficult question: What is the community? What are its boundaries? The semantic problem of giving a precise and unambiguous definition of the term "community" need not detain us here. The term applies to collectivities ranging from a tiny mountain village to the "world community" that mankind must achieve if it is to survive. The range of meaning includes

limited interest groups as well as the usually conceived population living in a local area and conducting overlapping and interdependent life activities that are perceived to bind the residents into a collective entity with which they are identified and to which they give a name. It is this more usual type of local community with which we are primarily concerned in this discussion. Such local groups will be found to vary in the degree to which they see themselves as community entities, and the degrees of "communityness" can be indexed in various ways. For practical purposes, it is not too difficult to determine the boundaries of a self-aware community. Once the boundaries are determined, the practical questions with which we are concerned are as follows. What conditions are necessary and what specific capabilities must be developed to enable the community to function competently as a community? What operations are required to provide the necessary conditions and capabilities?

So far as I know, there are presently no systematic, logically complete, empirically tested answers to these questions. The best we can do at the moment is to make a start by drawing on fragments of practical experience, observation, and relevant conceptualization to identify what appear to be essential conditions that must obtain to a substantial degree in the community if it is to function effectively as such. The conditions I shall discuss below represent just such a pragmatic distillation. No claim can be made that the list is exhaustive. The categories are not mutually exclusive and are heavily interrelated. For present purposes, the most useful way to regard them is as aspects of community functioning that could be the objects of concrete practical effort in a program designed to enhance community competence. Measures of change in these variables could well provide an index of the level of overall competence. Here then are some proposed essential conditions of community competence.

COMMITMENT

Commitment to the community as a valued relationship that is worthy of substantial effort to sustain and enhance is an essential condition of the capability of the community to act effectively. And the extent to which such commitment exists among constituents of the community is an important part of any measure of its competence. Precise identification of conditions that encourage and intensify commitment has not been made, but it does appear that people become genuinely committed to a community when: (1) they see that what it does and what happens to it has a vital impact on their own lives and values they cherish; (2) they find that they have a recognized significant role in it; and (3) they see positive results from their efforts to participate in its life. No ready-made general prescriptions for specific actions aimed to optimize commitment exist, but it is clear that this component will yield a range of specific targets for concrete programs. It is also clear that pseudocommitment based on empty slogans and artificial "boosting" campaigns will have little durable effect. It is encouraging that whatever the causes, people of all ranks and conditions often show that they are capable of becoming deeply committed to things of which they are a part, even under the most demanding and unpromising circumstances. It is a universal tendency to be attached in many ways to one's own locality, "be it ever so humble," but cheap, exploitative, manipulative use of this sentiment can turn into bitter rejection.

If commitment is based in part on consciousness of the degree to which one's interests and welfare are vitally involved in the functioning of the community, then programs directed to sharpening this awareness should affect commitment. However, such efforts will certainly back-fire if the negative and inimical aspects of the community are denied or glossed over. The negative aspects can be frankly dealt with as challenges and conditions that can be realistically attacked. Proposed remedies, of course, must be honest, and not make-believe promises that never get implemented.

Commitment comes with genuine involvement. Increasing the awareness of members of the significant roles they have in the collective life should enhance the sense of commitment. Here again, honesty in appraisal of the extent to which various segments have a vital share in the collective life is indispensable. Where appraisals reveal lack of significant roles, analyses of the barriers and programs in order to discover potential significant roles are indicated.

Commitment grows with realization that what one does makes a difference. People may be encouraged and helped to achieve what appear to be significant roles in the community, but if they do not find that they are actually making a significant impact on community processes and problems, the activity becomes meaningless. They then fall victims to that chronic sense of individual impotence peculiar to modern life. Alienation and reduced commitment result.

The reader will quickly perceive that the kinds of efforts suggested above to generate and enhance commitment will themselves, if successful, have substantial impact on the character of the community. The direction of this impact will, as we shall show later, be toward greater competence. Thus, in seeking to create committed people, the community itself may become created.

Other lines of endeavor can be suggested, but enough has been said to indicate this is no easy undertaking that can be accomplished by a few "civic parades," TV booster programs, and pious slogans by the local chamber of commerce and other promotional organizations. Nor can reliance be placed on a multiplicity of "services" by outside "experts" and dropped on the community.

SELF-OTHER AWARENESS AND CLARITY OF SITUATIONAL DEFINITIONS

Those who seek to control and exploit or to reduce the capacity of a community or some segments of it to act effectively will strive to blur identities and control perceptions of the situation in order to induce alignments and attitudes consonant with their special goals and interests. In our conception, a working hypothesis is that the degree to which communities can cope realistically with their problems is determined in considerable part by the clarity with which each component perceives its own identity and position on issues in the community context in relation to that of the other component parts. This includes awareness by each segment of its own interests and how these relate to the interests of the other elements—the degree of conflict or compatibility of interests as perceived, for example. Communities are unlikely to be very effective in identifying their real problems or in finding constructive working accommodations among their various groups if they try to work with blurred identities and conflicts, or communality of interests that are wittingly or unwittingly concealed. In the discussions, debates, and political struggles through which the community strives to arrive at working accommodations and to develop consensus on goals, policies, and programs, competence will increase to the degree that identities and their realistic positions are matters of clear self-other awareness. If such awareness is permitted to lead merely to confrontation and "nonnegotiable demands," then progress toward competent functioning is impeded.

The processes of increasing the realism and clarity of awareness of self and other and of their realistic situational position-ing, and of controlling and utilizing constructively the resulting intensification of discord and conflict, is the most misunderstood and harzardous phase of community development. It was this aspect of the work of the president's committee and later of the Office of Economic Opportunity that generated the most opposition from the local "Establishment" and the Congress, and was the cause of the most determined efforts to scuttle the whole community development movement.[3] The technology of helping people learn to make creative use of conflict is an undeveloped field, and it is indispensable for the development of competence of communities.

Difficult learning and unlearning is involved in achieving competence in realistic perception of self and other, and in the realistic appraisal of situations. People will have to unlearn habits of uncritical swallowing of whatever is dished out. They have to develop a healthy skepticism and skills in critical weighing of information, and at the same time retain a sensitivity to fresh ideas and perspectives. Conversion to doctrinaire ideologies is no substitute for the skills considered here. Practice in down-to-earth, realistic situational analyses of each concrete issue is the surest way of developing the capabilities called for.

ARTICULATENESS

Closely related to clarification of identity and interests is the ability of each segment of the community to articulate its views, attitudes, needs, and intentions, and, further, to articulate its perception of the relation of its position to that of the other segments of the community. Ordinarily the different groups in a community will vary widely in facility for

---

[3] See in this connection Huey Perry, *They'll Cut Off Your Project* (New York: Praeger, 1972)—an excellent parallel reading for this chapter and a must for those interested in community development.

articulate statement of a situation. Action programs aimed at increasing competence of the community will frequently have to include, for some groups, elementary training in communicative skills: speaking to an audience, conducting committee discussions, and formulating clear statements of a position on various issues.

COMMUNICATION

The factors of awareness and articulateness are reciprocally influential, and both are intimately related to capacity to communicate. As used here, communication refers to much more than mere emission and reception of oral or written symbols or indicative gestures and acts. Meaningful communication requires that the sender of the message take the role of the recipient and respond covertly, i.e., incipiently, to his own message in the way he anticipates that the other will respond. Unless he can do this, he literally does not know what he is saying, since the meaning of his message is given in the anticipated imagined response of the other. To be sure, his interpretation of the role of the other may be erroneous and his anticipation may not be fulfilled, but if interaction continues, erroneous perceptions will be corrected and the participants will become more accurate in their role taking. In this way the interacting population amasses its supply of common meanings upon which efficient communication must rest. This is what is meant when we remark that participants in a common enterprise learn to "speak the same language." The population of a community may speak the same language in a formal linguistic sense, but lack the communality of meanings referred to here. Communicative effectiveness and the accumulation of common meanings obviously depends on the ability to listen, to receive, quite as much as it does on the ability to send. To listen, to hear what the other is actually saying, also requires accuracy in taking his role and seeing the situation from his position. In an era of shouting and confrontation and din of mass media, it is increasingly rare to find competent listening with comprehension of what the other is saying. It is no accident that our words common, community, and communication stem from the same root, and the capability of a community to function effectively as such emerges with its skills and facilities for genuine two-way communication.

Adequate development of communicative skills and facilities should do much to aid in the identification and clarification of real issues and to facilitate productive discussion and debate. Such a development should aid greatly in reducing the bootless shouting, name calling, and obfuscating nondiscussion that so frequently passes for "community action." Enhancement of genuine communication is greatly aided by the design of effective channels of expression and discussion that are simple and readily accessible. The usual ones of press, politics, and other existing organizational channels are frequently inadequate, but could be greatly improved by deliberate effort. A network of connective, functional local forums and other discussional devices that actually aid discussion and crystallization of opinion, and funnel it undistorted to decision-making bodies, is badly needed in most communities. Some already established institutions can, by taking thought, be made to serve this function.

It is important at this point to take note of the fact that skill and accuracy in role taking do not necessarily lead to constructive "understanding" and collaborative effort. Accurate perception of the other's position and intentions can be used to outwit and exploit him, as skillful propagandists well know. These skills increase community competence only when they are used in an honest search for bases for collaborative endeavors to define common goals and collaborative means of implementing them.

CONFLICT CONTAINMENT AND ACCOMMODATION

Skills and capabilities implicit in the foregoing component conditions of competence do not ensure an absence of conflict. Indeed, as commitment increases, identities and situations become clarified, positions on issues become articulated, and communication becomes more effective, conflict may and frequently does become intensified. Furthermore, as conflict emerges, the interacting elements become less and less able to communicate effectively. What is required is a repertoire of procedures whereby open conflicts may be accommodated. All conflict tends to move toward some form of accommodated relation that enables the antagonists to live in relative peace, even though the bases for conflict may not be resolved.

The desideratum here is inventiveness in the development of procedures for working out accommodations that will keep conflict within bounds, while enabling the participants to continue efforts at resolutions of the sources of the conflict. Conflict is not something to be avoided or suppressed at all costs. Where it exists, it should be recognized and its sources made explicit. The competence required is that of accommodation and restoration of genuine communication, and a continued realistic search for resolution and reapprochement. Arbitration, civil procedures, and voting are forms of accommodative procedure. Labor contracts, segregation, and peace treaties can be seen as forms of accommodation in that they operate to reduce open conflict. Some forms of accommodation will obviously facilitate continued interaction more readily than others. The competent community will show a versatility and inventiveness in the use of established procedures and in the de-

velopment of new procedures that will produce forms conducive to continued and flexible interaction.

PARTICIPATION

If we pause at this point and look back over the alleged components of community competence just discussed, we can see that they are not clearly separable, independent factors but do in fact exercise a good deal of reciprocal influence on one another. In particular, effective communication quite obviously depends upon articulateness and self-other clarity, and they in turn are dependent upon communication. Or perhaps it is more accurate to say that all these emerge in a process of interaction in which they are both process and product. In any case, they and the motivational factors we have grouped and called commitment, are essential to participation in the processes of community life. Participation in the sense we are using that term is not the equivalent of competence, but it is an indispensable element of community competence. It is a developing process in which the person commits himself to a community in which he contributes to the definition of goals as well as to ways and means for their implementation and enjoyment. As a capability it develops with the development of the components described above, and participation in turn is a significant condition for their growth.

MANAGEMENT OF RELATIONS WITH THE LARGER SOCIETY

The foregoing conditions may be optimally present, but our community could nevertheless be rendered less than competent by conditions impinging upon it from the outside. No local community, of course, can be entirely autonomous. It is therefore necessary for a community to be aware of the context of relations in which it exists and to develop its capacity to adapt to those conditions—to utilize resources and supports which the larger social system makes possible and to act to reduce the threats to its life posed by larger social processes inimical to it. Any community can be mortally crippled or completely destroyed by overwhelming natural catastrophes or cultural, social, political, or economic forces too massive for it to cope with or adapt to. But, within a wide range of situations, knowledge of the social processes surrounding it and skill in utilizing them or managing their impact is possible with even modest understanding and technical talent directed to these factors. Upgrading these capabilities is an essential part of achieving competence.

It is in this area of problems that all elements of a community need to be especially alert and well informed. All too frequently, a community has accepted advice and decisions of various local, state, and federal "planning and development experts," only to discover that it has been sold down the river for exploitation by special interests which control these alleged public agencies, or by the self-perpetuating bureaucratic concerns of the agencies themselves.

Communities must learn to make full use of specialists who command technical knowledge and expertise. They will find it necessary to participate in continued planning to meet changing conditions and new problems generated both inside and outside the community. This need imposes the further necessity of learning how to use experts and specialists without being controlled by them. One important device is to structure the situation so that the experts are clearly subordinate to a broadly representative, tough-minded citizens' group which can be trusted to see that the technical issues are translated into terms the community can understand, and widely communicated and discussed in the framework of the long-run values and welfare of the whole community. No community can trust even the best-intentioned specialists to perform this function for it.

MACHINERY FOR FACILITATING PARTICIPANT INTERACTION AND DECISION MAKING

The processes of interaction required for achieving consensus and making decisions require rules and regularized modes of procedure. In small communities these may be quite simple and informal. As size increases, direct fact-to-face participation in all phases of consensus building and decision making becomes less and less feasible. More formal means for debate, discussion, and representative procedures are required. This means increased risk of inadequate commmunication and the development of rigid and unresponsive institutional machinery that frequently impedes the processes it is ostensibly designed to facilitate. Competent community performance requires constant scrutiny and review of procedures to insure optimal communication and interaction among all parts of the community's structure. Mere verbal assurances that our traditional institutions provide these necessary functions is not enough. Evidence of actual performance is necessary.

SOME GENERAL OBSERVATIONS

Some general comments may be of help at this point.

1. The component conditions presented as essential to the development of a competently functioning local community are not logical derivatives of a systematic general theory. Rather, they emerged from observations of practical efforts of local populations to develop capabilities necessary to function as communities in coping with local problems. Actually, the categories appeared as designations of types of

tasks that had to be addressed by staffs which sought to help the localities identify problems, define goals, and mobilize resources to cope and implement. At this state of development of theory and practice, it is probably wiser to continue to regard these and other potential categories as indicating things to do with and to local groups by way of increasing their capacity to act effectively as collective entities, rather than attempt to determine whether or not they can be encompassed in a general theory. These categories can also be used tentatively as criteria by which to measure progress toward improved competence. With increasing empirical experience, a more coherent and systematic conceptualization should emerge, thus providing a more incisive analysis of the critical processes involved.

2. No claim is made that the present tentative list of essential conditions is exhaustive. But action based on the present list should reveal other essential components. There are factors such as material resources, geographic location, population characteristics, cultural and political conditions, and so on, that certainly bear on the effectiveness with which a community can act as such. However, the ones we have selected here appear to be relevant under any condition under which the community may exist. They apply to a materially impoverished fishing community as well as to an affluent suburb. It is not a foregone conclusion that the high-consumption community would be found to be the more competent; it is quite possible for the fishing village to be highly competent. The other conditions just suggested may, in some sense, be viewed as modifiers of the tentative "essentials" we have proposed.

3. Obviously the categories are not mutually exclusive. Indeed, they are for the most part inextricably interrelated. The justification of attempting a separation is primarily to give practical handles for taking hold of and working with a complex phenomenon. Thus, instead of undertaking vague ad hoc and relatively unfocused efforts to increase the community's competence in general, specific, concrete programs can be mounted to increase genuine communicative capabilities and institutional devices for facilitating communication; promote greater clarity of analysis of the actual lines of interest cleavage and acting perspectives; encourage more participation in discussion, decision making, and action; and so on.

4. We reiterate that the conceptualizations attempted here are directed to the enhancement of competent functioning within a participant democratic framework. It is quite possible that a very different cultural context would require a different set of conditions for effective collective action. It would be interesting and useful for clarifying ideas about competence as here conceived to analyze the requirements for community competence under an authoritarian system.

5. It should be apparent to anyone reasonably familiar with a specific community that changes induced by efforts to enhance competence along lines suggested here would frequently be accompanied by a good deal of social and political turbulence. Indeed, unless great care, discretion, and skill are exercised and extended preparatory work is done, the situation can readily become explosive. In communities with long standing hostilities, deprivations, and repressed unresolved conflicts, progress toward greater awareness and articulateness frequently results in premature and destructive confrontations and violence. These situations may be precipitated by segments who see their power position threatened, or by disadvantaged groups who see no way of gaining power except by violent means. In this connection the reader is again referred to Huey Perry's excellent chronicle of the experience of Mingo County, West Virginia. The experiences recounted in that work do not

cover all conditions here regarded as essential to competent functioning, but they do illustrate the enormous productivity of, as well as intense reaction to, even partial efforts in the development of competence.

The grave risks involved in the kinds of programs suggested should not, indeed must not, be allowed to inhibit attempts to create competent communities if democracy itself is to survive.

6. Ideas and conceptualizations are useful to give structure and direction to action. But they must eventually rest on pragmatically tested operations for their implementation. The space limitations of a single chapter preclude any attempt to consider the "how-to-do-it" aspects of our problem. This must be left to later communications and to the gleanings of experience in community development practices that may be of relevance, even though not enjoying the focus provided by the present analysis.

However, a thoughtful consideration of each of the suggested component conditions of competence will readily suggest possible concrete steps that might be taken in any attempt to enhance the particular capability. These suggestions will occur especially to those who have engaged in even a limited amount of actual community development effort. Furthermore, experience indicates that when one line of action is undertaken with people (not imposed upon them), new possibilities emerge and can be evaluated and tried out.

Another encouraging word is that communities frequently demonstrate that they can learn from the experience of attempting to increase their abilities to function as such, provided, of course, that the experience is not too traumatic for the community to assimilate and continue to function, and also provided that the experience can be articulated and its significant components and "lessons" perceived by the participants.

7. Finally, it should be noted that in most instances communities will need assistance from personnel who are perceptive, skillful, and courageous, and who can work with and facilitate various community groups in developing the relevant capabilities without attempting to become the "leaders" or to become agents for imposing programs and services on the community. This partnership must be genuine and not a "slick trick" for putting something over on one or another group or on the community as a whole. If the latter is the case, the community will be left less competent than it was before it was exploited.

THE COMPETENT COMMUNITY AND MENTAL HEALTH

The relevance of the development of community competence for mental health may be viewed from the broad perspective of how the general level of competence of the community can condition the mental health of its population. Another perspective is that of considering the relevance of the competence level for the development of specific programs considered to be aids to improving mental health.

From the more general perspective, it could with substantial justification be claimed that development of the competence of the community as conceived here would itself be a program of mental health. (I have discussed elsewhere certain aspects of this approach at greater length.) There can be little doubt that the conditions of modern mass technological society tend increasingly to depersonalize and dehumanize much of our collective life. Persons perceive themselves to be living in an environment of enormous social, economic, and political forces that vitally affect their lives, yet over which they feel they have no control. The resulting alienation, devaluation of the self, and accompanying passivity, apathy, and loss of a sense of significance form a profound handicap to achieving a vigorous, sturdy mental health and to functioning as parents in developing mentally healthy children. The discovery that they and their neighbors can take effective collective action to cope with their common problems, that they can become meaningful and effective actors in the life of the community, is frequently found to be a powerful stimulus. Certainly, the recapture of at least some share in the determination of one's fate and a new sense of worth and potency should provide some of the necessary basis for mentally healthy development. To the extent that a community provides the arena for effective participation by the individual in the vital processes of his society, it is a significant factor in his mental health.

If the problem is viewed from a more specific perspective, it is clear that the level of competence of the community is highly relevant to the effectiveness of specific programs aimed at improving its mental health. Anyone who has sought to provide mental health facilities, services, promotional campaigns of information and education, and so on, knows that such enterprises require vigorous participation by the community itself in their development. If such participation is lacking, the program will subside into a relatively minor enterprise that falls far short of its potential. It may seem wasteful of time and effort to try to establish a mental health program by going through the hard work and sometimes stormy episodes of involving the significant elements of the community in the laborious task of looking at their situations, assessing their needs, identifying problems, achieving consensus on goals, and making hard decisions of what action to undertake with what priorities— all of which is attended by high risks of failure or at least some severe setbacks. It is especially embarrassing when some government bureaucratic funding agency is breathing down one's neck and demanding proof of RESULTS. It is of some comfort, however, to recognize that these apparently irrelevant operations and crises can themselves be part of the mental health-producing processes of building the competence of the community. For mental health is not a matter of the condition of that abstraction, the isolated individual. It is essentially the quality of and is inextricably bound up with the relations of the person with himself and with his fellows as individuals and as groups. The capacity for effective functioning in those intrapersonal, interpersonal, and intergroup relations is a measure of his mental health.

REFERENCES

Boardman, V. "School Absences, Illness and Family Competence." Ph.D. dissertation, University of North Carolina, 1972.

Cottrell, L. S., Jr. "New Directions for Research on the American Family." *Social Casework* 34 (1953), pp. 54–60.

――――. "Social Planning, the Competent Community and Mental Health." In *Urban America and the Planning of Mental Health Services*, Symposium no. 10, pp. 391–402. New York: Group for the Advancement of Psychiatry, 1964.

――――. "The Competent Community—A Long-Range View." Address to the Houston Community Leaders Forum, Houston, Texas, October 29, 1967. Mimeographed.

Foote, N. N., and Cottrell, L. S., Jr. *Identity and Interpersonal Competence*. Chicago: University of Chicago Press, 1955.

Inkeles, A. "Social Structure and the Socialization of Competence." *Harvard Educational Review* 36 (1966), pp. 265–83.

Knapp, D., and Polk, K. *Scouting the War on Poverty*. Lexington, Mass.; D. C. Heath, 1971.

Meade, G. H. *Mind, Self and Society*. Chicago: University of Chicago Press, 1934.

Perry, H. *They'll Cut Off Your Project*. New York: Praeger, 1972.

Smith, M. B. "Competence and Socialization." In *Socialization and Society*, ed. by John A. Clausen. Boston: Little, Brown, 1968, pp. 270–320.

Sullivan, H. S. "Tensions Interpersonal and International: A Psychiatrist's View. In *Tensions that Cause Wars*, ed. by Hadley Cantril. Urbana: University of Illinois Press, 1950, pp. 79–138.

White, R. W. "Motivation Reconsidered: The Concept of Competence." *Psychological Review* 66 (1959), pp. 297–333.

_____. *Competence and the Psychosexual Stages of Development*. Nebraska Symposium on Motivation, ed. by M. Jones. Lincoln: University of Nebraska Press, 1960, pp. 97–141.

42

Communes and commitment

Rosabeth Moss Kanter

The primary issue with which a utopian community must cope in order to have the strength and solidarity to endure is its human organization: how people arrange to do the work that the community needs to survive as a group, and how the group in turn manages to satisfy and involve its members over a long period of time. The idealized version of communal life must be meshed with the reality of the work to be done in a community, involving difficult problems of social organization. In utopia, for instance, who takes out the garbage?

The organizational problems with which utopian communities must grapple break down into several categories:

How to get the work done, but without coercion;

How to ensure that decisions are made, but to everyone's satisfaction;

How to build close, fulfilling relationships, but without exclusiveness;

How to choose and socialize new members;

How to include a degree of autonomy, individual uniqueness, and even deviance;

How to ensure agreement and shared perception around community functioning and values.

These issues can be summarized as one of commitment; that is, they reflect how members become committed to the community's work, to its values, and to each other, and how much of their former independence they are willing to suspend in the interests of the group. Committed members work hard, participate actively, derive love and affection from the communal group, and believe strongly in what the group stands for.

For communes, the problem of commitment is crucial. Since the community represents an attempt to establish an ideal social order within the larger society, it must vie with the outside for the members' loyalties. It must ensure high member involvement despite external competition without sacrificing its distinctiveness or ideals. It must often contravene the earlier socialization of its members in securing obedience to new demands. It must calm internal dissension in order to present a united front to the world. The problem of securing total and complete commitment is central.

Because communes consciously sepa-

Reprinted by permission of the publishers and author from pp. 64–74 of Rosabeth Moss Kanter, *Commitment and Community: Communes and Utopias in Sociological Perspective*, Cambridge, Mass.: Harvard University Press, Copyright 1972 by the President and Fellows of Harvard College. Footnotes have been renumbered.

rate from the established order, their needs for the concentration of members' loyalty and devotion are stronger than are those of groups operating with the support of society and leaving members free to participate in the larger system. The commitment problems of utopian communities resemble those of secret societies, as described by Georg Simmel: "The secret society claims the whole individual to a greater extent, connects its members in more of their totality, and mutually obligates them more closely than does an open society of identical content."[1] The essence of such a community is in strong connections and mutual obligations. Communal life depends on a continual flow of energy and support among members, on their depth of shared relationships, and on their continued attachment to each other and to the joint endeavor.

DEFINITIONS

For communal relations to be maintained, what the person is willing to give to the group, behaviorally and emotionally, and what it in turn expects of him, must be coordinated and mutually reinforcing. This reciprocal relationship, in which both what is given to the group and what is received from it are seen by the person as expressing his true nature and as supporting his concept of self, is the core of commitment to a community. A person is committed to a group or to a relationship when he himself is fully invested in it, so that the maintenance of his own internal being requires behavior that supports the social order. A committed person is loyal and involved; he has a sense of beloning, a feeling that the group is an extension of himself and he is an extension of the group. Through commitment, person and group are inextricably linked.

Commitment arises as a consideration at the intersection between the organizational requisites of groups and the personal orientations and preferences of their members. On the one hand, social systems must organize to meet their systemic "needs"; on the other hand, people must orient themselves positively and negatively, emotionally and intellectually, to situations. While the system is making specific demands for participation, group relatedness, and control, the people in it are investing more or less of themselves, are deciding to stay or to leave, are concentrating varying degrees of their emotional lives in the group, and are fervently obeying or finding ways to sabotage basic principles and rules of the system. For the group to get what it needs for existence and growth at the same time that people become positively involved requires organizational solutions that are simultaneously mechanisms to ensure commitment by affecting people's orientations to the group.

Commitment thus refers to the willingness of people to do what will help maintain the group because it provides what they need. In sociological terms, commitment means the attachment of the self to the requirements of social relations that are seen as self-expressive.[2] Commitment links self-interest to social requirements. A person is committed to a relationship or to a group to the extent that he sees it as expressing or fulfilling some fundamental part of himself; he is committed to the degree that he perceives no conflict between its requirements and his own needs; he is committed to the degree that he can no longer meet his needs elsewhere. When a person is committed, what he wants to do (through internal feeling) is the same as what he has to do (according to external demands), and thus he gives to the group what it needs to maintain itself

---

[1] Georg Simmel, "The Secret Society," in *The Sociology of Georg Simmel*, ed. Kurt H. Wolff (New York: Free Press, 1964), p. 366.

[2] This definition bears some similarity to Talcott Parson's notion of "institutionalization."

414

at the same time that he gets what he needs to nourish his own sense of self. To a great extent, therefore, commitment is not only important for the survival of a community, but also is part of the essence of community. It forms the connection between self-interest and group interest. It is that identification of the self with a group which Charles Horton Cooley considered essential for self-realization.

To determine the links between person and system that forge the bonds of commitment, one must first distinguish the three major aspects of a social system that involve commitment: retention of members, group cohesiveness, and social control.[3] Retention refers to people's willingness to stay in the system, to continue to staff it and carry out their roles. Group cohesiveness denotes the ability of people to "stick together," to develop the mutual attraction and collective strength to withstand threats to the group's existence. And social control involves the readiness of people to obey the demands of the system, to conform to its values and beliefs and take its dictates seriously.

Continuance, cohesion, and control are

three analytically distinct problems, with potentially independent solutions. A person may be committed to continuing his membership but be continually deviant within the group, disloyal and disobedient—that is, *un*committed to its control and unwilling to carry out the norms and values that represent system policy. A rebellious child may reject parental control but be unwilling or unable to withdraw from the family system; he may subvert the values of the system yet be committed to remain within it. Furthermore, a person may be highly attracted to a group within a social system but be uncommitted to continued participation in the system because of other circumstances. An office worker, for example, may take a better job even though his best friends work in his former office. The inmate of a prison may form close ties with fellow prisoners and even with guards, yet certainly wish to leave the system at the earliest opportunity. In specific social systems, one or another of these commitment problems may be of paramount importance. A business organization may concentrate on solving problems of continuance rather than cohesion; a T-group or encounter group may be concerned solely about cohesion; a religious organization may stress control. In other cases the three may be causally related, with solutions to all three problems mutually reinforcing and multiply determined. In a utopian community, for instance, which emphasizes all three aspects of commitment, the more members are attracted to one another, the more they also wish to continue their membership, and the more they are able to wholeheartedly support its values. Despite this possible overlap, however, for purposes of understanding the roots of commitment, continuance, cohesion, and control must be separated.

At the same time, a person orients himself to a social system instrumentally, affectively, and morally. That is, he orients himself with respect to the rewards and

---

[3] Although recruitment would seem at first glance to be as important as retention of people for continuation of a system, the two problems are distinct, requiring for solution different kinds of organization strategies. Recruitment does not necessarily require commitment but may be accomplished in many other ways with noncommitted actors (for example, birth, accident, and external organizational phenomena may serve to recruit uncommitted individuals). However, once a person has performed any single act within a system, the problem arises of committing him to further and future participation. Thus, the commitment necessary for continuation involves retaining participants, and recruiting them is not a commitment problem (though of course the ways in which they are recruited have implications for commitment). In very complex systems, it might also seem likely that group cohesiveness would be limited to peer groups. However, if cohesiveness is defined not in terms of sociability and mutual attraction but rather in terms of the ability to withstand disruptive forces and threats from outside the group ("sticking together"), it applies to systems of any degree of complexity. See Neal Gross and William Martin, "On Group Cohesiveness," *American Journal of Sociology* 57 (December 1952), pp. 533–46.

costs that are involved in participating in the system, with respect to his emotional attachment to the people in the system, and with respect to the moral compelling-ness of the norms and beliefs of the system. In the language of social action theory, he cognizes, cathects, and evaluates.[4] Cognitive orientations discriminate among objects, describing their possibilities for gratification or deprivation, and distinguishing their location and characteristics. Cathectic orientations represent an emotional state with respect to objects, the kind and amount of feeling they generate. Evaluative orientations refer to standards of judgment: good or bad, right or wrong. As a person relates to the world around him, he gives each element a "rating" on these three dimensions, and he chooses to behave toward it in accordance with his rating, the degree of its positive or negative value for him.

People orient themselves to social systems in the same way, and the value of a system in each of the three dimensions defines a person's behavior toward it. The system can organize in such a way as to ensure its positive value for the person around each orientation, and if it does, it gains commitment in the three areas that are essential to maintain the system. Each of the personal orientations has the potential to support one particular concern of the social system. Positive cognition can support continuance, positive cathexis can support group cohesion, and positive evaluation can support social control.

Commitment to continued participation in a system involves primarily a person's cognitive or instrumental orientations. When profits and costs are considered, participants find that the cost of leaving the system would be greater than the cost of remaining; "profit," in a net psychic sense, compels continued participation. In

a more general sense, this kind of commitment can be conceptualized as commitment to a social system role.' It may be called instrumental commitment. Commitment to relationships, to group solidarity, involves primarily a person's cathectic orientations; ties of emotion bind members to each other and to the community they form, and gratifications stem from involvement with all members of the group. Solidarity should be high; infighting and jealousy, low. A cohesive group has strong emotional bonds and can withstand threats to its existence; members "stick together." This quality may be called affective commitment. Commitment to uphold norms, obey the authority of the group, and support its values, involves primarily a person's evaluative orientations. When demands made by the system are evaluated as right, moral, just, or expressing one's own values, obedience to these demands becomes a normative necessity, and sanctioning by the system is regarded as appropriate.[5] This quality is here designated moral commitment. In some respects, commitment to norms and values resembles the concept of a superego, which binds the evaluative components of the self to the norms of a system through an internalized authority.

Each of the three kinds of commitment has different consequences for the system and for the individual. Ignoring for the moment all the other diverse sources of influence on group life, groups in which people have formed instrumental commitments should manage to hold their members. Groups in which people have formed affective commitments should report more mutual attraction and interpersonal satisfaction and should be able to withstand threats to their existence. Groups in which members have formed moral commitments should have less deviance, chal-

---

[4] Talcott Parsons and Edward A. Shils, eds., *Toward a General Theory of Action* (New York, 1962), pp. 4–6, 11.

[5] Social control is possible without moral commitments, of course, but it should not be as efficient or effective.

lenge to authority, or ideological controversy. Groups with all three kinds of commitment, that is, with total commitment, should be more successful in their maintenance than those without it.

At the same time, there are consequences for the person in making these commitments. If the group is such that a person feels he can make an instrumental commitment, he becomes invested in it and finds his membership rewarding. If the group is such that he can make an affective commitment, he gains strong social ties, relatedness, and a sense of belonging. If the group is such that he can make a moral commitment, he gains purpose, direction, and meaning, a sense that his acts stem from essential values. To some extent, a person's identity is composed of his commitments.

COMMITMENT-BUILDING PROCESSES

A group has a number of ways in which to organize so as to promote and sustain the three kinds of commitment. For each commitment, it needs to set in motion processes that reduce the value of other possible commitments and increase the value of commitment to the communal group—that is, processes both detaching the person from other options and attaching him to the community. The person must give up something as well as get something in order to be committed to a community; communes, like all other social systems, have their costs of membership. The person must invest himself in the community rather than elsewhere and commit his resources and energy there, removing them from wherever else they may be invested, or from whatever alternatives exist for commitment. Commitment thus involves choice—discrimination and selection of possible courses of action. It rests on a person's awareness of excluded options, on the knowledge of the virtues of his choice over others. A person

becomes increasingly committed both as more of his own internal satisfaction becomes dependent on the group, and as his chance to make other choices or pursue other options declines. This is commitment in Howard Becker's sense.[6] A course of action may involve more of a person's resources, reputation, or choices than he consciously chose to commit, with the result that the line of action simultaneously cuts him off from the chance to commit himself elsewhere. This process is similar, according to Becker, to the making of side bets, gambling on the fact that each step toward complete commitment will pay off. If the commitment is not sustained, and the line of action is not continued, the person then loses more than his original investment. Side bets, therefore, deriving from the fact that any choice may reduce the chances of ever taking up excluded choices, help to bring about commitment. These processes of giving up and getting make the group a clearly focused object for commitment. The clearer and more defined a group becomes to a person, the easier it is for him to concentrate his commitment there. This process contains the first principles of a "gestalt sociology": to develop maximum commitment in its members, a group must form a unity or a whole, coherent and sharply differentiated from its environment—a figure clearly distinguished from the ground, whether the ground is the outside society or excluded options for behavior. Commitment to social systems, concentrating the psychic energy in a group, may operate according to the same gestalt principles as object perception. According to these principles, the issue of commitment would occur primarily around the boundaries of a group. The group builds commitment to the extent that it clearly cuts off other possible objects of commitment, becomes an inte-

---

[6] Howard S. Becker, "Notes on the Concept of Commitment," *American Journal of Sociology* 66 (July 1960), pp. 32–40.

grated unity tying together all aspects of life within its borders, develops its own uniqueness and specialness, and becomes capable, by itself, of continuing the person's gratification. The strength of commitment, then, depends on the extent to which groups institute processes that increase the unity, coherence, and possible gratification of the group itself, at the same time that they reduce the value of other possibilities. The six commitment-building processes proposed do just that.

Commitment to continued participation involves securing a person's positive instrumental orientations, inducing the individual to cognize participation in the organization as profitable when considered in terms of rewards and costs. Cognitive orientations are those that rationally determine the positive or negative valences of relationships, perceiving their worth in energy and resources. In a purely cognitive judgment, no notion of emotional gratification (cathexis) or of morality (evalution) is attached to the group. For positive cognition to be acquired by a community, the system must organize so that participation is viewed as rewarding. The individual who makes an instrumental commitment finds that what is profitable to him is bound up with his position in the organization and is contingent on his participating in the system; he commits himself to a role. For the person there is a "profit" associated with continued participation and a "cost" connected with leaving. Thus, sacrifice (detaching) and investment (attaching) are among the components of instrumental commitments. Sacrifice involves the giving up of something considered valuable or pleasurable in order to belong to the organization; it stresses the importance of the role of member to the individual. Sacrifice means that membership becomes more costly and is therefore not lightly regarded nor likely to be given up easily. Investment is a process whereby the individual gains a stake in the group, commits current and

future profits to it, so that he must continue to participate if he is to realize those profits. Investment generally involves the giving up of control over some of the person's resources to the community.

Community is based in part on the desire for strong relations within a collectivity, for intense emotional feeling among all members, for brotherhood and sharing. Utopia is the place where a person's fundamental emotional needs can be expressed and met through the communal group. The community seeks to become a family in itself, replacing or subsuming all other family loyalties. It is this kind of relating, involving commitment to group cohesion, that enables the community to withstand threats to its existence, both as pressure from the outside and as tension and dissent from inside.

Commitment to group cohesion and solidarity requires the attachment of a person's entire fund of emotion and affectivity to the group; emotional gratification stems from participation in and identification with a collective whole. Emotional commitment becomes commitment to a set of social relationships. The individual commits himself to the group as his primary set of relations; his loyalty and allegiance are offered to all the members of the group, who together comprise a community. The group thus has tight social bonds cementing it together. In cases where strong ingroup loyalty is present, a community can stick together even though it is forcibly removed from its home, loses its crop, or is threatened with a lawsuit. Such intense family-like involvement also makes members more willing to work out whatever conflicts and tensions may arise among them. This kind of commitment is aided by renunciation (a detaching process) and communion (an attaching process). Renunciation involves giving up competing relationships outside the communal group and individualistic, exclusive attachments within. Whatever fund of emotion the individuals possess becomes concentrated in the group itself, gluing all members together, creating a cohesive unit. It is to this unit alone that members look for emotional satisfaction and to which they give their loyalty and commitment. Communion involves bringing members into meaningful contact with the collective whole, so that they experience the fact of oneness with the group and develop a "we-feeling."

The search for community is also a quest for direction and purpose in a collective anchoring of the individual life. Investment of self in a community, acceptance of its authority and willingness to support its values, is dependent in part on the extent to which group life can offer identity, personal meaning, and the opportunity to grow in terms of standards and guiding principles that the member feels are expressive of his own inner being. Commitment to community norms and values, or moral commitment, involves securing a person's positive evaluative orientations, redefining his sense of values and priorities so that he considers the system's demands right and just in terms of his self-identity, and supporting the group's authority becomes a moral necessity. The person making a moral commitment to his community should see himself as carrying out the dictates of a higher system, which orders and gives meaning to his life. He internalizes community standards and values and accepts its control, because it provides him with something transcendent. This commitment requires, first, that the person reformulate and re-evaluate his identity in terms of meeting the ideals set by the community. For this to occur, the group must first provide ways for an individual to reassess his previous life, to undo those parts of himself he wishes to change, and to perceive that identity and meaning for him lie not in an individualistic, private existence but in acceptance of the stronger influence of the utopian group. At the same time, the person must experience the greater power and meaning represented by the community, so that he will attach his sense of identity and worth to carrying out its demands and requirements. Thus, mortification (a detaching process) and transcendence (an attaching process) promote evaluative, moral commitments. Mortification involves the submission of private states to social control, the exchanging of a former identity for one defined and formulated by the community. Transcendence is a process whereby an individual attaches his decision-making prerogative to a power greater than himself, surrendering to the higher meaning contained by the group and submitting to something beyond himself. Mortification opens the person to new directions and new growth; transcendence defines those directions. Mortification causes the person to "lose himself"; transcendence permits him to find himself anew in something larger and greater.

Six processes are thus available to build commitment to communal groups. To the extent that groups develop concrete organizational strategies around these processes—commitment mechanisms—they should generate a stronger commitment than can those without such strategies. The number and kind of commitment mechanisms instituted should contribute to a community's success—its ability to endure and continue to satisfy its members.

43
New towns and communal values:
A new approach to the search
for communal ideals

Richard O. Brooks

Those new towns that are animated by communal ideals base their efforts on the fundamental belief that communal values arise spontaneously after the creation of settlements in which people live, work, and relax in proximity.

The study of Columbia casts serious doubt upon this belief, and a careful examination of the belief reveals its basic fallacy. *Urban civilization is a form of civilization in which the nexus between proximity of living and the achievement of communal values is broken.* Once the link between proximity and communal values is broken, one can no longer expect these values to arise from the creation of proximate settlements, whether in the form of new towns or neighborhood organizations.

Rather, one must plan carefully, within the full complexity of urban civilization, for the achievement of these values. Such a planning effort will require a more careful identification of the values, the use of theories to define them, the review of our present level of achievement of the values, a study of the way in which such values can be generated, and the design of new programs to achieve them. Guiding such a planning effort is the faith that a strengthened family, a sense of belonging, a respect for nature and tradition, and a sense of shared values can be maximized through rational planning rather than mis-

takenly hoped for as the product of the creation of new settlements.

THE ECLIPSE OF COMMUNITY

Probably the most prominent theoretical spokesman for the community ideologists is Maurice Stein. In his classic *The Eclipse of Community*,[1] Stein purports to document the decline of the local community, a decline oriented by the forces of bureaucracy, urbanization, and industrialization. Stein and the communitarian ideologists believe that such an "eclipse" has taken place. They view the forces of urbanization as fundamentally negative forces, destroying local communal life and leaving no settled social order in its place. A condition of urban anarchy is assumed, if not described. The assumption of such a chaotic condition makes reform through the creation of new communities imperative and relatively easy. Presumably an ordered community is to be preferred to "urban chaos" (a favorite term of the communitarians), and the presumed absence of a settled social order to resist reform efforts to "organize" the new community means that ultimate success is probable.

The recent failure of efforts to recreate or organize communities in general and the experience of Columbia in particular suggest that something may be seriously amiss with Stein's theory. The urban scene appears to be more impervious to commu-

[1] Maurice R. Stein, *The Eclipse of Community: An Interpretation of American Studies* (Princeton, N.J.: Princeton University Press, 1960).

nity organization efforts than the early communitarian theory supposed. Fortunately, more recent theories of urban community life have partly caught up with reality. These theories suggest that the "eclipse of the community" approach rests upon three fundamental fallacies.

First, the forces of urbanization do not simply destroy the local community but establish an alternative social system. There is no "eclipse," "social chaos," or "urban anarchy," but rather the creation of new urban forms. Second, the new urban social system cannot be identified as "local." The urban system extends across broad geographic bounds. Thus comes the startling conclusion that the local community may not be the only type of community but that there are more geographically extensive kinds of community. Third, there now is speculation that this new urban system can realize some or all of the communal values upheld by the communitarians. In short, there may be no necessary connection between local communities and communal values.

The three fallacies of the communitarian ideology provide the basis for an understanding of why there is resistance (such as that encountered in Columbia) to the attempt to deploy communitarian strategies. It is worthwhile looking at the three fallacies in more detail.

Urban civilization as an alternative social system

Roland L. Warren's *The Community in America*[2] marks the first step away from the oversimplifications of the communitarians and the work of Maurice Stein. In his treatment of the community as a "locality-relevant" combination of social units and systems, Warren recognizes that the community was not "eclipsed" by the forces of

urbanization or driven into anarchy but rather was modified by the penetration of vertical organizations and the work of the market system. Warren established a new meaning of community, by finding, at the local level, "horizontal patterns" of interaction between the different vertical organizations that had penetrated the local level. Following Warren, empirical studies of urban local communities began to stress not "urban chaos" but new organized patterns of community life that were developing at the local level of the urban system.

The decline of the importance of proximity

But even after Warren's contributions, the importance of proximity remained a crucial assumption in much community theory and urban study. The assumption that proximity was a significant property of "community" and "communal organization" lingered. For Warren, "proximity" was a crucial underlying characteristic of his "horizontal patterns" of local community life. In urban theory the spatial concept of density continued to play an important role in defining the urban scene.

Perhaps it was Jean Gottmann's *Megalopolis*[3] that broke the imaginative barriers to considering the urban community in new ways. In any case, the decline in the importance of proximity or "locality relevance" to the theory of community may be seen in the recent writings of many studying community. Despite the initial emphasis upon shared territory of the major community theorists (Warren, Kaufman, Hillery),[4] all of these authors, in the recent

---

[2] Roland L. Warren, *The Community in America* (Chicago: Rand McNally, 1963).

[3] Jean Gottmann, *Megalopolis* (Cambridge: MIT Press, 1961).

[4] Harold F. Kaufman, "Toward an Interactional Conception of Community," *Social Forces* 38, 1 (October 1959); George Hillery, *Communal Organizations: A Study of Local Societies* (Chicago: University of Chicago Press, 1968); and Roland L. Warren, *Truth, Love, and Social Change —and Other Essays on Community Change* (Chicago: Rand McNally, 1971).

development of their theories, have concentrated upon nonspatial aspects of community. Warren has moved to the study of organizational interaction, in which shared space may be only one of many variables affecting the nature and scope of interaction. Although Kaufman is interested in distinguishing interactions that have reference to locality and those that do not, he does not limit his use of the concept of community to the former. And Hillery, although retaining the concept of localization, views the neighborhood, the rural town, and the city as "communal organizations." The concept of "organization" emphasizes the community as composed of parts separate in function and mutually interdependent, rather than simply people in proximity.

When one turns to the major urban theories, one finds very little use being made of the territorial community theory by those studying the city. The reason for the apparent irrelevance of community theory to urban studies results in part from the assumption of "territoriality" made by the early community theorists. The assumption of shared territory as a base of the local community conflicts with the notion of a pattern of national interdependence resulting from urbanization. Students of the city, who see the constantly eroded boundaries of the city, and who are painfully aware of the national-local interdependencies of our urban world, tend to relegate the territorially bound "community" and its theory to an unimportant place in the study of the city. They fail to use the developed theory of community to guide their study of the city, because of its territorial assumptions. (One exception to this generalization is the field of urban geography.)

Instead, urban theorists have gropingly attempted to develop nonterritorial theories of the city. One classic essay by Melvin Webber argues that the quintessence of urbanization is not population density or agglomeration but specialization, the concomitant interdependence, and human interactions by which interdependencies are satisfied.[5] A similar approach to the city has been taken by Scott Greer. In his classic, *The Emerging City,* Greer views the city as a "differentiated part of our relatively large-scale society—the point at which the organizational output of one organization becomes the input of another."[6]

Behind the declining importance of space in the theories of urban community lies a shift in the basic definition of community. This basic definition is gradually separating proximity from the factors that contribute to the "commonality" of community. To understand what is happening, it is necessary to discuss briefly the definition of community. People may have "community"—something in common with one another—in several ways. As individuals, they may have a common characteristic such as the same income or race, and they may be aware of this situation. They may exchange goods and services with one another. They may be viewed and view themselves as functional parts of a larger unit, such as the family or a class system. They may pursue common purposes and be aware of that common pursuit. In modern society, all four aspects of community have been cut loose from spatial proximity of residence, work, and play. People may be alike in many essential ways but not live near one another, and exchange (economic and communicative) is now possible over great distances. People may view themselves as members of social systems extending across the nation and world. They may share common purposes that can be easily communicated across space. *Space has become relatively less important in all aspects of community.*

---

[5] Melvin Webber, "Order in Chaos: Community Without Propinquity," in Lowden Wingo, ed., *Cities and Space* (Baltimore: Johns Hopkins Press, 1963).

[6] Scott Greer, *The Emerging City* (Glencoe, Ill.: Free Press, 1964).

The declining importance of space as a central concept in the understanding of local and urban communities does not mean that space is still not an important factor in community or urban analysis. But it means that space may often not be the major independent variable of the presumed virtues of the small community or the problems of the large ones. Urban and community theorists have turned to new concepts—systems analysis, interorganizational fields, and communications theory in an attempt to understand urban interaction.

The disjunction between small proximate communities and communal values

One basic contribution of Simmel's classic essay on the city[7] was to argue that the city was not a cultureless anarchy but rather was possessed of an urban culture in which virtues such as punctuality, calculation, and objectivity were important. This conclusion of Simmel cast doubt upon whether urbanization meant simply the destruction of values, resulting in chaos. On the contrary, urbanization for Simmel meant the replacement of the local community values with new sets of "urban values"—a new shared culture.

Since Simmel's essay, a number of sociologists have argued that not only does urbanization bring a set of values, but mature urbanization results in the realization of many of the values previously attributed to the small community. These sociologists cite the development of the "personalized consumer," new patterns of family life in the city and its suburbs, new forms of security within mature bureaucratic occupations, the new role of mass communications in developing an urban consensus, and informal interaction within large organizations as examples of developing urban phenomena and institutions that can achieve communitarian goals.[8]

A NEW APPROACH TO PLANNING TO ACHIEVE COMMUNAL VALUES

Once the nexus has been broken between proximate communities and communal values, a completely new approach must be taken to the realization of those values within an urban context. If one cannot expect these values to be spontaneously produced by the creation of new towns, neighborhood organizations, or communes, then how can these values be achieved?

The first step requires a more careful definition of communal values themselves.

As stated above, the communal ideology—as exemplified in the writings pertaining to community development and organization, rural sociology, black power, and community decentralization—stresses a series of values that include love and respect for the land, respect for tradition, informal "face-to-face" relationships, economic self-determination, local political autonomy, shared values, a sense of belonging, and the recognition of the importance of the family.

[Earlier] I listed many specific attitudes, life-styles, and community conditions that constellate around each larger communal value. The identification of these many possible components of the communal ideal proves that the ideal is a complex concept. Its complexity is hidden by its simple appeal to basic feelings that we all share. But reflection upon the ideal and

---

[7] Georg Simmel, *The Great City and Cultural Life* (Dresden, 1903).

[8] Harold L. Wilensky and Charles N. Lebeaux, *Industrial Society and Social Welfare: The Import of Individualization on the Supply and Organization of Social Welfare Services in the United States* (New York: Russell Sage Foundation, 1958), p. 146 and following.

the study of attempts to achieve it in urban society lay bare the many nuances that the communal ideal may take and, as we have seen in the case of Columbia, the variety of ways by which its achievement may be frustrated.

As a consequence, a new approach must be taken to its realization. This approach requires a complex planning process, but no more complex than the intellectual efforts required to establish large-scale proximate communities such as Columbia. The first step in this new process is the clarification of the component values of the community ideal. Despite all the writing about the "community," few analyses of its component values have been set forth. There have been helpful analyses of the related ideals of "equality" and "love" by the Institute of Philosophical Research.[9] Discussion of related notions of "environmental quality" have been conducted without attention to the relationship between this notion and that of the respect for nature espoused by the communitarians. No systematic analysis of each component value and the relationship among values in the communitarian ideal has been carried out.

A second step is the assessment of the desirability of the various aspects of the communal ideal itself. Communitarians have been frequently attacked as naive, but there has been little reflective inquiry into the limits of the communitarian ideal as an ideal. One departure from this intellectual sterility is an essay by Roland Warren published in 1970, which raises fundamental questions about the communitarian assumptions pertaining to primary group relationships, autonomy, distribution of power, participation, commitment, homogeneity, local control, and absence of conflict. All the embarrassing questions come home to roost in this article. What

level of conflict do we want in our communities? What kind and degree of heterogeneity, and why? What kind of local commitment, and why? What degree of community participation can we expect and do we want?[10] These basic questions ware raised by James Rouse before he built Columbia. The behavioral scientists he gathered together to help him plan Columbia could not answer them, nor has the ongoing effort in Columbia answered them. So they remain to be asked again, and hopefully answered in the future.

A new level of understanding of the communal ideal can be achieved with the added assistance of social science theory and methods. These methods, however, have not yet been brought to bear systematically on the problem of achieving communal values within an urban society but have been diverted into the study of local communities. The important contributions of social science theory lie in the reformulation of communal ideals, the establishment of the relationship of these ideals to the entire structure of modern society, and the development of specific indicators for the ideals.

The reformulation of the communal ideals within the literature of social science has taken several directions. One approach has been to lay a basis for reinterpreting these ideals with concepts more appropriate to modern urban society. Thus, Werner Landecker has found the concept of "social integration" to be more useful than "community." Landecker has distinguished four different kinds of integration to be studied in society.[11] The virtue of the concept of "social integration" as opposed to "community" is that connotations of spatial proximity are not

---

[9] Robert Hazo, *The Idea of Love* (New York: Praeger Publishers, 1967).

[10] Roland L. Warren, "The Good Community: What Would It Be?" *Journal of Community Development Society*, no. 1 (Spring 1970), pp. 14–23.

[11] Werner Landecker, "Types of Integration and Their Measurement," *American Journal of Sociology* 56 (1951), pp. 332–40.

found in this concept. Moreover, distinguishing different kinds of integration suggests that widely different facets of societal life may be involved in the achievement of the ideal. Another new formulation of many of the concepts underlying the communal ideal may be found in Roland Warren's study of "interorganizational behavior." From this viewpoint, the communal ideal may be seen as positing the desirability of one of many possible patterns of interaction between institutions within society.

A second contribution of social science theory is the exploration of the relationship between communitarian ideals and institutions of the society at large. Thus, in her study of 19th-century communes from a sociological perspective, Rosabeth Kanter identifies the role of commitment mechanisms in terms of larger aspects of the social system.[12] Commitment is viewed as the linking of self-expressiveness to the social requirements of organizations to retain group members, secure group cohesiveness, and maintain social control. One frequently identified aspect of the communal ideal—commitment—is analyzed at a deeper level in terms of the needs of the individuals and the functions of the social system.

A third contribution of social science in the analysis of communal ideals lies in the development of social indicators relevant to components of the ideal. Empirical social science studies have led to the identification of specific indicators of societal activities that may be said to reflect the achievement of communal ideals. For example, Irving Rosow and others have measured the amount of informal interaction between certain groups.[13] Indexes for friendship and equality have been developed. The role of these indicators is not merely to measure the degree to which a society or institutions within that society achieve certain goals but also to clarify the meaning of the values and ideals, highlighting issues concerning their meaning.

The next step in a new planning approach to the redefinition and achievement of communal ideals within an urban setting lies in the recognition that these ideals will be achieved as the product of the workings of many institutions within society. Thus, these values are not the necessary product of the workings of local settlements but rather the result of a wide range of institutions, ranging from the federal government to intermediary groups between the individual and mass society.

For example, a "strengthened family" may be one of the ideals (admittedly vaguely defined) of the communal values. This "strengthened family" may be the result, in part, of a tacit or explicit set of policies pursued at the federal, state, and local governmental level. It may be helped or hindered by a variety of specialized urban institutions such as family counseling services. It may be affected by class behavior. Its composition may be defined in part by peer groups and friendships. Its functions may be influenced by the urban milieu in which it is situated.

Thus, the achievement of any given level of any particular communal value will very much depend upon the relative contribution of each institutional force. The precise estimation of these relative contributions will remain the province of the social sciences. But the use of social science conclusions to reach rough estimations of the effects of our current policies in a separate task that needs doing.

Thus, one can imagine a series of parallel inquiries pursuing the estimation of the influence of a wide variety of institutions upon selected communal values. But such

---

[12] Rosabeth Moss Kanter, *Commitment and Community: Communes and Utopias in Sociological Perspective* (Cambridge, Mass.: Harvard University Press, 1972).

[13] Irving Rosow, "The Social Effects of Physical Environment," *American Institute of Planners Journal* 27 (May 1961), pp. 127–33.

an approach would mean a complete re-definition of "community studies" as it is currently known and practiced in the social sciences. *Rather than a study of local settlements, the study of the contribution of local and nonlocal institutions to the achievement of communal values becomes the central focus of inquiry.*

The philosophical review of communal ideals, the use of social science theory to clarify these ideals and specify them with social indicators, the attempt to measure the contributions that various institutions make to the achievement of these ideals, are a necessary preface to the design of action and programs intended to maximize communal values. But when attention turns to the design of programs, the above approach suggests that little attention might be paid to the traditional community organization efforts that presume that local organization is the necessary way to promote communal values. Instead, the focus should be upon the strengthening of those institutions that are found to contribute most of the achievement of one or another specific communal value. If, for example, a certain level of income is found to promote positive family functioning, then some form of national family assistance plan may be the program pursued rather than the building of new towns, which were naively believed to have a beneficial impact on family life.

The approach I have outlined here is the approach of rational social policy analysis. The clarification of goals, the development of social indicators, the measurement of the present effects of programs and institutions upon those goals, and the design of programs in light of this analysis, is an approach that is often recommended but rarely followed. Although social policy analysis has been subjected to much recent questioning, the field is still too much in its infancy to estimate its future success or failure.

However, there are special obstacles to the application of policy analysis to the achievement of communal values. The professionals associated with communitarian efforts have been traditionally linked to efforts to promote local settlements. Their roles are often defined in terms of the creation and strengthening of local communities. As a consequence, these communitarians may be wedded by tradition, belief, and role to a continued faith in the efficacy of local settlements as the major vehicle for the achievement of communal values. The social client groups —the poor, the blacks, and others—that have been the object of community development efforts may also lack a perspective sympathetic to anything other than local community development efforts. Finally, many of the intellectuals who have devoted time and attention to community development thought appear to continue to concentrate on local development efforts.

Nevertheless, there is some hope for change. As indicated above, some intellectuals have moved away from local community development as the sole focus for achievement of communal values. With the current dissatisfaction with liberal doctrines, some may turn to communitarian ideals. Some members of minority groups have begun to realize the limitations of local community development efforts and are turning to national political alliances that favor other approaches to their problems. And with the waning domestic support for local community development programs, practitioners of community development may be willing to entertain drastic new alternatives.

The turn to rational social policy planning as the first step in the new search for the realization of communitarian values assumes that such planning will be necessary but not sufficient to reach these values. The roles of spontaneity, tradition, self-expression, love—components essential to communitarian ideals and not subject to rational planning—will have to intervene and flower along with the results of any planning effort. Nevertheless, planning directed at the careful definition of communal values and careful identifica-

tion of the institutional means to achieve these values appears far superior to the present approach, which seeks to recreate the traditional rural community anew.

44

A neighborhood of the future

David Morris and Karl Hess

Elroy Jones woke up at nine o'clock, remembering once more the old days when he had to wake up hours earlier to beat the commuter traffic into town. While leisurely eating breakfast, he savored the fine fruit that he had with his eggs. Both came from the greenbelt around the city which was established after the great famine of the late 1970s. Cliffdale, the neighborhood Elroy lived in, grew much of its own food. During the great famine, when the large food corporations forced out almost all the small family farmers, and then collapsed themselves, the neighborhood had gathered together to see how much food it could produce. It never amounted to more than 25 percent of its needs. Cliffdale was just too densely populated. But when the famine hit, the neighborhood had to do something. The Cliffdale Community Council, which had been negotiating lethargically with the city authorities for more power over local affairs, began telling residents to take direct action, to tear up paved streets that weren't absolutely essential for traffic and bring topsoil from areas where there was a "surplus," like city woods. Garbage and human wastes were collected to provide compost and fertilizer, and within only one season the street gardens had borne vegetables.

As in any crisis, unity was strong during that time. The city tried to stop the actions at first, but held off when other neighborhoods began imitating Cliffdale's policies. "How the world changes," Elroy mused. He could still remember the 1950s and 1960s, when there was a rush to pave over the cities, a frenzy so great that even private citizens joined in cementing over their backyards with terraces, covering their front yards with artificial grass.

Elroy went outside. He could easily walk to the community factory, where he worked assembling d.c. motors used in the electric cars which were everywhere in the community. But a light rain was falling, and he decided to take the minibus system for those 10 blocks. As he waited under the canopy for the bus, he glanced at the falling rain, glad that nature was providing for the sustenance of the neighborhood. Only a decade before, rain was considered a nuisance in the cities. In fact, there had been one plan put forward by a famous futurist (how strange the word seemed now, when everyone considered themselves futurists) that cities cover themselves with huge domes to keep away the rain and snow. Elroy understood the argument for such a plan. It had even made sense at the time. With the city paved over there had been nothing to catch the water, and it carried silt and leaf residue and auto exhaust to nearby water supplies, polluting them. In Washington,

Reprinted with permission of the authors and publishers from David Morris and Karl Hess, *Neighborhood Power: The New Localism* (Boston: Beacon Press, 1975), pp. 159–72.

D.C., where Cliffdale was located, the combined sewer system had made it necessary to open the gates when it rained because rain overloaded the sewage capacity, causing raw sewage to pour directly into the Potomac River. And, besides, people had forgotten what rain was for. Bus stops had no canopies then. Driving was hazardous in the rain. Domes sounded like a pretty good idea.

The minibus slid quietly into the bus stop and Elroy got on. He joked some with Pat, the driver, retelling stories about the factory where they had recently worked together. Pat, like most people in the neighborhood rotated through a number of jobs during his work lifetime. It had been discovered, by talking with workers, that they wanted three things. One was to control their work time, another was to have some feeling that they were making a whole product, some sense of craftsmanship. The third was that no one, not even on what some people would think was the best job of all, want to work at it for 50 years. So people tended to rotate. It had worked out pretty well, especially because people who worked at a number of jobs achieved an understanding of the pressures peculiar to each occupation.

Of course no system is ideal, Elroy thought, and this one still had its problems. Changing people's conceptions about employment was still going to take some time. For generations, even millennia, people worked so they could earn enough money to survive. The job, ideally, was interesting, but it was mainly a necessary evil used for supporting wife, family, and house. The idea that work should fill a social function, producing wealth for the community, was a relatively new concept. Elroy remembered the many experiments in resource allocation. The community, like many, had gone through a pro-Bellamy period, reverting to labor credits administered through a central office, but had found the system too favorable to a centralized state apparatus. They

had tried time units, basing the cost of an item on the amount of labor that went into it. This was more comfortable, because people could intuitively accept the fact that 40 hours of work was 40 hours of work; in fact, if one were to judge by the physical effort involved, surely the construction worker was working harder than the bank president. In the final analysis time was the essential common denominator for all humanity. Presently Cliffdale was working with a hybridized system, using a free market and monetary incentive for luxury items, and a guaranteed goods level for anything else.

There had been a time when people had taken advantage of such a system, and there were still many neighborhoods that carried on with the old market economy because they had had such problems with free goods. But in most communities, after people got over their initial impulse to just sit and do nothing, new work ethics arose and people decided they were too bored just sitting around. Besides, when the choice was no longer working for 40 or 50 hours a week at a menial job that one did not like and had no control over versus goofing off, but rather was a choice of 20 hours of work in a comfortable work environment with rotation of jobs and worker control, the whole appeal of work changed.

There still remained a few dirty jobs, but ingenuity had eliminated many of them. At first the community councils had rotated the more unattractive jobs, so that garbage collection, for example, was done by one person for only one week out of the year. Soon the neighborhood decided that the goal should be to eliminate the job. The neighborhood outlawed most packaging, and prohibited the use of nonreturnable containers. With in-house composting, garbage collection almost disappeared. The main item of collection currently was goods that had become worn out and newspapers, and even newspapers were diminishing as new electronic communication became more widespread and creative.

As the bus moved quietly along the city streets. Elroy remembered that in the old days the neighborhood had had almost 25 percent of its labor force unemployed. In fact, the figure was closer to 40 percent when you counted all the women who were staying at home taking care of one child apiece. The process in the old society was to take more and more people out of the labor force and provide for their sustenance from those who were working. It seemed ridiculous now, but at the time it was common practice for children to go to school at the age of 4 and stay there until the age of 25, never performing any socially useful work in those 21 years, but rather "learning" in some strange, mystical way. They would then take a job, work for approximately 30 years, and then retire on pensions. Those who were not so fortunate waited until age 60 and retired on social security. Some people had warned that this could not continue; even in the early 1960s there were voices of doom, but most of the attention was given to the prophets of plenty, who assured people that ever-expanding wealth would permit everyone to be taken care of. Ironically, it was money which was the underpinning and at the same time the burden of the system. The growth in those days caused a transiency in the population. Children no longer took care of their parents. Parents no longer took care of their children. Neighbors no longer talked with one another about disputes; they called the police. Families served very little of the traditional functions of education, protection, and acculturation. Children ran away from homes to be taken care of in runaway shelters. An increasing part of the population was in jail, or halfway houses.

Things that had been free no longer were. Disputes were often mediated by paid policemen and paid judges. Entertainment cost money. Old people were cared for in rest homes. All of this, plus the dwindling number of people who worked for a living, finally caused such a great strain on the system that people had to devise new ways of living. The first plans were no advance. They tried to get people to do menial work picking up garbage and beautifying streets. It didn't work because these underpaid laborers, working for government checks, began to compete with other paid workers, and added to the unemployment rolls.

Elroy wasn't sure what would have happened if the economy had not suddenly nosedived, throwing millions out of work and abruptly terminating the growth of the 1960s. The depression forced stability on neighborhoods. People became less transient. They relied on each other more, not out of altruism but out of necessity. And, finally, new definitions of work and public welfare arose. The school systems taught students in the factories and the communities themselves. The difference between vocational and academic training disappeared as technicians, laborers, engineers, and others worked together to redesign the neighborhood itself. Day-care centers flourished, with old people, who could recount the experiences of yesteryear, taking the main burden of caring for the children.

As the bus rolled on toward the factory, Elroy noticed the forest of windmills on the rooftops but gave them no special attention, ignoring them much as his father would have ignored the forest of TV antennas on rooftops of his time. He saw the sun glinting off the solar cells and solar collectors and remembered suddenly the bitter arguments that had occurred when solar energy was first introduced. It seemed that no one had thought about "sun rights," that is, the right not to have a building go up next door which cut off one's access to a certain number of hours of sunlight a day. Under the old system, there were court suits and zoning-commission hearings, but in most cases the owners of high-rise office buildings and apartment houses won their case. When zoning was left to the neighborhood, however, this stopped, and right now the line of equal rooftops was unbroken. With the coming of local control there was a certain sameness in architecture, but this sameness was forced on the people by nature's laws. Windows faced to the south, as did slanted rooftops. The solar cells and collectors were combined. Someone in a neighborhood in France had discovered the way to most efficiently combine the heating and electrical solar equipment, and that system was currently sweeping the world. Some fossil fuels were still needed to supplement sun and wind systems, but not much. Petroleum, which had been used primarily in internal-combustion engines, was now restricted by consent of all the people in the country to certain plastic materials and pharmaceuticals. It had taken a plague to convince people of that. In the late 1970s, with gasoline consumption still increasing, the cities ran out of energy-intensive chlorine supplies because it was not as profitable to supply the city water-purification system as it was to supply cars. As people began to get sick from drinking untreated water, the hospitals filled up, but there were not enough medicines available to treat the ill because so many of the medicines had a petroleum base. When the death toll ran into the thousands, people decided it was better to conserve the precious raw material for future generations' health and welfare than to burn it in inefficient car engines.

Transportation had become a much different affair in Cliffdale. Transportation systems that went from all areas of the city and suburbs to downtown had been pretty much done away with. Much of the transportation had been replaced by electronic communication of information. When the two-way communications systems had been installed in every home, and the wave-guide systems had permitted the number of communications channels to be almost infinite in number, travel to downtown had diminished considerably. Most of the physical transportation had been useful only as way to pass information along. The boss went downtown in order to spend most of the day in conference, dictating letters, or making phone calls. The secretary went downtown in order to type, answer the phone, and file correspondence. And so on. It seemed almost a miracle when someone suggested that an effective electronic communication system would pay for itself in less than a year, by saving on travel expenses and the deterioration of office buildings, not to mention wear and tear on nerves.

When electronic communication freed people, patterns of living began to change. Families could once more stay at home together. Initially there were many who left the cities altogether to live in isolated rural areas, doing their jobs by cathode-ray-computer screen and video phone. Some still stayed in those remote areas, but fairly soon people discovered that there was a need for physical presence, at least in social activities, that human beings are gregarious, and that communicating by electronics was psychologically debilitating.

When downtown became only an electronic pulse away, rather than an hour by freeway during rush hour, the sense of the city quietly altered. Factories were established in the neighborhoods. Transportation systems became locally oriented. It seemed ridiculous to think that in the old days it was easier to get downtown, a distance of some 10 miles, than it was to go sideways to another neighborhood, a distance of half a mile. Now the minibuses, the electric cars which were rented, not owned, by the neighborhood residents, and the bicycles took care of local transportation.

Elroy disembarked at the factory, a warehouse that had been used at one time to store office supplies. As he walked into the assembly area he noticed a group of co-workers gathered around a large TV screen. Walking over to them he saw that they were talking with workers in Sweden who had just discovered a more efficient method of manufacturing the d.c. motors which were the main product of the factory. Sven Palmer, a young electician working in the Swedish factory, had developed a way of winding the armature which increased efficiency by almost 10 percent. He was busy demonstrating the new winding technique to the American workers. Elizabeth Rhodes was the first to get the knack of it, and a cheer went up from the workers gathered around the screen when they realized that one more transfer of technology from people to people had been accomplished.

Realizing that the increased efficiency would produce a savings for the community, the workers decided to declare a holiday. In the old days an increase in efficiency of the product would probably have been ignored, and any increase in production techniques meant more products coming off the line in less time. Products were made to break quickly, for in the sales of parts and new products lay the profits of the firm. In Cliffdale the community decided how many d.c. motors it needed, and then worked long enough to produce that many. There were always some new ones needed, and there were also replacements needed. Whenever there was a breakthrough such as happened today, the old motors were taken in and rebuilt to increase their efficiency. But the factory would never produce more than was needed. So in that case an increase in efficiency probably meant a decrease in work hours. A celebration was in order, a holiday declared.

Elroy recalled with pleasure that the very television screen that had enabled them to learn the new armature winding had been built by a previous work group in the neighborhood which had done its work so well that it hadn't reconvened now for more than a year. Only its small transistor production unit, housed in the top floor of a building once used for real-estate speculators' offices, was active regularly. The holiday declared when the television production had been completed had been something special because it was accompanied by a neighborhood meeting in which it was decided that three people from the neighborhood would, voluntarily, of course, take a year away from the neighborhood to work at the regional facility where, by intercommunity agreement, TV transmission equipment was built and this area's participation in the global inter-neighborhood TV netork maintained.

This holiday, Elroy thought, they might take some time also to decide who wanted to work for a much shorter period of time on the installation, by community cooperative effort, of a new diesel-electric power plant in the locomotive used to maintain rail service between the towns of Atlantic seaborad with which Cliffdale joined in a transportation pool.

Elroy's own inclination at this point was to think more about a project far, far different from his usual activity, to satisfy his own need and desire for at least a short time of active life away from the community. Some people never left the community. Others were away almost half their lives, making it hard sometimes to regard them as resident in any one place. Elroy was inclined to stay put himself, but to enjoy a week away now and then.

Life used to be rigorously divided between work, travel, toil, and pleasure. Now it wasn't. It didn't have to be and no one in his right mind would want it to be, Elroy thought. Why had so many people put up with it for so long, he wondered. Histories have many answers but, obviously, he thought, the most reasonable ones had to do with the control of productive and natural resources by so few people, the absence of a truly free society in which people generally, and not a few in particular, used their own good common sense to make the decisions affecting their lives.

At any rate, what Elroy had been thinking about lately was signing up for one of the still vacant volunteer spots in the regional iron-ore cooperative, to do a week of mining. He'd hate to do such work day in and day out, of course, but for a short period it was bracing, helped restore some of the muscular vigor that too much time at an indoor job was bound to sap, and put him directly in touch with new people in a new environment.

Actually, the neighborhood was rather sharply divided on the matter of iron ore this year. The neighborhood's own amazingly successful recycling efforts had meant that iron and steel supplies (remelted in a solar-powered refractory furnace) were more than enough for the neighborhood's current production plans. There was a strong feeling that the figures on need projected by some were too high. At any rate, the neighborhood assembly had been unable to come anywhere near consensus on the matter, there was no widespread spirit in the neighborhood for volunteering and the matter now rested solely and informally with individuals who could, if they wanted, volunteer for the iron mining—or just forget it. (If the assembly *had* agreed, then there would have been neighborhood meetings, recruiting festivals, and public commendation for those who went.)

Elroy was persuaded that, overall, it would be better to step up ore production right now than wait until the needs were more apparent. Also, he had to confess to himself, he just plain welcomed a chance to get away for a while and to do some hard work. It would be a real vacation.

Meanwhile, Elroy joined Elizabeth in walking down to the day-care center to see her two children, ages two and three. The brightly painted, multicolored exterior was a far cry from the grey facade that had greeted the visitor a decade before. At that time it had been a bank, one of five in the neighborhood. As Cliffdale established its own bank and credit union and people began to put their money in that institution, the other branch banks moved out of the neighborhood to more profitable areas. The high-ceilinged banking area provided a perfect play area for children, with ladders and swings and even sandboxes ingeniously built in. As Elizabeth and Elroy came into the building, they were greeted by the subdued rumble of 40 children at play, painting, drawing, dancing, clowning around.

Most working parents visited their children at some time during the day, every day. Some parents, of course, elected to stay full time with their children, but few did so in isolation—working at a day-care center being a far more pleasurable answer than staying cooped up in a small house. Nursing mothers established a schedule after the first few months of feeding their children. But the everyday care was given over to those in the community who were most interested in children, who were patient, and who had some experience. The staff here were also studying child psychology in the local community college. Some would help in setting up new centers where the need arose. It had been discovered shortly after the day-care center opened that old people enjoyed very much sitting in the building and watching the children, and that the children enjoyed that attention. The tradition of story telling had been revived by old-timers who knew about the old days in ways that TV and radio didn't seem to capture.

As with most buildings in the community, this one was multipurpose. There was a laundromat in the basement (with its waste heat used to heat the day care center in winter). There was a lounge for the elderly and infirm. And there was a library-communication facility where people could browse through literature or use video channels to hook up with other communities or individuals around the world.

The idea, fairly successful at this point, was to bring the community together, especially those segments that had been isolated. Community centers had been the refuge of the young, the teenagers, replete with pool tables and bowling alleys or stages. The old were segregated in rest homes, the very young in nurseries. Just as the food market in Cliffdale was located very near the factories and schools, so this building housed different projects and activities to reduce the compartmentalizing that society had fallen into before.

Elizabeth took her two children out of the building, after checking with the supervisor on duty. It was late afternoon, and they would be going home soon in any case. The children loved to pick vegetables, so Elroy and Elizabeth went over to the garden their block used for growing their food. Probably a visitor to the neighborhood would have found the proliferation of greenhouses and vegetables and fruit trees the most awesome sight in the community. Although Cliffdale did not grow all its food within its borders, it seemed that everywhere one turned there were ripe tomatoes, or huge cabbages, or the beginnings of pumpkins. The children loved the pumpkins best, besides the sunflowers, and probably for the same reason—they were so big.

As the children played, Elroy and Elizabeth talked about the years immediately ahead for the children when they would move from the day-care center to whichever educational or apprenticeship pattern seemed best in light of their own temperaments, of their parents' inclinations, or even of the decisions of their friends in the current center. Since the society was free, since the neighborhood was, indeed, sovereign over itself and its resources, and since it was no longer necessary to beat down your neighbors in order to get what you wanted out of life (assuming that the "want" didn't include raw power or some sadistic desire to push people around), since, in short, the purpose of community was the well-being of its members rather than the profit of absentee owners, the early educational decisions of children

were nowhere near as binding or formative as in the past.

People could always change these days. Opportunities were, in effect, endless. Work was honored, waste was shunned, cooperation was the way of the world, and competition was reserved just for gala events such as music festivals, art shows, and the many trade and craft fairs at which people vied, but lovingly, to show the excellence of their work.

The real difference was that to be a winner, now, there did not have to be losers.

The honor was in trying. Excellence was freely admitted and admired without resentment and jealousy—everybody's reward, ultimately, being the same: work done as well as one could, whether a new process for suspending a bridge, or a poem.

Knowledge for the new life had become, simply, knowledge for life. Manipulative skills, the skills of exploitation and advantage, of wile and conniving, were no longer respected. There were no institutions to teach them. Schools, even university communities, formed now to engage people, teachers and students, senior and junior scholars, in processes of exploring knowledge of the natural world and the ethics of the human world in that nature.

For many young people this meant, mainly, joining the mainstream of the community as early as possible, becoming responsible and self-reliant young people. Basic skills, such as reading, rudimentary science, logic, knowledge of the ways of the neighborhood and of surrounding communities, were taught everywhere: in the day-care centers, at home, in groups that children formed themselves.

Other and more special skills—arts, crafts, specific sciences—could be approached in several ways. The neighborhood itself had formed an ongoing educational community for electrodynamics, an area that over time had become particularly important in this particular neighborhood. Senior skilled people, in this community, volunteered to work for certain times each day with young people interested in the subject, emphasizing the theoretical knowledge which, as soon as possible, would be given practical application in part-time apprenticeships to people actually working at production or research. Age was simply no longer a criterion for what a young person should do at any particular point. Skill, personal devotion, and direction were the measures now.

And, quite importantly, from the time a young person was accepted into full citizenship of the neighborhood assembly (the young person's neighbors applied for her or him, the assembly voted approval or not), the young person was fully participating in all the decisions not only of education and apprenticeships but of everything affecting the life of the neighborhood.

Elroy and Elizabeth had first met during the years of hottest debate over the nature of the assembly. Elroy had insisted then that the assembly needed to be subordinated to an executive council of key people who could direct the energies of the neighborhood. Elizabeth wisely, Elroy now happily admitted, had held out for the full sovereignty of the assembly and for the notion that only a fully self-reliant and self-responsible community could realize all the potential of its members, that any hard-and-fast delegations of responsibility to some just weakened the responsibility of the rest. That idea had prevailed, and the neighborhood now was fully free because the citizens were fully involved and fully responsible.

Beyond the neighborhood, of course, there also was a political life, but even it was carefully guarded so that power would never again, as it had in the past, accumulate in a few hands.

Elroy was a member of the city-wide council which did planning on a larger scale than the neighborhood. Each neighborhood controlled its own affairs. The city-wide council was made up of representatives chosen by the neighborhoods. All the members were subject to recall and, in fact, a parliamentary system had developed whereby, if the representative found that a majority of his or her constituents disagreed with a decision, he or she resigned pending a vote of confidence. The city-wide council had control over those areas of planning which did not lend themselves to just neighborhood decision making. For example, the creation of greenbelts, the discussion of basic manufacturing resources, the placement of hospitals, were all under the province of the city-wide council. Usually the city council made tentative decisions, for example, deciding how many hospitals were needed for a city of 500,000 and then the neighborhoods thrashed out where they would be located. Every neighborhood had its own clinics, which, by the way, also were multipurpose, hooked up with food markets, the links between nutrition and health.

Meetings were at a different neighborhood every month and were held once a week. Not very many people showed up unless there was a crisis period. Participation occurred as people felt decisions *had* to be made, or when decisions had to be *unmade*.

Now the children were running back to Elizabeth and Elroy. The growing field they had just left was gleaming in the late sun. Friends, neighbors, passed them, each with a greeting. Friends, neighbors, working at other times at freely chosen tasks, each with a productive place in the community—to feed it, provide its material needs, delight it, decorate it, enrich it in some way.

No wasted materials littered the common walkways. The air was clear. People did not fear one another. The most respected were not the most powerful but the most creative and the most cooperative. Art flourished as the creative practice of the entire community. Some excelled.

All participated. Music was the common delight of the community. Science was the common knowledge, letting everyone live in nature knowing of its and their limits as well as possibilities. Women, children, men, the aged, the idiosyncratic, were kind to one another, bound together not by laws but by their common human condition.

The laughter of the children glided like a stream of tiny bells through the neighborhood. Dusk was nearing. And tomorrow was beginning to form in the neighborhood once again.